This edition published 2006 by
John Wiley & Sons Australia, Ltd
42 McDougall Street, Milton Qld 4064

Typeset in New Baskerville Light 10/12, Univers Light 8.5/10

Authorised adaptation of the fifth edition by
John R. Schermerhorn, James G. Hunt and
Richard N. Osborn, *Managing Organizational Behavior*
(ISBN 0 471 577750 2), published by John Wiley & Sons,
New York, United States of America. Copyright © 1994
in the United States of America by John Wiley & Sons,
Inc. All rights reserved.

US edition © John Wiley & Sons, Inc. 1994
Australian edition © John Wiley & Sons Australia, Ltd 2006

The moral rights of the authors have been asserted.

National Library of Australia
Cataloguing-in-Publication data

Organisational behaviour: core concepts and applications.

  1st Australasian ed.
  Includes index.
  ISBN 978 0 47080 951 8.

  1. Organisational behaviour. I. Wood, J. M.
  (Jack Maxwell), 1945– .

302.35

Cover and internal design images: © PhotoAlto, © Photodisc, © Stockbyte

Edited by Sharon Nevile

Printed in China by
Printplus Limited

10 9 8 7 6 5

ORGANISATIONAL BEHAVIOUR: CORE CONCEPTS AND APPLICATIONS

WOOD ZEFFANE FROMHOLTZ FITZGERALD SCHERMERHORN HUNT OSBORN

FIRST AUSTRALASIAN EDITION

WILEY

John Wiley & Sons Australia, Ltd

BRIEF CONTENTS

PART 1 INTRODUCTION 1

1 What is organisational behaviour? 2

PART 2 MANAGING INDIVIDUAL BEHAVIOUR AND PERFORMANCE 39

2 Individual attributes and their effects on job performance 40

3 Motivation and empowerment 76

4 Learning, reinforcement and self-management 112

5 Job design, goal setting and flexible work arrangements 148

PART 3 MANAGING GROUP DYNAMICS AND TEAM PERFORMANCE 187

6 Groups and group dynamics 188

7 Teamwork and team building 226

PART 4 MANAGING ORGANISATIONAL PROCESSES AND PERFORMANCE 265

8 Organisational structure and design 266

9 Organisational culture 308

10 Power, politics and influence in organisations 342

11 Leadership 382

12 Decision making 418

13 Communication, conflict and negotiation in organisations 452

14 Organisational change and innovation 488

PART 5 CASE STUDIES 524

CONTENTS

Accompanying resources xv

Cases and real-world examples at a glance xvi

Tutorial activities at a glance xviii

How to use this book xix

Preface xxi

About the authors xxiii

Acknowledgements xxv

PART ONE   INTRODUCTION 1

CHAPTER 1   WHAT IS ORGANISATIONAL BEHAVIOUR? 2

Learning objectives *2*

Introduction *4*

What is organisational behaviour? *4*

Why do organisations exist? *6*

Organisations as open systems *7*

Managers in organisations *9*

What is an effective manager? *9*

Managing task performance *9*

Human resource maintenance *10*

The management process *12*

Contemporary themes in organisational behaviour *13*

Globalisation *14*

The changing nature of work *17*

The changing nature of the workforce *18*

The changing nature of employer–employee relations *22*

Ethics and values *26*

Why study organisational behaviour? *27*

Summary *28*

Chapter 1 study guide *30*

Key terms *30*

Review questions *30*

Application questions *30*

Research questions *31*

Running project *31*

Individual activity *31*

Group activity *32*

Suggested reading *34*

End notes *34*

- **What would you do?** *12*
- **The effective manager 1.1** *13*
  Moving from traditional to re-engineered values
- **The effective manager 1.2** *15*
  Ten attributes of the global manager
- **Counterpoint** *15*
- **International spotlight** *19*
- **Ethical perspective** *23*
- **Case study: Hubbard's Foods Ltd** *33*

PART TWO   MANAGING INDIVIDUAL BEHAVIOUR AND PERFORMANCE 39

CHAPTER 2   INDIVIDUAL ATTRIBUTES AND THEIR EFFECTS ON JOB PERFORMANCE 40

Learning objectives *40*

Introduction *42*

Individual performance factors *42*

   Individual attributes *42*

   Work effort *43*

   Organisational support *44*

Demographic differences among individuals *44*

Competency differences among individuals *45*

   Cognitive abilities *45*

   Physical abilities *45*

   Emotional competence *46*

Personality differences among individuals *47*

   Personality determinants *47*

   Personality traits *49*

Individual differences and workplace diversity *51*

Values *52*

   Sources and types of values *53*

   Patterns and trends in values *53*

Attitudes *55*

   Components of attitudes *55*

   Attitudes and behaviour *56*

   Attitudes and cognitive consistency *56*

   Job satisfaction as an attitude *57*

Job satisfaction and workplace behaviour *58*

   Job satisfaction, absenteeism and turnover *58*

   The link between job satisfaction and overall
      job performance *60*

Perception and the perceptual process *62*

   Factors influencing the perceptual process *63*

   Stereotyping *63*

Summary *65*

Chapter 2 study guide *67*

Key terms *67*

Review questions *67*

Application questions *67*

Research questions *68*

Running project *68*

Individual activity *68*

Group activity *69*

Suggested reading *71*

End notes *71*

- **Ethical perspective** *50*
- **The effective manager 2.1** *51*
  Working with workplace diversity
- **The effective manager 2.2** *58*
  Facets of job satisfaction (from the Job Descriptive Index)
- **What would you do?** *59*
- **Counterpoint** *61*
- **International spotlight** *61*
- **Case study: Drugs Inc.** *70*

CHAPTER 3   MOTIVATION AND EMPOWERMENT 76

Learning objectives *76*

Introduction *78*

Motivating and empowering the workforce *78*

   Contemporary issues affecting motivation and
      empowerment *78*

   The work motivation challenge *81*

Content and process motivation theories *82*

Content theories *82*

   Maslow's hierarchy of needs theory *83*

   Alderfer's ERG theory *84*

   McClelland's acquired needs theory *85*

   Herzberg's two-factor theory *87*

Process theories *90*

   Equity theory *90*

   Expectancy theory *92*

Integrating content and process motivation theories *96*

**Another perspective on motivation: self-concept and
   personal values** *98*

Empowerment *99*

Summary *102*

Chapter 3 study guide *104*

Key terms *104*
Review questions *104*
Application questions *104*
Research questions *105*
Running project *105*
Individual activity *105*
Group activity *107*
Suggested reading *109*
End notes *109*

- **International spotlight** *80*
- **The effective manager 3.1** *91*
  Steps for managing the equity process
- **Ethical perspective** *92*
- **What would you do?** *95*
- **The effective manager 3.2** *96*
  Tips for influencing the perceived valence of work outcomes
- **Counterpoint** *99*
- **Case study: Assistance at National Investment & Insurance** *108*

CHAPTER 4   LEARNING, REINFORCEMENT AND SELF-MANAGEMENT 112

Learning objectives *112*
Introduction *114*
Learning as a modification of work behaviour *114*
Classical conditioning *115*
Operant conditioning *116*
Cognitive learning *117*
Social learning *117*
Reinforcement as a strategy to modify work behaviour *120*
Positive reinforcement *121*
Negative reinforcement (avoidance) *124*
Punishment *124*
Extinction *126*
Organisational behaviour modification strategies — a summary *127*
Reinforcement perspectives *127*
Social learning theory and behavioural self-management *128*
Managing pay as an extrinsic reward *130*
Multiple meanings of pay *130*
Merit pay *131*
Creative pay practices *133*
The learning organisation *135*
The teaching organisation *137*
Summary *138*

Chapter 4 study guide *140*

Key terms *140*
Review questions *140*
Application questions *140*
Research questions *140*
Running project *141*
Individual activity *141*
Group activity *142*
Suggested reading *144*
End notes *145*

- **What would you do?** *119*
- **The effective manager 4.1** *124*
  Guidelines for allocating extrinsic rewards to ensure a positive reinforcement effect
- **The effective manager 4.2** *125*
  Guidelines for using punishment as a reinforcement strategy
- **Ethical perspective** *132*
- **International spotlight** *134*
- **The effective manager 4.3** *135*
  Creating a learning organisation
- **Counterpoint** *136*
- **Case study: A to Z Networking** *143*

CHAPTER 5   JOB DESIGN, GOAL SETTING AND FLEXIBLE WORK ARRANGEMENTS 148

Learning objectives *148*

Introduction *150*

Intrinsic motivation *150*

Job design *151*

Job simplification *151*

Job enlargement *152*

Job rotation *152*

Job enrichment *153*

The job characteristics model *155*

Individual differences: moderators of the job characteristics model *156*

Testing and the motivating potential score *157*

The research *157*

Socio-technical job design *160*

Social information and job design *160*

Multiskilling *161*

Goal-setting theory *162*

Goal setting: follow-up research *163*

Goal setting and MBO *164*

Key performance indicators *165*

Flexible work arrangements *165*

Major drivers of changing work arrangements *166*

Types of flexible work arrangements *168*

Summary *173*

Chapter 5 study guide *176*

Key terms *176*

Review questions *176*

Application questions *176*

Research questions *177*

Running project *177*

Individual activity *177*

Group activity *179*

Suggested reading *180*

End notes *180*

- **International spotlight** *156*
- **The effective manager 5.1** *158*
  Guidelines for implementing a program of job enrichment
- **Counterpoint** *159*
- **The effective manager 5.2** *165*
  Key issues for mutual goal setting in an MBO program
- **Ethical perspective** *167*
- **What would you do?** *171*
- **Case study: Port Kembla Coal Terminal** *179*
- **Part 2 case study: Getting RailCorp to run like a train** *184*

PART THREE   MANAGING GROUP DYNAMICS AND TEAM PERFORMANCE   187

CHAPTER 6   GROUPS AND GROUP DYNAMICS 188

Learning objectives *188*

Introduction *190*

What is a group? *190*

Types of group in organisations *190*

Purposes of groups in organisations *193*

Managing groups for effectiveness *196*

Groups and task performance *196*

Group effectiveness *197*

Groups as open systems *198*

Inputs into the group process *199*

Organisational setting *199*

Nature of the group task *201*

General membership characteristics   *202*

Group size   *205*

Group processes and group effectiveness   *206*

Stages of group development   *206*

Required and emergent behaviours   *209*

Group norms and roles   *210*

Emotions in groups   *211*

Group communication and decision making   *211*

Outputs of the group process — task performance and group maintenance   *211*

Group task performance   *212*

Group maintenance   *212*

Intergroup dynamics   *214*

Work flow interdependency and intergroup relations   *214*

Other factors affecting intergroup relations   *215*

Dynamics of intergroup competition   *216*

Summary   *217*

Chapter 6 study guide   *220*

Key terms   *220*

Review questions   *220*

Application questions   *220*

Research questions   *221*

Running project   *221*

Individual activity   *222*

Group activity   *222*

Suggested reading   *223*

End notes   *224*

- **The effective manager 6.1   *197***
  Ten characteristics of an effective group

- **What would you do?   *200***

- **International spotlight   *203***

- **Ethical perspective   *210***

- **Counterpoint   *213***

- **Case study: Workshops for organisational change at a global FMCG company   *222***

CHAPTER 7   TEAMWORK AND TEAM BUILDING 226

Learning objectives   *226*

Introduction   *228*

What are teams?   *228*

Groups versus teams   *228*

Teams and their effectiveness   *229*

Effective teams   *229*

Foundations of the team-building process   *230*

Team-building goals   *231*

Effective team leadership   *231*

Effective team facilitators   *233*

Teamwork activities and training   *233*

Timing and location of teamwork activities   *236*

Team performance and cohesiveness   *239*

Team norms   *239*

Team roles and role dynamics   *240*

Team cohesiveness   *240*

Influencing team cohesiveness   *241*

Types of workplace teams   *242*

Employee involvement teams   *244*

Problem-solving teams   *244*

Self-managing teams   *245*

Virtual teams   *247*

Future challenges for work teams   *249*

Empowerment through new technology   *250*

Trust   *250*

Accountability   *250*

Diversity   *250*

Team leadership   *252*

Summary   *253*

Chapter 7 study guide   *255*

Key terms   *255*

Review questions   *255*

Application questions   *255*

Research questions   *256*

Running project   *256*

Individual activity   *256*

Group activity   *257*

Suggested reading   *259*

End notes   *259*

- **The effective manager 7.1**   *231*
  How to build a high-performing team
- **The effective manager 7.2**   *232*
  Ten rules for team leaders to create effective teams
- **What would you do?**   *237*
- **The effective manager 7.3**   *239*
  Seven steps for leaders to encourage positive team norms
- **Ethical perspective**   *243*
- **International spotlight**   *249*
- **Counterpoint**   *251*
- **Case study: Life and death outcomes for the MET**   *258*
- **Part 3 case study: Teaming in Singapore's public service for the twenty-first century**   *261*

PART FOUR   MANAGING ORGANISATIONAL PROCESSES AND PERFORMANCE 265

CHAPTER 8   ORGANISATIONAL STRUCTURE AND DESIGN 266

Learning objectives   *266*

Introduction   *268*

Organisational structure and design   *268*

Factors influencing organisational design   *269*

Scale   *269*

Technology   *270*

Environment   *271*

Strategy   *272*

Organisational goals, control and coordination   *273*

Organisational goals   *273*

Control   *274*

Coordination   *278*

Vertical specialisation   *279*

Unity of command and span of control   *280*

Horizontal specialisation   *281*

Departmentalisation by function   *282*

Departmentalisation by division, geography and customer   *283*

Departmentalisation by matrix   *286*

Mixed forms of departmentalisation   *287*

Emerging forms of organisational design and workforce implications   *288*

The simple design   *288*

The bureaucracy   *290*

Divisionalised organisations   *292*

The conglomerate   *292*

The core–ring organisation   *293*

The adhocracy   *296*

Other structural arrangements   *296*

Summary   *298*

Chapter 8 study guide *300*

Key terms *300*

Review questions *300*

Application questions *300*

Research questions *301*

Running project *301*

Individual activity *302*

Group activity *302*

Suggested reading *304*

End notes *304*

- **International spotlight** *272*
- **The effective manager 8.1** *275*
  Signs of too much control
- **Ethical perspective** *277*
- **The effective manager 8.2** *279*
  Selecting personal coordination styles
- **What would you do?** *285*
- **The effective manager 8.3** *290*
  The natural dysfunctional tendencies
  of a bureaucracy
- **Counterpoint** *295*
- **Case study: Defence force recruiting** *303*

CHAPTER 9 ORGANISATIONAL CULTURE 308

Introduction *310*

The concept of organisational culture *310*

Understanding the connections between
  organisational and national cultures *310*

Levels of cultural analysis *311*

Subcultures and countercultures *312*

Imported subcultures and cultural diversity *313*

Observable aspects of organisational culture *314*

Stories, rites, rituals and symbols *314*

Cultural rules and roles *317*

Values and organisational culture *318*

Linking actions and values *318*

Common assumptions and organisational culture *319*

Common assumptions and management
  philosophy *319*

**What do organisational culture researchers
  investigate?** *320*

Alternative perspectives on organisational culture *321*

Integration perspective *321*

Differentiation perspective *322*

Ambiguity/fragmentation perspective *322*

The functions of organisational culture for its
  members *324*

**Managing organisational culture: building,
  reinforcing and changing culture** *326*

Ethics and organisational culture *329*

Summary *330*

Chapter 9 study guide *332*

Key terms *332*

Review questions *332*

Application questions *332*

Research questions *333*

Running project *333*

Individual activity *334*

Group activity *335*

Suggested reading *337*

End notes *338*

- **International spotlight** *316*
- **What would you do?** *317*
- **Counterpoint** *323*
- **The effective manager 9.1** *328*
  Using organisational culture to help
  the organisation compete
- **Ethical perspective** *329*
- **Case study: J&J's credo** *336*

CHAPTER 10   POWER, POLITICS AND INFLUENCE IN ORGANISATIONS 342

Learning objectives *342*

Introduction *344*

Power and influence *345*

Position power *346*

Personal power *349*

Power, authority and obedience *352*

The Milgram experiments *352*

Obedience and the acceptance of authority *353*

Obedience and the zone of indifference *354*

Managing with power and influence *355*

Acquiring managerial power *356*

Turning power into influence *357*

Exercising upward influence *359*

Empowerment *359*

Power keys to empowerment *360*

Empowering others *360*

The limits of empowering others *361*

Organisational politics *362*

The two traditions of organisational politics *362*

Organisational politics in action *364*

Office politics and the informal network *364*

Political action and the manager *365*

Political action and subunit power *366*

Political action in the chief executive suite *366*

The politics of empire building *368*

The consequences of power and politics *369*

The double-edged sword of organisational politics *369*

The ethics of power and politics *370*

Trust and managerial influence *372*

Summary *372*

Chapter 10 study guide *374*

Key terms *374*

Review questions *374*

Application questions *374*

Research questions *374*

Running project *375*

Individual activity *375*

Group activity *376*

Suggested reading *378*

End notes *379*

- **Ethical perspective** *347*
- **International spotlight** *349*
- **What would you do?** *350*
- **The effective manager 10.1** *355*
  Dealing with insubordinate employees
- **The effective manager 10.2** *361*
  Guidelines for implementing empowerment
- **Counterpoint** *363*
- **Case study: Making Memories** *377*

CHAPTER 11   LEADERSHIP 382

Learning objectives *382*

Introduction *384*

Leadership and management *384*

Development of theories on leadership *385*

Traditional leadership approaches: trait and behavioural theories *386*

Trait theory *386*

Behavioural theories *386*

Situational contingency theories of leadership *388*

Fiedler's leadership contingency theory *389*

House's path–goal theory of leadership *391*

Hersey and Blanchard's Situational Leadership® model *392*

Substitutes for leadership *393*

Emerging leadership perspectives *395*

Charismatic approaches *395*

Transactional and transformational leadership approaches *396*

The new leadership revisited *400*

Questions and answers concerning the new leadership *400*

Gender, age and cultural diversity — current issues in leadership *405*

Gender and leadership *405*

Leadership and age *406*

Leadership and culture *407*

Summary *407*

Chapter 11 study guide *409*

Key terms *409*

Review questions *409*

Application questions *409*

Research questions *410*

Running project *410*

Individual activity *411*

Group activity *412*

Suggested reading *414*

End notes *415*

- **The effective manager 11.1** *399*
  The four 'I's of transformational leadership
- **International spotlight** *399*
- **The effective manager 11.2** *401*
  20 characteristics of a strong leader
- **Counterpoint** *402*
- **Ethical perspective** *404*
- **What would you do?** *406*
- **Case study: Leadership challenge** *413*

CHAPTER 12 DECISION MAKING 418

Learning objectives *418*

Introduction *420*

Decision making in organisations *420*

Types of decisions made by managers *420*

Decision environments of managers *421*

Steps in the decision-making process *422*

Approaches to decision making *422*

The role of intuition *424*

The use of judgement heuristics *425*

Creativity *426*

Making a choice and implementing a decision *427*

Selecting problems carefully *427*

Strategies for involvement — who decides? *428*

Managing participation in decision making *429*

How groups make decisions *430*

The problem of escalating commitment *435*

Current issues in organisational decision making *436*

Culture and decision making *436*

Technology and decision making *436*

Ethical decision making *437*

Summary *442*

Chapter 12 study guide *444*

Key terms *444*

Review questions *444*

Application questions *444*

Research questions *445*

Running project *445*

Individual activity *445*

Group activity *446*

Suggested reading *448*

End notes *448*

- **International spotlight** *424*
- **Counterpoint** *425*
- **The effective manager 12.1** *429*
  Improving organisational problem-solving skills
- **The effective manager 12.2** *432*
  Guidelines for achieving group consensus

- **The effective manager 12.3** *434*
  Spotting the symptoms of 'groupthink'
- **What would you do?** *440*
- **Ethical perspective** *441*
- **Case study: Child protection** *447*

CHAPTER 13   COMMUNICATION, CONFLICT AND NEGOTIATION IN ORGANISATIONS 452

Learning objectives *452*

Introduction *454*

Communication in organisations *454*

Interpersonal communication *455*

Effective and efficient communication *457*

Communication channels *457*

Barriers to interpersonal communication *460*

Conflict *460*

What is conflict? *461*

Substantive and emotional conflicts *461*

Levels of conflict *463*

Conflict and culture *464*

Constructive and destructive conflicts *465*

Conflict situations faced by managers *466*

Conflict-management approaches *468*

Conflict-resolution styles *469*

Negotiation *472*

Four types of negotiation situations *472*

Negotiation goals and outcomes *473*

Different approaches to negotiation *474*

Managerial issues in negotiation *475*

Gaining integrative agreements *476*

Classic two-party negotiation *476*

Summary *480*

Chapter 13 study guide *482*

Key terms *482*

Review questions *482*

Application questions *482*

Research questions *483*

Running project *483*

Individual activity *483*

Group activity *484*

Suggested reading *485*

End notes *486*

- **Ethical perspective** *458*
- **The effective manager 13.1** *460*
  The habits of good communicators
- **The effective manager 13.2** *462*
  Communication that can lead to conflict
- **The effective manager 13.3** *466*
  How to prevent destructive conflict
- **The effective manager 13.4** *468*
  What can be done to better manage workplace conflict?
- **International spotlight** *471*
- **What would you do?** *477*
- **Counterpoint** *479*
- **Case study: Conflict over new business strategies** *485*

Learning objectives *488*

Introduction *490*

What is organisational change? *490*

Planned and unplanned change *491*

Leadership of change *491*

Forces of change *493*

Organisational targets for change *495*

Phases of planned change *496*

Change levers and change cycles *497*

Planned change strategies *500*

Top-down approach to change *500*

Force-coercion and planned change *501*

Rational persuasion and planned change *501*

Shared power and planned change *501*

Resistance to change *502*

Why people resist change *503*

How to deal with resistance to change *504*

Change and stress *506*

What is stress? *506*

Sources of stress *506*

Preventing or coping with stress *507*

Innovation in organisations *508*

The innovation process *508*

Features of innovative organisations *510*

Summary *512*

Chapter 14 study guide *514*

Key terms *514*

Review questions *514*

Application questions *514*

Research questions *515*

Running project *515*

Individual activity *515*

Group activity *516*

Suggested reading *518*

End notes *519*

- **The effective manager 14.1** *493*
  Effective and efficient change management

- **The effective manager 14.2** *494*
  Pathways to effective cultural change

- **Counterpoint** *499*

- **The effective manager 14.3** *502*
  Guidelines for effective change

- **Ethical perspective** *507*

- **The effective manager 14.4** *508*
  Promoting an innovation culture

- **International spotlight** *509*

- **What would you do?** *511*

- **Case study: Planning for change at Alpha Metal Products** *517*

- **Part 4 case study: The ups and downs of National Mutual/AXA** *521*

PART FIVE CASE STUDIES 524

Case study 1: Solutions Software Company *525*

Case study 2: Teams at Fisher & Paykel *527*

Case study 3: Queensland Health crisis *530*

Case study 4: Workout World *533*

Case study 5: KD Transport *536*

Glossary 538

Index 550

ACCOMPANYING RESOURCES

This textbook is just part of a total Organisational Behaviour resource package for students and instructors. Additional resources are as follows.

For instructors

- **Instructor's resource guide**, prepared by Andrew Creed (Deakin University). This guide includes a complete set of teaching tools. Each chapter in the guide is divided into three sections:
  1. Lecturer support material — includes a visual chapter overview, where learning objectives are linked to the related chapter headings, a chapter concepts map, a chapter synopsis, introductory statements/questions to stimulate thought about the topic, supplementary lecture issues/mini-topics, lecture stops and learning objectives
  2. Responses for text questions and exercises, including answers to 'What would you do?' and 'Counterpoint' questions; review, application and research questions; suggested answers to the 'Running Project' questions; and 'Individual activity', 'Group activity' and 'Case study' questions
  3. Materials for additional class activity, including supplementary lectures or mini-topics that may serve as the basis for additional lectures or other activities, and additional practical exercises on the chapter topic to extend students in tutorials or as written assignments or projects.
- **Test bank**, prepared by Sue Heap (Auckland University of Technology). The test bank provides more than 1300 carefully prepared test questions, including multiple-choice, true/false, scenario multiple-choice, fill-in and completion, connector, visual diagram, short-answer and essay questions. Each objective test question is accompanied by the correct answer, a textbook page reference and a brief answer description, and is coded either factual (for factual information found directly in the textbook) or applied (whereby students utilise knowledge gained to work out the appropriate answer).
- **PowerPoint (audio and video enhanced) teaching slides**, prepared by Dawn Edwards (Charles Sturt University). These visually appealing teaching slides have been enhanced with integrated audio and video content. The result is a state-of-the-art, easy-to-use instructor presentation tool that brings organisational behaviour concepts to life. Whether used in lectures, tutorials or workshops, these slides are guaranteed to stimulate student interest, analysis and discussion.
- **'OB at Work'**, updated quarterly. Organisational Behaviour at Work references recent articles from journals and magazines to relevant chapters in the textbook and provides an overview of each article, along with citation information and accompanying questions.
- **WebCT and Blackboard** support for Organisational Behaviour: Core Concepts and Applications is available for online teaching and learning designs supported by these systems. John Wiley & Sons Australia will provide content based on material that accompanies the textbook.

For students

An extensive student web site (www.johnwiley.com.au/highered/woodcore) has been developed in support of this textbook, both for classroom applications and distance-learning environments. It includes the following resources to enhance your learning experience:

- Interactive chapter revision quizzes
- Interactive self-assessments to assess your managerial style and competencies
- Glossary games to test your understanding of key terms and definitions.

CASES AND REAL-WORLD EXAMPLES AT A GLANCE

Chapter	Opening vignette	OB in action
1 What is organisational behaviour?	Vodafone	• Division of labour in fast-food restaurants • BreadTalk (Singapore) • Asian tourism • BHP Billiton • Siemens New Zealand • Real Recruitment (New Zealand) • NSW Department of Commerce • Outsourcing to India (AXA, ANZ, GE Capital) • Office location considerations • ING
2 Individual attributes and their effects on job performance	Link-up International	• Richard Branson • Women in management • Job satisfaction survey • ANZ
3 Motivation and empowerment	SalesForce (call centre)	• Rotorua Florist; Collision Repair Association • Commonwealth Bank; Western Australian Department of Premier and Cabinet; Victorian Department of Human Services • Di Lorenzo Ceramics • Jinjian Garment Factory • Compass & Foster's employee share ownership programs • Estee Lauder Group • Wilderness Society • Employee empowerment at Siemens New Zealand
4 Learning, reinforcement and self-management	CRG Medical Foundation	• New Zealand Leadership Development Centre • Bonus incentives • Mentoring in the legal profession • Centrelink • Royal Mail • Punishment • Extinction strategy • The Warehouse • Collingwood Football Club • Mercy Hospital for Women • Fred Hutchinson Cancer Research Center
5 Job design, goal setting and flexible work arrangements	Minter Ellison	• Defence Force Recruiting • Blue Chip (New Zealand) • Vector (New Zealand) • Westpac; Archives New Zealand • Woolworths • Phoenix Organic (New Zealand) • Telecom New Zealand
6 Groups and group dynamics	Coleambally Irrigation Co-operative Limited	• Airport Limousine (M) Sdn Bhd and Koperasi Jurupandu Usahawan Limosin Airport KLIA • Taronga Park Zoo • Living Nature (New Zealand) • ING; Hunter Water • St George Bank • Land Information New Zealand • Flight Centre
7 Teamwork and team building	ACT Brumbies	• GE Commercial Finance Australia and New Zealand • Executive Corporation • The Warehouse • Different explanations of teamwork • Personnel Psychology • Volunteer Service Abroad (New Zealand) • Digital • Medical research • Becton Dickinson Medical • Company board composition and performance
8 Organisational structure and design	Macquarie Bank	• Adidas-Salomon • Safe Hand Security • St George Bank • Wotif.com • Microsoft Australia • Commonwealth Bank • Wesfarmers • Kimberly-Clark • Warner Village Theme Parks • Coles Myer • Bank of Queensland; Edmen
9 Organisational culture	NSW State Rail Authority	• Office & General Cleaning Services; Deane Apparel (New Zealand) • ING • NatWest • Siebel Systems (CRM) • ADFA
10 Power, politics and influence in organisations	Dick Smith	• James Packer • Corporate governance (HIH, One.Tel) • National Australia Bank
11 Leadership	David Moffatt — Telstra	• Charismatic versus inspirational leaders • Air New Zealand • Australian emotional intelligence research • National Australia Bank • Gail Kelly (St George Group)
12 Decision making	Waterfall Inquiry	• Decision making in an uncertain environment • Saatchi & Saatchi • Sydney's second airport • *Challenger* space shuttle (NASA) • Individual vs artificial intelligence
13 Communication, conflict and negotiation in organisations	Comcare	• Noise in a university lecture • 3M • CEO forums • Dispute-resolution centres
14 Organisational change and innovation	Domino's Pizza	• BHP and Billiton merger • India Semiconductor Association

End of part cases	• RailCorp • The Singapore Government's 'Public Service for the 21st Century' strategy • National Mutual/AXA

Ethical perspective	Counterpoint	What would you do?	International spotlight	Case study
Paid maternity leave — whose responsibility is it?	Globalisation for good or evil?	The psychological contract	The dimensions of culture	Hubbard's Foods Ltd
The collapse of HIH	Incentive pay to motivate the workforce: is it working?	Sickies — staff absenteeism	Global managerial competencies	Drugs Inc.
Keeping secrets — who gets what?	Knowing and engaging our workers?	Motivation in the face of job loss	International labour	National Investment & Insurance
Paying for performance	The trouble with learning	Mentoring for better service in Sydney's hotels	Can performance incentives work for China?	A to Z Networking
Who will look after the casual workers?	Enrichment and work–life balance in the 'real world'	A proposal for maternity leave	Attracting and retaining talented global workers	Port Kembla Coal Terminal
Expected silence	Beyond groups and into the wider world	Too close for comfort?	Global education groups	A global FMCG company
Team versus personal values	Too friendly to be effective?	Adventures in team building	Cross-functional teams in the supply chain	MET — medical emergency teams
Battling fraud	Structure for the people — a workers' market?	Branch offices	Going global	Defence force recruiting
Censorship at work	Harmony and unity in culture — reality or myth?	Dress to express	Mary Kay Cosmetics in China	Johnson & Johnson's credo
Bullying and management competence	The perception of political behaviour	Working in a detention centre	News Corp	Making Memories
The accountability of company leaders	Servant leadership	Succession planning	Lessons from Jack Welch	ABC Accounting Associates — leadership challenges
Nestlé baby formula	Intuitive decision making	A sound decision?	The precautionary principle	Child protection
How much information to share	Verbal disputes in sports	Underlying conflict	Stakeholder engagement and conflict resolution	Conflict over new business strategies
Long hours and stress at work	'Resistance to change' revisited	Trouble in the accounts department	Innovation in Australia's food and agriculture sector	Planning for change at Alpha Metal Products

End of book cases • Solutions Software Company • Fisher & Paykel • Queensland Health • Workout World • KD Transport

TUTORIAL ACTIVITIES AT A GLANCE

Chapter	Individual activity	Group activity
1 What is organisational behaviour?	Global awareness	Management foundations
2 Individual attributes and their effects on job performance	Personal values	Building a more positive self-concept
3 Motivation and empowerment	Are you motivated to work hard at your studies?	What do you want from a job — motivators or hygienes?
4 Learning, reinforcement and self-management	What, when and how I learn	Getting creative with remuneration
5 Job design, goal setting and flexible work arrangements	Job design preference	Aligning personal goals with organisational goals
6 Groups and group dynamics	Analysing a group	Analysing your groups
7 Teamwork and team building	Identifying norms that influence teams	Brainstorming
8 Organisational structure and design	Vertical and horizontal specialisation: organising XYZ Paper Company	Assessing organisational structure and design
9 Organisational culture	Assessing your organisation's culture	Your university culture
10 Power, politics and influence in organisations	Influence tactics	Machiavellianism
11 Leadership	Survey of leadership	Leadership in action
12 Decision making	Decision-making biases	The fishing trip
13 Communication, conflict and negotiation in organisations	Disagreeing with your boss	Conflict resolution
14 Organisational change and innovation	Innovative attitude scale	Force field analysis

HOW TO USE THIS BOOK

Organisational Behaviour: Core Concepts and Applications, First Australasian Edition has been designed with you, the student, in mind. We aim to provide you with a tool that best communicates the subject matter and facilitates learning. The following elements have been developed to assist you.

 Learning objectives listed at the start of each chapter help you identify the essential elements of that chapter. For ease of study and navigation, these learning objectives are also signposted in the margin at the appropriate point in the body of the chapter itself, and are revisited in the chapter summary.

 These boxed features throughout the text show how people can make a difference in the way organisations operate by highlighting progressive or innovative practices from the real world.

 Ethical Perspective features highlight situations and dilemmas that may affect investor, consumer and staff attitudes, the long- and short-term economic viability of the organisation, and management practices.

 Counterpoint features provide an opposing view to stimulate discussion, analysis and the development of critical thinking skills.

 Regularly throughout the text, you will be asked to put yourself in the shoes of a decision maker and to propose a solution to an organisational issue.

 International Spotlight features elaborate on the management practices of organisations around the world, particulary focusing on those operating in the Asia–Pacific region.

 Practical tips and checklists provide advice on how to achieve high performance in dynamic and demanding work environments.

STUDY GUIDE

Each chapter concludes with an integrated study guide. Designed for self-study, it includes:
• a list of key terms • review, application and research questions • a running project
• individual and group activities • a case study.

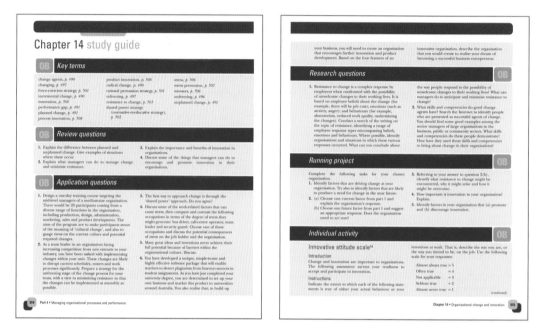

END OF PART AND END OF BOOK CASE STUDIES

Additional situational and real-life cases of varying lengths enable you to apply what you have learnt to key concepts from multiple chapters.

PREFACE

Organisational Behaviour: Core Concepts and Applications, First Australasian Edition is based on the popular *Organisational Behaviour, 3rd edition* by Wood et al. This core concepts edition has retained the key themes of the original work, while reflecting the content coverage of a typical one-semester organisational behaviour subject. Content is relevant and tightly focused, to engage rather than overwhelm students.

The text is divided into a flexible four-part structure that clearly articulates the importance of studying and understanding organisational behaviour as a discipline. Beginning with an explanation of organisational behaviour as a concept, the text progresses logically through managing the various organisational components of individuals, groups, teams and processes with a consistent theme of enhancing organisational *performance.*

In the information age, business prosperity is increasingly based on the intellectual capital of organisations. That is, the information in people's minds, rather than physical capital or the material resources within a country. The rapid pace of scientific and technological advances is enabling unprecedented communication and competition in the global marketplace.

This information revolution is creating information organisations. These emerging organisations are quite different from their predecessors. Typically, they are smaller and smarter; they have core, peripheral and outsourced staff; their keys to success are information and knowledge; their organisational structures are fluid and organic to make them more responsive to necessary changes; hierarchies are minimised; and expert teams of employees solve problems and make decisions. The Internet, videoconferencing and other communication technologies allow telecommuting to be a reality for some workers, for at least part of the working week.

Technology is not the only evolving variable for contemporary managers. A more culturally diverse workforce, with individual differences in traditions, values and attitudes across cultures is now more common in the workplace. This workforce is also becoming more flexible and demanding, wanting an environment where their work is interesting and challenging, where they have autonomy and are empowered to take responsibility. Managers must continually monitor and balance what an employee wants from an organisation, and what the organisation can offer and needs in order to be effective.

These changes are placing enormous pressures on all managers striving to make their organisations effective in the business environment of the twenty-first century. It is increasingly clear that new and modified managerial competencies are required to maintain a company's competitive edge. Flatter organisational structures signal a change in the use of power by managers; more emphasis has to be placed on communication, which is the life blood of any organisation; and managers and leaders with vision are required to transform their organisations in an ever-changing landscape. New structures and job designs are required to facilitate teamwork and learning in knowledge-based organisations, promoting efficiency and minimising conflict.

These transformations are seldom achieved easily. However, embracing and initiating change in an organisation is essential for achieving a competitive edge. Ultimately, management is about getting results — the right results. We live in an age where change is a constant, and this poses challenges. However, while the challenges are vast, this environment is also exciting.

Organisational Behaviour: Core Concepts and Applications, First Australasian Edition is designed to help intending managers to cope more effectively with the pressures and demands of the information age. It also updates the field of organisational behaviour to incorporate the new challenges associated with the emergence of the knowledge-based organisation and the global marketplace. Effective managers require a sound understanding of the organisational frameworks, theories and practices presented in this text if they are to meet the increasingly challenging performance targets associated with managerial life.

The author team would like to thank the many academics who have contributed so much to our total resource offering by way of reviews, case contributions and writing lecturer support material:

- Case contributors — Val Morrison (Southern Cross University), Ron Fisher (Griffith University)
- Lecturer support material — Andrew Creed (Deakin University), Dawn Edwards (Charles Sturt University), Sue Heap (Auckland University of Technology), Michele Fromholtz (Charles Sturt University).
- Reviewers — Dr Philip Reece (Murdoch University), Val Morrison (Southern Cross University), Ken Parry (Griffith University), Melanie Bryant (Monash University), Graham Elkin (Otago University), John Gilbert (Waikato University), Sunia Vosikata (University of the South Pacific), Kerry Unsworth (Queensland University of Technology), Brad Jackson (Victoria University of Wellington).

Thanks also to the authors who have worked over the years on the larger version of the text, which formed the basis of this edition: Joe Wallace, Judith Chapman and Val Morrison.

We would also like to thank the editorial team at John Wiley & Sons for their assistance in the development of this textbook and its associated resources. We trust that it will make the teaching and studying of Organisational Behaviour a rewarding experience.

Jack Wood
Rachid Zeffane
Michele Fromholtz
Anneke Fitzgerald

May 2006

ABOUT THE AUTHORS

Professor Jack Wood (PhD, Alberta, Canada) has held numerous senior management positions in higher education, including Deputy Vice-Chancellor International and Corporate at Central Queensland University; Professor of Management, Associate Dean International and Director of International Programs within the Faculty of Business and Economics at Monash University; MBA Director at both the University of Sydney and Monash University; and he was the Foundation Professor in Management at Monash–Mt Eliza Business School. He has published about ninety articles on management education, and is the author of and a contributor to a number of books in this field. His major research interests are knowledge management, the virtual workplace, work time options and improvements to the performance of Australian expatriate management, with special reference to Asia. He has been an Australian delegate to Asia–Pacific Economic Cooperation (APEC) meetings in Osaka, Japan, and has also worked as a consultant for the Organisation for Economic Co-operation and Development (OECD) in Paris and for the New Ways to Work organisation in San Francisco. Jack Wood has served as an executive member of the Australia and New Zealand Academy of Management (ANZAM) for a number of years.

Dr Rachid Zeffane BSc Economics (Algiers), MSc (Management) and PhD (Management and Organisational Behaviour) (Wales) is Associate Professor in Management and Organisational Behaviour at the College of Business Administration, University of Sharjah, United Arab Emirates. He was formerly Associate Professor in Management at the Bowater School of Management and Marketing, Deakin University, and has also held academic positions at Griffith University (Qld) and the University of Newcastle (NSW). He has extensive national and international experience in teaching and research in the areas of Organisational Behaviour and Management at both undergraduate and postgraduate levels, and has also led several executive programs. He has over fifty publications in international journals, including two papers selected for the prestigious *Classic Research in Management*, edited by Professor Derek Pugh (1998). His research work appears in leading international journals such as the *International Journal of Human Resource Management*, *Journal of Management Studies*, *Social Science Research*, *Organization Studies*, *Human Systems Management* and the *International Journal of Employment Relations*. He has also consulted to major Australian organisations on a variety of management-related issues and projects.

Michele Fromholtz is a lecturer in Organisational Behaviour and Public Sector Management at Charles Sturt University, New South Wales. She holds a Bachelor of Business (Business Administration), a Bachelor of Arts, a Master of Public Administration, and a Graduate Certificate in University Teaching and Learning. Currently on the board of directors of a local business enterprise centre, she has also undertaken consultancy work, and been directly employed in the public sector and involved with several community organisations. Her research interests include regional and community development, organisational culture and workplace folklore, and the decision-making behaviour of policy implementers in public sector organisations.

Dr Janna (Anneke) Fitzgerald is a senior lecturer and Research Studies Program Coordinator for the College of Business at the University of Western Sydney. She has a PhD in Management and was originally trained as a Registered Nurse. After many years as a health manager and educator she pursued an academic career in the discipline of Organisation Studies. Her research and writing interests include organisational decision making in the context of healthcare management. She is currently leading international research into professional identity influences on organisational decision making comparing triage systems in The Netherlands and New South Wales. In addition, she is leading a large research project investigating the relationship between working in synchronisation with natural drives and occupational wellbeing. She currently teaches Organisational Behaviour and Research Methodology and supervises several higher degree students in related areas of research.

ACKNOWLEDGEMENTS

The authors and publisher would like to thank the following copyright holders, organisations and individuals for permission to reproduce copyright material in this book.

Images

© Purestock: **3** (left), **118** (lower left), **403, 485, 525** • Newspix: **6, 51, 345** (photo)/Graham Crouch; **43** (photo)/Ross Schultz; **304**/AFP Photo/Australian Defence Department/HO; **350**/Cameron Richardson; **404**/Jon Hargest • Getty Images: **8** (top)/AFP/Roslan Rahman; **16**/Darren McCollester; **238**/Tim Barnett; **294**/Paul Broben; **527**/Michael Bradley • © Digital Stock: **8** (bottom), **80, 123, 263, 398, 419** (background), **437, 533** • Fairfax Photo Library: **14**/Jessica Hromas; **349**/Bryan Charlton; **383** (left)/AFR/Rob Homer • Copyright Clearance Center: **20** based on Hofstede's five dimensions of national cultures from the *Academy of Management Executive*, 'Cultural constraints in management theories' by Geert Hofstede, vol. 7, 1993; **43** (top) republished with permission of the *Academy of Management Review* from 'The missing opportunity in organizational research: some implications for a theory of work performance' by Blumberg & Pringle, vol. 7, 1982, p. 565. Both permission via the Copyright Clearance Center • © Banana Stock: **23, 132** • AAP Image: **25**/AP Photo/Gautam Singh; **343** (left)/Paul Miller; **479**/AFP Photo/Greg Wood • © PhotoDisc, Inc.: **33, 41** (top), **98, 108, 113** (left), **144, 152, 156, 200, 223, 245, 249, 258, 267** (left), **271, 274, 280, 311, 315, 317, 421, 441, 447, 456, 458, 474, 494, 499, 507, 509** (photo), **512** • © image addict.com.au: **57** © John Fairfax Publications Pty Limited • John Wiley & Sons Australia: **59, 120**; and **79, 92, 194, 234, 329, 347, 440**/photos by Kari-Ann Tapp • © Digital Vision: **70, 138, 149** (left), **193** (top), **328, 414, 477** (photo), **518, 530, 536** • © EyeWire Images: **77** (left) • Marc Wallace Jr: **85** from *Managing behavior in organizations* by Marc Wallace Jr & Andrew D. Szilagyi, © 1982, Scott, Foresman & Company. Reproduced with permission of the authors • Harvard Business School Publishing Corporation: **87** adapted and reprinted by permission of *Harvard Business Review*, exhibit 1 from 'One more time: how do you motivate employees?' by Frederick Herzberg, Sep–Oct 1987, © 2002 Harvard Business School Publishing Corporation. All rights reserved • Elsevier: **118** (top) adapted from *Organizational Dynamics*, Autumn 1984, Kreitner & Luthans, 'A social learning approach to behavioral management', p. 55, © 1984; **371** reprinted from *Organizational Dynamics*, August 1983, Velasquez, Moberg & Cavanagh, 'Organizational statesmanship and dirty politics', p. 73, © 1983. Both with permission from Elsevier • © The Warehouse (New Zealand): **128** • American Psychological Association: **155** adapted from J. Richard Hackman & Greg R. Oldham, 'Development of the job diagnostic survey', *Journal of Applied Psychology*, vol. 60 (1975), © 1975 by the American Psychological Association. Adapted with permission • © Corbis Corporation: **159, 309** (left), **428** • © DFR: **161**/Jeff Burnham • Blackwell Publishers: **163** from E. A. Locke & G. P. Latham, 'Work motivation and satisfaction: light at the end of the tunnel', *Psychological Science*, vol. 1, no. 4, July 1990. Reproduced with permission of Blackwell Publishing • Australian Picture Library: **180**/Lightstorm — S & B Kendrick; **185**/John Van Hasselt • Coleambally Irrigation Co-operative Limited: **189** • McGraw-Hill USA: **191** © R. Likert, *New patterns of management* (1961). Reproduced with the permission of The McGraw-Hill Companies, Inc.; **288** © Hodgetts & Luthans, *International management* (1997). Reproduced with the permission of The McGraw-Hill Companies, Inc.; **394** adapted from Fred Luthans, *Organizational behavior*, 6th edn, ch. 10 (© NY: McGraw-Hill, 1992) and ideas derived from Kerr and Jermier, 'Substitutes for leadership', *Organizational Behavior and Human Performance*, vol. 22 (1978), p. 387 • © IT StockFree: **196, 277, 377, 453** (left) • Pearson Education US: **208** Edgar Schein, *Process consultation*, vol. 1, 2nd edn, © 1998, pp. 81 & 82. Reprinted by permission of Pearson Education, Inc., Upper Saddle River, NJ • © Sport The Library: **227** (left)/Photosport • Collingwood Football Club: **243** reproduced with the permission of Collingwood Football Club and the Winners Sports Nutrition Company • John Wiley & Sons, Inc: **247, 509** (top); **392** adapted from *Organizational theory: an integrated approach* by R. Osborn, J. Hunt & L. Jauch, © 1980; **492** from *Corporate comeback* by Robert H. Miles, Jossey-Bass, © 1997; **498** (figures 14.4 and 14.5) adapted from *Managing strategic change: technical, political and cultural dynamics* by N. Tichy, © 1983. All reprinted with permission of John Wiley & Sons, Inc. • © Image Source: **316** • Johnson & Johnson: **336** (logo) reproduced courtesy of Johnson & Johnson • © Brand X Pictures: **367** • Grid International Inc.: **388** reproduced by permission from *Leadership dilemmas — grid solutions* © 1995. Gulf Publishing Company, Houston, TX. All rights reserved • © Flat Earth: **424** • © ImageState: **459** • Allyn & Bacon: **470** from R. Wayne Pace & Don F. Faules, *Organizational communication*, 3rd edn, published by Allyn & Bacon, Boston, MA. © 1994 by Pearson Education. Reprinted by permission of the publisher • © Stockdisc: **489** (left) • © Fancy Images: **523**.

Text

John Wiley & Sons, Inc.: **54–5** (table 2.1) from *Managing workforce 2000* by D. Jamieson & J. O'Mara, Jossey-Bass, © 1991; **445–6** (Individual activity) adapted from Max H. Bazerman, *Judgement in managerial decision making*, 3rd edn, Wiley, NY, © 1994. Both reprinted with permission of John Wiley & Sons, Inc. • McGraw-Hill USA: **68–9**, **69–70**, **107** © Robert N. Lussier, *Human relations in organizations: a skill building approach*, 2nd edn, Homewood, IL, Richard D. Irwin, 1993; **399–400** *Jack Welch and the GE way* by Robert Slater, 1999. Both reproduced with the permission of The McGraw-Hill Companies, Inc. • James Hall: **77** *AFR Boss*, July 2004 • Barry Fitzgerald: **95** *The Sydney Morning Herald*, 14 March 2005 • NIACE: **141–2** first published by NIACE, 1998, in 'Your life, your work, your future' • Tracey Evans: **149** Jane Cherrington, *Management Today*, May 2005 • Richard Hackman: **177–9** © *The job diagnostic survey: an instrument for the diagnosis of jobs and the evaluation of job redesign projects*, technical report 4, J. R. Hackman, G. R. Oldham • Carolyn Rance: **179–80** *HR Monthly*, September 2005 • © Text Pacific Publishing: **200–1** This article appeared in the September 2004 edition of Australia's leading magazine for managers: *Management Today* (published by Text Pacific Publishing for the Australian Institute of management) www.aim.com.au; **237–8** This article appeared in the May 2005 edition of Australia's leading magazine for managers: *Management Today* (published by text Pacific Publishing for the Australian Institute of management) www.aim.com.au • Jody Marshall for Response Design Group, Sydney: **222–3** 'Accommodating innovation', *HR Monthly*, May 2004 • Journalists Copyright: **227** John Stensholt, *BRW*, 16–22 June 2005; **267** Adele Ferguson, *BRW*, 25–31 August 2005. By permission of Journalists Copyright • Hardie Grant Magazines: **303–4** 'On manoeuvres' by Scott Latham, *HR Monthly*, April 2005, pp. 30–4. Reproduced with the permission of Hardie Grant Publishing • Debra Woog McGinty: **334–5** © 2001 — Connect2 Corporation and Blueprint. All Rights Reserved. Reproduced with the permission of the authors: Debra Woog McGinty and Nicole Moss • Johnson & Johnson: **336–7** reproduced courtesy of Johnson & Johnson • Australian Broadcasting Corporation: **350–2** extracts from the *Lateline* program 'Woomera detention centre doctor speaks out' first broadcast on ABC TV *Lateline* on 27 October 2004, reproduced by permission of the Australian Broadcasting Corporation and ABC Online. © 2004 ABC. All rights reserved. The full text is available at: http://www.abc.net.au/lateline/content/2004/s1229335.htm • Elsevier: **376–7** adapted from *Studies in machiavellianism* by Richard Christie and Florence L. Geis, p. 17, © 1970, with permission from Elsevier • Australian Business Limited: **401–2** reprinted with permission of leading business advisory group, Australian Business Limited/State Chamber, www.australianbusiness.com.au • Institute for Social Research: **411–12** adapted from *The survey of organizations*, © 1980 by The University of Michigan. Reprinted by permission of the Institute for Social Research • Pearson Education US: **412–13** David A. Kolb, Joyce S. Osland, Irwin M. Rubin, *Organizational behavior: an experiential approach*, 6th edn, © 1995. Reproduced by permission of Pearson Education, Inc., Upper Saddle River, NJ • Attorney General's Department, NSW: **419** reproduced with the permission of the Director General, Attorney General's Department of NSW • © Lee Hopkins: **462–3** from 'Minimising conflict with effective communication', from http://www.conflict911.com/guestconflict/minimizingconflict.htm • Newmont Mining Corporation: **471–2** • Commonwealth Copyright Administration: **489** www.innovation.gov.au, The National Innovation Council, Department of Industry, Tourism and Resources, © Commonwealth of Australia, reproduced by permission • Department of Agriculture: **509–510** from the Innovation Australia website © Stroudgate Australasia Pty Ltd, www.stroudgate.net/innovation and the Minister for Agriculture Fisheries and Forestry, The Hon. Peter McGauran MP and Commonwealth Department of Agriculture, Fisheries and Forestry • Blackwell publishers: **515–6** from J. E. Ettlie & R. D. O'Keefe, 'Innovative attitudes, values and intentions in organizations', *Journal of Management Studies*, vol. 19, 1982. Reproduced with permission of Blackwell Publishing • Andrew Penn: **521–3** adapted from Andrew Penn, 'Transformational change: a case study', Mt Eliza Business School, www.mteliza.com.au • Mary Mallon: **527–8** adapted from M. Mallon and T. Kearney, *Asia Pacific Journal of Human Resources*, 2001, 39 (1), pp. 93–106. Reproduced with the permission of the author.

Every effort has been made to trace the ownership of copyright material. Information that will enable the publisher to rectify any error or omission in subsequent editions will be welcome. In such cases, please contact the Permissions Section of John Wiley & Sons Australia, Ltd who will arrange for the payment of the usual fee.

PART 1

INTRODUCTION

1 What is organisational behaviour?   *2*

CHAPTER 1

What is organisational behaviour?

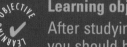

Learning objectives
After studying this chapter, you should be able to:

1. define organisational behaviour

2. explain why organisations exist

3. discuss the role of managers in organisations

4. discuss some of the key issues affecting organisations today

5. explain why managers, and organisational members generally, need a thorough understanding of organisational behaviour principles.

'You'll find plenty of conversation, noise and laughter as we bounce ideas off each other to find simple and clever ways of delighting our customers.'[1] That's how mobile phone operator Vodafone describes its work environment. Mobile communications is one of the fastest-changing and competitive industries. Success depends on providing innovative technology matched with high standards of customer service.

Vodafone Group is a multinational company with about 165 million customers worldwide. It was founded in the UK but now operates, either directly or with partners, in more than 40 countries.[2] Vodafone Asia Pacific has more than 19 million customers in Australia, New Zealand, Japan and Fiji.

Vodafone entered the New Zealand market in 1998 by purchasing BellSouth New Zealand. It has more than 55 per cent of the New Zealand mobile market and employs more than 1300 people.[3] Relatively few of those people are managers. Vodafone New Zealand has chosen a 'flat' structure to keep decisions closer to the customer, 'in the hands of those who need it'.[4] Giving its workers the power to make decisions means customers get faster service.

Vodafone New Zealand also seeks to reward its workers in innovative ways. As an example of this, Vodafone has its employees nominate coworkers as 'Legends' and then chooses winners who receive an international resort holiday. Increasingly, workers are not just seeking money in exchange for work. They want the work itself to be rewarding and they are looking for employers that offer more. Vodafone tries to offer rewards that will attract people it thinks are the right 'fit' for the company. Vodafone Australia's director of people and brand Wendy Lenton says: 'We're trying to attract a certain kind of person in the first place. You've got to fit in with the culture … every touch point needs to align with our values and culture.'[5] This approach extends to its communication with employees. Rather than issuing memos and email after email, Vodafone holds a monthly meeting called 'The Fatt' which involves quizzes, handouts and other interactive activities to introduce new policies, ideas and programs.[6]

Vodafone's New Zealand operation has to be considered a success, holding more than half the market. In fact, its former CEO Grahame Maher was brought to the Australian operation in 2001 to try to salvage the business, which was losing hundreds of millions of dollars a year. Within a few years under Maher, Vodafone Australia turned its first profit. Maher's solution was to reduce staff numbers by more than half, rely more on outsourcing and, in particular, change the culture of the company. Having successfully turned Vodafone Australia around, Maher left in 2005 to head Vodafone Sweden, saying he wanted to experience working in a non-English-speaking country.[7] This is another theme evident at Vodafone. When it comes to management and organisational culture, one size does not fit all, but there is much to be learned from people and organisations around the world. Being a global organisation, many employees are seconded to other countries to learn alternative ways of doing things.

Introduction

Recall how Vodafone describes itself: 'You'll find plenty of conversation, noise and laughter as we bounce ideas off each other to find simple and clever ways of delighting our customers.'[8] You couldn't say that about every organisation; perhaps for many organisations it wouldn't work. But it does seem to work for Vodafone and it reflects many of the fundamental ingredients of a successful organisation: its members are engaged and happy with their task; ideas are shared; workers are supported; the organisation is delivering a product that satisfies its customers; and the customers make the company profitable.

Throughout this book you will learn about the complex field of organisational behaviour — what people and groups do in organisations, and why. We will place a particular emphasis on learning the skills you will need to be an effective manager within the organisations of today and tomorrow. Organisations of all kinds depend on managers to help ensure the work experiences of others are both productive and satisfying. Managers must act and think in the right ways, and they must do so even as great changes take place in the environment. Some significant influences on organisations today are: globalisation, information and communications technology, the emergence of a knowledge-based economy, an increasingly diverse workforce, and some significant changes in how employers and employees view each other. These types of changes require managers and other organisational members who are committed to learning and practising effective organisational behaviour. We hope this book will help you along that path.

What is organisational behaviour?

Organisational behaviour defined

LEARNING OBJECTIVE 1

Formally defined, organisational behaviour is the study of individuals and groups in organisations. It emerged as an academic discipline during the late 1940s and has been prominent as an academic subject in business schools since then.

Organisational behaviour has strong ties to the behavioural sciences such as psychology, sociology and anthropology, as well as to allied social sciences such as economics and political science. It draws on this variety of scholarly vantage points to build concepts, theories and understandings about human behaviour in organisations. Organisational behaviour is unique in its focus on applying these diverse insights to create better understanding and management of human behaviour in organisations.

> **Organisational behaviour** is the study of individuals and groups in organisations.

Among the special characteristics of organisational behaviour are its:

- *Applied focus.* The ultimate goals of the field are to help people and organisations achieve high performance levels, and to help ensure all organisation members achieve satisfaction from their task contributions and work experiences.[9]
- *Contingency orientation.* Rather than assume that there is a universal way in which to manage people and organisations, organisational behaviour scholars adopt a contingency approach.[10] That is, they recognise that behaviour may vary systematically depending on the circumstances and the people involved. For example, organisational behaviour scholars recognise that 'cultural differences' among people may affect the way theories and concepts of management apply in different countries.[11] Management practices cannot simply be transferred from one part of the world to another without considering the cultural implications of the different settings in which they are to be applied.

> A **contingency approach** is the attempt by organisational behaviour scholars to identify how situations can be understood and managed in ways that appropriately respond to their unique characteristics.

- *Emphasis on scientific inquiry.* Organisational behaviour uses scientific methods to develop and empirically test generalisations about behaviour in organisations.[12] The three key characteristics of scientific thinking that underpin organisational behaviour research and study are: the controlled and systematic process of data collection; careful testing of the proposed explanations; and acceptance of only explanations that can be scientifically verified.

Organisational behaviour is not a static discipline. Managers are constantly seeking new insights and ideas to improve their effectiveness. Maybe you have already heard of some of these concepts: best practice, benchmarking, the learning organisation, the virtual workplace and knowledge management, to name a few. The study of organisational behaviour is improving our understanding of old and new concepts alike; such issues as stress, emotional intelligence and instinctive drive, all of which you'll learn about as you progress through this book.

The field of organisational behaviour helps managers both deal with and learn from their workplace experiences. Managers who understand organisational behaviour are better prepared to know what to look for in work situations, to understand what they find, and to take (or help others to take) the required action.

Effective managers need to understand the people that they rely on for the performance of their unit. While each person, team/group and organisation is complex and unique, an individual's, team's/group's or organisation's performance depends on their *capacity* to work, *willingness* to work and *opportunity* to work. This concept can be summarised by the performance equation (figure 1.1). The performance equation views performance as the result of the personal and/or group attributes, the work effort they make and the organisational support they receive.

Performance equation: Job performance = attributes × work effort × organisational support.

Job performance	=	attributes	×	work effort	×	organisational support

FIGURE 1.1 • The performance equation

This equation can be applied to the three different units of analysis that form the structure of this book: individual, group/team, and organisation. The multiplication signs indicate that all three factors must be present for high performance to be achieved. This means that each factor should be maximised for each unit of analysis (individual, group/team and organisation) in a work setting if the maximum level of accomplishment is to be realised. Every manager must understand how these three factors, acting either alone or in combination, can affect performance. We will use this equation as the theoretical guide for much of the material presented in this book. Part 2 looks at individual behaviour and performance. In chapter 2 we will address individual attributes required to generate performance *capacity*; chapters 3 and 4 deal with motivation and volition to generate a *willingness* to perform; and chapter 5 points at how organisations can provide individuals with the best *opportunity* to perform. Part 3 of the book looks at organisational performance from a group/team level and organisational level and Part 4 combines individual performance, group performance and organisational processes in the context of organisational behaviour. Even though these concepts are presented in different parts and chapters of this book, they are highly related. Remember the multiplication sign in the performance equation indicates that all three factors (attributes, work effort and organisational support) must be present to gain a high level of performance.

For practitioners, the performance equation raises the question of whether performance is predictable. It is suggested that cognitive ability, or intelligence (as measured by IQ), is a reasonable predictor of job performance.[13] However, many human resource managers would argue that additional testing is required to ensure a good fit between capability and expected performance. Over the past few years the concept of 'emotional intelligence' (EI or EQ) has surfaced, sparking hopes for creating another way to predict performance. Emotional intelligence is defined as a form of social intelligence that allows us to monitor and shape our emotions and those of others.

Emotional intelligence is a form of social intelligence that allows us to monitor and shape our emotions and those of others.

Daniel Goleman suggests that emotional competence is a learned capability, based on emotional intelligence, that results in outstanding work performance.[14] In these domains EI is considered to be a competency for performance. For example, a person with a level of emotional intelligence is competent in recognising their own strengths and weaknesses.

Reuven Bar-On developed a self-assessment instrument (emotional quotient inventory, or EQi)[15] measuring traits and abilities related to social knowledge. The EQi is a measure of psychological wellbeing and adaptation, and can be a measure related to performance. Jack Meyer and Peter Salovey profess that EI is composed of mental abilities and skills.[16] They see EI as a form of intelligence that processes and benefits from emotions. They believe that other measures of intelligence fail to take into account individual differences in the ability to perceive, process and manage emotions. Chapter 2 expands on the notion of emotional intelligence as one of the individual attributes as a predictor for the capacity to perform.

Why organisations exist

LEARNING 2 OBJECTIVE

Why do organisations exist?

Simply stated, organisations exist because individuals are limited in their physical and mental capabilities. Organisations are mechanisms through which many people combine their efforts and work together to accomplish more than any one person could alone.

The purpose of any organisation is to produce a product or service. Large and small businesses produce a diverse array of consumer products and services such as motor vehicles, appliances, telecommunications and accommodation. Not-for-profit organisations produce services with public benefits, such as health care and rehabilitation, public education and park maintenance.

A clear statement of purpose, or 'goal statement', is important to guide the activities of an organisation and its members. To illustrate, the following are goals of some prominent organisations:

- 'to be the world's mobile communications leader — enriching customers' lives, helping individuals, businesses and communities be more connected in a mobile world' (Vodafone Group)[17]
- 'to enhance our businesses and strengthen our position as a premier integrated communications services provider in the Asia Pacific region' (SingTel)[18]
- 'to maximise income and provide long-term sustainable returns to unit holders through the strategic acquisition, professional management and ongoing development of office, retail and industrial assets' (KIWI Income and Property Trust)[19]
- 'to create long-term value through the discovery, development and conversion of natural resources, and the provision of innovative customer and market-focused solutions' (BHP Billiton)[20]
- 'to put the customer first and let everything else, every business activity and consideration, flow from that principle' (The Warehouse).[21]

Division of labour is the process of breaking the work to be done into specialised tasks that individuals or groups can perform.

To achieve its purpose, any organisation depends on human effort. The division of labour is the process of breaking the work to be done into specialised tasks that individuals or groups can perform: it is a way of organising the efforts of many people to their best advantage.

OB in action

The division of labour and task specialisation will be quite clear in your favourite fast-food restaurant — McDonald's, Eagle Boys, Hungry Jacks, KFC, Ali Baba's and so on. Certain people take your order and your money, others cook the food, and still others clean after everyone else has gone home for the night. By dividing the labour and training employees to perform highly specialised tasks, these companies strive for excellence in task accomplishment.

A good division of labour helps an organisation mobilise the work of many people to achieve its purpose.

A well-functioning organisation with a clear purpose and appropriate division of labour, like those of fast-food restaurants, achieves synergy, which is the creation of a whole that is greater than the sum of its parts. Synergy in organisations occurs when people work well together while using available resources to pursue a common purpose. In psychology this is called a 'gestalt'.[22] Within an effective organisation, this 'gestalt' is created by the organisation's division of labour, task specialisation and hierarchy of authority, as well as by effective managerial behaviour.

Synergy is the creation of a whole that is greater than the sum of its parts.

Organisations as open systems

Organisations ultimately depend for their success on the activities and collective efforts of many people. People are the essential human resources of an organisation — the individuals and groups whose performance contributions enable the organisation to serve a particular purpose. But organisations need more than people if they are to survive and prosper. They also need material resources, which are the technology, information, physical equipment and facilities, raw materials and money necessary for an organisation to produce some useful product or service.

Many organisational behaviour scholars believe that organisations can be best understood as open systems that transform human and material resource 'inputs' received from their environment into product 'outputs' in the form of finished goods and/or services. The outputs are then offered to the environment for consumption. If everything works, measured via feedback, the environment accepts these outputs and allows the organisation to obtain the resource inputs it needs to continue operating in the future (figure 1.2).

Human resources are the individuals and groups whose contributions enable the organisation to serve a particular purpose.

Material resources are the technology, information, physical equipment and facilities, raw material and money that are necessary for an organisation to produce some product or service.

Open systems transform human and physical resources received from their environment into goods and services that are then returned to the environment.

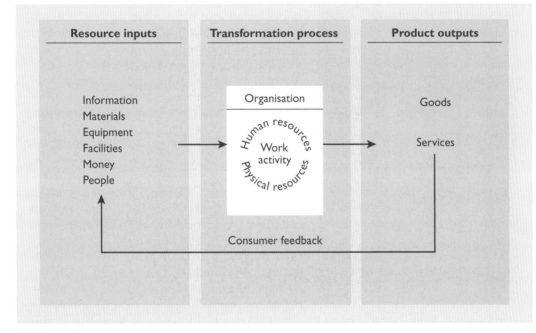

FIGURE 1.2 • How an organisation operates as an open system

Of course, things can go wrong; an organisation's survival depends on satisfying environmental demands. When the organisation's goods and/or services are not well received by the environment, it will sooner or later have difficulty obtaining the resource inputs it needs to operate.

One company that is responding to its environment is BreadTalk. Founded in 2000, BreadTalk has grown to become one of the most recognisable local brands in the food and beverage industry in Singapore. This is evidenced by its 'Singapore Promising Brand Award 2002'. The brand is known for the way it has revolutionised the culture of bread consumption in Singapore with its 'visually appealing, aromatic and unique-tasting products'. When the 'Floss bun' (a very sweet soft and fluffy bun) was first introduced in 2000 the BreadTalk brand was propelled to stardom and took Singapore consumers by storm. The brand has already gone regional with four franchised outlets in Jakarta, two wholly owned stores in Shanghai, and several more franchised outlets due to open in the Gulf Cooperation Council, Malaysia and the Philippines.[23] There is now hope to expand to Australia and New Zealand. Think about how BreadTalk's experience reflects the system in figure 1.2.

Just as business outcomes have an impact on the business environment and society as a whole, world events can also influence business survival. The tourism industry was greatly affected by the 2004 Boxing Day tsunami and the October 2002 and 2005 terrorism attacks in Bali. Although initially the tourism industry in Indonesia and Malaysia slumped as a result of these events, the industry responded by applying survival strategies and some improved their performance as a direct result of refocusing the market. For example, after the 2002 bombings, the Indonesian tourism authorities and commercial providers actively promoted Bali to markets that, unlike Australia, did not have an emotional association with the Bali bombings. This resulted in a boost for Bali, where visitors from Singapore to Bali lifted from 17 666 in 2002 to 26 881 in 2003.[24]

Other tourism businesses in the Asia–Pacific region responded to the change in business environment. After the Bali bombings, Australia promoted its destinations as 'safe' and the Philippines promoted its resorts as unaffected by the Boxing Day tsunami. Both countries seized upon the opportunity to attract tourists that might otherwise have travelled to Bali or the Malaysian coast.[25] Time will tell if these tourism businesses are able to sustain growth by attracting returning tourists in the future, or if loyal Bali and Malaysian coast patrons return to their previous preferred destinations.

Managers in organisations

Now that we share a basic understanding of organisations, we can speak more precisely about what it means to be a manager. A manager is a person in an organisation who is responsible for work that is accomplished through the performance contributions of one or more other people.

Today, the focus of both management research and practice is not so much on the manager as on the work team or unit. A work team or unit is a task-oriented group that includes a manager and his or her direct reports. Such groups are found in organisations of all types, and they can be small or large. Examples include departments in a retail store, divisions of a corporation, branches of a bank, wards in a hospital and teams in a manufacturing plant. Even a university class can be considered a work team; the lecturer is its manager and the students are team members. The study of such work teams has become a key area of organisational behaviour research.

What is an effective manager?

It is not easy to define what makes a manager an effective manager within a business context. The list of managerial competencies identified over the past few decades helps us understand more clearly the competencies required for effective management. However, such research also illustrates the difficulties in defining effective management because it is still hard to achieve expert consensus on what constitutes a basic core of competencies. It is even more difficult to find agreement on prioritised rankings of such competencies.[26] Many of the best-known writers in the management literature typically emphasise one managerial competence at the expense of all others. Tom Peters, for example, stresses that good managers are *doers*. (Wall Street says they 'do deals'.) Michael Porter emphasises that they are *thinkers*. Zalesnick and Bennis believe good managers are really *leaders*, whereas, historically, Fayol and Urwick have portrayed good managers as *controllers*.[27]

Fundamentally, any manager should seek two key results for a work unit or work team: task performance, which is the quality and quantity of the work produced or the services provided by the work unit; and human resource maintenance, which is the attraction and continuation of a capable workforce over time. This latter notion, while too often neglected, is extremely important. It is not enough for a work unit to achieve high performance on any given day; it must be able to achieve this level of performance every day, both now and into the future. Good human resource maintenance is a major concern of organisational behaviour. It directs a manager's attention to matters such as job satisfaction, job involvement, organisational commitment, absenteeism and turnover, as well as performance. Wendy Lenton, Vodafone director of people and brand, points out that 'The theory is that if you care for your people, your people will care for you, but if people feel unappreciated or unhappy at work, the anxiety manifests into ill health, low motivation, low productivity and absenteeism.'[28]

This book treats high performance and good human resource maintenance as results that any manager should seek. Indeed, the two results can be seen as the criteria for an effective manager — that is, a manager whose work unit achieves high levels of task accomplishment and maintains itself as a capable workforce over time. This concept of the 'effective manager' offers an important framework for understanding organisational behaviour and developing personal managerial skills. A special text feature, 'The effective manager', is used in this and later chapters to help remind us of these applications.

Managing task performance

Recall that task performance is the quality and quantity of the work produced or the services provided. An effective manager must be concerned with the 'productivity' of work units and their members. Formally defined, productivity is a summary measure of the

OBJECTIVE 3 LEARNING The role of managers

A **manager** is responsible for work that is accomplished through the performance contributions of others.

Work teams or **units** are task-oriented groups that include a manager and his or her direct reports.

Task performance is the quality and quantity of work produced.

Human resource maintenance is the attraction and continuation of a viable workforce.

An **effective manager** is a manager whose work unit achieves high levels of task accomplishment and maintains itself as a capable workforce over time.

Productivity is a summary measure of the quantity and quality of work performance that also accounts for resource use.

quantity and quality of work performance achieved (task performance) that also accounts for resource use. It is not acceptable simply to 'get a job done'; any job must be done with the best use of available resources — human and material. Productivity is a benchmark of managerial and organisational success.

The best organisations want value-added managers, whose efforts clearly enable their work units to achieve high productivity and improve 'bottom-line' performance. Value-added managers create high-performance systems in which individuals and groups work well together, to the benefit of the entire organisation and its clients or customers. Value-added managers are also the most likely to reap the rewards of satisfying careers. In an age of organisational restructuring and downsizing, often designed to reduce the number of management levels, value-added managers have little trouble justifying their jobs. The advice of consultant Tom Peters is worth considering: 'Middle Managers: Act like a consultant. Make friends with the line, create projects...Your job, salary, and esteem are all in mortal danger...are you ready?'[29] In many ways, this book is about you becoming a value-added manager.

Today's managers are confronted with a considerable dilemma. They are seeking ever-increasing added value from their stock of human capital. For example, Vodafone pursues this through a flat organisational structure and greater worker participation in decision making. On the other hand, while these approaches may improve worker productivity, they also have the potential to increase worker stress, burnout and absenteeism, and ultimately to result in a decline in worker productivity. To maximise the potential benefits of new initiatives, we must balance them against a careful consideration of quality of work life issues. One hallmark of a socially responsible organisation is its success not only in achieving high performance outcomes, but also in helping its members experience high levels of job satisfaction. The next section provides more detail on the broader issue of human resource maintenance.

Human resource maintenance

The need to ensure long-term and sustainable high performance helps to focus a manager's attention on the need to 'maintain' all of a work unit's resources (human and material resources alike). Just as managers should not allow a valuable machine to break down for lack of proper maintenance, they should never allow a valuable human contribution to be lost for lack of proper care.

Through their daily actions, the best managers in the new workplace will be able to create conditions in which people achieve their highest performance potential while experiencing a high quality of work life. The concept of quality of work life (QWL) gained deserved prominence in organisational behaviour study as an indicator of the overall quality of human experience in the workplace. It expresses a special way of thinking about people, their work and the organisations in which their careers are fulfilled. It establishes a clear objective that high productivity should be achieved along with job satisfaction for the people who do the required work. Vodafone says it takes 'a holistic approach to work and lifestyle'.[30]

QWL activities represent special applications of the many organisational behaviour concepts and theories discussed throughout this book. In particular, the following benchmarks of managerial excellence highlight true commitments to quality of work life:[31]

- *participation* — involving people from all levels of responsibility in decision making
- *trust* — redesigning jobs, systems and structures to give people more freedom at work
- *reinforcement* — creating reward systems that are fair, relevant and contingent on work performance
- *responsiveness* — making the work setting more pleasant and able to serve individual needs.

It is important to remember that a broader social value associated with work makes any manager's responsibilities more complex. QWL is an important component in the quality of life: negative work experiences can affect a person's non-working life. Some of the most worrisome social ills — for example, alcoholism and drug abuse— may be linked with the adjustment problems of people who are unable to find meaning and self-respect in their work.[32] The social importance of managers as major influences on the quality of work life experienced by other people is well established. The study of organisational behaviour recognises that poor management can decrease overall quality of life, not just the quality of work life. It also recognises that good management can increase both.

The psychological contract

You are probably familiar with the word 'contract' as it pertains to formal, written agreements such as a workplace agreement or an agreement between a union and an employer. Another, less formal contract deals with the 'relationship' between every employee and their organisation. We call this the psychological contract — specifically, what the individual and the organisation expect to give to and receive from each other in the course of their working relationship. This contract represents the expected exchange of values that encourages the individual to work for the organisation and motivates the organisation to employ that person. When the individual is being recruited by the organisation, this exchange is an anticipated one; later, during actual employment, expectations are either confirmed or denied. Part of the manager's job is to ensure that both the individual and the organisation continue to receive a fair exchange of values under the psychological contract.

The psychological contract specifies what the individual and the organisation expect to give to and receive from each other in the course of their working relationship.

Figure 1.3 depicts an exchange of values between the individual and the organisation, as expressed in the psychological contract. The individual offers contributions, or work inputs of value, to the organisation. These contributions — such as effort, skills, loyalty and creativity — make each employee a true human resource to the organisation. One important measure of any organisation's success is its ability to attract and maintain a high-quality workforce. In return for these contributions, the organisation gives the individual inducements — such as pay, benefits, status and job security — to encourage participation. These inducements are of value to the individual as ways of satisfying one or more important needs.

Contributions are individual work efforts of value to the organisation.

Inducements are what the organisation gives to the individual on behalf of the group.

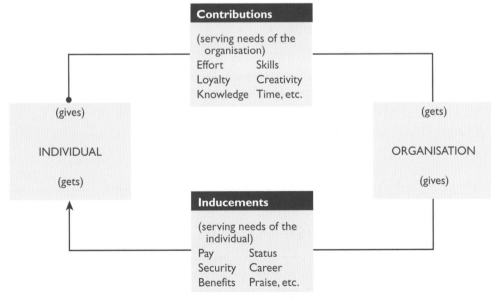

FIGURE 1.3 • A 'healthy' psychological contract means that inducements and contributions are in balance.

When the exchange of values in the psychological contract is felt to be fair, a balance exists between inducements and contributions. This ideal condition creates a healthy psychological contract — one that fosters job satisfaction by allowing individuals to feel good about their work and relationship with the organisation. When the exchange of values is perceived to be unfair, the psychological contract is unhealthy. Consequently, the individual may develop a poor attitude and lose the desire to work hard. These feelings can create absenteeism and unwanted job turnover, as otherwise good workers seek jobs elsewhere.

Some pressures in today's economic and business environment can make the management of psychological contracts a difficult task. Think about the sense of betrayed loyalty experienced by people who lose their jobs or who see others lose their jobs when an organisation is downsized or restructured to increase productivity.

WhatWould You**Do?**

Realigning the psychological contract

Most employees feel that their psychological contracts have been violated in some way by their employer at some time. Misunderstandings are often ignored. However, when a violation takes a serious form, such as a breach of promise and trust, feelings of betrayal can surface. According to Denise Rousseau,[33] there are four main courses of action an individual may take in response to a perceived violation of psychological contract:

- *Voice* is a constructive effort to change and focus on restoring trust by discussing issues of concern with a manager or other appropriate colleague/supervisor.
- *Silence* reflects a willingness to accept unfavourable circumstances in the hope that they may improve.
- *Destruction/neglect* is most common when voice channels do not exist or if there is a history of conflict. This often causes counterproductive behaviours including theft, slowing or stopping work and intentions to destroy relationships.
- *Exit* is often the last resort when dealing with contract violations and refers to voluntary termination of the relationship.

One of the challenges faced by many managers is how to keep aligning psychological contracts in a rapidly changing business environment. Change is almost always accompanied by increasingly complex systems and increased performance pressures on individual staff members. Managers need to be aware that increased performance pressures in formerly less complex organisations can be seen as a psychological contract violation for longer-tenured employees.

Imagine you are a manager in a company that recently experienced tremendous growth. You have been made aware that one of the administrative officers is complaining to coworkers about the increased work pressures he is experiencing as a result of sudden business growth. In addition, another long-term staff member has expressed her dissent with the introduction of a new computer system.

Questions

1. How would you label the response from the staff members to the psychological contract violation?
2. How would you (re)establish psychological contracts with your staff?

The management process

The **management process** involves planning, organising, leading and controlling the use of organisational resources.

Managers use the **management process** of planning, organising, leading and controlling the use of organisational resources to achieve high performance results in both task performance and human resource maintenance. These four functions of management are planning, organising, leading and controlling (see also figure 1.4).

1. Planning is the process of setting performance objectives and identifying the actions needed to accomplish these objectives.
2. Organising is the process of dividing up the work to be done and coordinating the results to achieve a desired purpose.
3. Leading is the process of directing the work efforts of other people to help them to accomplish their assigned tasks.
4. Controlling is the process of monitoring performance, comparing the results with the objectives and taking corrective action as necessary.

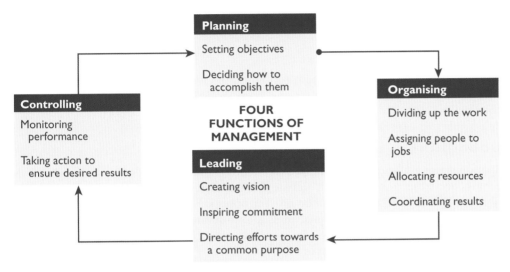

FIGURE 1.4 • Planning, organising, leading and controlling — four functions of management

There is no doubt that the task of managing both efficiently and effectively is becoming more complex. So far we have briefly discussed foundational organisational behavioural themes. In addition to these well-established organisational behaviour principles, today's business environment requires managers to deal with emerging and fast evolving challenges. The next part of this chapter will place the key concepts of organisational behaviour into the real world environment in which the managers of today and tomorrow will work.

Contemporary themes in organisational behaviour

Key issues affecting organisations

Among the biggest challenges that managers must deal with are: globalisation, the changing nature of work, the changing nature of the workforce, and the changing nature of the relationships between employers and employees. These in turn create another challenge: that of managing change itself. One approach is process re-engineering — formally defined as 'the fundamental rethinking and radical redesign of business processes to achieve dramatic improvements in critical contemporary measures of performance such as cost, quality, service and speed'.[34] The result involves a substantial shift in values, as shown in 'The effective manager 1.1'.

Moving from traditional to re-engineered values
Traditional work values
- The boss pays our salaries; keep the boss happy.
- To keep your job, stay quiet and don't make waves.
- When things go wrong, pass problems to others.

THE **Effective**Manager 1.1

We will briefly discuss some of the main contemporary issues in organisational behaviour. We will revisit these themes throughout the book as your knowledge of organisational behaviour builds.

Globalisation

Globalisation is the process of becoming more international in scope, influence or application.

Globalisation is not a new concept. The pros and cons — indeed the definition — of globalisation have been the topic of much debate for decades. We look at this debate in the 'Counterpoint' later in this chapter. For our purposes we will define globalisation as the process of becoming more international in scope, influence or application. In a business context, **globalisation** is characterised by networks that bind countries, institutions and people in an interdependent global economy.[35]

OB in action

BHP Billiton has 35 000 employees operating in 20 different countries. The head office is located in Melbourne with major corporate centres and stock exchange listings in London, Johannesburg and Houston. The company's operations include oil and gas interests in Australia, Pakistan, the United Kingdom, Algeria and the Gulf of Mexico, and aluminium interests in Australia, Brazil, Mozambique, South Africa and Surinam. In addition to this there are coal, diamonds, base metals, stainless steel and carbon steel interests in every continent of the world. In 2005 BHP Billiton had a turnover of A\$42.4 billion.[36]

Global management skills and competencies include understanding of international business strategy, cross-cultural management, international marketing, international finance, managing e-business and the Internet, risk management, managing sustainable organisations, re-engineering organisations, managing the virtual workplace, knowledge management, international economics and trade, and Asian languages.

Success in the increasingly global business environment will depend on a new breed of 'global manager' with global management skills and competencies. **Global management skills and competencies** include a strong and detailed understanding of international business strategy, cross-cultural management, international marketing, international finance, managing e-business and the Internet, risk management, managing sustainable organisations, re-engineering organisations, managing the virtual workplace, knowledge management, international economics and trade, and Asian languages. 'The effective manager 1.2' suggests ten important attributes of the successful global manager.

Ten attributes of the global manager

The global manager is able to:
1. negotiate effectively in different business environments
2. solve problems quickly and under different circumstances
3. motivate and communicate well with people from different cultures
4. understand different government and political systems
5. manage and create a sustainable environment
6. convey a positive attitude and enthusiasm when dealing with others
7. manage business in both traditional and virtual environments
8. view different economies as belonging to a single global market
9. be culturally sensitive and adaptable
10. manage the 'triple bottom line'— society, economy and the environment.

It is important for managers to study and learn about the management and organisational practices of their counterparts in other nations. What is being done well in other settings may be of great value at home, whether that 'home' is Australia, Singapore or anywhere else in the world. Whereas the world at large once looked mainly to the North Americans and Europeans for management insights, today we recognise that no one culture today possesses all of the 'right' answers to our management and organisational problems.

OB in action

New Zealand economic commentator Brian Gaylor says that 'New Zealand leadership was about standing on the fourth rung of the ladder and kicking anyone wanting to come up'; nowadays he acknowledges that things have changed, managers are now 'movers and motivators' and spend their time encouraging others to climb the rungs with them. Siemens New Zealand CEO Graeme Sumner believes that the days of the individual are gone, because in the large and fast moving global environment that his organisation operates in, decisions are often made after collaboration with many people who bring their own unique perspectives. Sumner believes that no-one has all the knowledge and so he has tried to instil a culture of honesty, openness and integrity to encourage 'better' decisions.[37]

COUNTER**POINT**

Globalisation for good or evil?

The impact of multinational corporations (MNCs) on their host countries almost always causes controversy. This is most noticeable in developing nations that find they are overpowered by sizeable MNCs. On many occasions, MNCs are offered lower tax rates, cheap labour and substandard working conditions in comparison to the developed nations' standards, and local workers are generally used only for the lower-scale positions. MNCs can subsequently face a public relations nightmare when stories of child labour, physical abuse of workers and slave wages come to the surface. On the other hand, for workers who are socially and economically impoverished, the arrival of these MNCs can improve the existence and survival of their families. The issues are complex and there are no easy solutions. Globalisation is expected to continue, particularly as more developing countries and formerly communist countries become more open to international trade and investment. But is this a positive or a negative development? Consider the debate surrounding what are colloquially known as sweatshops.

(continued)

A BBC television program, *Panorama*, aired a story about a factory in Cambodia that manufactured products for companies such as The Gap and Nike. Reportedly, in this factory children under the age of 15 were working more than 12 hours a day in terrible conditions on what Westerners would consider extremely low wages.[38] As a result of negative press, Nike and The Gap removed the production of their goods from Cambodia, costing hundreds of locals their jobs and the country millions of dollars in contracts. Similar pressures forced a German garment maker to lay off 50 000 child workers in Bangladesh. OXFAM later discovered that many of the children then became destitute and turned to prostitution and crime to sustain themselves, and some ultimately starved to death. Similarly in Nepal, after a crackdown in the carpet industry, UNICEF reported that thousands of young girls turned to prostitution to survive. In Pakistan, after a controversy regarding sweatshop soccer balls, manufacturers including Nike and Reebok shut down their plants, costing tens of thousands of workers their jobs. This resulted in the mean family income in Pakistan falling by more than 20 per cent.[39]

Of course MNCs have ethical duties in terms of their own actions and those of their subcontractors and suppliers. There are labour laws and standards for pay, safety and the use of coercion.[40] However, it is difficult to determine exactly what these standards are and who sets them. The question is: Should these be 'Western' standards or the standards of the country in which the factory operates?

International trade has increased 3000 per cent since the 1960s[41] and this has been accompanied by an increase in civil and political freedom worldwide.[42] Many developing nations are increasing their overall prosperity at a higher rate than the developed nations have been capable of doing. For example, China doubles its income per capita every 10 years, partly aided by a high prevalence of sweatshops. Compare this to Great Britain, where it took 58 years to do the same thing during the industrial revolution.[43]

Questions

1. Summarise the issues surrounding globalisation as presented above from the 'Western' perspective and from a local perspective.

2. From these summaries, prepare a case *for* globalisation and prepare a case *against* globalisation, integrating both the 'Western' and local perspectives.

The changing nature of work

Work itself is changing rapidly due to globalisation, advances in technology, the growth in the services sector, and especially an increasing reliance on knowledge to generate new products and services. These changes require workers with different skills to the workers of the past, including the ability to continuously learn new skills and adapt to changing needs. Managing such workers presents a number of new challenges for managers. We will look at some of the biggest changes in the following sections.

Technology

Technology has emerged as an ever-present, dominant force in our lives. Just as 100 years ago people could not have accurately predicted the technology that is commonplace now, we can not foresee all the technological advances ahead of us. What is certain is that continuing change in information and communications technology will have massive implications for workers, managers and organisations alike.

High technology allows machines to do many routine chores more cheaply and accurately than people can; it makes available more information for planning and control to more people at all levels of organisational responsibility; and it is causing both people and organisational structures to change old habits and adopt new ways of doing things. For example, the use of email has revolutionised office communication. It is a convenient medium among the more than 100 million email users worldwide.[44] However, email has potentially negative consequences in the workplace. The main problems are that written forms are more official, less easy to withdraw and suffer from the absence of other additional communication modes, such as body language and intonation of voice. In addition, there is a growing body of research that suggests email reduces a person's ability to build rapport and impairs the establishment of trust. These problems are exacerbated by cultural issues when email users are in different countries.[45] Nevertheless, email has proven to be a convenient communication medium that has changed work practices significantly.

Knowledge management

Another major driver of organisational change is the growth of the knowledge-based economy in which prosperity is built on 'intellectual capital' — the use of information in people's minds — rather than on physical resources. The OECD defines a knowledge-based economy as 'an economy in which the production, distribution and use of knowledge is the main driver of growth, wealth creation and employment across all industries — not only those industries classified as high tech or knowledge intensive'.[46]

> A **knowledge-based economy** is an economy in which the production, distribution and use of knowledge is the main driver of growth, wealth creation and employment across all industries — not only those classified as high tech or knowledge intensive.

Recognition of knowledge and the contribution that knowledge creation, distribution and use can make towards improved levels of performance and productivity is not new; economies have always relied on knowledge expansion and application through research and development to create new products and improvements in productivity. What is new is the speed at which knowledge is being created and the pace at which it is being transformed into new goods and services.

In a knowledge-based economy, the central questions for high-performing organisations are:
- What do we know and what knowledge do we have?
- How do we organise to make best use of this knowledge?
- Who can add value to what we know?
- How quickly can we learn something new?
- How quickly can we deliver this new knowledge into the global marketplace?

Much knowledge resides within employees, including their skills, creativity and experience. It also exists in other areas such as the organisation's systems, processes and structures, and in the relationships that organisations have with their customers, suppliers and other stakeholders. Knowledge management (KM) focuses on processes designed to improve an

> **Knowledge management** (KM) focuses on processes designed to improve an organisation's ability to capture, share and diffuse knowledge in a manner that will improve business performance.

organisation's ability to capture, share and diffuse knowledge in a manner that will improve business performance.

An important aspect of knowledge management is retaining people who possess the knowledge the organisation or the country needs. Workers are increasingly mobile and are taking their knowledge with them to their new workplaces across the globe. Such movement across national boundaries is commonly referred to as **brain drain**.

At just 3.5 per cent, New Zealand's unemployment rate is at an 18-year low. This has resulted in a skills shortage in areas such as accountancy, engineering and IT. The shortages have resulted in creative recruitment strategies as organisations fight to attract talent. One of the more interesting tactics used by recruitment organisation Real Recruitment involved mounting 500 posters in the toilets of one of the rugby stadiums during the 2005 Lions tour of New Zealand. The posters were aimed at attracting UK supporters, who are known as the 'Barmy Army', to immigrate to New Zealand. The poster's slogan was 'You'd be Barmy not to switch sides for a while'.[47]

The changing nature of the workforce

The composition of the workforce is changing. Managers must be aware of, and able to successfully manage in the context of, the following trends:[48]

- the size of the workforce is growing more slowly than in the past
- the average age of the workforce is rising
- more women are entering the workforce
- the proportion of ethnic minorities in the workforce is increasing
- the proportion of immigrants in the workforce is increasing
- workforce mobility is increasing
- 'labour packaging' is growing through short-term migrant labour importation in many Asian and Middle Eastern countries
- international careers and mobile managers are becoming commonplace
- international experience is becoming a prerequisite for career progression to many top-level management positions.

Perhaps the most notable change in the workforce is that it is more diverse than at any time in history. The term **workforce diversity** refers to the presence of demographic differences among members of a given workforce.[49] These differences include gender, race and ethnicity, culture, age and able-bodiedness.

In the sections below, we will look at the changing nature of the workforce in terms of culture, age and gender.

Culture

The workforce is becoming more multicultural as a result of migration, and as workforces increasingly span more than one country. Australia and New Zealand are among the most multicultural countries in the world. Almost one in three members of the workforce in major Australian cities such as Sydney and Melbourne was born outside Australia. About one in three people in the Auckland region of New Zealand was born overseas. Managers — whether or not they are directly involved in international business — must be able to effectively manage people from different cultures and make the most of the advantages that a diverse workforce can bring. For example, diversifying the workforce can be used as a market strategy. A diverse workforce can provide business with a competitive advantage by capitalising on language skills, cultural knowledge, business networks and knowledge of business practices in overseas markets, and intelligence about overseas markets, including intimate knowledge of consumer tastes and preferences. Businesses can use the skills to improve productivity and innovation in the workplace, developing domestic niche markets and entering new, or increasing market share in, overseas markets.[50]

Research has shown that styles of leadership, motivation and decision making, and other management roles vary among different countries.[51] For example:

- *Leadership.* A study of international airlines found substantial differences in leadership styles despite the fact that the technology, types of jobs, skills required and basic operations are very similar from one company to another.[52]

- *Motivation.* Managers must avoid being parochial or ethnocentric. They cannot assume all people will be motivated by the same things and in the same ways as they are. Most of the popular theories of work motivation have been developed in the United States. These theories may help explain the behaviour of North Americans, but serious questions must be raised about how applicable they are to other cultures.[53] While North Americans, for example, value individual rewards, Japanese people prefer group rewards.

- *Decision making.* Latin American employees may feel uncomfortable with a boss who delegates too much authority to them. In France, decisions tend to be made at the top of companies and passed down the hierarchy for implementation. In other cultures, such as the Scandinavian, employees want their managers to emphasise a participative, problem-solving approach. In Japan, many companies use the *ringi* system for making decisions. *Ringi* is a group decision approach whereby all affected company members affix their sign of approval to widely circulated written proposals. Culture may even play a role in determining whether a decision is necessary at all — that is, whether the situation should be changed. Australians and New Zealanders tend to perceive situations as problems to be solved; other cultures, such as the Thai and Indonesian, tend to accept situations as they are. Thus, an Australian is more likely to decide that a workplace problem exists and that something should be done about it.[54]

Geert Hofstede, a Dutch scholar and consultant, has identified five dimensions of national culture — power-distance, uncertainty avoidance, individualism–collectivism, masculinity–femininity and long-term–short-term orientation — which provide one way of understanding differences across national cultures.[55] Hofstede's dimensions of national culture are described in the following 'International spotlight'.

The dimensions of culture

International **SPOTLIGHT**

Hofstede's five dimensions of national culture can be described as follows:[56]

1. *Power-distance* — the degree to which people in a country accept a hierarchical or unequal distribution of power in organisations. Indonesia, for example, is considered a high power-distance culture, whereas the Netherlands is considered a relatively low power-distance culture.

2. *Uncertainty avoidance* — the degree to which people in a country prefer structured rather than unstructured situations. France, for example, is considered a high uncertainty avoidance culture, whereas Hong Kong is considered a low uncertainty avoidance culture.

3. *Individualism–collectivism* — the degree to which people in a country focus on working as individuals more than on working together in groups. Germany, for example, is considered a relatively individualistic culture, whereas Sweden is considered a more collectivist culture.

4. *Masculinity–femininity* — the degree to which people in a country emphasise so-called masculine traits, such as assertiveness, independence and insensitivity to feelings, as dominant values. Japan, for example, is considered a highly masculine culture, whereas the Netherlands is considered a more feminine culture.

(continued)

5. *Long-term–short-term orientation* — the degree to which people in a country emphasise values associated with the future, such as thrift and persistence, over values that focus on the past or present, such as social obligations and tradition. China, for example, is high on long-term orientation, while the United States is more orientated towards the short term.

Continuing research on these cultural dimensions examines how countries can be grouped into clusters sharing generally similar cultures. Scholars are interested in such cluster maps as they try to determine how management practices can and do transfer across cultures.

One such grouping is shown in figure 1.5. 'Anglo' countries tend to score quite low on the long-term–short-term dimension, whereas the Asian 'Dragons' — Hong Kong, Singapore, Japan, South Korea and Taiwan — score quite high on this dimension. Hofstede and Bond argue that the long-term value and influence of Confucian dynamism may, at least in part, account for the surge of economic successes by these Asian nations.[57]

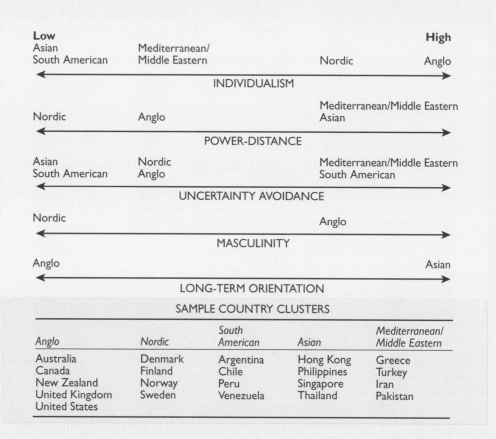

FIGURE 1.5 • A sample of 'country clusters' based on Hofstede's five dimensions of national cultures
Sources: Based on Geert Hofstede, 'Cultural constraints in management theories', *Academy of Management Executive*, vol. 7 (February 1993), pp. 81–94; and Betty Jane Punnett, *Experiencing international management* (Boston: PWS-Kent, 1989), p. 19.

Age

In Australia, almost 25 per cent of the population will be 65 years or older by 2051; almost 20 per cent may be 85 years or older.[58] New Zealand also has an ageing population. By 2051 half the New Zealand population will be older than 45 years, compared with a median age of 35 years in 2001.[59] Japan will have the most rapidly ageing population of any major power, and will experience an increasing shortage of labour. The ageing of the workforce has a number of important implications for organisations. These include:

- the possibility of a labour shortage – not enough workers with the right skills for the work that needs to be done
- a loss of 'organisational memory' as the baby boomer generation (born between 1946 and 1964) reaches retirement (from 2006) and leaves the workforce
- an increasing representation of generations X (born after 1964) and Y (born after 1978) at senior levels within organisations as the baby boomer generation retires
- the need for new types of employment relationships to meet the needs of generations X and Y. For example, workers from generations X and Y are looking for different types of rewards for their work — they are less focused on just pay and job security. Vodafone, for example, meets this need by offering incentives such as giving workers the day off on their birthdays, allowing casual dress and giving them access to a health and wellbeing program that includes such services as free massages.[60] Vodafone provides rewards and working conditions it believes will appeal to the type of employee it wants. The company also seeks to ensure its employees live with the technology and services they sell. (In fact, in 2005, a Vodafone Australia employee, James Trusler, 31 years old and from generation X, was the world record holder for TXT messaging — 2 minutes 6 seconds for a 160-character TXT message.)[61]
- greater workforce mobility and less loyalty to the organisation due to the different attitudes of members of generations X and Y. They expect to have a series of jobs and multiple careers over their working lives. This is in stark contrast to older generations who tended to work for one company, perhaps rising through the ranks over the years.
- the much higher levels of technical competence brought to the workplace by generation X and Y employees compared with their predecessors.

Gender

The past 40 years has been characterised by an increasing number of women entering the workforce, a breaking down of the traditional idea that some jobs are gender-specific (for example, nurses are women, mechanics are men), and increasing numbers of women in senior positions within organisations. For example, women now comprise 30 per cent of the three most senior levels of management. However, the top tier is still predominantly male orientated and 54 per cent of the top 200 Australian publicly listed companies do not have a female in an executive management role.[62] As you can see in table 1.1, the Australian labour force status (2005) shows significant gender differences for full- and part-time workers.

	Participation in the workforce (%)	Full-time ('000s)	Full-time (%)	Part-time ('000s)	Part-time (%)
Male	71.6	4526.8	66	781.7	29
Female	55.6	2313.6	34	1937.40	71
Total	63.5	6840.3	100	9559.50	100

TABLE 1.1 • Australian labour force status

Source: Extracted from Australian Bureau of Statistics, *Year book Australia 2005* (Labour force) (Canberra: ABS, 2005).

One of the greatest implications of increased female participation in the workforce is for organisations to learn how to manage work–family relations such as maternity leave; this will be discussed later. The increased female presence in the workforce has also influenced organisational behaviour in terms of employer–employee relations.

The changing nature of employer–employee relations

The relationship between employers and employees is changing in how the organisation views its members and how people view employers. In the new workplace, employment is cut and streamlined for operational efficiency, businesses have flatter and more flexible structures, and the workforce is more diverse and dispersed.

Globalisation has significantly altered the employment relationship, creating challenges for organisations, managers and employees. Wage earners find themselves working at home for foreign employers. More senior executives are arriving at their positions with the benefit of 'overseas experience'. And more junior executives are being asked and encouraged to take on such assignments. Consequently, today's managers must be able to both 'think globally' and 'act locally' in pursuing their opportunities.

Human rights and social justice are increasingly pursued in the new workplace, just as they are in the world at large. All managers must deal with growing pressures for self-determination from people at work. Workers want input into major decisions that have a direct effect on their working lives.[63] Workers want more freedom to determine how and when to do their jobs. They want the benefits of increased participation accrued through workplace initiatives such as industrial democracy, job enrichment, autonomous work groups, flexible working hours and family-friendly workplaces. All of these initiatives are changing the nature of day-to-day human resource management.

To create value-adding human capital, the twenty-first-century manager must be well prepared to deal with not only the pressures outlined above but also pressures for:

- *Employee rights.* People expect their rights to be respected on the job as well as outside their work environment, including the rights of individual privacy, due process, free speech, free consent, freedom of conscience and freedom from sexual harassment.
- *Job security.* People expect their security to be protected, including security of their physical wellbeing (in terms of occupational safety and health matters, as well as economic livelihood), guaranteed protection against layoffs and provisions for cost-of-living wage increases.
- *Employment opportunity.* People expect — and increasingly demand — the right to employment without discrimination on the basis of age, sex, ethnic background or disabilities. Among these demands are concerns to further the modest but important gains made in recent years by women and other groups that have been marginalised in the workplace. The concept of the 'glass ceiling' has been introduced into management vocabulary to describe the discriminatory barriers that women may face as they seek to advance their careers in organisations. Progress will be applauded, but it will not be accepted as a substitute for true equality of opportunity.
- *Equity of earnings.* People expect to be compensated for the 'comparable worth' of their work contributions. The fact that certain occupations (such as nursing) have been traditionally dominated by women, whereas others (such as carpentry) have been traditionally dominated by men is no longer accepted as justifying pay inequity. Equal pay for equal work, equity of rewards involving a comparison of inputs to output, and other related issues such as money and motivation continue to be widely discussed topics.

We will now briefly examine a few of the major issues in the changing employment relationship.

Work–life balance

Increasingly, workers are seeking balance between their work and the other aspects of their lives. Progressive organisations recognise the need to support their workforce to minimise stress levels and burnout, and to maximise work performance. Many companies recognise the increased pressures experienced in dual-income households, where both partners try to manage work and family commitments. Many companies are introducing initiatives to create a 'family-friendly workplace' to help employees better balance work and family commitments.

Workplace initiatives include work options such as job sharing, permanent part-time work and telecommuting, new leave provisions such as paid maternity and paid paternity leave, as well as supported child-care facilities.[64]

The New South Wales Department of Commerce recommends that small businesses implement a family-friendly workplace.[65] The department suggests that employees be allowed to bring their children to work occasionally if the need arises; for example, when an employee's regular child carer is not available, or when an alternative arrangement cannot be made for school-aged children on pupil-free days. Employees might also want their child to be at the workplace briefly after school or when they need to take the child to a medical appointment or other activity after work.

The department suggests the advantages of such an approach are:
- 'reduced absenteeism [as] employees can carry out their regular duties while knowing their children are safe
- increased ability to recruit quality staff
- improved staff morale, motivation and commitment to the organisation
- [it] presents a positive image of the business as a family-friendly organisation.'[66]

Disadvantages might include:
- 'possible concerns about the safety of the work environment for children
- possible concerns about privacy and confidentiality of the work
- unsupervised children may distract other employees from their work
- children with contagious illnesses could pose a work-related health risk to employees.'[67]

Paid maternity leave — whose responsibility is it?

In 1998 the International Labour Organisation (ILO) declared that 'More than 120 nations provide paid maternity leave'. By March 2005, Australia and the United States were the only OECD countries that still did not provide this assistance to women. The ILO has a minimum standard of 12 weeks' maternity leave, paid at 66 per cent of the woman's previous earnings (although it recommends 14 weeks).[68] The issue is important because it is expected that about 80 per cent of all women in industrialised countries will work outside the home throughout their child-rearing years.[69] What will happen to family income when women fall pregnant? There is now a growing body of evidence from around the world that the pay gap between mothers and child-less women is greater than it is between men and women generally.

One of the more vital and controversial questions in many countries is: 'Whose responsibility is it to pay for maternity leave?' There are three main options: the employee, the employer or the government. The most talked about option is to force employers to pay for maternity leave, like other types of leave. However, there are only two industrialised nations (Switzerland and Singapore) that require employers to bear the full costs of paid maternity leave.[70] In other countries this cost is shared between employer, employee and government.

(continued)

Australia's birth rate has declined to 1.7 per woman.[71] The government acknowledges some responsibility for child rearing in the form of a one-off maternity payment (A$3079), immunisation payments (A$200) and ongoing child-care payments, stay-at-home parental allowances and various family tax benefits from Centrelink.[72] However these payments do not meet the minimum standards under the United Nations' Convention on the Elimination of All Forms of Discrimination against Women (CEDAW), which Australia ratified in 1983. Australia currently has a reservation against Article 11(2)(b) of the convention and refuses to agree to provide adequate paid maternity leave entitlements for women, which clearly goes against current international standards.[73]

TABLE 1.2 • Maternity leave entitlements

Country	How much leave?	% of wages	Who pays?
Afghanistan	90 days	100%	Employer
Australia	1 year	Nil	n/a
Brazil	120 days	100%	Social Security
Canada	18 weeks	55% for 15 weeks	Unemployment insurance
Denmark	18 weeks	100% for 10 weeks	Social security
Ethiopia	90 days	100%	Employer
Germany	14 weeks	100%	Social security to a ceiling then employer pays the rest
Haiti	12 weeks	100% for 6 weeks	Employer
India	12 weeks	100%	Employer/social security
Iraq	62 days	100%	Social security
Italy	5 months	80%	Social security
Japan	14 weeks	60%	Social security/health insurance
Morocco	12 weeks	100%	Social security
New Zealand*	14 weeks	[100% up to a ceiling]	[Social security]
South Africa	12 weeks	45%	Unemployment insurance
Thailand	90 days	100% for 45 days then 50% thereafter	Employer for 45 days then social security
UK	1 year	90% for 6 weeks then a flat rate thereafter	Social security
USA	12 weeks	Nil	n/a

Source: Extracted from International Labor Organisation, '*More than 120 nations provide paid maternity leave*', ILO press release 98/7 (16 February 1998).

* New Zealand did not provide paid maternity leave at the time of the ILO survey, but now does.

Outsourcing

As we have already seen, countries, cultures and peoples around the world are increasingly interconnected. One result is that it is increasingly possible to transfer jobs from one country to another. Job migration (the transfer of jobs from one country to another) and global outsourcing (the replacement of domestic jobs with contract workers in another country) are popular to countries such as India, the Philippines and Russia, especially in IT-related jobs. With increasing use of virtual workspaces enabled by communications and information technology, it is easy to contract for many types of work anywhere in the world, at the lowest price. To remain competitive, organisations and workers themselves must continually change to achieve high performance.

India places a high value on education and many workers have one or two degrees. Through successful global marketing of its knowledge-based workforce, many companies in a variety of industries (IT, aerospace, finance, telecommunications) are now outsourcing their work to India. Often the workers are shown video footage from the country they service; they watch local television shows via cable and partake in accent reduction courses, all in an effort to 'fit' with the culture they are servicing. One of the largest growth areas is finance. AXA Asia Pacific has its back office functions and data entry work done in India, and part of the ANZ Bank's IT operations are also undertaken there. Organisations like GE Capital (which runs credit card operations for Coles Myer, Shell and Buyers Edge), HSBC Bank and American Express have relocated credit card fraud departments to India. Interestingly, whenever you call these organisations, irrespective of where you are in the world, your call will be answered by someone in either Delhi or Mumbai, the emerging call-centre capitals of the world. This human capital has proved a successful commodity for India: in 1995 the Indian outsourcing sector turned over about US$100 million; by 2002 that figure had increased to US$2 billion.[74] Many companies outsource labour to developing countries, where skills are often high and labour costs are significantly cheaper. However, companies must carefully consider both internal (cost) and external (customer experience) factors when outsourcing services, as many customers struggle to accept call centres that are not locally based and it could in turn affect a customer's trust in and loyalty to a certain brand, company or organisation.

Casualisation of the workforce

One of the key themes from the chapter so far has been that organisations and the environments in which they operate are rapidly changing. Organisations are seeking greater flexibility and adaptability to respond to these changes. Increasingly, organisations are seeking people who can adapt to changing needs. Another method has been to change the composition of their workforce to consist of core workers and contingent workers. The contingent workers are usually employed on a casual basis. **Casual work** is work where the number and schedule of work hours vary and there is little or no security of ongoing employment. The number of casual workers and casual jobs has increased greatly in Australia in recent years: in 1984, 15.8 per cent of the Australian workforce was employed casually, and in 2003 this number increased to 26 per cent.[75] While employing casual staff gives managers the ability to quickly increase or decrease the number of workers to meet demand, there are significant downsides for both employer and employees. For example, employees suffer a loss of job security and predictability of income; they may have less loyalty to their employer; and they may be less likely to invest in new skills or knowledge that could benefit the employer.[76]

Telecommuting

Telecommuting means working from a location other than the organisation's offices. It often refers to working from home. Telecommuting has become increasingly feasible due to technology (for example, mobile phones, email) that allows easy communication with the office and coworkers. While there are benefits to employees in terms of work–life balance (for example, saved travelling time and being able to work in their home environment), employees can become socially isolated and may miss out on opportunities for promotion and so on. An investigation by the New South Wales State Chamber of Commerce found that 23 per cent of survey respondents had employees who regularly worked from home or who worked via remote links. A further 24 per cent of respondents had employees who teleworked occasionally.[77]

Since the terrorist attack on the World Trade Center towers in New York on 11 September 2001, many companies have been reluctant to place all or most of their employees at one location. By having operations spread across different geographic locations — or even just different buildings — the risk of losing a large proportion of resources — human, physical or intellectual — in a terror attack or disaster such as an earthquake or fire is greatly reduced.

Vodafone also facilitates telecommuting. In fact it wants its workers to make the most of its mobile services — using mobile phones, laptops and Blackberry devices — to work and play whenever and wherever they are.

Ethics and values

With an increasingly interconnected world, the growing representation of generation X and Y employees and employers, and a greater appreciation of the fragility of the natural environmental, organisations, their members and the communities they exist within are placing more emphasis on ethical behaviour. The concepts of corporate social responsibility (that organisations have a responsibility to the societies that sustain them) and triple bottom line reporting (that organisations need to consider society and the environment as well as their economics) are among the most prominent organisational responses to the increased emphasis placed on ethics and values.

Formally defined, **ethical behaviour** is behaviour that is morally accepted as good and right, as opposed to bad or wrong, in a particular setting. Business scandals resulting in the collapse of high-profile companies such as HIH Insurance and telecommunications company One.Tel have highlighted the importance of ethics in managerial behaviour. Today a trend is clear: the public is demanding that government officials, managers, workers in general and the organisations they represent all act in accordance with high ethical and moral standards.

Ethical managerial behaviour is behaviour that conforms not only to the dictates of law but also to a broader moral code that is common to society as a whole. But exactly what moral code governs a person's choices is a subject of debate.

Corporate social responsibility refers to the notion that corporations have a responsibility to the society that sustains them. This responsibility includes such things as providing employment, caring for the environment, contributing to charities and operating in a way that meets the society's needs. Corporate social responsibility is not necessarily a concept that should be regulated. The Business Council of Australia (BCA) represents the top 100 companies in Australia who contribute 219 000 staff hours annually to community groups. The BCA is strongly opposed to new regulations aimed at mandating corporate social responsibility, as it is their belief that it will encourage organisations to simply comply with legislation rather than encouraging them to be truly socially responsible.[78]

> **Corporate social responsibility** refers to the notion that corporations have a responsibility to the society that sustains them.

ING Bank is collaborating with Habitat for Humanity to assist in providing shelter for over 100 families from the Baseco compound in Tondo, Manila. The company is encouraging its staff and managers to come to the site and assist in building the new homes as part of ING's commitment to corporate social responsibility. The site is close to where many ING employees work and it offers an opportunity for them to apply basic business values to real life situations, whilst helping a community in need.[79]

An ethical dilemma occurs when a person must make a decision that requires a choice among competing sets of principles. Such a situation may arise when a member of an organisation decides whether to do something that could be considered unethical, but that benefits the person or the organisation or both. Is it ethical, for example, to pay to obtain a business contract in a foreign country? Is it ethical to allow your company to dispose of hazardous waste in an unsafe fashion? Is it ethical to withhold information in order to discourage a good worker from taking another job? Is it ethical to conduct personal business on company time? Ethical dilemmas are common in life and at work. Research suggests that managers encounter such dilemmas in their working relationships not only with superiors and employees but also with customers, competitors, suppliers and regulators. Common issues underlying the dilemmas involve honesty in communications and contracts, gifts and entertainment, kickbacks, pricing practices and employee terminations.[80]

> An **ethical dilemma** occurs when a person must make a decision that requires a choice among competing sets of principles.

Why study organisational behaviour?

By now you should understand why it is important for managers — and every other member of an organisation — to have a good understanding of organisational behaviour.

The message is clear: the successful twenty-first-century manager will have to make the behavioural and attitudinal adjustments necessary to succeed in dynamic times. Robertson has outlined the attributes of the new-look Australian manager for the next decade:

> **OBJECTIVE 5 LEARNING**
> The need to understand organisational behaviour

Tomorrow's managers will come from any country or culture and experience many placements in a wide ranging career. They will also be super men and women: being graduates, possibly postgraduates, with a global focus, able to manage in both regulated and deregulated economies in an environment typified by rapid change. They would be surprised by anything more than a limited term, high pressure appointment, and their position would be results driven.[81]

Your learning about organisational behaviour may begin with this book and a course as part of your formal education. But it can and should continue in the future as you benefit from actual work experiences. Your most significant learning about organisational behaviour may come with time as your career progresses. But it will do so only if you prepare well and if you are diligent in taking maximum advantage of each learning opportunity that arises.

The learning and education of the future is perhaps best conceptualised by the terms 'lifelong learning' and 'recurrent learning'. The essence of these propositions is that education and learning should continue over the lifespan of the individual from the full variety of actual work and life experiences. It is both a personal responsibility and a prerequisite to long-term career success. Day-to-day work experiences, conversations with colleagues and friends, counselling and advice from mentors, training seminars and workshops, professional reading and videotapes, and the information available in the popular press and mass media all provide frequent opportunities for continual learning about organisational behaviour. In progressive organisations, supportive policies and a commitment to extensive training and development are among the criteria for organisational excellence. The opportunities for lifelong learning and recurrent education are there; you must make the commitment to take full advantage of them at all times.

Summary

Organisational behaviour defined

Organisational behaviour is the study of individuals and groups in work organisations. This body of knowledge assists managers to interact effectively with their employees and improve organisational performance. Effective managers need to understand the people that they rely on for the performance of their unit. An individual's, team's/group's or organisation's performance depends on their capacity to work, willingness to work and opportunity to work. This concept can be summarised by the performance equation which views performance as the result of the personal and/or group attributes, the work effort they make and the organisational support they receive.

Why organisations exist

Organisations are collections of individuals working together to achieve a common purpose or goal. Organisations exist because individuals are limited in their physical and mental capabilities. By working together in organisations, collections of individuals are able to achieve more than any individual could by working alone. The purpose of an organisation is to produce a product or to provide a service. To produce such outputs, organisations divide work into required tasks to organise the efforts of people to their best advantage. This process is termed 'division of labour'. Organisations can be portrayed as 'open systems' in that they obtain human and material inputs from their external environment, then transform these inputs into product outputs in the form of finished goods or services, which they then offer back to the external environment for consumption. If the environment values these outputs, then the organisation will continue to survive; if not, then it may fail to obtain subsequent inputs for future production and it may cease to operate.

The role of managers

A manager is responsible for work that is accomplished through the performance contributions of one or more other people. The management process involves planning, organising, leading and controlling. Managers should seek two key results for a work unit or work team: task performance, which is the quality and quantity of the work produced or the services provided by the work unit; and human resource maintenance, which is the attraction and continuation of a capable workforce over time. An effective manager's work unit achieves high levels of productivity and maintains itself as a capable workforce over time by keeping the psychological contract in balance. The psychological contract is individuals' expectations regarding what they and the organisation expect to give and receive from each other as an exchange of values. In a 'healthy' psychological contract, the contributions made to the organisation are believed to be in balance with the inducements received in return. The insights provided through the study of organisational behaviour can help managers help others maintain healthy psychological contracts with their employers. They can also help managers build and maintain work environments that offer their members a high quality of work life, which is marked by participation, independence, equity and responsiveness.

Key issues affecting organisations

Globalisation is the process of becoming increasingly international in character. A managerial career in today's work environment will sooner or later bring contact with international issues and considerations. Managing to perform effectively in a globalised marketplace requires many new skills and competencies.

Changes to the nature of work are largely due to globalisation, advances in technology, the growth in the services sector and, especially, an increasing reliance on knowledge to generate new products and services. These changes to the nature of work require workers and managers with new skills and abilities.

The workforce is becoming diverse: more multicultural, older, and there are more women working than ever before. Managing such a workforce requires new approaches.

Workers are seeking greater work–life balance. They are also seeking a greater variety of incentives for their work contribution. More workers expect to have a series of jobs or careers over their lifetime. Employers should not expect the same degree of loyalty as in the past. Employers are seeking a more flexible, adaptable workforce that can keep pace with the ever-increasing speed of change in the marketplace. Outsourcing and the use of casual workers are among the ways organisations are responding to this need.

Organisations are under increasing pressure to conduct themselves ethically and to acknowledge that they have a responsibility to the society that sustains them.

The need to understand organisational behaviour

Learning about organisational behaviour is both a personal responsibility and a prerequisite to long-term career success. The field of organisational behaviour helps managers both deal with and learn from their workplace experiences. Managers who understand organisational behaviour are better prepared to know what to look for in work situations, to understand what they find and to take (or help others to take) the required action.

Chapter 1 study guide

Key terms

brain drain, *p. 18*
casual work, *p. 26*
contingency approach, *p. 4*
contributions, *p. 11*
controlling, *p. 13*
corporate social responsibility,
   p. 27
division of labour, *p. 6*
effective manager, *p. 9*
emotional intelligence, *p. 5*
ethical behaviour, *p. 26*
ethical dilemma, *p. 27*
global management skills and
   competencies, *p. 14*

globalisation, *p. 14*
human resource maintenance,
   p. 9
human resources, *p. 7*
inducements, *p. 11*
knowledge-based economy, *p. 17*
knowledge management, *p. 17*
leading, *p. 13*
management process, *p. 12*
manager, *p. 9*
material resources, *p. 7*
open systems, *p. 7*
organisational behaviour, *p. 4*
organising, *p. 13*

performance equation, *p. 5*
planning, *p. 13*
process re-engineering, *p. 13*
productivity, *p. 9*
psychological contract, *p. 11*
quality of work life, *p. 10*
synergy, *p. 7*
task performance, *p. 9*
value-added managers, *p. 10*
work team, *p. 9*
work unit, *p. 9*
workforce diversity, *p. 18*

Review questions

1. What is organisational behaviour and why do managers need to understand it?
2. What are the factors that accelerate organisational change today?
3. What is an effective manager? What are the competencies an effective global manager requires?
4. Why is it important for managers to have a *global* view of learning in organisations?

Application questions

1. Why is human resource maintenance important to effective management? What negative effects on business performance may result from managers' neglect of people issues? Can managerial performance be measured using a single criterion? Explain your answer.
2. What is meant by the term 'global management'? What distinguishes it from other types of management?
3. How have developments in information technology changed the nature of the workplace and the practice of management? How do virtual organisations differ from other organisations?
4. What is the psychological contract? Why is it important to understanding employment? What major challenges to the quality of work life are presented by the conditions and environment of today's organisations?
5. Why is an understanding of cultural differences important to business? What are some steps that managers can take to develop greater cross-cultural awareness? How would you describe the Australian culture if you were attempting to attract foreign investment?
6. What is corporate social responsibility and how is this influencing organisational behaviour?

1. Write a report to answer the following question:

   In this time of dramatic changes in the business environment, how will organisations be managed in ten years' time? Give examples and suggestions.

   Your research on this question can pursue a wide variety of alternatives. At a minimum, you must support your report by readings from at least two business publications (for example, *Asian Business Review*, *Business Review Weekly*, *Bulletin Magazine*, *World Executive Digest*, *Asia Inc.* or *Asia Week*) approved by your lecturer and at least one journal (for example, *Australian Journal of Management*, *Management (NZ)*, *Asia Pacific Journal of Human Resources* or *Asian Journal of Management*) approved by your lecturer.

2. Training managers and employees to make the most of a diverse workforce can be extremely useful. Visit Diversity@work (www.work.asn.au) and find out how diversity can be good for business. Use the resources available at the site to test your knowledge of diversity awareness in the workplace.

Running project

The running project appears at the end of each chapter in this book. By completing the exercises in the running project you will gain important insights into organisational behaviour and management in the new workplace. Each exercise requires you to collect and analyse information relating to the material discussed in that chapter.

The first step is to choose an organisation to study. Remember that we will be asking you for information about a broad range of management approaches and processes at your chosen organisation, so you must choose an organisation for which this information is readily available. We suggest using one of the following approaches.

1. Choose a well-known company. This option means you are likely to have access to information through newspapers, magazines, the company's corporate web site and your library's resources.

2. Better still, choose a smaller company that you can access directly. This approach has much to offer if management will agree to talk to you at length (remember that you'll need to talk to them regularly throughout your study of this book). For example, you might choose the company you work for. For this approach, make sure you can secure substantial cooperation and information from your chosen company. Your instructor may have some guidance for you before you make a decision.

3. Your instructor may provide suggestions on which company to study.

Your task for chapter 1 is to choose the organisation you will study and to obtain enough information about that company to carry out the following instructions and answer the questions asked.

1. Identify the purpose or goals of the organisation.

2. Draw the organisation as an 'open system'. List the inputs, transformations and outputs.

3. What knowledge management processes does the organisation have in place to provide feedback?

4. Describe the business environment, both in terms of specific environment and general environment.

Individual activity

Global awareness

As we note in this chapter, the environment of business is becoming more global. The following assessment is designed to help you understand your readiness to respond to managing in a global context.

You will agree with some of the following statements and disagree with others. In some cases, you may find it difficult to make a decision, but you should force a choice. Record your answers next to each statement according to the scale on the following page.

(continued)

Strongly agree = 4   Somewhat disagree = 2
Somewhat agree = 3   Strongly disagree = 1

_____ 1. Some areas of Malaysia are very much like Indonesia.

_____ 2. Although aspects of behaviour such as motivation and attitudes within organisational settings remain diverse across cultures, organisations themselves appear to be increasingly similar in terms of design and technology.

_____ 3. Spain, France, Japan, Singapore, Mexico, Brazil and Indonesia have cultures with a strong orientation towards authority.

_____ 4. Japan and Austria define male–female roles more rigidly and value qualities like forcefulness and achievement more than Norway, Sweden, Denmark and Finland.

_____ 5. Some areas of Malaysia are very much like Brunei.

_____ 6. Australia, the United Kingdom, the Netherlands, Canada and New Zealand have cultures that view people first as individuals and place a priority on their own interests and values, whereas Colombia, Pakistan, Taiwan, Peru, Singapore, Mexico, Greece and Hong Kong have cultures in which the good of the group or society is considered the priority.

_____ 7. The United States, Israel, Austria, Denmark, Ireland, Norway, Germany and New Zealand have cultures with a low orientation towards authority.

_____ 8. The same manager may behave differently in different cultural settings.

_____ 9. Denmark, Canada, Norway, Singapore, Hong Kong and Australia have cultures in which employees tolerate a high degree of uncertainty, but such levels of uncertainty are not well tolerated in Israel, Austria, Japan, Italy, Argentina, Peru, France and Belgium.

_____ 10. Some areas of Malaysia are very much like the Philippines.

For interpretation, see page 37.

OB *Group activity*

Management foundations

Objectives

1. To understand the management foundations recommended by the American Assembly of Collegiate Schools of Business (AACSB). (These are the skills and personal characteristics that should be nurtured in university students of business for success in the new workplace of the twenty-first century.)

2. To assess your abilities in the ten management foundations

3. To select areas for development through planning

4. To examine diversity within the class members' responses

Total time: 10–20 minutes

Step 1: Self-assessment

Rate yourself by placing a number from 1 to 7 on the line before each of the ten management foundations to best describe how frequently you exhibit this behaviour. Be honest; you will not be asked to share your score in class.

Usually = 7
Frequently = 6
Often = 5
Sometimes = 4
Infrequently = 3
Seldom = 2
Rarely = 1

_____ 1. *Resistance to stress.* I get the job done under stressful conditions.

_____ 2. *Tolerance for uncertainty.* I get the job done under ambiguous and uncertain conditions.

_____ 3. *Social objectivity.* I act free of racial, ethnic, gender and other prejudices or biases.

_____ 4. *Inner work standards.* I personally set and work to high performance standards on my own.

_____ 5. *Stamina.* I work long, hard hours.

_____ 6. *Adaptability.* I am flexible and adapt to change.

_____ 7. *Self-confidence.* I am consistently decisive and display my personal presence.

_____ 8. *Self-objectivity.* I evaluate my personal strengths and weaknesses, and understand my motives and skills relative to tasks I need to do.

9. *Introspection*. I learn from experience, awareness and self-study. (I do not make the same mistake twice.)

10. *Entrepreneurism*. I address problems and take advantage of opportunities for constructive change.

Finally, consider this question: 'If I asked my friends and coworkers to answer these questions for me, would they select the same frequencies that I did?' You may want to ask them to select scores for comparison.

Step 2: Best practice manager
Repeat the process of rating against the ten management foundations, but this time assess how frequently you consider a 'best practice' manager should exhibit these behaviours.

Step 3: Gap analysis
Compare your self-assessment ratings with those for the best practice manager. Identify any significant differences (greater than one point) in the two sets of ratings. Select the three management foundations in which the greatest gaps were evident when you compared the ratings.

Step 4: Self-development
Review the three management foundations with the greatest gaps (identified in step 3). Develop some suggestions for self-improvement in each of these three areas.

Procedure for group discussion
1. The lecturer should determine the number of students who are most in need of improvement for each of the ten management foundations.

2. Discuss whether there is diversity, or whether all students elected the same foundations.

3. Beginning with those identified by the largest number of students, discuss how to improve performance against the management foundations.

4. Continue to discuss the foundations in priority order (from highest to lowest numbers identifies) until all ten are discussed, or the time runs out for the exercise.

Case study: *Hubbard's Foods Ltd*

Hubbard's Foods Limited is a cereal manufacturer based in Auckland, New Zealand. The company has an 18.5 per cent share of the New Zealand cereal market. CEO Dick Hubbard (who was elected as Mayor of Auckland in 2005), remembers clearly the early days when at one stage the company was three weeks away from entering receivership. Those early days have generated the principle of 'minimum waste and minimum fuss'.

Hubbard's Triple Bottom Line Report aims to provide sustenance for the mind, body and soul of everyone who has contact with the company. The company's key stakeholders include shareholders, employees, suppliers, customers and the community. At Hubbard's all stakeholders are looked after. For example, when the company outgrew its original factory, a new site was chosen on the outskirts of Auckland in a low-income, high-unemployment area to offer local unemployed employment opportunities. Hubbard aims to recruit and retain the best-performing staff. He values university education and offers scholarships to those who would like to begin a degree in food technology. Employees are valued, treated with respect and participate in a 10 per cent pre-tax profit-sharing scheme based strictly on years of service rather than income or job title. All employees were taken to Samoa for the long weekend to celebrate the company's ten-year anniversary. It is of no surprise to discover that Hubbard's has low staff turnover rates and absenteeism.

One of the more unusual features of Hubbard's commitment to its customers is that it has a very strict policy with respect to advertising. For example, the company does not advertise to children, it does not create unrealistic images, it will not play to individual fears, it will not denigrate the competition and, more importantly, it will inform. One area of advertising is the inclusion in each cereal box of the company newsletter, the *Clipboard*. Customers are kept informed via the *Clipboard*, with information about complaints, problems and controversies, and also good news and successes. Other community commitments include sponsorship to Outward Bound, World Vision's Kids for Kids concert

(continued)

and a variety of other local community and school projects.

Dick Hubbard is also a member of the New Zealand Business Council for Sustainable Development and the company currently recycles paper, cardboard, plastic shrink wrap, aluminum containers, plastic containers, raw material containers and toner cartridges. In addition, the company has a program of eliminating waste and educating customers about sustainable development.[82]

Questions

1. Under the headings 'Society', 'Economy', 'Environment', summarise what you think should appear in Hubbard's Triple Bottom Line Report.

2. Using the information in this chapter, what comments can you make about the nature of the employee–employer relationship at Hubbard's?

3. Use the performance equation on page 5 to predict the overall organisational performance by analysing organisational '*capacity x willingness x organisational support*'.

OB Suggested reading

David Blenkhorn and Craig Fleisher, *Competitive intelligence and global business* (Westport, CT: Praeger Publishers, 2005).

Stewart R Clegg, *Managing and organizations: an introduction to theory and practice* (London: Sage Publications, 2005).

Hans G Daellenbach, *Management science : decision making through systems thinking* (New York: Palgrave Macmillan, 2005).

Peter F Drucker, *The new realities* (New York: HarperCollins, 1989).

Ali F Farhoomand, *Managing (e)business transformation : a global perspective* (New York: Palgrave Macmillan, 2005).

Dallas Hanson and Peter Dowling, *Strategic management: competitiveness and globalisation*, Pacific Rim 2nd ed. (South Melbourne: Thomson Learning, 2005).

Robert F Hartley, *Management mistakes and successes*, 8th ed. (Hoboken, NJ: John Wiley & Sons, 2005).

Harvard Business School, *Management dilemmas: when people are the problem* (Boston: Harvard Business School Press, 2005).

Paul Keating, *Engagement: Australia faces the Asia Pacific* (Sydney: Macmillan, 2000).

Petra Kuchinka, *Levels of corporate globalization: developing a measurement scale for the global customer management* (New York: Palgrave Macmillan, 2005).

R Stewart, *Globalisation, the changing nature of employment, and the future of work: the experience of work and organisational change* (New York: Palgrave Macmillan, 2005).

K Ohmae, *The borderless world: power and strategy in the global marketplace* (London: HarperCollins, 1990).

Arvind Phatak, Rabi Bhagat, Roger Kashlak, *International management: managing in a diverse and dynamic global environment* (New York: McGraw-Hill, 2005).

John Saee, *Managing organizations in a global economy: an intercultural perspective* (Mason, Ohio: Thomson/South-Western, 2005).

Trevor Wilson, *Global diversity at work; winning the war for talent* (Toronto: John Wiley & Sons, 2001).

OB End notes

1. Vodafone Group, 'Working for Vodafone', http://www.vodafone.co.nz/aboutus/12.1.2.4_working.jsp?item=people&subitem=working (viewed 29 September 2005).

2. Vodafone Group, 'Company information', http://www.vodafone.co.nz/aboutus/12.1_the_vodafone_company.jsp (viewed 29 September 2005).

3. Vodafone Group, 'Company information', http://www.vodafone.co.nz/aboutus/12.1_the_vodafone_company.jsp (viewed 29 September 2005).

4. Vodafone Group, 'Our structure', http://www.vodafone.co.nz/aboutus/12.1.2.2_structure.jsp?item=people&subitem=structure (viewed 29 September 2005).

5. Lynette Hoffman, 'Mutual benefits', *Human Resources* (24 August 2005), http://www.humanresourcesmagazine.com.au/articles/B3/0C0357B3.asp?Type=60&Category=881 (viewed 6 October 2005).

6. Lynette Hoffman, 'Mutual benefits', *Human Resources* (24 August 2005), http://www.humanresourcesmagazine.com.au/articles/B3/

0C0357B3.asp?Type=60&Category=881 (viewed 6 October 2005).

7. 'Vodafone chief to leave in May', *Sydney Morning Herald* (14 April 2005), http://www.smh.com.au/news/Breaking/Vodafone-chief-to-leave-in-May/2005/04/14/1113251730778.html (viewed 4 October 2005).

8. Vodafone Group, 'Working for Vodafone', http://www.vodafone.co.nz/aboutus/12.1.2.4_working.jsp?item=people&subitem=working (viewed 29 September 2005).

9. See PR Lawrence and JW Lorsch, *Organisations and environment: managing differentiation and integration* (Homewood, IL: Richard D Irwin, 1967).

10. ibid.

11. Geert Hofstede, 'Cultural constraints in management theories', *Academy of Management Executive*, vol. 7 (1993), pp. 81–94. See also Geert Hofstede, *Culture's consequences* (Beverly Hills, CA: Sage, 1980).

12. See Uma Sekaran, *Research methods for managers*, 2nd ed. (New York: John Wiley & Sons, 1992).

13. John Arnold, *Work psychology. understanding human behaviour in the workplace*, 4th ed. (Edinburgh Gate, Harlow: Pearson Education Limited, 2005).

14. D Goleman, *Working with emotional intelligence* (New York: Bantam, 2000).

15. R Bar-On, *The emotional intelligence inventory (EQi): technical manual* (Toronto: Multi Health System, 1997).

16. JD Mayer and P Salovey, 'What is emotional intelligence?' in P Salovey and DJ Sluyter (eds), *Emotional development and emotional intelligence* (New York: Basic Books, 1997).

17. Vodafone Group, 'Vision & values', http://www.vodafone.com/article/0,3029,CATEGORY_ID%253D30304%2526LANGUAGE_ID%253D0%2526CONTENT_ID%253D21016,00.html (viewed 4 October 2005).

18. Singtel, 'Company profile', http://home.singtel.com/about_singtel/company_profile/vision_n_mission/companypro_visionmission.asp (viewed March 2005).

19. KIWI Income and Property Trust, 'Investment philosophy', http://www.kipt.co.nz/n129.html (viewed March 2005).

20. BHP Billiton, 'Charter', http://www.bhpbilliton.com/bb/aboutUs/charter.jsp (viewed 24 November 2005).

21. The Warehouse, 'Core purpose and values', http://www.thewarehouse.co.nz/ (viewed 24 November 2005).

22. M Wertheimer [an address before the Kant Society, Berlin, 7 December 1924], reprinted in WD Ellis, *Source book of Gestalt psychology* (New York: Harcourt, Brace And Co, 1938).

23. BreadTalk corporate web site, http://www.breadtalk.com/ (viewed March 2005).

24. Susan Kurosawa, 'Vulture tourists', *The Australian* [1st all-round country edition] (24 October 2005), p. 10.

25. ibid.

26. A Fish and J Wood, 'Cross-cultural management competence in Australian business enterprises', *Asia Pacific Journal of Human Resources*, vol. 35, no. 1 (1996), pp. 274–301.

27. Henry Mintzberg, 'Rounding out the manager's job', *Sloan Management Review* (Fall 1994), pp. 11–26.

28. Lynette Hoffman, 'Mutual benefits', *Human Resources* (24 August 2005), http://www.humanresourcesmagazine.com.au/articles/B3/0C0357B3.asp?Type=60&Category=881 (viewed 6 October 2005).

29. Tom Peters, *Thriving on chaos* (New York: Knopf, 1991).

30. Lynette Hoffman, 'Mutual benefits', *Human Resources* (24 August 2005), http://www.humanresourcesmagazine.com.au/articles/B3/0C0357B3.asp?Type=60&Category=881 (viewed 6 October 2005).

31. Ruth Champion-Hughes, 'Totally integrated employee benefits', *Public Personnel Management*, vol. 30, issue 3 (Washington, 2001); M Joseph Sirgy, David Efraty, Phillip Siegel, Dong-Jin Lee, 'A new measure of quality of work life (QWL) based on need satisfaction and spill-over theories', *Social Indicators Research*,. vol. 55, issue 3 (Dordrecht, September 2001).

32. M Joseph Sirgy, David Efraty, Phillip Siegel, Dong-Jin Lee, 'A new measure of quality of work life (QWL) based on need satisfaction and spill-over theories', *Social Indicators Research*,. vol. 55, issue 3 (Dordrecht, September 2001).

33. DM Rousseau, *Psychological contract inventory — technical report* (Pittsburg: Carnegie Mellon University, 2000).

34. Michael Hammer and James Champy, *Re-engineering the corporation* (New York: HarperCollins, 1993); Hammer and Champy, 'The promise of re-engineering', Fortune (3 May 1993), pp. 94–7.

35. Deresky, *International management: managing across borders and cultures*, 4th ed. (Prentice Hall, 2003).

36. BHP Billiton, 'Annual report 2005', http://annualreport.bhpbilliton.com/2005/plc/repository/financial/financialReview.asp (viewed 18 October 2005).

37. Vicki Jayne, 'The new leaders', *New Zealand Management* (February 2005), p. 29.

38. BBC News corporate web site http://news.bbc.co.uk/1/hi/programmes/panorama/archive/970385.stm (viewed 26 October 2005).

39. R Balko, 'Sweatshops and globalisation', http://aworldconnected.org/article.php/525.html (viewed 27 October 2005), also cited in M Street, *Taking sides: clashing views on controversial issues in management* (Iowa: McGraw-Hill, 2005), pp. 336–42.

40. D Arnold and N Bowie, 'Sweatshops and respect for persons', *Business Ethics Quarterly*, vol 13, no. 2 (2003), pp. 221–42.

41. M Street, *Taking sides: clashing views on controversial issues in management* (Iowa: McGraw-Hill, 2005), p. 306.

42. ibid.

43. R Balko, 'Sweatshops and globalisation', http://aworldconnected.org/article.php/525.html (viewed

27 October 2005), also cited in M Street, *Taking sides: clashing views on controversial issues in management* (Iowa: McGraw-Hill, 2005), pp. 336–42.

44. J Gottschalk, 'The risks associated with the business use of email', *Intellectual Property & Technology Law Journal*, vol. 17, no. 7 (July 2005), pp. 16–18.

45. N Eason, 'Don't send the wrong message, when email crosses borders, a faux pas could be just a click away', *Business 2.0*, vol. 6, no. 7 (August 2005), p. 102; S Harris, 'Uh oh', *Government Executive*, vol. 37, no. 1 (January 2005), pp. 66–71.

46. OECD, *The knowledge based economy* (Paris: OECD, 1996).

47. L Colquihoun, 'New Zealand on the lookout for skills — Employers are fighting an international "war for staff" as hiring expectations reach record levels despite a continuing brain drain to Australia and beyond', *Financial Times* (London, 18 August 2005), p. 9.

48. See also *Workforce 2000: competing in a seller's market. is corporate America prepared?* (Indianapolis: Tower Perrin/ Hudson Institute, 1990).

49. See John P Fernandez, *Managing a diverse workforce* (Lexington, MA: D. C. Heath, 1991); Julie O'Mara, *Managing workplace 2000* (San Francisco: Jossey-Bass, 1991).

50. Department of Immigration and Multicultural and Indigenous Affairs, 'Productive diversity: Australia's competitive advantage', http://www.immi.gov.au/facts/ 07productive.htm (viewed 25 October 2005).

51. See Geert Hofstede and Michael H Bond, 'The Confucius connection: from culture roots to economic growth', *Organizational Dynamics*, vol. 16 (1988), pp. 4–21; Geert Hofstede, 'Cultural constraints in management theories', *Academy of Management Executive*, vol. 7 (February 1993), pp. 81–94.; and Adler, op. cit.

52. Fritz Rieger and Durhane Wong-Rieger, 'Strategies of international airlines as influenced by industry, societal and corporate culture' *Proceedings of the Administrative Sciences Association of Canada*, vol. 6, part 8 (1985), pp. 129–41.

53. See Geert Hofstede, 'Motivation, leadership, and organization: do American theories apply abroad?', *Organizational Dynamics*, vol. 9 (Summer 1980), pp. 42–63; Nancy Adler (1991), op. cit., pp. 123–48.

54. Adler (1991), op. cit.

55. Geert Hofstede, *Culture's consequences: international differences in work-related values*, abridged ed. (Beverly Hills, CA: Sage, 1984); Geert Hofstede and Michael H Bond, 'The Confucius connection: from culture roots to economic growth', *Organizational Dynamics*, vol. 16 (1988), pp. 4–21.

56. Geert Hofstede, 'Cultural constraints in management theories', *Academy of Management Executive*, vol. 7 (February 1993), pp. 81–94.

57. Developed from Geert Hofstede, 'Motivation, leadership, and organization: do American theories apply abroad?', *Organizational Dynamics*, vol. 9 (Summer 1980), pp. 42–63;

Geert Hofstede and Michael H Bond, op. cit.; Geert Hofstede (1993), op. cit.

58. H van Leeuwen, 'Population could rise by 56 per cent', *Australian Financial Review* (23 July 1996), p. 5. See D Jackson, 'Australia's impending demographic revolution', *Australian Bulletin of Labour*, vol. 22, no. 3 (September 1996), pp. 194–211.

59. Information from Statistics NZ, 'National population projections (2001 (base) – 2051)', media release (24 October 2002), www.stats.gov.nz (viewed 24 March 2003).

60. Vodafone Group, 'Working for Vodafone', http:// www.vodafone.co.nz/aboutus/ 12.1.2.4_working.jsp?item=people&subitem=working (viewed 29 September 2005); Lynette Hoffman, 'Mutual benefits', *Human Resources* (24 August 2005), http:// www.humanresourcesmagazine.com.au/articles/B3/ 0C0357B3.asp?Type=60&Category=881 (viewed 6 October 2005).

61. Vodafone Australia, 'Facts & figures', http:// www.vodafone.com.au/rep/about/company/ facts_figures.jsp?gs=foryou&hd=about_vodafone&st=comp any_info&ss=facts_Figures (viewed 29 September).

62. A Horin and C Munroe, 'Looking down on the glass ceiling', *The Age* (Melbourne, 3 April 2004), p. 3.

63. E. Davis and R. Lansbury, *Managing together* (Sydney: Longman, 1996).

64. Majella J Albion , 'A measure of attitudes towards flexible work options', *Australian Journal of Management*, vol. 22, issue 2 (2004).

65. NSW Department of Commerce, Office of Industrial Relations, 'Family friendly ideas for small business', http: //www.industrialrelations.nsw.gov.au/workandfamily/ strategy/guidebook/guide_child.html (viewed 10 May 2005).

66. NSW Department of Commerce, Office of Industrial Relations, 'Family friendly ideas for small business', http: //www.industrialrelations.nsw.gov.au/workandfamily/ strategy/guidebook/guide_child.html (viewed 10 May 2005).

67. NSW Department of Commerce, Office of Industrial Relations, 'Family friendly ideas for small business', http: //www.industrialrelations.nsw.gov.au/workandfamily/ strategy/guidebook/guide_child.html (viewed 10 May 2005).

68. International Labor Organisation, '*More than 120 nations provide paid maternity leave*', ILO press release 98/7 (16 February 1998).

69. ibid.

70. ibid.

71. Farah Farouque, 'So will you do it for your country?', *The Age* (Melbourne, 15 May 2004).

72. Family Assistance Office, www.familyassist.gov.au (viewed 10 March 2005).

73. Human Rights and Equal Opportunity Commission, '*Commissioner calls on Government to remove Australia's reservation to CEDAW*', press release (30 June 2004), http://www.hreoc.gov.au/media_releases/2004/45_04.htm (viewed 10 March 2005).

74. Mark Lawson, 'Making the switch from Dubbo to Delhi', *Australian Financial Review* (20 March 2003), http://afr.com/specialreports/report1/2003/03/20/FFXXYTV9DDD.html (viewed 10 March 2005); AFP, 'India set to emerge as a major outsourcing hub for global aerospace industry' (13 February 2005), http://www.independent-bangladesh.com/news/feb/14/14022005bs.htm#A13 (viewed 10 March 2005).

75. Human Rights and Equal Opportunity Commission, *Report of the national pregnancy and work inquiry*, ch. 10 at p. 147, http://www.hreoc.gov.au/word/sex_discrim/pregnant_productive/part_c.doc (viewed 20 October 2005); Australian Bureau of Statistics, 'Social trends', ch. 2 of *Australia Now 2005*.

76. P Robinson, 'Exploding the myth of the happy casual worker', *The Age* (Melbourne, 28 July 2004), p. 2.

77. New South Wales State Chamber of Commerce, 'Getting a grip on IT' (May 2005), http://www.thechamber.com.au/homezone/policy/PDF/GettingaGriponITfinal.pdf (viewed 21 October 2005).

78. M Zonneveldt, 'Business lobby fights new rules', *Herald Sun* (Melbourne, 17 October 2005), p. 30.

79. 'ING Habitat for Humanity tie up to build homes for Baseco fire', *Businessworld* (Manila, 12 October 2005), p. 1.

80. See Steven N Brenner and Earl A Mollander, 'Is the ethics of business changing?', *Harvard Business Review*, vol. 55 (January/February 1977), pp. 50–7; Saul W Gellerman, 'Why "good" managers make bad ethical choices', *Harvard Business Review*, vol. 64 (July–August 1986), pp. 85–90; Barbara Ley Toffler, *Tough choices: managers talk ethics* (New York: John Wiley & Sons, 1986); Justin G Longnecker, Joseph A McKinney and Carlos W Moore, 'The generation gap in business ethics', *Business Horizons*, vol. 32 (September/October 1989), pp. 9–14; John B Cullen, Vart Victor and Carroll Stephens, 'An ethical weather report: assessing the organization's ethical climate', *Organizational Dynamics* (Winter 1990), pp. 50–62.

81. R Robertson, 'Super manager 2010: a profile', *Sydney Morning Herald* (12 April 1995).

82. J Kirkwood and D Ruwhui, 'Growth at Hubbard's Foods?', *Journal of the Australian and New Zealand Academy of Management*, vol. 9, no. 2 (2003), pp. 47–57; Hubbard's Foods Limited corporate web site, http://www.hubbards.co.nz/clipboards.php (viewed 24 October 2005).

Interpretation of 'Individual activity'

All of the statements are true. Thus, your score should be close to 40. The closer your score is to 40, the more you understand the global context of organisational environments. The closer your score is to 10, the less you understand the global context. For developmental purposes, you should note any particular items for which you had a low score and concentrate on improving your knowledge of those areas.

PART 2

MANAGING INDIVIDUAL BEHAVIOUR AND PERFORMANCE

2 Individual attributes and their effects on job performance   *40*

3 Motivation and empowerment   *76*

4 Learning, reinforcement and self-management   *112*

5 Job design, goal setting and flexible work arrangements   *148*

Part 2 case study: Getting RailCorp to run like a train   *184*

CHAPTER 2

Individual attributes and their effects on job performance

Learning objectives

After studying this chapter, you should be able to:

1. explain the individual performance equation

2. discuss the demographic characteristics that distinguish individuals

3. discuss competency characteristics that distinguish individuals

4. discuss personality characteristics that distinguish individuals

5. list some strategies that managers can adopt to capitalise on workforce diversity in their organisations

6. define and describe possible values and attitudes of workers

7. explain the importance of job satisfaction as a specific organisational attitude, and determine how this variable can affect job performance

8. describe the perceptual process and common perceptual distortion of stereotyping.

Paul Burgess, director of Link-up International[1], an Australian management consultancy, developed the Instinctive Drive System™. He says that the Instinctive Drive (ID)™ questionnaire measures the actions of individuals in organisations at a much deeper level than the personality typology tests that organisations commonly use to help improve performance. The ID System™ measures the 'why' of actions by combining a survey tool with follow-up counselling and exploring why participants act in a particular way.[2] Ongoing qualitative research into the perceptions of individuals regarding improvement of performance shows a common theme among interviewees: in many cases the discovery of an individual's instinctive drives allows them to feel 'normal, accepted and relieved'. For example, individuals who are found to be naturally driven towards 'improvise' now have a better insight into why they inherently reject planning and structure in the workplace. These improvisers *naturally* leave things till the last minute. Many stated they tried for years to change behaviour that was believed to be 'a bad habit'. After completing their ID™ questionnaire, workers with a natural drive towards 'improvise' felt acknowledgement for the different way in which they work from coworkers who are the opposite — 'avoid improvise'. The research has found that, since discovering their drives, workers with a drive towards 'improvise' concede that they may need to work according to a structure or plan as otherwise their (seemingly) disorganised way of working may impact negatively on the performance of others. Individuals who are 'avoid improvise' report that, since knowing their instinctive drives, they recognise that they need to be more flexible and, as a strategy, leave a portion of their day to deal with 'unexpected occurrences'.

The combination of different individuals each with different instinctive drives in the workplace is unavoidable, arguably necessary, and can be difficult to manage. Quantitative research suggests people who are driven towards 'improvise' are also more likely to be 'avoid verify'.[3] One interviewee, who knows she is naturally driven to 'verify', reported a lot of tension between herself and her colleagues, who are mostly driven to improvise. The colleagues claimed that the person who is driven to *verify* was always criticising their ideas by questioning and rethinking the feasibility of those suggestions. At the same time, the high verifier reported she was being ostracised by the group as she clearly behaved differently than her coworkers. Interviewees reported that since discovering their instinctive drives and applying the strategies, it is recognised by individuals in the group that the worker who is driven to verify has an important role to play in decision making. The verifier makes the improvisers stop and think about the details and consequences of their ideas. As a result, the improvisers are more accepting of criticisms, and the person driven to 'verify' expresses critique in a more positive way so as not to deny improvisers the scope to be creative.

Natural instincts are unchangeable. The ID System™ taps into individual motivational drives or instincts. When raising individual instinctive drives from the subconscious level to consciousness, individuals and their managers can strategise on how to achieve peak performance by allowing people to work within stride of their instinctive drives.[4]

Introduction

People are different! Contemporary organisations are dealing with some key issues that a manager must address when attempting to influence individual performance. Accordingly, it is important as managers that we stop and ask what makes them different. In this chapter we first examine in detail three broad categories important in our study of organisational behaviour: demographic or biographical characteristics; competency characteristics; and personality characteristics.

We then briefly address individual differences in planning strategies you can use to deal with the increasing diversity in the workforce. Next, as students or as managers of people, it is extremely important to understand your own values and how they differ from those held by others. This is especially the case in pluralist societies such as Australia and the United States. In a pluralist society we particularly need to understand differences in perceptions across cultures.

Consequently, in this chapter we examine values, attitudes and perceptions as they relate to the workplace. This includes a comprehensive discussion on job satisfaction and workplace behaviour. We also discuss perception as an attribute for work performance and reflect on the perceptual process and cognitive frameworks affecting perceptions. These concepts, together with demography, competency and personality, are critical to your understanding of the importance of responding to individuality in the workplace.

Individual performance factors

The individual performance equation

LEARNING 1 OBJECTIVE

In chapter 1 we presented the organisational behaviour model that should help us explain and predict human behaviour in the workplace. As discussed, the performance equation (see figure 2.1) views performance as the result of the personal attributes of individuals, the work effort they make and the organisational support they receive. The multiplication signs indicate the three factors must be present for high performance to be achieved. Every manager must understand how these three factors can affect performance results.

| Job performance | = | individual attributes | × | work effort | × | organisational support |

FIGURE 2.1 • The basic performance equation

We will use this equation as the theoretical guide for the material presented in this chapter. Notice that:
- individual attributes relate to a *capacity* to perform
- work effort relates to a *willingness* to perform
- organisational support relates to the *opportunity* to perform.[5]

Individual attributes

Several broad categories of attributes create individual differences that are important in the study of organisational behaviour. These include demographic or biographic characteristics (for example, gender, age or ethnic background); competency characteristics (aptitude/ ability, or what a person can do); personality characteristics (a number of natural and learned traits reflecting what a person is like, including individual innate or instinctive drives); values, attitudes and perceptions that influence how we interpret the world. The importance of these various attributes depends on the nature of the job and its task requirements. Managerially speaking, individual attributes must match task requirements to facilitate job performance (figure 2.2).

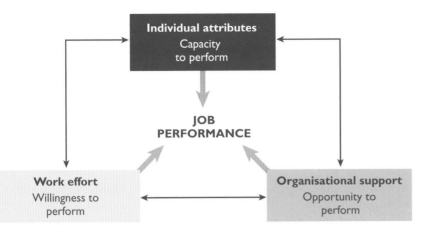

FIGURE 2.2 • Dimensions of individual performance factors

Source: Suggested by Melvin Blumberg and Charles D Pringle, 'The missing opportunity in organizational research: some implications for a theory of work performance', *Academy of Management Review*, vol. 7 (1982), p. 565.

Flamboyant billionaire Richard Branson used a reality TV show, *Quest for the Best*, to search for a possible successor for his Virgin business group. Sixteen eager young entrepreneurs followed him around the world competing against each other in business challenges and competitive adventures. One of the key components of Branson's list of individual traits is an ability to take calculated risks. In one episode, two contestants were challenged to create a world record by going over the Victoria Falls in a barrel. There was considerable risk involved and previous attempts had left people severely injured.

After weighing up the risks, one contestant chose not to do the challenge. The other contestant chose to go ahead. However, what he hadn't realised was that Branson was testing contestants' ability to assess risk — the contestant prepared to go over the falls failed and was sent home.

In the final episode, after receiving a cheque for $1 million, the last remaining contestant was to face yet another challenge. He was given a choice between keeping the money and flipping a coin. 'Heads' would result in the contestant receiving nothing and 'tails' would result in the contestant winning something 'far greater', which was not specified. After 45 minutes of agonising decision making, and against advice from past contestants, the winner decided to keep the cheque for a million dollars because he wasn't prepared to risk it. Branson was delighted and found the contestant had made the right decision. The reward was the million dollars and a three-month probation as the President of Virgin Worldwide. Branson had clearly found the contestant to be a *calculated* risk taker, a trait considered vital for a Virgin company president.[6]

Work effort

To achieve high levels of performance, even people with the right individual attributes must have the willingness to perform; that is, they must display adequate work effort. For many reasons different individuals display different levels of willingness to perform. Motivation to work describes the forces within an individual that account for the level, direction and persistence of effort expended at work. A highly motivated person works hard. *Level* of effort refers to the amount of energy that is put forth by the individual (for example, high or low level of effort to complete a task). *Direction* refers to an individual's choice when presented with a number of alternatives (for example, quality versus quantity) and *persistence* refers to the length of time a person is willing to persevere with a given action (trying to achieve a goal or abandon it when it is found difficult to attain the goal).

Organisational support

The third component of the individual performance equation is organisational support.[7] Even people whose individual characteristics satisfy job requirements and who are highly motivated to exert work effort may not be good performers because they do not receive adequate support in the workplace. Organisational behaviour researchers refer to such inadequacies as situational constraints and these may include: a lack of time; inadequate budgets; inadequate tools, equipment and supplies; unclear instructions; unfair levels of expected performance; and inflexibility of procedures.

Let us now turn to the first set of variables in our model — individual attributes — and examine three in particular: demography, competency and personality. The relevant part of the individual performance equation is shown in figure 2.3.

FIGURE 2.3 • Part of the individual performance equation

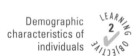
Demographic differences among individuals

Demographic characteristics, sometimes called *biographical characteristics*, are the background variables that help shape what a person has become. Key demographic characteristics are gender, age and racial background. Usually, demographic characteristics are easy to determine by appearance or from a person's personnel file. It is useful to think of these characteristics both in current terms (for example, a worker's current income) and in historical terms (for example, where and in how many places a person has lived, and family socioeconomic status).

In terms of gender differences and work performance, research suggests that men and women show no consistent differences in their analytical skills and problem-solving abilities. However, women tend to treat their staff in a less autocratic way than men, engage more in transformational behaviour and deliver more rewards for good performance.[8] Hence, there is a difference in leadership behaviour between men and women that may affect overall work performance.

In terms of age differences and work performance, older workers are often stereotyped to be set in their ways. On the other hand there is a positive relationship between seniority and performance because older persons have greater experience, resulting in higher skills and knowledge. In addition, more experienced workers tend to have lower turnover and less absenteeism.[9]

In terms of ethnicity and work performance, there is no evidence ethnicity is related to individual work performance providing ethnic groups are managed appropriately. This means that managers should be culturally aware and sensitive, be clear in their communication with workers from a non-English-speaking background (NESB) and recognise the potential for stereotyping and discrimination.[10]

Hair colour can be seen as an individual biological attribute. There is an abundance of jokes that surround the supposed incompetence of blondes and the fiery temperament of redheads. This recently prompted research in the United States. The hair colour of all the Fortune 500 CEOs was recorded: 2.2 per cent were naturally blonde and 3.4 per cent had red hair. These numbers are surprising as 20 per cent of the US population are naturally blonde and only 1 per cent have red hair. This shows that blondes were, relatively, grossly underrepresented and redheads were overrepresented among the CEOs. Interestingly, the results were the same even when minorities and women were removed from the data. Despite these surprising results, hair colour discrimination has not yet been made illegal.[11]

If we examine the individual performance equation again, we are suggesting that some demographic characteristics of individuals may affect the capacity to perform work, which in turn may affect the level of individual work performance. However, demography is not a good indicator in seeking individual–job fits; rather aptitude, personality, values, attitudes and perceptions are what count.

Competency differences among individuals

OBJECTIVE 3 LEARNING

Competency characteristics of individuals

The second category of individual attributes relates to competency. Competency is a broad concept relating to the aptitudes and abilities of people at work. Aptitude represents a person's capability to learn something. Ability reflects a person's existing capacity to perform the various tasks needed for a given job. Aptitudes are potential abilities, while abilities are the knowledge and skills that an individual already possesses.[12] In addition, emotional competence plays a role in the ability to handle the work pressures.

Aptitude is the capability to learn something.

In terms of our individual performance model, competency is an important consideration for a manager when selecting candidates for a job. Once people with the appropriate aptitudes or abilities have been selected, on-the-job and continuing education/training or professional development activities can be used to enhance their required job skills.

Ability is the capacity to perform the various tasks needed for a given job.

Many different aptitudes and abilities are recognised as relevant to work performance and some have been extensively researched in the workplace. As a result, various tests are currently available to measure individual capacity. We can categorise abilities as cognitive abilities, physical abilities and emotional intelligence.

Cognitive abilities

As a college or university student, you have probably taken some tests of cognitive abilities while at school or when you are applying for a job. Some provide a measure of general intelligence or the 'G Factor' (such as the Stanford-Binet IQ test); others represent capacity in more specific areas such as verbal comprehension, spatial ability, numerical ability and memory.[13] Researchers still disagree over the extent to which our intelligence is determined at birth. The consensus view is that genetics and life experience together shape our capacity, although we are all born with some limits to development in specific areas.

Cognitive abilities refer to our mental capacity to process information and solve problems.

Physical abilities

Tune in to the Olympics, the World Cup or the Asia–Pacific Games and it is soon apparent that we all differ in terms of our physical abilities. Different sports require different levels of speed, strength, flexibility and stamina. The same is true of many different jobs. Fire-fighters

Physical abilities refer to our natural and developed motor capacities for speed, strength, flexibility and so on, as well as our use of the five senses.

need strength and stamina to withstand extreme physical conditions. Electricians need colour-perfect vision to work with electrical circuitry (about 10 per cent of the male population is red–green colour blind, while only a small proportion of females are). Manual dexterity has long been recognised as a crucial skill for people engaged in detail work, such as microsurgery and jewellery making.

If a particular job has a certain physical requirement, it is important that it is measured objectively, rather than through the inappropriate use of stereotypes. For example, in the past, to become a mail officer at Australia Post, a person had to weigh a minimum of 45 kg. This requirement was based on the assumption that small people are incapable of lifting heavy objects. This has prevented many Asian women, who often weigh less than 45 kg, from seeking work as mail officers. The validity of this stereotypical criterion was successfully challenged in court.[14] These days, the criterion for assessing potential mail officers is that they must be able to lift up to 16 kg in weight.

Emotional competence

Until fairly recently emotions were given very little attention by researchers in organisational behaviour. Generally speaking, emotions were seen as impediments to sound decision making and an ordered approach to workplace relations. This kind of thinking is quickly being replaced by a view that sees emotions as a normal part of our workplace experiences. In fact, recent research has revealed the centrality of emotions to all areas of human functioning.[15] For example, to make decisions we are guided by our values, which are in turn based on our emotions. Reasoning and emotion are intertwined.

Emotional intelligence is one aspect of our emotional functioning that complements the cognitive form of intelligence already discussed. So what is emotional intelligence? It is a form of social intelligence that allows us to monitor and shape our emotional responses and those of others. For many people, it is even more important than cognitive intelligence for success in life. The concept of emotional intelligence was popularised by Daniel Goleman in 1995 with the publication of his book on the topic, although others had been researching the area for some time.[16]

We now turn to the specific dimensions that make up emotional intelligence. A sound place to start is with the research instruments that are under development to assess it. There are several of these, and each has a slightly different way of constructing and defining the dimensions or components of emotional intelligence. The oldest and most well-researched was developed by Reuven Bar-On as a self-report instrument of emotional wellbeing.[17] It includes various measures of self-awareness and regard, interpersonal competence, adaptability, stress management and general mood state. An instrument that focuses more closely on awareness and management of emotions is the Multifactor Emotional Intelligence Scale.[18] The four dimensions on the MEIS are as follows:

* identifying emotions — awareness of, and the ability to identify, the emotions you and others are feeling
* using emotions — the capacity to weigh up the emotional aspects of values and attitudes when confronting problems and making decisions
* understanding emotions — the ability to understand complex emotions and to recognise how emotions pass through stages over time
* managing emotions — the ability to exercise self-control and self-regulation, and to empathise with and influence others.

Emotion management is well and truly placed on the organisational agenda. Emotion is a valuable resource to be harnessed in order to gain employee commitment (willingness) and a competitive advantage. Some researchers have the pessimistic view that emotion can be commodified via a 'commercialisation of intimate life'.[19] Others celebrate the recognition of emotion as a vital part of organisational life, and harness these energies in a positive way to improve customer service and counteract employees' emotional exhaustion.[20]

Emotional intelligence is a form of social intelligence that allows us to monitor and shape our emotions and those of others.

Emotion management is exercising emotional self-control and self-regulation influenced by the context in which individuals find themselves

For example, on a recent Virgin Blue flight, the air crew were obviously having a good time. The customer service manager's commentary during the usually boring demonstration of air safety equipment was very humorous and set the scene for interpersonal relations between crew members as well as between crew members and passengers. There were smiles all around.

Emotion is a lived interactional experience with an organisational dark side. For example, emotional burnout in front-line service work, the everyday stresses and strains of organisational life, and the difficulty of working with bullies or harassers are a reality that managers face. However, not all emotion is controlled by the organisation. Employees are social beings who enter the organisation with life histories and experiences. They may take up organisationally prescribed roles, experience frustrations and often have to present themselves very differently to customers or clients. There is no clear divide between public and private worlds of emotion.[21]

Perhaps one of the most emotionally exhausting professions is nursing. Often nurses cannot show publicly their private emotions. For example, when a nurse cares for a particular patient during the process of dying, and especially when he or she has cared for this person for a long period of time, the nurse will experience a strong emotional response to the patient's death. At the same time, the nurse is likely to care for several other patients in the ward. In consideration of his or her other patients, the nurse cannot share the privately felt emotions publicly. Thus, to be effective, nurses need to be highly competent social actors and emotion managers.

Emotion constantly crosses boundaries between self and society, private and public, formal and informal. Employees continually juggle their mixed emotions in order to both enjoy and endure the rigours of organisational life.[22] Managing employee emotions in the workplace includes recognising the potential transformative power of human action, while managers also need to recognise the emotive forces that inhibit organisationally desirable behaviours. For this, managers themselves need to be emotionally competent. This is one reason why Victoria University in Wellington, New Zealand, has now introduced compulsory emotional intelligence development into its MBA program.[23]

Personality differences among individuals

LEARNING OBJECTIVE 4 Personality characteristics of individuals

The third basic attribute of individuals is personality. We use the term personality to represent the overall profile or combination of characteristics that capture the unique nature of a person as that person reacts and interacts with others. Personality combines a set of physical and mental characteristics that reflect how a person looks, thinks, acts and feels. Understanding personality contributes to an understanding of organisational behaviour by helping us to see what shapes individuals, what they can do (competency) and what they will do (motivation). We expect there to be a predictable interplay between an individual's personality and the tendency to behave in certain ways. A common expectation, for example, is that introverts (people who are more interested in their private thoughts and feelings than in their external environment) tend to be less sociable than extroverts. Personality is a vital individual attribute for managers to understand.

Personality is the overall profile or combination of traits that characterise the unique nature of a person.

Personality determinants

An important question in looking at personality is what determines it. Is personality inherited or genetically determined? Or are personality attributes determined by experience? You may have heard someone say something like, 'She acts like her mother'. Or someone may argue that: 'Michael is the way he is because of how he was raised' or indeed: 'She is a born leader'. These arguments illustrate the nature/nurture controversy — that is, is personality determined by heredity (or genetic endowment) or one's environment? Figure 2.4 shows that these two forces actually operate in combination. Heredity consists of those factors that

The **nature/nurture controversy** is the argument over whether personality is determined by heredity, or genetic endowment, or by one's environment.

are determined at conception, and includes physical characteristics and gender in addition to personality factors. Environment consists of cultural, social and situational factors.

FIGURE 2.4 • Heredity and environmental links with personality

Heredity

Psychologists acknowledge that the mind is made up of three domains: the cognitive domain (such as skills and learned behaviour); the affective domain (emotions); and the conative domain (instinctive approaches). Conative actions are those derived from striving instincts. Previous studies of components of the mind often ignored the notion of conation or instinct. **Instinct** is described as inherited patterns of unreasoned and unchangeable responses to particular actions and behaviours. At the beginning of modern psychology both emotion and conation were considered central to its study. However, interest in these topics declined as measuring overt behaviour and cognition received more attention. The notion of instinct as the primary source of motivation was abandoned for several reasons, the common one being that this may place human beings on the same level as other animals.[24] Striving instincts are subconscious and immeasurable. However, conative *actions* can be quantified.[25] One way of measuring these conative actions is via the Instinctive Drive System™.

The Instinctive Drive System™, as introduced at the beginning of this chapter, is a measure of an individual's natural drives that cannot be changed. So far, Australian research has identified four innate drives. These are the drive to verify, to authenticate, to complete and to improvise.[26] Individuals are either driven to fulfil or to avoid these drives. Measuring Instinctive Drive (ID)™ helps to explain why people with similar emotional affections and similar cognitions, such as experience and training, behave very differently. Once an individual's IDs™ are discovered, employees who work out of stride with their natural way of doing things can employ strategies to reduce occupational stress. Equally, managers who know the innate drives of their staff can adjust job design to ensure high levels of performance.

Personality measurement tools are heavily criticised for lacking statistical reliability and validity. However, *quantitative* validity and reliability may very well be irrelevant. The perceived outcomes of participating in a program that improves understanding of interpersonal relations at work (or the qualitative results of such participation) are clearly valued by many organisations, as can be seen by the success of the management consultancies running them.

Environment

Cultural values and norms play a substantial role in the development of an individual's personality and behaviours. For example, contrast the individualism of Australian culture with the collectivism of Mexican culture.[27] Social factors reflect such things as family life, religion and the many formal and informal groups in which people participate throughout their lives. Finally, situational factors can influence personality; for example, the opportunity to assume increasingly challenging goals or to come back from failure can help build a person's feeling of self-worth.

There is considerable debate concerning the impact of heredity on personality. The most general conclusion is that heredity sets the limits on just how much personality characteristics can be developed, whereas the environment determines development within these limits. The limits appear to vary from one characteristic to the next.

Instinct is made up of inherited patterns of unreasoned and unchangeable responses to particular actions and behaviours.

Personality traits

Organisational behaviour literature describes numerous personality traits and characteristics. In this section we will consider some of the personality traits that have been linked with behaviour in organisations. Firstly, we will outline the 'big five personality dimensions', and we will follow this with a discussion of other key characteristics that have attracted considerable research interest.

Five key dimensions of personality

In a fascinating study of how we describe people's personalities, researchers identified 17 953 English-language terms that had been used over the years. They sorted the terms into groups with similar meanings, and finally distilled them into five key dimensions of personality.[28] Research has generally confirmed the relevance of each dimension to behaviour in organisations:

- *extroversion–introversion:* the degree to which individuals are oriented to the social world of people, relationships and events, as opposed to the inner world. Extroverts tend to be outgoing, talkative and sociable, while introverts are quiet and are happier spending time alone or with a few close friends.
- *conscientiousness:* the extent to which individuals are organised, dependable and detail focused, versus disorganised, less reliable and lacking in perseverance.
- *agreeableness:* the extent to which individuals are compliant, friendly, reliable and helpful, versus disagreeable, argumentative and uncooperative. One measure of this dimension is the Employee Reliability Scale.[29] Low-reliability individuals tend to be hostile towards rules, have feelings of detachment from others, and are thrill-seeking, impulsive and socially insensitive. Those with high scores have favourable attitudes to teamwork, helping others and punctuality, and are more adaptable.
- *emotional stability:* the degree to which individuals are secure, resilient and calm, versus anxious, reactive and tending to mood swings.
- *openness to experience:* the extent to which individuals are curious, open, adaptable and interested in a wide range of things, versus resistant to change and new experiences, less open to new ideas and preferring routine.

The five key dimensions of personality are extroversion–introversion; conscientiousness; agreeableness; emotional stability; and openness to experience.

Turn back to this chapter's opening. You may wonder if and how InstinctiveDrive™ differs from personality. A pilot study undertaken at the University of Western Sydney suggests that subconscious innate behaviour (instinctive drives) is linked with personality on just one dimension (openness to experience). If it is instinctive drives that ultimately govern people's behaviour when they are left to their own volition, then testing the motivational drive of individuals will help managers quickly understand 'what makes their staff tick'. The research team at the University of Western Sydney concluded that the Instinctive Drive System™ could therefore act as a springboard for communication between managers and staff.[30]

Locus of control

One widely used instrument is Rotter's locus of control, which measures the internal–external orientation of a person — that is, the extent to which a person feels able to affect his or her life.[31] People have general conceptions about whether events are controlled by themselves primarily, which indicates an internal orientation, or by outside forces or their social and physical environment, which indicates an external orientation. Internals, or persons with an internal locus of control, believe they control their own fate or destiny. In contrast, externals, or persons with an external locus of control, believe much of what happens to them is beyond their control and is determined by environmental forces.

For example, *internals* would agree with statements like 'people's misfortunes result from the mistakes they make' and 'by taking an active part in political and social affairs, people can control world events'.

Locus of control is the internal–external orientation — that is, the extent to which people feel able to affect their lives.

Internals are persons with an internal locus of control, who believe they control their own fate or destiny.

Externals are persons with an external locus of control, who believe what happens to them is beyond their control.

On the other hand, *externals* would agree with statements such as 'many of the unhappy things in people's lives are partly due to bad luck' and 'as far as world affairs are concerned, most of us are the victims of forces we can neither understand nor control'.

In the work context and generally speaking, internals seek more information, experience stronger job satisfaction, perform better on learning and problem-solving tasks, have greater self-control and are more independent than externals.

Authoritarianism/dogmatism

Both 'authoritarianism' and 'dogmatism' deal with the rigidity of a person's beliefs. A person high in authoritarianism tends to adhere rigidly to conventional values and to obey recognised authority. This person is concerned with toughness and power. People high in dogmatism see the world as a threatening place. They often regard legitimate authority as absolute, and accept or reject others according to how much they agree with accepted authority. Superiors possessing these latter traits tend to be rigid and closed.[32]

We may expect highly authoritarian individuals to present a special problem because they are so susceptible to obey authority that they may behave unethically in their eagerness to comply.[33] Authoritarianism has been directly linked with 'crimes of obedience' and unethical behaviour.[34] For example, authoritarianism is a required trait in military organisations throughout the world. One recent example of a crime of obedience was the abuse of Iraqi prisoners by US soldiers at Abu Ghraib, and there have been many historical examples including Jewish genocide during World War II and the 1968 My Lai massacre in Vietnam.[35] However, authoritarianism is not confined to the military; for example, under instruction, Arthur Andersen employees shredded documents to cover up the impending corporate scandal that allegedly led to the demise of one of the US's largest accountancy organisations and sparked the ENRON scandal.[36]

Machiavellianism

Another interesting personality dimension is Machiavellianism, which owes its origins to Niccolo Machiavelli. The very name of this sixteenth-century author evokes visions of a master of guile, deceit and opportunism in interpersonal relations. Machiavelli earned his place in history by writing *The prince*, a nobleman's guide to the acquisition and use of power.[37] From its pages emerges the personality profile of a Machiavellian — that is, someone who views and manipulates others purely for personal gain.

Manipulation is a basic drive for some people in social settings. And although some people view manipulation of others as being deceitful and sinful, others see manipulation as an important attribute for succeeding in an organisation. Thus, it is easy to see why Machiavelli's ideas have been both so avidly read and so heavily criticised over the years.[38]

ETHICAL
Perspective

The collapse of HIH

Researcher Susan Key has found that there is a connection between personality traits, such as locus of control, and a tendency for managers to behave ethically in organisations.[39] Locus of control is a measure of an individual's belief in the extent to which they can affect external events. An individual attributes control over events to either themselves (internal) or to other factors in their external environment (external). Individuals with an internal locus of control are more likely to perceive they have the discretion to act. When managers perceive that they have discretion to act, they are more likely to intervene in organisational processes when moral, social or legal issues are at stake. However, using this discretion can be very costly to individuals and to the shareholders involved.

For example, moral, social and legal indiscretions caused the collapse of the Australian insurance company HIH — to date, Australia's largest corporate failure. The collapse forced 41 companies into liquidation and inflicted losses and hardship on the Australian community. The liquidation process is expected to take 10 years, with a negligible return to the creditors. The former board director, Rodney Adler, has faced civil and criminal penalties. Adler's actions included disseminating false and misleading information, lying to other board members and failing to disclose that the outcome of some of his decisions benefited him personally in terms of financial gain.[40] Adler is banned from company directorship for 20 years, he must pay compensation of A$7 million and he must spend a minimum of two and a half years in jail. In addition, Adler has handed back the Order of Australia award that he received in 1999 for his philanthropic services to Australia.[41] So on the one hand, Adler used his discretion to break the law in order to gain significant personal financial benefits. On the other hand, he used that same discretion to donate large sums of money to charity — this raises questions about Adler's moral code. When Adler handed back his award he acknowledged that in light of the criminal convictions it would have been inappropriate to keep it. Some would think this was the 'right' thing to do, while others saw this action more as a strategic move on Adler's behalf, trying to win back some of the public appreciation he has lost.

Individual differences and workplace diversity

Capitalising on workplace diversity

Increasing diversity is creating unparalleled workplace challenges. Significant variations are occurring in skill levels, education, physical abilities, cultural backgrounds, lifestyles, personal values, individual needs, ethnicity and social values. This increasing diversity is changing the mix of skills required to effectively manage the workforce.

Organisations that can incorporate the opportunities created by diversity into their business strategies and management practices can gain a significant competitive advantage.

Working with workplace diversity

Implementing a diversity management program

THE **Effective**Manager 2.1

- Examine current structures and processes — do they harbour any systemic biases to disadvantage some groups? Whose priorities do they reflect? Who is excluded (for example, from decisions made in corridors or on the golf course)?
- Take a long-term view — attitudes may need to change and this will not happen overnight.
- Get support for change from the top (commitment, resources, money, time), as nothing will change without it.
- Get the involvement of all those who will be affected by change.

(continued)

Benefits of a workplace that is open to diversity

- With shortages of skilled labour in some occupational areas, recruitment of staff is easier for organisations that welcome diversity.
- Diverse workplaces have contacts with customers and business partners from a wider range of cultures and groups.
- Diverse perspectives bring creativity and innovation.
- Problems are solved using a wider range of ideas and perspectives.

Essentially, managers need to ensure everyone in the organisation is sensitive to individual differences and to seek innovative ways to match increasingly diverse workers with job requirements. This may mean developing innovative recruiting strategies to attract new sources of labour and creating flexible employment conditions to better use the increasingly diverse range of workers.

The organisation also needs to utilise various aspects of education and training in working with diverse employees, using a broad range of programs — from basic skills to workshops designed to encourage managers and employees to value those with different demographic backgrounds. Note that training should be ongoing. Some organisations involve managers in conducting the training, to help provide a feeling of responsibility for making workplace diversity successful.

Turn back to figure 2.3 on page 44. Notice that in figure 2.5 we now add the other three important individual attribute variables:

1. values
2. attitudes
3. perception.

We will now discuss these variables.

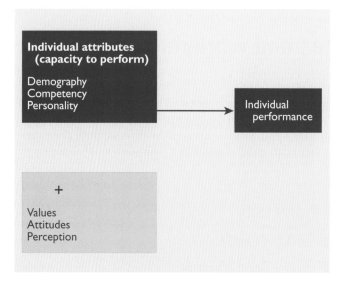

FIGURE 2.5 • The individual performance equation

Values and attitudes

Values

Values can be defined as broad preferences concerning appropriate courses of action or outcomes. As such, they reflect a person's sense of right and wrong, or what 'ought' to be.[42]

'Equal rights for all' and 'people should be treated with respect and dignity' are examples of values held by people. Values tend to influence attitudes and behaviour. If, for example, you value equal rights for all and you work for an organisation that treats its managers much better than it does its workers, you may form the attitude that your organisation is an unfair place to work, and you may seek employment elsewhere.

Values are global beliefs that guide actions and judgements across a variety of situations.

Sources and types of values

People's values develop as a product of the learning and experiences they encounter in the cultural setting in which they live. Because learning and experiences differ from one person to another, value differences result. Such differences are likely to be deep-seated and difficult (although not impossible) to change; many have their roots in early childhood and the way in which a person was raised.[43]

Psychologist Gordon Allport and his associates developed a classification of human values in the early 1930s.[44] However, although that classification had a major impact on the literature, it was not specifically designed for people in a work setting. More recently Meglino and associates have developed a values schema aimed at people in the workplace.[45] There are four values in this classification:

1. *Achievement* — getting things done and working hard to accomplish difficult things in life
2. *Helping and concern for others* — being concerned with other people and helping others
3. *Honesty* — telling the truth and doing what you feel is right
4. *Fairness* — being impartial and doing what is fair for all concerned.

The Meglino framework was developed from information obtained in the workplace, where these four values were shown to be especially important. Thus, the framework should be particularly relevant for studying organisational behaviour.

Patterns and trends in values

Values are important to managers and to the field of organisational behaviour because they have potential to influence workplace attitudes, behaviours and outputs. In addition, values can be influential through **value congruence**, which occurs when individuals express positive feelings on encountering others who exhibit values similar to their own. When values differ, or are incongruent, conflicts may result over such things as goals and the means to achieve them. The Meglino value schema was used to examine value congruence between leaders and followers. The researchers found greater follower satisfaction with the leader when there was such congruence in terms of achievement, helping, honesty and fairness values.[46]

Value congruence occurs when individuals express positive feelings on encountering others who exhibit values similar to their own.

Some value incongruencies can be traced to differences in the time periods during which people grew up and their values were set. The needs, values and expectations of different generations in the workplace can present a challenge to managers.

There are four generations identified in the workforce:
- older generation, aged 60 and over: 21 per cent of the workforce
- baby boomers, aged 40–59: 29.5 per cent of the workforce
- generation X, aged 29–40: 42 per cent of the workforce
- generation Y, aged 16–28: 7.5 per cent of the workforce.[47]

The greatest value difference among the generations is between the baby boomers and generation X. Baby boomers are stereotyped as being the original rebels and social activists, changing the world. However, baby boomers still 'bought into' the traditional values of the older generation. It is the baby boomers who are credited with founding the '60 hour working week'; they are supposedly driven, hardworking, loyal, and respectful to seniority and traditional workplace values. Baby boomers still see a distinction between managers and workers; they are union members and are often naturally authoritarian in their leadership styles.[48]

In contrast, generation X are stereotyped as being self-reliant, they value autonomy, they dislike supervision and demand better balance of work life and home life. They are savvy and information driven and tend to be more cynical than other generations. This explains their aversion to political activism; they prefer to focus on what's real and achievable in a practical way. There is no organisational loyalty as their careers have been dominated by downsizing and layoffs, so if they are not learning or growing they will simply move on. This generation have not bought into the 'manager versus worker' polarised view; they see organisations as a partnership and so prefer teamwork and conciliation rather than dictatorship and militancy.[49]

Interestingly, generation Y have been described as generation X on steroids! This generation's expectations, performance, self-esteem and maintenance are all high. Generation Y demand flexibility from day one; they are results driven and have no respect for past accomplishments; their only interest is today and the future. Generation Y in particular are empowered and have grown up in an era where rights were entrenched in the workplace, hence they generally see no place for unions.[50]

Of course these characterisations are just that! Managers need to be aware of value incongruence when working with different generations. However, they also need to be careful not to create stereotypes. We will discuss stereotyping in more detail later in this chapter.

Research suggests that individual rewards systems are the key to managing the different generational values and this may require a much more hands-on approach to management, with monitoring of work performance and expectations spelled out.[51]

Now turn to table 2.1. The values reported here are based on responses from a sample of US managers and human resource professionals.[52] The responding organisational specialists were asked to identify the work-related values they believe to be most important to individuals in the workforce, both now and in the near future. The nine most popular values are listed in the table. Even though individual workers place their own importance on these values, and many countries have diverse workforces, this overall characterisation is a good place for managers to start when dealing with employees in the new workplace.

However, we should be aware of applied research on value trends over time. Values change as the world is changing. For example, the 9/11 tragedies will have changed value ranking. When employees talk about security, this is no longer assumed to be financial security but also personal security at work.

TABLE 2.1 • The top nine work-related values		
1	Recognition for competence and accomplishments	People want to be seen and recognised, both as individuals and teams, for their value, skills and accomplishments. They want to know that their contribution is appreciated.
2	Respect and dignity	This value focuses on how people are treated — through the jobs they hold, in response to their ideas, or by virtue of their background. The strong support for this value indicates that most people want to be respected for who they are; they want to be valued.
3	Personal choice and freedom	People want more opportunity to be free from constraints and decisions made for and about them by authorities. They want to be more autonomous and able to rely more on their own judgement. They wish to have more personal choice in what affects their lives.
4	Involvement at work	Large portions of the workforce want to be kept informed, included and involved in important decisions at work, particularly where these decisions affect their work and quality of life at work.
5	Pride in one's work	People want to do a good job and feel a sense of accomplishment. Fulfilment and pride come through quality workmanship.

6 Lifestyle quality	People pursue many different lifestyles and each person wants theirs to be of high quality. Work policies and practices have a great impact on lifestyle pursuits. The desire for time with family and time for leisure were strongly emphasised.
7 Financial security	People want to know that they can succeed. They want some security from economic cycles, rampant inflation or devastating financial situations. This appears to be a new variation on the desire for money — not continual pursuit of money, but enough to feel secure in today's world, enjoy a comfortable lifestyle and ride out bad times.
8 Self-development	The focus here is on the desire to improve continually, to do more with one's life, to reach one's potential, to learn and to grow. There is a strong desire by individuals to take initiative and to use opportunities to further themselves.
9 Health and wellness	This value reflects the ageing workforce and increased information on wellness. People want to organise life and work in ways that are healthy and contribute to long-term wellness.

Source: D Jamieson and J O'Mara, *Managing workforce 2000* (San Francisco: Jossey-Bass, 1991), pp. 28–9.

Attitudes

Like values, attitudes are an important component of organisational behaviour. Attitudes are influenced by values, but they focus on specific people or objects, while values have a more general focus. 'Employees should be allowed to participate' is a value; 'your positive or negative feeling about your job as a result of the participation it allows' is an attitude. Formally defined, an attitude is a predisposition to respond in a positive or negative way to someone or something in our environment. When you say that you 'like' or 'dislike' someone or something, you are expressing an attitude. One important work-related attitude is job satisfaction. This attitude expresses a person's positive or negative feelings about various aspects of their job and/or work environment.

Regardless of the specific attitude considered, it is important to remember that an attitude, like a value, is a concept or construct; that is, one never sees, touches or actually isolates an attitude. Rather, attitudes are *inferred* from the things people say (informally or formally) or do (their behaviour).

> An attitude is a predisposition to respond in a positive or negative way to someone or something in your environment.

> The cognitive components of an attitude are the beliefs, opinions, knowledge or information a person possesses.

Components of attitudes

Study figure 2.6 carefully. This shows attitudes as accompanied by antecedents and results. The beliefs and values antecedents in the figure form the cognitive component of an attitude: the beliefs, opinions, knowledge or information a person possesses. Beliefs represent ideas about someone or something, and the conclusions people draw about them; they convey a sense of 'what is' to an individual. 'My job lacks responsibility' is a belief shown in figure 2.6. Note that the beliefs may or may not be accurate. 'Responsibility is important' is a corresponding aspect of the cognitive component that reflects an underlying value.

> Beliefs represent ideas about someone or something and the conclusions people draw about them.

> The affective components of an attitude are the specific feelings regarding the personal impact of the antecedents.

The affective component of an attitude is a specific feeling regarding the personal impact of the antecedents. This is the actual attitude, such as 'I do not like my job'. The behavioural component is an intention to behave in a certain way based on specific feelings or attitudes. This intended behaviour is a predisposition to act in a specific way, such as 'I am going to quit my job'.

> The behavioural components of an attitude are the intentions to behave in a certain way based on a person's specific feelings or attitudes.

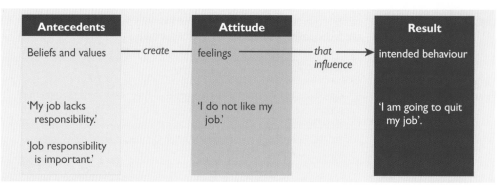

FIGURE 2.6 • A work-related example of the three components of attitudes

In summary, the components of attitudes systematically relate to one another as follows:[53]

$$\text{Beliefs and values} \xrightarrow[]{\text{create}} \text{attitudes} \xrightarrow[\text{predispose}]{\text{that}} \text{behaviour.}$$

Attitudes and behaviour

Look again at figure 2.6. It is essential to recognise that the link between attitudes and behaviour is tentative. An attitude results in intended behaviour. This intention may or may not be carried out in a given circumstance. For example, a person with a favourable attitude towards unions would have an attitude predicting such intentions as saying positive things about unions. However, other practical factors in a given situation may override these intentions. For example, hearing a good friend say negative things about unions may lead to the suppression of the tendency to say something positive in the same conversation. The person has not changed his favourable attitude in this case, but nor has he carried out the associated intention to behave.

Even though attitudes do not always predict behaviour, the link between attitudes and potential or intended behaviour is important for managers to understand. Think about your work experiences or conversations with other people about their work. It is not uncommon to hear concerns expressed about someone's 'bad attitude'. These concerns typically reflect displeasure with the behavioural consequences with which the poor attitude is associated. As we will show, unfavourable attitudes in the form of low job satisfaction can result in costly labour turnover. Unfavourable attitudes may also result in absenteeism, tardiness and even impaired physical or mental health. One of the manager's responsibilities, therefore, is to recognise attitudes and to understand both their antecedents and their potential implications.

Attitudes and cognitive consistency

One additional avenue of research on attitudes involves cognitive consistency; that is, the consistency between a person's expressed attitudes and actual behaviour. Let us go back to the example depicted in figure 2.6. A person in this illustration has an unfavourable attitude towards a job. She knows and recognises this fact. Now assume that her intentions to leave are not fulfilled and that she continues to work at the same job each day. The result is an inconsistency between the attitude (job dissatisfaction) and the behaviour (continuing to work at the job).

Festinger, a noted social psychologist, uses the term cognitive dissonance to describe a state of inconsistency between an individual's attitudes and his or her behaviour.[54] Let us assume that you have the attitude that recycling is good for the economy but you do not recycle.

> **Cognitive dissonance** is a state of perceived inconsistency between a person's expressed attitudes and actual behaviour.

Festinger predicts that such an inconsistency results in discomfort and a desire to reduce or eliminate it. There are three ways of achieving this reduction or elimination.

- *Changing the underlying attitude.* You decide that recycling really is not very good after all.
- *Changing future behaviour.* You start recycling.
- *Developing new ways of explaining or rationalising the inconsistency.* Recycling is good for the economy, but you do not recycle because the plastic recycling bags and procedures require more resources than are saved through recycling.

Job satisfaction as an attitude

Formally defined, job satisfaction is the degree to which an individual feels positively or negatively about work. It is an emotional response to one's tasks as well as to the physical and social conditions of the workplace. As a concept, job satisfaction also indicates the degree to which the expectations in someone's psychological contract are fulfilled.

Job satisfaction is the degree to which individuals feel positively or negatively about their jobs.

On 26 July 2004 the *Sydney Morning Herald* reported that Australians like work because of what they do and who they do it with. Compiled for the Job Futures network, the survey of 1000 people found that 88 per cent of participants are satisfied with their jobs. Of these, 34 per cent particularly enjoyed the nature of the work and 22 per cent enjoyed relationships with their coworkers.[55]

Men and women generally had the same reasons for job satisfaction except in two key areas. Eighteen per cent of men said it was their colleagues who were the cause of their satisfaction — for women it was 25 per cent. Pay was ranked by 18 per cent of men as the cause for their satisfaction, compared to 11 per cent of women.

Two attitudes closely related to job satisfaction are 'organisational commitment' and 'job involvement'. Organisational commitment refers to the degree to which a person strongly identifies with, and feels a part of, the organisation. Job involvement refers to the degree to which a person is willing to work hard and apply effort beyond normal job expectations.

Job satisfaction is among the important attitudes that influence human behaviour in the workplace. Thus, organisational behaviour researchers are interested in accurately measuring job satisfaction and understanding its consequences for people at work. On a daily basis, managers must be able to infer the job satisfaction of others by careful observation and interpretation of what they say and do while going about their jobs. Among the many available job satisfaction questionnaires, two popular ones are the Minnesota Satisfaction Questionnaire (MSQ) and the Job Descriptive Index (JDI).[56] The MSQ measures satisfaction with working conditions, opportunities for advancement, freedom to use one's own judgement, praise for doing a good job and feelings of accomplishment, among others.

Organisational commitment is the degree to which a person strongly identifies with, and feels a part of, the organisation.

Job involvement is the degree to which a person is willing to work hard and apply effort beyond normal job expectations.

'The effective manager 2.2' shows five important facets of job satisfaction from the JDI that summarise the factors that can influence whether people develop positive feelings about their work.

Job satisfaction

LEARNING OBJECTIVE 7

Job satisfaction and workplace behaviour

It is helpful to view job satisfaction in the context of two decisions people make about their work. The first is the decision to belong — that is, to join the organisation, attend work regularly and remain with the organisation. The second is the decision to perform — that is, to work hard in pursuit of high levels of task performance.

Job satisfaction, absenteeism and turnover

Absenteeism is the failure of people to attend work on a given day.

Job satisfaction influences absenteeism, or the failure of people to attend work. In general, satisfied workers are more regular in attendance and are less likely to be absent for unexplained reasons. Job satisfaction can also affect turnover, or decisions by people to terminate their employment: satisfied workers are less likely to leave, while dissatisfied workers are more likely to leave when they can.[57]

Turnover is the decision by people to terminate their employment.

In addition to job satisfaction, both absenteeism and turnover are of major concern to managers as a part of their human resource maintenance responsibility. The costs of turnover, especially, are high. They include the expenses of recruiting, selecting and training replacements, as well as productivity losses caused by any operational disruptions and low morale.

Clearly, the intention to remain or belong (the notion of organisational commitment which we referred to earlier) is closely related to job satisfaction. However, how these two are related is not totally clear as yet. Does job satisfaction produce commitment? Or, if we are committed to the organisation, will that lead to satisfaction with our work? Look at figure 2.7 closely — which way do you think it is?

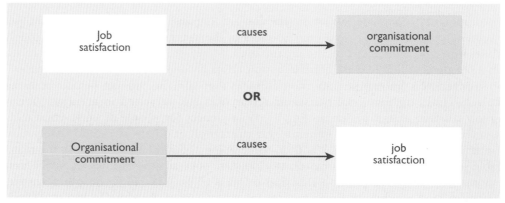

FIGURE 2.7 • Hypothesised links between job satisfaction and organisational commitment

Sickies — staff absenteeism

A 'sickie' occurs when an employee fails to turn up for work without a legitimate reason. Worker absenteeism can have a significant impact on a business's bottom line. Surveys show almost half of all Australian workers take the odd sickie.[58] Unscheduled absences that are not due to illness are estimated to cost Australian employers more than A$7 billion a year in lost productivity and disruption. However, sickies are not only an Australian phenomenon; unauthorised absenteeism occurs internationally. Asia and Africa have the lowest rates of absenteeism, whereas the United States and Western European countries such as Germany and France have the highest rates, with Australia and New Zealand falling in the middle.[59]

Caring for (sick) family members and worker job dissatisfaction are cited by most workers as the main causes of absenteeism. Some reasons for taking a sickie are far less obvious; for example, an Air New Zealand employee was sacked because she took a sick day to see a Robbie Williams concert. She would not have been caught had she not flown from Auckland to Wellington using her staff discount on the air fare![60]

In some countries legislation supports an employer's right to request a medical certificate for the purpose of establishing the genuineness of an application for paid sick leave — even for a single sick day.[61] However, organisational psychologist Dr Peter Cotton asserts that everyone at some stage wakes up in the morning and just doesn't feel like going to work, for a variety of reasons. Cotton's belief is that employers should sanction 'doona days' twice a year so that for those rare mornings, employees can just put the doona back over their head and not go into work. The belief is that this will help to reduce stress, particular in an era where up to 20 per cent of workers in Australia and New Zealand work more than 50 hours per week.[62]

Questions

1. In a small group, brainstorm some 'real' reasons for single-day absenteeism.
2. What are some strategies that managers can employ to reduce the financial impact of 'sickies'?

The link between job satisfaction and overall job performance

Performance is a summary measure of the quantity and quality of task contributions made by an individual or group to the work unit and organisation.

Recall the performance equation. **Performance** is defined as the quantity and quality of individual, group or organisational accomplishments. What is the relationship between job satisfaction and performance? This question assumes that satisfaction and performance may be related but does not say how. There is considerable debate on this issue — sometimes called the job satisfaction–performance controversy — which involves three alternative points of view,[63] and is by no means solved.[64]

(a) Satisfaction causes performance (S→P).

(b) Performance causes satisfaction (P→S).

(c) Rewards cause both performance and satisfaction (R→P, S).

Argument A: satisfaction causes performance

If job satisfaction causes high levels of performance, the message to managers is quite simple: to increase people's work performance, make them happy. However, research indicates that there is no simple and direct link between individual job satisfaction at one point in time and work performance at a later point in time. This conclusion is widely recognised among organisational behaviour scholars, even though some continue to argue that the S→P relationship may exist to various degrees, depending on the exact situation; for example, some evidence suggests an S→P relationship is more likely for professional or higher-level employees than for non-professionals or those at lower job levels.[65] These alternative views continue to be debated.

Argument B: performance causes satisfaction

If high levels of performance cause job satisfaction, the message to managers is quite different. Rather than focusing first on people's job satisfaction, attention should be given to helping people experience high performance accomplishments. From this outcome, job satisfaction would be expected to follow. Research indicates that an empirical relationship exists between individual performance measured at a certain time and later job satisfaction. A model of this relationship, based on the work of Edward E Lawler and Lyman Porter,[66] is presented in figure 2.8.[67] In the figure, performance accomplishment leads to rewards that, in turn, lead to satisfaction. Rewards in this model are *intervening variables* — that is, they 'link' performance with later satisfaction. In addition, a *moderator variable* — perceived equity of rewards — further affects the relationship. The moderator indicates that performance will lead to satisfaction only if rewards are perceived as equitable. If individuals feel their performances are unfairly rewarded, the P→S effect will not hold.

This viewpoint is important for managers to understand, not because it resolves the job satisfaction–performance controversy, but because it highlights the importance of rewards in the management process.

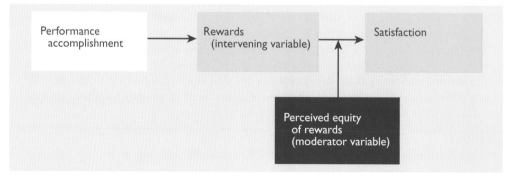

FIGURE 2.8 • Simplified version of the Porter–Lawler model of the performance–satisfaction relationship

Argument C: rewards cause both satisfaction and performance

This final argument in the job satisfaction–performance controversy is the most compelling. It suggests that a *proper* allocation of rewards can positively influence both performance and satisfaction. Research indicates that people who receive high rewards report higher job satisfaction. But research also indicates that performance-contingent rewards influence a person's work performance.[68] Large rewards are given for high performance; small or no rewards are given for low performance. Additionally, while giving a low performer only small rewards may lead to initial dissatisfaction, the expectation is that the individual will make efforts to improve performance to obtain greater rewards in the future.

The point is that managers should consider satisfaction and performance as two separate but interrelated work results that are affected by the allocation of rewards. Whereas job satisfaction alone is not a good predictor of work performance, well-managed rewards can have a positive influence on both satisfaction and performance.

COUNTER**POINT**

Incentive pay to motivate the workforce: is it working?

Many businesses believe that incentive programs are a popular tool to motivate and reward employees. For example, in the mid-1990s, the insurer Colonial Mutual created an incentive program to motivate and reward franchisees. The incentive scheme operated like an airline's frequent-flyer program, with points awarded each month for sales, attending seminars and workshops, attending external courses and so on. Franchisees joined the scheme as bronze members and progress to silver and gold. This incentive program has kept Colonial Mutual's insurance sales team happy and helped increase revenue as the company underwent a restructuring.[69]

However, others argue that it is *certain* that any benefits gained in the short term will be more than lost in the long term. Incentives are used to trigger a short-term burst of output. However, according to some, the next time such a burst is required, the reward will no longer be looked at as an 'incentive', but as an 'expected'.[70]

Questions

1. In your opinion, does a reward system, such as incentive pay, cause *sustained* motivation and satisfaction? Why or why not?
2. Will incentive pay or other rewards have the same effect on each individual worker? Why or why not?
3. Once such a reward system is introduced, what consequences will it have if the organisation has to withdraw the scheme?
4. What are the ethical implications of award schemes? In discussing this question consider the factors affecting the decision-making processes; for example, managerial control and punishment, loyalty, personality differences and personal threats that employees and employers may experience.

Global managerial competencies

International
SPOTLIGHT

Global managers must understand and respond to customers, governments and competitors across the world. To be successful, global managers must develop key global and cultural competencies: cultural self-awareness, cultural consciousness, ability to lead multicultural teams, ability to negotiate across cultures and a global mindset.[71]

- *Cultural self-awareness.* The starting pointing for cultural sensitivity is an understanding of the influence of one's own culture. A clear appreciation of one's own

(continued)

cultural values, assumptions and beliefs is a prerequisite for developing an appreciation of other cultures.[72]

- *Cultural consciousness.* A critical requirement for global managers is the ability to adapt to cultural requirements and manage cultural diversity.[73]
- *The ability to lead multicultural teams.* This requires working collaboratively with people with different cultural perspectives and developing cultural sensitivity.[74]
- *The ability to negotiate across cultures.* Global managers are required to negotiate with people from different countries and cultures. Negotiating styles and approaches vary substantially with each culture.[75]
- *A global mindset.* An essential global management competency has been described as 'global thinking', a 'global mindset' or a 'global perspective'. Managers need to appreciate the strategic implication of global business and develop a long-term orientation. A global mindset allows a manager to scan the global environment from a very broad perspective.[76]

Universities and colleges must help to develop these competencies. Cant (2004) asserts that, in the United States, many undergraduate business students have a limited knowledge of other societies and are naive about the effect that cultural differences may have on the conduct of international business. This may also apply to other countries around the Pacific Rim. If business courses are to adequately prepare students for global assignments, they must assist students to develop these global cultural competencies by offering specifically prepared courses in cross-cultural management and international business.[77] In Australia and New Zealand, providers of diplomas, undergraduate bachelor degrees, majors and masters programs are actively preparing students for global business and global management.

Thus far we have discussed individual differences in terms of demography, competency, personality, values and attitudes. This last section focused on job satisfaction as an attitude and we have expanded on that by linking job satisfaction and workplace behaviour, arguing the links between satisfaction and performance. Now turn back to the individual performance equation on page 42. Employees' capacity to perform is dependent on individual attributes (demography, personality and competency) that are influenced by values, attitudes and perceptions. The next section outlines the perceptual process and includes stereotyping as a way for individuals to select, organise, interpret, retrieve and respond to information from the world around them.

The perceptual process

LEARNING OBJECTIVE 8

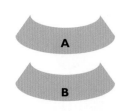

Perception and the perceptual process

Look at the two shapes on the left and compare them. Objectively, A and B are the same length, but they do not look that way to most people. Now think back to the last soccer, basketball or netball game you watched. How similarly did you and a friend supporting the other team see the game? What about the referee's calls in close situations? Did you agree with them?

This example illustrates the notion of perception, or how we select, organise, interpret and retrieve information from the environment.[78] As the example shows, perception is not necessarily the same as reality; nor are the perceptions of two people necessarily the same when describing the same event. The process is outlined in figure 2.9.

Through perception, people process information inputs into decisions and actions. Perception is a way of forming impressions about oneself, other people and daily life experiences. It is also a screen or filter through which information passes before having an effect on people.

Perception is the process through which people receive, organise and interpret information from their environment.

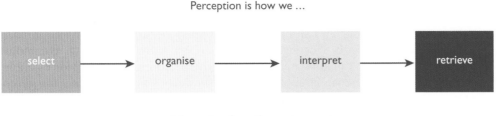

Perception is how we ...

select → organise → interpret → retrieve

... information from the environment.

FIGURE 2.9 • The perceptual process

Factors influencing the perceptual process

A number of factors contribute to perceptual differences and the perceptual process among people at work. These include the characteristics of the perceiver, the setting and the perceived.

- *The perceiver.* A person's needs or motives, past experiences, values, attitudes and personality may all influence the perceptual process. A person with a negative attitude towards unions, for example, may look for antagonism even during routine visits by local union officials to the organisation.

- *The setting.* The physical, social and organisational context of the perceptual setting can also influence the perceptual process. Hearing a subordinate call the boss by his or her first name may be acceptable in Australia and New Zealand, but not in Germany or Malaysia.

- *The perceived.* Characteristics of the perceived, such as contrast, intensity, size, motion and repetition or novelty, are also important in the perceptual process. A bright red sports car will tend to stand out from a group of grey sedans; whispering or shouting will stand out from ordinary conversation; very small or very large people will tend to be perceived differently from and more readily than average-sized people; and moving objects will stand out from those not moving.

Perceptions are influenced by values and attitudes and, in turn, influence behaviour; for example, a manager feels that employees are not performing well and perceives the reason to be a lack of effort (an internal factor). This manager is likely to respond with attempts to 'motivate' the employees to work harder. However, exploring the possibility of changing external, situational factors to remove job constraints and providing better organisational support may be ignored. This oversight could sacrifice major performance gains.

Perceptual distortions can make the perceptual process inaccurate and affect the response. For example, a halo effect occurs when one attribute of a person is used to develop an overall impression (smiling person is nice), and usually occurs at the organisation stage of perceptual process. Another example of perceptual distortion is projection, where one's personal attributes are assigned to other individuals. This usually occurs at the interpretation stage of perception. A common perceptual distortion is stereotyping.

Stereotyping occurs when information is being organised and sorted in different 'categories' or stereotypes. This process is heavily influenced by schemas or cognitive frameworks that represent organised knowledge about a given concept developed through experience. Stereotypes obscure individual differences. They can prevent managers from accurately assessing people's needs, preferences and abilities.

Schemas are cognitive frameworks developed through experience.

Stereotyping

As stated earlier, demographic differences between individuals can influence work performance; for example, length of service may indicate greater knowledge and skill. Different demographic characteristics, such as gender, age and ethnicity, are particularly important to managers in light of equal employment opportunity and workforce diversity management.

Demographic variables in particular are often the source of inappropriate generalisations, misconceptions and perceptions — for example, 'young people today are lazy and lack motivation', or 'men are cold and insensitive'. *Stereotyping* occurs when an individual is assigned to a group or category (for example, old people) and the attributes commonly associated with the group or category are assigned to the person in question (for example, old people are not creative). Demographic characteristics may serve as the basis for stereotypes that obscure individual differences, preventing people from getting to know others as individuals and from accurately assessing their potential performance. Someone who believes that older people are not creative, for example, may mistakenly decide not to appoint a very inventive 60-year-old person to an important job.

Perceptions about age and performance

There is a common stereotype or misconception concerning age, in relation to learning and flexibility. Many people associate older people with a sense of inertia. However, the truth is that this depends on the individual. Many older people have shown themselves to be flexible. Further, age and performance have been found to be unrelated; that is, older people are no more likely than younger people to be unproductive.[79] In addition, older workers are less likely than younger workers to leave a job, so there is a managerial advantage if they are performing well. Overall, contrary to common opinion, the data suggest that most older workers are likely to be good workers.[80]

The research findings on age are particularly important, given that the workforce is ageing. The figures on the changing age demographic in Australia show that important shifts are occurring. There are currently 170 000 new entrants into the workforce every year; however, it is estimated that by 2030 this figure will drop to 125 000 new entrants. Currently, for every person over 65 there are 5.3 people of working age (usually considered to be from ages 15 to 64). By 2022 the figure is expected to drop to 3.5, and in 2042 it will be even lower at 2.5.[81]

However, ageism is prevalent in the workplace in many Western countries. In Australia and the United States, research shows that older managers are more at risk of being retrenched and, if retrenchment occurs, that the older worker will have more difficulty in finding new employment that matches his or her old job in terms of income or security.[82] Increasingly in Japan, once workers reach 50 they are being pushed into early retirement.[83] However, in rural China agricultural workers continue their employment until well in their seventies.[84] This reflects the more traditional views in Asia that older workers are to be respected, not disparaged.[85]

OB in action

The Australia and New Zealand (ANZ) Bank has numerous programs aimed at recruiting, retaining and supporting mature-aged employees. Some of the more outstanding features of the organisation's program include communication and training programs on age-related matters; financial planning for retirement; a career extension program that emphasises flexible work options; and an open door policy for retired workers to return. In addition, the bank strives to create a competitive rivalry between branches which helps employees recognise and value the experience of their coworkers. In 2004, the ANZ Bank was the recipient of the 'Employment and Inclusion of Mature Aged Workers' award,[86] sponsored by the Australian Government Department of Health and Ageing and administered by Diversity@Work, a social enterprise committed to making organisations stronger through diversity.

Perceptions about gender and performance

Perceptions about gender and performance have been difficult to combat, particularly for women. As mentioned earlier, there are few gender-related differences affecting performance; nevertheless there are still inequalities.

The fight for equal pay between men and women continues. Since 1972, Australian women have received equal pay for equal work — that is, if they perform the same work as a man. According to the National Women's Consultative Council report, this is estimated to have benefited 18 per cent of adult female employees. However, despite equal pay and anti-discrimination legislation, women still earn less than men in all categories of earnings, all components of earnings, all major occupational groupings and all industries. Regardless of the figure used, or the comparisons made, women's average earnings are consistently and demonstrably lower than those of their male counterparts (table 2.2).

	Males ($)	Females ($)	F/M ratio
Adult employees:			
— full-time ordinary weekly earnings	1028.80	873.80	0.85
— full-time total weekly earnings	1096.20	887.90	0.81
All employees: weekly total earnings	910.90	606.00	0.67

TABLE 2.2 • Average weekly earnings for male and female adult employees and the female/male earnings ratio

Source: Australian Bureau of Statistics, *Average weekly earnings, Australia*, cat. no. 6302.0 (Canberra: ABS, 2004).

The gap between male and female earnings is narrowing. However, what seems to be consistently ignored is the earnings difference between women with children and women without children, where the gap is significant and increasing.[87] There is evidence that the family responsibilities of women are having a significant effect on their earning ability because their work choices are based on working flexibility rather than high income.[88]

Perceptions about ethnicity and performance

A growing proportion of the new workforce is composed of an increasingly broad spectrum of employees from differing ethnic backgrounds.[89] This is particularly true of the Asia–Pacific region, where many organisations have multicultural workforces. Dealing with diverse ethnicities in the workplace is a contemporary management issue that strongly rejects the notion of ethnic stereotyping. Stereotyping can easily result in discrimination, which is against the law.

Good managers try to make decisions and take action with a true understanding of the work situation. A manager who is skilled in influencing the perceptual process will try to have a high level of self-awareness, seek information from various sources to confirm or contradict personal impressions of a decision situation, and be empathetic — that is, be able to see a situation as it is perceived by other people and avoid common perceptual distortions that may bias his or her views of people and situations. In addition, good managers are aware of various kinds of interpretive schemas of their employees and their possible impact, avoid inappropriate actions and actively influence the perceptions of other people.

Summary

The individual performance equation
The individual performance equation views performance as the result of the personal attributes of individuals, the work efforts they put forth and the organisational support they receive. Individual performance factors are highlighted in the equation: performance = individual attributes × work effort × organisational support. Individual attributes consist of demographic, competency and personality characteristics. Work effort is reflected in the motivation to work. Organisational support consists of a wide range of organisational support mechanisms, such as tools, resources, instructions and the like, that provide the opportunity for an individual to perform if they have the capacity and willingness.

Demographic characteristics of individuals

Demographic characteristics of individuals are background variables that help shape what a person has become. Some demographic characteristics are current (for example, a worker's current health status); others are historical (for example, length of service).

Competency characteristics of individuals

Competency characteristics among individuals consist of aptitude (the capability to learn something) and ability (the existing capacity to do something). Aptitudes are potential abilities. Abilities can be classified as cognitive abilities, physical abilities and emotional intelligence.

Personality characteristics of individuals

Personality captures the overall profile or combination of characteristics that represent the unique nature of a person as that person reacts and interacts with others. We expect there to be a predictable interplay between an individual's personality and a tendency to behave in certain ways. Personality traits important in organisational behaviour are problem-solving style, locus of control, authoritarianism/dogmatism, Machiavellianism, and the 'big five' personality dimensions.

Capitalising on workplace diversity

Increasing diversity is creating workplace challenges. Significant variations are occurring in skill levels, education, physical abilities, cultural backgrounds, lifestyles, personal values, individual needs, and ethnic and social differences. Workplaces that are open to diversity create a diversity management plan.

Values and attitudes

Values are global concepts that guide actions and judgements across a variety of situations. Values are especially important in organisational behaviour because they can directly influence outcomes, such as performance or human resource maintenance; they can also have an indirect influence on behaviour by means of attitudes and perceptions. While treated as characteristics of individuals in this chapter, values can also reflect differences among various societal and organisational cultures. Attitudes are influenced by values but focus on specific people or objects; in contrast, values have a more global focus. Attitudes are predispositions to respond in a positive or negative way to someone or something in one's environment. They operate through intended behaviour to influence actual behaviour or other variables.

Job satisfaction

Job satisfaction is a specific attitude that indicates the degree to which individuals feel positively or negatively about their jobs. It is an emotional response to one's tasks as well as to the physical and social conditions of the workplace. Often, job satisfaction is measured in terms of feelings about various job facets, including the work, pay, promotion, coworkers and supervision. Job satisfaction is related to employee absenteeism and turnover, but the relationship to performance is controversial. Current organisational behaviour thinking rejects the notion that satisfaction causes performance, and instead argues that rewards influence both satisfaction and performance.

The perceptual process

Individuals use the perceptual process to select, organise, interpret and retrieve information from their environment. Perceptions are influenced by a variety of factors, including social and physical aspects of the situation as well as personal factors such as needs, experience, values, attitudes and personality. A manager who is skilled in influencing the perceptual process will be able to see a situation as it is perceived by other people and avoid common perceptual distortions that may bias his or her views of people and situations. In addition, managers must avoid stereotyping as this can have social and legal implications.

Chapter 2 study guide

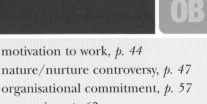

Key terms

ability, *p. 45*

absenteeism, *p. 58*

affective components, *p. 55*

aptitude, *p. 45*

attitude, *p. 55*

authoritarianism, *p. 50*

behavioural components, *p. 55*

beliefs, *p. 55*

cognitive abilities, *p. 45*

cognitive components, *p. 55*

cognitive dissonance, *p. 56*

demographic characteristics, *p. 44*

dogmatism, *p. 50*

emotion management, *p. 46*

emotional intelligence, *p. 46*

externals, *p. 49*

five key dimensions of personality, *p. 49*

instinct, *p. 48*

internals, *p. 49*

job involvement, *p. 57*

job satisfaction, *p. 57*

locus of control, *p. 49*

Machiavellians, *p. 50*

motivation to work, *p. 44*

nature/nurture controversy, *p. 47*

organisational commitment, *p. 57*

perception, *p. 62*

performance, *p. 60*

personality, *p. 47*

physical abilities, *p. 45*

schemas, *p. 63*

situational constraints, *p. 44*

turnover, *p. 58*

value congruence, *p. 53*

values, *p. 53*

Review questions

1. Describe and explain the individual performance equation used in this chapter.
2. Name the factors influencing an individual's capacity to perform.
3. List and briefly explain the five key dimensions of personality.
4. Name the factors that influence the perceptual process and explain each of them.

Application questions

1. Personality testing is widely used as a recruitment and selection strategy. What are the advantages and disadvantages of such a strategy and why? In your answer please use examples.
2. The year is 2015 and you are employed by the 'Commission of Inquiry into the Ageing Workforce'. Your role is to prepare a report on current employment trends in relation to age; their broader implications for the economy and society; and creative strategies to address problem issues. What would you write?
3. Colleges and universities are 'workplaces' for generating, acquiring and sharing new knowledge. There is great diversity within the student population, but this may not be used in the classroom teaching strategies that you experience. Develop a 'diversity management program' suitable for use by teachers and lecturers in the classroom that would reflect the diversity of the student group, and capitalise on its potential within this group to enhance learning. Explain the ideas behind your diversity management program.
4. Explain the relevance of emotional intelligence and emotional management to the workplace. Illustrate your answer with examples.
5. Read the 'International spotlight' starting on page 61. What values and attitudes do individuals need to develop to become successful *global* managers? How do these values and attitudes differ from what a *local* manager must develop?
6. 'Workplace values and attitudes typically undergo significant change from one generation of workers to the next.' Do you agree? Explain and give examples.

1. Review the discussion of diversity in terms of the basic attributes of individuals in organisations. Write a report that answers the following questions.
   (a) Research and describe the current diversity of the Australian workforce.
   (b) Select at least five items for comparison and compare data on Australian workforce diversity with data from at least three other developed countries. Present your findings in a table. What were facilitators and barriers to the comprehensiveness of your analysis? Can you draw a conclusion on how well 'diversity' is understood in other developed countries?
   (c) When comparing different developed countries, can you conclude if Australia's workforce is more or less diverse than those of other countries? Why or why not?
   (d) What is the implication of workforce diversity in terms of *global* business management?

2. Search the Internet for an organisation in the transport, health, hospitality, banking or retail industry and notice the values that it espouses in its mission or goal statement and related materials. Do you think that these values are the most appropriate for this organisation? Can you find any evidence that this organisation is putting its values into practice? How does the organisation monitor the values and attitudes of its staff through surveys or other measures?

OB *Running project*

Using the information you have available about your organisation, perform the following activities.

1. What does management look for in potential employees to ensure a good fit between the employee and the job requirements?

2. Identify the types of organisational support provided to employees.

3. How diverse is the workforce of your organisation? Assess the strategies your organisation has in place to encourage and benefit from workforce diversity.

4. Determine what management and employees do to ensure job satisfaction.

OB *Individual activity*

Personal values[90]

For the following 16 items, rate how important each one is to you.
Write a number between 0 and 100 on the line to the left of each item.

Not important				Not important				Very important		
0	10	20	30	40	50	60	70	80	90	100

____ 1. An enjoyable, satisfying job
____ 2. A high-paying job
____ 3. A good marriage
____ 4. Meeting new people; social events
____ 5. Involvement in community activities

<pre>
___   6. My religion
___   7. Exercising, playing sports
___   8. Intellectual development
___   9. A career with challenging opportunities
___ 10. Nice cars, clothes, home etc.
___ 11. Spending time with family
___ 12. Having several close friends
___ 13. Volunteer work for not-for-profit organisations, like the cancer society
___ 14. Meditation, quiet time to think, pray etc.
___ 15. A healthy balanced diet
___ 16. Educational reading, television, self-improvement programs etc.
</pre>

Below, transfer the numbers beside each of the 16 items to the appropriate column, then add the two numbers in each column.

	Professional	Financial	Family	Social
	1. ____	2. ____	3. ____	4. ____
	9. ____	10. ____	11. ____	12. ____
Totals	____	____	____	____
	Community	Spiritual	Physical	Intellectual
	5. ____	6. ____	7. ____	8. ____
	13. ____	14. ____	15. ____	16. ____
Totals	____	____	____	____

The higher the total in any area, the higher the value you place on that particular area. The closer the numbers are in all eight areas, the more well-rounded you are.

Think about the time and effort you put into your top three values. Is it sufficient to allow you to achieve the level of success you want in each area? If not, what can you do to change? Is there any area in which you feel you should have a higher value total? If yes, which area? What can you do to change?

Group activity

OB

Building a more positive self-concept[91]

Objective
To develop a more positive self-concept
Total time: 5–15 minutes

Preparation
The objective of this activity is to develop a more positive self-concept. According to humanistic theory, the self-concept is important in the development of personality. This may not be an easy exercise for you, but it could result in improving your self-concept, which has a major impact on your success in life. Complete the following three-step plan for building a positive self-concept.

You may be asked to share your plan with a person of your choice in class. (Your lecturer should tell you if you will be asked to do so.) If so, do not include anything you do not wish to share; write a second set of plans that you are willing to share.

Step 1: Identify your strengths and areas for improvement
What do you like about yourself? What can you do well (reflect on some of your accomplishments)? What skills and abilities do you have to offer people and organisations? What are the things about yourself or your behaviour that you could improve to help build a more positive self-concept?

(continued)

Step 2: Set goals and visualise them

Based on your areas of improvement, write down some goals in a positive, affirmative format; three to five is recommended as a start. Once you achieve these goals, go on to others — for example, 'I am positive and successful' (not 'I need to stop thinking/worrying about failure') or 'I enjoy listening to others' (not 'I need to stop dominating the conversation'). Visualise yourself achieving your goals; for example, imagine yourself succeeding without worrying, or visualise having a conversation you know you will have, without dominating it.

Step 3: Develop a plan and implement it

For each of your goals, state what you will do to achieve it. What specific action will you take to improve your self-concept by changing your thoughts or behaviour? Number your plans to correspond with your goals.

Procedure for group discussion

Break into teams of two or three members. Try to work with someone with whom you feel comfortable sharing your plan.

Using your prepared plan, share your questions and responses one at a time. It is recommended that you each share one question/answer before proceeding to the next. The choice is yours, but be sure you get equal 'air time': for example, one person states 'what I like about myself' and the other person follows with their response. After you both share, go on to cover 'what I do well', and so on. During your sharing you may offer each other helpful suggestions, but do so in a positive way; remember, you are helping one another build a more positive self-concept. Avoid saying anything that could be considered confronting or critical.

OB Case study: Drugs Inc.

Drugs Inc. is a fully owned subsidiary of a large pharmaceutical company. It manufactures a wide range of medicines. The company also invests heavily in research and development (R&D), in the hope of becoming a world player in pharmaceuticals.

The board of directors and executive management posts are occupied by older males. The rest of the workforce consists of around 60 staff members, including scientists and technicians involved with R&D, skilled pharmaceutical workers and a general factory workforce with 12 different nationalities represented. In addition, administration is supported by four female clerks.

Recently business has not been going well. Drugs Inc. has been finding it difficult to compete with overseas companies who manufacture medicines more cheaply. At the moment, 95 per cent of the skilled pharmaceutical workers in the plant are full-time permanent employees. To cut costs, senior managers have decided that the skilled pharmaceutical workers must work on a more flexible basis. The plan is to make 50 per cent of those workers casual employees, which will result in a decrease of direct costs. The general factory workforce will be reduced by 30 per cent. In addition, Drugs Inc. plans to set up an Internet business so that it can sell medicines directly to the public, both in Australia and overseas, in the hope that it can cut more staff, including two of the clerks.

Questions

1. Refer to the individual performance equation in the early part of this chapter. Use this equation to identify the possible causes of the problems facing Drugs Inc.

2. What behaviours are you expecting from the skilled workers in response to the strategies proposed by the managers?

3. You are at the beginning of your studies in organisational behaviour. What additional knowledge about human behaviour would help you to better understand the problems at Drugs Inc. and to pose suitable solutions?

Suggested reading

S Bolton, *Emotion management in the workplace* (Basingstoke: Palgrave McMillan, 2005).

S Clegg, M Kornberger and T Pitsis, *Managing and organizations: an introduction to theory and practice* (Thousand Oaks, CA: Sage, 2005).

Charles J Cranny, Patricia C Smith and Eugene F Stone, *Job satisfaction: how people feel about their jobs and how it affects their performance* (New York: Lexington Books, 1992).

SO Daatland and S Biggs, *Ageing and diversity: multiple pathways and cultural migrations* (Bristol: Policy Press, 2004).

John P Fernandez, *Managing a diverse workforce* (Lexington, MA: Lexington Books, 1991).

J Woldfogel, 'Understanding the family gap in pay for women with children', *Journal of Economic Perspectives*, vol. 12, no. 1 (Winter 1998), pp 137–56.

End notes

1. Link-Up International corporate web site, http://www.linkup.com.au/

2. P Burgess, *The ID Impact Survey. A measure of actual improvement in leadership, capability and team effectiveness* (Link-up International, 2003); P Burgess (ed.), *The development of the ID system including reliability and validity (version 2.1)* (Miranda, NSW: Link-Up International, 2003).

3. J Fitzgerald, N Ferres, K Hamilton and J Fitzgerald, 'What makes people tick: The instinctive drive as a means to improve team performance', paper presented to the ABBSA conference, Cairns, 2005.

4. ibid.

5. Melvin Blumberg and Charles D Pringle, 'The missing opportunity in organizational research: some implications for a theory of work performance', *Academy of Management Review*, vol. 7 (1982), pp. 560–9.

6. 'The rebel billionaire, quest for the best', http://www.tvtome.com/tvtome/servlet/EpisodeGuideSummary/showid-27223/The_Rebel_Billionaire_Bransons_Quest_for_the_Best/ (viewed 10 April 2005).

7. See Thomas N Martin, John R Schermerhorn, Jr and Lars L Larson, 'Motivational consequences of a supportive work environment', in *Advances in motivation and achievement: motivation enhancing environment*, vol. 6 (Greenwich, CT: JAI Press, 1989), pp. 179–214.

8. R Schemerhorn, J Hunt and R Osborn, *Organizational behavior*, 9th ed. (Hoboken: John Wiley & Sons, 2005).

9. ibid.

10. ibid

11. M Takeda, M Helms, P Klintworth, J Sompayrac, 'Hair colour stereotyping and CEO selection: can you name any blonde CEOs?', *Equal Opportunities International*, vol. 24, issue 1 (2005), pp. 1–13.

12. C Jaffee, 'Measurement of human potential', *Employment Relations Today*, vol. 27, issue 2 (Summer 2000), p. 15; E Smith, 'Communities of competencies: new resources in the workplace', *Journal of Workplace Learning*, vol. 17, issue 1/2 (2005), p. 7.

13. C Spearman, *The abilities of man* (New York: Macmillan, 1927).

14. *Dao v Australian Postal Commission* (1987) 162 CLR 317.

15. E Smith, 'Communities of competencies: new resources in the workplace', *Journal of Workplace Learning*, vol. 17, issue 1/2 (2005), p. 7; S Perkel, 'Primal leadership: realizing the power of emotional intelligence', *Journal of Management Consultancy*, vol. 15, issue 3 (September 2004), p. 56; K Petrides, A Furnham and Martin G Neil, 'Estimates of emotional and psychometric intelligence: evidence for gender-based stereotypes', *The Journal of Social Psychology*, vol. 144, issue 2 (April 2004), p. 149; L Herkenhoff, 'Culturally tuned emotional intelligence: an effective change management tool?', *Strategic Change*, vol. 13, issue 2 (March/April 2004), p. 73.

16. D Goleman, *Emotional intelligence* (New York: Bantam, 1995); D Goleman, *Working with emotional intelligence* (New York: Bantam, 2000).

17. R Bar-On, 'Emotional intelligence and self-actualization' in J Ciarrochi, J Forgas and JD Mayer (eds), *Emotional intelligence in everyday life: a scientific inquiry* (New York: Psychology Press, 2001).

18. JD Mayer and P Salovey, 'What is emotional intelligence?' in P. Salovey and DJ Sluyter (eds), *Emotional development and emotional intelligence* (New York: Basic Books, 1997).

19. A Hochschild, *The commercialization of intimate life* (Berkley, Los Angeles: University of California Press, 2003).

20. N Kinnie, S Hutchinson and J Purcell, 'Fun and surveillance: the paradox of high commitment management in call centres', *International Journal of Human Resource Management*, vol. 11, no. 5 (2000), pp. 967–85.

21. S Bolton, *Emotion management in the workplace* (Basingstoke: Palgrave McMillan, 2005).

22. ibid.

23. R Stock, 'Watch those emotions — they're the new IQ', *Sunday Star Times* (Wellington, New Zealand, 21 December 2003), p. D8.

24. K Kolbe and D Kolbe, 'Management by instinct leads the way to change' (1999). www.kolbe.com (viewed 1 February 2004).

25. P Burgess, *The ID Impact Survey. A measure of actual improvement in leadership, capability and team effectiveness* (Link-up International, 2003); P Burgess (ed.), *The development of the ID system including reliability and validity* (version 2.1) (Link-Up International, 2003).

26. ibid.

27. See Geert Hofstede, *Culture's consequences: international differences in work-related values*, abridged ed. (Beverly Hills, CA: Sage, 1984).

28. G Allport and H Odbert, 'Trait names: a psycholexical study', *Psychological Monographs*, vol. 47 (1936), pp. 211–14.

29. See J Hogan and R Hogan, 'How to measure employee reliability', *Journal of Applied Psychology*, vol. 74 (1988), pp. 273–9.

30. JA Fitzgerald and N Ferres. *Report on the validation of Instinctive Drive™ system* (Sydney: University of Western Sydney, 2005).

31. JB Rotter, 'Generalized expectancies for internal versus external control of reinforcement', *Psychological Monographs*, vol. 80 (1966), pp. 1–28.

32. Don Hellriegel, John W Slocum, Jr and Richard W Woodman, *Organizational behavior*, 5th ed. (St Paul: West, 1989), p. 46.

33. See John A Wagner III and John R Hollenbeck, *Management of organizational behavior* (Englewood Cliffs, NJ: Prentice Hall, 1995), ch. 4.

34. V Lee Hamilton and Herbert C Kelman, *Crimes of obedience: towards a social psychology of authority and responsibility* (London: Yale University Press, 1990).

35. Herbert C Kelman, 'The policy context of torture: a social-psychological analysis', *International Review of the Red Cross*, vol 87., no. 857 (March 2005).

36. P Waldmeir, 'Anderson conviction overturned', *Financial Times* (London, 1 June 2005), p. 15.

37. Niccolo Machiavelli, *The prince*, trans. George Bull (Middlesex: Penguin, 1961).

38. K Cyriac and R Dharmaraj, 'Machiavellianism in Indian management', *Journal of Business Ethics*, vol. 13, no. 4 (April 1994), pp. 281–6; Myron Gable and Martin T Topol, 'Machiavellian managers: do they perform better?', *Journal of Business and Psychology*, vol. 5, no. 3 (Spring 1991), pp. 355–65.

39. S Key, 'Perceived managerial discretion: an analysis of individual ethical intentions', *Journal of Managerial Issues*, vol. 14, no. 2 (2002), p. 218.

40. Australia Securities and Investment Commission, 'Rodney Adler pleads guilty', media release 05-29 (16 February 2005), http://www.asic.gov.au/asic/asic_pub.nsf/ byheadline/05-29+Rodney+Adler+pleads+guilty? openDocument (viewed on 10 April 2005).

41. 'Rodley Adler hands back gong', *Sydney Morning Herald* (11 April 2005), http://smh.com.au/news/Business/ Rodney-Adler-hands-back-gong/2005/04/10/ 1113071849111.html (viewed 11 April 2005).

42. See PE Jacob, JJ Flink and HL Schuchman, 'Values and their function in decisionmaking', *American Behavioral Scientist*, vol. 5 (supplement 9, 1962), pp. 6–38.

43. See M Rokeach and SJ Ball Rokeach, 'Stability and change in American value priorities, 1968–1981', *American Psychologist* (May 1989), pp. 775–84.

44. Gordon Allport, Philip E Vernon and Gardner Lindzey, *Study of values* (Boston: Houghton Mifflin, 1931).

45. Bruce M Meglino, Elizabeth C Ravlin and Cheryl L Adkins, 'Value congruence and satisfaction with a leader: an examination of the role of interaction', unpublished manuscript (University of South Carolina, 1990), pp. 8–9; Bruce M Meglino, Elizabeth C Ravlin and Cheryl L Adkins, 'The measurement of work value congruence: a field study comparison', *Journal of Management*, vol. 1, no. 1 (1992), pp. 33–43.

46. ibid.

47. P Kitchen, 'HR staffers learn about generational difference at Woodbury NY conference', *Knight Ridder Tribune Business News* (Washington, 14 May 2005), p. 1.

48. P Kitchen, 'HR staffers learn about generational difference at Woodbury NY conference', *Knight Ridder Tribune Business News* (Washington, 14 May 2005), p. 1; Jason Rawlins, 'Work values change with new generations of workers; revolution in the workplace', transcript of Australian Broadcasting Corporation radio program AM (23 October 2004), p. 1; AR Earls, 'Clash of generations in workplace genxers, boomers seen as having different life goals, values, career expectations,' *Boston Globe* (Boston, Mass, 10 August 2003), p. G1.

49. ibid.

50. ibid.

51. ibid.

52. See D Jamieson and J O'Mara, *Managing workforce 2000* (San Francisco: Jossey-Bass, 1991), pp. 28–9.

53. See Martin Fishbein and Icek Ajzen, *Belief, attitude, intention and behavior: an introduction to theory and research* (Reading, MA: Addison-Wesley, 1975).

54. Leon Festinger, *A theory of cognitive dissonance* (Palo Alto, CA: Stanford University Press, 1957).

55. http://www.smh.com.au/articles/2004/07/26 (viewed April 2005).

56. The Job Descriptive Index (JDI) is available from Dr Patricia C Smith, Department of Psychology, Bowling Green State University; the Minnesota Satisfaction Questionnaire (MSQ) is available from the Industrial Relations Center and Vocational Psychology Research Center, University of Minnesota.

57. For job satisfaction trends, see *Work in America: report of a special task force to the Secretary of Health, Education, and Welfare* (Cambridge, MA: MIT Press, 1973); George H Gallup, *The Gallup Poll*, 1972–1977, vol. 1 (Wilmington, DE: Scholarly Resources, 1978); Charles N Weaver, 'Job satisfaction in the United States in the 1970s', *Journal of Applied Psychology*, vol. 65 (1980), pp. 364–7; 'Employee satisfaction', Inc. (August 1989), p. 112; Alan Farnham, 'The trust gap', *Fortune* (4 December 1989), pp. 56–78.

58. The Hallis Turnover and Absenteeism Survey was released in early 2004.

59. http://www.cch.com.au/ (viewed April 2005).

60. 'Sick worker went to concert', *Dominion Post* (Wellington, New Zealand, 9 November 2002), p. A20.

61. For example *Workplace Relations Act 1996* (Cth), Schedule 1A, 1C (1) in Australia.

62. C Larmer, 'Doona days', *Sunday Telegraph* (Sydney, 8 May 2005), p. 2.

63. Charles N Greene, 'The satisfaction–performance controversy', *Business Horizons*, vol. 15 (1972), p. 31; Michelle T Iaffaldano and Paul M Muchinsky, 'Job satisfaction and job performance: a meta-analysis', *Psychological Bulletin*, vol. 97 (1985), pp. 251–73; Greene, op. cit., pp. 31–41; Dennis Organ, 'A reappraisal and reinterpretation of the satisfaction-causes-performance hypothesis', *Academy of Management Review*, vol. 2 (1977), pp. 46–53; Peter Lorenzi, 'A comment on Organ's reappraisal of the satisfaction-causes-performance hypothesis', *Academy of Management Review*, vol. 3 (1978), pp. 380–2.

64. B El-Bedayneh and S Sonnad, 'An analysis of the self-rated job performance and job satisfaction relationships in Jordanian hospitals' (1990), http://www.mutah.edu.jo/userhomepages/nurses.pdf (viewed April 2005).

65. See Stephen P Robbins, *Organizational behavior*, 6th ed. (Englewood Cliffs, NJ: Prentice Hall, 1993), p. 188.

66. E Lawler and L Porter, 'The effects of performance on job satisfaction' *Industrial Relations*, vol. 7 (1967), pp. 20–8.

67. Lyman W Porter and Edward E Lawler III, *Managerial attitudes and performance* (Homewood, IL: Richard D. Irwin, 1968).

68. P Podsakoff, W Todor and R Skov, 'Effect of leader contingent and non-contingent reward and punishment behaviours on subordinate performance and satisfaction' *Academy of Management Journal*, vol. 4 (1982), pp. 810–21.

69. *Business Review Weekly* (15 July 1996), http://www.uow.edu.au/arts/sts/bmartin/dissent/documents/health/mayne_smedley_refs.html (viewed 10 April 2005).

70. For more on incentive pay please read John Belcher, *How to design and implement a results oriented variable pay system* (AMACOM, 1996); Richard Henderson, *Compensation management in a knowledge-based world*, 8th ed. (Englewood Cliffs, NJ: Prentice Hall 2000).

71. AG Cant, 'Internationalizing the business curriculum: developing intercultural competence', *Journal of American Academy of Business*, vol. 5, issue 1/2 (2004), pp. 177–82.

72. NJ Adler, *International dimensions of organizational behavior*, 4th ed. (Canada: South-West, 2002); RT Moran and JR Ricsenburger, *The global challenge: building the new worldwide enterprise* (London: McGraw-Hill, 1994); S Sokuvitz and AM George, 'Teaching culture: the challenges and opportunities of international public relations', *Business Communications Quarterly*, vol. 66 (June 2003), pp. 97–106.

73. MW McCall and GP Hollenbeck, *Developing global executives: the lessons of international experience* (Boston: Harvard Business School, 2002); RT Moran and JR Ricsenburger, *The global challenge: building the new worldwide enterprise* (London: McGraw-Hill, 1994).

74. NJ Adler and S Bartholomew, 'Managing globally competent people', *The Academy of Management Executive*, vol. 6, no. 3 (1992), pp. 52–65; RT Moran and JR Ricsenburger, *The global challenge: building the new worldwide enterprise* (London: McGraw-Hill, 1994); ME Mendenhall, TM Kuhlman and OK Stahl (eds), *Developing global business leaders: policies, processes and innovations* (Westport, CT: Quorum, 2001).

75. NJ Adler, *International dimensions of organizational behavior*, 4th ed. (Canada: South-West, 2002); NJ Adler and S Bartholomew, 'Managing globally competent people', *The Academy of Management Executive*, vol. 6, no. 3 (1992), pp. 52–65; RT Moran and JR Ricsenburger, *The global challenge: building the new worldwide enterprise* (London: McGraw-Hill, 1994).

76. NJ Adler and S Bartholomew, 'Managing globally competent people', *The Academy of Management Executive*, vol. 6, no. 3 (1992), pp. 52–65; RM Kanter, 'Afterward: what thinking globally really means' in RS Barnwik and RM Kanter (eds), *Global strategies* (Boston: Harvard Business Press, 1994), pp. 227–32; RT Moran and JR Ricsenburger, *The global challenge: building the new worldwide enterprise* (London: McGraw-Hill, 1994).

77. AG Cant, 'Internationalizing the business curriculum: developing intercultural competence', *Journal of American Academy of Business*, vol. 5, issue 1/2 (2004), pp. 177–82.

78. HR Schiffmann, *Sensation and perception: an integrated approach*, 3rd ed. (New York: John Wiley & Sons, 1990).

79. M Aadomt, *Applied industrial/organizational psychology*, 4th ed. (Southbank Vic.: Thomson, 2004).

80. S Saunders, 'A certain age — job market discrimination', *Weekend Australian* (18 October 2003), p. C12.

81. 'Looming labour crisis puts the focus on grey force', *Sydney Morning Herald* (2 October 2002), p. 4.

82. Human Rights and Equal Opportunity Commission, *Age matters: a report on age discrimination* (Sydney: Commonwealth of Australia, May 2000).

83. William Holstein, 'Japan rises again', *Chief Executive*, issue 182 (October 2002), pp. 50–2.

84. L Pang, A de Brauw, S Rozelle, 'Working until you drop: the elderly of rural China', *The China Journal*, issue 52 (July 2004), pp. 73–94.

85. R Hoar, 'Seven over 70', *Management Today* (October 2003), p. 60.
86. See 'Diversity@work Awards 2004 winners', http://diversityatwork.com.au/strategic/awards/2004/winners.cfm?Category=1#category1 (viewed 8 April 2005).
87. J Woldfogel, 'Understanding the family gap in pay for women with children', *Journal of Economic Perspectives*, vol. 12, no. 1 (Winter 1998), pp. 137–56.
88. A Berstein, 'Women's pay: why the gap remains a chasm; a new study spells out the costly impact of family obligations', *Business Week* (New York, 14 June 2004), p. 58; J Humphries, 'Towards a family-friendly economics', *New Political Economy*, vol. 3, issue 2 (July 1998), p. 223.
89. See Taylor H Cox and Stacy Blake, 'Managing cultural diversity: implications for organizational competitiveness', *Academy of Management Executive*, vol. 5, no. 3 (1991), p. 45; P Burns, A Myers and A Kakabadse, 'Are natural stereotypes discriminating?', *European Journal of Management*, vol. 13, no. 2 (1995), pp. 212–17.
90. Robert N Lussier, *Human relations in organizations: a skill building approach*, 2nd ed. (Homewood, IL: Richard D. Irwin, 1993). Used by permission.
91. ibid.

Chapter 3
Motivation and empowerment

1. discuss the complexities of motivating and empowering today's workforce

2. explain the difference between the two main types of motivation theories — content and process

3. outline the major theoretical contributions from the content theories of motivation of Maslow, Alderfer, McClelland and Herzberg

4. explain the process theories of motivation, including equity theory and expectancy theory

5. explain how managers can use an integrated model of content and process motivation theories to enhance productivity and human resource maintenance

6. explain how self-concept and personal values may add to our understanding of individual motivation

7. discuss empowerment and explain how the empowerment process works.

At SalesForce there's 'stuff' going on all the time [says managing director Kevin Panozza]. 'If you didn't have a very good social life before you started working here, you'd be thrilled.'

The 'stuff' includes concerts, cook-offs and, recently, an art show. Panozza says creative people are drawn to the company's non-hierarchical, laid-back atmosphere. Letting people express themselves and encouraging their creative side keeps them happy.

He also thinks call-centre workers have a right to take the power back. Too many have been sworn at or patronised by cranky customers — few of whom realise what a vital role they play in the modern economy. The industry may not have its own union right now — with only a minority belonging to other unions — but if every call-centre worker in Australia went on strike tomorrow, business as we know it would grind to a halt.

SalesForce is opposing the ACTU's attempts to introduce a standard award for call-centre workers. Panozza uses performance-based pay as his major motivating force and says he would struggle to keep doing so under an award.

The base pay rate at SalesForce is no better than at its competitors, but some high performers, he claims, earn double what they would under the proposed award. He says performance-based pay recognises people for a job well done. SalesForce also hands out certificates signed by senior management, as well as days out and gifts.

'We spend a lot of time getting every member of the team to communicate with each other and with senior management,' Panozza says. 'We have forums where people can express themselves and come up with ideas. We have one-on-ones every couple of weeks. We spell the job out to them very clearly.'

'We prepare people properly for what they are doing so they are confident and competent. That's a big issue [in phone work], because if you're struggling to find out what you're supposed to do and what you're expected to achieve, you can't be happy and confident.' Panozza also strives to recognise what people do and don't want. Call-centre work is shift-based. Clients need a certain number of agents to be available at any one time, and plenty are 24/7 operations. That means work–life balance has to be tackled with common sense, says Panozza. The company tries to fit people's hours around their lifestyles, so those who aren't so good at getting out of bed in the morning might be offered shifts running from midday to evening.

Working parents are not asked to work outside school hours if they don't want to. Fitting around people's lifestyles is easier when you have a pool of 2600 staff, but he says it's really about 'being very flexible and understanding in how you manage your people'.

If you do that, he says, you will eliminate many of the work–life balance issues that plague the modern workplace.

Source: Extract from James Hall, 'Call me', *Australian Financial Review BOSS Magazine*, issue 7 (24 July 2004), pp. 26–27.

Introduction

One of the keys to effective management lies in harnessing the motivation of employees in order to achieve the organisation's goals and objectives. Motivation is therefore a key topic in the study of organisational behaviour. This chapter discusses several motivation theories and the concept of empowerment in terms of how they may contribute towards increasing both productivity and the quality of working life. The theories in this chapter are an important foundation for the ideas to be developed throughout the rest of this book. Before looking at the separate theories, two key points should be made. First, motivation to work refers to forces within an individual that account for the level, direction and persistence of effort expended at work. Within this definition of work motivation:

- *level* refers to the amount of effort a person puts forth (for example, a lot or a little)
- *direction* refers to what the person chooses when presented with a number of possible alternatives (for example, to exert effort on achieving product quality or product quantity)
- *persistence* refers to how long a person sticks with a given action (for example, to try for product quantity or quality, and to give up when it is difficult to attain).

Second, it is important to emphasise that motivation to work (or willingness to perform) is one of three components of the individual performance equation (the other two are the capacity to perform and organisational support) which was presented in chapter 2. High performance in the workplace depends on the combination of these three individual performance equation factors (as will be emphasised later in the chapter when motivation theories are integrated).

Motivation to work refers to the forces within an individual that account for the level, direction and persistence of effort expended at work.

Motivating and empowering the workforce

Motivating and empowering today's workforce

LEARNING OBJECTIVE 1

Each employee is different, each organisation's workforce may have different characteristics, and at different times or in different locations there may be different circumstances that affect motivation and empowerment strategies in different ways. In order to meet the challenge of motivating employees, managers must be concerned with the context in which this is being done. Managers also need to understand the challenges of the work effort–motivation cycle.

Contemporary issues affecting motivation and empowerment

Organisations that fail to recognise contextual factors and their implications for workplace motivation risk losing their best people to more exciting, satisfying or rewarding opportunities elsewhere. The contemporary issues of job security, labour shortages and ageing population, and workforce mobility are briefly summarised below.

Job security

The prevalence of 'downsizing' or 'rightsizing' in the 1990s in many organisations resulted in substantial and widespread job losses. While the downsizing has not continued at the same pace it still remains a possibility in organisations. For example, in 2005, the National Australia Bank was planning cutbacks of as many as 1700 jobs in its UK banks[1] and announced 253 job cuts in its back-office functions in Australia, with speculation about more.[2] Late in the same year, Telstra announced its intention to cut up to 12 000 jobs over the next five years.[3] As a result of these historical and current events, many workers retain a fear of retrenchment while many others find themselves left to work harder to take up the work of those already retrenched. As many as 20.2 per cent of Australian workers thought it was very or somewhat possible that they would be retrenched in 2004.[4] This atmosphere of uncertainty, insecurity and fear of future retrenchment can condition performance, making it difficult to sustain high levels of employee commitment, loyalty or motivation.

Labour shortages and an ageing workforce

The retrenchments discussed above suggest an excess of labour in organisations. Now many organisations are likely to be concerned with labour shortages. There are two key contributing factors — the shortage in skilled employees and the ageing workforce. In Australia, there are shortages, for example, in electrotechnology, engineering, retail motor, food trades including commercial cookery, rural work, building and construction, emerging technologies, retail, road freight transport, aerospace, marine manufacturing, nursing and accounting. Such shortages can be cyclical (especially in building) and regional (such as in information technology, which affects New South Wales but not elsewhere).[5] Skills shortages in New Zealand are the main constraint for around 25 per cent of organisations and are particularly prevalent in the services and building sectors. Other areas of shortages are in vehicle and engine service, engineering, drivers, media, fishing, and food and hospitality.[6] As the following example shows, the shortages are already being felt in some areas of New Zealand.

Over about three months, Pamela Jenkins unsuccessfully advertised in towns and cities around New Zealand for a florist for her store, Rotorua Florist. Eventually, to fill the vacancy, she heard through a friend of a German florist who was interested, and Jenkins queued at the Immigration Service to get her a work permit. In Hamilton, Jill Robinson is the region's delegate to the Collision Repair Association. She says that businesses in this area report spending thousands of dollars advertising for workers, without success. She and her husband have given up advertising for staff in their panel and motor repair business.[7]

In conjunction with the skills shortage, the ageing population is leading to a potential 'experience deficit' as older workers retire.[8] It appears that organisations are slow to respond to these looming shortages. For example, a survey of chief executives in Australia found that they are still less likely to hire mature-age workers than their younger counterparts.[9] However, there is some planning as the following examples show.

The Commonwealth Bank began studying its employee age profile in late 2002 and found that a significant portion of employees intended to leave before they turned 60 and some before they turned 55. These people indicated that more flexible working conditions, phased retirement and a better work–life balance would encourage them to stay, so the bank developed new initiatives to support them. These include options to buy extra annual leave and the opportunity to participate in community projects.[10]

Public sector organisations are also gearing up for the change. Studies show that unless they adopt planning strategies they will not be able to sustain the levels and quality of service they currently provide. The Western Australian Government, including the Department of Premier and Cabinet, and the Victorian Department of Human Services are looking at ways to understand the problems and to increase their labour pool using devices like scenario planning.[11]

As labour shortages increase there will be a growing need for organisations to carefully consider employee needs and expectations and what they can do to attract and retain highly trained and skilled workers and older employees.

Workforce mobility

Another feature of many workplaces is the mobility of the workforce. This relates to the willingness of workers to move from job to job and from organisation to organisation. A Newspoll survey showed that more than one-third of Australian employees were looking for a new job in 2005.[12] Many young people opt to travel and work overseas for extended periods. Mobility also relates to the trend for organisations to seek whole workforces from other locations (such as different states or provinces or countries). Many organisations are already familiar with multicultural workforces, either domestically or in various global locations. Motivation of different cohorts within the workforce may require local or cross-cultural knowledge and an understanding of the psychological bond an employee has with the organisation. The following 'International spotlight' provides some examples of how workforces are being sourced from other locations.

International
SPOTLIGHT

Bring in the workers

In some areas organisations have problems attracting sufficient workers and, once they have them, it can be difficult to retain them. In a more globalised world, a solution that is growing in popularity is sourcing labour from other countries. For example, in the Mildura region of Victoria many of the 8000 fruitpicking jobs available in the area each year are not filled, despite efforts to entice Australian workers. Pay rates that give pickers the opportunity to earn more than $1000 a week during the season have not alleviated the shortage. In response, the Sunraysia Mallee Economic Development Board (SMEDB) and Dali International Co-Operative Company have signed a memorandum to seek approval from the Australian Government to bring in experienced Chinese fruit pickers to the Mildura area.[13] In China itself there are growing shortfalls of up to 2 million workers for factories in Guangdong and Fujian provinces. In the past, these factories could recruit workers from other provinces because they were desperate for work and willing to live hundreds of kilometres from their homes and families. Now those workers have the ability to negotiate better rewards and conditions in other, more economically successful, provinces[14] that may have the equivalent of US middle class incomes by 2007–2010.[15] New Zealand farms are also suffering, with one rural recruitment business bringing in about 100 people a year to work on dairy, beef and sheep farms. The workers come mainly from Britain, South Africa and Zimbabwe. The business would recruit even more, if recruits could be found.[16]

Malaysia has been heavily dependent on foreign workers coming mostly from Indonesia, as well as the Philippines, Myanmar, Bangladesh, Sri Lanka and India. The country has a total of about 10.5 million in its workforce, with around 2.6 million being foreign workers. Figures are not certain, but it is estimated that about 1.5 million of these foreign workers are 'legal'. It is thought that at least another 500 000 illegal workers still remained after a three-month amnesty period that ended in March 2005 caused an estimated 400 000 illegal immigrants to leave the country. At the same time that the government is pursuing these illegal workers, it is also wrestling with the problem of filling labour shortages of approximately 200 000 workers in the manufacturing sector, 150 000 in construction, 50 000 in plantations and another 20 000 in the services sector. Plans exist to begin recruiting workers legally from Pakistan, India, Myanmar, Nepal and Vietnam.[17]

While such readymade workforces can appear to provide an easy fix, they can also create other problems. Not only are there political and legal problems relating to immigration or visas, there is also an increasing requirement for the managers of such workers to be alert to cultural differences in motivation.

The work motivation challenge

Managers in organisations affected by such changes and pressures must build or rebuild loyalty and commitment, and create a positive organisational climate in which employees are motivated to achieve at high levels of work performance.

This challenge is examined in more detail in figure 3.1. The figure shows how an individual's willingness to perform is directly related to the needs, expectations and values of the individual, and their link to the incentives or aspirations presented by the organisational reward system. Rewards fulfil individual goals such as financial remuneration and career advancement.

The degree of effort expended to achieve these outcomes will depend on:
- the individual's willingness to perform, and his or her commitment to these outcomes in terms of the value attached to a particular outcome
- the individual's competency or capacity to perform the tasks
- the individual's personal assessment of the probability of attaining a specific outcome
- the opportunity to perform (which is central to empowerment, discussed later in the chapter).

A number of organisational constraints or barriers, if not minimised, may restrict high levels of individual performance.

Figure 3.1 shows that if the outcome or goal is attained, then the individual experiences a reduction in pressure or tension, and goal attainment positively reinforces the expended effort to achieve the outcome. As a result of this positive experience, the individual may repeat the cycle. On the other hand, if the outcome is frustrated after a reasonable passage of time (for example, when no career progression has occurred), then the individual experiences goal frustration and arrives at a decision point. The individual is presented with three alternatives:
1. exit from the organisation
2. renew attempts at goal achievement, or modify or abandon the goals
3. adopt a negative response to the frustration experience, and perform at below-optimum levels.

The challenge for managers is to create organisations in which the opportunities to perform through competency building and empowerment are maximised and the impediments to performance are kept to a minimum to avoid the negative consequences of goal frustration. Figure 3.1 shows the complexity of the work motivational process, and emphasises the importance of individual needs, expectations and values as key elements of this process. Some of these issues are addressed in the rest of this chapter.

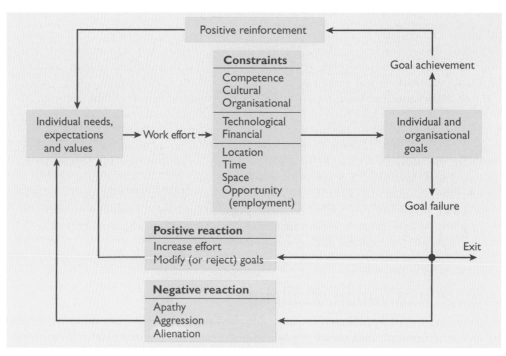

FIGURE 3.1 • Understanding the work effort–motivation cycle

Difference between content and process motivation theories

LEARNING OBJECTIVE 2

Content and process motivation theories

Two main approaches to the study of motivation are known as the content and process theories. A more recent approach, based on personal values and self-concept, is also presented later in the chapter.

Content theories offer ways to profile or analyse individuals to identify the needs that motivate their behaviours.

Content theories are primarily concerned with what it is within individuals or their environment that energises and sustains behaviour. In other words, what specific needs or motives energise people? We use the terms 'needs' and 'motives' interchangeably to mean the physiological or psychological deficiencies that one feels a compulsion to reduce or eliminate. If you feel very hungry (a physiological need), you will feel a compulsion to eliminate or satisfy that need by eating. If you have a need for recognition (a psychological need), you may try to satisfy that by working hard to please your boss. Content theories are useful because they help managers understand what people will and will not value as work rewards or need satisfiers.

Process theories seek to understand the thought processes that take place in the minds of people and that act to motivate their behaviour.

The process theories strive to provide an understanding of the cognitive processes that act to influence behaviour. Thus, a content theory may suggest that security is an important need. A process theory may go further by suggesting how and why a need for security could be linked to specific rewards and to the specific actions that the worker may need to perform to achieve these rewards. Process theories add a cognitive dimension by focusing on individuals' beliefs about how certain behaviours will lead to rewards such as money or promotion; that is, the assumed connection between work activities and the satisfaction of needs.[18]

Content theories of motivation

LEARNING OBJECTIVE 3

Content theories

Maslow, Alderfer, McClelland and Herzberg proposed four of the better-known content theories. Each of these content theories has made a major contribution to our understanding of work motivation. Some have provided a basis for more complex theorising in later years.

Maslow's hierarchy of needs theory

Abraham Maslow's hierarchy of needs theory (figure 3.2) identifies higher-order needs (self-actualisation and esteem) and lower-order needs (social, safety and physiological requirements). Maslow's formulation suggests a prepotency of these needs; that is, some needs are assumed to be more important (potent) than others, and must be satisfied before the other needs can serve as motivators. Thus, the physiological needs must be satisfied before the safety needs are activated, and the safety needs must be satisfied before the social needs are activated, and so on.

The physiological needs are considered the most basic; they consist of needs for such things as food, water and the like. Individuals try to satisfy these needs before turning to needs at the safety level, which involve security, protection, stability and so on. When these needs are active, people will look at their jobs in terms of how well they satisfy these needs.

The social needs of a sense of belonging and a need for affiliation are activated once the physiological and safety needs are satisfied. The higher-order needs depicted in figure 3.2 consist of the esteem and self-actualisation needs — that is, being all that one can be. Here, challenging work and recognition for good performance assume centre stage.

> **Higher-order needs** are esteem and self-actualisation needs in Maslow's hierarchy.

> **Lower-order needs** are physiological, safety and social needs in Maslow's hierarchy.

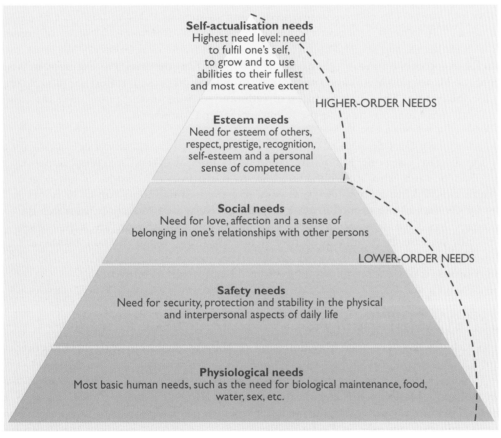

FIGURE 3.2 • Maslow's hierarchy of needs

Maslow: the research

Some research suggests that there is a tendency for higher-order needs to increase in importance over lower-order needs as individuals move up the managerial hierarchy.[19] Other studies report that needs vary according to a person's career stage,[20] the size of the organisation[21] and even geographic location.[22] However, there is no consistent evidence that the satisfaction of a need at one level will decrease its importance and increase the importance of the next higher need.[23] Some people find that working in smaller organisations can fulfil more than one need, as the following example suggests.

Yvonne Boecker left a computer manufacturer with 250 employees to work as accounts manager at Di Lorenzo Ceramics, a small tile-importing company in Sydney. Yvonne enjoys the challenges of working in a smaller, friendlier organisation where she has more work variety, feels less like a number, and is free from the politics and competition of big corporations.[24]

To what extent does Maslow's theory apply only to Western culture? In many developing nations the satisfaction of lower-order needs, such as basic subsistence and survival needs, consumes the entire lifetimes of many millions of individuals, with little opportunity to progress to higher-level need satisfaction. But in societies where regular employment is available, basic cultural values appear to play an important role in motivating workplace behaviour. In those countries high in Hofstede's uncertainty avoidance, such as Japan or Greece, security tends to motivate most employees more strongly than does self-actualisation. Workers in collectivist-oriented countries such as Pakistan tend to emphasise social needs.[25] In general, a person's frame of reference will determine the order of importance of their needs, and societal culture influences that frame of reference.[26] We must also be careful to consider ethnic or other cultural groups within countries. For example, in New Zealand the Maori, non-Maori and other ethnic groups could present different cultural contexts for motivation. The circumstances of different sections of the population may also make a difference to motivation, as the following example shows.

In the Jinjian Garment Factory in Shenzen, China, workers are predominantly unskilled peasants who are willing to come to the province to work for low wages, endure crowded living conditions and work uneven seasonal hours (up to 12 hours a day for 28 days of the month in peak season). Because of production pressures the company has tried penalising workers by deducting pay for quality deficiencies, especially because there appears to be a deliberate slowdown in rate among them.[27] However, due to a shortage in experienced workers caused by high employee turnover, the company is now looking for ways to motivate and retain its employees.

Alderfer's ERG theory

ERG theory categorises needs into existence, relatedness and growth needs.

Clayton Alderfer has developed a modification of Maslow's hierarchy with the ERG theory (figure 3.3).

ERG theory is more flexible than Maslow's theory in three basic respects.[28] First, the theory collapses Maslow's five need categories into three: **existence needs** relate to a person's desire for physiological and material wellbeing; **relatedness needs** represent the desire for satisfying interpersonal relationships; and **growth needs** are about the desire for continued personal growth and development. Second, while Maslow's theory argues that individuals progress up the hierarchy as a result of the satisfaction of lower-order needs (a satisfaction–progression process), ERG theory includes a 'frustration–regression' principle, whereby an already satisfied lower-level need can become activated when a higher-level need cannot be satisfied. Thus, if a person is continually frustrated in their attempts to satisfy growth needs, relatedness needs will again surface as key motivators. Third, according to Maslow, a person focuses on one need at a time. In contrast, ERG theory contends that more than one need may be activated at the same time.

Existence needs are about the desire for physiological and material wellbeing.

Relatedness needs are about the desire for satisfying interpersonal relationships.

Growth needs are about the desire for continued personal growth and development.

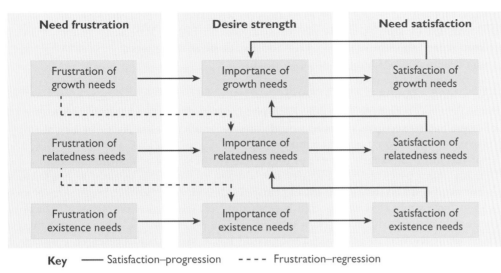

Key —— Satisfaction–progression ---- Frustration–regression

FIGURE 3.3 • Satisfaction–progression, frustration–regression components of ERG theory
Source: Marc J Wallace, Jr, and Andrew D Szilagyi, Jr, *Managing behavior in organizations* (Glenview, IL: Scott, Foresman, 1982).

ERG: the research

Research on ERG theory is relatively limited and includes disclaimers.[29] One article provides evidence for the ERG need categories and reports additional findings — for example, growth needs were greater for respondents with more highly educated parents, and women had lower strength of existence needs and higher strength of relatedness needs than men.[30]

Additional research is needed to shed more light on its validity, but the supporting evidence on ERG theory is stronger than that for Maslow's theory. For now, the combined satisfaction–progression and frustration–regression principles provide the manager with a more flexible approach to understanding human needs than does Maslow's strict hierarchy. Importantly, Alderfer's theory emphasises that performance constraints outside the control of the individual (see figure 3.1), or innate disposition (such as lack of competence or low intrinsic work motivation) may cause a decline in effort or negative behaviour. Managers need to examine the workplace environment continually to remove or reduce any organisational constraint that will restrict opportunities for personal growth and development.

McClelland's acquired needs theory

In the late 1940s the psychologist David McClelland distinguished three themes or needs that he feels are important for understanding individual behaviour. These needs are:

- the **need for achievement (nAch)** — that is, the desire to undertake something better or more efficiently, to solve problems or to master complex tasks
- the **need for affiliation (nAff)** — that is, the desire to establish and maintain friendly and warm relations with others
- the **need for power (nPower)** — that is, the desire to control others, to influence their behaviour or to be responsible for others.

McClelland's basic theory is that these three needs are *acquired* over time, as a result of life experiences. People are motivated by these needs, which can be associated with different work roles and preferences. The theory encourages managers to learn how to identify the presence of nAch, nAff and nPower in themselves and in others, and how to create work environments that are responsive to the respective need profiles of different employees.

McClelland and his colleagues began experimenting with the Thematic Apperception Test (TAT) as a way of measuring human needs.[31] The TAT is a projective technique that asks people to view pictures and write stories about what they see. In one case, using projective

The **need for achievement (nAch)** is the desire to do something better, solve problems or master complex tasks.

The **need for affiliation (nAff)** is the desire to establish and maintain friendly and warm relations with others.

The **need for power (nPower)** is the desire to control others, influence their behaviour and be responsible for others.

techniques, McClelland tested three executives on what they saw in a photograph of a man sitting down and looking at family photos arranged on his work desk. In terms of nAch, McClelland scored the stories given by the three executives as follows.[32]

- person dreaming about family outing — nAch = + 1
- person pondering new idea for gadget — nAch = + 2
- person working on bridge-stress problem — nAch = + 4.

To provide a more complete profile, each picture would also be scored in terms of nAff and nPower. Each executive's profile would then be evaluated for its motivational implications based on the three needs in combination.

One of the most important aspects of McClelland's theorising is that he challenges and rejects many other psychological theories that suggest the need to achieve is a behaviour that is only acquired and developed during early childhood. Alternatively, psychologists such as Erickson have supported a view that the learning of achievement-motivated behaviour can only occur during critical stages of a child's development; if it is not obtained then it cannot be easily learned or achieved during adult life.[33] McClelland's research contradicts this viewpoint; he maintains that the need to achieve is a behaviour that an individual can acquire through appropriate training in adulthood.

McClelland: the research

Research lends considerable insight into nAch in particular and includes some interesting applications in developing nations. McClelland trained business people in Kakinda, India, for example, to think, talk and act like high achievers by having them write stories about achievement and participate in a business game that encouraged achievement. The business people also met with successful entrepreneurs and learned how to set challenging goals for their own businesses. Over a two-year period following these activities, the people from the Kakinda study engaged in activities that created twice as many new jobs as those who did not receive training.[34]

Other research also suggests that societal culture can make a difference in the emphasis on nAch. Anglo-American countries such as Australia, the United States, Canada and the United Kingdom (countries weak in uncertainty avoidance and high in masculinity) tend to follow the high nAch pattern. In contrast, strong uncertainty, high femininity countries, such as Portugal and Chile, tend to follow a low nAch pattern. There are two especially relevant managerial applications of McClelland's theory. First, the theory is particularly useful when each need is linked with a set of work preferences (table 3.1). Second, if these needs can truly be acquired, it may be possible to acquaint people with the need profiles required to succeed in various types of jobs. For example, McClelland found that the combination of a moderate to high need for power and a lower need for affiliation enables people to be effective managers at higher levels in organisations. Lower nAff allows the manager to make difficult decisions without undue worry of being disliked.[35] High nPower creates the willingness to have influence or impact on others, though misuse of that power may result in sabotage by those mistreated or prevented from rising to the top of the organisation.[36]

TABLE 3.1 • Work preferences of persons high in need for achievement, affiliation and power

Individual needs	Work preference	Example
High need for achievement	Individual responsibility; challenging but achievable goals; feedback on performance	Field salesperson with a challenging quota and the opportunity to earn individual bonus; entrepreneur
High need for affiliation	Interpersonal relationships; opportunities to communicate	Customer service representative; member of a work unit that is subject to a group wage bonus plan
High need for power	Influence over other persons; attention; recognition	Formal position of supervisory responsibility; appointment as head of special task force or committee

Herzberg's two-factor theory

Frederick Herzberg's research was based on in-depth interview techniques learned during his training as a clinical psychologist. This interview approach — called a 'critical incident technique' — has been the subject of considerable debate among academics over many decades, but the findings of his theory have been valuable. Herzberg began his research on motivation by asking workers to comment on two statements:[37]

1. 'Tell me about a time when you felt exceptionally good about your job.'

2. 'Tell me about a time when you felt exceptionally bad about your job.'

After analysing nearly 4000 responses to these statements (figure 3.4), Herzberg and his associates developed the two-factor theory, also known as the motivator–hygiene theory. They noticed that the factors identified as sources of work dissatisfaction (subsequently called 'dissatisfiers' or 'hygiene factors') were different from those identified as sources of satisfaction (subsequently called 'satisfiers' or 'motivator factors').

The motivator–hygiene theory distinguishes between sources of work dissatisfaction (hygiene factors) and satisfaction (motivators); it is also known as the two-factor theory.

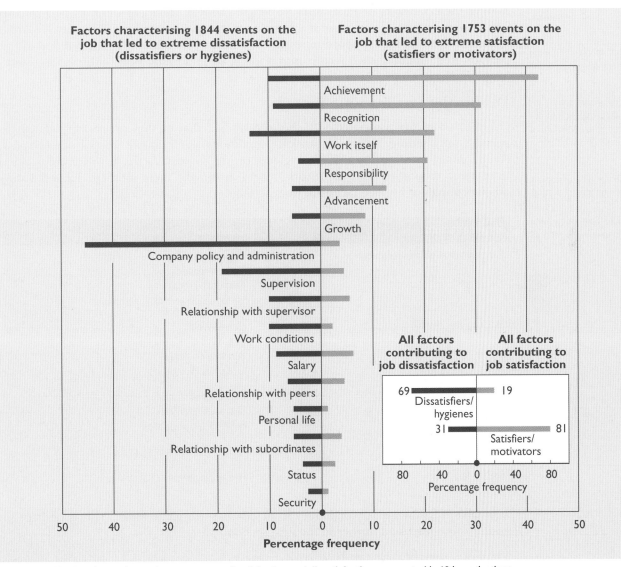

FIGURE 3.4 • Herzberg's two-factor theory: sources of satisfaction and dissatisfaction as reported in 12 investigations

Source: Adapted from Frederick Herzberg, 'One more time: how do you motivate employees?', *Harvard Business Review*, exhibit 1 (September/October 1987). © 2002 Harvard Business School Publishing Corporation. All rights reserved.

According to Herzberg's two-factor theory, an individual employee could be simultaneously both satisfied and dissatisfied because each of these two factors has a different set of drivers and is recorded on a separate scale. According to Herzberg's measurement the two scales are:

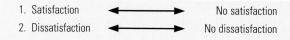

1. Satisfaction ⟷ No satisfaction
2. Dissatisfaction ⟷ No dissatisfaction

Effective managers have to achieve two distinct outcomes as discussed below: to maximise job satisfaction and, simultaneously, to minimise job dissatisfaction.

Satisfiers or motivator factors

To improve satisfaction, a manager must use motivator factors as shown on the right side of figure 3.4. These factors are related to job content — that is, what people do in their work. Adding these satisfiers or motivators to people's jobs is Herzberg's link to performance. These cover such things as sense of achievement, recognition and responsibility. According to Herzberg, when these opportunities are absent, workers will not be satisfied and will not perform well. Building such factors into a job is an important topic and it is discussed at length in chapter 5.

Dissatisfiers or hygiene factors

Hygiene factors are associated with the job context; that is, they are factors related to a person's work setting. Improving working conditions (for example, special offices and air conditioning) involves improving a hygiene, or job context, factor. It will prevent people from being dissatisfied with their work but will not make them satisfied. Table 3.2 shows other examples of hygiene factors in work settings.

Motivators (motivator factors) are satisfiers that are associated with what people do in their work.

Job content refers to what people do in their work.

Hygienes (hygiene factors) are dissatisfiers that are associated with aspects of a person's work setting.

Job context refers to a person's work setting.

TABLE 3.2 • Sample hygiene factors found in work settings

Hygiene factors	Examples
Organisational policies, procedures	Attendance rules Holiday schedules Grievance procedures Performance appraisal methods
Working conditions	Noise levels Safety Personal comfort Size of work area
Interpersonal relationships	Coworker relations Customer relations Relationship with boss
Quality of supervision	Technical competence of boss
Base salary	Hourly wage rate or salary

As table 3.2 shows, salary or money is included as a hygiene factor. This is perhaps surprising and is discussed further in the next section.

Money: motivator or hygiene factor

Herzberg found that low salary makes people dissatisfied, but that paying people more does not satisfy or motivate them. It is important to bear in mind that this conclusion derives from data that found salary had considerable cross-loading across both motivators and hygiene factors (see the bars that cross the central vertical line at zero percentage frequency in figure 3.4). Because most of the variance could be explained within the hygiene or job context group of factors, Herzberg concluded that money was not a motivator.

New ideas are constantly being explored to link money and motivation. Direct employee involvement in the financial future of the organisation is being widely encouraged through Employee Share Ownership Programs (ESOPs).[38] The most recent Australian Bureau of Statistics figures from 1999 show that around 5.5 per cent of employees were involved in employee share ownership in their main jobs or occupations. In 2000 the value of those shares was estimated to be between A$9 billion and A$12 billion.[39] Schemes exist in organisations such as Compass, Foster's and Palm Springs.

OB in action

> Food and hospitality company Compass has a sharesafe program that allows employees to commit to a monthly savings contribution that is banked and earns interest. Employees have the choice of the period (3–5 years). At the end of the period they are given a gift of shares equal to what their accumulated savings represent. In this way they have a vested interest in the performance of the business. Brewer and wine company Foster's has 80 per cent of its eligible employees (those who have worked with the company for at least a year) participating in its share loan plan to encourage a sense of connection between the organisation and its performance. They give a 50 cent discount on up to 2000 shares interest free (saving employees around $1000).[40]

It is difficult to explain the impact of such schemes on work motivation within Herzberg's framework, because these schemes have an impact on Herzberg's job content factors (such as responsibility and accountability) but also have a direct impact on money and its link to work motivation and performance. The link between money, ESOPs and work motivation remains complex and inconclusive to date.

Some Australian studies have found that the link between money and motivation also depends on other key factors, such as the work status of the employee. One study found that casual workers employed on a part-time basis placed a higher value on job security than on monetary reward. The implications of this finding are far reaching because the growth in the part-time workforce in Australia and New Zealand is far greater than the growth of the full-time workforce.

Herzberg: the research and practical implications

Organisational behaviour scholars debate the merits of the two-factor theory.[41] While Herzberg's continuing research and that of his followers support the theory, some researchers have used different methods and are unable to confirm the theory. It is therefore criticised as being method-bound — that is, supportable only by applying Herzberg's original method. This is a serious criticism because the scientific approach requires that theories be verifiable when different research methods are used. The critical incident method used by Herzberg may have resulted in respondents generally associating good times in their jobs with things under their personal control, or for which they could give themselves credit. Bad times, on the other hand, were more often associated with factors in the environment, under the control of management.

Herzberg's theory has also met with other criticisms.
1. The original sample of scientists and engineers probably is not representative of the working population.
2. The theory does not account for individual differences (for example, the similar impact of pay regardless of gender, age and other important differences).
3. The theory does not clearly define the relationship between satisfaction and motivation.[42]

Such criticisms may contribute to the mixed findings from research conducted outside the United States. In New Zealand, for example, supervision and interpersonal relationships were found to contribute significantly to satisfaction and not merely to reducing dissatisfaction. And certain hygiene factors were cited more frequently as satisfiers in Panama, Latin America and a number of countries other than the United States. In contrast, evidence from countries such as Finland tends to confirm US results.[43] In view of globalising workforces, these distinctions may have significant importance for managers endeavouring to motivate their employees.

However, the theory does have value. For example, it may help to identify why a focus on job environment factors (such as special office fixtures, piped-in music, comfortable lounges for breaks and high base salaries) often do not motivate. It also draws strong attention to the value of job design and motivation as discussed in chapter 5.

Process theories of motivation
LEARNING OBJECTIVE 4

Process theories

As useful as they are, content theories still emphasise the 'what' aspect of motivation — that is, 'If I have a security deficiency, I try to reduce or remove it'. They do not emphasise the thought processes concerning 'why' and 'how' people choose one action over another in the workplace. For this, we must turn to process motivation theories. Two well-known process theories are equity theory and expectancy theory.

Equity theory

Equity theory is based on the phenomenon of social comparison and posits, because people gauge the fairness of their work outcomes compared with others, that felt inequity is a motivating state of mind.

Equity theory is based on the phenomenon of social comparison and is best known through the writing of J Stacy Adams.[44] Adams argues that when people gauge the fairness of their work outcomes compared with those of others, felt inequity is a motivating state of mind. That is, when people perceive inequity in their work, they experience a state of cognitive dissonance, and they will be aroused to remove the discomfort and to restore a sense of felt equity to the situation. Inequities exist whenever people feel that the rewards or inducements they receive for their work inputs or contributions are unequal to the rewards other people appear to have received for their inputs. For the individual, the equity comparison or thought process that determines such feeling is:

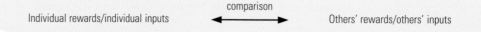

Individual rewards/individual inputs ← comparison → Others' rewards/others' inputs

Resolving felt inequities

Felt negative inequity exists when individuals feel they have received relatively less than others have in proportion to work inputs.

A **felt negative inequity** exists when an individual feels that they have received relatively less than others have in proportion to work inputs. **Felt positive inequity** exists when an individual feels that they have received relatively more than others have.

Felt positive inequity exists when individuals feel they have received relatively more than others have.

Both felt negative and felt positive inequity are motivating states. When either exists, the individual will likely engage in one or more of the following behaviours to restore a sense of equity:

1. change work inputs (for example, reduce performance efforts)
2. change the outcomes (rewards) received (for example, ask for a raise)
3. leave the situation (for example, quit)
4. change the comparison points (for example, compare self with a different coworker)
5. psychologically distort the comparisons (for example, rationalise that the inequity is only temporary and will be resolved in the future)
6. act to change the inputs or outputs of the comparison person (for example, get a co-worker to accept more work).

Equity theory predicts that people who feel either under-rewarded or over-rewarded for their work will act to restore a sense of equity.

Adams's equity theory: the research

The research of Adams and others, accomplished largely in laboratory settings, lends tentative support to this prediction.[45] The research indicates that people who feel overpaid (feel positive inequity) have been found to increase the quantity or quality of their work, while those who are underpaid (feel negative inequity) decrease the quantity or quality of their work. The research is most conclusive about felt negative inequity. It appears that people are less comfortable when they are under-rewarded than when they are over-rewarded.

Managing the equity dynamic

Figure 3.5 shows that the equity comparison intervenes between a manager's allocation of rewards and their impact on the work behaviour of staff. Feelings of inequity are determined solely by the individual's interpretation of the situation.

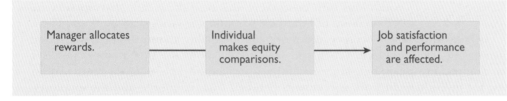

FIGURE 3.5 • The equity comparison as an intervening variable in the rewards, satisfaction and performance relationship

Thus, it is incorrect to assume all employees in a work unit will view their annual pay rise as fair. It is not how a manager feels about the allocation of rewards that counts; it is how the recipients perceive the rewards that will determine the motivational outcomes of the equity dynamic. Managing the equity dynamic therefore becomes quite important to the manager who strives to maintain healthy psychological contracts — that is, fairly balanced inducements and contributions — among staff.

Rewards that are received with feelings of equity can foster job satisfaction and performance. In contrast, rewards that are received with feelings of negative inequity can damage these key work results. The burden lies with the manager to take control of the situation and make sure that any negative consequences of the equity comparisons are avoided, or at least minimised, when rewards are allocated. 'The effective manager 3.1' below shows how you can deal with these concerns.

Steps for managing the equity process
- Recognise that an employee is likely to make an equity comparison whenever especially visible rewards, such as pay, promotions and so on, are being allocated.
- Anticipate felt negative inequities.
- Communicate to each individual your evaluation of the reward, an appraisal of the performance on which it is based, and the comparison points you consider to be appropriate.

THE **Effective**Manager 3.1

Managing the equity dynamic across cultures can become very complex. Western expatriates working in multinational corporations typically adopt an individual frame of reference when making equity comparisons. For local employees in Eastern cultures, the value placed on rewards and the weighting attributed to a specific outcome may vary considerably from Western norms. The group, not the individual, is the major point of reference for such equity comparisons and if a multinational corporation tries to motivate by offering individualised rewards, employees may not respond as expected.[46]

The following 'Ethical perspective' examines how people may perceive inequity in the context of individual pay conditions where the rewards of others are not clearly known but perceptions of inequity may still occur.

Keeping secrets — who gets what?

While industrial awards have historically allowed Australian workers to know what other workers are paid, changing conditions make this less likely. Organisations can pay above-award rates, for example, giving individuals a higher pay than legally required. Since people do not generally discuss their pay conditions with co-workers, this typically means that workers are often unaware of how their pay compares with that of others. There is increasingly more secrecy and more confidentiality about worker rewards and outcomes in the workplace, which can have implications for how workers perceive their comparative treatment. More recently, Australian workplace agreements (AWAs) allow for individualised work agreements between each employee and the employer. For many employers these offer the advantage of overriding most of the provisions of industrial awards that previously governed most employees — awards remain but cover minimum conditions restricted to a small number of allowable matters.

AWAs are thought to provide more flexibility in work hours and wages. Individual AWAs are checked and approved by the Office of the Employment Advocate and must pass a 'no-disadvantage' test. The total package of conditions cannot be less favourable for the employee than the equivalent in the relevant award, though it is possible that some individual conditions may be less favourable. Employees must be given time to consider the agreement and have dispute processes available to them. AWAs tend to be short-term contracts, though they continue after expiration until terminated or replaced by a new AWA. Some have no provisions for wage increases during the period of the agreement. Importantly, they are secret contracts of employment and as such there is a strong concern that people in similar jobs (for example, nurses) may end up receiving different wages and conditions despite doing the same work.[47] While this may reduce employees' capacity to compare their workplace inputs and outputs with each other, it does raise concern about the fairness and transparency of workers' rewards in organisations. When a sense of equity and expectation of rewards for comparable work underpins motivation, these are important considerations for managers.

Expectancy theory

Victor Vroom's expectancy theory[48] seeks to predict or explain the task-related effort expended by a person. The theory's central question is: 'What determines the willingness of an individual to exert personal effort to work at tasks that contribute to the performance of the work unit and the organisation?'

Figure 3.6 illustrates the managerial foundations of expectancy theory. Individuals are viewed as making conscious decisions to allocate their behaviour towards work efforts and to serve self-interests. The three key terms in the theory are as follows.

1. **Expectancy:** the probability that the individual assigns to work effort being followed by a given level of achieved task performance. Expectancy would equal '0' if the person felt it was impossible to achieve the given performance level; it would equal '1' if a person was 100 per cent certain that the performance could be achieved.

Expectancy is the probability that the individual assigns to work effort being followed by a given level of achieved task performance.

2. Instrumentality: the probability that the individual assigns to a given level of achieved task performance leading to various work outcomes that are rewarding for them. Instrumentality also varies from '1' (meaning the reward outcome is 100 per cent certain to follow performance) to '0' (indicating that there is no chance that performance will lead to the reward outcome). (Strictly speaking, Vroom's treatment of instrumentality would allow it to vary from −1 to +1. We use the probability definition here and the 0 to 1 range for pedagogical purposes; it is consistent with the basic instrumentality notion.)

3. Valence: the value that the individual attaches to various work reward outcomes. Valences form a scale from −1 (very undesirable outcome) to +1 (very desirable outcome).

Expectancy theory argues that work motivation is determined by individual beliefs about effort–performance relationships and the desirability of various work outcomes from different performance levels. Simply, the theory is based on the logic that people *will do* what they *can do* when they *want to*.[49] If you want a promotion and see that high performance can lead to that promotion, and that if you work hard you can achieve high performance, you will be motivated to work hard. Estee Lauder, a leading skin care, fragrance and hair care company, is an example of a business where promotion within is well entrenched, thereby increasing employee belief that performance may lead to promotion.

The Estee Lauder Group in Australia encourages the retention and promotion of employees; 60 per cent of employees have been with the company for more than ten years. Managing Director Penny Thompson believes that people within the organisation, even on the front line, have a great deal to contribute. She says: 'We have an unspoken policy that, yes, you can take someone from the outside, but if you take someone from the inside they already know the challenges'.[50]

Multiplier effects and multiple outcomes

Vroom posits that motivation (M), expectancy (E), instrumentality (I) and valence (V) are related to one another by the equation: $M = E \times I \times V$.

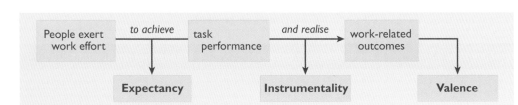

FIGURE 3.6 • Expectancy theory terms in a managerial perspective

This relationship means that the motivational appeal of a given work path is sharply reduced whenever any one or more of these factors approaches the value of zero. Conversely, for a given reward to have a high and positive motivational impact as a work outcome, the expectancy, instrumentality and valence associated with the reward must all be high and positive.

Suppose a manager is wondering whether the prospect of earning a merit pay rise will be motivational to a subordinate. Expectancy theory predicts that motivation to work hard to earn the merit pay will be low if the person:

1. feels they cannot achieve the necessary performance level (expectancy)

2. is not confident a high level of task performance will result in a high merit pay rise (instrumentality)

3. places little value (valence) on a merit pay increase

4. experiences any combination of these.

Side notes:

Instrumentality is the probability that the individual assigns to a level of achieved task performance leading to various work outcomes.

Valence represents the values that the individual attaches to various work outcomes.

Expectancy theory argues that work motivation is determined by individual beliefs about effort–performance relationships and the desirability of various work outcomes from different performance levels.

Expectancy theory is able to accommodate multiple work outcomes in predicting motivation. As shown in figure 3.7, the outcome of a merit pay increase may not be the only one affecting the individual's decision to work hard. Relationships with coworkers may also be important, and they may be undermined if the individual stands out from the group as a high performer. Although merit pay is both highly valued and considered accessible to the individual, its motivational power can be cancelled out by the negative effects of high performance on the individual's social relationships with coworkers. One of the advantages of expectancy theory is its ability to help managers account for such multiple outcomes when trying to determine the motivational value of various work rewards to individual employees.

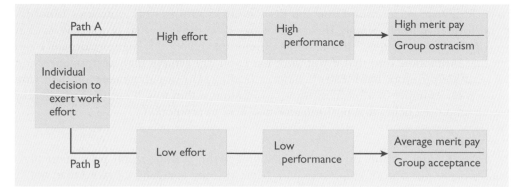

FIGURE 3.7 • An example of individual thought processes, as viewed by expectancy theory

Vroom: managerial implications

The managerial implications of Vroom's expectancy theory are summarised in table 3.3. Expectancy logic argues that a manager must try to understand individual thought processes, then actively intervene in the work situation to influence them. This includes trying to maximise work expectancies, instrumentalities and valences that support the organisation's production purposes. In other words, a manager should strive to create a work setting in which the individual will also value work contributions serving the organisation's needs as paths towards desired personal outcomes or rewards.

TABLE 3.3 • Managerial implications of expectancy theory

Expectancy term	The individual's question	Managerial implications
Expectancy	'Can I achieve the desired level of task performance?'	Select workers with ability; train workers to use ability; support individual ability with organisational resources; identify performance goals
Instrumentality	'What work outcomes will be received as a result of the performance?'	Clarify psychological contracts; communicate performance–reward possibilities; confirm performance–reward possibilities by making actual rewards contingent on performance.
Valence	'How highly do I value the work outcomes?'	Identify individual needs or outcomes; adjust available rewards to match these.

Expectancy theory might also be considered in the context of uncertainty in the workplace. In the following 'What would you do?' feature, WMC Resources workers may have difficulty believing that there will be instrumental links between their current performance and valued outcomes if their jobs are insecure.

Motivation in the face of job loss

More than 650 white-collar workers at WMC Resources are spending Victoria's Labour Day long weekend worrying about the future of their jobs, due to the uncertainty flowing from BHP Billiton's expected success in its A$9.2 billion takeover of the Melbourne mining house.

BHP has yet to say how many of WMC's white-collar workers will retain their jobs on completion of the takeover, which has the WMC board's blessing.

But the white-collar workers fear the worst because nearly all of their positions are duplicated within BHP.

Those fears appear well based given that BHP has put aside A$120 million to cover one-off costs to 'eliminate duplicate functions' in WMC's nickel and copper business, marketing and other corporate functions. On an annual basis, BHP estimates annual 'corporate costs efficiencies' of A$115 million.

The first of BHP's 'transition' teams visited WMC's Southbank head office last week. BHP prides itself on the 'proven systems and processes' that eliminated duplication and extracted cost-savings in the 2001 merger with the London-based Billiton.

WMC has two offices in Melbourne. The head office at Southbank employs 230 people. Another 170 people work in the group's centralised supply and contracts services division and administration services in St Kilda Road. Another 250 white-collar jobs are at WMC's Belmont office in Western Australia.

Not expected to suffer big job losses are 55 nickel business positions at the Belmont office and the small number of white-collar jobs in Adelaide associated with the Olympic Dam copper–uranium mine in the far north of South Australia.

WMC managing director Andrew Michelmore has scheduled staff meetings for tomorrow at both the Southbank and St Kilda Road offices. While BHP has said it would honour job contracts, the issue of job security is expected to dominate the briefings.

Because it has long been a takeover target, WMC has a minimum six-months redundancy payment system. It was established to attract new staff concerned that their jobs would disappear on the group falling to a takeover bid. Beyond that arrangement, redundancy is at industry standards.

An insight into how WMC's board and senior management will fare once WMC disappears will come with the expected release before Easter of the group's 2004 annual report. The report will detail the arrangements and contracts covering their employment.

On Friday, BHP managing director Chip Goodyear would not put a number on the likely job losses at WMC were BHP's bid to succeed, saying only that 'there will be job losses as a result of this'.

'There are positions that will be duplicated by the process and, as a result, there will be reduction in some overhead costs for sure,' he said. But he did offer some hope for WMC's brightest stars.

'We are a growing organisation. We've done 24 projects in the last three years around the world. We've got 26 under way now. So we continue to grow and expand our business quite significantly, and that always requires first-class people,' Mr Goodyear said.

He cited the A$1.76 billion being pumped into its existing Australian nickel business.

Source: Barry Fitzgerald, 'WMC workers fear for jobs', *The Sydney Morning Herald* (14 March 2005), p. 38.

Questions

1. If you were a WMC manager and responsible for some of these employees, how would you go about clarifying performance–reward relationships to manage their motivation in the short term?

2. What other approaches would you use to maintain the motivation of employees?

In terms of outcome valence, the manager can identify individual needs or outcomes important to each individual, then try to adjust available rewards to match these. In this sense the theory can be universally applied. Each individual may be different, though different cultural patterns of values will affect valence of rewards across cultures. It may also be possible to change the individual's perceptions of the valence of various outcomes, as shown in 'The effective manager 3.2'.

THE **Effective**Manager 3.2

Tips for influencing the perceived valence of work outcomes

- Find out the currently valued outcomes for each employee.
- Determine the outcomes that are currently available to them.
- Discuss how well the two sets match, and examine similarities between each individual's list and your list.
- Show how some available outcomes may be more desirable or less undesirable than the worker thinks (for example, promotion may be available, but the employee currently does not desire it because he or she feels uncomfortable with it).

Vroom: the research

There is a great deal of research on expectancy theory, and good review articles are available.[51] Although the theory has received substantial support, specific details (such as the operation of the multiplier effect) remain subject to question. Rather than charging that the underlying theory is inadequate, researchers indicate that problems of method and measurement may cause their inability to generate more confirming data. Thus, while awaiting the results of more sophisticated research, experts seem to agree that expectancy theory is a useful insight into work motivation.

One of the more popular modifications of Vroom's original version of the theory distinguishes between extrinsic and intrinsic rewards as two separate types of possible work outcomes.[52] Extrinsic rewards are positively valued work outcomes that the individual receives from some other person in the work setting. An example is pay. Workers typically do not pay themselves directly; some representative of the organisation administers the reward. In contrast, intrinsic rewards are positively valued work outcomes that the individual receives directly as a result of task performance; they do not require the participation of another person. A feeling of achievement after accomplishing a particularly challenging task is one example. The distinction between extrinsic and intrinsic rewards is important because each type demands separate attention from a manager seeking to use rewards to increase motivation. We discuss these differences more thoroughly in chapters 4 and 5.

Extrinsic rewards are positively valued work outcomes that the individual receives from some other person in the work setting.

Intrinsic rewards are positively valued work outcomes that the individual receives directly as a result of task performance.

Integrating content and process motivation theories

LEARNING OBJECTIVE 5

Integrating content and process motivation theories

Each of the theories presented in this chapter is potentially useful for the manager. Although the equity and expectancy theories have special strengths, current thinking argues for a combined approach that points out where and when various motivation theories work best.[53] Thus, before leaving this discussion, we should pull the content and process theories together into one integrated model of individual performance and satisfaction.

First, the various content theories have a common theme, as shown in figure 3.8. Content theorists disagree somewhat as to the exact nature of human needs, but they do agree that:

$$\text{Individual needs} \xrightarrow{\text{activate}} \text{tensions} \xrightarrow[\text{influence}]{\text{that}} \text{attitudes and behaviour.}$$

The manager's job is to create a work environment that responds positively to individual needs. Poor performance, undesirable behaviours and/or decreased satisfaction can be partly explained in terms of 'blocked' needs, or needs that are not satisfied on the job. The motivational value of rewards (intrinsic and extrinsic) can also be analysed in terms of 'activated' needs to which a given reward either does or does not respond. Ultimately, managers must understand that individuals have different needs and place different importance on different needs. Managers must also know what to offer individuals to respond to their needs and to create work settings that give people the opportunity to satisfy their needs through their contributions to task, work unit and organisational performance.

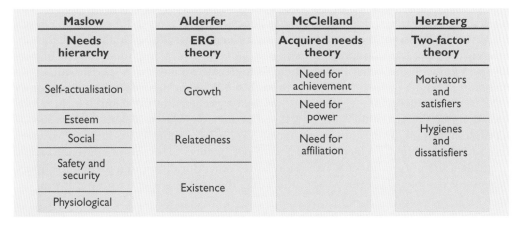

FIGURE 3.8 • Comparison of content motivation theories

Figure 3.9 is a model that goes further to integrate content and process theories. The model, as proposed by Lyman W Porter and Edward E Lawler, is an extension of Vroom's original expectancy theory.[54] The figure is based on the foundation of the individual performance equation (see chapter 2). Individual attributes and work effort, and the manager's ability to create a work setting that positively responds to individual needs and goals all affect performance. Whether a work setting can satisfy needs depends on the availability of rewards (extrinsic and intrinsic). The content theories enter the model as the manager's guide to understanding individual attributes and identifying the needs that give motivational value to the various work rewards allocated to employees. Managers are also interested in promoting high levels of individual satisfaction as a part of their concern for human resource maintenance. You may recall that we concluded our chapter 2 review of the satisfaction–performance controversy by noting that when rewards are allocated on the basis of past performance (that is, when rewards are performance contingent), they can cause both future performance and satisfaction. Motivation can also occur when job satisfactions result from rewards that are felt to be equitably allocated. When felt negative inequity results, satisfaction will be low and motivation will be reduced. Thus, the integrated model includes a key role for equity theory and recognises job performance and satisfaction as separate, but potentially interdependent, work results.[55]

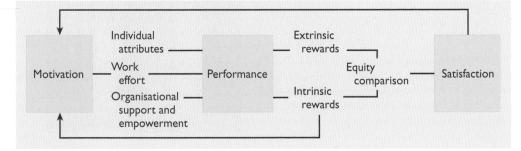

FIGURE 3.9 • Predicting individual work performance and satisfaction: an integrated model

Another perspective on motivation: self-concept and personal values

In recent years a new body of work has developed to explain other dimensions of motivation that do not seem to be covered by content and process theories. For example, people often offer their services voluntarily or engage in altruistic deeds for no anticipated rewards (intrinsic or extrinsic). Personal value systems and the idea of self-concept, discussed in chapter 2, underly this approach. **Self-concept** is the concept that individuals have of themselves as physical, social and spiritual or moral beings.

The self-concept approach comes from personality theory. It focuses on using the concept of the self as an underlying force that motivates behaviour, that gives it direction and energy and sustains it. Self-concept is derived from many influences including family, social identity and reference groups, education and experience. Generally speaking, these aspects of personality are a guide to our behaviour and help us to decide what to do in specific situations. So, for example, young people may choose to study medicine or dentistry at university, or to enter the family trade, because that is what was always expected of them and has therefore become an important part of their identity. Rewards such as money and status may be secondary considerations. Many acts are done out of a sense of responsibility, integrity or even humour, which relate to the self-concept aspect of personality.[56] This sort of approach would help to explain the nurse who waits with the relatives of a critically injured patient for hours after his shift is completed; or the person who works the shift of a friend who is studying for exams.

In contrast to a focus on needs or cognitive thought processes to explain motivation, the self-concept approach relies on other ways of understanding motivation to explain the full range of motivated behaviour. People may also draw on the values they hold, and the way that these values are a guide to behaviours that seem right or appropriate for them. For example, people internalise values that are espoused by the professional group (or the organisation) to which they belong. Behaviours consistent with such values might include saving lives and property at considerable personal risk, exposing unethical financial practices despite censure from management, or facing personal hardship like Fiona McCrossin.

Having identified many content and process theories, and an integrated model of these two approaches, as well as the ideas of self-concept and personal values in motivation, it is a good time to reflect on how managers may be able to realistically implement all these in the workplace. The following 'Counterpoint' raises some points about the complexity and difficulties of motivating employees.

Self-concept is the concept that individuals have of themselves as physical, social and spiritual or moral beings.

OB in action

Fiona McCrossin is an individual who is motivated by her personal values in relation to the environment. Fiona worked as a teacher after completing a degree in marine biology. She became a member of the Wilderness Society and eventually made a career transition to that organisation because she was so passionate about saving forests on the south coast of New South Wales. McCrossin regularly faces financial difficulties, pays bills late and gets eviction notices. But it seems that she is willing to work seven days a week for just $200 a week because she feels it is the most important thing she can do for her children.[57]

Knowing and engaging our workers?

When managers or scholars discuss workplace motivation, they tend to talk about it as if work, and a single workplace, is the only place where people exert effort towards fulfilling needs, achieving rewards and/or living life according to their self-concept. The idea that you can get to know your employees and work out what motivational needs they have, and then find ways to help them satisfy those needs can over-ascribe the importance of work in motivating people, and simplify the complex circumstances and working arrangements that exist in today's workforce.

It is to be expected that employers would want some return on their motivational strategies. To do so employers need to invest time, money and other resources into employees who are 'engaged' with the company. The idea of 'employee engagement' helps to link up motivation with the workplace attitudes of organisational commitment, job satisfaction and advocacy (those who speak highly of their own organisation as an employer and of its products, services and brand). Studies in the United States and Canada reveal that companies with disengaged employees have significant productivity losses, while those with engaged employees have higher revenue, customer loyalty and profits.[58]

The idea that in the new-style workplace employees are all engaged may be problematic since many remain for only a short time, have links with more than one organisation and/or have mixed feelings about their employment. These include an increasing number of casual or part-time employees, which in turn includes the 'well-heeled itinerants' who are working multiple jobs (such as some university academics who hold three or more concurrent jobs).[59] Loosely engaged professionals often move from one contracted job to another, many working as free agents. Older workers may be torn between the pressures to continue working, at least part-time, and their desire to retire. At the other end of the age spectrum, a recent Australian survey of generation Y employees (those born between 1978 and 1994) found that they were very likely to change jobs if their expectations were not met in an organisation.[60]

People who work remotely or operate in a virtual workplace may lack engagement with the organisation. For example, 4000 software consultants at Wipro, an Indian IT company, operate from and between customer sites outside of India.[61]

Also, it is important to remember that people do not spend all their lives at work, and other things in their lives may drive behaviour as much as their work. Whether they play sport, work in their gardens, act in a voluntary capacity in a community organisation or pursue further study, they are involved in motivation outside the workplace.

Questions

1. How might an employee's needs be satisfied outside the workplace and, if this occurs, how would it impact upon the needs that employees seek to satisfy in the workplace?

2. Why might casual employees, those with multiple jobs, older employees, generation Y workers, and virtual and professional workers be less engaged than other employees and what could an employer do to seek to motivate these different cohorts?

Empowerment

OBJECTIVE 7
LEARNING

Empowerment and the empowerment process

Much of the motivational theory discussed in this chapter has addressed the question of what management can do to ensure employees positively contribute to the achievement of organisational goals. In the workplace in the twenty-first century, the worker is searching for recognition, involvement and a heightened sense of self-worth and the employer is often looking for a 'can do' mentality among employees that lessens the need for managerial control.

Empowerment can do this. Empowerment is the process by which managers delegate power to employees to motivate greater responsibility in balancing the achievement of both personal and organisational goals. The key question for managers is how to facilitate employees' individual and joint contributions to the organisation and their own development. Empowerment focuses on liberating, not controlling, human energy, and on balancing the achievement of personal and organisational goals. Managers commonly attempt these processes by delegating more power to employees and encouraging them to take on leadership roles in the organisation.

The concept of empowerment is founded on the belief that everyone has an internal need for self-determination and a need to cope with environmental demands directly. This suggests that appropriate empowerment strategies can raise the perception of low self-efficacy. Self-efficacy refers to a person's belief that they can perform adequately in a situation. It refers to a state of mind or mentality,[62] which is why its relationship with empowerment strategies is important (self-efficacy is discussed in more depth in chapter 4). Empowerment strategies are designed to improve self-efficacy by providing employees with greater autonomy and by increasing knowledge and control over factors directly related to job performance.

Some work on empowerment has identified the following stages (see figure 3.10) in the empowerment process.[63]

- *Stage 1* Identify the conditions contributing to low self-efficacy. This could include organisational factors (such as poor communication systems and an impersonal bureaucratic climate); supervisory style factors (such as authoritarianism, an emphasis on failure or lack of communication of reasons for action or inaction); reward factors (such as rewards that are not performance-based, or the low incentive value of rewards); and job design factors (such as unclear roles, unrealistic goals, low levels of participation and low job enrichment).

- *Stage 2* Employ empowerment strategies and techniques that help to vest substantial responsibility in the hands of the individual who is closest to the problem requiring a solution.
  - *Cultivate a 'service wisdom'.* Trained and multiskilled employees should be able to handle non-routine situations, to understand the bigger picture and how their role affects other employees and the achievement of organisational goals.
  - *Encourage job mastery.* Provide coaching, training and appropriate experiences to ensure successful job performance.
  - *Create a freedom to act.* Treat employees as if they own their jobs, devolving power so employees can adequately resolve problems. Managers should set appropriate boundaries to the freedom to facilitate successful employee job performance without creating inappropriate licence.
  - *Provide emotional support.* Employees must feel that if they act within the designated boundaries, then managers will support their actions even if they make mistakes. Such support helps reduce stress and anxiety through clearer role definition, task support and concern for employee wellbeing.
  - *Provide appropriate feedback.* Employees need regular and detailed feedback so they know how they are performing against managerial expectations.
  - *Share the power.* Share as much power as possible, allowing for employee experience, education and task difficulty.
  - *Demonstrate active listening skills.* Learn to listen to feedback from experienced employees, because the person performing the task often has the best ideas on process improvement.
  - *Learn how to let go.* Treat employees as partners and equals rather than as subordinates and know when to let go when their work is successfully helping the business move in the right direction.
  - *Encourage diversity of approach.* Employees should have the discretion to use various job styles and methods provided they meet agreed organisational standards for the work.

- *Develop participative management skills.* Encourage employees to participate in major decisions that directly affect their daily working lives.
  - *Encourage modelling.* Employees should be able to observe and model their work on examples of 'best practice' performance in particular skills and competency-based areas relevant to their own work assignments.
  - *Create job enrichment.* Enrich jobs by making employees more accountable and responsible for key aspects of their work performance.
- *Stage 3* Provide self-efficacy information directly to the employee. This stage focuses on modifying employee behaviour and increasing the self-efficacy belief. Four approaches have been identified.
  - *Competency building.* Structure training and organisational learning so that employees acquire new skills through successive, moderate increments in task complexity and responsibility.
  - *Encouragement and persuasion.* Use verbal feedback and other persuasive techniques to encourage and reinforce successful job performance.
  - *Emotional support.* Provide emotional support for employees and minimise emotional arousal states such as anxiety, stress and the fear associated with making mistakes. Mistakes should be seen as part of the learning process.
  - *Modelling.* Allow employees to observe workers who perform successfully on the job.

Both stages 2 and 3 are designed to remove and eradicate the conditions identified in stage 1, and to develop the positive feelings of self-efficacy within the individual employee.

- *Stage 4* Create a 'can do' mentality and an empowering experience for the employee. If stages 2 and 3 are successful then they will increase the employee's effort–performance understanding. As we saw earlier in the chapter, expectancy theories of motivation are essential for high and sustained levels of performance. Here, performance is linked directly to the positive mentality of the individual.

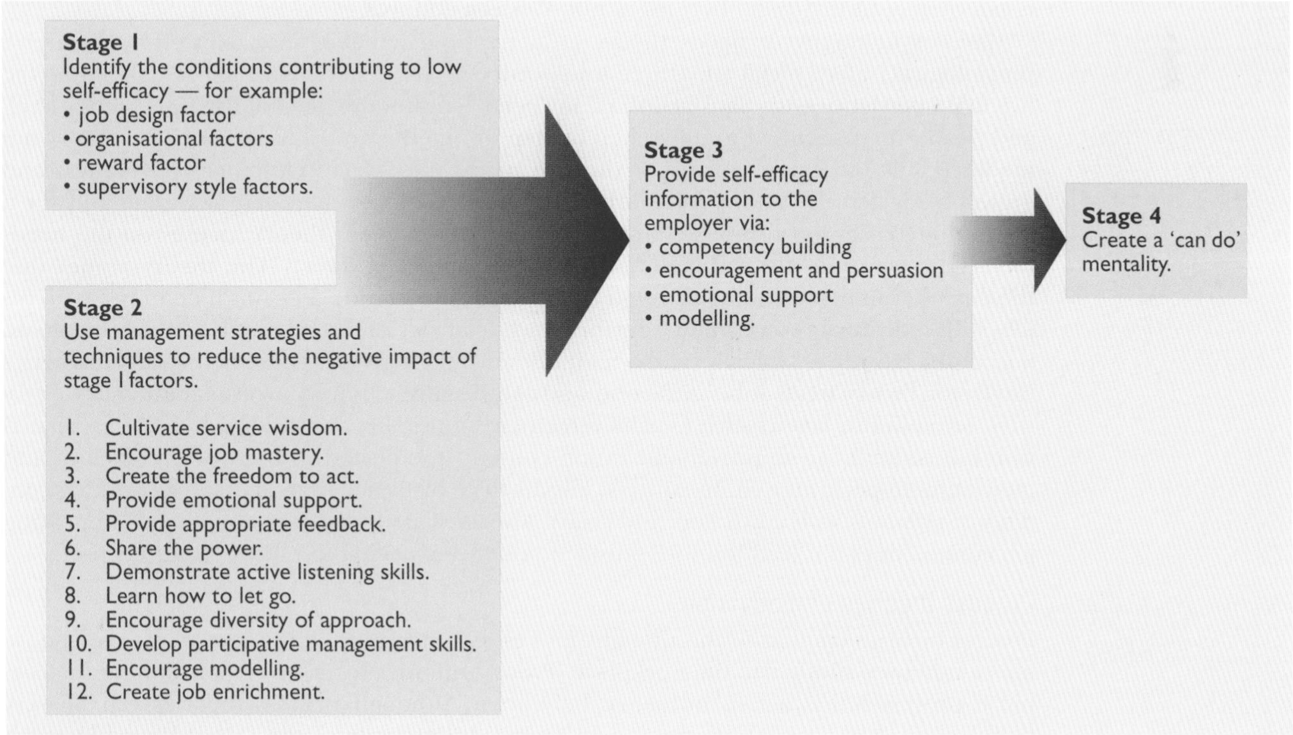

Stage 1
Identify the conditions contributing to low self-efficacy — for example:
• job design factor
• organisational factors
• reward factor
• supervisory style factors.

Stage 2
Use management strategies and techniques to reduce the negative impact of stage 1 factors.

1. Cultivate service wisdom.
2. Encourage job mastery.
3. Create the freedom to act.
4. Provide emotional support.
5. Provide appropriate feedback.
6. Share the power.
7. Demonstrate active listening skills.
8. Learn how to let go.
9. Encourage diversity of approach.
10. Develop participative management skills.
11. Encourage modelling.
12. Create job enrichment.

Stage 3
Provide self-efficacy information to the employer via:
• competency building
• encouragement and persuasion
• emotional support
• modelling.

Stage 4
Create a 'can do' mentality.

FIGURE 3.10 • Modelling the empowerment process

Some of these techniques and strategies are evident in Siemens in New Zealand.

CEO of Siemens New Zealand Graeme Sumner believes that the organisation runs on the knowledge and skills of its employees and that they must be empowered to operate effectively and to make decisions. The organisation has crews that travel globally and need to be able to make decisions as they go. This offers potential but also involves risk. The company has a framework that supports its empowerment approach. This includes a high level of integrity, collaboration, valuing and respecting people's opinions and trusting that people know what they are doing.[64]

Summary

Motivating and empowering today's workforce

In the contemporary world a key challenge is to motivate and empower workers towards productive performance. With ageing populations, labour shortages and mobile workforces, organisations will need to understand how to motivate and empower employees in order to attract and retain them and to enhance performance.

Difference between content and process motivation theories

There are two main types of motivational theories — content and process. Content theories examine the needs that individuals have. Their efforts to satisfy those needs are what drive their behaviour. Process theories examine the thought processes that people have in relation to motivating their behaviour.

Content theories of motivation

The content theories of Maslow, Alderfer, McClelland and Herzberg emphasise needs or motives. They are often criticised for being culturally biased, and caution should be exercised when applying these theories in non-Western cultures.

Maslow's hierarchy of needs theory arranges human needs into a five-step hierarchy: physiological, safety, social (the three lower-order needs), esteem and self-actualisation (the two higher-order needs). Satisfaction of any need activates the need at the next higher level, and people are presumed to move step by step up the hierarchy. Alderfer's ERG theory has modified this theory by collapsing the five needs into three: existence, relatedness and growth. Alderfer also allows for more than one need to be activated at a time and for a frustration–regression response. McClelland's acquired needs theory focuses on the needs for achievement (nAch), affiliation (nAff) and power (nPower). The theory argues that these needs can be developed through experience and training. Persons high in nAch prefer jobs with individual responsibility, performance feedback and moderately challenging goals. Successful executives typically have a high nPower that is greater than their nAff. Herzberg's two-factor theory treats job satisfaction and job dissatisfaction as two separate issues. Satisfiers, or motivator factors such as achievement, responsibility and recognition, are associated with job content. An improvement in job content is expected to increase satisfaction and motivation to perform well. In contrast, dissatisfiers, or hygiene factors such as working conditions, relations with coworkers and salary, are associated with the job context. Improving job context does not lead to more satisfaction but is expected to reduce dissatisfaction.

Process theories of motivation

Process theories emphasise the thought processes concerning how and why people choose one action over another in the workplace. Process theories focus on understanding the cognitive processes that act to influence behaviour. Although process theories can be very useful in explaining work motivation in cross-cultural settings, the values that drive such theories may vary substantially across cultures and the outcomes may differ considerably.

Equity theory points out that people compare their rewards (and inputs) with those of others. The individual is then motivated to engage in behaviour to correct any perceived inequity. At the extreme, feelings of inequity may lead to reduced performance or job turnover. Expectancy theory argues that work motivation is determined by an individual's beliefs concerning effort–performance relationships (expectancy), work–outcome relationships (instrumentality) and the desirability of various work outcomes (valence). Managers, therefore, must build positive expectancies, demonstrate performance-reward instrumentalities, and use rewards with high positive valences in their motivational strategies.

Integrating content and process motivation theories

The content theories can be compared, with some overlap identified. An integrated model of motivation builds from the individual performance equation developed in chapter 2 and combines the content and process theories to show how well-managed rewards can lead to high levels of both individual performance and satisfaction.

Self-concept, personal values and motivation

Theories that focus on self-concept and personal values seek to describe motivation that cannot be readily explained by content and process theories. Self-concept is an aspect of personality that describes the concept individuals have of themselves as physical, social and spiritual or moral beings. This self-conception guides their behaviour. Personal values can guide behaviour in the same way.

Empowerment and the empowerment process

Empowerment is the process by which managers delegate power to employees to motivate greater responsibility in balancing the achievement of personal and organisational goals. For employees who experience low self-efficacy, managers can implement strategies to improve the employees' feelings of self-worth and their capacity to improve their performance.

Chapter 3 study guide

OB ## Key terms

content theories, *p. 82*

empowerment, *p. 100*

equity theory, *p. 90*

ERG theory, *p. 84*

existence needs, *p. 84*

expectancy, *p. 92*

expectancy theory, *p. 93*

extrinsic rewards, *p. 96*

felt negative inequity, *p. 90*

felt positive inequity, *p. 90*

growth needs, *p. 84*

higher-order needs, *p. 83*

hygienes (hygiene factors), *p. 88*

instrumentality, *p. 93*

intrinsic rewards, *p. 96*

job content, *p. 88*

job context, *p. 88*

lower-order needs, *p. 83*

motivation to work, *p. 78*

motivators (motivator factors), *p. 88*

motivator–hygiene theory, *p. 87*

need for achievement (nAch), *p. 85*

need for affiliation (nAff), *p. 85*

need for power (nPower), *p. 85*

process theories, *p. 82*

relatedness needs, *p. 84*

self-concept, *p. 98*

self-efficacy, *p. 100*

valence, *p. 93*

Review questions

1. Define 'work motivation' and identify the role of motivation in the individual performance equation.
2. Compare the 'needs' in Alderfer's and McClelland's theories of motivation.
3. Explain the key differences between the expectancy and the equity theories of motivation.
4. Describe each of the four stages in the empowerment process.

Application questions

1. What challenges might there be in motivating (a) young unskilled workers and (b) highly talented and experienced middle-aged workers?
2. Assuming that an organisation successfully retains its older employees, what can it do to motivate them?
3. 'It is impossible to know what employees want but if you give them good salaries or wages they can use the money to find ways to fulfil their own needs. Employers do not need to worry about anything else.' Discuss (debate) this statement.
4. Explain the application of the integrated model of motivation to each of the following occupational groups at an early career stage: police officers and marketing research professionals.
5. Discuss ways in which (a) a major retail store could empower its retail assistants in their jobs and (b) a bank could empower its tellers in their work.
6. Imagine that you are the manager of a small furniture design and manufacturing company. Several of the staff members have complained that the rewards and benefits provided by the company are inequitable. What practical steps can you take to evaluate current policies and practices, or to ensure that perceptions of inequity are rectified?

Research questions

1. 'The need theories of motivation are culturally based.' Discuss this statement, examining in detail one of the need theories of motivation. In answering this question, you are encouraged to read an original work of the theorist associated with the theory you chose, such as David McClelland's *The achieving society*, or the works of Douglas McGregor and Abraham Maslow, given in the 'suggested reading' for this chapter.

2. Many companies in the service sector — large hotels and resorts, for example — are implementing empowerment strategies to improve the quality of service provided to residents and guests. Search the Internet for an example of such a company, with particular emphasis on strategies used to empower front-line staff.

Running project

Using the information you have available about your organisation, answer the following questions.
1. How does management try to motivate employees?
2. Based on your answer to question 1, does this vary between permanent and casual employees? How and why?
3. To what extent does management use money, both wages/salary and performance-based pay, as a motivator? Are the self-concepts or personal values of individuals likely to have an impact on their efforts at work?
4. How does the organisation manage the equity process?
5. How does management empower the organisation's employees?

Individual activity

Are you motivated to work hard at your studies?

Complete the questions in this exercise, based on your work as a university or college student. This exercise should help to explain the level of effort you put into your studies at university or college, while also clarifying the way the expectancy theory of motivation is intended to work.

Connection 1: Expectancy (probability that your effort will result in a certain level of performance)

How often is it true for you personally that the first factor leads to the second factor in your studies?

	Never	Sometimes	Often	Always
Spending twice as many hours on an assignment results in a higher grade.				
Studying consistently throughout the semester leads to better results.				
Participating in class activities enhances my understanding of the subject or improves my grades.				
Being organised helps me handle the demands of being a student				

(continued)

Connection 2: Instrumentality (probability that your performance will result in various rewards and outcomes)

How likely are you to receive the following rewards if you work hard (put in the hours, study consistently, participate, try to be organised)?

	Never	Not very likely	Fairly likely	Very likely
A better academic record/transcript				
More/better employment options				
Peer acceptance				
Sense of accomplishment				
Building my knowledge/skills				
Feeling good about myself				
Avoidance of pressure and stress				
A 'pat on the back' from my parents/family				
Reward — holiday, dinner out, etc.				
Other (specify)				

Connection 3: Valence (value of the reward outcome to you)

How important are each of the following rewards to you?

	Not important	Moderately important	Fairly important	Very important
A better academic record/transcript				
More/better employment options				
Peer acceptance				
Sense of accomplishment				
Building my knowledge/skills				
Feeling good about myself				
Avoidance of pressure and stress				
A 'pat on the back' from my parents/family				
Reward — holiday, dinner out, etc.				
Other (specify)				

After you have completed the questions, review your answers in the light of what expectancy theory tells us about motivation:

- What do your answers in the 'expectancy' section tell you about your level of confidence in your abilities, or the things that have discouraged/encouraged you in the past?

- Refer to your responses in the 'instrumentality' section. What do they tell you about the rewards you experience from your studies? Are they predominantly extrinsic, intrinsic or a mix of both?
- Compare the rewards you experience (or expect to experience) from your studies with the rewards you value from the 'valence' section. How well do they match one another? Are there any rewards that you value highly but do not expect to receive?
- Assess the 'multiplier effect' to explain the level of effort you put into your studies. Compare your results with those of others in the class. If your motivation to study is low, what can you do to improve it?

Group activity

OB

What do you want from a job — motivators or hygienes?[65]

Objectives

1. To help you better understand how job factors affect motivation
2. To help you realise that people are motivated by different factors
3. To better understand Herzberg's motivation theory and determine if you agree with it

Total time: 10–30 minutes

Preparation

Complete the following 'Motivators or hygienes' assessment before coming to class.

Most workers want job satisfaction. The following 12 job factors may contribute to job satisfaction. Rate each according to how important it is to you. Place a number on a scale of 1 to 5 on the line before each factor.

Very important	Somewhat important			Not important
5	4	3	2	1

_____ 1. An interesting job

_____ 2. A good boss

_____ 3. Recognition and appreciation for the work I do

_____ 4. The opportunity for advancement

_____ 5. A satisfying personal life

_____ 6. A prestigious or status job

_____ 7. Job responsibility

_____ 8. Good working conditions (nice office)

_____ 9. Sensible company rules, regulations, procedures and policies

_____ 10. The opportunity to grow through learning new things

_____ 11. A job I can do well and at which I can succeed

_____ 12. Job security

To determine if hygienes or motivators are important to you, place your scores below.

Hygiene factors	Score	Motivational factors	Score
2.	_____	1.	_____
5.	_____	3.	_____
6.	_____	4.	_____
8.	_____	7.	_____
9.	_____	10.	_____
12.	_____	11.	_____
Total points	_____	Total points	_____

Add each column vertically. Did you select hygienes or motivators as being more important to you?

Procedure for class discussion

1. Break into groups of five or six members and discuss the job factors selected as important by group members. Come to a consensus on the three factors that are most important to the group. If the group has other factors not listed in the activity, you may add them.

2. Select a representative from your group to write the group's three most important job factors on the board.

3. The lecturer can then identify the most important job factors for the entire class.

4. Are the class selections motivators or hygienes? As a class, discuss whether you agree with Herzberg's two-factor theory.

Chapter 3 • Motivation and empowerment

107

Ninety assistance officers (AOs) work in the IT support (ITS) section of National Investment & Insurance (NII), a company whose main business is selling and servicing insurance and financial packages for both individual and corporate customers. An AO's role is to respond to requests by their 'customers' — any of the 19 500 employees of the company whose jobs depend on the effective use of computers.

Customers can email for help, use an internal telephone number or a free-call number from outside. The service runs 24 hours, seven days a week, with 15 AOs working between 7 am and 7 pm. Between 7 pm and 11 pm the unit is scaled back to four workers, with only two workers between 11 pm and 7 am. On weekends, six AOs work during the day, with just two at night between 11 pm and 7 am. Almost all jobs are remedied remotely or if a visit is necessary it is done by arrangement. There is always an 'on-call manager' available to come in and resolve a problem, or to talk an AO through a difficult problem. When they begin this job, new AOs only work during the day shift so that they can be supported by supervisors on duty until they learn the business and its systems.

Eighty per cent of the AOs are casual employees, paid an hourly rate, who work four- to eight-hour shifts. Many are IT students from a nearby university. Some continue working to get extra money after they graduate, favouring the after-hours shifts so they can work at other jobs during the day. The remaining 20 per cent are full-time employees, mostly supervisors or managers who have gained their positions after being casual employees.

Casual AO positions are advertised several times a year since staff turnover is high. Full-time AO positions are infrequently available. Once employed full-time, AOs are given annual pay increments, are eligible to participate in training programs and, after a year, apply for further promotion. Most go on to higher-level positions in the ITS.

A recent survey of workers in NII showed that AOs do not usually resolve their requests quickly enough (they often take one to two days); that they are not friendly; and that the customers sometimes feel like they are talking to a machine. Data recording the requests dealt with reveal that 95 per cent of the problems are small and are often related to poor user knowledge rather than equipment or software failures. To begin to improve performance and motivation, Brendan, the manager of the ITS, held a meeting with all the AOs — their first ever common meeting. Up to this time, communication of requirements had involved word of mouth, sticky paper notes or email newsletters. At the meeting, after outlining his aims and asking for comments, Brendan found that a number of common issues emerged. Many AOs find it difficult to help people who seem to know 'absolutely nothing' about computing. In other cases the employees who ring up become demanding or abusive and act like they know a lot more than the AOs (and the AOs admit, sometimes they do). The casual AOs say many of them don't bother applying for positions because they don't know what it takes to get one of the full-time positions — they just know that some do and some don't when they apply. The casual AOs also feel that the full-time AOs (including managers and supervisors) do less because their jobs are safe.

Questions

1. What ways can AOs at NII satisfy higher-order needs in the current context and what could be done to improve their opportunities to do so?

2. Assume that casual workers prefer full-time employment at NII. Describe how a casual worker could use expectancy theory to work out how to gain full-time employment. How can NII send clearer messages to its casual workers about the way to get a full-time job there?

3. Compare employee motivation for full-time and casual employees at NII. Explain why they might be different.

Suggested reading

Mike Applegarth, *Leading empowerment: a practical guide to change* (Oxford: Chandos, 2005).

Ken Blanchard, John P Carols, Alan Randolf, *Empowerment takes more than a minute* (San Francisco: Berrett Koehler, 2001).

Judy Cameron and W David Pierce, *Rewards and intrinsic motivation: resolving the controversy* (Westport, Conn: Bergin & Garvey, 2002).

Miriam Erez, Uwe Kleinbeck and Henk Theirry (eds), *Work motivation in the context of a globalizing economy* (Mahwah, NJ: Lawrence Erlbaum Associates, 2001).

Bruno S Frey and Margit Osterloh (eds), *Successful management by motivation: balancing intrinsic and extrinsic incentives* (New York: Springer, 2002).

James R Lucas, *Balance of power: authority or empowerment? How you can get the best of both in the 'interdependent' organization* (New York: AMACOM, 1998).

Abraham Maslow, *Motivation and personality*, 2nd ed. (New York: HarperCollins, 1970).

Douglas McGregor, *The human side of enterprise* (New York: McGraw-Hill, 1960).

Lyman W Porter, Gregory A Bigley and Richard M Steers, *Motivation and leadership at work* (Boston: McGraw-Hill, 2003).

Johnmarshall Reeve, *Understanding motivation and emotion* (New York: Wiley, 2005).

Kenneth W Thomas, *Intrinsic motivation at work: building energy and commitment* (San Francisco: Berrett Koehler, 2002).

Janelle Wells, *Just rewards* (Sydney: Allen & Unwin, 2004).

End notes

1. Lisa Murray, 'Who's next? NAB axes 1700 jobs in Britain', *Sydney Morning Herald* (31 March 2005), p. 21.
2. Lisa Murray, 'Bank sees scope to cut jobs in back office', *Sydney Morning Herald* (7 April 2005), p. 20.
3. Michael Sainsbury and Michael West, 'Bourse rebuffs Telstra Revolution', *The Australian* (16 November, 2005), p. 23.
4. Leon Gettler, 'Decade of getting the sack still churns Australians' stomachs', *Sydney Morning Herald* (6 May 2004), p. 24.
5. Department of Employment and Workplace Relations, *Workforce tomorrow: adapting to a more diverse Australian labour market*, (Canberra: Commonwealth of Australia, 2005), available at www.workplace.gov.au. See also 'Skills in demand lists 2005', www.workplace.gov.au.
6. Department of Labour (New Zealand), 'Skills in the labour market — September 2005', www.dol.govt.nz/publications/lmr/lmr-Skills.asp.
7. Bronwyn Sell, 'Skills shortage takes a high toll on employment', *The New Zealand Herald* (14 April 2005).
8. Derek Parker, '[Skill shortage:] crisis ahead', *Management Today* (August 2004), pp. 26–9.
9. Craig Donaldson, 'CEOs close door on older workers', *Human Resources* (5 April 2005), pp. 1 and 12.
10. Fred Pawle, '[Filling the] jobs gap, *Management Today* (August 2004), p. 31.
11. Suzanne Keen, 'Work in progress', *HR Monthly* (February 2005), pp. 18–24.
12. '2005: a year for job hopping?', *Human Resources*, issue 72 (25 January 2005), p. 4.
13. Sue Neales, 'Growers seek Chinese labour', *The Weekend Australian* (29 December 2004 – 3 January 2005), p. 4.
14. 'Labour shortfall puts pressure on Chinese wages', *Sydney Morning Herald* (5 April 2005), p. 22.
15. Robin Pratt (CEO Ngāi Tahu Holdings) in Ruth Le Pla, 'Lionising business: five CEOs on a changing China', *Management* (New Zealand, November 2005), pp. 24–32.
16. Bronwyn Sell, op. cit.
17. Several articles on this issue were reported in the Asian media around 17 March to 10 April 2005 including 'Malaysia must reduce dependence on foreign workers' (21 March 2005), 'Malaysia to hire 100,000 Pakistanis to plug labour vacuum' (18 March 2005), 'Malaysia's illegal labour solution backfires — again' (10 April 2005), all at Channelnewsasia.com; and 'KL may ask firms to reserve 51% of jobs for locals', Asiaone, http://www.asia1.com.sg/st/st_200050411.html.
18. See John P Campbell, Marvin D Dunnette, Edward E Lawler III and Karl E Weick, Jr, *Managerial behavior performance and effectiveness* (New York: McGraw-Hill, 1970), ch. 15.
19. Lyman W Porter, 'Job attitudes in management: II. Perceived importance of needs as a function of job level', *Journal of Applied Psychology*, vol. 47 (April 1963), pp. 141–8.
20. Douglas T Hall and Khalil E Nougaim, 'An examination of Maslow's need hierarchy in an organizational setting',

Organizational Behavior and Human Performance, vol. 3 (1968), pp. 12–35.

21. Lyman W Porter, 'Job attitudes in management: IV. Perceived deficiencies in need fulfillment as a function of size of company', *Journal of Applied Psychology*, vol. 47 (December 1963), pp. 386–97.

22. John M Ivancevich, 'Perceived need satisfactions of domestic versus overseas managers', *Journal of Applied Psychology*, vol. 54 (August 1969), pp. 274–8.

23. Mahmoud A Wahba and Lawrence G Bridwell, 'Maslow reconsidered: a review of research on the need hierarchy theory', *Academy of Management Proceedings* (1974), pp. 514–20; Edward E Lawler III and J Lloyd Shuttle, 'A causal correlation test of the need hierarchy concept', *Organizational Behavior and Human Performance*, vol. 7 (1973), pp. 265–87.

24. Peter Vincent, 'Greener pastures', *The Sydney Morning Herald*, My Career section (18–19 September 2004), p. 1.

25. See Nancy J Adler, *International dimensions of organizational behavior*, 2nd ed. (Boston: PWS-Kent, 1991), p. 153; Richard M Hodgetts and Fred Luthans, *International management* (New York: McGraw-Hill, 1991).

26. Adler, op. cit., ch. 11.

27. Tieying Huang, Junping Liang and Paul W Beamish 'Jinjian Garment Factory: motivating go-slow workers' in Gerard H Siejts, *Cases in organizational behavior*, (Thousand Oaks, CA: Sage, 2006), pp. 30–5.

28. See Clayton P Alderfer, 'An empirical test of a new theory of human needs', *Organizational behavior and human performance*, vol. 4 (1969), pp. 142–75; Clayton P Alderfer, *Existence, relatedness, and growth* (New York: The Free Press, 1972); Benjamin Schneider and Clayton P Alderfer, 'Three studies of need satisfaction in organizations', *Administrative Science Quarterly*, vol. 18 (1973), pp. 489–505.

29. Lane Tracy, 'A dynamic living systems model of work motivation', *Systems Research*, vol. 1 (1984), pp. 191–203; John Rauschenberger, Neal Schmidt and John E Hunter, 'A test of the need hierarchy concept by a Markov model of change in need strength', *Administrative Science Quarterly*, vol. 25 (1980), pp. 654–70.

30. Clayton P Alderfer and RA Guzzo, 'Life experiences and adults enduring strength of desires in organizations', *Administrative Science Quarterly*, vol. 24 (1979), pp. 347–61.

31. Sources pertinent to this discussion are David C McClelland, *The achieving society* (New York: Van Nostrand, 1961); David C McClelland, 'Business, drive and national achievement', *Harvard Business Review*, vol. 40 (July/August 1962), pp. 99–112; David C McClelland, 'That urge to achieve', *Think* (November/December 1966), pp. 19–32; GH Litwin and RA Stringer, *Motivation and organizational climate* (Boston: Division of Research, Harvard Business School, 1966), pp. 18–25.

32. George Harris, 'To know why men do what they do: a conversation with David C. McClelland', *Psychology Today*, vol. 4 (January 1971), pp. 35–9.

33. EH Erikson, *Childhood and society*, 2nd ed. (New York: Vintage, 1963).

34. P Miron and DC McClelland, 'The impact of achievement motivation training in small businesses', *California Management Review* (Summer 1979), pp. 13–28.

35. David C McClelland and David H Burnham, 'Power is the great motivator', *Harvard Business Review*, vol. 54 (March–April 1976), pp. 100–10; David C McClelland and Richard E. Boyatzis, 'Leadership motive pattern and long-term success in management', *Journal of Applied Psychology*, vol. 67 (1982), pp. 737–43.

36. Charles M Kelly, 'The interrelationship of ethics and power in today's organizations', *Organizational Dynamics*, vol. 5 (Summer 1987); Christopher Farrell, 'Gutfreund gives Salmon's young lions more power', *Business Week*, vol. 32 (20 October 1986); Jolie Solomon, 'Heirs apparent to chief executives often trip over prospect of power', *Wall Street Journal*, vol. 29 (24 March 1987).

37. The complete two-factor theory is well explained by Herzberg and his associates in Frederick Herzberg, Bernard Mausner and Barbara Bloch Synderman, *The motivation to work*, 2nd ed. (New York: John Wiley & Sons, 1967); and Frederick Herzberg, 'One more time: how do you motivate employees?', *Harvard Business Review*, vol. 46 (January/February 1968), pp. 53–62.

38. E Davis and R Lansbury (eds), *Managing together* (Melbourne: Longman, 1996).

39. Australian Government, Department of Employment and Workplace Relations, 'Trends and statistics on ESO [employee share ownership] in Australia', www.workplace.gov.au/workplace/Category/SchemesInitiatives/ESO (viewed 14 April 2005).

40. This information comes from case studies, online videos and general information at Australian Government, Department of Employment and Workplace Relations, 'Employee share ownership', www.workplace.gov.au/eso (viewed 14 April 2005).

41. See Robert J House and Lawrence A Wigdor, 'Herzberg's dual-factor theory of job satisfaction and motivation: a review of the evidence and a criticism', *Personnel Psychology*, vol. 20 (Winter 1967), pp. 369–89; Steven Kerr, Anne Harlan and Ralph Stogdill, 'Preference for motivator and hygiene factors in a hypothetical interview situation', *Personnel Psychology*, vol. 27 (Winter 1974), pp. 109–24.

42. See Nathan King, 'A clarification and evaluation of the two-factor theory of job satisfaction', *Psychological Bulletin* (July 1970), pp. 18–31; Marvin Dunnette, John Campbell and Milton Hakel, 'Factors contributing to job satisfaction and job dissatisfaction in six occupational groups', *Organizational Behavior and Human Performance* (May 1967), pp. 143–74; House and Wigdor, op. cit.

43. Adler, op. cit., ch. 6; Nancy J Adler and JT Graham, 'Cross cultural interaction: the international comparison fallacy', *Journal of International Business Studies* (Fall 1989), pp. 515–37; Frederick Herzberg, 'Workers needs: the same

around the world', *Industry Week* (27 September 1987), pp. 29–32.

44. See, for example, J Stacy Adams, 'Toward an understanding of inequality', *Journal of Abnormal and Social Psychology*, vol. 67 (1963), pp. 422–36; J Stacy Adams, 'Inequity in social exchange' in L Berkowitz (ed.), *Advances in experimental social psychology*, vol. 2 (New York: Academic Press, 1965), pp. 267–300.

45. See 'Toronto Sun Publishing Corporation', *Wall Street Journal* (9 March 1990), pp. B1–B2.

46. P Dowling, R Schuler and D Welch, *International dimensions of human resource management* (Melbourne: Wadsworth, 1994).

47. This information derives from Mike Toten, 'Workplace agreements for small business: what are the options?', *Australian CPA*, vol. 71, no. 1 (February 2001), p. 44; Australian Nursing Federation, 'Australian workplace agreements: important information', reproduced in *Australian Nursing Journal*, vol. 5, no. 7 (February 1998), p. 7; Paul J Gollan, 'Formalised individual agreements in Australia', *Employee Relations*, vol. 26, no.1/2 (2004), pp. 44–61; Kristin van Barnevald and Peter Waring, 'AWAs: a review of the literature and debates', *Australian Bulletin of Labour*, vol. 28, no. 2 (June 2002), pp. 104–19.

48. Victor H Vroom, *Work and motivation* (New York: John Wiley & Sons, 1964).

49. For an excellent review, see Richard T Mowday, 'Equity theory predictions of behavior in organizations' in Richard M Steers and Lyman W Porter (eds), *Motivation and work behavior*, 4th ed. (New York: McGraw-Hill, 1987), pp. 89–110.

50. Elizabeth King, 'The beauty bosses', *Australian Financial Review BOSS Magazine* (September 2004), pp. 20–6.

51. Gerald R Salancik and Jeffrey Pfeffer, 'A social information processing approach to job attitudes and task design', *Administrative Science Quarterly*, vol. 23 (June 1978), pp. 224–53.

52. See Terrence R Mitchell, 'Expectancy models of job satisfaction, occupational preference and effort: a theoretical, methodological, and empirical appraisal', *Psychological Bulletin*, vol. 81 (1974), pp. 1053–77; Mahmoud A Wahba and Robert J House, 'Expectancy theory in work and motivation: some logical and methodological issues', *Human Relations*, vol. 27 (January 1974), pp. 121–47; Terry Connolly, 'Some conceptual and methodological issues in expectancy models of work performance motivation', *Academy of Management Review*, vol. 1 (October 1976), pp. 37–47; Terrence Mitchell,

'Expectancy-value models in organizational psychology' in N Feather (ed.), *Expectancy, incentive and action* (New York: Erlbaum, 1980).

53. Mitchell (1982), op. cit.

54. Lyman W Porter and Edward E Lawler III, *Managerial attitudes and performance* (Homewood, IL: Richard D. Irwin, 1968).

55. This integrated model is not only based on the Porter and Lawler model but is consistent with the kind of comprehensive approach suggested by Evans in a recent review. See Martin G Evans, 'Organizational behavior: the central role of motivation' in JG Hunt and JD Blair (eds), *1986 yearly review of management of the Journal of Management*, vol. 12 (1986), pp. 203–22.

56. For further explanation of alternatives to process and content theories of motivation, see N Leonard, L Beauvais and R Scholl, 'Work motivation: the incorporation of self-concept-based processes', *Human Relations*, vol. 52, no. 8 (1999), pp. 969–98; R McKenna, 'Identity, not motivation: the key to employee–organisation relations' in R Wiesner and B Millett, *Management and organisational behaviour* (Brisbane: John Wiley & Sons, 2000), pp. 35–45.

57. Stephanie Peatling, 'It's not easy being green', *The Sydney Morning Herald*, My Career section (5–6 February 2005), p. 1.

58. Kelly Samson, 'Research off the map', *HR Monthly* (December 2004 – January 2005), pp. 34–5.

59. Deidre Macken, 'My job-juggling career', *The Weekend Australian Financial Review* (6–7 March 2004), p. 25.

60. Craig Donaldson, 'Managers drop the Generation Y ball', *Human Resources* (5 April 2005), p. 9.

61. John Lui, 'Asia Pacific 25: not by price alone', *Managing Information Strategies*, special annual issue (2004), pp. 73–86.

62. ME Gist, 'Self-efficacy: implications in organizational behavior and human resource management', *Academy of Management Review*, vol. 12 (1987), pp. 472–85; A Bandura, 'Self-efficacy mechanism in human agency', *American Psychologist*, vol. 37 (1987), pp. 122–47.

63. Jay A Conger and Rabindra N Kanungo, 'The empowerment process: integrating theory and practice', *Academy of Management Review*, vol. 13, no. 3 (1988), pp. 471–82.

64. 'The new leaders', *New Zealand Management* (February 2005), pp. 29–35.

65. Robert N Lussier, *Human relations in organizations: a skill building approach*, 2nd ed. (Homewood, IL: Richard D. Irwin, 1993). Used by permission.

Chapter 4
Learning, reinforcement and self-management

Learning objectives
After studying this chapter, you should be able to:

1. outline the four general approaches to learning

2. explain organisational behavioural modification and how reinforcement strategies are involved in it

3. discuss social learning theory and behavioural self-management

4. explain how to manage pay as an extrinsic reward

5. discuss the concepts of the learning organisation and the teaching organisation.

The CRG Medical Foundation helps to develop *communities of competence* with the aim of reducing the thousands of deaths that occur each year due to medical mistakes and medication errors.

CRG fosters confidential reporting of all hazardous conditions and near-miss events. The reporting of accidents and incidents helps individuals and organisations learn from past experiences and develop solutions for improved patient safety. This includes ongoing and routine reporting, education and the redesign of healthcare systems, including the development of policies and procedures.[1] CRG brings together knowledge and skill from different entities to form a community of competence.

For example, the knowledge and skills of CRG, a medications study group and a substance-abuse rehabilitation facility were pooled to develop a national registry to help with the collection and safe disposal of unused and expired medications. The registry supports national efforts to remove excess medications in the home in a bid to reduce childhood overdoses, medication abuse and medication error.[2]

According to Elizabeth Smith, executive director CRG, communities of competence bring the 'separate strengths and core competences of individuals, groups, and organizations into a meaningful, goal oriented whole'.[3] Smith argues that the individuals' abilities, skills, knowledge or overall competence are, in practice, often not the basis for work group and team formation. Smith asserts that if closer attention is paid to the fit between the job requirements and an individual's competencies, then productivity, job satisfaction and overall work quality can be improved by creating a community of competence. The communities of competence can reshape work groups by combining notions of communities of practice, sociology, socialisation, self-organising systems, systems approaches and systems thinking.

Communities of competence are also said to be excellent catalysts for change as they can aid in breaking down existing barriers that prevent the open sharing of knowledge and expertise. Communities of competence facilitate the exchange of knowledge among members that is required for organisational learning. As a form of learning organisation, communities of competence are an excellent way to enable the sharing of knowledge, and encourage individuals to work together.[4]

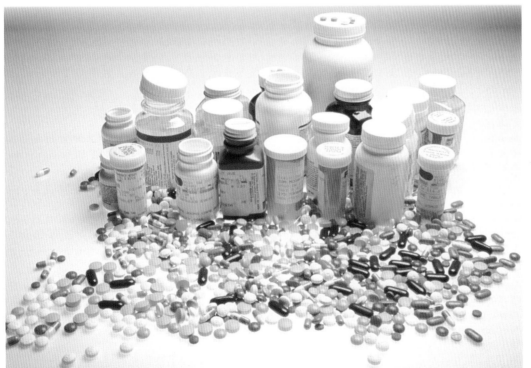

Introduction

The explosive growth in the amount of new information available for consumption, together with the speed at which current knowledge becomes obsolete, makes learning a critical factor for the survival of both the individual and the organisation.

In this chapter, we address three major questions.

1. *How do people acquire the knowledge, skills and competencies they need to be valuable participants in the workplace?* To answer this question, we need to understand the four different learning methods. These methods explain how we learn from our experiences of acting, thinking, observing and reflecting on our behaviour and interaction with others.

2. *How can a manager allocate extrinsic rewards, including pay, so desired work behaviours are encouraged and facilitated, rather than discouraged and inhibited?* To examine this question we need to be especially familiar with learning and the management of various forms of reinforcement and rewards. It is possible to use extrinsic rewards very effectively; they are an important part of any broad-based motivational strategy.

3. *What is organisational learning?* In this section we introduce and critically assess some of the elements necessary to combine individual learning and create a learning organisation. The notion of the teaching organisation reminds us that the continual renewal of all organisational structures and processes is now essential for organisations to maintain competencies.

At the individual level, learning, reinforcement and self-management are important building blocks in organisational behaviour. In addition, rewards systems may help the modification of behaviours to a desired state. In this chapter, we discuss each of these topics and some ways in which managers can use them in the organisations of today and tomorrow.

At the organisational level, much is written about organisational learning and the learning and teaching organisation. We will briefly introduce these concepts at the end of this chapter after examining the importance of learning for the individual.

Learning as a modification of work behaviour

Four general approaches to learning

LEARNING OBJECTIVE 1

Behaviourists study *observable* behaviours and consequences of behaviour, and reject subjective human psychological states as topics for study.

There is no doubt that what people *do* is critical to organisational success and the scientific study of human behaviour has a central role in understanding and potentially influencing behaviours at work. Therefore, it can be argued that 'behaviour', rather than thought processes or feelings, is the unit of analysis in organisational behaviour research.[5] This is a philosophical stance adopted by behaviourists, who generally argue that to understand human behaviour, scientists must focus on observational behaviour *deriving* from internal psychological processes.

Behaviourists argue that any construct that cannot be directly observed, such as internal psychological states, emotions and feelings, will fail to provide a systematic understanding of human behaviour. Rather, external exhibitions and the consequences of behaviour are given priority. For example, BF Skinner and other learning theorists argue that behaviour is environmentally controlled.[6] While work psychologists believe that this represents a rather limited view of human psychology, behaviourist ideas have been successfully applied in organisations and many behavioural concepts are being incorporated into related theories, such as social cognitive theory. These areas of applied research help managers modify behaviours and influence the *willingness* of workers to improve overall performance. With this in mind, refer back to the performance equation in chapter 1, page 5.

Learning is a relatively permanent change in behaviour that occurs as a result of experience.

Learning is defined as a relatively permanent change in behaviour resulting from experience. Learning is the process by which people acquire the competencies and beliefs that affect their behaviour in organisations. An understanding of basic learning principles will deepen your perspectives on the concepts and theories of motivation discussed in chapter 3. Managers with such awareness are well positioned to influence the willingness of their employees, necessary to achieve maximum positive outcomes from their work.

It is important to differentiate between learning and performance. Learning refers to the process of acquiring the capacity to perform through attaining the requisite skills or competencies. *Performance* implies that the individual, in addition to acquiring these requisite skills or competencies, is motivated to engage in the appropriate behaviour to apply the learning.

Learning in organisations can occur in many ways, and there are many different approaches attempting to maximise learning in the workplace. New employees often introduce new skills and competencies that have been acquired in a former workplace or through formal education. In addition, many organisations invest considerable sums of money in improving the skills and competencies of their workforce through formal training programs. For example, management development training and education has attracted significant investment globally.

The New Zealand Government recently invested NZ$20 million to establish a leadership development centre aimed at the management development of New Zealand public service employees. The central government provides ongoing funding of NZ$2.5 million a year, while various departments contribute a similar amount on a user-pays basis.[7]

However, it is important to emphasise that much learning in organisations occurs informally in an unstructured and haphazard manner.

There are four general approaches to learning:
1. classical conditioning
2. operant conditioning
3. cognitive learning
4. social learning.

Each approach offers potentially valuable insights to managers and the field of organisational behaviour.

Classical conditioning

Classical conditioning is a form of learning through association. This type of learning involves the manipulation of a stimulus (or stimuli) to influence behaviour (figure 4.1). We define a stimulus as something that incites action. Classical conditioning associates a previously neutral stimulus — that is, one that has no effect on behaviour — with another stimulus that does affect behaviour. The former thus becomes a conditioned stimulus, which, when it occurs, also draws forth the now conditioned response. This process is illustrated by the well-known experiments conducted by Ivan Pavlov, the Russian psychologist who 'taught' dogs to salivate (conditioned response) at the sound of a tone (conditioned stimulus) by ringing a bell just prior to feeding the dogs. The sight of the food caused the dogs to salivate. Eventually, the dogs 'learned', through the association of the bell with the presentation of meat, to salivate at the ringing of the bell alone. Classical conditioning is often termed *stimulus–response learning*.

Involuntary and reflexive behaviours of humans are also susceptible to classical conditioning. These are often associated with strong emotional reactions or vivid and painful experiences. For example, after witnessing a car crash at a certain intersection, passing this intersection again is likely to bring back this vivid memory, resulting in an emotional response.

The same principle of classical conditioning, where two previously unrelated things (the stimulus and the response) are brought together in the mind of the person, applies in the work setting. However, both the manager and the employee may take a long time to figure

Classical conditioning is a form of learning through association that involves the manipulation of stimuli to influence behaviour.

Stimulus is something that incites action.

out the stimulus and response connection shown in figure 4.1. In addition, classical conditioning at a higher order takes place where a second or third stimulus is introduced. Pavlov introduced a shape to the tone and, after several trials, dogs salivated to the shape alone. This is known as second-order conditioning. Humans may be conditioned to third or even higher orders. For example, consider the car crash already described. When the crash was seen there was a certain piece of music playing. Hearing the music can cause a strong emotional response (fear and anxiety) that leads to altered driving behaviour. Now imagine it was raining at the time. The automated response of fear and anxiety is created when passing the place of the accident, when hearing the music and when it rains. The classical conditioning approach helps managers to gain a better understanding of the emotional reactions of their staff. Further, the general stimulus–response notion sets the stage for operant conditioning.

Operant conditioning

Operant conditioning is the process of controlling behaviour by manipulating its consequences.

Operant conditioning is learning that is achieved when the consequences of a behaviour lead to changes in the probability of its occurrence. You may think of operant conditioning as learning through reinforcement. Figure 4.1 clarifies how this operant, or behaviourist, approach contrasts with classical conditioning. The former approach views behaviour as 'operating' on its environment to produce consequences that affect its future occurrence. Operant conditioning is often termed response–stimulus learning that produces behaviour that will not appear spontaneously.

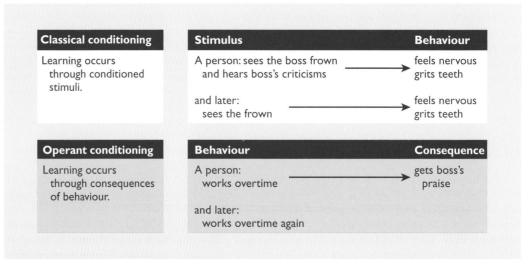

FIGURE 4.1 • Differences between the classical and operant conditioning approaches to learning

The noted psychologist BF Skinner popularised operant conditioning as a way of controlling behaviour by manipulating its consequences.[8] The method consists of a three-component framework: antecedents–behaviour–consequences, sometimes called ABC contingencies or 'if/then' relationships. Returning to figure 4.1, the antecedent (A) — the condition leading up to behaviour — may be an agreement between the boss and the employee to work overtime as needed. If the employee engages in the overtime behaviour (B), the consequence (C) — the result of the behaviour — is the boss's praise.

Whereas classical conditioning works only on behaviours that are involuntary in nature, operant conditioning has a broader application to almost any human behaviour. Therefore, according to some behaviourists, operant conditioning has substantial applications in the workplace, whereas others protest that people are much more self-controlled and thinking (a process also known as cognitive learning).

Many modern organisations offer incentives to achieve desired behaviours. For example, monetary bonuses may be offered to those employees who demonstrate a certain level of care in the workplace by alerting managers to potential hazards. This bonus incentive can result in employee behaviour that includes a higher awareness of workplace safety issues. Hence, there is a direct connection between the incentive, the behaviour as a result of the incentive and, ultimately, the consequences of the behaviour,[9] which may include a safer workplace and reduction in insurance premiums. Other examples of bonus incentives in the workplace are rewards associated with a low sick-leave rate, and consistent levels of performance and/or output; or rewards for loyalty in the form of long-service leave and company recognition for years of service.

Cognitive learning

Cognitive learning is learning that is achieved by thinking about the perceived relationship between events and individual goals and expectations. The process motivation theories reviewed in chapter 3 help to illustrate how this learning perspective is applied to the work setting. These theories are concerned with explaining how and why people decide to do things, by examining the ways in which people come to view various work activities as perceived opportunities to pursue desired rewards, to eliminate felt inequities and the like. These cognitive explanations of learning differ markedly from the behaviourist explanations of operant conditioning.

Now refer back to the example on incentives when reporting safety issues at work. Can you think of *why* the employees take more care with workplace safety issues? Do the employees modify their behaviour to receive the bonus, to impress their manager or from a sense of social responsibility? These reasons are based on cognitive thought and play an important part in why and how people learn.[10]

> Cognitive learning is a form of learning achieved by thinking about the perceived relationship between events and individual goals and expectations.

Social learning

Social learning is learning that is achieved through the reciprocal interactions among people, behaviour and environment. Social learning theory is expressed in the work of Albert Bandura[11] and uses such reciprocal interactions to integrate operant and cognitive learning approaches; that is, environmental determinism and self-determinism are combined. Behaviour is seen not simply as a function of external antecedents and consequences, or as being caused by only internal needs, satisfaction or expectations (see chapter 3), but as a combination of the two. Social learning theory stresses our capacity to learn from re-enforcement and punishments experienced by other people and ourselves. Figure 4.2 illustrates and elaborates on this reciprocal interaction notion.

In figure 4.2, the individual uses modelling or vicarious learning to acquire behaviour by observing and imitating others. The person then attempts to acquire these behaviours by modelling them through practice. The 'models' could be the person's parents, friends or even well-known celebrities. In the work situation, the model may be a manager or coworker who demonstrates desired behaviours. Mentors or senior workers who befriend more inexperienced protégés can also be very important models. There has been interesting psychology-based work that investigates the link between television and real-life professional practice. As a result, the Resource Centre for Women in Science, Engineering and Technology (SET) is hoping to capitalise on this research by offering funding to television script writers who incorporate in their plot lines women with non-traditional occupations such as science, technology and engineering. The aim is to encourage higher participation rates of women in these occupations through modelling the occupations on television.[12]

> Social learning is learning that is achieved through the reciprocal interaction between people and their environments.

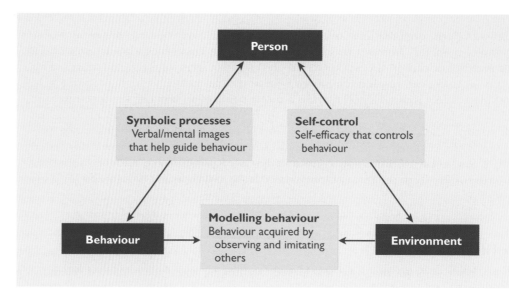

FIGURE 4.2 • Social learning model

Source: Adapted from R Kreitner and F Luthans, 'A social learning approach to behavioral management: radical behaviorists "mellowing out"', *Organizational Dynamics* (Autumn 1984), p. 55.

Although mentors or role models may come from diverse sources, the shortage of appropriate mentors or role models is often a concern in the contemporary workplace. Indeed, some have argued that a shortage of mentors for women in management is a major constraint on their progression up the career ladder. It is also a leading reason why many women are leaving the corporate world and moving into self-employment.[13]

If management structures are to reflect the diversity of the workforce in countries such as Australia, then establishing mentoring programs is important.

Female law graduates now outnumber their male counterparts 60 to 40. However, despite the increase in female solicitors, only 16 per cent of the partners at law firms are female.[14] In addition, significantly fewer females than males are members of the Bar, with just 4 per cent of women making it to the coveted position of senior counsel.[15]

The NSW Law Society, the NSW Bar Association, NSW Young Lawyers and the Women Lawyers' Association of NSW have introduced mentoring schemes in an attempt to redress the inequalities within the legal profession.[16] The NSW Office for Women established the Lucy Mentoring Scheme with the specific purpose of increasing the numbers of women in middle and senior management and on corporate boards. The scheme is set up to coach final-year undergraduate female students in law, accounting, finance and business to provide them with specific leadership experience and allow collaboration on field projects. Student participants are required to spend a total of 35 hours in their mentor's workplace and complete a reflective journal of their experiences.[17] In 2005 the Lucy program was extended to include male mentors as well as female.[18]

Self-efficacy and social learning

The symbolic processes depicted in figure 4.2 are also important in social learning. Words and symbols used by managers and others in the workplace can help communicate values, beliefs and goals and therefore serve as guides to a person's behaviour. A 'thumbs up' or other symbol from the boss, for example, lets you know your behaviour is appropriate.

At the same time, an individual's self-control is important in influencing his or her behaviour. Self-efficacy is an important part of such self-control. People with high self-efficacy believe that:

- they have the necessary ability for a given job
- they are capable of the effort required
- they are motivated to perform the required behaviour
- no outside events will hinder them from obtaining their desired performance level.[19]

In other words, high self-efficacy people believe they can manage their environmental cues and consequences and their cognitive processes to control their own behaviour. People with low self-efficacy believe that no matter how hard they try, they cannot manage their environment well enough to be successful. If you feel self-efficacious as a student, for example, a low grade on one test will encourage you to study harder, talk to the lecturer or do other things to enable you to do well the next time. In contrast, a person low in self-efficacy might drop the course or give up studying.

Even people who are high in self-efficacy do not control their environment entirely. As a manager, you can have an impact on the environment and other factors shown in figure 4.2 (even though the impact is less than in the operant approach). This is especially the case in influencing another person's self-efficacy. A manager's expectations and peer support can go far in increasing a worker's self-efficacy and feelings of control.

Here are some key points for managers to consider in applying social learning theory.[20]

- Identify appropriate job behaviours.
- Help employees select an appropriate behavioural model for behavioural modelling.
- Work with employees to meet the requirements of the new behaviours.
- Structure the learning situation to enhance learning of the necessary behaviours.
- Provide appropriate rewards (consequences) for workers who perform the appropriate behaviours.
- Engage in appropriate managerial actions to maintain the newly learned behaviours.

If management structures in the twenty-first century are to reflect the diversity of the workforce in countries such as Australia and New Zealand, then establishing mentoring programs is important.

Mentoring for better service in Sydney's hotels

Mentoring is a management development technique that involves an experienced individual teaching and training someone with less knowledge in a particular area.[21] Mentoring takes place on the job and involves close relationships between experienced organisational members and the protégé (the learner). Protégés observe, question and explore, while mentors demonstrate, explain and model.

A recent study in luxury hotels in Sydney found that one of the impediments to achieving service quality is a lack of formal and informal mentoring of new supervisors and managers. Hoteliers realise customer satisfaction leads to customer retention, and that the competitive advantage in a saturated market is determined by the quality of service. Hoteliers also know that their existence may be threatened unless they invest sufficient resources. This investment is particularly important in terms of human capital. As the major contributors to meeting and exceeding customer expectations, supervisors and managers of hotels need to be nurtured through formal and informal mentoring. However, mentoring is almost entirely absent in Sydney's luxury hotels.[22]

(continued)

Researchers found that several factors contribute to a lack of mentoring within the hotel sector:
- a continued trend to flatten the organisational structure of hotels, where the most senior managers may be located at another hotel within the chain
- a generally very young and inexperienced local management team
- an ongoing loss of experienced leaders, who take positions in other sectors of the service industry.[23]

The hotel sector in Sydney exists in a highly competitive environment. This requires hotels to make greater efforts to meet and exceed customers' expectations.

Questions
1. Can you think of some other industry-specific reasons why mentoring may be largely absent from luxury hotels in Sydney?
2. If you were a manager, how would you identify future leaders?
3. How would you nurture and motivate young managers to become seasoned leaders in the hotel industry?

Organisational behaviour modification and reinforcement strategies

LEARNING OBJECTIVE 2

The **law of effect** refers to Thorndike's observation that behaviour that results in a pleasant outcome is likely to be repeated; behaviour that results in an unpleasant outcome is not likely to be repeated.

Extrinsic rewards are positively valued work outcomes that the individual receives from some other person in the work setting.

Reinforcement as a strategy to modify work behaviour

Reinforcement plays a key role in the learning process. The foundation for this relationship is the law of effect, as stated by EL Thorndike: behaviour that results in a pleasant outcome is likely to be repeated, while behaviour that results in an unpleasant outcome is not likely to be repeated.[24]

The implications of the law of effect are rather straightforward. Rewards are outcomes or environmental consequences that are considered by the reinforcement perspective to determine individual behaviour. In chapter 5 we discuss both intrinsic and extrinsic rewards. In terms of operant learning and reinforcement, our interest is in the latter.

Recall that extrinsic rewards are positively valued work outcomes that the individual receives from some other person. They are important external reinforcers or environmental consequences that can substantially influence people's work behaviours through the law of effect. Table 4.1 presents a sample of extrinsic rewards that managers can allocate to their staff.[25]

Some are contrived or planned rewards that have direct costs and budgetary implications, such as pay increases and cash bonuses. (Various forms of pay are of such importance as planned extrinsic rewards that we devote a later section of this chapter to managing pay as an extrinsic reward.) A second category includes natural rewards that have no cost other than the manager's personal time and efforts; examples are verbal praise and recognition in the workplace.

TABLE 4.1 • Sample of extrinsic rewards allocated by managers

Contrived rewards (some direct cost)		Natural rewards (no direct cost)
Refreshments	Promotion	Smiles
Piped-in music	Trips	Greetings
Nice offices	Company car	Compliments
Cash bonuses	Paid insurance	Special jobs
Merit pay increases	Stock options	Recognition
Profit sharing	Gifts	Feedback
Office parties	Sport tickets	Request for advice

Organisational behaviour modification brings together the application of the previously mentioned operant conditioning, reinforcement and extrinsic reward notions. You can think of it as the systematic reinforcement of desirable work behaviour and the non-reinforcement or punishment of unwanted work behaviour. Organisational behaviour modification includes four basic reinforcement strategies:

1. positive reinforcement
2. negative reinforcement (or avoidance)
3. punishment
4. extinction.

Let us look at each of these strategies in some detail.

> Organisational behaviour modification is the systematic reinforcement of desirable work behaviour and the non-reinforcement or punishment of unwanted work behaviour.

Positive reinforcement

BF Skinner and his followers advocate positive reinforcement: the administration of positive consequences that tend to increase the likelihood of the desirable target behaviour being repeated in similar settings. For example, a manager may nod to express approval to a staff member after she makes a useful suggestion during a sales meeting.

> Positive reinforcement is the administration of positive consequences that tend to increase the likelihood of repeating the behaviour in similar settings.

To use positive reinforcement well in the work setting, you must first be aware of what has potential reward value (table 4.1). In using these rewards for reinforcement purposes, you must remember several points.

Positive reinforcers and rewards are not necessarily the same. Recognition is both a reward and a positive reinforcer if a person's performance later improves. However, some apparent rewards turn out not to be positive reinforcers; for example, a supervisor may praise a staff member in front of other group members for finding errors in a report, but the group members may then give the worker the silent treatment so the worker stops looking for errors. In this case, the supervisor's 'reward' does not serve as a positive reinforcer.

To have maximum reinforcement value, a reward must be delivered only if the desired behaviour is exhibited; that is, the reward must be contingent on the desired behaviour, as in the contingent ABC model. This principle is known as the law of contingent reinforcement. In the previous example, the supervisor's praise was contingent on the subordinate's finding errors in the report, even though this praise did not turn out to be a positive reinforcer.

> The law of contingent reinforcement is the view that for a reward to have maximum reinforcing value, it must be delivered only if the desired behaviour is exhibited.

OB in action

Finally, the reward must be given as soon as possible after the desired behaviour. This is known as the **law of immediate reinforcement**.[26] If the supervisor praised the worker as soon as the errors were found, that praise would be consistent with this law.

> Employee reward programs are a form of social recognition, which is an excellent form of employee motivation.[27] Centrelink, Australia's social security office, places great emphasis on the recognition of employee achievements and successes. Centrelink's *national* awards recognise outstanding achievement for Change Management; Excellence in Youth Servicing; Customer Service; and Outstanding Achievement. In addition, Centrelink has Australia Day awards for staff that have shown outstanding dedication. Centrelink also puts nominees forward for the national Public Service Medal, CEO Service Medal and Order of Australia awards.
>
> In addition, many awards schemes are in place at a local level. For example, in Centrelink's 'North Central Victoria' area, awards are given twice a year for Customer Service, Supporting Centrelink People, Achievement of Key Performance Indicators and 'Getting It Right'. This area also has annual cluster awards for 'helping our customers move forward; outstanding achievement through innovation or change; working in partnership with the community and business; Indigenous servicing; and efficiency and effectiveness of operations and procedures'.[28]
>
> Centrelink also publishes the *Centrelink People* magazine which is available to all employees. The magazine features many of the awards success stories, and includes a section for customer feedback. An important feature of the rewards program is ongoing monitoring of staff morale. Twice yearly, Centrelink surveys staff and asks the question: 'Do you receive recognition and praise for good work?'[29]

The behaviours in the above example were fairly general in nature. Sometimes, if the desired behaviour is more specific and difficult to achieve, another form of positive reinforcement, called shaping, will be used. **Shaping** is the creation of a new behaviour by the positive reinforcement of successive approximations to the desired behaviour. We attempt to mould individuals' behaviour by guiding their learning in a series of small graduated steps towards targeted behavioural outcomes.

If an employee constantly arrives at work 40 minutes late, but today arrives only 20 minutes late, under a shaping strategy to modify this behaviour we would reinforce this improvement. The frequency of the reinforcement would increase as the employee moves closer to the desired behavioural outcome.

Scheduling of positive reinforcement

Positive reinforcement can be given according to continuous or intermittent schedules. **Continuous reinforcement** administers a reward each time a desired behaviour occurs. **Intermittent reinforcement** rewards behaviour only periodically.

These alternatives are important because the two schedules may have very different impacts on behaviour.

1. Continuous reinforcement draws forth a desired behaviour more quickly than does intermittent reinforcement, but continuous reinforcement is more costly in the consumption of rewards and more easily extinguished when reinforcement is no longer present.
2. Behaviour acquired under intermittent reinforcement lasts longer when reinforcement is discontinued than does behaviour acquired under continuous reinforcement. In other words, it is more resistant to extinction.

As shown in table 4.2, intermittent reinforcement can be given according to fixed or variable schedules. The variable schedules are considered to result in more consistent

---

The law of immediate reinforcement states that the more immediate the delivery of a reward after the occurrence of a desirable behaviour, the greater the reinforcing effect on behaviour.

Shaping is the creation of a new behaviour by the positive reinforcement of successive approximations to the desired behaviour.

Continuous reinforcement is a reinforcement schedule that administers a reward each time a desired behaviour occurs.

Intermittent reinforcement is a reinforcement schedule that rewards behaviour only periodically.

patterns of desired behaviours than result from fixed reinforcement schedules. Fixed interval schedules provide rewards at the first appearance of a behaviour after a given time has elapsed; fixed ratio schedules result in a reward each time a certain number of the behaviours has occurred. A variable interval schedule rewards behaviour at random times, while a variable ratio schedule rewards behaviour after a random number of occurrences.

Reinforcement schedule	Example
Fixed interval — give reinforcer after specific time passes	Weekly or monthly pay cheques
Fixed ratio — give reinforcer after specific number of responses	Piece rate pay or sales commissions
Variable interval — give reinforcer at random times	Occasional praise by boss on unscheduled 'walk arounds'
Variable ratio — give reinforcer after a random number of responses	Random quality checks with praise for zero defects

TABLE 4.2 • Four ways to schedule intermittent positive reinforcement

Many innovations using reinforcement schedules have been introduced in recent years to attempt to reduce the costs associated with high levels of employee absenteeism. For example, Royal Mail usually has approximately 10 000 of its 170 000 employees off sick at any one time and has an average absentee rate of 12 days per employee per year. Although it is fairly common in modern organisations to offer bonuses to employees who take less than a certain number of sick days per year, Royal Mail has added a new spin. Each employee who had perfect attendance over a six-month period was entered in a raffle. Raffle prizes included 37 cars and 75 holiday vouchers (worth about A$4800).[30] The scheme is controversial because it could be perceived as discriminating against the genuinely ill who are not able to participate because of their illness.[31] However it did manage to get an extra 1000 people to show up for work each day and Royal Mail had its best performance in ten years. The next time the scheme was run, the prizes were scaled back to holiday vouchers worth A$670, but the number of prizes increased to 390. It is clear that the organisation is still trying to find the right balance with its reinforcement strategies.[32] Although this positive reinforcement approach is still controversial it appears to be far more widely accepted than the decision of Australia Post several years ago to force employees who were persistently sick to see the company doctor instead of their own.[33]

Let us summarise this section on positive reinforcement by looking at 'The effective manager 4.1' guidelines.

THE **Effective**Manager 4.1

Guidelines for allocating extrinsic rewards to ensure a positive reinforcement effect
1. Clearly identify the desired behaviours.
2. Maintain an inventory of rewards that have the potential to serve as positive reinforcers for these people.
3. Recognise individual differences in the rewards that will have positive values for each person.
4. Let each person know exactly what must be done to receive a desirable reward. Set clear target antecedents and give performance feedback.
5. Allocate rewards contingently and immediately upon the appearance of the desired behaviours. Make sure the reward is given only if the desired behaviours occur.
6. Allocate rewards wisely in terms of scheduling the delivery of positive reinforcement.

The consequences associated with work behaviours are not always positive in nature. Often adverse consequences are put in place to influence employee motivation and behaviour. The following section deals with ways of manipulating adverse consequences.

Negative reinforcement (avoidance)

Negative reinforcement is the withdrawal of negative consequences, which tends to increase the likelihood of the behaviour being repeated in similar settings; it is also known as avoidance.

Negative reinforcement, or avoidance, is the withdrawal of negative consequences, which tends to increase the likelihood of the desirable behaviour being repeated in similar settings. There are two aspects here: first, the negative consequences, then the withdrawal of these consequences when desirable behaviour occurs. The term 'negative reinforcement' comes from this withdrawal of the negative consequences. This strategy is sometimes called avoidance because its intent is for the person to avoid the negative consequence by performing the desired behaviour; for instance, a worker who prefers the day shift is allowed to return to the day shift if they perform well on the night shift.

Both positive and negative reinforcement seek to encourage desirable behaviour. The first type of reinforcement provides pleasant consequences; the second provides unpleasant consequences, followed by their withdrawal when the desired behaviour occurs.

Punishment

Punishment is the administration of negative consequences or the withdrawal of positive consequences, which tends to reduce the likelihood of repeating the behaviour in similar settings.

Unlike positive reinforcement and negative reinforcement, punishment is not intended to encourage positive behaviour but to discourage negative behaviour. Formally defined, **punishment** is the administration of negative consequences or the withdrawal of positive consequences, which tends to reduce the likelihood of the behaviour being repeated in similar settings. For example, stimuli to weaken behaviours can include written and verbal reprimands, assignment of unpopular tasks, performance measurements and evaluation, transfer or dismissal.

There are major reservations about using punishment as a motivational tool. Research on punitive manipulation in the workplace is scarce. This may be because punishment is seen by the workers as arbitrary and capricious and leads to low satisfaction as well as low performance.[34]

Problems with the punishment strategy

Problems such as resentment and sabotage may accompany a manager's use of punishment. It also is wise to remember the following issues.

- Although a behaviour may be suppressed as a result of punishment, it may not be permanently abolished.
- The person who administers punishment may end up being viewed negatively by others.
- Punishment may be offset by positive reinforcement received from another source. Peers may reinforce a worker at the same time that the manager administers the punishment. Sometimes, the positive value of such peer support may be strong enough to cause the individual to put up with the punishment. Therefore, the undesirable behaviour continues; for example, a student may be verbally reprimanded many times by a lecturer for being late to class yet the grins offered by other students may justify the student's continuing tardiness.
- The behavioural response to punishment is typically less predictable and therefore may be less effective as a behavioural modification strategy.

In addition, the generational differences referred to in chapter 2 (pages 53–4) need to be taken into account when applying reinforcement strategies. Using the stereotypical classification of generations in organisations, punishment is considered to be increasingly ineffective for generation Y people. They are more likely to change their behaviour by simply moving on. Hence, positive reinforcement and extinction may be better strategies when managing staff from generation Y.[35]

OB in action

Punishment can take many forms. For example, people who do not show appropriate behaviours can be forced to work at an undesirable desk or checkout; a person may be given monotonous tasks for a period of time; a person may be forced to commence work very early in the morning, or be expected to stay back on a Friday night. The problem with these types of punishment is that managers need to be aware of an individual's likes and dislikes. Some people may like to start work early or work on a Friday night. If managers are not aware of staff preferences, the risk is that the punishment may inadvertently be rewarding. For example, in universities and colleges teaching on a Friday night is often considered desirable as classes are notoriously small and very relaxed, and often pizza is ordered in...hardly a punishment.[36]

If you are going to administer punishment, 'The effective manager 4.2' provides some useful guidelines.[37]

THE **Effective**Manager 4.2

Guidelines for using punishment as a reinforcement strategy

1. *Tell the individual what is being done wrong.* Clearly identify the undesirable behaviour that is being punished.
2. *Tell the individual what is right.* Clearly identify the desirable alternative to the behaviour that is being punished.
3. *Punish in private.* Avoid the public embarrassment that comes with punishing someone in front of others.
4. *Punish in accord with the laws of contingent and immediate reinforcement.* Make sure that the punishment is truly contingent on the undesirable behaviour and that it follows its occurrence as closely as possible.
5. *Make sure the punishment matches the behaviour.* Be fair in equating the magnitude of the punishment with the degree to which the behaviour is truly undesirable.

When evaluating the merits of punishment, we need to consider organisational justice. Punishment that is viewed by employee observers to be unfair may affect others' attitudes and commitment. At the same time, punishment may be important for the maintenance of positive attitudes, by way of demonstrating organisational justice.[38] The notion of organisational justice is highly related to process theories for motivation (chapter 3) and, in particular, Adams's equity theory that stems from the principle of social comparisons and balance. Further, a range of procedural justice theories have influenced research into organisational justice.[39]

Extinction

Extinction is the withdrawal of the reinforcing consequences for a given behaviour.

Extinction is a reinforcement strategy that deals with the withdrawal of the reinforcing consequences for a given behaviour. For example, Jack is often late for work, and his coworkers cover for him (positive reinforcement). The manager instructs Jack's coworkers to stop covering for him, withdrawing the reinforcing consequences. The manager has deliberately used extinction as a means to stop an undesirable behaviour. This strategy decreases the frequency of, or weakens, the behaviour. The behaviour is not 'unlearned'; it simply is not exhibited. No longer reinforced, the behaviour will reappear if reinforced again. Whereas positive reinforcement seeks to establish and maintain desirable work behaviour, the goal of extinction is to weaken and eliminate undesirable behaviour. Consider the following true story.

OB in action

> One day a manager of a leading supermarket walked into the storeroom and discovered a problem with several of her junior workers. One worker, a 16-year-old boy, was constantly being teased and tormented by an obviously popular 17-year-old colleague. Every time the teasing occurred, several other workers would join in with the torment by laughing and supporting the 17-year-old boy's jokes and comments. Both the boys were excellent workers.
>
> The manager was faced with the problem of trying to alter the behaviours of *all* of the workers. She could have publicly punished the 17-year-old by showing her displeasure at his inappropriate behaviour, but instead she chose to be a little more astute. She sent both the 16- and 17-year-old boys out of the storeroom to the shop floor. She then explained to the remaining workers how they were directly responsible for the 17-year-old boy's behaviour and made an agreement with them that they would discontinue this behaviour. Without the others supporting him, the 17-year-old stopped teasing the 16-year-old boy within one week. In addition, the manager increased the frequency of her positive comments to both the 16- and 17-year-old boys, complimenting them on how well they appeared to be getting on, rewarding them to be responsible for improving and reinforcing a congenial work atmosphere.[40]

As this example shows, extinction can be especially powerful when combined with positive reinforcement. Extinction caused the 17-year-old to stop his bullying. However, because the manager was still concerned that he maintained his otherwise useful organisational contributions, she provided him with immediate acknowledgement and approval where appropriate, including comments on his relationship and maturity in relation to the 16-year-old. These extrinsic rewards have a positive reinforcing effect on desirable behaviour. The combined strategy of extinction and positive reinforcement in this instance proved to be a most useful tool for this manager.

Organisational behaviour modification strategies — a summary

Figure 4.3 summarises the use of each organisational behaviour modification strategy using the ABC framework. Each is designed to direct work behaviour towards practices desired by management. Both positive and negative reinforcement are used to strengthen the desirable behaviour of improving work quality when it occurs. Punishment is used to weaken the undesirable behaviour of high error rate, and consists of either administering negative consequences or withdrawing positive consequences. Likewise, extinction is used deliberately to weaken the undesirable, high-error-rate behaviour when it occurs. However, extinction is also used inadvertently to weaken the desirable, low-error-rate behaviour. Finally, do not forget that these strategies may be used in combination as well as independently.

FIGURE 4.3 • Applying the ABC framework in a work setting

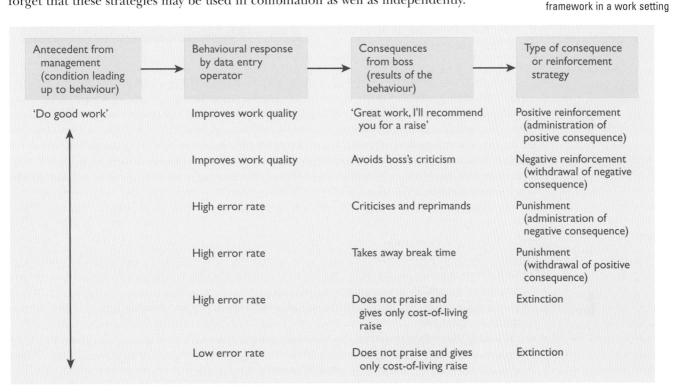

Antecedent from management (condition leading up to behaviour)	Behavioural response by data entry operator	Consequences from boss (results of the behaviour)	Type of consequence or reinforcement strategy
'Do good work'	Improves work quality	'Great work, I'll recommend you for a raise'	Positive reinforcement (administration of positive consequence)
	Improves work quality	Avoids boss's criticism	Negative reinforcement (withdrawal of negative consequence)
	High error rate	Criticises and reprimands	Punishment (administration of negative consequence)
	High error rate	Takes away break time	Punishment (withdrawal of positive consequence)
	High error rate	Does not praise and gives only cost-of-living raise	Extinction
	Low error rate	Does not praise and gives only cost-of-living raise	Extinction

Certain aspects of behaviour modification theory need further research. Much of the research in this area is predicated on the use of positive reinforcement to modify behaviour. Less is known about the effects of punishment. The reactions to punishment would appear to be less predictable and less understood by researchers, and one only has to look at the penal systems in many countries to understand the need for further research in this area.

Reinforcement perspectives

The effective use of reinforcement strategies can assist in the management of human behaviour at work. Testimony to this effect is found in the application of these strategies in many large companies, including Westpac, Coles-Myer and government departments such as the Health Insurance Commission. Smaller companies also use strategies to reward and retain good staff. For example, the boutique networking firm discussed in the case study at the end of this chapter regularly uses a variety of reinforcement strategies, including a sliding scale of bonuses for individuals who bill out more than 100 hours in a month. In addition, high-activity workers may take extra leave days (with pay) at their convenience and, in return for displaying excellent customer service, individuals are regularly taken out for lunch.[41]

Reinforcement strategies are also supported by the growing number of consulting firms that specialise in reinforcement techniques.

OB in action

Under Stephen Tindall, New Zealand's 'The Warehouse' had very effective reinforcement strategies for employees. These included significant bonuses, a discounted medical scheme and, among other benefits such as birthdays off on full pay, staff share purchases and attendance with a spouse at the annual nationwide conference.[42]

However, we must recognise that managerial use of these approaches is not without criticism. Some reports on the 'success' of specific programs are single cases that have been analysed without the benefit of scientific research designs. It is hard to conclude definitively whether reinforcement dynamics caused the observed results. One critic argues that the improved performance may well have occurred only as a result of the goal setting involved; that is, because specific performance goals were clarified and workers were individually held accountable for their accomplishment.[43] Another concern is whether it is ethical to use behaviour modification strategies.[44]

We expect that continuing research will primarily refine our knowledge of the reinforcement strategies rather than dramatically change existing insights. The worth of such strategies in work settings seems clearly established. Future research will probably tell us, as managers, how better to use the various reinforcement strategies. The fact that we should be using them already seems well established, but we should temper such use with a strong managerial emphasis on employee involvement wherever possible, and by explicit efforts to avoid exploitation. In other words, we should always pursue reinforcement from strong ethical foundations.

It is also clear that much of the work on reinforcement and learning has been based in Western cultures. As the global business world gathers pace, greater understanding of how to modify behaviour across cultures will become important.

More cross-cultural comparative research is needed to examine whether the research findings from Western cultures are supported in other cultures. If a Japanese manager were to use positive reinforcement to shape the behaviour of a Japanese worker, for example, would such a public display be accepted by the worker and/or their coworkers?

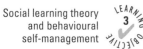
Social learning theory and behavioural self-management
LEARNING OBJECTIVE 3

Social learning theory and behavioural self-management

Social learning theory is applied in the workplace to encourage employees to help manage or lead themselves. Table 4.3 shows some possible self-management strategies. Notice how these strategies build on social learning theory to emphasise both behavioural and cognitive focuses. Their use is designed to enhance self-efficacy and the worker's feeling of self-control. For example, 3M (the company that manufactures Post-It Notes) encourages employees to apply behavioural self-management actions (such as those listed in table 4.3) wherever possible. People are encouraged to 'work outside the box' to facilitate new product innovations.[45] Many high-profile sporting organisations throughout the world use sports psychologists to teach players the strategies listed in table 4.3.[46]

TABLE 4.3 • Self-management strategies

Behaviour-focused strategies	
Behaviour	**Strategy**
Self-setting goals	Setting goals for your own work efforts
Managing cues	Arranging and altering cues in the work environment to facilitate your desired personal behaviours
Rehearsing	Physically or mentally practising work activities before you actually perform them
Self-observing	Observing and gathering information about specific behaviours that you have targeted for change
Self-rewarding	Providing yourself with personally valued rewards for completing desirable behaviours
Self-punishing	Administering punishments to yourself for behaving in undesirable ways (This strategy is generally not very effective.)
Cognitive-focused strategies	
Building natural rewards into tasks	Redesigning where and how you do your work to increase the level of natural rewards in your job. Natural rewards that are part of, rather than separate from, the work (that is, the work, like a hobby, becomes the reward) result from activities that cause you to feel: – a sense of competence – a sense of self-control – a sense of purpose
Focusing thinking on natural rewards	Purposely focusing your thinking on the naturally rewarding features of your work
Establishing constructive thought patterns	Establishing constructive and effective habits or patterns in your thinking (for example, a tendency to search for opportunities rather than obstacles embedded in challenges) by managing your: – beliefs and assumptions – mental imagery – internal self-talk

Self-management is a social learning theory that can be applied by behaviour-focused strategies and cognitive-focused strategies. However, self-management for an organisational member includes managing inconsistencies between individual and organisational expectations and goals.

It is evident that self-management includes self-reflection or introspection, where individuals contemplate their thoughts, feelings and actions. In the organisational context, self-reflection can lead to the discovery of incongruence between organisational goals and personal expectations. These intrapersonal conflicts often involve actual or perceived pressures from incompatible goals or expectations of the following types. *Approach conflict* occurs when a person must choose between two positive and equally attractive alternatives. An example is having to choose between a valued promotion in the organisation or a desirable new job with another organisation. *Avoidance conflict* occurs when a person must choose between two negative and

Intrapersonal conflict is conflict that occurs within the individual as a result of actual or perceived pressures from incompatible goals or expectations.

equally unattractive alternatives. An example is being asked either to accept a job transfer to another town in an undesirable location or to have your employment with an organisation terminated. *Approach–avoidance conflict* occurs when a person must decide to do something that has both positive and negative consequences. An example is being offered a higher-paying job, but one whose responsibilities will entail unwanted demands on your time.

This chapter has emphasised workers as individuals. However, many of the self-management strategies can also be extended to self-managed teams, which are discussed later in the book. Managers are seeking strategies designed to increase the use of human potential in the workplace. Many Western organisations have experienced the downsizing of the past decade, and now they are giving increased attention to new approaches designed to increase worker productivity. Organisations are being designed to have flatter structures, provide increased worker empowerment and offer greater opportunities for self-management — all strategies designed to increase the use of the workplace's human resource.

Managing pay as an extrinsic reward

LEARNING OBJECTIVE 4

Managing pay as an extrinsic reward

The earlier part of this chapter focused on different kinds of reinforcement and extrinsic reward. Table 4.1 showed various forms of pay as one of these extrinsic rewards and reinforcers. Pay is an especially complex extrinsic reward. It can help organisations attract and retain highly capable workers, and it can help satisfy and motivate these workers to work hard to achieve high performance. But if workers are dissatisfied with the salary, pay can also lead to strikes, grievances, absenteeism, turnover and sometimes even poor physical and mental health. The various aspects of pay make it an especially important extrinsic reward.[48]

Multiple meanings of pay

To use pay effectively as a reward a manager must understand why it is important to people. Various organisational behaviour theories recognise multiple meanings of pay and the potential of these meanings to vary from one person or situation to another. When it comes to the relationship between pay and job satisfaction, for example, each of the following theories (with which you are already familiar) offers a slightly different perspective.

According to Maslow's hierarchy of needs theory, pay is a unique reward that can satisfy many different needs. It is used directly to satisfy lower-order needs, such as the physiological need for food, and it is of symbolic value in satisfying higher-order needs, such as ego fulfilment.

According to McClelland's acquired needs theory, pay is an important source of performance feedback for high-need achievers. It can be attractive to persons with a high need for affiliation when offered as a group bonus, and it is valued by the high need-for-power person as a means of 'buying' prestige or control over others.

According to Herzberg's two-factor theory, pay in the form of base wage or salary can prevent dissatisfaction but cannot lead to motivation (although merit pay rises given as special rewards for jobs done well can cause increased satisfaction and motivation). However, Herzberg's research does show that pay cross-loads across both his hygiene and motivating factors. This finding recognises that many of the respondents in Herzberg's research perceived money as a motivating factor.

Expectancy and equity theories, as well as the various reinforcement strategies, give additional insight into the multiple meanings of pay and their potential relationships to job performance. These ideas (summarised in table 4.4) show how pay can serve as a motivator of work effort, when properly managed. This phrase is the real key; for pay to prove successful as a reward that is truly motivational to the recipient, it must be given:

1. contingent on the occurrence of specific and desirable work behaviours, and

2. equitably.

Merit pay and a variety of emerging creative pay practices are applications that need to be dealt with in more detail.

Theory	The meaning of pay
Equity theory	Pay is an object of social comparison. People are likely to compare their pay and pay increases with those received by others. When felt inequity occurs as a result of such comparisons, work effort may be reduced in the case of negative inequity, or increased in the case of positive inequity.
Expectancy theory	Pay is only one of many work rewards that individuals may value at work. When valence, instrumentality and expectancy are high, pay can be a source of motivation. However, the opportunity to work hard to obtain high pay will be viewed in the context of other effort–outcome expectancies and the equity dynamic.
Reinforcement theory	Pay is one of the extrinsic rewards that a manager may use to influence the work behaviour of employees. Through the techniques of operant conditioning, pay can be used as a positive reinforcer when the laws of contingent and immediate reinforcement are followed.

TABLE 4.4 • The multiple meanings of pay as viewed from a performance perspective

Merit pay

Edward Lawler is a management expert whose work has contributed greatly to our understanding of pay as an extrinsic reward. His research generally concludes that for pay to serve as a source of work motivation, high levels of job performance must be viewed as the path through which high pay can be achieved.[49] **Merit pay** is defined as a compensation system that bases an individual's salary or wage increase on a measure of the person's performance accomplishments during a specified time period. That is, merit pay is an attempt to make pay contingent on performance.

For some time now, research has supported the logic and theoretical benefits of merit pay, but it also indicates that the implementation of merit pay plans is not as universal or as easy as we may expect.[50]

To work well, a merit pay plan must:
- be based on realistic and accurate measures of individual work performance
- create a belief among employees that the way to achieve high pay is to perform at high levels
- clearly discriminate between high and low performers in the amount of pay reward received
- avoid confusing 'merit' aspects of a pay increase with 'cost-of-living' adjustments.

These guidelines are consistent with the basic laws of reinforcement and the guidelines for positive reinforcement discussed earlier in the chapter.

However, total quality management guru W Edwards Deming has long been a critic of pay-for-performance schemes. Deming argues, because performance is difficult to measure, that all employees should receive a traditional salary or wage, and that all future pay rises should be administered uniformly across the company to encourage cooperation and teamwork.

There are potential problems in linking pay to performance. However, many human resource experts and headhunters emphasise the importance of rewarding high performers for a private company's ability to attract top talent in a competitive global marketplace. As a result, a large number of Australian companies in the private sector (and a growing number of companies in New Zealand) maintain pay-for-performance schemes. A Morgan and Banks survey of 2100 businesses Australia-wide revealed that 70.2 per cent of these companies had some form of performance-based pay system for senior executives and a further 60.5 per cent had a similar scheme for middle managers. Only 40.4 per cent of the same sample of companies had implemented any performance-based pay scheme for non-managerial employees.[51] Such schemes have many critics, because some Australian chief executive officers have received bonus payments of shares even when their performance has been less than meritorious.[52]

Merit pay is a compensation system that bases an individual's salary or wage increase on a measure of the person's performance accomplishments during a specified time period.

By nature, performance-related pay is context and time related — so rewarding public servants is much more problematic than company CEOs. For example, in New Zealand the situation for public service chief executives is complicated because of the lag between performance measured and outcomes reported. It can take years for new policies to take effect and produce improved measurable achievements. In addition, government executives are often restricted in implementing radical changes by existing government policies, including policies related to funding. Further, apart from measurable financial efficiencies, quality of (governmental) services is difficult to measure. The New Zealand State Services Commission is dedicated to working on solutions for this complex problem.[53]

ETHICAL
Perspective

Paying for performance

The concept of linking pay with performance is controversial. Most employers would agree that quality employees deserve higher pay than underperforming employees. However, exactly what constitutes a 'quality employee' is problematic. Performance measurements are largely based on the perceptions of immediate supervisors; they are subjective and not based on specific criteria, and therefore can cause a sense of unfairness for many employees.

In response to the Australian public's expectation of higher teaching standards, there is a move to link teachers' pay with their performance under the assumption that quality teachers improve academic outcomes. Advocates of teacher 'pay for performance' plans argue that the profession will be able to attract and retain good-quality teachers. Proponents of a performance-linked pay system believe that student academic outcomes are an objective measure for teacher performance. These proponents deem teacher award payments (where teachers are paid according to their level of experience) to be inequitable, because some high-performing teachers demonstrably engage more effectively with their students and generate improved academic outcomes.[54] Pay schemes linked to student outcomes have been used in the United States and, more recently, in the United Kingdom.

Research from the United Kingdom shows that performance-linked pay makes little to no difference to student outcomes. However, the program may not have been implemented for long enough to draw any definitive conclusions. Research in the United States shows a slight difference in performance when teachers are paid according to student outcome measures. One significant difference between the UK and US programs is the involvement of teachers throughout the implementation phase of the US program, whereas in the United Kingdom only principals were consulted.[55]

In New South Wales, opponents of a performance-linked pay scheme point out that teaching effectiveness is only one of many variables affecting student outcomes. For example, variables such as competence, demographic differences (in particular, socio-economic status and gender), personality, motivation, and support from school and family, may also affect student performances. This multi-variability was recognised by the then state premier Bob Carr, who opposed linking teachers' pay with performance because of the impossibility of taking all variables into account in an equitable and fair manner when measuring teachers' performance.[56]

In addition, it can be argued that performance-linked pay makes strong assumptions about monetary rewards and motivation for performance, whereas teachers in particular display a relatively high level of *intrinsic* motivation.[57]

Creative pay practices

Merit pay plans are but one attempt to enhance the positive value of pay as a work reward and to use it as a positive reinforcer. Indeed, some argue that merit pay plans are not consistent with the demands of today's organisations because they fail to recognise the high degree of task interdependence among employees, as illustrated particularly in total quality management programs. Still others contend that the nature of any incentive scheme should be tied to the overall organisational strategy and the nature of the desired behaviour; for example, the pay system of an organisation that needs highly skilled individuals in short supply should emphasise employee retention, rather than performance.[58]

Many organisations facing increased competition, in an attempt to become more competitive by getting more from their workers, use varying creative incentive schemes either singly or in combination. Such non-traditional practices are becoming more common in organisations with increasingly diverse workforces and a growing emphasis on total quality management or similar setups.[59] These creative schemes can include skill-based pay, gain-sharing plans, lump-sum pay increases, bonus share schemes and flexible benefit plans.

Pay practice	Description
Skill-based pay	A pay system that rewards people for acquiring and developing job-relevant skills that relate to organisational needs
Gain-sharing plans	A pay system that links pay and performance by giving workers the opportunity to share in productivity gains through increased earnings.
Lump-sum pay increases	A pay system in which people elect to receive their annual wage or salary increase in one or more lump-sum payments
Bonus share schemes	A share plan to reward high-performing executives
Flexible benefit plans	Pay systems that allow workers to select benefits according to their individual needs

TABLE 4.5 • Creative pay practices

There is a growing trend away from rewarding performance solely by financial outcomes. Many companies are now incorporating non-financial outcomes, such as a flexible benefit plan, into this performance-based pay equation. Additional criteria such as improved customer service, employee satisfaction with managerial style and increased market share are being added to the equation to obtain a clearer and more comprehensive profile of the measurement of effective managerial performance.[60]

The following 'International spotlight' looks at how the effectiveness of incentives varies with different cultural and economic contexts.

International
SPOTLIGHT

Can performance incentives work for China?

Incentives used to motivate employees to increase performance are a typically Western concept. Hence, we must assume that the concept of incentives is not considered in the same manner in other areas of the world and, in some cases, it could be considered offensive to entice workers to perform better.

For example, in China, traditionally employees are paid according to the legislated national wage scales as a blue- or white-collar worker, with little differences in pay between workers and their supervisors. Bonuses are usually paid to a group that exceeded predetermined performance targets, where the individual members of that group benefit from the bonus. More recently, attempts to introduce individual performance-based incentives are becoming more common. However, it has been suggested that this will be a very difficult transition due to the deep-rooted collectivism in the Chinese culture.

Diverse opinions about performance incentive schemes in the West and the East have significant consequences for Chinese multinational corporations (MNCs) operating in countries such as Australia, New Zealand, the United States or the United Kingdom. This means that individual wages for comparable positions across different countries will be very different. In addition to deep-seated cultural underpinnings, differences arise from complex legal and economic issues. For example, one major legal issue is that in Australia, Chinese firms have to pay holiday pay, which is an unknown concept in China. In addition, Chinese MNCs in Western countries compete with the local labour market and generally are forced to offer higher wages to attract better-skilled staff. Further, the art of negotiating a wage contract is very much a Western concept and avoided by Chinese executives. Interestingly, the Chinese head offices appear to be unaware of salary practices that are in place overseas, as these are often determined locally by the subsidiaries and are not necessarily declared.

What happens to those Chinese who elect to work for MNCs outside China? The dilemma for Chinese MNCs is that they need to conform to international standards while still being faithful to their national practices. Many organisations do this by treating their global employees differently, based on their national backgrounds and managerial status. Hence, Chinese MNCs use a mixture of fixed and flexible performance-based payments for their non-Chinese workers, while retaining standard wages for their expatriate Chinese employees. This may not be an ideal situation in terms of equity, which may be the reason for the apparent ignorance of global diverse wage practices at the head office.

Nevertheless, Chinese MNCs are found to conform to international best practice; they are found to be internally equitable, externally competitive and actively enabling organisations to optimise their total wages packages.[61]

The learning organisation

The human race has experienced more rapid changes in the past 25 years than in the rest of humanity's existence. During the next 20 years or so, this pace of change is likely to accelerate. The challenge for organisations in this rapidly changing environment is to be flexible and adaptable enough to cope, because not only growth but, perhaps more importantly, organisational survival depends on these responses. This section introduces the concepts of the learning organisation and the teaching organisation.

The 'learning organisation' was popularised by Peter Senge in his book, *The fifth discipline*.[62] He argued that a learning organisation is a medium to enhance the development and use of knowledge at an individual level and, consequently, at an organisational level. Such knowledge will lead to organisational change. Learning organisational models are attempting to harness this potential for change in order to achieve competitive advantage. Now refer back to the story on communities of competence that began this chapter. You can see that in addition to achieving a competitive advantage for business, learning organisations can also enhance social services.

Organisational learning refers to the process of becoming a learning organisation and can be conceptualised as acquiring or developing new knowledge that modifies or changes behaviour and improves organisational performance. Underlying the concept of a learning organisation is a belief that organisations can be transformed by improving communication processes and techniques so as to enrich relationships among members.

Organisational learning is acquiring or developing new knowledge that modifies or changes behaviour and improves organisational performance.

Creating a learning organisation

Managers can create a learning organisation by:

- building a powerful shared vision of future growth that will provide the focus for learning and a benchmark for future achievements
- developing strategies and action plans that will inspire the commitment of all personnel to achieve the future goals of the organisation
- making extensive use of a continuous process of consultation to achieve consensus and unity of thought
- encouraging continual renewal of all organisational structures and processes
- employing systems thinking to ensure the organisation focuses on both internal and external factors driving the change
- creating self-directed teams of employees that are supported to make decisions at appropriate levels.

The degree to which an organisation can successfully create a learning environment can be measured by examining:

- the relationship between the employee and the organisation
- the value placed on the employee and their organisational contribution
- employee ownership and acceptance of responsibility, and
- employee empowerment.[63]

THE **Effective**Manager 4.3

Certain preconditions are essential if a successful learning environment is to be created through these new communication processes.[64]

1. *Trust.* All organisational members must believe they can rely on an individual's word (spoken or written). Trust permeates all organisational relationships and strongly influences all aspects of coordination and control. Managerial actions — such as encouraging supportive rather than defensive behaviour, aligning goals among and between organisational members, managing information flows and avoiding stereotyping — assist in building a trusting environment.

2. *Commitment.* The company must develop an emotional and intellectual commitment to its actions and achievements.

3. *Perceived organisational support.* Organisational support reinforces a bond between the organisation and its employees, and creates a sense of involvement with organisational objectives. An emphasis on relationship building and organisational support also reinforces the growth of trust and commitment.

Again referring to the discussion at the beginning of this chapter, you can see that organisational learning is about deliberately and continuously acquiring, processing and disseminating knowledge in order to transform the organisation to be more effective and/ or competitive. This sounds rather attractive in theory, but more recent research is questioning the prescriptive nature and apparent ease of transformation into a learning organisation in much of the management literature.[65] This research indicates that the process of learning in organisations is much more problematic than first understood and is presented in the 'Counterpoint' to follow. Despite these concerns, there are examples of organisations that are adaptive and that foster a collective learning environment of trust, commitment and organisational support.

From 1995 to 2000, The Mercy Hospital for Women in Melbourne went through five chief executive officers and four nursing directors. The last appointees inherited a situation where 40 per cent of the nurses were about to leave their positions and another 41 per cent were considering leaving the profession entirely. The new health-care managers chose to appoint a team of 14 nurses whose task was to find innovative ideas for change and improvement. The team was encouraged to be independent and was given full decision-making authority. This empowered team spent much of its time developing team skills and competencies, as well as getting to know the needs and wants of the Mercy staff. All employees were involved in creating a shared vision and making changes accordingly. Within a period of 18 months there was a significant reduction in the number of nurses wanting to leave. Mercy Hospital is considered to be an example of a learning organisation.[66]

COUNTER**POINT**

The trouble with learning

What do the terms 'learning' and 'learning organisation' mean? In common usage, people generally equate them with acquiring facts. However, acquired information needs to be interpreted and translated into usable knowledge. For organisations, knowledge acquisition is tied up with systems for codifying and disseminating information. But the real meaning of learning is much broader than this. It encompasses the subtle changes that take place when people, individually or collectively, reinterpret or *reframe* their experiences, and modify their behaviour accordingly.

Learning organisations can only enable competitive advantage via learning if 'knowledge' exists and can be identified as important to the organisation. In addition, this knowledge then needs to be *transferable* and a learning organisation needs to do this better than comparable organisations.[67] Knowledge acquisition and transfer is problematic, as gaining knowledge tends to be self-referential (based on what is known within the organisation). Knowledge sharing is vitally important to a learning organisation, as having a 'shared vision' underpins the collective nature of the organisational learning process. The problem is that when organisational members are all moving the same way, they may very well move in the wrong direction and 'actively damage the future direction of the company'.[68] This means that despite all intentions of being 'open' to external feedback, and responsive to the specific and general organisational environments, organisational decision making is likely to be reactive. This reactivity is in direct contrast to an organisational learning process that is meant to be proactive. Therefore, knowledge development to enable competitive advantage, on the scale anticipated by learning organisations, is somewhat idealistic. The process may legitimate ineffective and circular processes and may hinder the desire to become a learning organisation — it is unlikely that transformation will occur.

Difficulties may also occur with learning and well-intentioned attempts to create a 'learning organisation' because existing mental models limit our ability to be adaptive.[69] Mental models can provide a link between individuals and collectives as they provide a context for interpretation of knowledge. Recent research in the United Kingdom, regarding the role of strongly held mental models in a team environment, asserts that individual and organisational mental models ultimately may prevent desired creativity for innovation.[70] Strongly shared mental models are potentially 'closed' to new stimuli; little new knowledge can emerge, and radically different and creative ideas are likely to be rejected. Hence, behaviour modification is unlikely to be achieved.

Learning is a subjective process encompassing the absorption of new knowledge through emotional, intuitive and reflective filters and mental models. Real learning is a lifelong process and requires the skills of self-management, self-knowledge and self-evaluation.

Questions

1. Identify barriers and facilitators for organisational learning.
2. How can individual learning be transformed into organisational learning?
3. Think of an organisation where you have worked (or use your knowledge of your university or college). To what extent is the organisation a 'learning organisation'? Identify the facilitators and barriers to learning in these particular organisations.

The teaching organisation

The 1990s saw the rise to prominence of the learning organisation. Learning is a necessary competence, but it is insufficient to assure market leadership. The companies that have outperformed competitors and increased shareholder returns have been those able to move beyond being learning organisations to become teaching organisations.

The two types of organisation have many similarities. Fundamental to both is the common objective that every person within the organisation continually acquires new knowledge and appropriate skills. However, the distinguishing aspect of a teaching organisation is its ability to be more agile and to build more continuity into its successes. This is a direct consequence of a teaching organisation's added focus on passing on learning experiences and knowledge; that is, a teaching organisation aims to convey learning experiences to others, thereby allowing the organisation to achieve and maintain success. Leaders in teaching organisations feel responsible for sharing their knowledge with other staff as a means of helping the organisation to develop a knowledge base rapidly and accurately, infused with hands-on experience.

> A **teaching organisation** aims to pass on learning experiences to others, thereby allowing the organisation to achieve and maintain success.

Reflecting on the CRG Medical Foundation discussed at the beginning of this chapter, we could classify it as a teaching organisation because it facilitates the process of learning by connecting experts in a particular field. CRG brings together potential members of a community of competence, who are assessed on their achievement motivation, emotional intelligence, self-efficacy and their ability to share the workload.

The constant focus on developing people to become leaders allows a teaching organisation to become more agile and responsive to changes, because its members are always armed with the necessary knowledge and know-how to deal with new situations. An added benefit is the continuity of smooth leadership successions, preventing the potential disruption that a leadership change can entail.

The Fred Hutchinson Cancer Research Center is a rapidly growing research organisation whose employees share a strong commitment to preventing, diagnosing and curing cancer. Not satisfied with traditional methods for continuous quality improvement, the centre introduced a pilot peer mentoring program using 'management learning groups'. Comprising about eight senior managers, each group helps its members to learn from each other by sharing their knowledge, experience, wisdom and resources. The focus is on solving real problems as they arise and developing a better mutual understanding of the organisation's culture, systems and politics. While the groups meet monthly, the members also contact one another informally to provide ongoing coaching and support. Anecdotal evaluation of the pilot program indicates that the management learning groups provide a valuable forum that complements conventional management development programs while also building the capacity of the Fred Hutchinson Center as a successful research organisation.[71]

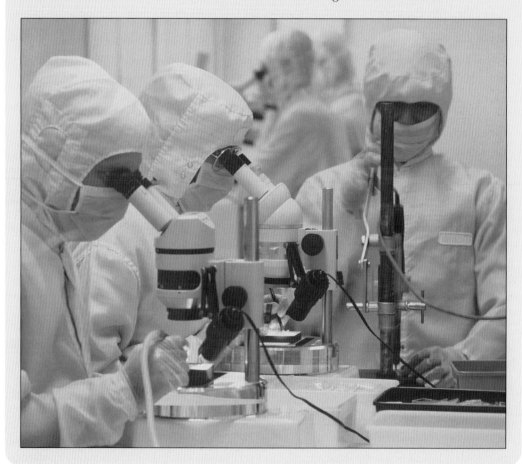

Summary

Four general approaches to learning

Learning is a relatively permanent change in behaviour resulting from experience. It is an important part of rewards management. The four general approaches to learning are classical conditioning, operant conditioning, cognitive learning and social learning. Modern managers need to understand the principles of cognitive learning, which relate to the motivational theories discussed in chapter 5; operant conditioning, which is achieved when the consequences of behaviour lead to changes in the probability of its occurrence; and social learning.

Organisational behaviour modification and reinforcement strategies

Reinforcement is the means through which operant conditioning takes place. Its foundation is the law of effect, which states that behaviour will be repeated or extinguished, depending on whether the consequences are positive or negative. Reinforcement is related to extrinsic rewards (valued outcomes that are given to the individual by some other person) because these rewards serve as environmental consequences that can influence people's work behaviours through the law of effect.

Organisational behaviour modification uses four reinforcement strategies to change behaviour: positive reinforcement, negative reinforcement (avoidance), punishment and extinction. Positive reinforcement is used to encourage desirable behaviour; the administration of positive consequences tends to increase the likelihood of a person repeating a behaviour in similar settings. Positive reinforcement should be contingent (administered only if the desired behaviour is exhibited) and immediate (as close in time to the desired behaviour as possible).

Negative reinforcement, or avoidance, is used to encourage desirable behaviour; the withdrawal of negative consequences tends to increase the likelihood that a person will repeat a desirable behaviour in similar settings.

Punishment is the administration of negative consequences or the withdrawal of positive consequences, which tends to reduce the likelihood of a given behaviour being repeated in similar settings. Punishment is used to weaken or eliminate undesirable behaviour, but problems can occur. Therefore, one must be especially careful to follow appropriate reinforcement guidelines (including the laws of contingent and immediate reinforcement) when using it. Punishment is likely to be more effective if combined with positive reinforcement.

Extinction is the withdrawal of the reinforcing consequences for a given behaviour. It is often used to withhold reinforcement for a behaviour that has previously been reinforced. This is done to weaken or eliminate the undesirable behaviour. It is an especially powerful strategy when combined with positive reinforcement.

Social learning theory and behavioural self-management

Social learning theory advocates learning through the reciprocal interactions among people, behaviour and environment. Therefore, it combines operant and cognitive learning approaches. Behavioural self-management builds on social learning theory to emphasise both behavioural and cognitive foci with a special emphasis on enhancing a worker's self-efficacy and feeling of self-control. Self-management is useful in treating workers both as individuals and as part of self-managed teams.

Managing pay as an extrinsic reward

Managing pay as an extrinsic reward is particularly important because pay has multiple meanings — some positive and some negative. As a major and highly visible extrinsic reward, pay plays a role in reinforcement and in the motivation theories discussed previously. Its reward implications are especially important in terms of merit pay. Other pay practices that are important and offer creative reward opportunities are skill-based pay, gain-sharing plans, lump-sum pay increases and flexible benefit plans.

Learning organisations and teaching organisations

A learning organisation is one in which members recognise the importance of communicating new knowledge for the benefit of the organisation. Such an environment can be encouraged if trust, commitment and a perception of organisational support exist. A teaching organisation is highly similar to a learning organisation; the difference lies in the focus on continuity in the passing on of necessary knowledge and know-how from leaders to other members of the organisation. This ensures that a teaching organisation is always agile and able to maintain its success.

Chapter 4 study guide

OB ## Key terms

behaviourists, *p. 114*
classical conditioning, *p. 115*
cognitive learning, *p. 117*
continuous reinforcement, *p. 122*
extinction, *p. 126*
extrinsic rewards, *p. 120*
intermittent reinforcement,
  p. 122
intrapersonal conflict, *p. 129*

law of contingent reinforcement,
  p. 121
law of effect, p. *120*
law of immediate reinforcement,
  p. 122
learning, *p. 114*
merit pay, *p. 131*
negative reinforcement, *p. 124*
operant conditioning, *p. 116*

organisational behaviour
  modification, *p. 121*
organisational learning, *p. 135*
positive reinforcement, *p. 121*
punishment, *p. 124*
shaping, *p. 122*
social learning, *p. 117*
stimulus, *p. 115*
teaching organisation, *p. 137*

Review questions

1. Explain the 'law of effect'.
2. What are extrinsic rewards and how are these related to learning and reinforcement?

3. Distinguish between 'negative reinforcement' and 'punishment'.
4. Summarise the main features of a learning organisation.

Application questions

1. Describe the classical conditioning process and provide examples of its impact on behaviours and emotions.
2. Mentoring, based on social learning theory, is often used to teach less experienced managers new skills. Discuss the operation and efficacy of mentoring programs in the contemporary workplace.
3. Punishment strategies should be used sparingly by managers. Explain why.

4. What are some of the ethical issues to consider when linking pay and performance?
5. Turn back to the 'International spotlight' on page 134. What are some cultural issues to consider when using incentives for the purpose of achieving greater performance?
6. Critically analyse the difference between 'a learning organisation' and 'organisational learning'.

Research questions

1. As you have read in this chapter, punishment is a management tool that continues to be used in the workplace despite increasing concerns about its effectiveness. Using the library and other resources you have access to, research the following questions and either write a 1000-word report on your findings, or complete a 20-minute presentation of your findings to the class.

Thinking of your own workplace (or one you are familiar with):

(a) How frequently is punishment used? Give examples.
(b) Explain the behavioural and emotional response to punishment.
(c) How does punishment prevent undesirable behaviour from reoccurring?

(d) Do you think that punishment has a place in modern workplaces? Why or why not?

2. Find an organisation online that publicises its employee rewards. How does the organisation motivate its employees? Would you like to work for this organisation? Why or why not? Compare your answer with those from others in your class and discuss why your answers may be the same or different.

Running project

Complete the following activities for your organisation.

1. Identify at least one example of each of the four approaches to learning.
2. Describe the formal and informal mentoring processes in place. If there aren't any, why are they thought unnecessary?
3. What extrinsic rewards does management use?
4. How does management deal with unwanted work behaviour exhibited by employees?
5. Identify whether your organisation exhibits elements of a learning or teaching organisation. Describe them. If the organisation is not a learning or teaching organisation, has this disadvantaged the organisation?

Individual activity

What, when and how I learn[72]

Objective

To gain a greater understanding of what, when and how individuals learn

Total time: 40 minutes

Instructions

Think of *four* different things that you have learned that were, and still are, important to you.

Now, for each one, think carefully about *what* you learned, *when* you learned, *how* you learned and, lastly, what it was that most *helped you learn it*. To help you with this, you might like a few ideas. What you learned and when are straightforward, but how and what helped most are a little more complicated!

In terms of how, think about this:

Did you learn whatever it was by reading about it, being told about it, being shown how to do it, by trial and error, by practising it, by thinking about it, from film or video or any other medium, by research or by a combination of these or any other ways of learning? Were you taught by somebody else, or did you learn it on your own? Were you in a group, was the process formal or informal and did you have to undergo some kind of testing or accreditation? Did you learn in a way not written here — what was it?

For what helped you learn it, decide what factors you believe most helped you to learn. Was it your interest, did you have a particularly inspiring teacher or instructor, was there some kind of reward or sanction to be applied if you did or did not succeed? Or perhaps it was a target that you set yourself? Is there anything else that you can define that caused you to *want* to learn, helped you to keep learning and supported your successful learning? It will be worthwhile considering which factors were internal (that is, from within yourself) and which were external, from the job, peer pressure, fashion or anything else.

Now, fill out the following table.

What I learned	When I learned it	How I learned it	What most helped me to learn it

(continued)

To help you think about how you learn, tick the box that describes you best.

	Always	Most times	Seldom	Never
I memorise things easily				
I work out the meaning of things				
I notice what is around me				
I ask questions and think about the answers				
I use sources of information (the media, libraries, etc.)				
I measure what I find out against things I know				
I see links between things				
I choose how best to do things				
I use information and experience to choose solutions				
I act when I have decided				
I think about consequences				
I select important bits of information				
I enjoy learning new things				
I share what I learn				

To get a better understanding of how you learn, think about these questions:
- How do I learn best — alone, in a group, with an instructor, from books, by doing, by watching, by any other way or by a lot of different ways?
- What makes me want to learn?
- What gets me started on learning?
- What keeps me learning?
- What stops me learning?
- How do other people affect my learning?

Now reflect on how you learn. How can you improve the way you are learning?

OB   *Group activity*

Getting creative with remuneration

Total time: 30 minutes

Objectives

1. To provide an experience of choices faced by managers when they make remuneration decisions
2. To help you review some of the theoretical issues involved in attempts to motivate employees though learning, reinforcement and flexible benefit plans
3. To apply these issues in a realistic and practical work setting

Instructions

In groups, you are to select a remuneration package that best fits each of the following employees' needs (they are listed under the employee profiles). When you have finished, one member of each group will report to the class their groups' remuneration selections for each employee. In the report the speaker must justify each selection made by using relevant theory and case knowledge.

Employee profiles

'The Nut House' is altering its pay structure to a more creative and flexible one to assist with employee motivation. However, each employee has at least 40 per cent of their package as a base salary. At the moment, all packages are paid as salary, and no performance bonuses are paid. Any additional hours worked by employees are not paid; instead, they receive time-in-lieu, which is to be taken one day at a time, on a Tuesday or Wednesday.

Fred

Fred is a middle manager who has been with the organisation for eight years. During that time he has never had a pay rise or a promotion. Fred is not skilled and obtained his position on the basis of bringing several very large customers to the organisation. Fred is unhappy at work. Fred has an aggressive manner when communicating with people. Fred has expressed no interest in learning new skills. Current salary package = $75 000.

Huong

Huong is an administrative officer who has been with the organisation for two years. She was looking for a slower-paced life where she could do her job and spend more time on her hobbies. Huong is well respected and an excellent worker who is keen to expand her knowledge at every opportunity. Current salary package = $35 000.

Carlos

Carlos is a middle manager who has been in the organisation for six years. Carlos is highly skilled and cannot be replaced easily; he is one of the hardest workers in the organisation and puts in long hours on the job. He is very well respected by everyone in the organisation and clients adore him. He never seems to take the time-in-lieu that he has accumulated. Carlos is looking for another job, where he can spend more time at home and to have an opportunity to undertake training and development. Current salary package = $90 000.

June

June is a 63-year-old lady who has been with the organisation since anyone else can remember. She worked two days per week. Although June is very good at her job, she has been taking more and more time off due to illness and other 'personal reasons', which is beginning to frustrate other members of staff. Current salary package = $18 000.

Kim

Kim is a 25-year-old marketing graduate who has worked in the sales department for three years. Kim intends working hard and being an executive by the time she is 30 years old. She has high aims that involve earning a lot of money, travel and driving a luxury car. Her current performance is average: she makes the sales margins, but there are also some complaints about her lack of customer service. Current salary package = $45 000.

Flexible options

Following are some of the more usual benefits available. This is not an exhaustive list and you may choose any other options that you think appropriate for the individual; be as creative as you can.

- Base salary
- Superannuation top-ups (no more than 20 per cent of total package)
- Gym membership $600
- Four-day working week $2000
- Part-time university education $2000
- Performance-linked salary
- Car allowance $10 000 (tax free)
- Provision of lunch $3500
- 25 per cent pay cut per annum, for every fifth year off with full pay
- Holiday accommodation vouchers up to $2000
- Skill-based salary
- ASX 100 shares of the employee's choice $5000
- Medical benefits: single $2000, family $4000
- Mobile phone $1200
- Child-care/elder-care payments up to $4000 per annum per child/elder

Case study: A to Z Networking[73] OB

A to Z Networking, a Sydney-based small enterprise, came into being in 1999. Twelve colleagues, just made redundant because their former employer went into bankruptcy, discussed a plan to buy the client list from the liquidators and start up their own business.

Two employees, Paul and Malcolm, set up the company and appointed themselves as directors. Paul, a network engineer, had considerable savings to invest, but had no management experience. Malcolm, the network manager, had earned credibility and trust

(continued)

with clients. Malcolm also had experience running a company.

A to Z is very successful. The client list grew quickly through word of mouth and within six months new employees were being hired.

During this period of growth, little thought was given to cash flow, rewards and other human resource maintenance issues as the two directors and the employees were 'mates'. Malcolm and Paul presumed their employees remained grateful for having a job. However, as the company grew and new staff members entered the company, the atmosphere changed. The original twelve were no longer a 'bunch of mates' working together. A hierarchy developed with Malcolm and Paul, as directors, firmly in charge. Some of the original twelve employees didn't like the changes and all but one left within 18 months.

The new employees enjoyed working at A to Z; Malcolm was a charismatic leader who developed a collegial atmosphere amongst the engineers. Tacit and explicit knowledge accumulated and was freely shared via an intranet. Engineers were empowered to make autonomous decisions, order stock as necessary and organise their own work day. They took advantage of training and development provided and enjoyed industry comparable rewards. During this time Paul worked as an engineer.

By 2003, the business had grown significantly. The company now operated nation-wide, and Malcolm's and Paul's roles changed accordingly. Malcolm spent much of his time flying interstate to meet corporate clients. There would be months when he did not meet any of the engineers. Consequently, Paul managed the day-to-day running of the business and the office. Paul's leadership style appeared to be vastly different than Malcolm's charismatic style, which was identified by many office workers and engineers as a source for work dissatisfaction.

Business became increasingly busy and engineers were regularly expected to work 60 hours or more per week. Due to the significant skills shortage of experienced engineers in the IT industry, Paul and Malcolm began routinely turning away new clients. To retain experienced engineers, their salaries were increased significantly above industry average. Today, two years later, the company is facing another massive staff turnover.[74]

Questions

1. What lessons can Paul and Malcolm learn from their experiences over the past six years in terms of staff behaviour modification strategies?

2. Using the organisational learning theory, what advice would you give to Paul and Malcolm to achieve transformational change?

3. Design a reward and benefits plan for the network engineers of A to Z that will help to retain and motivate them. What other strategies can Malcolm and Paul employ to reduce staff turnover?

4. Form into groups and brainstorm what Malcolm and Paul should do to ensure A to Z's organisational survival.

OB *Suggested reading*

Michael G Aamodt, *Applied industrial/organisational psychology*, 4th ed. (Southbank Vic.: Thomson, 2004).

John Arnold, *Work psychology. understanding human behaviour in the workplace*, 4th ed. (Edinburgh Gate, Harlow: Pearson Education Limited, 2005).

Schon Beechler and Allen Bird, *Japanese multinationals abroad: individual and organizational learning* (New York: Oxford University Press, 1999).

Deborah Blackman and Steve Henderson, 'Why learning organisations do not transform', *The Learning Organization Journal*, vol. 12, no. 1 (2005), pp. 42–56.

Donald Brown and Don Harvey, *An experiential approach to organization development*, 7th ed. (Upper Saddle River, NJ: Pearson Education, 2006).

Simon Crainer, *Key management ideas: thinkers that changed the management world* (Harlow: Prentice Hall, 1998).

Alfie Kohn, *Punished by rewards: the trouble with gold stars, incentive plans, A's, praise, and other bribes* (Boston: Houghton Mifflin, 1999).

Edward E Lawler III, *Strategic pay: aligning organizational strategies and pay systems* (San Francisco: Jossey-Bass, 1990).

Fred Luthans and Robert Kreitner, *Organizational behavior modification and beyond* (Glenview, IL: Scott, Foresman, 1985).

Michael J Marquardt, *Action learning in action: transforming problems and people for world class organizational learning*, 1st ed. (Palo Alto, CA: Davie-Black Publishers; and Alexandria, VA: American Society for Training and Development, 1999).

M O'Driscoll, P Taylor and T Kalliath, *Organisational psychology in Australia and New Zealand* (Melbourne: Oxford University Press, 2003)

Peter Senge, Art Kleiner, George Roth, Charlotte Roberts, Bryan Smith and Richard Ross, *The dance of change: the challenges to sustaining momentum in a learning organization* (New York: Doubleday, 1999).

Patricia K Zingheim and Jay R Schuster, *Pay people right! Breakthrough reward strategies to create great companies*, Jossey-Bass Business and Management Series (San Francisco: Jossey-Bass, 2000).

End notes

OB

1. CRG Medical Foundation for Patient Safety, 'Community of competence', www.communityofcompetence.com/articles/COFC.htm (viewed 30 September 2005).
2. CRG Medical Foundation for Patient Safety, 'Registries', www.communityofcompetence.com/sections/Registry.htm (viewed 30 September 2005.
3. EA Smith, 'Communities of competence: new resources in the workplace', *Journal of Workplace Learning*, vol. 17, issue 1/2 (2005), p. 9.
4. ibid.
5. See TR Davis and F Luthans, 'A social learning approach to organisational behaviour', *Academy of Management Review*, vol. 5 (1980), pp. 281–90.
6. For some of BF Skinner's works, see *Walden two* (New York: Macmillan, 1948); *Science and human behavior* (New York: Macmillan, 1953), *Contingencies of reinforcement* (New York: Appleton-Century-Crofts, 1969).
7. 'Government invests $20 million in budding leaders', *New Zealand Management*, (August 2003), p. 7.
8. BF Skinner's works, see *Walden two* (New York: Macmillan, 1948); *Science and human behavior* (New York: Macmillan, 1953), *Contingencies of reinforcement* (New York: Appleton-Century-Crofts, 1969).
9. M Aamodt, *Applied industrial/organisational psychology*, 4th ed. (Southbank Vic.: Thomson, 2004).
10. M Aamodt, *Applied industrial/organisational psychology*, 4th ed. (Southbank Vic.: Thomson, 2004).
11. A Bandura, *Social learning theory* (Englewood Cliffs, NJ: Prentice Hall, 1977).
12. 'TV drama seen as key for women engineers', *Professional Engineering*, vol. 17, issue 19 (10 November 2004), p. 9.
13. M Mattis, 'Women entrepreneurs: out from under the glass ceiling', *Women in Management Review*, vol. 19, issue 3 (2004), p. 154.
14. The Law Society of New South Wales, '2004 profile of the solicitors of NSW' (January 2005), www.lawsociety.com.au/uploads/filelibrary/
1107730500680_0.7314083026742801.pdf (viewed 10 May 2005).
15. The NSW Bar Association, 'Statistics update — 29 September 2004', http://www.nswbar.asn.au/Public/About%20us/statistics/StatsIntro2.htm (viewed 10 May 2005).
16. S Moran, 'Women mentors put student lawyers in the picture', *Sydney Morning Herald* (26 November 2004), p. 28.
17. Office for Women, NSW Premiers Department. 'Lucy mentoring program for young women', www.women.nsw.gov.au/Working/Working_YoungW_Lucy.htm (viewed 10 May 2005).
18. A Patty, 'Girls put the men in mentoring', *The Daily Telegraph* (22 April 2005), p. 26.
19. T Peterson and R Amn, 'Self-efficacy: the foundation of human performance' *Performance Improvement Quarterly*, vol. 18, no. 2 (2005), pp. 5–18.
20. See JD Zalesny and JK Ford, 'Extending the social information processing perspective: new links to attitudes, behaviors and perceptions', *Organizational Behavior and Human Decision Processes*, vol. 47 (1990), pp. 205–46; ME Gist, C Schwoerer and B Rosen, 'Effects of alternative training methods of self-efficacy and performance in computer software training', *Journal of Applied Psychology*, vol. 74 (1989), pp. 884–91; DD Sutton and RW Woodman, 'Pygmalion goes to work: the effects of supervisor expectations in a retail setting', *Journal of Applied Psychology*, vol. 74 (1989), pp. 943–50; ME Gist, 'The influence of training method on self-efficacy and idea generation among managers', *Personnel Psychology*, vol. 42 (1989), pp. 787–805.
21. G Dessler, J Griffiths, B Lloyd-Walker and A Williams, *Human resource management* (Australia: Prentice Hall, 2003).
22. R Presbury, JA Fitzgerald and R Chapman, 'Impediments to improvements to service quality in luxury hotels', *Managing Service Quality*, vol. 15, no. 4 (2005).

23. R Presbury and JA Fitzgerald, 'Achieving service quality — managers' perceptions of mentoring' (forthcoming).

24. EL Thorndike, *Animal intelligence* (New York: Macmillan, 1911), p. 244.

25. Based on Fred Luthans and Robert Kreitner, *Organizational behavior modification and beyond* (Glenview, IL: Scott, Foresman, 1985).

26. 'Paying employees not to go to the doctor', *Business Week* (21 March 1983), p. 150; 'Giving goodies to the good', *Time* (21 November 1985), p. 98; 'Incentive plans spur safe work habits, reducing accidents at some plants', *Wall Street Journal* (27 January 1987), p. 1.

27. M Aamodt, *Applied industrial/organisational psychology*, 4th ed. (Southbank Vic.: Thomson, 2004).

28. Australian Public Service Commission web site, www.apsc.gov.au/values/casestudy31.htm (viewed 5 June 2005).

29. ibid.

30. M Farquharson, 'Carrot vs stick', *Human Resources* (London, November 2004), p. 26.

31. ibid.

32. PK Yuk, 'Royal Mail continue rewarding healthy staff', *Financial Times* (London, 26 April 2005), p. 5.

33. S O'Brien, 'Postal staff sickies face crackdown', *Herald Sun* (Melbourne, 31 July 2003), p. 15.

34. AR Korukonda and James G Hunt, 'Pat on the back versus kick in the pants: an application of cognitive inference to the study of leader reward and punishment behavior', *Group and Organization Studies*, vol. 14, no. 3 (1989), pp. 299–324.

35. P Kitchen, 'HR staffers learn about generational difference at Woodbury NY conference', *Knight Ridder Tribune Business News* (Washington, 14 May 2005), p 1; Jason Rawlins, 'Work values change with new generations of workers: revolution in the workplace', transcript of the Australian Broadcasting Corporation radio program *AM* (23 October 2004), p. 1; AR Earls, 'Clash of generations in workplace genxers, boomers seen as having different life goals, values, career expectations,' *Boston Globe* (10 August 2003), p. G1.

36. M Aamodt, *Applied industrial/organisational psychology*, 4th ed. (Southbank Vic.: Thomson, 2004).

37. Hamner, op. cit.

38. GA Ball, LK Trevino and HP Sims, 'Just and unjust punishment: influences on subordinate performance and citizenship', *Academy of Management Journal*, vol. 37 (1994), pp. 299–322. Also see ch. 16 on organisational justice in M O'Driscoll, P Taylor and T Kalliath, *Organisational psychology in Australia and New Zealand* (Melbourne: Oxford University Press, 2003).

39. For an overview see M O'Driscoll, P Taylor and T Kalliath, *Organisational psychology in Australia and New Zealand* (Melbourne: Oxford University Press, 2003), ch. 16.

40. Personal communication exchanged on 12 June 2005.

41. Westpac Banking Corporation, www.westpac.com.au (viewed 5 June 2005); BHP Billiton, www.bhpbilliton.com (viewed 5 June 2005); National Australia Bank, 'NAB markets: Woolworths', www.nabmarkets.com/downloads/public/11287_0.pdf (viewed 5 June 2005); The Health Insurance Commission, www.hic.gov.au/providers/incentives_allowances/pip.htm (viewed 5 June 2005); pers. comm. with managing director of networking company on 10 May 2005.

42. The Warehouse, 'The 2004 triple bottom line report', www.thewarehouse.co.nz (viewed 30 September 2005). For further information, see BG Jackson and KW Parry, *The hero manager: learning from New Zealand's top chief executives* (Auckland: Penguin, 2001).

43. Edwin A Locke, 'The myths of behavior mod in organizations', *Academy of Management Review*, vol. 2 (October 1977), pp. 543–53. For a counterpoint see Jerry L Gray, 'The myths of the myths about behavior mod in organizations: a reply to Locke's criticisms of behavior modification', *Academy of Management Review*, vol. 4 (January 1979), pp. 121–9.

44. The concern is raised in Robert Kreitner, 'Controversy in OBM: history, misconceptions, and ethics' in Lee Frederiksen (ed.), *Handbook of organizational behavior management* (New York: John Wiley & Sons, 1982), pp. 71–91.

45. Charles C Manz and Henry P Sims, Jr, *Superleadership* (New York: Berkley, 1990).

46. T McLean, 'How to find the right frame of mind', *Financial Times* (London, 22 April 2000), p. 22; A Johnson and J Gilbert, 'The psychological uniform: using mental skills in youth sport', *Strategies*, vol. 18, no. 2 (2004), pp. 5–9; 'Improving the performance of expert workers', *The Journal for Quality and Participation*, vol. 27, no. 1 (2004), pp. 9–11.

47. Collingwood Football Club official web site, http://collingwoodfc.com.au (viewed 30 September 2005).

48. MA Spinelli and GR Gray, 'How important is compensation for job satisfaction of retail trainers? Some evidence', *Employee Benefit Plan Review*, vol. 58, no. 5 (November 2003), p. 29.

49. Edward E Lawler III, *Pay and organization development* (Reading, MA: Addison-Wesley, 1981).

50. For complete reviews of theory, research and practice, see Edward E Lawler III, *Pay and organizational effectiveness* (New York: McGraw-Hill, 1971); Lawler (1981), op. cit.; Edward E Lawler III, 'The design of effective reward systems' in Jay W Lorsch (ed.), *Handbook of organizational behavior* (Englewood Cliffs, NJ: Prentice Hall, 1987), pp. 255–71; K Bartol and A Srivastava, 'Encouraging knowledge sharing: the role of organisational reward systems', *Journal of Leadership & Organisational Studies*, vol. 9, no. 1 (2002), pp. 64–76; S Appelbaum and B Shapiro, 'Pay for performance: implementation of individual and group', *Management Decision*, vol. 30, no. 6 (1992), pp. 86–91.

51. M. Lawson, 'Incentive schemes used mainly for chiefs', *Australian Financial Review* (13 May 1996), p. 2.

52. Australian Council of Superannuation Investors Inc, 'CEO pay in the top 100 companies: 2002' (May 2003), www.acsi.org.au (viewed 7 June 2003); J McConvill, 'Money can't buy you...performance', *The Age* (10 June 2005).

53. State Services Commission, www.ssc.govt.nz/display/home.asp (viewed 30 September 2005).

54. The Association of Independent Schools of Queensland Inc, *AISQ Research Brief*, issue 3/02 (June 2002).

55. EC Wragg, GS Haynes, CM Wragg and RP Chamberlain, *Performance-related pay: the views and experiences of 1000 primary and secondary head teachers* [Teachers' Incentives Pay Project], occasional paper no. 1 (Exeter: School of Education, University of Exeter, UK, 2001).

56. Parliament of New South Wales, 'Teachers' performance pay', NSW Legislative Council *Hansard* (2 March 2005), p. 14394.

57. The Association of Independent Schools of Queensland Inc, *AISQ Research Brief*, issue 3/02 (June 2002).

58. Jone L Pearce, 'Why merit pay doesn't work: implications from organization theory' in David B Balkin and Luis R Gomez-Mejia (eds), *New perspectives on compensation* (Englewood Cliffs, NJ: Prentice Hall, 1987), pp. 169–78; Jerry M Newman, 'Selecting incentive plans to complement organizational strategy' in David R Balkin and Luis R Gomez-Mejia (eds), *New perspectives on compensation* (Englewood Cliffs, NJ: Prentice Hall, 1987), pp. 214–24; Edward E Lawler III, 'Pay for performance: making it work', *Compensation and Benefits Review*, vol. 21, no. 1 (1989), pp. 55-60.

59. See Daniel C Boyle, 'Employee motivation that works', *HR Magazine*, vol. 37, no. 10 (October 1992), pp. 83–9. Kathleen A McNally, 'Compensation as a strategic tool', *HR Magazine*, vol. 37, no. 7 (July 1992), pp. 59–66.

60. N Weinberg, 'Hidden treasure', *Forbes* (New York, 28 October 2002), p. 58.

61. J Shen, 'Compensation in Chinese multinationals', *Compensation and Benefits Review*, vol. 36, no. 1 (January/February 2004), pp. 15–26.

62. P Senge, *The fifth discipline* (Sydney: Random House, 1992).

63. Randolph T Barker and Martin R Camarata, 'The role of communication in creating and maintaining a learning organisation: preconditions, indicators and disciplines', *Journal of Business Communication*, vol. 35, no. 4 (1998), pp. 443–67.

64. D Blackman and S Henderson, 'Why learning organisations do not transform', *The Learning Organization Journal*, vol. 12, no. 1 (2005), pp. 42–56; L Lee-Kelley and D Blackman, 'More than shared goals: the impact of mental models on team innovation and learning', *Journal of Innovation and Learning*, vol. 2, no. 1 (2005), pp. 11–25; D Blackman, 'Is knowledge acquisition and transfer realisable?', *Electronic Journal of Radical Organization Theory*, vol. 7, no. 1 (March 2001), http://www.mngt.waikato.ac.nz/research/ejrot.

65. ibid.

66. JE Collette, 'Retention of nursing staff — a team based approach', *Australian Health Review*, vol. 28, no. 3 (2004), pp. 349–56.

67. Deborah Blackman and Steve Henderson, 'Why learning organisations do not transform', *The Learning Organization Journal*, vol. 12, no. 1 (2005), pp. 42–56.

68. ibid.

69. L Lee-Kelley and D Blackman, 'More than shared goals: the impact of mental models on team innovation and learning', *Journal of Innovation and Learning*, vol. 2, no. 1 (2005), pp. 11–25.

70. ibid.

71. E Wallach, 'Management learning groups: continuous quality improvement for managers', *Journal for Quality and Participation* (Summer 2001), pp. 30-3.

72. Extracted from National Institute of Adult Continuing Education, 'Your life, your work, your future', http://www.niace.org.uk/research/EDP/leonmatall2.doc (viewed 7 June 2005).

73. Please note that the name of this Sydney-based privately owned company, and the names of the individuals involved, have been changed.

74. Adapted from personal communication with directors of this company, June 2005.

Chapter 5
Job design, goal setting and flexible work arrangements

Learning objectives
After studying this chapter, you should be able to:

1. explain the concept of intrinsic motivation

2. compare and contrast the alternative job design strategies and link them to intrinsic work rewards

3. discuss the job characteristics model employing job diagnosis techniques as a newer approach to job enrichment

4. explain how goal-setting theory is linked to job design

5. discuss how flexible work arrangements contribute to workforce flexibility.

The nature of work, the design of jobs and the arrangements of when and where we work are all undergoing change. Flexible work arrangements can be difficult to implement but, as is the case with Minter Ellison, the gains for both employee and employer can be substantial.

If flexible work options can survive the pressure-cooker environment of a major law firm, it could be argued they're suitable for any business.

Minter Ellison introduced a new package of flexible work arrangements for both partners and staff about four years ago. The firm provides opportunities for people to work part-time, job-share and work remotely from home. It provides paid parental leave, runs parenting programs, has breastfeeding facilities available in the office and assists its people with information about child-care facilities.

One result is that the number of staff returning to work after parental leave has almost doubled from 47 per cent in 2001 to 80 per cent now.

'Our product is our people and their knowledge, really,' says Robert Marriott, Minter Ellison's HR director. 'The thing is, when you've got a very valuable, experienced lawyer who wants to take time out for various reasons — be it family or other — it's always useful to be able to retain their services. That means you've still retained that knowledge and avoided the costs of replacement, potentially, as well.'

'Minter Ellison has embraced flexible work arrangements because they reflect the firm's values,' says Marriott. 'One of our values is something we call "balance" which is respecting each other's needs outside work and the diverse contributions people can make to improve the firm internally.'

Marriott says the move is also about remaining competitive. 'There are other firms beginning to move in this area — some more than others — but that's only one side of the equation for us.'

Source: Jane Cherrington, 'Open all hours [Legal options]', *Management Today* (May 2005), pp. 40–3.

Introduction

In chapter 3 we discussed motivation in relation to intrinsic and extrinsic rewards. We built on that treatment in chapter 4, emphasising various aspects of reinforcement and different kinds of pay plans as extrinsic rewards. In this chapter we give special emphasis to intrinsic rewards and how to use job design, goal setting and flexible work arrangements to improve intrinsic job satisfactions.

Our society and the nature of workplaces are continuously changing, generating forces that impact upon how workers experience their work and their workplaces. Within the workplace, there is a deeper appreciation of how the job itself can affect an individual's motivation and job satisfaction. Organisations have moved well beyond simply trying to improve worker performance by offering limited extrinsic rewards such as higher wages or promotion. There is more focus now on responding to the intrinsic rewards that workers get from doing their jobs, and on the goals that can help to guide and motivate them in their work. Designing the work to maximise employee outcomes is fundamental to this process. The theoretical aspects of job design are explained and job design theories or approaches (such as job characteristics, socio-technical, socio-information and multiskilling) are examined to demonstrate how the design of jobs can have an impact on workers. The alignment and achievement of organisational goals through a process of goal setting is also considered, since this impacts upon employees' jobs and their motivation, satisfaction and performance within them. Finally, a discussion of flexible work arrangements explores how the very arrangements in which workers are employed are being reconsidered and modified. These new arrangements take into account the demands that employees experience; they enhance the quality of their working lives and also enhance their capacity to work productively for their organisations.

Intrinsic motivation

LEARNING OBJECTIVE 1

Intrinsic motivation

Intrinsic work rewards were defined in chapter 3 as those rewards that an individual receives directly as a result of task performance. One example is the feeling of achievement that comes from completing a challenging project. Such feelings are individually determined and integral to the work. The individual is not dependent on an outsider, such as a manager, to provide these rewards or feelings. This concept is in direct contrast to extrinsic rewards, such as pay and conditions, which are externally controlled. The unique nature of intrinsic rewards can be seen when a social worker says: 'My working conditions are bad and my coworkers are boring, but I get a sense of satisfaction out of helping my clients'.[1]

Intrinsic work rewards[2] are a very important part of motivating and satisfying employees in the workplace. Herzberg's two-factor theory of motivation in chapter 3 particularly draws attention to the importance of intrinsic job content factors in improving satisfaction in the job (while extrinsic job context factors can lead to dissatisfaction). His ideas will be discussed further in this chapter when job enrichment is considered. Intrinsic work rewards play a key part in effective job design. The example above illustrates that people can be motivated simply because they enjoy the experience of accomplishing tasks. This is described as intrinsic motivation, which is a desire to work hard solely for the pleasant experience of task accomplishment.

When we discussed extrinsic rewards in the last chapter, we saw the manager as responsible for allocating extrinsic rewards such as pay, promotion and verbal praise to employees, and for controlling general working conditions. To serve in this capacity, a manager must be good at evaluating performance, maintaining an inventory of valued work rewards and giving these rewards to employees contingent upon work performance.

Managing intrinsic work rewards presents an additional challenge for the manager. Still acting as an agent of the organisation, the manager must design jobs for individual employees so that intrinsic rewards become available to them as a direct result of feedback gained from working on assigned tasks. That is not to say that every manager should design

Intrinsic motivation is a desire to work hard solely for the pleasant experience of task accomplishment.

every job to provide every employee with the maximum opportunity to experience intrinsic work rewards. This chapter will help you to understand:

- when people may desire intrinsic work rewards
- how to design jobs for people who desire greater intrinsic work rewards
- how to motivate those people who do not desire intrinsic work rewards.

Job design

LEARNING OBJECTIVE 2 · Job design strategies and intrinsic work rewards

A **job** is one or more tasks that an individual performs in direct support of an organisation's production purpose. When a job is properly designed, it should facilitate both task performance and job satisfaction, partly through intrinsic motivation. Additional aspects of human resource maintenance, such as absenteeism, commitment and turnover, may also be influenced.

Job design involves the planning and specification of job tasks and the work setting designated for their accomplishment. This definition includes both the specification of task attributes and the creation of a work setting for these attributes. It includes all the structural and social elements of the job, and their impacts on employee behaviour and performance. The objective of job design is to help make jobs meaningful, interesting and challenging. The manager's responsibility is to design jobs that will motivate the individual employee. Figuratively speaking, this is properly done when:

Individual needs + task attributes + work setting *lead to* performance and satisfaction.

Between 1900 and 1950 there were many developments in management theories that ranged from scientific studies of job efficiency to studies that were more concerned with the human response to the job. Four major approaches to job design were identified. Each approach was prescriptive in nature and assumed that all workers would respond to the strategies in the same manner. None of these approaches made allowance for variation in the motivational potential of the individual worker. The approaches were:

1. job simplification (job engineering)
2. job enlargement
3. job rotation
4. job enrichment.

> **Jobs** are one or more tasks that an individual performs in direct support of an organisation's production purpose.
>
> **Job design** is the planning and specification of job tasks and the work setting in which they are to be accomplished.

Job simplification

Job simplification, often termed job engineering, involves standardising work procedures and employing people in clearly defined and specialised tasks. The machine-paced car assembly line is a classic example of this job design strategy.

This approach, deriving from the scientific managers such as Frederick Taylor, involves simplified jobs that are highly specialised and usually require an individual to perform a narrow set of tasks repetitively. The potential advantages include increased operating efficiency (which was the original intent of the job simplification approach), low-skill and low-cost labour, minimal training requirements and controlled production quantity. Some possible disadvantages of this 'de-skilling' include loss of efficiency due to low-quality work, high rates of absenteeism and turnover, and the need to pay high wages to get people to do unattractive jobs. For most people, simplified job designs tend to be low in intrinsic motivation. The jobs lack challenge and lead to boredom.

In today's high-technology age, a natural extension of job simplification is complete **automation** — allowing a machine to do the work previously accomplished through human effort. This approach increasingly involves the use of robots and sophisticated computer applications based on expert systems and artificial intelligence. The Walgreens pharmacy chain in the United States increased the rate of packing shipments from its distribution centre to its stores by more than 800 per cent with its use of robots.[3] More recently, computer applications such as menus on telephone help lines and the directed prompts and menus of bank automatic telling machines have replaced tasks previously done by human effort.

> **Job simplification** is standardising work procedures and employing people in clearly defined and specialised tasks.
>
> **Automation** is a job design that allows machines to do work previously accomplished by human effort.

Job enlargement

Job enlargement emerged in the 1950s when many managers sought a job design strategy to reduce the boredom associated with the job engineering approach. The aim is to increase the breadth of a job by adding to the variety of tasks performed by a worker. Task variety is assumed to offset some of the disadvantages of job simplification, thereby increasing job performance and satisfaction for the individual. Job enlargement increases task variety by combining into one job two or more tasks previously assigned to separate workers. The only change in the original job design is that a worker now does a greater variety of tasks.

Often job enlargement has not lived up to its promise. For example, if a graphic designer who has been designing business brochures and posters is also given the task of preparing book cover layouts, the job has been enlarged even if the same basic technique of using computer design software is utilised. The designer's supervisor would still secure the business, conduct meetings with the client and oversee the tasks, so there is no more responsibility. Job enlargement may add variety and alleviate boredom with mundane tasks but there may be limits to how much it might stimulate and satisfy the designer.

Job enlargement involves increasing task variety by combining into one job tasks of similar skill levels that were previously assigned to separate workers.

Job rotation

Job rotation involves increasing task variety by periodically shifting workers among jobs involving different tasks at similar levels of skill.

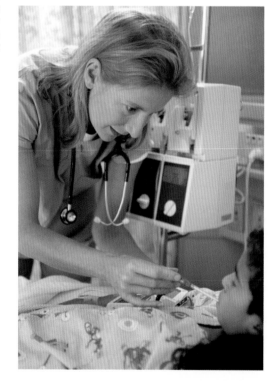

Like job enlargement, job rotation increases task variety but generally it does so by periodically shifting workers among jobs involving different tasks at similar skill levels. Job rotation can be arranged around almost any time period, such as hourly, daily or weekly schedules. For example, a nurse may be rotated on a monthly basis, looking after geriatric patients one month, surgical patients the next and rehabilitation patients each third month. However, as with job enlargement, the results have sometimes been disappointing. If a rotation cycle takes employees through a series of the same old jobs, the employees simply experience many boring jobs instead of just one. The nurse may still be doing the same repetitive tasks of checking pulses and taking blood pressure and temperatures in each ward. In different wards there may be different tasks such as checking and changing wound dressings or feeding patients in geriatrics, but overall the tasks may still seem routine.

While job rotation may decrease efficiency because people spend more time changing, it can add to workforce flexibility. Staff can be moved from one job to another and this is currently often the primary purpose of job rotation. Employers have a more adaptable workforce to accomplish work tasks when employees are on sick or recreation leave, or when they move from the organisation.

Perhaps the greatest weakness in the application of job rotation in the 1950s was that workers tended to be rotated horizontally (expanding the scope of the job) — that is, across tasks that demanded similar skill profiles. In other words, just as with enlargement, there was a horizontal loading of tasks, which means the breadth of the job is increased by the addition of a variety of tasks. Since the mid-1970s, job rotation has become an important part of work experience and corporate acculturation. New employees are often rotated

Horizontal loading involves increasing the breadth of a job by adding to the variety of tasks that the worker performs.

around the company and across different divisions to gain a better understanding of the corporate structure and corporate work and communication networks. At Robert Bosch Australia, a producer of automotive parts, new apprentices are taken through a program of planned job rotation after their initial basic training.[4] Job rotation can often involve vertical loading, which enables increasing job depth by adding responsibilities, like planning and controlling, that were previously held by supervisors. Such experience often contributes to employee development and helps overcome many limitations of the earlier approaches to job rotation. China, for example, has used rotation schemes to send employees from central urban locations into rural areas to keep in touch with the needs of rural communities.[5] Global companies in China such as Kone, Standard Chartered and Schering all offer job rotation as a feature of employment on their careers pages.[6] Vertical loading is a key aspect of job enrichment.

Vertical loading involves increasing job depth by adding responsibilities, like planning and controlling, previously held by supervisors.

Job enrichment

Frederick Herzberg, whose two-factor theory is discussed in chapter 3, suggests that it is illogical to expect high levels of motivation from employees whose jobs are designed according to the rules of simplification, enlargement or rotation (with horizontal loading). Herzberg asks, '[Why] should a worker become motivated when one or more "meaningless" tasks are added to previously existing ones or when work assignments are rotated among equally "meaningless" tasks?'[7] Rather than pursuing one of these job design strategies, Herzberg recommends that managers practise job enrichment.

Job enrichment is the practice of building motivating factors into job content. This job design strategy differs from the previous ones in that it seeks to expand job content by adding planning and evaluating duties (normally performed by the manager) to the employee's job. The changes that increase the 'depth' of a job involve vertical loading of the tasks, as opposed to the horizontal loading involved in job enlargement and much job rotation.

Job enrichment is the practice of building motivating factors into job content.

The seven principles guiding Herzberg's approach to job enrichment are listed in table 5.1. Each principle is an action guideline designed to increase the presence of one or more motivating factors. Remember, in the job enlargement and rotation strategies, managers tend to retain all responsibility for work planning and evaluating; in contrast, the job enrichment strategy involves vertical loading, which allows employees to share in these planning and evaluating responsibilities, as well as do the actual work.

Principle	Motivators involved
1. Remove some controls while retaining accountability	Responsibility and achievement
2. Increase the accountability of individuals for their own work	Responsibility and recognition
3. Give a person a complete natural unit of work (module, division, area and so on)	Responsibility, achievement and recognition
4. Grant additional authority to employees in their activities; provide job freedom	Responsibility, achievement and recognition
5. Make periodic reports directly available to the worker rather than to the supervisor	Recognition
6. Introduce new and more difficult tasks that the individual has not previously handled	Growth and learning
7. Assign to individuals specific or specialised tasks; enable them to become experts	Responsibility, achievement, recognition and advancement

TABLE 5.1 • Herzberg's principles of job enrichment

On the face of it, job enrichment seems appealing. However, it has some problems.

- Little, if any, diagnosis of the jobs is undertaken before they are redesigned.
- Cost–benefit data pertaining to job enrichment are not often reported and it may not always be worth it. Much of the time it is expensive to implement, especially if work flows need to be redesigned and facilities or equipment changed.
- Situational factors specifically supporting job enrichment have often not been systematically assessed.
- Many reports of the success of job enrichment have been evangelical in nature — that is, the authors overstate benefits and understate problems. There are few reported failures in the literature, possibly as a result of such bragging.
- Evaluations of job enrichment programs too often have not been conducted rigorously using the appropriate scientific method.
- Many trials of job enrichment have been undertaken with hand-picked employees, rather than a random sample of employees representing differing skill profiles and job environments.
- Job enrichment theory fails to recognise and emphasise that individuals may respond differently to job enrichment and that not all individuals will like it.
- Job enrichment falls into that category of workplace innovations that is much talked about but not widely practised. Despite the plethora of literature defining job enrichment, only a small number of case studies have actually been reported.[8]

The various strategies of job design are summarised on a continuum in figure 5.1. This figure shows how the strategies differ in their degree of task specialisation and as sources of intrinsic work rewards. The availability of intrinsic rewards is lowest for task attributes associated with simplified jobs, and highest for enriched jobs. Task specialisation is higher for simplified jobs and lower for enriched jobs.

The four basic approaches to job design (simplification, enlargement and rotation, and enrichment), as shown in figure 5.1, have provided vital insights into the complexity of effective job design. Collectively, they are an important platform for later theorists. However, the common factor underlying these approaches is that they are 'static'; that is, they assume that all individuals will respond in the same, positive manner to these approaches. They fail to recognise the 'dynamic' nature of individual behaviour — that workers can, and will, respond in a variety of ways to the implementation of any innovative job design approach. To be effective, a manager needs to be able to understand, identify and predict how an individual worker will respond to any job redesign approach.

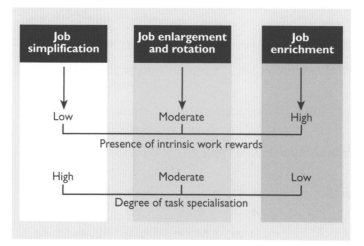

FIGURE 5.1 • A continuum of job design strategies

The job characteristics model

Pioneering work by Turner and Lawrence and Hulin and Blood in the 1960s began to look at the role of individual differences in job design.[9] They were trying to understand how an individual would respond to job redesign. That work led to the diagnostic approach — a technique developed by Richard Hackman and Greg Oldham, and which is the basis of their job characteristics model (sometimes abbreviated to JCM). This model addresses job design in a contingency fashion.[10] The diagnostic job design approach, which generated considerable research in the 1980s, recognises that there will be differences in the way any group of individuals responds to a change in the design of their jobs.

The current version of this newer approach to job enrichment, as depicted in Hackman and Oldham's **job characteristics model**, is shown in figure 5.2. Five core job characteristics are identified as task attributes of special importance in the diagnosis of job designs. A job that is high in these core characteristics is said to be enriched. The core job characteristics are:

1. *skill variety* — the degree to which the job requires an employee to undertake a variety of different activities and use different skills and talents
2. *task identity* — the degree to which the job requires completion of a 'whole' and identifiable piece of work (that is, it involves doing a job from beginning to end with a visible outcome)
3. *task significance* — the degree to which the job is important and involves a meaningful contribution to the organisation or society in general
4. *autonomy* — the degree to which the job gives the employee substantial freedom, independence and discretion in scheduling the work and determining the procedures used in carrying it out
5. *job feedback* — the degree to which carrying out the work activities results in the employee obtaining direct and clear information on how well the job has been done.

Hackman and Oldham state further that three critical psychological states must be realised for people to develop intrinsic work motivation. These are:
- experienced meaningfulness in the work
- experienced responsibility for the outcomes of the work
- knowledge of actual results of the work activities.

These psychological states represent intrinsic rewards that are believed to occur and to influence later performance and satisfaction when the core job characteristics are present in the job design.

> The **job characteristics model** identifies five core characteristics (skill variety, task identity, task significance, autonomy and job feedback) as having special importance to job designs.

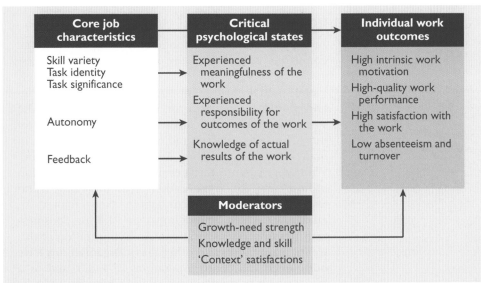

FIGURE 5.2 • Core job characteristics and individual work outcomes

Source: Adapted from J Richard Hackman and Greg R Oldham, 'Development of the job diagnostic survey', *Journal of Applied Psychology*, vol. 60 (1975), p. 161.

Individual differences: moderators of the job characteristics model

The job characteristics model recognises that the five core job characteristics do not affect all people in the same way. Unlike many earlier theories of job design, the job characteristics model recognises individual differences in response to changes in job design. A number of factors will influence the manner in which any individual employee responds to changes in the design of his or her job. These factors are called 'job design moderators'. Figure 5.2 shows three important individual difference moderators.

- *Growth-need strength.* This is the degree to which a person desires the opportunity for self-direction, learning and personal accomplishment at work. It is similar to Maslow's esteem and self-actualisation and Alderfer's growth needs. The theory predicts that people strong in growth-need will respond positively to enriched jobs, experiencing high internal motivation, high growth satisfaction, high-quality performance and low absenteeism and turnover. On the other hand, people low in growth-need strength will have negative reactions and will find enriched jobs a source of anxiety. They are likely to be at risk of being 'overstretched' in the job and possibly baulking at doing the job.[11]
- *Knowledge and skill.* Those with the knowledge and skill needed for performance in an enriched job are predicted to respond positively to the enrichment. Once again, we see how important a sense of competency or self-efficacy can be to people at work.
- *Context satisfaction.* This is the extent to which an employee is satisfied with the kind of contextual factors emphasised by Herzberg. For example, those satisfied with salary levels, supervision and working conditions are more likely than their dissatisfied colleagues to support job enrichment.

This list of moderators of the work outcome relationship of the job characteristics model is not intended to be exhaustive, because many other variables (such as high-order needs and workers' value systems) have also been examined as potential moderators of reactions to these job dimensions.[12] In general, people whose capabilities match the requirements of an enriched job are likely to experience positive feelings and to perform well; people who are inadequate or who feel inadequate in this regard are likely to have difficulties.

The following 'International spotlight' looks at the increasing importance of having jobs that will attract and retain talented global workers.

International
SPOTLIGHT

Attracting and retaining talented global workers

Increasing levels of globalisation involving international companies and markets are now part of the business world we operate in. Workers are also increasingly mobile, and there are skills shortages in many countries and global competition for knowledge workers. The so-called 'brain drain' has caused major shortages of information technology and e-business professionals in many countries, including Australia and New Zealand. With other labour shortages such as in the construction industry and skilled trades there is an increasing trend towards importing foreign labour (see chapter 3), attracting skilled immigrants or shifting business activities to overseas locations. As an illustration of this trend, many banks and other major organisations have outsourced call centre operations to India, and to a lesser extent to the Philippines and China.[13]

There can be considerable incentives for mobile workers to move to where the best jobs can be found — there is often competition between countries for the best workers. For example, proposed reductions in Australian tax rates in 2005 caused an immediate concern in New Zealand that there would be an increase in the 'brain drain' to Australia.[14] Other countries, including Australia, have also been concerned that their best and most talented workers move from the country to other, more attractive work.

Attracting 'talent' and retaining good employees, as is widely discussed in contemporary business literature, is important to organisations. In this context job design is important. Knowledge-based economies can contribute towards changing job designs so that organisations can offer jobs that will attract the most talented workers. These workers are often highly qualified and can afford to seek out jobs that offer them meaning, responsibility and opportunities for personal advancement and improvement. For the organisation that invests in these employees it is important to be sure that the job offered is sufficiently enriched, satisfying and motivating to retain the employees into the future, though this cannot be guaranteed as talented workers may continue to seek new opportunities. For example, president of ANZ China Andrew McGregor says that the bank's really good people are headhunted at least weekly. At ANZ China (in locations such as Shanghai), many Chinese workers have gained 'Western' experience in the bank. In order to retain these workers, he tries to promote exchanges with Australian bank workers to enhance their global experience. In the context of mobile global workers there will also be a need to consider cultural differences for workers from different backgrounds in any job placement or design. McGregor, for example, has found that, while his Chinese workers adapt to less hierarchical organisational structures, it is difficult to foster feedback and open discussion with them because of their respect for people in higher positions.[15]

Testing and the motivating potential score

Hackman and Oldham developed the job diagnostic survey questionnaire to test each of the dimensions in their job characteristics model, as shown in figure 5.2. They also developed a motivating potential score (MPS) to summarise a job's overall potential for motivating those in the workplace. You can calculate this score using the following formula:

$$MPS = (variety + identity + significance)/3 \times autonomy \times feedback$$

The scores for each of the dimensions come from the job diagnostic survey and show the great importance of autonomy and feedback in providing the results shown in figure 5.2. The MPS is especially useful for identifying low-scoring jobs that may benefit most from redesign.

A job diagnostic survey is a questionnaire used to examine each of the dimensions of the job characteristics model.

A motivating potential score is a summary of a job's overall potential for motivating those in the workplace.

The research

Considerable research has been done on the job characteristics approach. The approach has been examined in a variety of work settings, including banks, dentists' offices, corrective services departments, telephone companies, and such organisations as IBM and Texas Instruments. Job-design studies using this approach have also been reported in Australia.[16] A comprehensive review of the approach shows that:[17]

- on average, job characteristics affect performance, but not nearly as much as they affect satisfaction
- it is important to consider growth-need strength. Job characteristics influence performance more strongly for high growth-need employees than for low growth-need employees. The relationship to growth-need is about as strong as that to job satisfaction.

- employee perceptions of job characteristics are different from objective measures and from those of independent observers. Positive results are typically strongest when an overall performance measure is used, rather than a separate measure of quality or quantity.

'The effective manager 5.1' summarises some guidelines for implementing a job enrichment program and for reviewing the process.

Guidelines for implementing a program of job enrichment

Consider a job to be a candidate for job enrichment only when evidence exists that job satisfaction and/or performance is either deteriorating or open for improvement. Use a diagnostic approach and proceed with actual job enrichment only when:
- employees view their jobs as deficient in one or more of the core job characteristics
- extrinsic rewards and job context are not causing dissatisfaction
- cost and other potential constraints do not prohibit job design changes necessary for enrichment
- employees view core job characteristics positively
- employees have needs and capabilities consistent with new job designs.

Whenever possible, conduct a careful evaluation of the results of job enrichment to discontinue the job design strategy (if necessary) or to make constructive changes to increase its value. Expect that enrichment will also affect the job of the supervising manager, because duties will be delegated. Do not feel threatened or become anxious or frustrated. If needed, get help for required personal work adjustments.

Experts generally agree that the job diagnostic approach that is the basis for Hackman and Oldham's job characteristics model is useful. A series of implementation concepts for the enrichment of core job characteristics is outlined in figure 5.3 and some impacts of enriching core job characteristics are listed in table 5.2. However, these experts urge caution in applying the technique, emphasising that it is not a universal panacea for job performance and satisfaction problems. It can fail when job requirements are increased beyond the level of individual capabilities and/or interest. It can also raise issues of changes in remuneration — if employees are taking on more responsibility, should they be paid more? In summary, jobs high in core characteristics (especially as perceived by employees) tend to increase both satisfaction and performance, particularly among high growth-need employees. The following 'Counterpoint' looks at how job enrichment may overtax employees and increase the imbalance between the working and personal lives of employees (work–life balance is also discussed further under flexible work arrangements later in the chapter).

FIGURE 5.3 • Implementation concepts and the core job characteristics

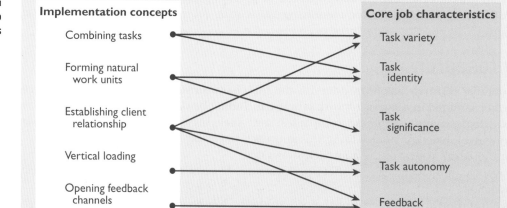

Source: Derived from J Richard Hackman, Greg Oldham, Robert Janson and Kenneth Purdy, 'A new strategy for job enrichment', *California Management Review*, vol. 17, no. 4 (1975), p. 62.

	Enriched	Unenriched
Skill variety	Decided own strategy for performing task and changed strategy at will	Were provided with explicit instructions for task to perform and strategy to use (e.g. 'first, open letters')
Task identity	Formed into groups of ten; performed all necessary operations on a certain proportion of customer requests	As an individual, performed just one of these operations on all requests
Task significance	Were briefed about importance of their jobs and how they fitted into the organisation as a whole	Received no formal instruction
Autonomy	Chose length and timing of breaks. Performed own inspections at intervals they determined	Except for breaks, stayed at workplace throughout the day. Had work periodically checked by inspectors
Feedback	Saw productivity posted on scoreboards at end of each day	Received no specific information about performance level

TABLE 5.2 • Sample core job characteristics for enriched and unenriched jobs

COUNTER**POINT**

Enrichment and work–life balance in the 'real world'

The notion of job design and job enrichment transforming the working lives of people is commendable. However, in reality there are much more complicated factors involved and the job experience for many people, while perhaps more stimulating, challenging and satisfying, may also be much more stressful and difficult.

The suggestions for job enrichment in table 5.2 look very reasonable. The opportunity for developing more skills, for completing more parts of the task, for having autonomy and feedback and viewing your job as significant in the organisation are commendable. Many people are experiencing enriched jobs in many organisations. More skills are acquired and required to do the job. Jobs are less routine and more autonomous and people take responsibility for much of their own work. They are often given a sense of identity with the task and feel their work is significant. But how does this fit into the real world of longer working hours and pressures for balance between work and home?

While endeavouring to improve jobs on the one hand, it would appear that organisations can also be major contributors to making individual workers' lives very difficult. In many countries people are being required to work longer hours. One survey by APM Training Institute in Australia illustrates this very clearly. It shows that our young graduates who may aspire to rewarding jobs appear to be unprepared for the 'real world' that will confront them. The survey found that 58 per cent of employers expected graduates to work up to 50 hours a week. These employers see overtime as a part of the job and only 8 per cent would pay extra wages. The graduates from school, college and university did not expect to work these hours. For example, only 45 per cent of those from university expected to work these hours and, of these, 78 per cent expected additional pay for the work.[18]

(continued)

While companies might talk actively about enriched jobs and work–life balance, we need to take some stock of how these changes really affect people. Given more responsibility in enriched jobs, many people will worker harder to do what is required of the job, even when it involves working longer hours. Another study conducted by the Voice Project team at Macquarie University found that work–life balance became an issue of concern for employees when they started to work more than about 50 hours a week. It also found that increasing hours to in excess of 15 hours overtime a week was linked to reduced feelings of wellness and ability to handle work with acceptable levels of stress. However, increasing hours were also linked to increasing employee consultation, involvement in decision making, career opportunities and awareness of organisational direction. On this point the study concludes that when there is some 'say' in their work and a desire for career success, workers may be more prepared to work long hours and sacrifice some balance between their work and lives.[19]

Questions

1. How and why would an enriched job cause an employee to work longer hours?
2. What responsibility do managers have to ensure their employees do not work excessive hours and experience excessive stress?
3. Is there any value in organisations providing flexible work arrangements if, at the same time, they are encouraging employees (intentionally or unintentionally) to work longer hours? Explain.

Socio-technical job design

Socio-technical job design is the design of jobs to optimise the relationship between the technology system and the social system.

Technology can sometimes constrain the ability to enrich jobs. Socio-technical job design recognises this problem and seeks to optimise the relationship between the technology system and the social system. This is achieved by designing work roles to integrate with the technology system. Best known is the semi-autonomous work group approach, by which self-managed or autonomous work teams perform a job previously done on the assembly line (these teams are discussed in chapter 7).

Because it is difficult and costly to modify technology in an existing plant, and to change work practices and job design across the entire organisation, the socio-technical approach often works more effectively in a 'greenfield' site (that is, a new site with no established work practices).

Over the past decade some managers have begun to question the costs of maintaining and developing this socio-technical approach in some plants because of the rising costs associated with rapid knowledge obsolescence and multiskilling the workforce. However, this is not always a problem, or organisations can take action to minimise this effect. For example, while Boeing has different cockpits on its different aircraft, Airbus's strategy is to have the same cockpit on all the models in its fleet. This means that pilots require much less re-skilling when they move between different aircraft models. More research on the costs and benefits of the approach in contemporary environments, and of strategies to minimise problems, is needed to address such criticisms.

Social information and job design

The **social information-processing approach** argues that individual needs, task perceptions and reactions are a result of socially constructed realities.

Gerald Salancik and Jeffrey Pfeffer have reviewed the literature on the job diagnostic approach to job design.[20] They question whether jobs have stable and objective characteristics that individuals perceive and to which they respond predictably and consistently. As an alternative, their social information-processing approach argues that individual needs, task perceptions and reactions are a result of socially constructed realities. Thus, social information in the workplace influences workers' perceptions of the job and their responses to it.

It is much like a student's perception of a class. Several of the student's friends may tell her that the lecturer is bad, the content is boring and the class requires too much work. The student may then think that the critical characteristics of the class are the lecturer, the content and the workload, and that they are all bad. All of this may take place before the student has even set foot in that class, and may substantially influence the student's class perception and response, regardless of the characteristics in the job characteristics approach.

Research on the social information-processing approach provides mixed results. Essentially, the results show that social information processing does influence task perceptions and attitudes, but the kinds of job characteristics described earlier remain very important.

Multiskilling

Multiskilling programs help employees become members of a flexible workforce and acquire an array of skills needed to perform multiple tasks in a company's production or customer service process. The cross-training and multiskilling of employees allow them to assume broader responsibilities so they are better equipped to solve problems. When a team member is absent, there is always someone who can take over the role. When suggestions for process improvements are required, members of the team have the requisite skills and expertise to make highly valued contributions. The 'operational cells' in the example below illustrate this.

Multiskilling helps employees acquire an array of skills needed to perform the multiple tasks in an organisational production or customer service process.

OB in action

The Australian Defence Force recently collaborated with Manpower to form Defence Force Recruiting (DFR). DFR was established to outsource the recruiting function from the army, the navy and the air force. Within DFR, workers (including workers from Manpower and the three services) perform their functions in units called operational cells. Within these, staff are coached and mentored to operate in a range of roles and functions. In the unit they become 'all rounders' who can easily be retrained and/or redeployed. This also gives the units the capacity to be flexible and responsive in any situation. Emphasis is not on 'roles' such as major or corporal, as might be expected in the army, for example, but rather on what the group is doing. Focus is also on participating in the work, work flow and reward systems instead of on hierarchical reporting, representation and strategy.[21]

Multiskilling is an innovative work practice that has helped improve organisational performance by 30 to 40 per cent in some cases. Strong links between a multiskilled workforce and improved productivity have been identified. More recently, the skills matrix has been used to measure employees' skill levels and compare them to the desired levels, which are often an upward moving target.

Overall, employees in a flexible workforce benefit from having a challenging and varied work experience, more control over their work environment, higher skill levels, higher pay opportunities and greater marketability in the job market.

Goal-setting theory

For any employee a reasonable question to ask the employer is: 'What is it you want me to do?' Without clear and appropriate goals, employees may suffer a direction problem and be unable to channel their work energies towards the right goal. The case of 'Sarah' illustrates this.

> Sarah (whose name has been changed) sought help from New Zealand coaching company Blue Chip because she was having trouble getting results from some of her teams whose job it was to implement projects. After personal coaching and analysis of the problem, Sarah came to realise that it was her own lack of confidence about some jobs that was being reflected in her teams' performance. When she knew what the job was about she was able to communicate requirements confidently to her team. However, when she was out of her depth with a project, and not confident that she could deliver, she failed to find out from the client enough about the project to clarify her understanding because she did not want to appear ignorant. When this happened she became stressed and could not inspire her team to achieve the task well. However, once she identified the problem and learnt how to handle it, Sarah was able to stop, ask the right questions of the client and then retain her focus on the task. This allowed her to clarify goals and task requirements and confidently lead and direct her teams to success.[22]

Similar problems are found in many work settings. Proper setting and clarification of task goals can eliminate, or at least reduce, these and other problems. Goal setting involves building challenging and specific goals into jobs and providing appropriate performance feedback.

Goal setting is the 'process of developing, negotiating and formalising the targets or objectives that an employee is responsible for accomplishing'.[23] Expanding job design to include goal setting results in specific task goals for each individual. These task goals are important because they have a link with task performance. Over a number of years, Edwin Locke developed a set of arguments and predictions concerning this link. This set of predictions serves as the basis for goal-setting theory. Locke's research, and that of others, provides considerable support for the following predictions.[24]

Goal setting is the process of developing, negotiating and formalising an employee's targets and objectives.

1. *Difficult goals are more likely to lead to higher performance than are less difficult ones* because they encourage effort that leads to greater outcomes. However, if the goals are seen as too difficult or as impossible, the relationship with performance no longer holds. An individual is likely to cease trying if the goal is unattainable.
2. *Specific goals are more likely to lead to higher performance than are no goals or vague or general ones.* Setting a specific goal of selling ten refrigerators a month should lead to better performance than a simple 'do your best' goal.
3. *Task feedback, or knowledge of results, is likely to motivate people towards higher performance by encouraging the setting of higher performance goals.* Feedback lets people know where they

stand and if they are on or off course in their efforts; for example, think about how eager you are to find out how well you have done in an examination.

4. *Goals are most likely to lead to higher performance when people have the abilities and the feelings of self-efficacy required to accomplish them.* Individuals must believe that they are able to accomplish the goals and feel confident in their abilities.

5. *Goals are most likely to motivate people towards higher performance when they are accepted and there is commitment to them.* One way of achieving such acceptance or commitment is by participating in the goal-setting process. You then feel a sense of 'ownership' of the goals. However, Locke and Latham report that goals assigned by someone else can be equally effective. The assigners are likely to be influential authority figures. Also, the assignment implies that the employee can actually reach the goal. Third, assigned goals are often a challenge. Finally, assigned goals help define the standards people use to attain personal satisfaction with their performance.[25] According to Locke and Latham, assigned goals only lead to poor performance when they are curtly or inadequately explained.[26]

Goal setting: follow-up research

Research using and extending the five predictions discussed is now quite extensive. Indeed, there is more research for goal setting than for any other theory related to work motivation.[27] Nearly 400 studies have been conducted in several countries, including Australia, the United Kingdom, Germany, Japan and the United States.[28] Locke and Latham and their associates have been at the forefront of this work, and have recently integrated their predictions into a more comprehensive framework that links goals to performance. We show a simplified version of the Locke and Latham framework in figure 5.4.

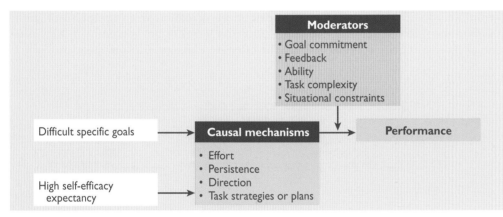

FIGURE 5.4 • Simplified Locke and Latham goal-setting framework
Source: Adapted from Edwin A Locke and Gary P Latham, 'Work motivation and satisfaction: light at the end of the tunnel', *Psychological Science*, vol. 1, no. 4 (July 1990), p. 244. Reprinted by permission of Blackwell Publishers.

Starting at the left we see the difficult, specific goals mentioned earlier in predictions 1 and 2. These are joined by high self-efficacy (mentioned in prediction 4 and emphasised in chapters 3 and 4) and high expectancy (discussed as a part of expectancy motivation theory in chapter 3). The argument is that these factors operate through the linking mechanisms of effort, persistence, direction, and task strategies or plans to affect performance. At the same time, the moderators of goal commitment (prediction 5), feedback (prediction 3), ability (prediction 4), task complexity and situational constraints also operate to strengthen or weaken the relationship between goals and performance.

Locke's predictions concerning goal setting are still relevant. However, they have now been embedded in the simplified framework in figure 5.4. That framework includes some ideas discussed in the motivation chapter and relates to concepts from expectancy theory, as shown in our discussion in the previous paragraph of the role of expectancy and self-efficacy.

Further, while our simplified framework does not show it, Locke and Latham argue that the instrumentality concept from expectancy theory (that is, that performance leads to rewards) operates through the link between challenging goals and valued rewards.[29] Again, the basic tenets of expectancy theory prove useful in explaining work behaviour. This relationship has sometimes led to the treatment of goal-setting theory as a process motivation theory, in addition to the equity and expectancy theories discussed in chapter 3. Further, the task-complexity notion discussed earlier suggests a link with job enrichment. As more enrichment is built into a job, the job becomes more complex and probably calls for new task strategies or plans. Finally, Locke's fourth prediction links goal-setting theory with ability as an individual attribute and with self-efficacy, which is so important in social learning theory.[30]

Goal setting and MBO

When we speak of goal setting and its potential to influence individual performance at work, the concept of management by objectives (MBO) immediately comes to mind. This approach has been widely used in many large organisations in both the public and private sectors.[31] In Australia and New Zealand many senior executives employed within the public service have performance-based contracts that identify clear goal-achievement milestones for each year.

MBO involves managers working with their employees to establish performance goals and plans that are consistent with higher-level work unit and organisational objectives.[32] When this process is followed throughout an organisation, MBO helps to clarify the hierarchy of objectives as a series of well-defined means–end chains.

Figure 5.5 shows a comprehensive view of MBO. The concept is consistent with the notion of goal setting and its associated principles (as already discussed). Notice how joint supervisor–employee discussions are designed to extend participation from the point of initial goal establishment to the point of evaluating results in terms of goal attainment. Key issues for mutual goal setting are summarised in 'The effective manager 5.2' on page 165.[33]

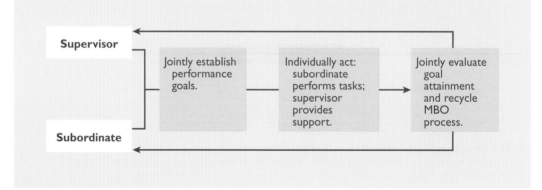

FIGURE 5.5 • The management-by-objectives (MBO) process

In addition to the goal-setting steps previously discussed, a successful MBO system calls for careful implementation. This means that the previous steps are translated into the kinds of strategies or plans, mentioned earlier, that will lead to goal accomplishment. Employees must have freedom to carry out the required tasks; managers may have to do considerable coaching and counselling. As with other applied organisational behaviour programs, managers should be aware of MBO's potential costs as well as its benefits.

Despite substantial research based on case studies of MBO success, such research has not always been rigorously controlled and it reports mixed results.[34] In general, and as an application of goal-setting theory, MBO has much to offer. But it is not easy to start and keep going. MBO may also need to be implemented organisation-wide if it is to work well.[35]

Key issues for mutual goal setting in an MBO program

- What must be done? Start with higher-level goals, job descriptions stating tasks to be performed, outcomes expected, necessary supplies and equipment, and so on.
- How will performance be measured? Time, money or physical units may often be used to measure performance. If the job is more subjective, emphasise behaviours or actions believed to lead to success.
- What is the performance standard? Start with previous performance or the average performance of others doing this job. Where these measures do not exist, use mutual supervisor–subordinate judgement and discussion.
- What are the deadlines for the goals? Discuss deadlines in terms of daily, weekly or longer terms.
- What is the relative importance of the goals? Not all goals are equally important. The manager and employee should decide the goal ranking together.
- How difficult are the goals? Watch especially for high task complexity and multiple goals. Come up with a clearly agreed decision.

Key performance indicators

The concept of individual goal setting has been further developed over the past few years to introduce the concept of key performance indicators (KPIs) — standards against which individual and organisational performance can be measured.

Such measurement is a step in the benchmarking process taken by companies wanting to achieve superior performance in a formal and structured way. In the annual Australian Quality Awards for Business Excellence, high performance has been linked to improved business performance, which has been strongly associated with improvements in recognising and using an organisation's key performance indicators.[36] Similar programs exist in New Zealand and other countries.

The use of such indicators in employee remuneration packages has been popular.[37] Using performance appraisals, an employee's pay is structured according to their achievement of individual key performance indicators that cascade down from organisational ones. The individual's contribution to the organisation can thus be measured, because the indicators provide a benchmark against which an employee can be judged. The use of performance appraisals holds employees accountable for their achievements. For example, in New Zealand, dairy company Fonterra makes use of its KPIs in annual incentive plans for employees. The KPIs include net profit after tax, milk payout, economic profit, organic growth, working capital efficiency, new product development and people development.[38]

A key performance indicator must therefore be Specific, Measurable, Achievable, Realistic and Time-framed (SMART).[39] It depends on the nature of the employee's job, the industry in which the employee works, the strategic direction and goals of the company, and the bottom line of the organisation.

The common use of key performance indicators to measure quantifiable targets also extends to qualitative issues, such as staff initiative and communication skills. For example, the Australian National Maritime Museum's KPIs include quantitative targets, such as number of visitor interactions, as well as qualitative ones, such as reputation (assessed by focus groups).[40]

Key performance indicators are standards against which individual and organisational performance can be measured.

Flexible work arrangements

Attempting to enhance worker satisfaction through job redesign involves mostly intrinsic factors relating to *doing the job*. Worker satisfaction (as well as avoidance of dissatisfaction) can

LEARNING OBJECTIVE 5 ✓ Flexible work arrangements

also be achieved by changing job conditions, such as the timing or number of working hours and work location. For example, the employee may experience a more acceptable working environment (extrinsic change) if working hours are flexible enough to allow the achievement of other (personal) goals. This, in turn, may affect the employee's levels of work motivation and performance (intrinsic changes), because they are more satisfied with their job environment. The key drivers and practices of flexible work arrangements are now presented.

Major drivers of changing work arrangements

In 2005 Access Economics, in conjunction with the Australian Computer Society, recommended that employers support flexible work arrangements such as teleworking, job sharing, part-time work and parental leave arrangements.[41] Organisations that utilise flexible strategies in the workforce have the potential to reap many benefits including:
- higher retention of staff and thus higher retention of organisational knowledge
- less absenteeism
- more capacity to meet peak demand and more capacity to service client demands outside normal hours
- more contented, productive, committed and motivated employees
- more diverse and qualified workforces.[42]

Flexible work practices can assist individual workers to deal with their work in the context of the following drivers.

Changing family lifestyles and work–life balance

The prevalence of households where both partners are working (dual-income families) and the rising number of one-parent families, along with increasing hours worked, exacerbate the problems of balancing work and life pressures. Substantial benefits can be gained for both employees and employers in considering the work–life balance for workers in very many different ways, as the following examples show.

OB in action

> The EEO Trust's 2005 Work & Life Awards (large organisation) New Zealand winner was Vector, one of the country's largest network infrastructure companies. With 300 people and a 24/7 business, the CEO Mark Franklin says people do their best work when they have the freedom to be able to take care of other important issues in their lives. The business offers flexible work hours, teleworking, generous leave and loans for unexpected hardships. The winner of the First Steps award was Harrison Grierson, which provides engineering, planning and surveying services. In its New Zealand and Australian offices, this business employs 300 people. The company works on its supportive workplace culture and offers a range of flexible working options and generous sick leave to its diverse workforce. It also has sports teams, social clubs, discounted medical insurance and a range of health initiatives such as free cholesterol checks and stress management seminars.[43]
>
> Even simple measures can reduce the pressures on staff as they struggle to fulfil personal and work goals in the limited time available to them. For example, car parts manufacturer Autoliv has set up a prayer room in its workplace to assist its many Muslim workers to participate in necessary religious activities.[44]

Occupational stress

With the emphasis on cost cutting and downsizing that has prevailed over the past two decades, employees in many organisations are expected to 'do more with less'. Employment models in most organisations operate on the basis that most employees are working standard hours (around 35–40 hours per week) and have standard working conditions.

However, such models are increasingly inappropriate. Research shows that, although one-third of the Australian labour force still, formally, works standard hours, the majority of full-time workers work extended hours (often without extra pay).[45] The real working conditions of so many employees, with increased pressure to work harder and longer, are associated with rising levels of work stress and burnout. Some organisations are responding by offering extended breaks from the workplace, such as sabbatical leave, to help employees cope more effectively.[46]

Changing levels and modes of employment

Throughout the 1980s and into the 1990s, rising levels of unemployment dominated and impacted on work security and workload. More recently, unemployment figures have stabilised or decreased (though there is some dispute about the way in which figures are measured). For example, in New Zealand in March 2003 there was a fall of 1.3 per cent in unemployment from the previous year.[47] However, the shift from traditional full-time permanent to casual or part-time jobs has been substantial in some countries, as has been an increase in the number of fixed-term contracted positions. About 25 per cent of the Australian labour force can be classified as working part-time. The following 'Ethical perspective' examines conditions for casual workers, whose needs are not normally as well 'looked after' as are those of permanent full-time workers.

ETHICAL
Perspective

Who will look after the casual workers?

While much is done in relation to increasing workplace flexibility for permanent employees of organisations, little is said about the situation in which casual workers find themselves. Some people have particular reasons for preferring casual work, but for many, being part of the 'irregular workforce' (as they have been labelled)[48] means their work is 'precarious'.[49] While they may receive higher wages per hour than their permanent counterparts, they do not get extra benefits, such as annual and sick leave. They have predominantly poorer conditions in terms of job variety, access to training, the chance of 'having a say' on organisational issues and of being consulted about workplace change. They have uncertain jobs, and cannot normally rely on regular hours or a regular income. They have lower than average earnings and lack access to workplace benefits such as career paths and work arrangements that enable them to balance family and work. They have been found to return less to the business because of the nature of their employment, and generally to have lower skill levels, commitment, efficiency and quality of service, and increased long-term costs.[50] So the increasing casualisation of the workforce means that this particular cohort not only misses out on the advantages to be gained by regular and reliable employment, but also on some of the flexible conditions that enhance a worker's life. While many casual workers may be younger people[51] who have fewer family and other commitments, we should still be concerned about the work–life imbalance and workplace stress that casual workers generally may experience in our workforce.

Ageing population and changing retirement patterns

The population is ageing and this means increasing pressure on social services, so flexible work options are being explored to retain the productive skills of many older workers while simultaneously offering them a new balance between work and lifestyle. In Australia, the proportion of people aged 65 and over will increase from 13 per cent (in 2002) to between 27 and 30 per cent in 2051.[52] Many corporations are examining retirement phasing schemes through which admission to full retirement is staggered across a number of years, rather than occurring abruptly at a certain age.[53] It will be critical to retain as many older employees as possible in the workforce especially as, proportionally, the pools of younger applicants will be decreasing.

Offering them part-time work, phased retirement or contracted work will also help to retain older workers.[54] Organisations such as Australia Post and Aurora Energy are developing age management approaches,[55] as are many other organisations. Westpac and the New Zealand public sector have strategies underway, as the following examples illustrate.

OB in action

Westpac announced in 2002 that over a three-year period it would actively seek to hire people over 45 years. Thirty per cent of these workers were recruited into its call centres. They were much older than the call-centre industry average, so the bank conducted age balance training to assist in intergenerational interaction among workers. The bank also gained commercial benefits from its strategy, one of the main reasons being that the older call-centre workers corresponded in age with many of the centre's customers. Many older customers felt that an advisor with life experience was more able to relate to the caller's situation, resulting in improved customer experiences.[56]

As part of New Zealand's Positive Ageing Strategy, government agencies are involved in various programs. Archives New Zealand is developing more family-friendly policies through its human resources section. The aim is to have a family-friendly policy that is appropriate for all staff, to eliminate ageism and to promote flexible work options. Inland Revenue is focusing on a retention strategy to encourage older workers to stay in the workforce and also on leadership through mentoring, with a program being introduced to encourage older workers to act as mentors. It aims to eliminate ageism and to promote flexible work options. The State Services Commission is working to ensure older workers in the public service have choices to continue their working lives in ways that are adapted to their situation as they age.[57]

Changing technology and the capacity to work remotely

Information technology enables many changes to the way in which work is organised and located. Work can often be location independent, and often there is no need for the employee and the employer to meet regularly. Teleworking and working remotely from the office have been extensively discussed over many years[58] and, despite a slow take-up, have been increasing in popularity.

Types of flexible work arrangements

Some of the important work options to emerge from the trends already outlined include a compressed work week, flexitime or flexiyears, job-sharing, V-time and teleworking or working remotely. Nearly all these options are designed to influence employee satisfaction and to serve as both extrinsic and intrinsic motivating devices by helping employees to balance the demands of their working and non-working lives. In our fast-changing society these arrangements are becoming more important as a way of dealing with our increasingly diverse workforce.

The compressed work week

A **compressed work week** is any scheduling of work that allows a full-time job to be completed in fewer than the standard five days. The most common form of compressed work week is the 'four–forty'; that is, forty hours of work accomplished in four ten-hour days. Added time off is a major feature for the worker. The individual often benefits from increased leisure time, more three-day weekends, free week days to pursue personal business, and lower commuting costs. The organisation can benefit, too, through reduced energy consumption during three-day shutdowns, lower employee absenteeism, improved recruiting of new employees, and the extra time available for building and equipment maintenance, though results are inconsistent.[59]

A **compressed work week** is any scheduling of work that allows a full-time job to be completed in fewer than the standard five days.

The potential disadvantages of the compressed work week include increased fatigue from the extended work day and family adjustment problems for the individual; and for the organisation, increased work scheduling problems and possible customer complaints due to breaks in work coverage. Possible constraints on the use of compressed work week schedules include union opposition and laws that require some organisations to pay overtime for work that exceeds eight hours of individual labour in any one day. Proposed legislation to increase the accepted 'normal' hours of work may enhance employers' capacity to expand compressed working week strategies in Australia. One study found that reaction to the compressed work week was most favourable among employees who had participated in the decision to compress the work week, who had had their jobs enriched as a result of the new schedule, and who had strong higher-order needs. The enrichment occurred because fewer employees were on duty at any one time and job duties were changed and enriched to accommodate this reduction.[60] A further interesting finding is employees' reluctance to once more seek employment under the typical standard-hours model of five days/40 hours once they have experienced the lifestyle changes associated with a compressed work week.[61]

Flexible working hours or flexiyears

Flexible working hours (flexitime) is defined as 'any work schedule that gives employees daily choice in the timing of work and non-work activities'.[62] Flexitime is perhaps the most widely adopted work option in Western economies such as Australia, though data on it is not always clear. In November 2003, 34 per cent of workers did not have fixed start and finish times but, of these, 11.5 per cent were not able to choose their times. For those who did have fixed start and finish times some were, and some were not, negotiated with the employer. Those with flexibility, therefore, may number just 22 per cent, with 24 per cent of full-time workers and 19 per cent of part-time workers having freedom to choose their own start and finish times.[63] The potential advantages are listed in figure 5.6.

> **Flexible working hours (flexitime)** is any work schedule that gives employees daily choice in the timing of work and non-work activities.

Organisational benefits	Individual benefits
Lower absenteeism	More time for leisure and personal business, e.g. dentist, bank and better timing of commuting
Reduced tardiness	Less commuting time
Reduced turnover	Higher job satisfaction
Higher work commitment	Greater sense of responsibility
Higher performance	Easier personal scheduling

FIGURE 5.6 • Organisational and individual benefits of flexible working hours

Proponents of this scheduling strategy argue that the discretion it allows workers in scheduling their own hours of work encourages them to develop positive attitudes and increased commitment to the organisation. Research tends to support this position.[64] The growing demand for working hours flexibility in the Australian workplace is clearly reflected in a recent survey of a cross-section of 200 Australian organisations including small, large and multinational companies. The survey found that flexitime, rostered days off and paid overtime would be critical 'pull factors' in attracting people to jobs. It also found that 50 per cent of the companies surveyed had implemented a flexitime system for employees, 47 per cent offered rostered days off to employees, and 54 per cent offered paid overtime.[65]

In Austria and Germany several firms have considered the possibility of a **flexiyear** or **annual hours** model of employment. Workers decide on the number of hours they want to work in the coming year, then can allocate them as they see fit. Their pay is equalised each month, but their hours can vary.[66] Such a system can reduce the need for overtime, match staff to fluctuating workloads such as those caused by seasonal demand, can reduce

> **Flexiyear** or **annual hours** is a system whereby total agreed annual hours are allocated by workers as they see fit.

absenteeism since options for taking time off are available, and can remove the need for bringing in casual staff.[67]

Job sharing

Another work-setting alternative is job sharing, whereby one full-time job is assigned to two or more people, who then divide the work according to agreements made between or among themselves and with the employer.[68] Under this scheme a job can be 'shared', which may require a high degree of coordination and communication between the job-sharing partners, or it may be 'split', which requires little cooperative interaction and coordination. Some jobs require a careful job-sharing approach, whereas in other cases a job split approach can work effectively. Work options such as job sharing and permanent part-time help facilitate better balance between work and family responsibilities. Job sharing often entails each person working half a day, although it may also be a weekly or monthly arrangement.

Job sharing has a lot to offer for the creation of a 'family-friendly workplace'. Organisations benefit from job sharing when they are able to attract talented people who would otherwise be unable to work. An example is the qualified teacher who also is a parent. Some teachers cannot be away from the home a full day but are able to work half a day. Through job sharing, two staff members can be employed to teach one class. Many other opportunities for job sharing exist.

Some job sharers report less burnout and claim they feel recharged each time they report for work. Finding the right partnerships is very important, however, because the 'sharers' must work well with each other.[69]

Reduced working hours and voluntary reduced work time (V-Time)

Voluntary reduced work time, or V-Time, is also known as time–income tradeoffs. Proposed by Fred Best[70] in 1979, it was considered that work sharing could be achieved through encouraging employees to trade either current or future work and income for leisure on a voluntary basis by packaging leisure in a way that best suited the needs of an individual. In a bid to reduce unemployment, the French Government led this approach, but made the work time reduction (10 per cent) *compulsory* rather than *voluntary*.[71] In Best's studies and in subsequent studies conducted in Australia by Mills and Wood and Bullock and Wood, the leisure packages available for trading were a reduced work day, a reduced work week, additional annual leave, sabbatical leave and earlier retirement.[72] For example, a 2 per cent reduction in 'current income' could be traded for any of the following:
- 10 minutes off each working day
- 50 minutes' reduction in one work day each week
- five days' added paid vacation each year
- seven weeks' paid leave after six years of work
- earlier retirement at the rate of five working days for every year worked until retirement.

This tradeoff could also be financed from 'future income', so that the employee takes a 2 per cent pay increase as an equivalent leisure package in one of the forms identified instead of as a salary increment.

V-Time has many potential advantages. From an employee's perspective, it provides major opportunities to improve the quality of work life and family life by establishing a new balance between work and leisure goals. From the employer's point of view, it provides opportunities for employees to self-fund periods away from the workplace, thereby reducing problems associated with depreciation of human capital (such as stress and burnout). However, if people are already working unpaid overtime it is unlikely that such a scheme could work effectively. Given that a Senate inquiry in Australia was told that 'if all the nation's unpaid overtime was converted into paid work for new employees, unemployment would virtually disappear'[73] it seems difficult to imagine how V-Time would effectively benefit employees.

However, there can be many other ways of assisting employees (though not necessarily the unemployed) through the provision of reduced working hours. For example, many women are keen to resume work in a part-time capacity after maternity leave. Being able to do this is not always easy, with some organisations being more and some less supportive, as the following example of Woolworths in New Zealand illustrates. Compare this with the case in 'What would you do?' that follows it.

Woolworths supermarket chain in New Zealand employs thousands of part-time workers. Where possible, Woolworths endeavours to accommodate the needs of all its workers. For example, when women return to work after parental leave they are given different working hours if they desire it. Many of them return to a 3- to 4-hour shift in the evenings and then move to day shifts as their children get older.[74]

A proposal for maternity leave

A full-time manager who had been on maternity leave with International Cargo Express was refused part-time work when she was ready to come back to work. She had worked for the company for five years prior to taking a year's maternity leave from June 2001. When ready to return to work, the woman submitted a proposal to her employer. She wanted to return to work three days a week, working from 7.30 am to 4 pm, because she could not get child care (she had her name on several waiting lists) and had to rely on her mother who lived 25 kilometres away from her. She chose the proposed working hours to avoid peak traffic and so that she could be at home to get her child ready for dinner and bed. She also offered to work Mondays, Tuesdays and Thursdays because these were the busiest days in her work, and to be on call on the other days if urgent issues should arise. The company claimed that her former position was full-time and she was not entitled to part-time work. While employees are not automatically entitled to part-time work, organisations should *properly consider* such requests and alternatives. In this case the company did not and the New South Wales Administrative Decisions Tribunal found that the organisation had indirectly discriminated against their employee by failing to fully and properly consider her proposal. The tribunal awarded the woman $15 000 damages for emotional distress and $1385 for loss of income during the time between when she would have returned to work with International Cargo Express and when she found alternative employment.[75]

Questions

1. What would you have done to fully and properly consider the employee's proposal?
2. What advantages and disadvantages for the employer might be possible in such a scenario when a full-time employee wants to come back from maternity leave to part-time work?
3. What strategies could you have taken to maximise the outcomes for both the woman and the organisation?

Remote working and the virtual office

It is now clear that the traditional office is no longer the sole focal point of employee activity.[76] Advances in communication and information technology, as well as changing attitudes towards trusting employees, are leading to more work being undertaken in 'virtual offices' *remote* from the central workplace. Workers can work from home, work while on the road, overseas or and in any other location. Despite lack of physical proximity to each other, workers in different locations are able to interact extensively with each other.

There are numerous options and forms of teleworking. The most common is working from home, but other options enable workers to work from well-equipped hotels, resorts, offices, telecentres and vehicles. All these options involve telework principles whereby a worker is enabled, for various reasons but especially information technology, to work remotely from the central organisation.

There are many successful examples of teleworking as the following two demonstrate.

Telework principles relate to work conducted remotely from the central organisation using information technology.

Phoenix Organic salespeople work in trucks around Auckland, Wellington and Christchurch. While they are filling an order at the customer's premises, they can hook up to a printer in the truck, automatically generating an invoice and proof of delivery. Outside Auckland, the reps send the orders immediately by mobile phone, check inventory and check on any prices or information customers require.

Rocom, also in New Zealand, once had a buzzing harbourside office but now encourages workers to be out of the office and nearer to the customers. Service calls go through a Message Master Enterprise Alert, which sends an SMS message (or email or paging) to the mobile phone of the best person to deal with the job. Chief executive Grant Crawshay explains that smartphones, pocket PCs and software enable workers to check merchandise and inventory, register sales, check compliance and do a range of other tasks remote from the main workplace.[77]

Measures of who qualifies in any statistical count of remote workers need further definition, and data collection must become more accurate. Trying to gain an accurate picture is difficult. In Australia, in 2005, the Australian Telework Advisory Committee suggested that around 2.4 million Australians work from home, with around 1.4 million of these being employees (the others may be self-employed, such as farmers, and those offering property, personal and communications services). A more narrow interpretation indicates that around one million worked all or most of their hours of work at home, or had an arrangement with their employer to work at home. Most of the one million workers are managers, administrators (male dominant) and advanced clerical and service workers (female dominant), and the most common age group represented in these 'at home' workers is 35–44 years.[78]

Statistics from New Zealand show that 15 per cent of working hours in the country were undertaken at home and 3 per cent occurred in vehicles or on foot, while workers were travelling (82 per cent of working hours were spent in traditional workplaces).[79] While many home workers operate home-based enterprises and/or are self-employed, employees also work at home, especially corporate managers and professionals. In many cases the work is done in the evening or on weekends, suggesting that these people take work home in addition to working at the 'office'.[80] The example opposite illustrates two such workers.

Teleworkers work in *virtual* workplaces or offices. In virtual workplaces, productivity can rise substantially as a result of fewer interruptions and a quieter, more focused environment. The virtual office can offer more flexible work schedules, allowing employees to do work when and where they are most productive, whether early in the morning or late in the evening. It also fosters better customer service, because virtual workers are constantly in the field in direct contact with their clients.

It is vital to match the right people to remote work. They must have disciplined work habits and the knowledge and technical skills to be able to work effectively without supervision. They must also be motivated to continually improve their work skills on their own, and to know when to call on outside support. Use of email, Internet and software for work and work meetings is involved. The employee will benefit by saving in commuting time and expense and reducing personal expenditure on lunches, work clothes, laundry and so on.

However, they may feel isolated from other employees and the workplace. They may be overlooked for training opportunities and promotions because they do not have a presence in the workplace. Managers and coworkers often do not believe that employees can work effectively at home without being supervised. Employees may be expected to work harder to prove the effectiveness of the arrangement and/or because working at home blurred the hours of attending to home and work duties. There can also be an expectation that being at home means workers can work at any time.[81] It can be unclear who should bear the cost of infrastructure for telework in the home (computers, printers, wireless or Internet broadband, airconditioning, heating, lighting, etc). It does appear that workers are often not knowledgeable enough to provide adequate data security and that technology failure can be a strong cause for terminating telework arrangements (with inability to download large files being an example of the problems that arise).[82]

OB in action

Roy Hanrahan, with a background in marine engineering and industrial relations, was able to enjoy the benefits of teleworking when offered a job by Telecom in New Zealand. Roy's role was to help former employees who had been seconded to a contractor to carry out design, building and maintenance work. He was to help them with their grievances, mediations etc. and to help them decide issues for themselves. As a teleworker, Roy enjoyed being able to wear casual clothes at home. He also had free use of a company car, and was required to travel often (and could enjoy his wife's company). He was allocated a desk in the HR section but was not required to attend meetings. Instead of being measured in terms of how many hours he works, Roy is assessed in terms of whether he gets the job done so he can, if he can manage it, work fewer hours and have more time for his own life.[83] Heather Jones, who is a communications manager for IBM, works two days at home and three days at the office. She has been able to maintain the benefits of working in the workplace (collegiate atmosphere and involvement in meetings and social events) but has also been able to be around to watch her 14-month-old child's development (such as when she started walking).[84]

When an employee becomes a teleworker, advantages accrue to the community through the reduction of travel, traffic and pollution, as well as by returning patterns of consumption to local neighbourhoods instead of city centres.[85] For the organisation, advantages include increased employee productivity and satisfaction; lower costs in providing office space and parking (providing ICT in the home or elsewhere can be much cheaper); and access to a larger pool of highly skilled workers, many of whom may not be willing to cope with the demands of the traditional office environment (those in carer roles or with a physical disability, for example). The potential business costs and problems may include insurance, security, local government zoning laws, office safety, remote support and supervision. Insurance issues involving the home office can be complex because responsibilities are not always clear. Others are data confidentiality and security, because employees often have confidential client information in their home office and must be responsible for security and backing up data to the main office's network.[86]

Summary

Intrinsic motivation

Intrinsic motivation is the desire to work hard solely for the pleasant experience of task accomplishment. It builds upon intrinsic work rewards, or those rewards that an individual receives directly as a result of task performance. They are self-motivating and do not require external reinforcement. Together these can be important components of job design.

LEARNING OBJECTIVE 1

Job design strategies and intrinsic work rewards

In theory, job design involves the planning and specification of job tasks and the work setting in which they are to be accomplished. The manager's responsibility is to fit individual needs with task attributes and the work setting so both performance and human resource maintenance are facilitated. Job design strategies include four broad alternatives. Job simplification standardises work procedures and employs people in clearly defined and specialised tasks. Job enlargement increases task variety by combining two or more tasks previously assigned to separate workers. Job rotation increases task variety by periodically rotating employees among jobs involving different tasks. Job enrichment builds motivating factors into job content by adding planning and evaluating duties. The intrinsic work rewards made available by these strategies range on a continuum from low (job simplification) to high (job enrichment).

The job characteristics model and the diagnostic approach to job enrichment

The job characteristics model and the diagnostic approach to job enrichment recognise that not everyone wants an enriched job. Rather, they consider those with high and low growth needs and related concerns. They then look at the effect of five core job characteristics (ranging from skill variety to feedback from the job itself) on intervening critical psychological states that influence motivation, performance and satisfaction. The socio-technical approach to job design is also known as the semi-autonomous work group. The impact and role of technology is viewed as a factor in designing jobs, and steps are taken to optimise the relationship between technology and the social system to which employees belong. The social information-processing model argues that individual needs, tasks perceptions and reactions are a result of social constructions of reality. Multiskilling promotes the learning of a wide array of skills needed to perform multiple tasks within a company. Employees who are multiskilled are better equipped to shoulder greater responsibilities, and to take over when another employee is absent.

Goal-setting theory and job design

Goal setting is the process of developing, negotiating and formalising the targets or objectives that an employee is responsible for accomplishing. It includes predictions that link it to job design and that serve as the basis for goal-setting theory. These predictions emphasise challenging and specific goals; knowledge of results; ability and a feeling of self-efficacy to accomplish the goals; and goal commitment or acceptance. A managerial technique that applies goal-setting theory is management by objectives (MBO). A manager and subordinate mutually agree on individual goals that are consistent with higher-level ones. A process is then implemented to monitor and assist the subordinate in task accomplishment, and the subordinate's performance is evaluated in terms of accomplished results. If implemented well, many positive aspects of goal-setting theory can be realised from MBO, but effective MBO systems are difficult to establish and maintain. Key performance indicators provide a benchmark against which employees' goals can be measured.

Flexible work arrangements

There are a number of flexible work arrangements. The compressed work week allows full-time work to be completed in less than five days. Flexible working hours allow employees a daily choice in timing work and non-work activities. Job sharing occurs when two or more people divide one full-time job according to an agreement among themselves and the employer. Flexiyear, annual hours, job sharing and V-Time are all designed to enable workers to balance the competing demands on their time of work, leisure and education. These flexible work arrangements are becoming more important as a way of obtaining the services of an increasingly diverse workforce requiring a family-friendly workplace in our rapidly changing society. Information and communication technologies have had a significant impact on organisational design. The capabilities of this technology and lessening costs mean that the technology can often be taken with the worker or to the worker.

This enables workers to work while travelling and/or from their homes. Such teleworking allows work to be conducted remotely from the central organisation using information technology. These methods have several potential benefits, especially for those with child-care or other care duties, or for those with physical disabilities. For all employees it can involve reductions in employee expenditure on travel to work, lunches and work clothes, as well as saving on time. The potential costs are increased isolation of employees, and poorer communication and knowledge sharing, as well as costs like insurance and establishment of home offices. Data confidentiality and security and local government zoning laws can also present potential problems.

Chapter 5 study guide

Key terms

automation, *p. 151*
compressed work week, *p. 168*
flexible working hours (flexitime),
   p. 169
flexiyear (annual hours), *p. 169*
goal setting, *p. 162*
horizontal loading, *p. 152*
intrinsic motivation, *p. 150*
job characteristics model, *p. 155*
job design, *p. 151*

job diagnostic survey, *p. 157*
job enlargement, *p. 152*
job enrichment, *p. 153*
job rotation, *p. 152*
job sharing, *p. 170*
job simplification, *p. 151*
jobs, *p. 151*
key performance indicators, *p. 165*
motivating potential score, *p. 157*
multiskilling, *p. 161*

social information-processing
   approach, *p. 160*
socio-technical job design, *p. 160*
telework principles, *p. 172*
vertical loading, *p. 153*
voluntary reduced work time
   (V-Time or time–income
   tradeoffs), *p. 170*

Review questions

1. What is the difference between intrinsic rewards and extrinsic rewards?
2. Explain the difference between job enlargement and job enrichment.
3. List and define the core job characteristics.
4. Explain the differences between job-sharing and voluntary reduced work time.

Application questions

1. Consider a situation in which you performed a duty for someone — for example, doing an assignment, doing a job for your supervisor or even doing a favour for a friend. List the rewards you obtained from completing the duty. Distinguish between the intrinsic and extrinsic rewards.
2. Assume you are a university lecturer in this subject who is designing an assignment for students — consider the assignment design as being a job design. Use the job characteristics model to design an assignment that will maximise the intrinsic motivation for students doing the assignment. Explain the advantages of your assignment design.
3. Think about and explain how much your current 'job' (studying at college or university) involves social information processing. Provide two examples.
4. In view of the listed predictions on goal setting provided in the chapter, how would you set goals for

yourself in completing a subject in your course? How would you think your instructor could be involved in this process of goal setting for you?
5. Consider the principles of teleworking. How much of your study requires you to be located at your college or university and how much of it do you undertake remotely? Explain the role that information technology plays in enhancing this process. Discuss, based on your experience as a student, whether you think you would work effectively as a teleworker or telecommuter in the workforce.
6. Think about a job you have some familiarity with (for example, a bank teller, shop assistant, your teacher). Explain what advantages or disadvantages you would see for (a) that person, (b) the employer and (c) you as the customer if that person was working flexible hours.

1. Many organisations have strongly developed conditions to support workplace flexibility for employees. Find two organisations in your community and investigate what flexible work arrangements they provide for their employees, and evaluate their apparent effectiveness.
2. Hewitt Associates, a global HR outsourcing company, announces each year the 'best employers' list for countries such as China, Hong Kong, India, the Philippines, Malaysia, Singapore, Thailand, Australia and New Zealand — and for Asia in general. In 2004, for Australia and New Zealand, Salesforce topped the list, with Bain International, Cisco Systems, Flight Centre and Seek also ranked as highly commended. Analyse the characteristics of these 'best' employers (from your country of interest) in terms of their jobs and job-related practices. (Note that there are other relevant or similar awards, such as *Fortune* magazine's best employers and *Human Resources* HR awards for work–life balance.)

Running project

Try to find the answers to the following questions about your organisation.

1. Has the nature of work, including technology utilised and/or the formal educational qualifications required for positions at the organisation increased over the past ten years? If so, has there been a corresponding change in job design and rewards? Explain. If not, why have the requirements increased? Do the requirements seem to match the job?
2. What intrinsic rewards do the employees at the organisation obtain from their work? If you have direct access to the organisation, it might be useful to speak directly with the employees.
3. Have any of the four approaches to job design been implemented? What was the outcome?
4. How does the organisation set goals for its employees? How does it communicate these goals and assess whether they are being met?
5. Describe any flexible work arrangements the organisation offers its employees. Assess the outcomes of these arrangements for both employees and the organisation.

Individual activity

Job design preference

Instructions

People differ in what they like and dislike about their jobs. Listed below are 12 pairs of jobs. For each pair, indicate which job you would prefer. Assume that everything else about the jobs is the same — pay attention only to the characteristics actually listed for each pair of jobs. If you would prefer the job in column A, indicate how much you would prefer it by putting a check mark in a blank to the left of the Neutral point. If you would prefer the job in column B, check one of the blanks to the right of Neutral. Check the Neutral blank only if you find the two jobs equally attractive or unattractive. Try to use the Neutral blank sparingly.

(continued)

Column A		Column B
1. A job that offers little or no challenge.	Strongly Neutral Strongly	A job that requires you to be completely isolated from coworkers.
2. A job that pays well.	Strongly Neutral Strongly	A job that allows considerable opportunity to be creative and innovative.
3. A job that often requires you to make important decisions.	Strongly Neutral Strongly	A job in which there are many pleasant people to work with.
4. A job with little security in a somewhat unstable organisation.	Strongly Neutral Strongly	A job in which you have little or no opportunity to participate in decisions that affect your work.
5. A job in which greater responsibility is given to those who do the best work.	Strongly Neutral Strongly	A job in which greater responsibility is given to loyal employees who have the most seniority.
6. A job with a supervisor who sometimes is highly critical.	Strongly Neutral Strongly	A job that does not require you to use much of your talent.
7. A very routine job.	Strongly Neutral Strongly	A job in which your coworkers are not very friendly.
8. A job with a supervisor who respects you and treats you fairly.	Strongly Neutral Strongly	A job that provides constant opportunities for you to learn new and interesting things.
9. A job that gives you a real chance to develop yourself personally.	Strongly Neutral Strongly	A job with excellent vacation and fringe benefits.
10. A job in which there is a real chance you could be laid off.	Strongly Neutral Strongly	A job that offers very little chance to do challenging work.
11. A job that gives you little freedom and independence to do your work in the way you think best.	Strongly Neutral Strongly	A job with poor working conditions.
12. A job with very satisfying teamwork.	Strongly Neutral Strongly	A job that allows you to use your skills and abilities to the fullest extent.

Interpretation

People differ in their need for psychological growth at work. This instrument measures the degree to which you seek growth-need satisfaction. Score your responses as follows:

For items 1, 2, 7, 8, 11 and 12, give yourself the following points for each item:

1	2	3	4	5	6	7
Strongly prefer A			Neutral			Strongly prefer B

For items 3, 4, 5, 6, 9 and 10, give yourself the following points for each item:

7	6	5	4	3	2	1
Strongly prefer A			Neutral			Strongly prefer B

Add up all of your scores and divide by 12 to find the average. If you score above 4.0, your desire for growth-need satisfaction through work tends to be high and you are likely to prefer an enriched job. If you score below 4.0, your desire for growth-need satisfaction through work tends to be low and you are unlikely to be satisfied or motivated by an enriched job.

Source: Reprinted by permission from JR Hackman and GR Oldham, *The job diagnostic survey: an instrument for the diagnosis of jobs and the evaluation of job redesign projects*, technical report 4 (New Haven, CT: Yale University, Department of Administrative Sciences, 1974).

Group activity OB

Aligning personal goals with organisational goals

Objectives

1. To help you develop a framework that will enable you to distinguish between personal goals and organisational goals
2. To develop an understanding of the 'big picture'

Total time: 20–30 minutes

Procedure

1. In the context of the class in session, list your personal goals for this class. These could take the form of what you hope to learn from the class, what grade you hope to obtain, or how you plan to apply the lessons you learn to your personal life.
2. Placing yourself in the position of the instructor, list objectives you think he or she would have for this class.
3. Compare your lists from steps 1 and 2 (that is, your personal goals and class objectives). Identify the areas in which the two lists align and those in which they differ. Where there are differences, consider why these differences exist.
4. In groups of three or four, attempt to map out the 'big picture' — that is, the goals of the class — and suggest how you can align your personal goals with this big picture.

Case study: *Port Kembla Coal Terminal* OB

Privatised by the NSW state government in 1990, Port Kembla Coal Terminal is managed by BHP Billiton on behalf of a consortium of coal mining companies that now own the facility.

Its former HR manager Leila Hogan, now organisation development manager at BHP Billiton's Illawarra Coal, believes restructured work practices and the introduction of family-friendly policies have played a significant part in boosting efficiency and ending the industrial relations disputes that used to plague terminal operations.

'Life was very adversarial before the introduction of our family-friendly initiatives and team-based system of work in 1996. There were many strikes even after privatisation,' she says. 'We haven't had one since we initiated the changes.'

With only three women in a workforce of 94, few employees are likely to take up the negotiated paid maternity leave provisions, but everyone benefits from the flexible approach to hours. 'People can bank hours and then take them off at times that suit their team and themselves. Performance-based discretionary leave can be awarded if people need time off for surgery or to care for family members.'

Men in heavy industry blue-collar jobs have traditionally missed out on attending events at their children's schools, says Hogan. 'Now they have the opportunity to manage their work hours in a flexible way so they can take a few hours off to go to a school play or assembly, or take their child to the doctor.

'When we talk about equity between the sexes, our system of work enables fathers and partners to participate in family life. Often in the past their role as a breadwinner has prevented them fully participating.'

(continued)

The company makes clear that it does not expect workers to forget their other responsibilities when they arrive at work. It provides phones for keeping in touch with home when necessary and it contributes to the home phone bills of workers who are often on call.

'The self-management of hours has been successful and improved morale has contributed to lower absenteeism as well as the dramatic decrease in IR disputes.'

Port Kembla coal Terminal was finalist in the ACCI/BCA Work and Family Awards last year. Hogan has since been in demand to speak at conferences and to other HR practitioners.

Source: Carolyn Rance, 'Port Kembla coal terminal: lightening the loads', case study in 'About time', *HR Monthly* (September 2005), pp. 22–9.

Questions

1. How do the family-friendly policies of Port Kembla Coal Terminal help employees deal with their work–life balance?

2. Explain how the restructured work practices of the organisation alter the job design of the employees.

3. How do these changes impact on work outcomes of employees and human resource maintenance in the organisation?

OB Suggested reading

Australian Telework Advisory Committee (ATAC), *Telework in Australia*, paper II (March 2005), www.workplace.gov.au.

D Clayton, *Leadershift: The work life balance program* (Melbourne: Acer Press, 2004).

Department of Labour, *Achieving balanced lives and employment: what New Zealanders are saying about work-life balance*, the Work Life Balance Project (Wellington: NZ Government, July 2004).

Don Edgar, *The war over work: the future of work and family* (Melbourne: Melbourne University Press, 2005).

Turid Horgen, Donald A Schon, William L Porter and Michael L Joroff, *Excellence by design: transforming workplace and work practice* (New York: John Wiley & Sons, 1998).

Diane Houston (ed.), *Work-life balance in the 21st century* (Basingstoke: Palgrave Macmillan, 2005).

Edwin A Locke and Gary P Latham, *A theory of goal setting and task performance* (Englewood Cliffs, NJ: Prentice Hall, 1990).

Sharon Parker and Toby Wall (eds), *Job and work design: organizing work to promote well-being and effectiveness* (Thousand Oaks, CA: Sage, 1998).

Daniel Petre, *What matters: success & work–life balance* (Paddington, NSW: Jane Curry, 2004).

Richard Pettinger, *Managing the flexible workforce* (Mankato, USA: Capstone, 2002).

Brendan R Read, *Home workplace: a handbook for employees and managers* (San Francisco: CMP Media, 2005).

Steve Shipside, *Flexible and virtual working* (Mankato, USA: Capstone, 2001).

Douglas K Smith, *Making success measurable! A mindbook-workbook for setting goals and taking action* (New York: John Wiley & Sons, 1999).

Marilyn Zelinsky, *New workplace for new workstyles* (New York: McGraw-Hill, 1998).

OB End notes

1. Ramon J Aldag and Arthur P Brief, 'The intrinsic-extrinsic dichotomy: toward conceptual clarity', *Academy of Management Review*, vol. 2 (1977), pp. 497–8.

2. See HL Tosi, John R Rizzo and Stephen J Carroll, *Managing organizational behavior*, 2nd ed. (New York: Harper & Row, 1990), ch. 8.

3. Based on an example presented in Edward E Lawler III, *Motivation in work organizations* (Monterey, CA: Brooks/Cole, 1973), pp. 154–5.

4. New Apprenticeships, 'Robert Bosch Australia', www.newapprenticeships.gov.au/stories/Emloyer_SuccessJune05/RobertBoschAust.asp?location=rural.

5. *Hong Kong Standard* (August 1990), p. 6.

6. Kone China, 'Careers — working at Kone', www.kone.com (viewed 9 January 2006); Standard Chartered, 'Careers — building your career' (2006), http://www.standardchartered.com.cn/career/byc_tra.html (viewed 9 January 2006); Schering China, 'Career — FAQs', www.schering.com.cn (viewed 9 January 2006).

7. Frederick Herzberg, 'One more time: how do you motivate employees?', *Harvard Business Review*, vol. 46 (January/February 1968), pp. 53–62.

8. See J. Richard Hackman, 'On the coming demise of job enrichment' in EL Cass and FG Zimmer (eds), *Man and work in society* (New York: Van Nostrand, 1975).

9. See Charles L Hulin and Milton R Blood, 'Job enlargement individual differences, and worker responses', *Psychological Bulletin*, vol. 69 (1968), pp. 41–55; Milton R Blood and Charles L Hulin, 'Alienation, environmental characteristics and worker responses', *Journal of Applied Psychology*, vol. 51 (1967), pp. 284–90; AN Turner and PR Lawrence, *Industrial jobs and the worker: an investigation of responses to task attributes* (Boston: Harvard Graduate School of Business Administration, 1965).

10. For a complete description and review of the research, see J Richard Hackman and Greg R Oldham, *Work redesign* (Reading, MA: Addison-Wesley, 1980).

11. See J Richard Hackman, Greg Oldham, Robert Janson and Kenneth Purdy, 'A new strategy for job enrichment', *California Management Review*, vol. 17, no. 4 (1975), p. 60.

12. See discussion on research into job design moderators in E Luthans, *Organizational behavior* (New York: McGraw-Hill, 1985).

13. Malcolm Maiden, 'Banks want to do the mess for less', *The Sydney Morning Herald*, Business & Money section (5–6 February 2005), p. 46.

14. Bernard Hickey, 'Aussie tax cuts may speed up NZ's "brain drain"', *The Press* (12 May 2005).

15. Carolyn Rance, 'The Long March', *HR Monthly* (April 2005), pp. 22–9.

16. T Thomas, 'Every man is a manager at BHP's Queensland mill', *Business Review Weekly*, vol. 14, no. 3 (January 1992), pp. 56–7.

17. See J Richard Hackman and Greg Oldham, 'Development of the job diagnostic survey', *Journal of Applied Psychology*, vol. 60 (1975), pp. 159–70.

18. 'Graduates not in the real world', *HR Monthly* (December 2004 – January 2005), p. 7.

19. Peter Langford and Louise Parkes, 'Debunking the myths around work/life balance', *Human Resources* (3 May 2005), p. 14.

20. See Gerald Salancik and Jeffrey Pfeffer, 'An examination of need–satisfaction models of job attitudes', *Administrative Science Quarterly*, vol. 22 (1977), pp. 427–56; Gerald Salancik and Jeffrey Pfeffer, 'A social information processing approach to job attitude and task design', *Administrative Science Quarterly*, vol. 23 (1978), pp. 224–53.

21. Scott Latham, 'On manoeuvres', *HR Monthly* (April 2005), pp. 30–4.

22. Carmel Byrne, 'Getting to know me!', *Management Woman* (NZ, April 2005), p. 21.

23. See Edwin A Locke, Karyll N Shaw, Lise M Saari and Gary P Latham, 'Goal setting and task performance: 1969–1980', *Psychological Bulletin*, vol. 90 (July/November 1981), pp. 125–52. See also Gary P Latham and Edwin A Locke, 'Goal setting — a motivational technique that works', *Organizational Dynamics*, vol. 8 (Autumn 1979), pp. 68–80; Gary P Latham and Timothy P Steele, 'The motivational effects of participation versus goal-setting on performance', *Academy of Management Journal*, vol. 26 (1983), pp. 406–17; Miriam Erez and Frederick H Kanfer, 'The role of goal acceptance in goal setting and task performance', *Academy of Management Review*, vol. 8 (1983), pp. 454–63.

24. ibid.

25. See Edwin A. Locke and Gary P. Latham, 'Work motivation and satisfaction: light at the end of the tunnel', *Psychological Science*, vol. 1, no. 4 (July 1990), pp. 240–6.

26. ibid.

27. ibid.

28. For a complete review of goal-setting theory and research see Edwin A Locke and Gary P Latham, *A theory of goal setting and task performance* (Englewood Cliffs, NJ: Prentice Hall, 1990).

29. See EA Locke and GP Latham, 'Work motivation and satisfaction', *Psychological Science* (July 1990), p. 241.

30. Locke and Latham, op. cit., pp. 240–6.

31. F Schuster and K Kendall, 'Where we stand — a survey of Fortune 500', *Human Resources Management* (Spring 1974), pp. 8–11.

32. For a good review of MBO, see Anthony P Raia, *Managing by objectives* (Glenview, IL: Scott, Foresman, 1974); Steven Kerr summarises the criticisms well in 'Overcoming the dysfunctions of MBO', *Management by Objectives*, vol. 5, no. 1 (1976).

33. Fred Luthans, *Organizational behavior*, 5th ed. (New York: McGraw-Hill, 1989), p. 282.

34. Craig C Pinder, *Work motivation theory, issues, and applications* (Dallas, TX: Scott, Foresman, 1984), p. 169.

35. Based on Cypress Semiconductor Corporation, *Harvard Business Review* (July/August 1990), pp. 88–9.

36. Peter Roberts, 'Awards indicate real success', *Australian Financial Review* (6 November 1998), p. 20.

37. Peter Roberts, 'Sharing the secrets of success', *Australian Financial Review* (3 July 1998), p. 42.

38. Fonterra (To Lead in Dairy), *2004 Annual Report* (April 2005), http://www.fonterra.com/pdfs/Fonterra_Annual_Report_2004-2005.pdf.

39. Anne-Maree Moodie, 'Career surfing now the new wave', *Australian Financial Review* (22 May 1998), p. 58.

40. Australian Maritime Museum, 'Strategic plan 2003–2006', www.anmm.gov.au/stratplan.htm.

41. 'Ending long hours in dark towers', *Human Resources* (5 April 2005), p. 8.
42. The Work and Age Trust, 'Flexible employment', www.eeotrust.org.nz/worklife/flex_employment.shtml, p. 6.
43. EEO Trust, 'Work-life leaders: 2005 EEO Trust work & life awards winners', http://www.eeotrust.org.nz/awards/leaders.cfm?content_id=524.
44. Jane Wells, *Just rewards* (Sydney: Allen & Unwin, 2004), p. 37.
45. Ron Callus and Russell D Lansbury (eds), *Working futures: the changing nature of work and employment relations in Australia* (Sydney: The Federation Press, 2002), p. 245.
46. J Wood and J Duffie, 'Sabbatical: a strategy for creating jobs', *New Ways to Work Newsletter*, vol. 2, no. 1 (Winter 1982), pp. 5–6; J Wood and J Duffie, 'Sabbatical: a strategy for creating jobs' (part II), *New Ways to Work Newsletter*, vol. 2, nos 2–3 (Spring/Summer 1982), pp. 5–6.
47. Helen Sears, Labour Market Statistics Division, Statistics New Zealand, *Labour market overview 2003* (Statistics New Zealand, 2004), p. 2.
48. ACIRRT (Australian Centre for Industrial Relations Research and Training), *Australia at work: just managing* (Sydney: Prentice Hall, 1999), quoting Bittman, p. 138.
49. Bettina Cass, 'Employment time and family time; the intersection of labour market transformation and family responsibilities in Australia' in Ron Callus and Russell D Lansbury (eds), *Working futures: the changing nature of work and employment relations in Australia* (Sydney: The Federation Press, 2002), citing Campbell, p. 157.
50. Diannah Lowry, 'The casual management of casual work: casual workers' perceptions of HRM practices in the highly casualised firm', *Asia Pacific Journal of Human Resources*, vol. 39, no. 1 (2001), pp. 42–62; ACIRRT, op. cit., p. 141.
51. Mark Wooden, 'The changing labour market and its impact on work and employment relations' in Callus and Lansbury, op. cit, p. 59.
52. Australian Bureau of Statistics 'Population projections, Australia', cat. no. 3222.0 (2 September 2003), www.abs.gov.au/ausstats.
53. B O'Hara, *Put work in its place: how to redesign your job to fit your life,* (Victoria, BC: Work Well, 1988).
54. Future of work, 'Population ageing: where will it take us?', www.dol.govt.nz/futureofwork/workforce-ageing.asp.
55. Craig Donaldson, 'CEOs close door on older workers', *Human Resources* (5 April 2005), pp. 1 and 12.
56. Craig Donaldson, 'Business, boldness and benefits: how Westpac tackled the ageing workforce', *Human Resources* (8 February 2005), pp. 12–13.
57. Office for Senior Citizens, Ministry of Social Development (NZ), *The New Zealand positive ageing strategy action plan (1 July 2004 to 30 June 2005)* (Wellington, NZ: Office for Senior Citizens, Ministry of Social Development, 2004), pp. 12, 19–20 and 62.
58. J Nilles, *The telecommunications–transportation tradeoff: options for tomorrow* (New York: John Wiley & Sons, 1976).
59. JC Latack and LW Foster, 'Implementation of compressed work schedules: participation and job redesign as critical factors for employee acceptance', *Personnel Psychology*, vol. 38 (1985), pp. 75–92.
60. Allen R Cohen and Herman Gadon, *Alternative work schedules: integrating individual and organizational needs* (Reading, MA: Addison-Wesley, 1978), pp. 38–46. See also Jon L Pearce and John W Newstrom, 'Toward a conceptual clarification of employee responses to flexible working hours: a work adjustment approach', *Journal of Management*, vol. 6 (1980), pp. 117–34.
61. J Wood, Altered work week study, unpublished PhD thesis, Department of Educational Administration, University of Alberta, Canada (1977).
62. 'France aims to make job sharing work', *The Australian* (23 August 1996).
63. Australian Bureau of Statistics, *Year book Australia. Labour — working arrangements*, Australia, cat. no. 1301 (Canberra: ABS, 2005).
64. See Jon L Pearce, John W Newstrom, Randall B Dunham and Alison E Barber, *Alternative work schedules* (Boston: Allyn & Bacon, 1989).
65. See Sarah Norris, 'Building flexibility', *Australian Financial Review* (14 January 2003), www.brw.com.au/stories/20030130/17687.asp (viewed February 2003).
66. B Teriet, 'West German firms experiment with flexible working years', *Management Review* (April 1989), p. 29; 'Norsk Hydro's new approach takes root', *Personnel Management* (January 1988), pp. 37–40.
67. CMB South Yorkshire, 'Annual/annualised hours' fact sheet, http://www.cmb.org.uk/files/annual-hours.pdf (viewed 10 January 2006).
68. J Wood and G Wattus, 'The attitude of professionals towards job sharing', *Australian Journal of Management*, vol. 12, no. 2 (1987), pp. 103–21.
69. 'Job shares can mean two brains for the price of one', *Management Today* (August 1998), p. 10.
70. F Best, 'Exchanging earnings for leisure: findings on an exploratory national survey on work time preferences', R&D monograph (Washington: US Department of Labor Employment and Training Administration, 1979); F Best, *Flexible life scheduling: breaking the education–work–retirement lockstep* (New York: Praeger, 1980).
71. 'France aims to make job sharing work', *The Australian* (23 August 1996), p. 29.
72. A Mills and J Wood, 'Attitudes of NSW employers towards voluntary reduced worktime', *Human Resources Management Australia*, vol. 24, no. 2 (May 1986), pp. 38–46; J Wood and F Bullock, 'Time–income tradeoffs: establishing a new equity between work, income and leisure' in R Castle, D Lewis and J Managan (eds), *Work, leisure and technology* (Melbourne: Longman Cheshire, 1986).

73. Carolyn Rance, 'Lost in transition', *HR Monthly* (March 2005), p. 22.

74. EEO Trust, 'Flexible employment', www.eeotrust.org.nz/worklife/flex_employment.shtml, p. 15.

75. Carol Louw, 'Win for right to part-time work', *HR Monthly* (December 2004–January 2005), p. 16; Sally Bolton, 'A bumpy path: returning to work after maternity leave', *Human Resources* (3 May 2005), pp. 22–3.

76. M Gray, N Hodson and G Gordon, *Teleworking explained* (New York: John Wiley & Sons, 1993).

77. Adam Gifford, 'Breaking the chains to the desk', *New Zealand Herald* (21 March 2005).

78. Australian Telework Advisory Committee (ATAC), *Telework in Australia*, paper II (March 2005), www.workplace.gov.au. These data draw from previous years and other studies such as the Household, Income and Labour Dynamics in Australia (HILDA) survey (2003) and Australian Bureau of Statistics (ABS) 'Location at work' survey. The paper is part of a taskforce activity by ATAC to identify trends and uptake of telework in Australia.

79. Paul Callister, 'The future of work within households: understanding household-level changes in the distribution of hours of paid work' (Department of Labour, New Zealand, 2001), www.dol.govt.nz/publication-view.asp?ID=198.

80. Paul Callister, 'The future of work within households: understanding household-level changes in the distribution of hours of paid work' (Department of Labour, New Zealand, 2001), www.dol.govt.nz/publication-view.asp?ID=198.

81. Australian Telework Advisory Committee (ATAC), op. cit., pp. 17–18.

82. Australian Telework Advisory Committee (ATAC), op. cit., pp. 19–20.

83. EEO Trust, 'Flexible employment', www.eeotrust.org.nz/worlife/flex_employment.shtml, pp. 10–11.

84. Christine Long, 'No workplace like home', *The Sydney Morning Herald*, My Career section (30–31 October, 2004), p. 1.

85. Telework New Zealand, 'Alternatives and choices', www.telework.co.nz/Alternatives.htm.

86. 'Wired to the desk', *Fortune* (Summer 1999), pp. 164–75; RH Kepczyk, 'Evaluating the virtual office', *Ohio CPA Journal*, vol. 58, no. 2 (April/June 1999), pp. 16–17; KA Edelman, 'Open office? Try virtual office', *Across the Board*, vol. 34, no. 3 (March 1997), p. 34.

Part 2
case study

Getting RailCorp to run like a train

Introduction

RailCorp provides state-owned passenger train services throughout New South Wales. It was created in 2004 by the merger of the State Rail Authority (SRA) and the metropolitan functions of the Railway Infrastructure Corporation. RailCorp, like any service organisation, must be prepared for constant change to ensure that it stays in tune with the requirements of its customers, which are chiefly the provision of an on-time and safe service. The economic sustainability of the business depends largely on ensuring trains run on time, but there is an obvious potential tension between passenger safety and running the trains strictly to timetable.

The Waterfall train disaster

The Waterfall train disaster that occurred in January 2003 was a catalyst for ongoing review of passenger and staff safety. On a busy Friday morning, a double-decker train on the way from Sydney to Port Kembla left the rails and smashed into a sandstone cutting at Waterfall in the Royal National Park. The train driver and six other people died and more than 40 passengers were injured, 21 of them seriously. Surviving passengers reported that the train picked up speed when heading into a sweeping bend and it was estimated that the train was doing twice the recommended speed limit for that part of the track. The vibrations are said to have woken passengers. The train left the tracks and pulled down two overhead stanchions. The front of the train lifted into the air, tearing the side out of the front carriage and tipping the last two carriages onto their sides.[1]

A special commission of inquiry was asked to report on the causes and contributing factors of the accident and the adequacy of safety management systems, and to put forward recommendations for necessary safety procedures.

One cause of the disaster was found to be a design fault of the 'deadman' brake. Although the brake was designed to stop the train unless the train driver exerted a set degree of pressure, the State Rail Authority was aware that an incapacitated driver of more than 110 kg could hold the foot pedal in the set position by the static weight of his legs. The most likely scenario was found to be that the 118 kg train driver suffered a heart attack and collapsed, while the train continued its travel. It was concluded that SRA safety management had serious shortcomings. In addition to this finding, many other contributing factors and errors were discovered. The commission produced a report containing 127 recommendations.[2]

Among many other things, recommendations in the Waterfall report included statements about implementing risk control procedures, improving communications at all levels of the organisation, improving maintenance of equipment, improving emergency response, periodic medical examinations and drug testing for all staff, more extensive training for staff, and instilling a safety culture by improving safety awareness, management systems and employing safety regulations.

Since the Waterfall disaster investigation, RailCorp has taken into account many of the recommendations. RailCorp proposes to deliver safe, clean and reliable passenger services by sharing a common set of values that provide a framework for service delivery.[3]

Organisational support for implementing change is extensive as many contributing factors were *systemic* problems and a result of inadequate disaster planning. For example, the 'deadman brake' failed due to poor design and there was no contingency for failure. After the accident had occurred, the guard relied on his personal phone to alert authorities as he had been very strongly directed not to use the guard phone. Rescue was delayed because emergency services had no way of identifying the exact location of the derailed train. The crash site environment was extremely dangerous as there was no clear procedure to access and disconnect electrical supply. In addition, surviving passengers were trapped in the train as there was no clear signage on how to open the train doors. Many passengers reported the accident via personal mobile phones, but emergency services found it difficult to distinguish between emergency calls and hoaxes. Also, gates to rail tracks and access roads were locked, delaying assistance to the victims.[4]

The government response to this accident report[5] is to support and implement most of the recommendations made by the commission. Some examples include the development of the RailCorp Incident Management Framework in consultation with emergency services, to assess accidents and incidents. In addition, a risk management framework has been implemented, a comprehensive program of safety science training for senior managers has begun, and regular review of equipment has begun. On an operational level, communication procedures have been standardised. A digital train radio system has been implemented and data loggers are in place on trains to monitor any incident or accident and to generally monitor a driver's performance. Further, a national standard for medical health assessments for the rail industry has been put in place and extensive training programs have commenced for train drivers and guards. RailCorp has also undertaken to review the current supervisory structure to ensure individual train drivers' needs are met.[6]

In response to damning reports on the contributing factors that were of an organisational cultural nature,[7] the RailCorp safety culture program is promising to attack areas including the inherent distrust between management and operational staff; the existing culture of blame; the lack of accountability and responsibility of individuals for the safety of the activities they undertake; the lack of ability to assess whether their level of safety performance is satisfactory; and the apparent lack of tracking of safety issues. It is intended that the RailCorp safety culture program will replace the present culture of on-time running with a culture encouraging safe, efficient and reliable provision of rail services.[8] This was further enforced by the introduction of a new timetable on 4 September 2005. The intentions of RailCorp to learn from this accident are impressive. However, RailCorp employs managers and operational staff who previously worked for the State Rail Authority and it cannot be assumed that all embrace the changes. However, the commissioner believes that with appropriate dedication RailCorp can achieve public safety *and* operational efficiency, because 'good safety management is not only a moral obligation, it is good business practice'.[9]

Questions

1. How does the Waterfall train accident affect individual job performance of the operational staff?
2. What strategies would you put in place to measure operational staff performance?
3. How did the Waterfall train accident and inquiry affect employee empowerment?
4. What strategies would you put in place to align managers' and operational staff's goals?
5. How would you evaluate whether the strategies implemented by RailCorp have improved organisational performance in a year's time?

End notes

1. NSW Ministry of Transport, *Waterfall train crash report* (2003).
2. PA McInerney, QC, *Special Commission of Inquiry into the Waterfall Rail Accident: final report*, vol. 1 (2005).
3. RailCorp, *RailCorp corporate plan 'at a glance'* (2004).
4. NSW Ministry of Transport 2003, op. cit.
5. NSW Ministry of Transport, *Waterfall Special Commission of Inquiry final report: government response*, report (2005).
6. ibid.
7. McInerney, op. cit.
8. RailCorp, op. cit.
9. McInerney, op. cit, p. ii.

PART 3

MANAGING GROUP DYNAMICS AND TEAM PERFORMANCE

6 Groups and group dynamics *188*

7 Teamwork and team building *226*

Part 3 case study: Teaming in Singapore's public service for the twenty-first century *261*

CHAPTER 6
Groups and group dynamics

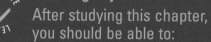

Learning objectives

After studying this chapter, you should be able to:

1. define a group and explain what types of groups exist in organisations

2. explain how groups meet individual and organisational needs

3. list and describe some of the key concepts that underpin managing effective groups

4. explain the inputs to groups that may contribute towards group effectiveness

5. define the dynamics and processes that occur within groups

6. describe the outputs of groups in terms of task and maintenance activities

7. explain the key features of intergroup dynamics and why it is important that managers understand them.

Coleambally Irrigation Co-operative Limited (CICL) operates in the Coleambally Irrigation Area (CIA) in southern New South Wales. It was formed in 2000, replacing a government agency. CICL delivers water allocations and administers requirements of two government licences. The organisation employs a CEO, Murray Smith, and approximately 35 other people and it has a board of directors (comprising both landholders and independent directors). Working within CICL, the board executive section consists of the CEO, the company secretary and an executive assistant. There are four other groups or sections, each with a manager and five to nine workers. These sections are: Operations (incorporating information systems and total channel control), Finance and Administration Services, Planning and Maintenance, and Natural Resources and Environment.

CICL is responsible for delivering up to 629 gigalitres of irrigation water to its member landholders (growers of rice, cereals and a diverse mix of other crops), although there is never any guarantee that full entitlements will be delivered to the region or to the landholders. Landholders may receive only a small percentage of their full entitlement (especially when water is in short supply). Some landholders, coping with constant structural adjustment to the industry and with government requirements, have demonstrated considerable anxiety and sometimes frustration towards CICL. To retain the rights to the water delivery, CICL must comply with the many requirements of the two licences it holds from the NSW Government and must implement its three land and water management plans, which typically require

CICL to manage the CIA's water and land. Requirements relate to soil suitability, seepage and water loss, salinity management, water recycling and on-farm storage, quality of outflows (for salt and chemicals), and a range of other factors. The future of water supply for the area depends on improving productivity levels through improved land and water management, and this must be achieved collectively by CICL and its member landholders. This is done, in part, through the operation of 'administrative regions'. Due to funding restrictions, the original five regions have been reduced to three: Kerarbury, Coleambally and Coleambally Outfall District (COD). Each area has a 'regional group' of landholder/farmers with a 'leader', and a 'regional administration officer' who is employed by the organisation. These groups hold meetings, engage in educational programs and other activities with the support and involvement of CICL staff. While not all landholders are actively involved in the regional groups, they ultimately will not be able to exempt themselves from the legal compliance requirements associated with their water delivery. Active 'compliers' are encouraged by incentive payments for improvements, and by an overall concern for the future of the CIA and their own farms. Considerable investment in water channel infrastructure has grown in recent years with the increasingly automated channel management called Total Channel Control.

As a whole, CICL also engages in other programs and projects that involve farmers and employees working with groups of people from other organisations. For example, the Biodiversity Benchmarking Survey also involves groups of researchers from the Australian Museum and Charles Sturt University. The Farm Management Champions Program is run in conjunction with the Rice Growers Association and the Murray Darling Basin Commission, and the Water Use Efficiency Project involves the CSIRO. In CICL's day-to-day operations, members of its staff also interact constantly with the Department of Environment and Conservation and the NSW Department of Primary Industries.[1]

Introduction

Group life is fundamental to the existence of the human species. We work in groups in our families, neighbourhoods, communities and political systems. Individuals seldom, if ever, behave without being influenced by the groups to which they belong. As we saw in the opening to this chapter, groups exist in organisations too and they are usually an important part of the organisation's operations and success. It is important to understand groups and the interactions between group members involved in the pursuit of organisational goals. The reality is that all organisations involve interrelationships among groups, both within and outside the organisation.

The best organisations tap the full potential of groups as an important human resource. They understand what groups can contribute and the problems sometimes associated with groups, and they have managers who are comfortable leading and participating in groups of all types and sizes. The benefits of people working cooperatively apply to any organisation. However, groups have to be understood and managed skilfully if they are to produce quality results. Just putting people together does not guarantee success.

In the workplace, the use of small groups is increasingly viewed as a prescription for success. Therefore, an understanding of group processes is important in dealing with human behaviour in organisations. This chapter introduces you to the basic attributes of groups as they are found in organisations, and examines group and intergroup dynamics to provide you with the knowledge and skills to work in and manage groups better. The next chapter, on teams and teambuilding, is closely linked.

What is a group?

Groups and types of groups

LEARNING OBJECTIVE 1

Groups are collections of two or more people who work with one another regularly to achieve one or more common goals.

Formally defined in an organisation context, a group is a collection of two or more people who work with one another regularly to achieve one or more common goals. There is absolutely no restriction on the size of a group. In the right circumstances, 50 individuals in a theatre production unit may see themselves as a group. However, 20 is commonly considered the upper limit, because beyond this number interaction and/or unity become more difficult and the group tends to split into smaller subgroups. This does not necessarily mean that a group of 20 people is always effective. Group effectiveness depends on a number of factors that will be discussed in the chapter.

In essence, a group is more than just a collection of people — say, passengers waiting to board a Qantas or Singapore Airlines flight, or a crowd watching a street procession. In a true group, members consider themselves mutually dependent to achieve common goals, and they interact with one another regularly to pursue those goals over a sustained period of time. In this chapter we will examine different work groups such as formal groups, informal groups and psychological groups. In the next chapter we will deal with a type of group called a team — while a group is a number of people who interact with one another for a common purpose, a team is a group of people who function as a unit.

Types of group in organisations

Groups appear in various forms in organisations. All groups within organisations have purposes and we will consider some of these later. Regardless of these, it is useful to classify groups into different types. A common managerial distinction is between formal groups and informal groups.

Formal groups

Formal groups are 'official' groups that are designated by formal authority to serve a specific purpose.

A formal group is an 'official' group that is designated by formal authority to serve a specific purpose. Employees become members of formal groups because they are formally assigned to them. Within these groups, people are assigned positions, such as leading hand or supervisor.

Another perfect example is the work unit headed by a manager and consisting of one or more people reporting directly to the manager. Such a group has been created by the organisation to perform a specific task. This 'task' may be described in general terms as the transformation of various resource inputs (such as ideas, materials and objects) into certain product outputs (such as a report, decision, service or commodity).

A manager is responsible for the group's performance while depending on the group's members to do the required work. Such challenges are found at all levels of managerial responsibility because any manager is responsible for the performance of at least one group. A popular view of organisations depicts them as interlocking networks of work groups. As shown in figure 6.1, this view identifies the important 'linking-pin' function of managers first described by Rensis Likert. Likert points out that managers actually create the network structure by simultaneously serving as superiors in one work group and as subordinates in another at the next higher level. Whereas the manager of a branch bank is 'in charge' of the branch, he or she is also one of several branch managers who report to the person at the next higher level. All work groups are thus seen as interconnected, working together to create the 'total' organisation.

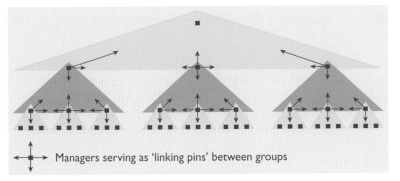

Managers serving as 'linking pins' between groups

FIGURE 6.1 • Likert's linking-pin model of an organisation as a complex network of interlocking groups

Source: Rensis Likert, *New patterns of management* (New York: McGraw-Hill, 1961). Reproduced with the permission of The McGraw-Hill Companies.

There are different types of formal groups in organisations; some are relatively permanent and others are more temporary in nature.

1. **Permanent formal work groups**, or command groups, often appear on organisation charts as departments (for instance, market research department) or divisions (for instance, consumer-products division), among other possibilities. Such groups can vary in size from small departments of just a few people to large divisions employing 100 or more people. However, in all cases, permanent formal work groups are officially created to perform a specific function on an ongoing basis. They continue in existence until a decision is made to change or reconfigure the organisation for some reason.

   Permanent formal work groups perform a specific function on an ongoing basis.

2. In contrast, **temporary formal work groups** (or task groups) are created for a specific purpose — to solve a specific problem or to perform a defined task — and typically disband once that purpose has been accomplished.[2] Good examples are the temporary committees and task forces that are important components of any organisation. Indeed, today's organisations tend to make considerable use of task forces for special problem-solving efforts. The managing director of a company, for example, may convene a task force to examine the possibility of implementing flexible work hours for non-managerial employees. Usually, such temporary groups appoint chairpersons or heads who are held accountable for results, much like the manager of a work unit. The head of a temporary group may be given a deadline or due date for submitting formal recommendations and/or for achieving a particular task. There are other ways of using groups in organisations too. For example, an organisation may use a 'focus group' to survey its employees, clients or customers about organisational products or processes.

   Temporary formal work groups are created for a specific purpose and typically disband once that purpose has been accomplished.

Informal groups

Social psychologists make an important distinction between the formal groups just discussed and informal groups. The latter emerge unofficially and are not formally designated as parts of the organisation. The key difference is that formal groups are officially defined in the organisational structure, whereas informal groups come into existence spontaneously and without formal endorsement. Most formal groups include one or more informal groups that have emerged within them. Alternatively, informal groups can exist in organisations but overlap different formal groups. For example, members of different formal groups may belong to a single informal group such as a Friday night social club. While they might not seem important to the organisation, these informal group links may affect members' behaviour in positive and negative ways. Sometimes wider sharing of information and support occurs through such informal group memberships. In other cases, informal groups can have political goals and their activities may destabilise the organisation or challenge its operations. Covertly, an informal group of executives engaging in nepotistic support for one another in promotion decisions, or coalitions to influence other key decisions, may undermine the organisation's capacity to achieve its goals effectively. Strikes by industrial unions are an overt example. Sometimes the organisation can endeavour to control informal groups and must deal with external groups as the following examples demonstrate.

A group of about 80 airport limousine drivers in Putrajaya, Malaysia, staged a protest at the Ministry for Human Resources and the Prime Minister's Department in December 2004. They claimed that their employer, Airport Limousine (M) Sdn Bhd, was using 'strong-arm' tactics to discourage drivers from joining a recently approved cooperative. The cooperative, called Koperasi Jurupandu Usahawan Limosin Airport KLIA, would be able to help look after the welfare of the drivers. Of the 700 drivers in the company, 379 were registered as members of the cooperative but it was claimed that three drivers had been suspended and three others had been asked to provide 'show cause' letters for joining the cooperative and for failing to follow company orders not to attend cooperative meetings.[3]

The Department of Infrastructure, Planning and Natural Resources and Taronga Park Zoo anticipated a battle with a zoo carpark action group in Mosman, Sydney, when plans for a new three-storey zoo carpark were made public in a development application to the department. The action group's objections to the zoo's plans were that the carpark was environmentally irresponsible and that it would scar the landscape (the zoo is surrounded by green parklands). On the other hand, the zoo needs much more parking since the existing facilities are completely inadequate.[4]

Two common types of informal groups are friendship groups and interest groups. Friendship groups consist of people with natural affinities for one another; they may tend to work together, sit together, take breaks together, and even do things together outside the workplace. Interest groups consist of individuals who share common interests; they may be job-related interests, such as an intense desire to learn more about computers, or non-work interests, such as community service, sports or religion.

There are at least two reasons for the emergence of informal groups in organisations. First, they help people get their jobs done. Informal groups offer a network of interpersonal relationships with the potential to 'speed up' the work flow or 'gain favours' in ways that formal lines of authority fail to provide. Second, informal groups help people to satisfy individual needs (these are discussed more in the next section).

Figure 6.2 illustrates how informal groups add complexity to the linking-pin model of organisations shown earlier. These groups create a vast array of informal but very real networks that further relate people from various parts of the organisation to one another. Accordingly, managers must be skilled at understanding and working with groups in both their formal and informal forms.

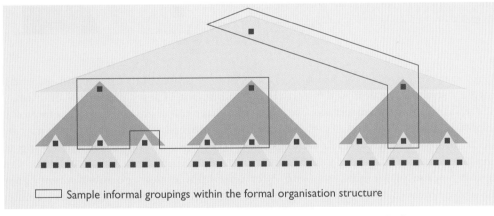

☐ Sample informal groupings within the formal organisation structure

FIGURE 6.2 • How informal groups add complexity to Likert's linking-pin model of organisations

Purposes of groups in organisations

OBJECTIVE 2 LEARNING

How groups meet individual and organisational needs

Groups can have a major impact on their members and on the organisation. In the workplace a prime managerial concern is to help groups influence members' attitudes and behaviours in positive ways. Managers also aim to enhance collective member contributions to effective performance through groups and also through allowing group members to satisfy their individual needs. Thus, it is clear that groups have two key purposes in organisations.

1. *Groups can help to meet organisational needs.* The following examples give an indication of some of the many ways in which this may occur. Groups provide the context in which many people learn how to do their jobs. The job skills and knowledge of group members can be shared. This shared knowledge can be used to help solve difficult and unique problems, and it can be especially helpful to newcomers who require advice and assistance in their jobs. In an effective group, members are quick to offer support and performance feedback.

This kind of support helps group members acquire job competencies and may even make up for deficiencies in the formal training and education practices of an organisation. How group members behave in the workplace serves as a 'model' for newcomers to follow. Group members communicate work performance expectations to one another, influencing one another's attitudes and beliefs about various aspects of the work setting. This influence may be positive or negative; that is, it may encourage or discourage high levels of work effort. A new employee soon learns from coworkers who are 'good' and 'bad' supervisors and who can be 'trusted'. These influences may even extend to how individuals feel about their job and the organisation; for example, a coworker may indicate that 'this is a good job to have and a great place to work' or 'this is a lousy job and you are better off looking for something else'. Naturally, managers would all like such influence within groups to be as positive and supportive of organisational goals as possible. The following example illustrates groups of employees who are dedicated to achieving organisational purposes.

Living Nature is a New Zealand cosmetics company that employees almost 100 people globally and produces around 300 products. According to the founder Suzanne Hall there is a finance department whose members are passionate about what they do, a despatch group that is extremely committed to getting orders out on time and a core group, mainly women, who are driven to make the business successful.[5]

2. *Groups can satisfy the needs of their individual members.* Groups, both formal and informal, provide social interaction and interpersonal fulfilment. They can provide individual security in the form of direct work assistance and technical advice, or offer emotional support in times of special crisis or pressure. In informal groups, individuals may be able to find sympathy for their feelings and receive task assistance without having to reveal uncertainties to managers. By participating in group activities members can acquire a sense of identification and offer opportunities for ego involvement. They can also achieve a sense of belonging from being with people who share similar values, attitudes and goals. In many ways, group involvement provides members with the full range of need satisfactions discussed in chapter 3 on motivation in the workplace.

Effective managers will attempt to use groups in ways that benefit both the group members and organisations. Contemporary organisations use groups in many creative and productive ways. Examples of the efficacy of groups can be found in many settings, as managers increasingly recognise the usefulness of groups in organisations. The scholar Harold J Leavitt points out the following reasons in support of groups.[6]

- Groups can help foster innovation and creativity.
- Groups sometimes make better decisions than individuals do, and can help gain commitments needed to implement such decisions.
- Groups can guide members and exert control over them.
- Groups help offset the negative effects of increasing organisation size.
- Groups can help organisations accomplish important tasks.

Even so, not all groups are problem free and not all of them necessarily benefit both group and individuals, as the following example shows.

Call centres have a reputation for high turnover and poor worker conditions. Some call-centre employees talk about working in head-high cubicles where they cannot see anyone else all day. They talk also of the pressure of having to meet specified daily call targets. While the members of these groups work with each other regularly to accomplish organisational tasks and goals, it would appear that some centres provide little in the way of filling social or higher-order needs; nor do they encourage their workers to work together. Some call centres do recognise these problems however. At ING Bank's Sydney call centre, employees can schedule their own breaks and working hours and take calls alongside their managers.[7] Hunter Water, a water, sewerage and drainage provider in New South Wales, ensures that its call centre employees spend 50 per cent of their time off the phones. The organisation encourages 'horizontal competence' in employees' careers and reduces boredom and stress by having them spend half their time in the back office areas of accounts-adjustments, or face-to-face with customers.[8] This can help ensure employees have a wider understanding of what they are trying to achieve.

While groups serve useful purposes in organisations, they can have various advantages and disadvantages. Table 6.1 summarises some these.

Advantages of groups	Disadvantages of groups
Groups bring together people for a specific purpose.	Some groups' specific purposes may conflict with the objectives of the organisation or with those of other groups.
Groups can achieve positive synergy.	Groups may result in negative synergy, especially when there are disruptive behaviours, ambiguous roles or interpersonal conflicts between group members.
Groups can become highly cohesive and high-performance entities.	Groups can become highly cohesive but work against organisational work goals.
Individuals can collaborate to achieve a joint goal.	Some people may be able to 'loaf' in groups while others do the work.
Groups of people with complementary skills, attitudes, experiences and viewpoints may enhance task accomplishment and decision making.	Groups of people with similar opinions and viewpoints may make uncreative or poor decisions while groups of people with extreme differences, or with strong subgroups, may experience dysfunctional levels of conflict in decision making.
People from collectivist societies are likely to work well in groups.	People from individualistic societies may not work well in groups.
Organising people into groups clarifies goals and activities and enables people to work together on large and complex tasks.	The more people are organised into specific task-related activities, the more they may become different from other groups working on different goals and activities, leading to problematic intergroup relations.
Groups can be an ideal collection of people to work on particular tasks.	Groups can be the wrong size or combination of people to accomplish what is necessary.
Informal groups can enable informal networks of individuals who support one another towards achieving organisational goals.	Informal groups can have members whose goals and behaviours conflict (intentionally or unintentionally) with organisational goals.

TABLE 6.1 • Potential advantages and disadvantages of groups

The success of organisations depends upon the success of its groups as well as the way networks of groups interlock and work with each other. Like individuals, groups must succeed for the organisation to prosper over the long run. At this point it is useful to highlight the issue of this 'network' of groups since workplace groups do not operate in isolation.

Managing groups for effectiveness

Managing for group effectiveness

LEARNING OBJECTIVE 3

Managers are concerned with productive workplace activity. Productive workplaces require efficient and effective performance activities at individual, group and organisational levels. In order to understand group effectiveness we need to consider what groups do and how they operate, and what might support or undermine group effectiveness.

Groups and task performance

In order to function, and continue functioning, a group must achieve two things:
- *task performance* — achieving the group's task or tasks
- *group maintenance* — maintaining the social system of the group itself.

These two group activities are examined more fully when the outputs of group activity are described later in the chapter. However, it is appropriate to highlight at the outset why they are important. When properly managed, groups are conducive to achieving synergy — the creation of a whole that is greater than the sum of its parts. When synergy occurs, groups accomplish more than the total of their members' individual capabilities. Therefore, organisations and their managers have much to gain through the effective use of groups as human resources. Research shows that groups often have three performance advantages over individuals acting alone.

Synergy is the creation of a whole that is greater than the sum of its parts.

1. When the presence of an 'expert' is uncertain, groups seem to make better judgements than those of the average individual operating alone.
1. When problem solving can be handled by a division of labour and the sharing of information, groups are typically more successful than individuals.
2. Given their tendencies to make more risky decisions, groups can be more creative and innovative than individuals in accomplishing their tasks.

Groups can also have problems. In essence, group problems can result in 'negative' synergy. A manager should endeavour to avoid these effects. The very word 'group', for example, produces both positive and negative reactions. It is said that 'two heads are better than one', but we are also warned that 'too many cooks spoil the broth'. The issue here is how well group members work together to accomplish a task. This includes a concern about social loafing, also called the 'Ringelmann effect'.[9] Ringelmann, a German psychologist, pinpointed this effect by asking people to pull as hard as they could on a rope, first alone and then in a group. He found that average productivity dropped as more people joined the rope-pulling task. Thus, the Ringelmann effect acknowledges that people may tend not to work as hard in groups as they would individually. There are two reasons: their contribution is less noticeable, and they prefer to see others carry the workload.

Social loafing is the tendency of people not to work as hard in groups as they would individually.

Social loafing is also another name for freeloading, which occurs when a person is placed in a group and removed from individual accountability. Because of differences in the degree of individualism or collectivism in different national cultures (see chapter 1), it is possible that social loafing might occur more in individualist societies than in collectivist societies where people focus on working together in groups. Obviously, one of a manager's interests in studying organisational behaviour is to learn how to minimise social loafing and maximise the performance contributions of any group.

Disruptive behaviour is any behaviour that harms the group process.

Other disruptive behaviours can affect group performance and functions and should be avoided. Disruptive behaviours are any behaviours that harm the group process. A good group member avoids (and helps other group members avoid) the following behaviours.

- lack of direction or uncertainty of purpose
- being overly aggressive towards other members
- infighting
- lack of respect and/or trust for each other
- withdrawing and refusing to cooperate with others
- shirking of responsibilities for group tasks or processes
- playing around when there is work to be done
- using the group as a forum for self-confession
- talking too much about irrelevant matters
- trying to compete for attention and recognition.

Awareness of such dysfunctional group behaviours is vital for managers. Knowing the potential problems can help them to take actions that will discourage or overcome such behaviours. Some of the ways in which behaviour within a group can affect group effectiveness will be discussed later in the chapter, especially in the section on group processes and group dynamics.

Group effectiveness

We can conclude that an **effective group** is one that achieves high levels of both task performance and human resource maintenance over time. Practically speaking, an effective group gets its job done and takes good care of its members in the process. Being part of an effective group is motivating and rewarding for an individual. In terms of task performance, an effective group achieves its performance goals in the standard sense of timely and high-quality work results. For a permanent work group, such as a manufacturing section or division, this may mean meeting daily work targets. For a temporary group, such as a new policy task force, this may involve submitting a draft of a new organisational policy to the company managing director. In terms of human resource maintenance, an effective group is one whose members are sufficiently satisfied with their tasks, accomplishments and interpersonal relationships to work well together on an ongoing basis. For a permanent work group, this means that the members work well together day after day; for a temporary work group, it means that the members work well together for the duration of the assignment.

A classic listing of the characteristics of an effective group is found in 'The effective manager 6.1'. For groups to be effective, managers need to be the key supports to help them get started and stay focused. Jaques, in his book which surveys the work on 'learning in groups', identifies approaches to improving group behaviour that focus on the development of the teaching staff to enable them to direct student groups.[10] However, there is little mention of explicit training in group dynamics and group skills for the students; yet without these skills the students' effectiveness in group learning will be reduced.

Effective groups are groups that achieve high levels of both task performance and human resource maintenance.

Ten characteristics of an effective group

THE **Effective**Manager 6.1

1. A sense of urgency and direction; purpose and goals
2. A lot of work at the start, setting a tone, setting a 'contract' and/or specifying a clear set of rules
3. A broad sense of shared responsibility for the group outcomes and group process
4. Effective approaches to recognising problems and issues and making decisions
5. A high level of commitment and trust among members
6. A balance in satisfying individual and group needs
7. A climate that is cohesive yet does not stifle individuality
8. An ability to confront differences and deal with conflict
9. An ability to deal with minority opinions effectively
10. Communication patterns with a proven track record

In practice, it is normal in the beginning for groups to address issues and problems they can manage most easily. Later, the problems become more difficult to solve and the groups may grow disinclined to change the perfect systems they have already worked out. This stage of group development can be difficult to endure. Mature groups may expand or change group membership and question well-established roles and processes as new problems arise. There is more about the stages of group development later in the chapter.

Groups as open systems

One way to gain a better understanding of what it takes to become effective as a group — and to remain so — is to view the group as an 'open system'. Consider the model presented in figure 6.3. This perspective depicts a group as an open system that interacts with its environment to transform group resource inputs into group outputs (a similar model is typically applied to organisations as open systems).

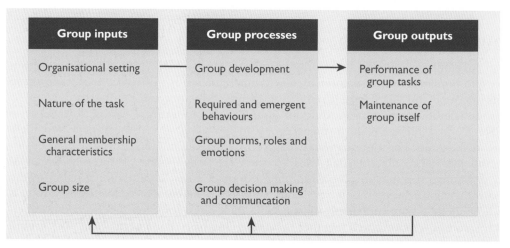

FIGURE 6.3 • The work group viewed as an open system — transforming group inputs into group outputs

For present purposes, the environment of any given group consists of other individuals and groups with whom the group interacts within the organisation. The group depends on these elements to provide the resources, or inputs, it needs to operate. In return for these resources, the group is expected to give something back to the environment — group outputs, or work results, of real value. Once again, the interlocking nature of groups in organisations is clear. The many groups of an organisation are interdependent; they depend on one another to provide the support needed for their operating success.

To be truly effective, therefore, a group must achieve its goals in such a way that other groups are also helped to attain theirs. Of course, this does not always happen. Sometimes, groups emphasise their own needs and neglect those of others. Sub-goal optimisation occurs when a group achieves its goals at the expense of the goals of others. The group identifies strongly with its own sub-goals and puts its efforts to achieving those. In doing so it has lost an appreciation of the fact that all the various groups should be working collectively for higher common goals, of which the group's sub-goal is just a part. For example, a marketing department may increase sales by offering customers special product designs that are difficult for manufacturing to produce — marketing looks good because it achieves a high sales record, but manufacturing looks bad because it has cost overruns. This is a tendency that must be avoided. An effective group should serve the needs of the total organisation, not just its own. It should establish and maintain good input–output relations with other parts of the larger system, both individuals and groups. This give and take helps the group gain the resource inputs it needs from the environment. It also helps the group perform in a manner that truly assists, rather than hinders, the performance efforts of other components of the organisation.[11]

Sub-goal optimisation occurs when a group achieves its goals at the expense of the goals of others.

Inputs into the group process

The effectiveness of a group, as in all open systems, will depend in part upon the inputs to the system. The better the group inputs, the better the chance of group effectiveness. When considering inputs, we are considering both the inputs to the tasks the group performs and also the inputs to the maintenance of the group itself. We need to be concerned with the way in which a group operates if we wish to have the group continue as an effective entity in the organisation. Group inputs are the initial 'givens' in a group situation. They set the stage for all group action. If all the inputs are satisfactory, the group has a strong foundation for pursuing effectiveness. But if even some of the inputs are unsatisfactory, efforts to achieve effectiveness will suffer from the problems and shortcomings tracing back to the input insufficiencies. An informed manager can avoid many of these difficulties by remaining aware of how these major categories of group input factors — organisational setting, nature of the task, membership characteristics and group size — may influence group operations and outcomes.

> **Group inputs** are the initial 'givens' in a group situation that set the stage for all group processes.

Organisational setting

The organisational setting can affect the way in which a group operates and what it accomplishes. Specifically, research suggests that the setting can influence whether group members become psychologically close to one another, the extent to which they cooperate and/or compete with one another, and how well they communicate with one another.[12]

Organisational policies, procedures and cultures that focus on individualism could act as barriers to group effectiveness. Groups rely more heavily on collective effort and evolve better in organisational settings that nurture and encourage that culture. Naturally, managers should create the most supportive settings possible to maximise the effectiveness of groups in which they are involved. Managers should build a shared sense of responsibility, develop vision alignment and provide opportunities for group collective development. Relevant parameters for a group setting include: goals and rewards; resources, spatial arrangements and technologies; and cultures and structures.

Goals and rewards

Many of the insights we discussed in chapters 3, 4 and 5, and in particular those about goals, needs and rewards can be applied to the group as well as the individual level of analysis. Appropriate goals and well-designed reward systems can help establish and maintain the 'motivation' for group members to work hard together in support of group-level accomplishments. On the other hand, groups can suffer if goals and rewards are focused too much on individual outcomes. As in the case of individuals, a group's performance can suffer when goals are:

- unclear
- insufficiently challenging
- arbitrarily imposed from the outside.

Sometimes unclear goals and individualised rewards can have very negative consequences and this highlights the need to consider who is responsible for ensuring that a group has clearly stated goals, is closely monitored in its activities and has appropriate reward practices.

Resources, spatial arrangements and technologies

The supporting resources, spatial arrangements and technologies of the group are important. Organisational resources important to the work group include adequate budgets, the right facilities, good work methods and procedures, and the best technologies.

These and related items provide groups with the background support needed to take optimum advantage of their performance opportunities. Any person, working alone or as part of a group, must be well supported to achieve maximum success. A good manager, for example, 'supports' a work group by making sure the members have the resources they need to use their talents fully and achieve high performance results. This includes the right technologies to help them do their jobs effectively and the right spatial arrangements to enable communication and interaction to achieve work outcomes and maintain group social systems. The following 'What would you do?' feature illustrates some issues that may relate to open-plan offices.

Even where groups are physically dispersed, technological or other solutions must enable them to communicate and collaborate in their group activities; for example, groups in which teleworkers may feel ostracised from their fellow group members unless efforts are made to include them. Another example from St George Bank also illustrates this point.

OB in action

St George Bank has 7400 staff and more than 400 branches across Australia that are, in effect, subgroups of the larger groups in the bank. Their HR head Brett Wright is very aware that, unless effort is made, people in branches may feel forgotten. St George has a program where senior managers take on a mentoring role. Mentors such as Wright try to make sure they are visible, listen to branch employees' concerns and visit them to show that they are part of the larger group.[13]

When support is absent or minimal, the performance of a group is likely to suffer and additional side effects may occur. When monetary resources are scarce, for example, groups may engage in unhealthy competition to obtain them. Such intergroup competition can be dysfunctional in terms of the accomplishment of higher-level organisational goals.

WhatWould YouDo?

Too close for comfort?

A recent study has found a very high level of employee dissatisfaction with open-plan workspaces. A survey of 1317 employees, conducted by human resources advice firm Talent2 Works, found that a remarkable 76 per cent of respondents believe that open-plan offices negatively impact on workplace productivity. The key reason, mentioned by 65 per cent of respondents, was that the design infringes too much on employee privacy.

'This is a very surprising finding,' says Mark Brayan, CEO of Talent2 Works. 'It raises some disturbing questions for many companies. There has long been a belief that open-plan environments are good for supporting better communication and team working, and they can certainly be cost-effective for employers. I found it especially surprising at the personal level, since the office that I work in is open plan, and every sign we have is that everyone here sees it as a very positive aspect of the company.

'But the survey shows that employees who are likely to have their concentration disrupted by noise or traffic, or who are uncomfortable with having their personal space limited, may not be able to work to their full potential in an open-plan office. This will need to be addressed.'

Brayan admits that there are situations which require more privacy than that available in a 'pure' open-plan office: staff issues such as performance reviews and discipline, as well as projects which demand commercial confidentiality. One answer, he suggests, is to mix open-plan design with rooms that can be used for specific tasks, such as meetings, interviews or client liaison. These offices should also be available to staff on an occasional basis, for work that requires concentration.

'The technology of the workplace has changed, and that can be important,' he notes. 'You can wire an office so that an employee can take a laptop computer or mobile phone and plug it in at different locations. The infrastructure that used to come with a desk is no longer so rigid.'

Source: Derek Parker, 'Planning the workspace [open design or cultural trapdoor?]', *Management Today* (September 2004), pp. 26–9. This article appeared in the September 2004 edition of Australia's leading magazine for managers: *Management Today* (published by Text Pacific Publishing for the Australian Institute of Management, www.aim.com.au).

Questions

1. What are the possible advantages and disadvantages of having group members work closely together in an open-plan workspace?

2. Use these findings to consider the appropriateness of open-plan workspace design for the following groups:
   (a) a group of creative advertising designers working on a new campaign
   (b) a group of accounting clerks entering data for client tax returns
   (c) a group of engineers, architects and other specialists working together to design a major public building.

Cultures and structures that value and support group activity and interaction

The 'cultures' of some organisations tend to be very individualistic; that is, they emphasise individual performance, individual advancement and individual rewards. This emphasis can make it more difficult to develop truly effective work groups. In contrast, groups can prosper more easily in cultures that place a high value on individual contributions to group accomplishments. Because of the mounting intransigence of local organisational cultures, and the changing work environment that makes cultural learning more urgent, groups have become important resources in sensitising managers and their employees to the cultural dimensions of their work.

Structure counts too. Every group will develop an internal structure as it goes about its daily operations. In some groups, this structure may be 'tight' and 'rigid'; in others, it may be 'loose' and more 'flexible'. Neither one structure nor the other is by nature good or bad. Circumstances often dictate which form of group structure works best and it will also depend upon the organisational structure in which it must operate, including interaction with other groups. A rigid organisation structure, for example, can constrain a group that is trying to operate in a flexible manner; yet a group with a rigid structure may encounter difficulties working within organisational structures that are more flexible in nature.

Nature of the group task

Like organisational setting, the nature of the task to be performed is an important factor in group input. Different tasks place different demands on a group. A basic rule of thumb is that the difficulty of achieving group effectiveness increases with the degree of task complexity.[14]

In other words, it is harder to accomplish complex tasks than to accomplish simple tasks. To master complex tasks, group members must apply and distribute their efforts more broadly than they do on simple tasks. They must also cooperate more to achieve desired results. When group members are successful in doing so, they usually experience high levels of satisfaction from knowing that they are able to accomplish complex tasks. This often has a positive roll-on effect and works as a further reinforcer of group effectiveness.

Task complexity can be understood along technical and social lines. In terms of technical demands on a group, the key issues are: How unusual is the task that is to be accomplished? How difficult is the task? And how dispersed is the information needed to accomplish the task? Compared with simple tasks, complex tasks are technically more demanding. They require high performance on unique and difficult tasks, and they require more information processing to make this performance possible. In terms of social demands on a group, the key issues relate to ego involvement and agreements on issues of ends and means; that is, compared with simple tasks, complex ones are more socially demanding. They are very ego involving, but they also make it more difficult to reach agreement on either the ends or the means for accomplishing them.[15]

- *Ego involvement* refers to the degree to which members strongly and personally identify with the group tasks. Ego-involving tasks relate to deeply rooted personal values, affect personal lives and/or engage personal skills.
- *Ends agreement* refers to members' agreement on what they are trying to accomplish and the criteria for defining 'success'. Ends agreement is easier to achieve when the group task is clear and the outcomes are measurable.
- *Means agreement* refers to members' agreement on how the group should go about performing its task. Means agreement is easier for tasks in which one approach is clearly the best; it is much harder to attain when many alternatives exist.

General membership characteristics

The attributes of individual group members are also important inputs that may affect both the way in which the group operates and what it accomplishes. The competency, demographic and psychological characteristics of the members are all important. Having the right competencies available within the membership can be a great asset to group performance. Although these talents alone cannot guarantee success, they establish an important baseline of potential performance accomplishments. And, if the input competencies are insufficient in any way, a group will operate with performance limits that are difficult to overcome. If group members suffer from too much personality conflict, for example, it is likely that critical energies — ones that otherwise might be used to enhance task accomplishment — will be drained as members deal with these issues. In the case of a new task force, a good manager carefully chooses the membership to avoid such problems and the performance limitations that may accompany them.[16] To this end, the demographic and psychological makeup of a group becomes important. If members have difficulty getting along, talents may be wasted as energies and attention are devoted to interpersonal problems. Whether this happens may depend in part on membership diversity and on how well this diversity is handled. Workforce diversity has already been examined in this book as an important issue in organisational behaviour. In the present context, it may be addressed from the perspective of diversity in the demographic and psychological characteristics of group membership. Important considerations include interpersonal compatibilities, membership heterogeneity and status.

The following 'International spotlight' demonstrates the importance of groups in international educational ventures and shows that national diversity and physical distance may be elements of many groups in our increasingly globalised world.

Global education groups

The growth in international educational partnerships has been substantial over recent years. Students in many countries can take advantage of arrangements in which local institutions operate in partnership with universities in other parts of the world. In Malaysia, in addition to some innovative local institutions (such as the Limkokwing University College of Creative Technology), there are numerous colleges, university colleges and other institutions that have arrangements with universities in the United Kingdom, the United States, Canada and Australia. For example, students studying at HELP University College can work towards degrees with the University of London, the University of Queensland and several others. Students in many institutions, such as Sunway University College, can also work towards matriculation (such as Canadian or Australian matriculation or a transfer to a US degree in Western Michigan University) or professional courses that lead to accreditation in areas such as accounting and marketing. INTI College has similar arrangements with several UK and Australian universities. Singapore also offers similar arrangements, with links to universities such as the Massachusetts Institute of Technology, the Wharton School of the University of Pennsylvania, Shanghai Jiao Tong University and the Technical University of Munich. Other institutions to offer education in Singapore include one of the world's leading business schools, INSEAD (France), and the Chicago Graduate School of Business. Similar arrangements exist in other countries, including China.

In order to enable these programs, there are many groups of teaching, management and administrative employees from the different institutions who must work together to achieve the desired educational outcomes. For example, there is a group of international lecturers who work full time at Monash University Malaysia. Some universities offer educational packages delivered by local teachers, and they send their teachers to the country to deliver part of the program as intensive teaching sessions and/or to assess the students' work and determine their final grades in the courses. In some cases reciprocal exchanges for the 'local' teaching staff are also available and help them to gain experience and familiarity with the university partner. In the meantime, management groups develop these programs and groups of administrative staff in both countries support these activities, largely through electronic communication methods such as email and fax. In all cases, the employees of the partner organisations must work together to achieve the common goals of the educational partnerships.[17]

Interpersonal compatibilities

The ability of diverse people to work well together in groups can be understood through the FIRO-B (fundamental interpersonal orientation) theory.[18] This theory helps explain how people orient themselves towards one another based on their needs to express and receive feelings of inclusion, control and affection. These needs can be measured by an instrument called the FIRO-B scale. They are defined as follows:

- the *need for inclusion:* the desire to be given prominence, recognition and prestige in the eyes of others
- the *need for control:* the tendency to exert control and to rebel or refuse control by others, or the tendency to be compliant and submissive
- the *need for affection:* the desire to be friendly and to seek close emotional ties with others.

FIRO-B theory points out that groups whose members are 'compatible' on these needs are more likely to be effective than groups whose members are more 'incompatible' on them.

Symptoms of harmful incompatibilities include the presence of withdrawn members, open hostilities, struggles over control, and domination by a few members. William Schutz, the author of the FIRO-B theory, states the management implications this way: 'If, at the outset, we can choose a group of people who can work together harmoniously, we shall go far toward avoiding situations where a group's efforts are wasted in interpersonal conflicts'.[19]

Membership homogeneity–heterogeneity

Homogeneous groups are groups whose members have similar backgrounds, interests, values, attitudes and so on.

Heterogeneous groups are groups whose members have diverse backgrounds, interests, values, attitudes and so on.

Groups whose members have similar backgrounds, interests, values, attitudes and so on are called homogeneous groups. Groups whose membership is more diverse on these dimensions are called heterogeneous groups. The degree of homogeneity or heterogeneity within a group can affect its operations and results.

The effect of member diversity on group performance is inconclusive. One reason for this is that heterogeneity or homogeneity can be considered on many different criteria. For example, a group may be homogeneous in age, but heterogeneous in terms of professional background of its members. It may be homogeneous in terms of ethnic background but heterogeneous in terms of member values. The value of group diversity may depend upon what the group is trying to achieve. For instance, a group with a heterogeneous membership often has a wide variety of skills and experiences that it can bring to bear on complex problems or tasks that require creativity or innovation. Alternatively, as the following example shows, greater diversity may help the group to engage with its client base.

OB in action

> Land Information New Zealand (LINZ) is an 18-member group that provides the Landonline public information service. The group has members with different sexual orientations, physical capabilities, language backgrounds and ethnic origins. While the diversity of the group might to some seem a potential problem for group cohesiveness, in fact it encourages and helps members to deal with diverse clients' needs.[20]

A group may have some difficulty getting diverse members to work together to make success like this possible. The more heterogeneous the membership, the more that manager, group leader and/or group members may need to work to encourage interaction and communication.[21] In a more homogeneous group, the chances for harmonious working relationships among members may be higher, but the group may find that complex tasks are hard to accomplish if the skills and experiences of the members are limited or narrow in focus.

In other words, although management of interpersonal relations is easier in homogeneous groups, the group may suffer performance limitations as a result of a narrow range of talents. In most cases, strong group homogeneity tends to be more beneficial in situations where group tasks are relatively simple and focused. In contrast, group diversity tends to provide better results in situations where group tasks are complex and highly varied. It is important, therefore, for managers to use good judgement when selecting members for work groups, committees and task forces to ensure the most productive mix of people is chosen.

Status

Status is the indication of a person's relative rank, worth or standing within a group.

A person's status is an indicator of his or her relative rank, worth or standing in terms of prestige and esteem within a group. This standing can be based on any number of factors, including a person's age, work seniority, occupation, education, work accomplishments or status in other groups. A degree of status incongruence may occur when people operate in more than one group and there is a perceived difference in their status in one group compared to that in another. Status incongruence occurs when a person's expressed status within a group is inconsistent with his or her standing on these factors in another context. For example, in high power-distance cultures, such as Hong Kong and Malaysia, status incongruence is expected if the chair of a committee is not the highest-ranking or senior member of the group.

Status incongruence occurs when a person's expressed status within a group is inconsistent with his or her standing in another context.

In a low power-distance culture, this sort of status incongruence may be more acceptable, though there can still be problems; for example, if a young graduate is hired to supervise a group of experienced workers. This is important if members of the group are to be comfortable and harmonious when working together. When there is status incongruence, problems such as stress, dissatisfaction and frustration can occur. The way members deal with these issues can affect group performance.

Group size

The size of a group, defined as the number of its members, can make a difference to its effectiveness. One study looked at 80 work groups in a financial services firm and found group size was positively related to effectiveness.[22] As noted earlier, there is no hard and fast 'magic number' for group size. Some warning signs could indicate when groups, perhaps as a result of their numbers, have outgrown the cohesiveness among members. These warning signs become apparent when it is difficult to unite the group, either physically or verbally. Further, if group meetings are governed by a rigid agenda designed to make sure that a maximum number of issues are communicated, and yet little is discussed, then the group may be too big.

Although it is difficult to pinpoint an ideal group size, a few general guidelines regarding the relationship between size and performance are recognised. Figure 6.4 depicts some of the possible tradeoffs. As a group becomes larger, more potential human resources are available to divide up the work and accomplish needed tasks. This relationship can boost performance, and member satisfaction also tends to increase — up to a point. As a group continues to grow larger, communication and coordination problems begin to set in among members. Satisfaction may dip and tendencies for more turnover and absenteeism increase, as do opportunities for more social loafing. Even logistical matters, such as finding time and locations for meetings, become more difficult with larger groups, causing performance problems.[23]

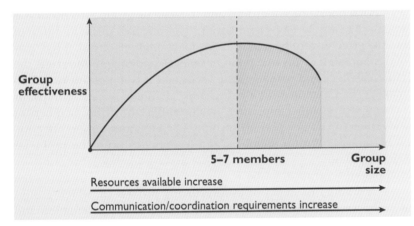

FIGURE 6.4 • Tradeoffs between group size and group effectiveness

In terms of general guidelines, the following patterns in group size can be noted. In problem-solving groups of fewer than five members, there are fewer people to share responsibilities. This typically results in more personal discussions and more participation by all members. In problem-solving groups of more than seven members, there tend to be fewer opportunities for participation, and members may be more inhibited in offering their contributions. There is also the possibility of domination by aggressive members and a tendency for the larger group to split into subgroups.[24] Thus, it appears that the best size for problem-solving groups is between five and seven members. In addition to the homogeneity–heterogeneity issue, this size guideline is useful for managers when they are forming committees and task forces to solve specific problems.

Another aspect of group size to consider is whether the number of members is odd or even. Groups with an even number of members seem more prone to sustained disagreement and conflict while working on tasks. One explanation is that the even number makes it harder for a dominant coalition to form, or for one position to get a majority if a vote is taken. In contrast, it seems easier for members in odd-numbered groups to form coalitions and to take majority votes to resolve disagreements. Where speed is required, this form of conflict management behaviour is useful and odd-numbered groups may be preferred. But where careful deliberations are required and the emphasis is more on consensus (such as in jury duty or complex problem solving), even-numbered groups may be more effective — that is, if the members do not deadlock.[25] Again, the choices made by the manager when initially forming the group may have an important impact on its eventual effectiveness.

Group processes and group dynamics

LEARNING OBJECTIVE 5

Group processes and group effectiveness

Group dynamics are the forces operating in groups that affect group performance and member satisfaction.

According to the 'open systems' group model described earlier, group dynamics are the forces operating in groups that affect task performance and human resource maintenance. If the group is an open system that transforms group inputs into group outputs, then group dynamics are the 'processes' through which this transformation is accomplished. In organisational behaviour and in management practice, it is common to use the term 'group processes' interchangeably with 'group dynamics'; both refer to the internal operations of a group. In this section we will consider the stages of group development, emergent and required behaviours, norms and roles, and emotions, and finally, we will briefly acknowledge group communication and decision making.

Stages of group development

One way to improve the internal operations of groups and to facilitate group effectiveness is to recognise different stages of group development. Groups typically pass through different stages in their life cycles. Any given group, be it a work group, committee or task force, may be in a different stage of development at any one point in time. Depending on the stage, the group may have different challenges and management needs and it is important to understand these to either manage or function within the group. Members of new groups, or groups with significant changes of membership, often behave differently from members of groups that have been together for longer periods of time. In both cases, group effectiveness may be influenced by how well group members and leaders deal with the problems typical to each stage of development.

Models of group development tend to describe it as a sequential process (in which the development goes through a number of steps) or as a recurring process (in which groups tend to return to or move between different group concerns such as task orientation and emotional expression).[26] The five sequential stages of Tuckman's model will now be discussed,[27] followed by an explanation of Gersick's 'punctuated equilibrium' model.

Forming stage

The forming stage is the first stage of group development, in which the primary concern is the initial entry of members to the group.

In the forming stage of group development, a primary concern is the initial entry of members to a group. At this point, individuals ask a number of questions as they begin to identify with other group members and with the group itself: What can the group offer me? What will I be asked to contribute? And can my needs be met at the same time as I contribute to the group? People are interested in discovering what is considered acceptable behaviour, determining the real task of the group and defining group rules. All this is likely to be more complicated in the workplace than in other settings. Members of a new task force, for example, may have been in the organisation for a substantial period of time.

Such factors as multiple group memberships and identifications, prior experience with group members in other contexts, and impressions of organisation philosophies, goals and policies may affect how these members initially behave in the newly formed task force.

Storming stage

The storming stage of group development is a period of high emotion and tension among the group members. Hostility and infighting may occur during this stage. Typically, the group experiences many changes. Membership expectations (the required activities) tend to be clarified and elaborated. Attention begins to shift towards obstacles standing in the way of group goals. Individuals begin to understand one another's interpersonal styles and make efforts to find ways in which to accomplish group goals while also satisfying individual needs. Outside demands, including premature expectations for performance results, may create pressures at this time. Depending on the group's size and membership composition, coalitions or cliques may appear in the form of emergent and informal subgroups. Conflict may develop over leadership and authority, as individuals compete to impose their preferences on the group and to achieve their desired status position. At this stage, discussions about the task, alternatives and possible actions occur. Group members may acknowledge their emotional responses to the task and attempt to justify their legitimacy.

> The storming stage is the second stage of group development, which is marked by a period of high emotion and tension among group members.

Initial integration stage

The initial integration stage of group development (sometimes referred to as the norming stage) is the point at which the group begins to come together as a coordinated unit. At this point, the interpersonal probes and jockeying behaviours of the storming phase give way to a precarious balancing of forces. In their pleasure at the new sense of harmony, group members will most likely strive to maintain this balance. The group as a whole will try to regulate individual behaviour towards this end; minority viewpoints and tendencies to deviate from or question group directions will be discouraged. Initial integration provides group members with a preliminary sense of closeness; consequently, members will want to protect the group from disintegration. Indeed, holding the group together may become more important than successfully working on the group's tasks. Therefore, some group members may wrongly perceive this stage as a stage of ultimate maturity. In fact, the sense of premature accomplishment needs to be carefully managed as a stepping stone to a higher level of group development and not an end in itself.

> The initial integration stage is the third stage of group development, at which the group begins to come together as a coordinated unit; it is sometimes called the norming stage.

Total integration stage

The total integration stage of group development (sometimes referred to as the performing stage) sees the emergence of a mature, organised and well-functioning group. The integration begun in the previous stage is completed during this period. The group is now able to deal with complex tasks and to handle membership disagreements in creative ways. Group structure is stable, and members are motivated by group goals and are generally satisfied. The primary challenges of this stage relate largely to continuing work on human resource maintenance and task performance, but with a strong commitment to continuing improvement and self-renewal. An effective group at this stage of development is made up of members who:
- continue to work well together
- understand their individual and collective responsibilities to other groups and to the larger organisation
- are able to adapt successfully as opportunities and demands change over time.

> The total integration stage is the fourth stage of group development, which sees the emergence of a mature, organised and well-functioning group; it is also referred to as the performing stage.

A group that has achieved the level of total integration typically scores high on the criteria of group maturity shown in figure 6.5.

A mature group possesses:

1. Adequate mechanisms for getting feedback

Poor feedback mechanisms	1	2	3	4	5	Excellent feedback mechanisms
			Average			

2. Adequate decision-making procedure

Poor decision-making procedure	1	2	3	4	5	Very adequate decision making
			Average			

3. Optimal cohesion

Low cohesion	1	2	3	4	5	Optimal cohesion
			Average			

4. Flexible organisation and procedures

Very inflexible	1	2	3	4	5	Very flexible
			Average			

5. Maximum use of member resources

Poor use of resources	1	2	3	4	5	Excellent use of resources
			Average			

6. Clear communication

Poor communication	1	2	3	4	5	Excellent communication
			Average			

7. Clear goals accepted by members

Unclear goals — not accepted	1	2	3	4	5	Very clear goals — accepted
			Average			

8. Feelings of interdependence with authority persons

No interdependence	1	2	3	4	5	High interdependence
			Average			

9. Shared participation in leadership functions

No shared participation	1	2	3	4	5	High shared participation
			Average			

10. Acceptance of minority views and persons

No acceptance	1	2	3	4	5	High acceptance
			Average			

FIGURE 6.5 • Ten criteria for measuring the maturity of a group

Source: E Schein, *Process consultation*, vol. 1, 2nd ed. 1998, figure 6.1, pp. 81 and 82. Reprinted by permission of Pearson Education Inc. Upper Saddle River, NJ.

Adjourning stage

A well-integrated group is able to disband, if required, when its work is accomplished. Thus, it is sometimes appropriate to address a fifth stage, the adjourning stage, of group development.[28] This is an especially important stage for the many temporary groups that are increasingly common in the new workplace, including task forces, committees and the like. Members of these groups must be able to convene quickly, do their jobs on a tight schedule and then adjourn, often to work together again in the future. The willingness of members to disband when the job is done and to work well together in future responsibilities, group or otherwise, is an important long-run test of group success.

Gersick's[29] idea of punctuated group development or 'equilibrium' suggests that groups tend to undergo two long phases of inertia 'punctuated' by a concentrated period of change that is more revolutionary or transitional. This occurs about midway through the life cycle of a group with a fixed task, usually when complacency and a sense of having time is lost to the panic accompanied by an approaching deadline. Depending on the urgency and nature of the task(s), and the life cycle of the group, such groups will experience different patterns of development and change.

There are links between Gersick's and Tuckman's models. It can be argued that the mid-point transition of Gersick's model occurs after the forming, storming and initial integration stages of Tuckman's model. At this point the group receives a 'wake-up alarm' and has to rapidly reassess its goals and direction, perhaps because this was not sufficiently undertaken in the storming stage. Once the new direction is established the group is likely to move into the total integration stage.[30]

Figure 6.5 provides some measures for examining a group and considering what level of maturity it has reached.

The **adjourning stage** is the fifth stage of group development, in which members of the group disband when the job is done.

Required and emergent behaviours

George Homans[31] believes that it is useful to distinguish among the activities, sentiments and interactions of group members. He also believes that it is useful to examine the required and emergent forms of each. Required behaviours are those contributions the organisation formally requests from group members as a basis for continued affiliation and support. They may include such work-related behaviours as being punctual, treating customers with respect and helping coworkers.

Emergent behaviours are those things that group members do in addition to, or in place of, what is formally asked of them by the organisation. Whereas required behaviours are formally designed with the group's purpose in mind, emergent behaviours exist purely as matters of individual or group choice. They are what people do that extends beyond formal job requirements but helps get the job done, such as telephoning an absent member to make sure they are informed about what happened during a group meeting. As figure 6.6 illustrates, emergent behaviours exist as a 'shadow' standing beside the required system.

Required behaviours are those contributions the organisation formally requests from group members as a basis for continued affiliation and support.

Emergent behaviours are those things that group members do in addition to, or in place of, what is formally asked of them by the organisation.

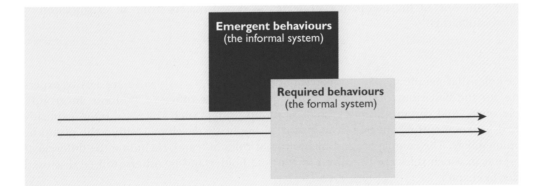

Emergent behaviours
(the informal system)

Required behaviours
(the formal system)

FIGURE 6.6 • The two faces of group dynamics: emergent behaviours and the informal system as a 'shadow' for required behaviours and the formal system

Group norms and roles

Two concepts that are helpful in understanding the processes within groups are norms and roles. These, especially group norms, are discussed more fully in chapter 7. Here, they are briefly summarised to set the foundations for understanding group behaviour.

Group norms are a vital part of understanding group behaviour. They are the standards of behaviour that group members are expected to display. They are important in many ways, but particularly because a group may require everyone to maintain certain levels of performance. In some cases, members are discouraged from working too hard since it may make others look bad or force them to work harder too. Norms can also relate to a range of other group behaviours such as greetings, breaks, dress codes and social participation. For example, it might be expected that group members attend morning tea, or that group members stick together in any conflict between ordinary workers and management. Group norms are not written down but can have an impelling effect on the behaviour of individuals. Not all group norms are positive and can result in ethical dilemmas, as the following 'Ethical perspective' reveals.

ETHICAL
Perspective

Expected silence

There is some concern about the quality of corporate governance occurring in boardrooms in Australia and New Zealand.[32] This relates to what is a well-accepted norm of behaviour of either 'keeping quiet' or 'not going public'. For some boards this is explicit policy; for example, at Wesfarmers what happens in the boardroom is not talked about outside.[33] While directors may express disagreement within meetings they seldom make their feelings known to the public, and seldom resign. Their silence often allows what they see as a poor decision to go ahead whereas some public airing might give the shareholders and others a further chance to influence the decision. The board members may face ethical dilemmas because they are trying to meet different types of expectations:

- competing interests of employees' working lives, shareholders' economic returns and corporate social responsibility[34]
- ensuring poor or potentially disastrous board decisions are not made even if that means having to go outside the boardroom to achieve this
- wanting to keep the appearance of a stable and harmonious company and board (public exposure of conflict on boards can bring about its own detrimental effects to reputation and business success)
- wanting to protect their own personal reputations and careers as directors, especially as there is a limited pool of people who appear to be chosen as directors.[35]

One person who did resign from a board was Carolyn Hewson. She was unhappy with AMP's attempt to buy a financially troubled life insurance company in China (her reasons were not made public but were later found out). Another is Sir Ross Buckland, who resigned from the board of Mayne in March 2004 because he did not agree with one of the company's strategies to buy products from an organisation called aaiPharma.[36]

The roles that people play in groups are also important. **Group roles** are sets of expectations for the behaviour of a person holding a particular office or position. In groups, people often hold certain positions, such as group leader. Such roles are often explicitly defined in statements of duties, but may also be implicitly developed within the group by group members. The complexity and difficulties of roles in teams, including the differences in the way in which roles are perceived by the role holder and by others, will be discussed further in chapter 7.

Group 'roles' sometimes refer more generally to how a person is expected to behave in order to achieve group goals, including task performance or group maintenance. We are able to use these expected roles to describe whether a person is helping or hindering the performance or continuation of the group. For example, in a group situation, whenever we make a suggestion or offer a comment in a meeting, we are playing a role. Because these types of roles are important in analysing the outputs of groups, in terms of whether they support the task performance or group maintenance, we consider these later in the chapter as 'task activities' and 'maintenance activities'.

Emotions in groups

The role of emotion in group dynamics has been a constant although often only implicit theme in the social psychological and organisational behaviour literatures.[37] Emotions are an essential and unavoidable element of group life. Disappointment, happiness, sadness, fear and dissatisfaction are just some emotions that can be found in a group situation. Given that emotions are an inseparable part of task activity in group situations, managers must embrace them rather than prevent their expression; this approach will help improve group effectiveness and therefore organisational effectiveness. Given the somewhat pejorative view of emotion in group situations, only a limited range of emotional expression tends to be socially acceptable. Expressions of negative emotion, such as anxiety, fear or anger, tend to be unacceptable except under fairly circumscribed conditions. It is frequently accepted that a high-status group member can convey impatience with a low-status group member, for example, but it is not generally accepted in reverse. Often, group tensions are fuelled by affective or expressive concerns that have little to do with task-focused issues, and minor disagreements can quickly escalate into major conflicts, with the group polarised into rival camps. In groups that are charged with negative emotions, intergroup conflict — whether over ends, means or resources — may generate distrust and hostility such that the conflict becomes the group's focal concern and initial goals are forgotten.

Group communication and decision making

Within groups communication and decision making are important functions. However, they are also important processes in the organisation as a whole, and for this reason they are each the subject of a separate chapter in part 4. It is important for us to acknowledge here that the dynamics of groups will affect the quality of decision making and communication; and also that the functioning of groups (both in terms of task performance and group maintenance) will be affected by decision making and communication. One particular problem that can occur with group decision making is 'groupthink', when members of a highly cohesive group seek to conform, come to think alike and/or become unwilling to be critical of one another's ideas and suggestions. This can result in poor, and sometimes very costly, decision errors. This and other group decision-making issues are discussed at length in chapter 12. In terms of communication, the structure of groups and how group members work on tasks — that is, in an interactive, coactive or counteractive way — will relate closely to the types of communication networks that exist in the group; decentralised, centralised or restrictive, respectively (see chapter 13).

Outputs of the group process — task performance and group maintenance

LEARNING OBJECTIVE 6 — Groups' task and maintenance outputs

Group outputs are the results of the transformation of group inputs through group processes.

Earlier in the chapter, when groups were described as open systems, group outputs were described as the products of the group process. A formal group has the purpose in an organisation of fulfilling one or more organisational tasks, and managers are typically concerned with ensuring the group does so. From the perspective of group members (including leaders or managers within groups), groups need to enable them to fulfil these task needs and also to fulfil their human maintenance needs.[38] These are necessary group outputs if groups are to function successfully in organisations. Every member of a group can and must assist in the group's development by doing things that specifically respond to group task and maintenance needs. Although a person in a position of formal authority, such as chairperson or department head, should also do these things, the responsibility is shared by and distributed among all group members. Any and all group members should be able to recognise when task needs and/or maintenance needs must be met; they should also possess the skills needed to step in and help meet these needs at any time. This sharing of responsibility for fulfilling group task and maintenance needs is sometimes called distributed leadership in group dynamics. As this term suggests, all members of effective groups help lead these groups by contributing towards both task and maintenance activities in the group process.[39]

> **Distributed leadership** is the sharing of responsibility for fulfilling group task and maintenance needs.

Group task performance

Group task performance is a vital output of the group process. It is expected that groups use the resources they have (including group inputs like membership and emotions) to achieve their task goals effectively and efficiently. This is a major output of the group, but contributing to that will be task-oriented behaviours that members of the group exhibit. Thus all groups need members who are able and willing to perform task activities. These are the various things members do that directly contribute to the performance of important group tasks. As already mentioned, they are not tasks that only the leader, chair, head or manager of the group should do; rather, they are tasks that all members should be doing. If task activities are not adequate, group process will suffer and the group will have difficulty accomplishing its objectives. In an effective group, by contrast, members will enhance group process by contributing these and other important task activities as needed:[40]

> **Task activities** are the various things members do that directly contribute to the performance of important group tasks.

- *initiating* — offering new ideas or ways of defining problems; suggesting solutions to group difficulties
- *seeking information* — attempting to clarify suggestions in terms of factual accuracy; asking for ideas of others
- *giving information* — offering authoritative and relevant information and facts
- *clarifying* — clarifying relations among various suggestions or ideas; attempting to coordinate member activities
- *summarising* — assessing group functioning; raising questions about the logic and practicality of member suggestions.

Group maintenance

Maintaining the group and the group members is another important group output and much group activity is directed towards that. Whereas task activities advance the task agenda of a group, maintenance activities support the social and interpersonal relationships among its members. 'Maintenance' activities do just that: they help maintain the group as an ongoing social system. If maintenance activities are not performed well, group processes will suffer as members become dissatisfied with one another and their group membership. In such cases, emotional antagonisms and conflicts may develop and drain energies that could otherwise help advance group purposes. Depending on the past experiences of the group and the problems to be solved, the proportion of maintenance roles to task roles will vary. Some groups, such as a bridge club, may only perform group maintenance roles. Their sole purpose is sociability. A church-building committee, on the other hand, has an assigned purpose and would probably show a preponderance of group task roles. The members of an effective group are aware of the need for maintenance activities and are able to provide them in ways that help build good interpersonal relationships and enhance the ability of the group to stay together over time.

> **Maintenance activities** are activities that support the emotional life of the group as an ongoing social system.

At this point, it is important to introduce a key concept of groups. In a group, cohesiveness (or group cohesion) is the degree to which members are attracted to and motivated to remain part of the group. The cohesiveness of the group is useful in explaining group behaviour in many contexts (for example, its relationship to group diversity and group norms), but is mentioned here because it has direct relevance to the social and interpersonal relations of group members. The concept is so important that it is discussed at length in chapter 7 (see page 240). Cohesiveness helps us to understand the following examples of important group maintenance activities. They include:[41]

- *encouraging* — praising, accepting or agreeing with other members' ideas; indicating solidarity and warmth
- *harmonising* — mediating squabbles within the group; reconciling differences; seeking opportunities for compromise
- *compromising* — maintaining group cohesion by 'coming halfway' or admitting an error; sacrificing status to maintain group harmony (The major difference between the harmoniser and the compromiser is that the compromiser is one of the parties in a conflict.)
- *gatekeeping* — encouraging participation of group members; trying to keep some members from dominating
- *setting standards* — expressing standards for the group to achieve or use in evaluating group process
- *following* — going along with the group; agreeing to try out the ideas of others.

Having considered the inputs, processes and outputs of groups, it is worth considering the usefulness of these concepts in a wider context. The following 'Counterpoint' addresses some of the issues that emerge when we consider a more complex world of multiple groups and networks.

> **Cohesiveness** is the degree to which members are attracted to and motivated to remain part of the group.

COUNTER**POINT**

Beyond groups and into the wider world

How connected are people in work groups? Isn't the concept now outdated? In contemporary organisations people are more focused on networking, on accomplishing tasks and fulfilling their own personal needs by working freely with many individuals or people or collections of people on a range of fronts. They belong to groups inside and outside work as well as network with a range of people. How can we pinpoint their behaviours to their membership of a particular group?

In highly individualistic cultures, people might largely ignore the processes of the groups in which they are operating, or at least often seek other ways of achieving their aims. Management in contemporary organisations can place too much emphasis on the dynamics of groups, treating them as if they had a unity and strength that blindly ignores individuality or multiple group membership. There is no magic black box that transforms these people away from their individual personalities, attitudes and values once they become part of a group. Even in a group, dominant or highly political individuals may really dictate the processes of the group. Outside of the group structures, political and personal networks may have more impact on what members of a group do than fellow group members.

Organisational structures also make individuals' networks more complex. In the public sector the idea of 'joined up' governments is very popular. It moves beyond old ideas of bureaucratic hierarchies to a complex and flexible model that involves networks of private contractors, non-profit organisations and government agencies all working together to deliver public services and policies. There are complex and multiple webs of connections among people that cross organisations and span the public and the private sectors.[42] Information and communication technologies enhance the possibility of these complex connections, while in the business world global activity necessitates it.

(continued)

The idea of neat, unified groups that act collectively is unlikely in our complex world of networks. Writers such as Mark Granovetter draw our attention to the way in which our social networks have subtle but important influence on individuals' economic choices. He finds that groups that are dense and cohesive are more able to overcome 'free-rider' behaviour because people in such close-knit groups tend to internalise norms of behaviour and members can feel the pressures of approval or disapproval from these groups very strongly. However, people often acquire valuable information from their weakest links.[43] This being so, managers should think far beyond understanding how individuals are affected by 'groups' in the workplace. Even when we have a clearly designated group of people working together constantly for common goals, there is no guarantee that other network links and/or events on a day-to-day basis will not change the dynamics of individuals in the work group. A group is, after all, only a set of individuals who are influenced by many forces around them. People can be influenced by events in their lives, their moods, changing abilities and motivations, changes to group membership when people come and go, and intergroup connections and networks. All these keep group dynamics in an unpredictable state of flux.

Questions

1. How can we come to terms with the definition of a group when individuals belong to many groups and are affected by them in various ways and to varying degrees?
2. Should managers now be more concerned with understanding networks and, if so, what phenomena should they be considering?

Intergroup dynamics

Intergroup dynamics

Before leaving this discussion of group dynamics, we need to look once again at the organisation itself as a network of many interlocking groups. In this complicated setting, intergroup dynamics become very important. They are the dynamics that operate between two or more groups.

Intergroup dynamics are the dynamics that take place between groups, as opposed to within groups.

The organisation ideally operates as a cooperative system in which the various groups are willing and able to help one another as needed. An important managerial responsibility is to make sure that groups work together to the benefit of the total organisation. Yet, by their nature, intergroup dynamics can be competitive as well as cooperative. Although there may be times when a bit of competition can help groups maintain their creative edge, too much competition can work to the detriment of the larger system. When intergroup rivalries and antagonisms detract from the ability of the groups to cooperate with one another, the organisation will lose the desired synergy. Progressive managers are able to build and maintain effective intergroup relations.[44]

Work flow interdependency and intergroup relations

Work flow interdependency is the way work flows in an organisation from one group to the next.

The way in which work flows in an organisation from one group to the next — that is, the nature of work flow interdependency — affects intergroup dynamics. Figure 6.7 depicts how pooled, sequential and reciprocal interdependencies affect the ways in which groups work together to achieve their goals.

Not much attention to the management of intergroup relationships is needed in *pooled interdependency*. The groups seldom, if ever, meet and they perform their respective tasks quite independently. As long as each group does its job in accordance with organisational goals, then the activities of other groups are of little concern.

What other groups do becomes more important when there is *sequential interdependency* of the work flows. This means that one group's outputs become another group's inputs.

The second group depends on the first group and cannot do its job unless the first group provides it with needed inputs in a timely and high-quality fashion. Naturally, this type of interdependency is prone both to more contact between the groups and to more potential problems in the intergroup relations. This creates a need for managerial attention to intergroup relations.

Things become even more complicated when there is *reciprocal interdependency* in the work flow. In this situation, many groups interact in input–output relationships, much as do members of the decentralised communication networks mentioned earlier in this chapter. With frequent and varied interactions among many groups in the normal day-to-day course of work, the intergroup dynamics become complex. They are also extremely important because a breakdown at any point will have spillover effects to other points. Managers in such settings must be good at helping multiple groups build and maintain good working relationships with one another.

These interdependencies exist in all organisations in various combinations and to various degrees. The relationship between front office and back office employees at Flight Centre is just one example.

In early 2005, Flight Centre announced a review of its operations in the light of increased competition. The review identified that the 'front office' workers — the various groups who run each shopfront outlet for the company — were not to lose jobs. However, under threat of reductions were the 'back office' staff — the groups of people in the business who organise and make available to shopfront workers all the relevant information about travel products, and who also provide the automated systems on which the shopfront workers check and sell products. If the back office is not organised or is weak in its preparation of this information and its maintenance of the systems, shopfront staff will be affected since they are dependent upon this work output.[45]

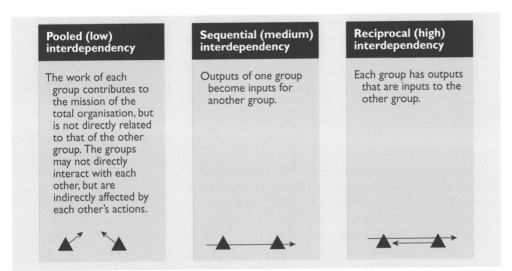

Pooled (low) interdependency	Sequential (medium) interdependency	Reciprocal (high) interdependency
The work of each group contributes to the mission of the total organisation, but is not directly related to that of the other group. The groups may not directly interact with each other, but are indirectly affected by each other's actions.	Outputs of one group become inputs for another group.	Each group has outputs that are inputs to the other group.

FIGURE 6.7 • Types of work flow interdependency and their impact on intergroup relationships

Other factors affecting intergroup relations

Many other factors may affect intergroup dynamics, some of which will now be discussed. The way in which they impact may vary according to the particulars of each situation.

The group status or prestige of one group compared with that of others may be important, particularly in sequential or reciprocal work flow interdependencies. For example, if a lower-status group must wait for the output of the higher-status group, the lower-status group may have little power to demand faster work from the other group. Groups may also differ in the ways in which they deal with time and goals. The time orientation of a group is based on the length of time needed to obtain necessary information and to accomplish tasks. When some groups are able to operate on shorter time horizons than other groups with whom work flow interdependencies exist, these differences can complicate intergroup relations. For example, nurses concerned for patient recovery may wish to extend the duration of patients' stay in hospital, while admissions staff, who focus mainly on the brief task of scheduling and admitting patients, may agitate for quicker discharges to free up beds.

The reward system under which a group performs can have a strong impact on intergroup relations. For example, if a group of concreters in a construction firm is being rewarded for the amount of concreting done per week (rather than its quality), that may cause potential problems for the group that is responsible for quality and safety of construction. The rewards are likely to reinforce the different goals of the two groups and exacerbate difficulties in intergroup relations.

Finally, groups differ in available resources. If a resource-rich group has frequent dealings with one that is, or perceives itself to be, resource poor, then intergroup problems can easily arise. For example, if a research and design group is well-resourced with funds and/or staff but must work with a poorly-resourced production unit to trial its designs, the production unit may be resistant to cooperating. The underlying issue has much to do with the equity theory of motivation discussed in chapter 3. Sometimes, groups need to share resources to get their jobs done. When the shared resource is in scarce supply and/or when there is no clear agreement on how it is to be allocated, intergroup problems are prone to develop.

Dynamics of intergroup competition

We pointed out earlier that the ideal organisation is a cooperative system in which people and groups always work together harmoniously. But, as the last two sections have indicated, the real world of the organisation as an interlocking network of groups may be far from perfect.

There are many ways and reasons for intergroup problems to develop. Competition occurs as well as cooperation. When this occurs, the dynamics depicted in figure 6.8 are also likely to occur.

There are two approaches to managing the dynamics of intergroup competition.[46] The first is to deal with the competition after it occurs. Recommended ways for controlling existing competition include:
- identifying a common enemy that can unite the groups
- appealing to a common goal that can unite the groups
- initiating direct negotiations between the groups
- training members of the groups to work cooperatively.

The second approach for managing intergroup competition is to take action before it occurs — that is, to prevent its occurrence in the first place. Recommended ways for preventing the emergence of destructive intergroup competition include:
- rewarding groups for their contributions to the total organisation
- avoiding win–lose competitions for important rewards
- rewarding groups for giving help to one another
- stimulating frequent interactions between members of different groups
- preventing groups from withdrawing and becoming isolated from one another
- rotating members among different groups.

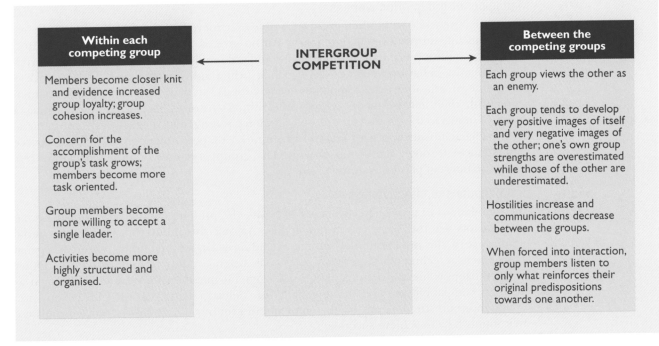

FIGURE 6.8 • What happens within and between groups engaged in intergroup competition

The potential disadvantages of intergroup competition are numerous. The competition may divert energies away from the performance of important tasks, as members focus on dealing with the other groups. Also common is the emergence of grudges, animosities or biased and selective viewpoints of one group towards another. The result is poor intergroup coordination. Therefore, the suggestions listed become quite important. Managers at all levels in organisations walk a thin line as they try to avoid the disadvantages of intergroup competition while still enjoying its advantages.

Those managers who are successful with intergroup dynamics can tap the potential advantages of intergroup competition. When groups compete with others, they may work harder, become more focused on key tasks, develop more internal cohesion and satisfaction, and achieve a higher level of creativity in problem solving. When properly harnessed, such dynamics of intergroup competition can be strong assets for an organisation.

Summary

Groups and types of groups

A group is formally defined as a collection of people who interact with one another regularly to attain common goals. Groups in organisations fall into two major categories. Formal groups are 'official' groups — work units, task forces, committees and so on that are created by a formal authority to achieve a specific purpose. Many such groups can be identified on organisation charts. Informal groups are 'unofficial'. They emerge spontaneously and are not designated by the organisation to serve any purpose. They may work for or against organisational needs, but tend to satisfy important individual needs.

How groups meet individual and organisational needs

One way to view an organisation is as an interlocking network of groups. From this perspective, the results accomplished by each group should add up in building-block fashion to fulfil organisational needs for task accomplishment. Any group offers the potential to satisfy important individual needs for social interaction, security and so on.

Managing for group effectiveness

Group effectiveness occurs when groups are able to achieve high levels of both task performance and human resource maintenance. Within groups, synergy occurs when a group is able to accomplish more than its members would accomplish individually. However, disruptive or negative behaviours such as social loafing (when individual members do not work as hard as they might otherwise) sometimes occur. Groups can be viewed as open systems interacting with their environments. Group effectiveness involves success in transforming a variety of inputs to the group (such as organisational setting, nature of the task, group membership characteristics and size) into group outputs (task performance and human resource maintenance) through the group process. The group processes or group dynamics represent the internal processes of the group.

Group inputs and effectiveness

The foundations of group effectiveness begin with the presence of the right inputs. Group input factors set the stage for group action. Among the inputs of special managerial significance is the organisational setting, including available operating resources, spatial arrangements, technologies, rewards and goal systems, cultures and structures. Other important inputs are the nature of the task; general membership characteristics such as member compatibilities and homogeneity or heterogeneity; status; and group size. Optimum group size depends on the context and group goals. Highly effective groups use their inputs fully to achieve success.

Group processes and group dynamics

Group dynamics are the forces operating within groups that affect task performance and human resource maintenance. They are the internal processes through which members work together to accomplish the transformation of group inputs into group outputs. The terms 'group dynamics' and 'group processes' are often used interchangeably. The behaviours within groups may be required or they may be emergent, additional behaviours. All groups pass through various stages in their life cycles. Five different stages of group development pose somewhat distinct management problems. Groups in the forming stage have problems managing individual entry. The storming stage introduces problems of managing expectations and status. Groups in the initial integration stage have problems managing member relations and task efforts. Groups in the total integration stage encounter problems managing continual improvement and self-renewal. Groups in the adjourning stage have problems managing task completion and the process of disbanding. Group norms or standards of behaviour will impact upon the behaviour of all group members. Group roles relating to particular positions in the group describe the expected behaviours for individuals in those roles. Emotions and patterns of communication and decision making are also elements of group dynamics.

Groups' task and maintenance outputs

Groups have two broad sets of needs that must be met if they are to operate successfully. First, group members contribute a variety of task activities, such as initiating and summarising, that make direct contributions to the group's task performance. Second, group members must contribute to the fulfilment of maintenance needs. These include other activities, such as encouraging and gatekeeping, that specifically help to maintain the social fabric of the group over time. Both task activities and maintenance activities must be accomplished in any group. The principle of distributed leadership points out that these activities can and should be provided, as needed, by all group members, not just by those formally designated as leaders. Groups are capable of providing many advantages to organisations but can also result in disadvantages.

Intergroup dynamics

Intergroup dynamics are the forces that operate between two or more groups. Although groups are supposed to cooperate in organisations, things do not always work this way.

Groups can become involved in dysfunctional conflicts and competition. Sometimes, the origins of these conflicts lie in work flow interdependencies; at other times, the origins can be traced to differing group characteristics. Such things as status, time and goal orientations, reward systems and resource availabilities can all make a difference in the way in which groups work together. Managers must be aware of the potential for problems in intergroup relations and know how to deal with them, even as they recognise that some competition can be good. The disadvantages of intergroup competition can be reduced through management strategies to direct, train and reinforce groups to pursue cooperative actions instead of purely competitive actions.

Chapter 6 study guide

Key terms

adjourning stage, *p. 209*
cohesiveness, *p. 213*
disruptive behaviour, *p. 196*
distributed leadership, *p. 212*
effective groups, *p. 197*
emergent behaviours, *p. 209*
formal groups, *p. 190*
forming stage, *p. 206*
friendship groups, *p. 192*
group dynamics, *p. 206*
group inputs, *p. 199*
group norms, *p. 210*

group outputs, *p. 211*
group roles, *p. 210*
groups, *p. 190*
heterogeneous groups, *p. 204*
homogeneous groups, *p. 204*
informal groups, *p. 192*
initial integration stage, *p. 207*
interest groups, *p. 192*
intergroup dynamics, *p. 214*
maintenance activities, *p. 212*
permanent formal work groups,
    p. 191

required behaviours, *p. 209*
social loafing, *p. 196*
status, *p. 204*
status incongruence, *p. 204*
storming stage, *p. 207*
sub-goal optimisation, *p. 198*
synergy, *p. 196*
task activities, *p. 212*
temporary formal work groups,
    p. 191
total integration stage, *p. 207*
work flow interdependency, *p. 214*

Review questions

1. Outline the different types of groups that can exist in organisations and provide your own example of each.
2. Explain how group size might affect group processes and effectiveness.
3. Explain the difference between initial integration and total integration in the group development stages.

4. Compare the three different types of work flow interdependency and discuss how the level of interdependency might relate to the degree of conflict between such groups.

Application questions

1. If groups are to create positive synergy in the accomplishment of organisational tasks, what must managers do to overcome disruptive behaviours?
2. Your product marketing group consists of two people in their 40s (one male, one female) and two people in their 20s (one male, one female) who must work together to find the best ways to market your organisation's products. What aspects of group membership might have an impact on the likely effectiveness of the group?
3. Until recently your group of seven members has been operating successfully and you felt that it was achieving high levels of effectiveness. However, since two members left your team (and the organisation) to go

to other jobs and you replaced them with two new members (one from outside the organisation and one from another organisational section), there is less group cohesion and more conflict. Discuss the reasons why these changes might have occurred and use theories and concepts about groups to explain them.

4. Roslyn is managing a completely new group of seven people, comprising two women and five men. The group is responsible for implementing a new risk-management strategy in the organisation over the next 12 months. Four of the people in the group are completely new to the organisation but have strong backgrounds in risk management, while the three from the organisation have a strong knowledge of the

organisation and its processes. How is the group likely to develop and what problems might eventuate?

5. The BluePot organisation is currently working on its enterprise agreement. The organisation has established a group of senior managers and employee representatives from various parts of the organisation to negotiate with the union representatives (employees of the organisation with help from the external union organisation) on the agreement. What types of groups are involved in this negotiation process?

6. Your organisation operates with four key groups: corporate services, sales, finance and production. Recently there have been problems with achieving its production targets because there is a shortage of workers; the corporate services group has been unable to replace departing employees rapidly enough. Sales is unhappy because they are unable to meet orders for stock, while finance is becoming increasingly stressed about the lack of cash flow in the business. What are the likely work flow relationships between each group and why might they cause problems?

Research questions

1. Investigate your own university or college and look for evidence of groups. They could be in the teaching faculty or department which manages your course or in other parts of the organisation, such as administrative sections or sections that support student activities. Find out what you can about the groups that exist by talking to people and investigating documents such as brochures, handbooks and web pages. You might also observe some groups who engage in non-work activities, or who work together on fundraising activities. You might find groups such as teaching staff and non-teaching staff, research teams or centres, groups from different disciplines (such as economics, management and law) and various committees. Discuss your findings, noting:
   (a) the different types of groups that exist
   (b) how members of one group might also belong to another
   (c) what formal decision-making groups exist

   (d) what group member characteristics exist (for example, numbers of men and women, economists versus accountants, senior versus lower-level staff).

   Draw some conclusions about the nature of group behaviour in your university/college faculty or department.

2. Search the web site of a major company looking for depictions of the company structure — either an organisational chart or lists of sections and departments in the company. Use this information to draw up a profile of *formal* groups within the organisation, labelling different types of groups and links between them. Analyse the groups, as much as you can from the information available, in terms of their likely features (size, homogeneity, position roles within them, resources, goals and decision-making functions). Repeat the process for another company and compare the two.

Running project

Complete the following tasks relating to your organisation.
1. Refer back to any earlier work you did on the structure of your organisation. Also try to obtain an organisational chart for the organisation. Describe how the organisation uses groups to structure the workplace.
2. If you have direct access to the organisation, try to find out about informal groups. Try to determine why these groups formed.

3. Choose one group in the organisation and draw a diagram of the group as an open system. List the most important outputs of the group and explain how the manager, group leader or group members would know whether the group is effective at any given time.
4. Choose two different groups within the organisation. Describe how these groups work with each other. If you have direct access to the organisation, ask management how it deals with intergroup conflict.

Individual activity

Analysing a group

Objective
To better understand the basic attributes of groups

Activity
For this exercise, select a specific group with whom you work or have worked, or a group you are familiar with from an organisation in your local community. Answer the following questions as they relate to the group.

1. Is the group a formal or an informal group? Explain why.
2. Is the group an open system? Explain why by discussing:

(a) its inputs

What is the organisational setting (resources, technology, spatial arrangements, reward systems and goals, structure, size and culture)? What is the nature of the group task? What are general membership characteristics (interpersonal compatibilities, membership homogeneity–heterogeneity, status)? What is the group size?

(b) its processes

What are some of the required and emergent behaviours of the group? How does communication occur? How are decisions made?

(c) its outputs

How does it satisfy task and maintenance needs?

Group activity

Analysing your groups

Objective
To show the relevance and pervasiveness of formal and informal groups within your lives:
- in your 'organisational' environment at university/college
- outside that environment (social and other organisations)

Procedure
Individually

List all of the various groups to which you belong currently.

In groups

1. Discuss the groups you have listed as individuals and place them into categories — formal or informal.
2. Are there some types of groups to which you all, or several of you, belong? Why?
3. What conclusions can you draw about the number of groups to which you individually and collectively belong?
4. Do you behave differently in different groups?

Case study: Workshops for organisational change at a global FMCG company

When a global FMCG (fast moving consumer goods) company refurbished its Australian office and manufacturing sites, the company was looking for one magical element that could transform its physical environments into places of innovation.

It found it by communicating with employees, understanding their needs, and working to create a 'balanced' working environment.

A series of 'alternative thinking and communication' workshops were held with groups of employees with varying backgrounds, ages and skills to help put together a 'people-driven' project brief.

The workshops were to free the participants' minds and stimulate creativity, and to encourage open communication while breaking down any hierarchy. In keeping with this, the settings were void of references to the participants' typical work surroundings.

Because people learn in different ways, the workshops combined aural, written and visual exercises. In interpreting the 1992 work of Honey and Mumford,

Sarah Cornelius has suggested that learning styles could be categorised into four types: activists (requiring a range of activities to keep them occupied), reflectors (deep thinkers who engage in the opportunity for learning), pragmatists (who need opportunities to trial what they have learnt) and theorists (who need time to explore links between ideas and situations).

The initial workshops were conducted one day a week for three weeks. The time in between allowed participants to gather data and reflect on what had already been done.

The workshops included exercises with individual employees to suit the different learning styles. Later there were exercises for small teams and finally exercises for the whole workshop group. Exercises included describing the working day, selecting images for collages to convey the organisation's culture, identifying and evaluating role model organisations, and anything-goes brainstorming.

Common themes began to appear. Through discussions and brainstorming, the group found that not one but three elements needed to be collectively addressed to achieve what they perceived as a balanced working environment: the physical, the cultural and the technological. The common themes were grouped accordingly, then arranged into tangible and non-tangible.

Ideas, themes and suggested solutions were refined for an initial brief for the new workplace environment, which management reviewed to ensure it aligned with the company's direction.

Management decided to pick up the momentum and address issues raised in the workshops. It added more people and in-house performance-driven workshops to the program. Subjects included disruptive innovation, associate needs, business direction, wellbeing, technological developments, and internal and external benchmarking.

Undertaking physical workplace change is of little benefit if an organisation's culture doesn't support it, or if personnel can't perform efficiently with the technology provided. Similarly, when technology is upgraded, the culture and workplace must be adapted.

Even minor changes in workplace environments can alienate those affected if the reasons are not understood. People typically resist change, usually due to fear of the unknown.

Through communication and by involving those most affected — the employees — change at the global FMCG company tended to be embraced by all rather than seen as negative. All those involved were aware of the potential results and they united to steer in the same direction.

The alternative thinking and communication workshops were empowering for individuals and the organisation. They promote ownership of ideas and solutions, ideas are cross-fertilised, and interaction is instigated or promoted across different groups and levels.

The global FMCG company is currently planning its roll-out of the balanced environment on a three-year timeline throughout Australia and New Zealand.

Source: Jody Marshall (for Response Design Group, Sydney), 'Accommodating innovation', *HR Monthly* (May 2004), pp. 38–9.

Questions

1. What types of groups were used at the global FMCG company in its project on achieving a change to innovation and what purposes did they fulfil for the organisation and individuals?
2. The duration of the workshops' 'group' activity was relatively short. What implications might this have for group processes, including group development and the development of group norms?
3. How effective was the activity of the groups and how did the group inputs affect the group?

Suggested reading

OB

Gerard M Blair, *Starting to manage: the essential skills* (London: Chartwell-Bratt, 1996).

Rupert Brown, *Group processes*, 2nd ed. (Oxford: Blackwell, 2000).

Ross Cross and Andrew Parker, *The hidden power of social networks: understanding how work really gets done in organizations* (Boston: Harvard Business School Press, 2004).

Judith Hoover, *Effective small group and team communication* (Belmont, CA: Thomson/Wadsworth, 2005).

David W Johnson and Frank P Johnson, *Joining together: group theory and group skills*, 7th ed. (Boston: Allyn & Bacon, 2000).

Gay Lumsden and Donald Lumsden, *Communicating in groups and teams: sharing leadership* (Belmont, CA: Wadsworth/Thomson, 2004).

Marshall Scott Poole and Andrea B Hollingshead (eds), *Theories of small groups: interdisciplinary perspectives* (Thousand Oaks, CA: Sage, 2005).

Alistair Rylatt, *Learning unlimited: practical strategies and techniques for transforming learning in the workplace*, 2nd ed. (Sydney: Business and Publishing, 2000).

Marlene E Turner (ed.), *Groups at work: theory and research* (Mahwah, NJ: Erlbaum, 2001).

T Tyson, *Working with groups*, 2nd ed. (Melbourne: Macmillan, 1998).

Alvin Zander, *The purposes of groups and organizations* (San Francisco: Jossey-Bass, 1985).

OB End notes

1. Coleambally Irrigation (CICL), 'About us', 'Business structure', 'Staff' (2005), www.colyirr.com.au; John Spriggs, Barbara Chambers, Tony Dunn and Michele Fromholtz, 'Beyond economic rationalism in rural Australia: a new approach to socio-economic change in the Coleambally Irrigation Area', Strategic Partnership with Industry – Research and Training Scheme (SPIRT) grant with Coleambally Irrigation Cooperative Ltd (CICL) (2001–02); John Spriggs, Barbara Chambers, Tony Dunn and Michele Fromholtz, 'Socioeconomic change in the Coleambally Irrigation Area', paper contributed to the 46th annual conference of the Australian Agricultural and Resource Economics Society, Canberra, 15 February 2002.

2. Little is written specifically on task forces, but one useful reference is W Alan Randolph and Barry Z Posner, *Getting the job done! Managing project teams and task forces for success* (Englewood Cliffs, NJ: Prentice Hall, 1992).

3. 'Drivers cry foul over co-op ban', *New Straits Times* (15 December 2004), p. 18.

4. Carolyn Cummins, 'Zoo car park sparks row', *The Sydney Morning Herald* (28–29 May 2005), p. 70.

5. Vicki Jayne, 'Suzanne Hall: at face value', *New Zealand Management* (October 2004), pp. 12–15.

6. Harold J Leavitt, 'Suppose we took groups seriously' in Eugene L Cass and Frederick G Zimmer (eds), *Man and work in society* (New York: Van Nostrand Reinhold, 1975), pp. 67–77.

7. Peter Vincent, 'Remember who's the boss', *The Sydney Morning Herald*, My Career section (19–20 February 2005), p. 1.

8. Julia Connell and Zeenobiyah Hannif, 'Tough calls', *HR Monthly* (July 2005), pp. 30–2.

9. Bib Latane, Kipling Williams and Stephen Harkins, 'Many hands make light the work: the causes and consequences of social loafing', *Journal of Personality and Social Psychology*, vol. 37 (1978), pp. 822–32; E Weldon and GM Gargano, 'Cognitive effort in additive task groups: the effects of shared responsibility on the quality of multi-attribute judgments', *Organizational Behavior and Human Decision Processes*, vol. 36 (1985), pp. 348–61.

10. David Jaques, *Learning in groups* (London: Kogan Page, 1991).

11. For further insights see J Richard Hackman, 'The design of work teams' in Jay W Lorsch (ed.), *Handbook of organizational behavior* (Englewood Cliffs, NJ: Prentice Hall, 1987), p. 343.

12. Linda N Jewell and H Joseph Reitz, *Group effectiveness in organizations* (Glenview, IL: Scott, Foresman, 1981), pp. 149–50.

13. Cameron Cooper, '[Making the outposts feel like] part of the team', *Management Today* (April 2004), pp. 30–2.

14. This discussion is developed from D Herold, 'The effectiveness of work groups' in Steven Kerr (ed.), *Organizational behavior* (Columbus, OH: Grid Publishing, 1979), pp. 99–103.

15. ibid.

16. James Ware, 'Managing a task force', note 478002 (Boston: Harvard Business School, 1977).

17. Information for this item comes from anonymous articles in the *New Straits Times*, Excel with Education supplement (15 December 2005): 'HELP yourself to good education', p. 13; 'Singapore's top collaborations', p. 17; 'Global approach at Monash', p. 12; from anecdotal accounts from lecturing employees at Australian universities; and also from Ooi Tee Ching, 'Creative Limkokwing varsity', *Business Times* (18 December 2004), p. B24.

18. William C Schutz, *FIRO: a three-dimensional theory of interpersonal behavior* (New York: Rinehart and Co., 1958).

19. William C Schutz, 'The interpersonal underworld', *Harvard Business Review*, vol. 36, no. 4 (July/August 1958), p. 130.

20. Vicki Jayne, 'Beating time' (incorporating 'The queen of diversity'), *New Zealand Management* (September 2004), p. 28.

21. Michael A Hitt, J Stewart Black and Lyman W Porter, *Management*, international ed. (Upper Saddle River NJ: Pearson Prentice-Hall, 2005), pp. 456–7.

22. MA Campion, GJ Medsker and AC Higgs, 'Relations between work group characteristics and effectiveness: implications for designing effective work groups', *Personnel Psychology*, vol. 46 (1993) pp. 823–50.

23. See Jon R Katzenbach and Douglas K Smith, 'The discipline of teams', *Harvard Business Review* (March–April 1993), pp. 111–20.

24. EJ Thomas and CF Fink, 'Effects of group size' in Larry L Cummings and William E Scott (eds), *Readings in organizational and human performance* (Homewood, IL: Richard D. Irwin, 1969), pp. 394–408.

25. See Marvin E Shaw, *Group dynamics: the psychology of small group behavior*, 2nd ed. (New York: McGraw-Hill, 1976).

26. David W Johnson and Frank P Johnson, *Joining together: group theory and group skills*, 7th ed. (Boston: Allyn & Bacon, 2000), p. 30.

27. This approach is based on J Steven Heinen and Eugene Jacobson, 'A model of task group development in complex organizations and a strategy of implementation', *Academy of Management Review*, vol. 1 (October 1976), pp. 98–111; Bruce W Tuckman, 'Developmental sequence in small groups', *Psychological Bulletin*, vol. 63 (1965), pp. 384–99; Bruce W Tuckman and Mary Ann C Jensen, 'Stages of small group development revisited', *Group and Organization Studies*, vol. 2 (1977), pp. 419–27.

28. Tuckman, op. cit.; Tuckman and Jensen, op. cit.

29. Trevor Tyson, *Working with groups*, 2nd ed. (Melbourne: Macmillan, 1998), pp. 11–12.

30. Stephen Linstead, Liz Fulop and Simon Lilley, *Management and organization* (Basingstoke: Palgrave Macmillan, 2004), pp. 377–8.

31. George C Homans, *The human group* (New York: Harcourt Brace, 1950).

32. David James and Emily Ross, 'New broom for boardroom', *Business Review Weekly* (26 May – 1 June 2005), pp. 58–61; 'Diversity on company boards', *New Zealand Management* (November 2004), pp. 80–1.

33. David James, 'Strong, silent types' *Business Review Weekly* (25 August – 14 September 2005), p. 58.

34. Catherine Walter, 'What makes an admirable board?', *Business Review Weekly* (25 August – 15 September 2005), p. 59.

35. James and Ross, op. cit., pp. 58–61.

36. Elizabeth Knight, 'Drunk with power but no bottle', *The Sydney Morning Herald* (10 March 2004), pp. 19–20.

37. BE Ashforth and RH Humphrey, 'Emotion in the workplace: a reappraisal', *Human Relations*, vol. 48, no. 2 (1995), p. 97.

38. Robert F Bales, 'Task roles and social roles in problem-solving groups' in Eleanor E Maccoby, Theodore M Newcomb and EL Hartley (eds), *Readings in social psychology* (New York: Holt, Rinehart and Winston, 1958).

39. For a good description of task and maintenance functions see John J Gabarro and Anne Harlan, 'Note on process observation', note 9–477–029 (Boston: Harvard Business School, 1976).

40. This discussion is developed from Edgar H Schein, *Process consultation*: vol. I, 2nd ed. (New York: Addison-Wesley, 1988), pp. 49–53; Rensis Likert, *New patterns of management* (New York: McGraw-Hill, 1961), pp. 166–9.

41. ibid.

42. Ruth Le Pla, 'Governing by network: joining the joined up club', *New Zealand Management* (May 2005), pp. 36–7.

43. Ross Gittins, 'It's not who you know, it's the networks you know', *The Sydney Morning Herald* (23–24 April 2005), p. 40, citing the work of Granovetter.

44. For a good discussion of intergroup dynamics see Schein, op. cit., pp. 106–15.

45. Andrew Fraser, 'The travel agent that had to find a new flight path', *The Weekend Australian* (2–3 April 2005), p. 23.

46. Schein, op. cit.

CHAPTER 7
Teamwork and team building

Learning objectives

After studying this chapter, you should be able to:

1. define teams and explain the difference between teams and groups

2. explain how teams operate and what makes them effective

3. discuss a range of team-building activities and approaches

4. explain the factors that affect team performance and cohesiveness

5. describe the main types of teams that exist in organisations

6. list and explain some future challenges for work teams.

The ACT Brumbies rugby union team uses an unusual structure and style of play. The team's inaugural coach Rod Macqueen, who coached Australia to victory in the 1999 rugby world cup, was an integral part of the Brumbies' beginning. He oversaw the implementation of a system of player empowerment in which the team had a large influence on many facets of the organisation.

Players in the first Brumbies squad had input into the team's playing style, training routine, the analysis of opposing teams, the team uniform, off-field clothing and even the team song. Many of the tactics used on the field were, and still are, suggested and refined by the players. It was a far cry from previous years and other sports, where players have usually been expected to merely follow instructions.

In his book *One step ahead*, Macqueen says: 'Everything we were doing was breaking new ground. This was because we were going through a revolutionary process. Most businesses and sports have an evolutionary process where changes take place naturally, but we were in a situation where existing structures were unable to cope. We had to start from the beginning and think laterally to solve the problems as they arose. It was fortunate for us that we were starting a brand new side. We didn't have the baggage that a lot of the traditional sides were carrying coming into the new professional era.'

[Chief Executive] Clarke says the team values as set out in 1996 are still in use today, although they have been tweaked and refined in some areas. Commentators have occasionally been critical of 'player-power' at the Brumbies, particularly the players' role in the departure of their coach, David Nucifora, after the team won the Super 12 title in 2004.

But Clarke says that listening to and implementing player ideas means a sense of responsibility and loyalty is bred within the team. 'None of them like to be sat in a corner and told, "Go out and do this" and have no input into it. It is all about enjoying and progressing, learning and developing, and becoming more experienced and a more rounded person. And you can only do that if you are in a collaborative environment that supports that sort of collegiate approach.

'From day one, when new players come into the organisation they get told and they see in practical ways how their ideas and thoughts can be put on the table for discussion, and then picked up and implemented. We encourage them not to sit back and be spoon-fed. We encourage people to actively participate in everything from development of programs, training principles and schedules, and playing strategies. Having them actively involved really does help reinforce the accountability of them delivering on the field,' Clarke says.

Source: John Stensholt, 'A field of their own', *Business Review Weekly* (16–22 June 2005), pp. 76–7.

Introduction

Increasingly, successful medium and large companies are relying on their employees to work in teams to find solutions to productivity and customer service problems. Teams are pervasive in organisations, with many companies putting their employees through team-building activities or adopting team approaches as described in the chapter opening. The Brumbies and the Collingwood Football Club (see 'Ethical perspective' on page 243) have real business interests in the benefits of effective teams. Organisations often use teamwork as part of their employee involvement program.[1] The increase in the use of teamwork is evident in many countries and organisations of many kinds. For example, in New Zealand, whitegoods producer Fisher & Paykel has introduced 'everyday workplace teams', which support project teams to gain the benefits of greater employee involvement (see case study 2 in part 5 of this book). In Australia, teams at Melbourne Water develop their own plans for safety improvement, efficiencies and activities to support business priorities.[2] Team approaches to work can foster top-quality products, individual employee concern for enhancing production, increased efficiency and high employee morale. Research has shown that teams consistently outperform individuals or random groups, especially when diverse skills, judgements and experiences can improve results. Teams generally work their magic by encouraging the individuals who comprise them to build new skills, and by raising organisational performance. Teams can add value to organisations committed to a set of core values that ensure quality performance.[3] Teamwork is increasingly considered one of the benchmarks of a successful organisation, while the ability to build effective teams is increasingly considered one of the benchmarks of a successful manager.

Given the rise of teamwork and a shift to flatter management structures, communication, compassion and a 'sharing, caring' approach to business leadership are paramount. To enhance the contributions of teams it is essential to understand teams and how to manage and lead them. This chapter introduces the concept of teams and their differences compared with groups. It examines a range of team-building approaches and goals, and several types of teams that exist in organisations.

What are teams?

Formally defined, a **team** is a small group of people with complementary skills, who work together as a unit to achieve a common purpose for which they hold themselves collectively accountable. In an employment situation or business setting, a team is a group of employees at any level in the organisation who are charged with working together to identify problems, form a consensus about what to do, and implement necessary actions in relation to a particular task or set of tasks. The management team at GE Commercial Finance is an example of an accountable team.

OB in action

Steve Sargent is the chief executive of General Electric Commercial Finance Australia and New Zealand. Sargent says the organisation has a measurement-driven culture which is visible to all employees. Sargent meets once a month with his team of key business unit managers and they discuss issues that might affect the business. While the reviews may often be light-hearted and fun, they are also focused on ensuring everyone is clear about the issues. As Sargent says, 'You flex your management style as appropriate . . . The team knows we have a high degree of accountability.'[4]

Groups versus teams

In the previous chapter we looked at groups. We saw that a group is made up of individuals who see themselves, and who are seen by others, as a social entity. The group is interdependent as a result of the tasks that the group members perform. The group is also embedded in one or more larger social systems, such as a community or an organisation, and it performs tasks that affect others, such as customers or coworkers. In recent years, the concept of the team has largely replaced that of the group in much organisational behaviour literature. Is this simply a matter of wording? Or are there more substantive differences between groups and teams?

As we saw in chapter 6, a **group** is a number of people who interact with one another for a common purpose, whereas a team is a group of people who function as a unit. When we think of the word 'team', sporting teams may come to mind — a football, netball or cricket team, for example. But work groups can also be teams. Groups do not become teams because that is what someone calls them. Nor do teamwork values ensure team performance. The essence of a team is *shared commitment*. Without it, groups perform as individuals; with it, they become a powerful unit of *collective performance*. Another fundamental distinction between teams and other forms of working groups hinges on performance. A working group relies on the individual contributions of its members for group performance. However, a team strives for something greater than its members could achieve individually. An effective team is always worth more than the sum of its parts. (Refer to the concept of synergy, discussed in chapter 6.) Some suggest that groups and teams form a continuum with groups at one end, being collections of people whose individual efforts combine 'additively' towards the achievement of a goal. Teams, at the other end, are collections of people whose efforts combine, synergistically, towards the achievement of the team's particular goals as well as the goals of the organisation.[5]

Teams can be extremely powerful when they work well, but transforming a group of individuals into a team can be hard work. The stages of group formation (forming, storming, initial integration, total integration and adjourning) discussed in chapter 6 also apply to the development of teams, and much of this chapter focuses on the building of teams.

Groups are collections of two or more people who interact with one another for a common purpose.

Teams and their effectiveness

OBJECTIVE 2 · LEARNING Teams and their effectiveness

Teams operate on three levels:

- *Team task level.* Teams are organised to carry out a specific task or to achieve a goal. Frequently, the team is so conscious of the need to accomplish this task that it is unaware of the other levels of need that operate simultaneously.
- *Individual needs level.* Every individual member brings to the team a particular set of needs that impinge on the team and its task. Teams are most likely to be found wanting at this level, for individual needs are often well hidden behind the task drive of the team, or behind the personal drive of the team leader or facilitator. Each individual on a team — member or leader — has a responsibility to ensure the successful working of the team.
- *Team maintenance level.* As people work together on a task, they also constantly interact in a shifting network of relationships. To accomplish its task, a team needs to have an awareness of itself as a team, and to recognise the need to maintain the relationships within it. Many of these responsibilities fall on the team leader or facilitator.

Effective teams

Typically, *teams that make or do things* are the effective groups discussed in chapter 6. They perform ongoing tasks, such as marketing or manufacturing, and are considered permanent; that is, they operate without scheduled dates for disbanding. Members of these teams must have long-term working relationships as well as good operating systems and the external support needed to achieve effectiveness over a sustained period of time.

Teams that run things consist of the leaders at the top of an organisation or at the top of major organisational subunits. Although otherwise referred to as 'top management groups', these groups must also perform as true teams. Key issues for such teams include identifying overall organisational purposes, goals and values, and helping others fulfil them. It is increasingly common today to find such teams formally designated in the top management structure of organisations. This approach receives support from management consultants and scholars and also well-regarded executives.[6]

Organisational direction and purpose is a key value for teams. There must be clarity about the task, even if there is considerable latitude in the means of achieving it. Quality relationships exist only when people can argue without the team falling apart. They should be able to disagree without creating resentment. Each member must recognise that the team exists to complete a task that is more than an individual can manage. 'Pulling together' can be facilitated by developing and supporting a common language and culture. While individual goals are important, they must be compatible with the team's goals. To unify a team, members must know their goals and roles, and work out relationships with other team members. Some of the problems affecting group effectiveness, discussed in chapter 6, also apply to teams. Compared with employees who work individually, effective teams tend to have:

- higher morale
- higher productivity
- greater pride in the job
- greater pride in the company.

Effective teams understand the value of working together instead of against each other. For a team to be effective, its members must include the necessary experts or those most familiar with the problem, and any team needs members with the right mix of skills if it is to achieve high levels of performance. Skills are group input factors that can make a large difference in the ability of the team to accomplish its tasks properly.

The most effective teams have a blend of styles, strengths and skills — a blend that fosters interdependence. If team members are expected to believe the whole is greater than the sum of its parts (that is, synergy), then the leader must make each individual aware of the big picture by fostering pride not only in the individual job, but in the team's results and its impact on the overall success of the organisation.

Every team needs to have certain roles assumed by or assigned to its members. If team members' roles are well planned, participants will have a clear idea of what they are doing. Team meetings are one aspect of team activity where these principles apply. Some of the most frequent organisational barriers to team performance are:

- inadequate rewards and compensation systems
- inadequate personnel and human resources development systems
- a lack of appropriate information systems
- a lack of top management commitment
- an ambiguous organisational alignment
- difficulties in personal mind shift (or lateral thinking)
- inadequate individual abilities and characteristics
- an inadequate team size and other membership factors.

Team-building approaches

Team building is a sequence of planned action steps designed to gather and analyse data on the functioning of a group, and to implement changes to increase its operating effectiveness.

Teamwork is when members of a team work together in a way that represents certain core values that promote the use of skills to accomplish certain goals.

Foundations of the team-building process

Formally defined, team building is a sequence of planned activities designed to gather and analyse data on the functioning of a group, and to initiate changes designed to improve teamwork and increase group effectiveness.[7] The essence of the team-building process is teamwork. Formally stated, teamwork occurs when members of a team work together in a way that represents certain core values that promote the use of skills to accomplish common goals. These values have been described as 'listening and responding constructively to views expressed by others, giving others the benefit of the doubt, providing support and recognising the interests and achievements of others'.[8] Teamwork does not always happen naturally; it is something that team members and leaders must work hard to achieve. Also, it is a continuous process, so the effort at maintaining teamwork is ongoing. Efforts within the team must relate to team maintenance as well as task performance. Thus, the core values that underpin teamwork that is effective in accomplishing team goals should be clearly understood and communicated.

Successful team building and teamwork are assisted by clear goals, and are accomplished by members of the team and their leaders, sometimes with the assistance of facilitators. Teams need to work on their teamwork skills and can be assisted in this by training and team-building approaches that are designed to assist people operate as teams. These particular aspects of teams are now discussed in more detail.

Team-building goals

In addition to its general emphasis on improving teamwork and group effectiveness, team building is useful for:[9]
- clarifying core values to guide and direct the behaviour of members
- transforming a broad sense of purpose into specific performance objectives
- developing the right mix of skills to accomplish high-performance results
- enhancing creativity in task performance.

Values are an important ingredient in the organisational or corporate culture, as discussed in chapter 9. The same holds true at the level of the work group or team. Good values help guide members' attitudes and behaviours in directions consistent with the team's common purpose. These values act as an internal control system for the group or team, and they can substitute for outside direction that a supervisor may otherwise have to provide. Team building is one way in which core values can be identified, encouraging commitment on the part of group members. It can help the team to assess and develop the goals, values and skills of its membership and determine what must be done to maximise this input factor. Team building is also a way for ongoing groups to assess themselves periodically and to make the constructive changes necessary for the group to keep up with new developments.

Creating and sustaining a high-performing team is a challenging task in any setting. 'The effective manager 7.1' offers some guidelines for meeting this challenge.

How to build a high-performing team[10]
- Communicate clear high-performance standards.
- Set the tone in the first team meeting.
- Create a sense of urgency; set a compelling context for action.
- Make sure team members have the right skills.
- Establish clear rules for behaviour by the team.
- As team leader, 'model' the expected behaviours.
- Identify specific objectives that can be achieved to create early 'successes'.
- Continually introduce new facts and information to the team.
- Make sure the team members spend a lot of time together.
- Give positive feedback; reward and recognise high-performance results.

THE **Effective**Manager 7.1

Effective team leadership

Skilled team leaders are essential to the operation of effective teams. While team leaders are involved in the day-to-day leadership of the team, they are also involved in team building, either at the time of establishment or when the team is endeavouring to refresh or renew its teamwork skills. Team leaders need competencies in a range of areas, including an ability to:
- build trust and inspire teamwork
- facilitate and support team decisions
- expand team capabilities
- create a team identity
- make the most of team differences
- foresee and influence change.

The team leader or manager's role is to make it easy for the team to define goals, develop plans and solve problems. Effective team leaders work to bring the team together and keep it focused on resolving one issue before moving on to the next. For teams to be effective, team leaders often need training in the right skills, roles and styles for teams as well as in conducting team development activities and meetings. Mike O'Neill was aware of his role as a team leader, as the following example shows.

Mike O'Neill was the CEO of Whirlpool Australia prior to becoming CEO of the Executive Corporation (an international organisation of chief executives who work at increasing their effectiveness). O'Neill said his leadership was like being the captain of a football team; he knew when to lead from the front and when to step back. He says, 'In football we see the captain set the example and then go back into the team and let someone else step forward...A great leader is a person who can blend into the background while the team keeps moving forward.'[11]

Leaders should be able to supply essential information and clarify issues. Awareness and self-assessment can enable team leaders to evaluate the way in which they communicate with team members. When team leaders listen attentively, they appear open and interested in what people are saying. By asking for and carefully considering advice, leaders allow employees to participate in decisions that affect them. Leaders should avoid domineering practices such as being impatient with alternative views and interrupting people. However, avoiding arguments by not responding to disagreements could be misinterpreted as agreement, disregard or lack of fortitude. By merely listening during meetings, leaders send a message that they have nothing to contribute to the team and may fail to keep the team on track with their tasks.

In teamwork, traditional top-down leadership is replaced by a situation in which:
- the team is an interacting and collective unit rather than a set of individuals
- responsibility for team performance and maintenance is shared by all team members
- position and power is diminished in team leadership
- expressions of members' needs and feelings are not discouraged, but dealt with openly in team meetings.

'The effective manager 7.2' suggests ten rules for team leaders to follow to avoid needless mistakes.

Ten rules for team leaders to create effective teams[12]

1. Use the organisation's strategy to guide team actions and plans.
2. Do not tolerate undesirable behaviour, because it will undermine team morale and performance.
3. Do not allow your self-interest to dominate team interest, because resentment, competition and conflict will ensue.
4. Do not allow fear to influence team behaviour.
5. Do not allow cliques to develop that will undermine the unity of the team.
6. Deal with conflict promptly so team morale does not suffer.
7. Refuse to recognise lack of trust as an excuse, but seek to develop trust on an ongoing basis.
8. Encourage risk taking by all members of the team.
9. Share information so the team retains its shared sense of purpose.
10. Manage processes carefully.

Effective team facilitators

Facilitating team building is a challenging task and one that should not be taken lightly. Whether organisations use outside facilitators or internal facilitators (such as facilitators from the human resources area or from within the team itself), it is important that the facilitator is trained and competent to do the job. Facilitators who have team-building and development skills can help teams become more viable and productive organisational entities. Team-building facilitators structure their interventions to gain:

1. appreciation and understanding of the complexity and dynamics of the team-building process
2. identification of team needs in order to build greater proficiency in the approaches and skills necessary to help the team develop
3. a safe and open forum for discourse in which team members can ask tough questions and share deep concerns that have been plaguing them and inhibiting their team's progress.

A trained facilitator or management consultant contributes to improving the corporate team process by fostering interdependence, leader support, willingness to try new ideas and to suggest new options, and open and improved communication.

A part of facilitating teamwork is encouragement to make the necessary choices, even if these are unpopular. There must be a belief by senior leaders and team members that the positive results of change are worth the challenge of disrupting the status quo. The following example illustrates that teams sometimes have to make tough decisions.

The New Zealand-based 'The Warehouse Group' is known for its successful business 'Red Sheds', but at the end of 2004 was mystified by its lack of success in a similar business it ran in Australia, 'Yellow Sheds'. One of the priorities, according to new CEO Ian Morrice, was to build a management team that was capable of confronting the challenges that the business faced. While Australian operations improved in 2005 — they made a loss of A$5.4 million compared with A$32.3 million the previous year — the new team was willing to confront this situation with a long-term and strong, overall business perspective even though the loss had lessened. Between June and September 2005 the management team had shifted its way of dealing with the challenge from a potential merger to a potential sale to Millers' Crazy Clarks and Go Lo.[13]

While facilitators can work to encourage teamwork through playful and constructive activities (light-side team-building), sometimes there is a need to address the 'dark side' too. Real issues emerge and sometimes they are not pleasant to deal with and can frighten not only the participants but their team facilitators as well. If team members hear a facilitator sidestep real issues to stay positive, they may distrust the facilitator and the process. It is rare to find a team facilitator who feels equally comfortable and skilled at both the light side and the dark side of team building. What may work well in these situations is a partnership between two consultants — one who is skilled and comfortable with the light-side activities, and one who is effective on the dark side. Team members who work on both sides have a better chance to address their fears about working as a team.

Effective team facilitators observe and listen to the team, and assess its needs. They may then apply models and theoretical perspectives from a stock of models with which they are familiar.

Teamwork activities and training

There are numerous methods, games and training techniques that help teams, their leaders and/or their facilitators improve teamwork, broaden perspectives, maximise ideas and reach consensus. An organisation's training department and/or external consultants can provide managers with assistance for team building, whether it is when the team is first formed or later, when the team members need revitalisation with their teamwork. As the following University of Queensland example indicates, many people have a poor understanding of what teamwork entails and training may be one way of improving this situation.

The University of Queensland used a workshop to train a group of 81 graduate entry students from several professions (occupational therapy, physiotherapy, speech pathology and audiology). These four types of professionals work together with children with development coordination disorder (DCD). However, while the participants indicated teamwork was important in many cases, overall it seems that they had only a superficial knowledge of teamwork. In order to be able to train professionals so that they can understand teamwork and work effectively in teams, the researchers sought to understand how the student/professionals explained it. They found different professional training backgrounds resulted in different explanations of teamwork. For example, occupational therapy students were less likely to mention that team members should share 'similar goals' or that team members were required to 'cooperate'. Audiology students had a strong emphasis on 'team spirit'.[14]

Most of the many possible approaches to team building have the common steps shown in figure 7.1. In other words someone in or out of the team notes a problem, then team members work together to gather and analyse data about the problem, to plan actions for improvement, to implement action plans, and to monitor and evaluate results and take further action if required.

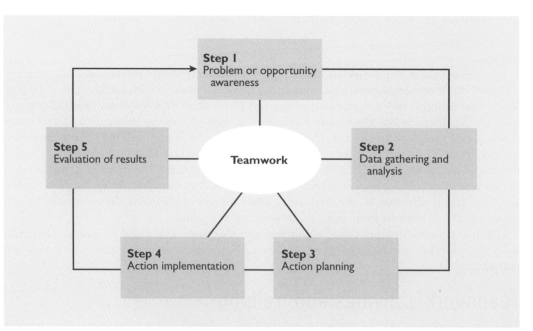

FIGURE 7.1 • How team members work together in a typical team-building activity

The team-building process just described is a cooperative one. There is an emphasis on team members working together to accomplish various team-building tasks. Throughout the process, everyone is expected to participate, as group effectiveness is evaluated and decisions are made on what needs to be done to maintain or improve this effectiveness in the future. Then everyone shares in the responsibility for implementing the agreed action plans and evaluating action results.

Effective management principles and good team-building skills go hand in hand. The team's objectives should be defined and the team members should understand why they are important. In addition, the team members should understand how they benefit individually. Any team must be made up of members who feel responsible for actively working together to accomplish important tasks, whether those tasks involve recommending things, making or doing things, or running things; that is, the members must feel 'collectively accountable' for what they accomplish through 'teamwork'. Three of many possible types of teamwork activities are now described: experiential activities, challenging viewpoints and reaching consensus through brainstorming. It is important to note that these methods are not exclusive of each other and different methods or approaches can accomplish similar outcomes.

Experiential activities

To enhance the quick formation of teams, facilitators may resort to experiential approaches, including 'games'. The games are designed to encourage participants to process information actively, rather than receiving it passively. They are intended to build on the motivational qualities of cooperation and competition among team members as well as trust. A good example is the game referred to as 'learning teams',[15] which involves two types of activity: the cooperative learning session and the competitive tournament session.

An example of a 'cooperative' learning session game involves the team receiving an identical set of 15 objects, which are arranged on a table and hidden from view. After viewing half of the objects, each team is asked to duplicate the exact arrangement of the objects, using its own set of matching objects. The team that accomplishes the task in the least amount of time wins a prize. Each group is told that either team might have one or two saboteurs who would work against their own team to keep it from winning. The deciding factor in the game is the amount of time and energy a team spends dealing with the idea of a saboteur in their midst. Teams that are most concerned with saboteurs always lose. The results of the game show that trust is critical for meeting team goals.[16]

Challenging viewpoints

Some team-building approaches work on breaking down team members' viewpoints, either individually or collectively, since these may impede team performance. One approach is called the *devil's advocate* process, which helps team members overcome resistance to change. Playing the devil's advocate means taking an oppositional stance in an argument to force others to strengthen their position and clarify their reasoning. Other approaches can also help to shift people from their usual roles to look at the problem differently. For example, sometimes it is not easy to break down the usual roles of team managers, as a management consultant found in the following example.

In trying to build teams and develop skills, team managers typically feel under considerable pressure since they are responsible for the team. Yet, often they cannot clearly express what it is that is required from the team-building process, and their employees claim there is poor communication and insufficient contact; lack of feedback, trust and clear direction; and a focus on negatives. This creates an 'us and them' scenario and fails to achieve the outcomes desired. Keith McGregor, management psychologist from the firm Personnel Psychology has developed a team-building

(continued)

model that seeks to overcome these difficulties. It is based on a customer–supplier model and frames the manager as the customer and the staff as the suppliers. Staff must act as concerned suppliers who seek feedback from their customer (the manager) about what is needed. Viewing the boss as a customer for whom they are delivering a service has the effect of giving staff a greater sense of control and everyone a strong sense of responsibility for the outcomes of the team-building exercise and the work of the team in general.[17]

Reaching consensus through brainstorming

Team consensus is general agreement that all members of a team support. Consensual decision making is more effective than other types of decision making. It forces the team to consider more aspects of a problem and to be alert to objections. Team consensus does not just happen; it results from following careful guidelines, including:

- working towards a common goal through brainstorming
- using quiet time to allow for personal reflection
- avoiding voting
- not expecting unanimous agreement on all reasons for making a particular decision.

We discuss decision making in further detail in chapter 12, but the important issue here is that reaching consensus means that people are making a true team decision.

In **brainstorming**, team members actively generate as many ideas as possible, and they do so relatively quickly and without inhibitions. Members of a brainstorming team follow these four rules:

1. *All ideas are acceptable.* All criticism is ruled out. No-one is allowed to judge or evaluate any ideas until the idea-generation process has been completed.
2. *'Freewheeling' is welcomed.* The emphasis is on creativity and imagination; the wilder or more radical the idea, the better.
3. *Quantity is wanted.* The emphasis is also on the number of ideas; the greater the number, the more likely that a superior idea will be raised.
4. *'Piggy-backing' is good.* Everyone is encouraged to suggest how others' ideas can be turned into new ideas, or how two or more ideas can be joined into still another new idea.

The core of brainstorming rests with the ban on evaluation during the idea-generation process. This approach tends to reduce members' fears of criticism or failure. Typical results include enthusiasm, involvement and a free flow of ideas. Researchers consider brainstorming superior to open-group discussions when the goals are creative thinking and the generation of alternative solutions to identified problems. Therefore, this time-honoured technique still has important practical applications in the modern workplace.

Employee brainstorming sessions can be a valuable way in which to produce great ideas. But before convening a session, the group should establish goals. A goal may be to gather information, solve a problem, make a decision, deal with change or plan a project. Once the group decides on the goal, it should choose a specific agenda or topic. Participants should have time to think about the topic before the session. And a generous amount of time should be allowed for the actual session, which should take place in a comfortable, non-threatening setting.

Timing and location of teamwork activities

Some of the broad foundations and particular activities of team building have already been discussed. With these in mind, we can also talk about some different choices that are made about when to conduct team-building activities, and where to locate them. While many factors can impinge on these decisions, the following represent some common approaches. These are: formal retreats, continuous improvement and outdoor experiences.

Brainstorming is a technique by which team members generate as many ideas as possible, without being inhibited by other team members.

Formal retreats

In the formal retreat approach, the team-building activities take place during a 'retreat' that is organised off site. During this retreat, which may last from two to seven or more days, the members of a team work intensively on a variety of planning and experiential activities. These activities are often initiated by a review of data gathered through surveys, interviews or group activities such as the nominal group technique. Formal retreats are typically held with the assistance of a consultant who is either hired or made available by in-house staff. Team-building retreats offer opportunities for intense and concentrated efforts to examine team problems and future directions. In this context, organisations often seek the help of outside facilitators.

Continual improvement

Not all team building is done in a formal retreat format, or with the assistance of consultants. Indeed, in light of the new workplace's emphasis on teams, a continual improvement approach to team building is important. Here the manager, team leader and/or team members take responsibility for regularly engaging in the team-building process. This method can be as simple as periodic meetings that implement the team-building steps; it can also include self-managed retreats such as those just described. In all cases, team members are committed to monitoring team development and accomplishments continually, and to taking collective responsibility for making the day-to-day changes needed to ensure team effectiveness.

From a total quality management perspective, continual improvement of work teams through team building is certainly an important concept. Any informed manager should be able to assist teams in fulfilling this responsibility, and team building should become a regular element in the annual or semi-annual task agendas of any team. Many quality improvement programs rely on team efforts. The internal goals of such teams are for members to trust one another, work together to solve problems, help enhance one another's performance and aspire to feel like winners. The external goals are for these teams to identify their customers and suppliers, gain commitment from their customers and suppliers, focus on team performance and project the image of winners.

Outdoor experiences

The outdoor experience approach is an increasingly popular team-building technique that may be performed on its own or in combination with the data-feedback and continual improvement approach just described. For a group that has never experienced team building, an outdoor experience can be a high-powered way to begin the process; for teams experienced with team building, it can be a way of enriching and varying the process over time. The essence of any outdoor experience involves putting group members in a variety of situations in which they need to work collectively to overcome physical tests that may be beyond individual capabilities. By having to work together in the face of such obstacles, both individual character and commitments to teamwork can be developed. A popular sponsor of such team building is the Outward Bound Leadership School, but many others exist. As indicated in the following 'What would you do?' feature, team-building 'retreats' and 'experiences' can be be fraught with problems.

Adventures in team building

Sharon Davis's last team-building 'adventure', a training day on a maxi-yacht racing outside the heads of Sydney Harbour, had a number of outstanding moments. There was a storm, seasickness and sunburn, and a moment of realisation when a competitive colleague pulled on a pair of white leather sailing gloves in a symbolic gesture of strength and supremacy at the outset.

(continued)

'It was my worst nightmare,' recalls Davis, a survivor of many similar team events. The physical rigours presented less of a challenge for her than trying to see how they translated to practical application at work on a day-to-day basis.

Needless to say, Davis, who now heads human resources for AMP Financial Services — an organisation with 2800 employees — is no supporter of the great outdoors methods of developing team cohesion that once dominated the corporate landscape. Like many others, she prefers to keep the development of highly functional teams on dry land and, most often, within the business context as part of strategic and operational planning.

Not so long ago, the mention of team-building typically conjured up images of colleagues edging down cliff faces with nothing but a rope and the goodwill of fellow workers preventing them from plunging into a ravine, careering at high speed down rapids, vanishing into caves or spraying their buddies with paint from a gun. Cosier group bonding activities also presented an option, from cooking to dot painting, theatre sports and song-writing sessions.

Depending on your bent, or glee at seeing a difficult colleague disappear down a river without a paddle, the experiences invariably delivered 'war stories' of hilarity and terror, with a widely questioned benefit to the team at the real coalface, back at the office.

Approaches to team building have broadened. While some of the rugged, extreme style of 'bonding' that allows outward displays of trust, problem-solving capabilities, overcoming fear and physical prowess still feature on many management agendas, today's trends show a line of thinking that owes more to hard-core business planning and less to re-enacting the corporate version of the TV hit, *Survivor*.

There's a new scenario. As organisations have developed, the nature of teams has shifted. The trend to working cross-functionally, and breaking away from operating in confined spaces, brings people together in various configurations at many levels, from the relative simplicity of a sales or call-centre team to the many facets of a supply chain with one common goal, to satisfy the customer.

Source: Deborah Tarrant, '[Building a] better team', *Management Today* (May 2005) pp. 25–7. This article appeared in the May 2005 edition of Australia's leading magazine for managers: *Management Today* (published by Text Pacific Publishing for the Australian Institute of Management, www.aim.com.au).

Questions

1. Your manager has asked you to organise an outdoor adventure as a team-building exercise for your team. What would you do if you felt such exercises were potentially dangerous and ineffective in translating team skills into the workplace?

2. On an outdoor retreat for which you are responsible, one of the participants becomes (a) very frightened of the exercise about to be performed; and (b) injured. What would you do to deal with the situation for the individual and other team members?

Team performance and cohesiveness

While many factors will influence team cohesiveness and performance, norms and roles are two key areas for consideration. We will also examine the important relationship between norms, performance and team cohesion.

Team norms

Norms of behaviour can occur in many subsets of the organisation. For example, in chapter 6 we defined group norms and in chapter 9 you will see that cultural norms of behaviour also operate in the organisation. So the norms that occur in teams are defined in the same way. A team norm is an idea or belief about the behaviour that team members are expected to display. **Norms** are often referred to as 'rules' or 'standards' of behaviour that apply to team members.[18] They help clarify membership expectations in a team. Norms allow members to structure their own behaviour and to predict what others will do; they help members gain a common sense of direction; and they reinforce a desired team or organisational culture.

Norms are rules or standards about the behaviour that group members are expected to display.

When a member of a team violates a team norm, other members typically respond in ways that attempt to enforce the norm. Time and energy can be saved if team members take the time in the beginning to write a code of conduct establishing the basic principles and rules that will determine the power, duties and rights of both the team and its members. Every team's code will be unique to the set of circumstances of its project. The code of conduct should deal with the 'soft' issues — philosophies, principles and values. These are difficult concepts to deal with and yet, if the team's views on them are resolved, this could yield the greatest payoff for the team in the long run. The code of conduct should also deal with organisational detail, and may include responses to direct criticisms, reprimands, expulsion, social ostracism and the like. For instance, Livia, an enthusiastic employee, may enter a team as a highly capable and highly motivated worker. But her efforts to achieve high performance are met with 'pressure' from other team members who want her to reduce her efforts and conform to the team's low performance norm. Livia gives in to the pressure, accepts the norm, and agrees to work at far less than her true performance potential. Another example may be the subtle pressure by fellow team members to attend or participate in certain social functions.

Teams operate with many types of norm. Among these norms are those regarding expected performance, attendance at meetings, punctuality, preparedness, criticism, social behaviours and so on. Other common norms in work teams deal with relationships with supervisors, colleagues and customers, as well as honesty, security, personal development and change. Norms are essentially determined by the collective will of team members, so it is difficult for organisations and their managers to dictate which norms a given team will possess. The concerned manager must try to help team members adopt norms supportive of organisational goals. A manager or team leader can take a number of steps to encourage the development of positive team norms; some are shown in 'The effective manager 7.3'.[19]

Seven steps for leaders to encourage positive team norms

- Act as a positive role model.
- Hold team meetings to gain agreement on desired behaviours.
- Recruit and select new members who can and will perform as desired.
- Train and orient new members in the desired behaviours.
- Reinforce and reward the desired behaviours.
- Hold team meetings to discuss feedback and review performance.
- Hold team meetings to plan ways to increase effectiveness.

THE **Effective**Manager 7.3

Team roles and role dynamics

A **role** is a set of expectations for the behaviour of a person holding a particular office or position.

Roles were discussed in chapter 6, but here we extend this to a team context. Membership expectations can create problems for any member of any team. In teams, the term **role** describes a set of expectations for the behaviour of a person holding a particular office or position. Often these expectations are unclear, and this uncertainty raises anxieties and creates problems. This can occur in newly formed teams, when new members join an existing team, or in teams whose members have reached the total integration stage of development, as discussed in chapter 6.

In chapter 13 we discuss some of the issues involved in the communication of role expectations. In the specific context of a work group or team, role dynamics that involve uncertainties and stress can create problems. **Role ambiguity** occurs when a member of a work group or team is unsure about what other members expect of them. This uncertainty raises anxieties and creates problems. **Role conflict** occurs when a member is unable to respond to the expectations of one or more members. This conflict may be due to overload or incompatibility. Just as in the case of ambiguity, the stress and anxiety associated with role conflicts of both types can cause problems for both the individual member and the team as a whole. The team-building techniques discussed earlier are designed to address these types of problem.

Role ambiguity is the uncertainty about what other group members expect of a person.

Role conflict occurs when a person is unable to respond to the expectations of one or more group members.

Team cohesiveness

Cohesiveness is the degree to which members are attracted to and motivated to remain a part of a team.

The extent to which members of a team conform to the team's norms is strongly influenced by the level of cohesiveness in the team; that is, the degree to which members are attracted to, and motivated to remain part of, a team.[20] Cohesiveness tends to be high when:

- team members are homogeneous in age, attitudes, needs and backgrounds
- team members respect one another's competencies
- team members agree on common goals
- team tasks require interdependent efforts
- the team is relatively small
- the team is physically isolated from other groups
- the team experiences performance success
- the team experiences a performance crisis or failure.

Cohesive teams are good for their members. Members of highly cohesive teams are concerned about their team's activities and achievements. In contrast to persons in less cohesive teams, they tend to be more energetic when working on team activities, they are less likely to be absent, and they tend to be happy about performance success and sad about failures. Cohesive teams generally have stable memberships and foster feelings of loyalty, security and high self-esteem among their members; they satisfy a full range of individual needs. Sometimes tough experiences and survival of them, as well as isolation, can be very influential in developing high team cohesiveness. The example of a volunteer team in Africa (see page 241) illustrates this.

Cohesive groups or teams may or may not be good for the organisation. The critical question is: 'How does cohesiveness influence performance?' Figure 7.2 helps answer this question by showing the relationship between team cohesiveness and team performance. Typically, the more cohesive the team, the greater the conformity of members to team norms. As you would expect, the performance norm is critical for any team. Thus, when the performance norm is positive, high conformity to it in a cohesive team should have a beneficial effect on task performance; when the performance norm is negative in a highly cohesive team, undesirable results may be experienced.

Notice in figure 7.2 the performance implications for various combinations of cohesiveness and norms. Performance is highest in a very cohesive team with positive performance norms. In this situation, members encourage one another to work hard on behalf of the team.

The worst situation for a manager is a highly cohesive team with negative performance norms. Again, members will be highly motivated to support one another, but the organisation will suffer as the team restricts its performance consistent with the negative norm. Between these two extremes are mixed situations, in which a lack of cohesion fails to ensure member conformity to the guiding norm. The strength of the norm is reduced, and the outcome is somewhat unpredictable but is most likely to be on the moderate or low side.

Debbie Snelson is head of Volunteer Service Abroad (VSA) in New Zealand. She is someone who has considerable experience working in teams in difficult locations, having also been a director for the African Wildlife Foundation for 15 years. She can tell stories about teams of park rangers who have had to work together in encounters with gorillas, bomb blasts and even hostility on international borders. At VSA, volunteer teams are often engaged in a project for one to two years. People leave their comfort zones and work together in locations without the daily comforts they are used to. They are challenged in physical, cultural and psychological ways. According to Snelson, there is usually no organisational hierarchy to lean on and their work can have a huge impact on the lives of a whole community, so they are typically very focused on, and aware of, outcomes. This was the case in one recent farm project in Africa, where the team's work really did mean the difference between the community going hungry or not.[21]

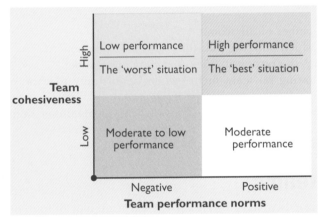

FIGURE 7.2 • How team cohesiveness and performance norms can influence team performance

Influencing team cohesiveness

Look again at figure 7.2. How would you feel with a team that falls into any cell other than the high-performance one? To deal with these possibilities, a manager must recognise that there will be times when steps should be taken to build cohesiveness in a team, such as when the team has positive norms but low cohesiveness. There may be other times when steps must be taken to reduce cohesiveness, such as when the members of a highly cohesive team are operating with negative performance norms and when previous efforts to change these norms have failed. Managers must be prepared to deal with both situations. As shown in figure 7.3, managers can take steps to increase or decrease team cohesiveness. These include making changes in team goals, membership composition, interactions, size, rewards, competition, location and duration.

Trust is a very important ingredient for team cohesiveness and performance. The higher the level of trust in a team, the greater the cohesiveness, satisfaction and effectiveness. The genuine sharing of information can also greatly contribute to the building of trust; this simple act can demonstrate a strong commitment to the team.

Targets		
How to *decrease* cohesion		**How to *increase* cohesion**
Create *disagreement*	Goals	Get agreement
Increase *heterogeneity*	Membership	Increase homogeneity*
Restrict within team	Interactions	Enhance within team
Make team bigger	Size	Make team smaller
Focus within team	Competition	Focus on other teams
Reward individual results	Rewards	Reward team results
Increase contact with other teams	Location	Isolate from other teams
Disband the team	Duration	Keep team together

*Increased homogeneity may result in other negative effects such as groupthink or lack of diverse opinions.

FIGURE 7.3 • How to increase and decrease cohesiveness in a work team

Conflict is a frequently unavoidable part of teamwork. It is not necessarily detrimental and can lead to creative solutions. However, if not managed, it can destroy team cohesiveness. You can manage conflict by:[22]

- giving ample recognition to each member of the team
- focusing on a win–win situation, in which both the individual and the team benefit
- establishing a team charter that states the responsibilities of each team member
- mediating personal differences, allowing all team members an opportunity to express their views
- finding areas of agreement to allow team members to focus on team goals rather than areas of conflict
- helping team members to address personal behaviours that will facilitate change.

Types of teams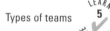

Types of workplace teams

There is no ready-reckoner to tell us exactly what category a particular team may fit into, or for giving a precise picture of the types of teams that operate in organisations and how successful they are. While some broad types of teams are recognisable, there are many subtle variants, many terms used to label them and many degrees of success. However, we do know that managers in contemporary organisations are adopting many innovative ways of better using teams as human resources of organisations. The watchwords of these approaches are empowerment, participation and involvement. More recently, technology enables physically remote membership of teams. A short case from a manufacturing plant (in the 'OB in action' on page 243) illustrates some aspects of these approaches.

We cannot comprehensively cover all types of teams or all developments in team theory. However, for the rest of this section four common types of teams are outlined: employee involvement teams, problem-solving teams, self-managing teams and virtual teams. Despite classifying them into types, it must be accepted that every team is different and may have features that overlap the types discussed here. For instance, it is possible to have a problem-solving team that is also an employee involvement team, or a self-managing team that is also a virtual team. You will come across many other terms to describe teams and/or types of teams, such as cross-functional teams (see the 'International spotlight' on page 249) and world-class teams. The following 'Ethical perspective' also illustrates that teams can be formed when two or more organisations engage in some form of joint venture.

Some time ago, Mahmood Mohajer, a production supervisor at a Digital plant, realised that his work team was two weeks behind in an important production run. In the past, Mahmood would have immediately put everyone on an overtime schedule. This time, he did things differently. He first met with the production teams and outlined the problem. He then asked them to come up with a solution. 'It was a real risk', he says of the approach. 'I was so nervous I had to trust them.'

Mahmood got the team's response the following Monday. Everyone decided to work the entire weekend to catch up on the production schedule. They had accepted responsibility for meeting the production goals and came up with a way of doing so that would meet their needs as well as those of the firm. It was still an overtime schedule but somewhat different from the one Mahmood might have set. Yet, theirs would also work...perhaps even better than his. Because it was their idea, team members were highly motivated to make their solution a real success.

Mahmood says that his new team approach requires a 'coaching' rather than a 'policing' role. One of his workers told him, 'We wanted to tell you how to fix some problems before, but you wouldn't listen to us'.[23]

Team versus personal values

ETHICAL
Perspective

Pure Bliss Foods was an unknown start-up business run by Ashley Salisbury and Robert Boyd. The business could not afford a big advertising campaign for its health bars. When Collingwood Football Club offered to form a new company, Winners Sports Nutrition, with shared ownership and shared profits, their business took off. Salisbury and Boyd develop the products while Collingwood's marketing team ensures the brand reaches the consumers and has successfully reached global markets. While the players loved the product, one player had thought the bars would be off limits due to the team's diet.[24] Fortunately, the 'health' bars were not a problem, but it does raise the question of how often team members are challenged by what they are required to do for the team. Collingwood players are  the visible advertising presence for the product, as it is assumed that fans will be influenced by what the players choose to eat. In other teams, such as research teams, members may be expected to be involved in research that is funded by corporations with records of environmental or health damage (such as cigarette makers). Individual team members may have value conflicts and other issues that may affect the team as a whole and it may be a challenge for team leaders to manage around these issues.

Employee involvement teams

Employee involvement teams are teams of workers who meet regularly outside their normal work units for the purpose of collectively addressing important workplace issues.

Many of the creative developments applied to the use of teams in organisations fall into the category of employee involvement teams. This term applies to a wide variety of settings in which teams of workers meet regularly outside their normal work units for the purpose of collectively addressing important workplace issues. The goals of an employee involvement team often relate to total quality concepts and the quest for continuous improvement in all operations. Typically consisting of five to ten members, these teams regularly spend time discussing ways to enhance quality, better satisfy customers, raise productivity and improve the quality of work life.

Employee involvement teams are mechanisms for participation. They allow workers to gain influence over matters affecting them and their work. They also allow the full advantages of team decision making to become a part of everyday organisational affairs. These advantages include bringing the full extent of worker know-how to bear on problems and gaining the commitment of these workers to implement fully any problem-solving approaches that may be selected.

For employee involvement to succeed, traditional managers like Mahmood Mohajer must make sincere commitments to participation and empowerment. The opportunities for the workers to have an influence on what happens to them must be real. When accomplished, true employee involvement offers the potential for contributing positively to performance accomplishments in the new workplace. It also offers employees the advantages of filling higher-order needs such as achievement, recognition and growth (see chapter 3).

Problem-solving teams

Some teams are created for the specific purpose of generating solutions to problems — for example, quality circles, task forces and autonomous work teams. Developed as a means of generating ideas that would raise product quality by reducing defects and error rates, quality circles were a precursor to the total quality movement.[25] A quality circle is a small group of people who meet periodically (for example, for an hour or so once per week) to discuss and develop solutions for problems relating to quality, productivity or cost.

Quality circles are groups of workers who meet periodically to discuss and develop solutions for problems relating to quality, productivity or cost.

For the circles to be successful, members should receive special training in information-gathering and problem-analysis techniques. Quality circle leaders should emphasise democratic participation in identifying and analysing problems and choosing action alternatives. After proposed solutions are presented to management, implementation should be a joint effort between the quality circle and management.

Quality circles cannot be looked on as panaceas for all of an organisation's ills, however. Indeed, a number of conditions must be met to keep quality circles from becoming just another management 'gimmick'. These include the following:
- an informed and knowledgeable workforce
- managerial willingness to trust workers with necessary information
- the presence of a 'team spirit' in the quality circle group
- a clear emphasis on quality in the organisation's goals
- an organisation that encourages participation.

Task forces are temporary teams created to fulfil a well-defined task within a fairly short period of time.

The task force is another kind of team created to solve problems. Task forces are temporary, created with a relatively well-defined task to fulfil. They have a more limited time horizon than that of quality circles; once the task is accomplished, the task force is disbanded.

Other 'teams' might include the 'skunkworks' and 'hotgroups' that may be formed to solve important problems or to develop new ideas. The intention is to remove these teams from the pressures and demands of day-to-day work. However, it is important to acknowledge that some hotgroups or skunkworks are so intensely involved in their task that individual needs and group maintenance activities are neglected. In this sense, they would fail to live up to the criteria of being high-performing and trusting over a long period. In other contexts, specific teams might be set up within an organisation, but with the task of investigating a problem in the society in which it operates. The following research team is an example of such a team.

A research team at the University of New South Wales was awarded $7.125 million to research how 'good' lipoproteins can protect people from atherosclerosis (narrowing of the arteries — a common cause of death in Australia). The team is made up of internationally recognised experts in basic, clinical and public health research related to cardiovascular disease. In investigating the action of 'good' lipoproteins, the team will be hoping to provide insights into how lifestyle factors, physiological processes and pathological situations relate to the cells lining blood vessels and the susceptibility of individuals to atherosclerosis.[26]

Autonomous work teams perform highly related or interdependent jobs, and they are given significant authority and responsibility for many aspects of their work, such as planning, scheduling, assigning tasks to members and making decisions with financial consequences.[27] They were the precursor to the self-managing work team, which we will examine in the next section.

Autonomous work teams are teams given significant authority and responsibility over their work in contexts of highly related or interdependent jobs.

Self-managing teams

Many companies across the world have moved towards the concept of self-managed work teams in which employees work together as equals to solve problems and improve operations. Every self-managed team needs members with three different strengths:

- technical or functional expertise
- problem-solving and decision-making skills
- interpersonal skills.[28]

Formally defined, **self-managing teams** are small groups of people empowered to manage themselves and the work they do on a day-to-day basis.[29] They are also referred to as 'self-directed teams'. Typically, a self-managing work team is one in which the members themselves:

- make decisions on how to divide up tasks within the team
- make decisions on scheduling work within the team
- are able to perform more than one job for the team
- train one another in jobs performed by the team
- evaluate one another's job performance on the team
- are collectively held accountable for the team's performance results.

Self-managing teams are small groups of people empowered to manage themselves and the work they do on a day-to-day basis.

What differentiates self-managing teams from more traditional work groups is the fact that their members have substantial responsibility for a wide variety of decisions involved in the accomplishment of assigned tasks. Indeed, the very purpose of the self-managing work team is to take on duties previously performed by traditional supervisors — that is, such things as quality control, work scheduling and even performance evaluation. The example of BDM illustrates these features.

OB in action

Becton Dickinson Medical (BDM) manufactures hypodermic syringes, needles and cannulas, and other similar supplies for pharmaceutical industries. It prides itself on achieving its goals through mutual trust and respect and, accordingly, manages its 300-plus employees in teams. These are self-managing teams though subdivided into a steering team, resource teams and process teams. As their name suggests, resource teams provide resources and are focused on achieving technical improvements, better quality, cost reduction and improvements in waste management and efficiency. Their members come from across the organisation, offering a range of skills and expertise. The process teams directly produce the products and their members include technicians, programmers, auditors, storemen, clerks and administrative assistants. Team leaders encourage participation, decision making and focus on performance, targets and evaluation of results. They have authority and responsibility to prioritise their activities, change methods and procedures, to meet standards, safety and customer requirements, to schedule their own activities and maintenance and many other aspects of their work.[30]

Well-designed, step-by-step methods of developing self-managed work teams can move authority and responsibility to all levels, allow employees to manage their own activities and help managers feel more comfortable with the process of empowering employees. This typically assumes that the proper foundations have been laid and the proper culture exists to allow an organisation to begin this process.[31]

The establishment and implementation of the concept requires a number of steps. These may include:

1. learning about the self-managing work team concept
2. conducting a readiness assessment to determine if teams are right for the culture
3. communicating to employees the organisation's vision and values as they relate to empowerment and teams
4. taking the organisation through the workplace redesign process
5. implementing the redesign
6. evaluating the progress of self-managing work teams.

Organising into self-directed work teams requires planning, selecting the right team members and leaders, designing teams for success, training continually, and carefully managing the shift of power and responsibilities from leaders to team members.

Self-managing teams operate with fewer layers of management than do traditional organisational structures. Research shows that, in comparison with individuals with no participation in a team, members of self-directed teams are significantly more likely (than non-members) to report that teams have increased profits, improved customer service and boosted the morale of both employees and management.[32]

When self-managing teams are added to an organisation, a number of benefits are expected. Among the advantages that may be realised are:[33]

- improved productivity and production quality, and greater production flexibility
- faster response to technological change
- fewer job classifications and fewer management levels
- lower employee absenteeism and turnover
- improved work attitudes.

Because a self-managing team really does manage itself in many ways, there is no real need for the former position of supervisor. Instead, a team leader usually represents the team when dealing with higher-level management. The possible extent of this change is shown in figure 7.4, where the first level of supervisory management has been eliminated and replaced by self-managing teams. Note also that many traditional tasks of the supervisor are reallocated to the team. Thus, for persons learning to work in such teams for the first time, and for those managers learning to deal with self-managing teams rather than individual workers, the implications can be quite substantial.

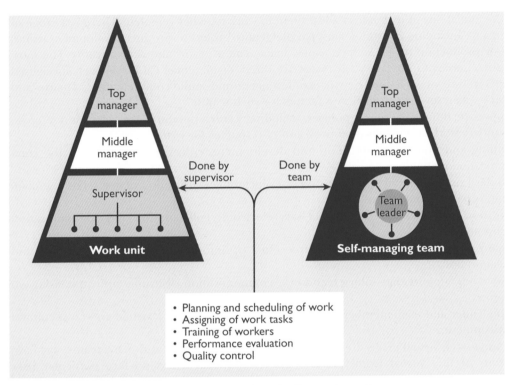

FIGURE 7.4 • Organisational and management implications of self-managing work teams

Perhaps the most important prerequisite is for team members' jobs to be interdependent. Administrative systems must be able to record performance based on team accomplishments. At the same time, these systems should also enable rewards to be given to team members over time periods that may vary depending on the nature of team assignments. Self-managed work teams differ from traditional work groups in that the team, rather than the first-line supervisor, controls the critical management processes that typically include:

- planning
- organising
- directing
- staffing.

Typically these teams move through five stages of development as they grow from new creations to mature, fully functioning groups over a period. To reach a fully functioning stage, teams may need to undergo training that includes communication, administrative and technical skills. Progressive levels of training in these areas through each of the stages of development become the driving force for team growth and development.

Virtual teams

Alongside the changing trends towards teamwork in organisations, other important developments have resulted in the emergence of virtual teams. A **virtual team** is one whose members work interdependently towards the achievement of a common goal across space and time.[34] Such teams can also work across organisational boundaries. They have developed in the context of new forms of organisational structure, the rapid and ongoing advances in information and communication technologies (ICTs), and globalisation.

A **virtual team** is one whose members work interdependently towards the achievement of a common goal across space and time.

Virtual teams rely particularly on ICTs to enable communication and team activity, since they are physically separate. The degree of separation may range from being on separate floors of a large building to being located in different countries around the world. While those in the same building might get together more often, their dislocation from each other and the availability of technology allow them to work together remotely. There is a range of such teams, including network teams, parallel teams, project or product-development teams, work or production teams, service teams, management teams and action teams. The most typical technologies used by such teams are direct email, email via list servers, specialised group software or 'groupware', videoconferencing and audio-conferencing.[35] Duarte and Snyder explain seven critical success factors for such teams:[36]

- supportive human resource policies including career development, rewards for cross-boundary work and results, and provision of resources for virtual work
- training and on-the-job education and development, especially in the use of the communication technology
- standard organisational and team processes including clarification of goals, costing, planning, reporting and controlling
- provision and maintenance of necessary electronic collaboration and communication technology
- organisational culture that allows free flow of information, shared leadership and collaboration
- leadership support that values teamwork, communication, learning and capitalising on diversity
- team-leader and team-member competencies for operating in a virtual and cross-cultural environment.

In some ways virtual teams are no different from other teams, and many teams may have elements of the 'virtual team' present. However, virtual teams do face particular risks because of the context in which they operate. The crucial areas in which they differ from other teams are:

- *Dependence on technology.* Participation may be inhibited if a team member is uncertain of the technology or if equipment is inadequate.
- *Absence of non-verbal cues in communication.* Misunderstandings in communication may occur as words are read or heard in the absence of facial expression and body gestures, for example.
- *Place of interaction.* Outside the context of a particular place, and often a particular culture or subculture, there may be fewer initial shared assumptions and values among team members.
- *Timing of interaction.* Communication may be synchronous (real time) or asynchronous as members respond in their own time.
- *Degrees of public and private communication.* In a team that physically meets there is more chance that conflict, domination and other aspects of human interaction are visible and unavoidable, whereas in virtual teams it is possible that private communications between some team members, in addition to full team shared communications, may influence behaviour.
- *Recording of the group process.* The electronic media used tend to record the group process automatically, whether or not the participants desire it, which may sometimes lead to team members exhibiting extra caution about what they are willing to 'say' in writing.[37]

Virtual teams can bring together a range of members with diverse contributions without requiring that those members be located in the same place. They have the ability to transcend borders and organisational structures. However, as for any other team, there are many other requirements for team success. Hackman[38] argues that virtual teams have the same needs and potential problems as any other team (as discussed throughout this chapter), but that it is even harder to create the right conditions for success in virtual teams.

Cross-functional teams in the supply chain

Supply chain management is an increasingly important operation in large and globalising corporations. For example, major supermarket chains such as Woolworths and Coles in Australia and Foodstuffs in New Zealand manage very closely the supply of produce for their stores. They can also be very closely involved in contracting growers to grow produce of a particular type and quality.

In managing supply chains — and such organisations may have very many suppliers — there are often teams of people involved in transport and logistics, including warehousing, inventory control, marketing and product development. Teams may operate within the organisation and/ or across it and other businesses that have a contractual link. Managing the tasks involved in sourcing produce through the supply chain as well as the relationships involved requires teamwork and team management skills. Freelance supply chain specialist Brad Harrison advises that the supply chain management team should be managed by a supply chain professional. He says that there is a need for cross-functional project-based teams to improve the supply chain operation. Managing a supply chain team involves collaborative action among members of the team (including any non-corporate members such as agents or suppliers). There may not be the opportunity for day-to-day contact and much of the activity of any team may be conducted in geographical isolation, with the key physical link being the shift of products from producer to the organisation. In view of the huge growth in supply chain management these are important issues for team management. One example of an effective supply chain arrangement is Singapore-based Flextronics, which built industry parks near its suppliers to improve productivity and which, in turn, became an important supplier to Microsoft.[39]

Future challenges for work teams

Work teams will continue to present various challenges in organisations. These challenges relate to use of technology, trust, accountability, diversity and the nature of leadership within the teams. While challenges are likely to be applicable to teams of all kinds, sometimes one is particularly relevant to a certain type of group, and this is reflected in the following discussion.

Empowerment through new technology

Empowerment strategies play a crucial role in team development and maintenance. A new technology, group support systems, can assist managers as they strive to improve team performance while fostering effective and productive team member behaviours. These systems involve software that supports activities such as brainstorming, idea consolidation, alternative evaluation and voting. Status liabilities confronting those of lesser rank in corporate groups are diminished by input anonymity, concurrent access to participation, and the capability of the group support system's voting tool to promote and restrict decision making through group consensus. The structure of the electronic meeting room where the group support system technology is housed promotes equitable interaction and suggests a commitment to task. Because verbal discussion is an integral part of the group support system process, effective leadership is essential. The group support system's tools complement the session leader's facilitation activities by contributing directly to the management and automation of the meeting process.

Trust

To build trust, members usually need face-to-face contact. Trust is important in all teams but it can often be missing. For example, a self-managing team might be undermined by a lack of trust when team leaders or other groups within the organisation try to control their behaviour by resorting to hierarchical authority. Employee involvement teams may feel distrust if they have worked hard to provide a recommendation to solve a problem only to find that it is ignored. There are particular issues for trust in virtual teams. Management author Charles Handy argues that this is the challenge and key difficulty for virtual teams, because people develop trusting relationships mainly through personal interactions.[40] A lack of daily personal contact can heighten misunderstandings and undermine a team's effectiveness.[41]

Virtual teams therefore need to develop a high level of trust and work hard at maintaining it. Handy suggests that to build trust among dispersed team members, creating a shared sense of purpose is paramount. He also suggests that the first meeting of the team should occur face-to-face rather than online, if this is possible. As he notes, 'Virtuality requires trust to make it work — technology on its own is not enough'.[42]

Accountability

As more organisations adopt self-managed teams, autonomous work groups and cross-functional teams, the question of accountability often arises, and answers are usually difficult to find. Most managers have a good idea of what it means to hold an individual accountable, but they do not always know how to apply accountability to a team. As we have already shown, there is much evidence to suggest that work teams can accomplish far more than individuals working separately. However, much of the potential of a team is wasted unless it is harnessed through an appropriate structure and monitored through individual accountability.

Diversity

There can be many difficulties in managing diverse teams in organisations. These occur whether the organisation is located in one country or transcends national borders. Diversity can occur across a range of criteria such as gender, profession and different religious, ethnic and national cultures. In the case of culture, the impact of diversity will depend in part on the balance of team membership. Some teams may have just one representative from a minority culture (for example, an Australian team may have one Aboriginal representative), some may have two distinct cultures (a New Zealand team may have a mix of representatives from European and Maori cultures), and yet others will embrace several cultures (a Malaysian team may include those from Malay, Chinese, Indian and European backgrounds).

Other diversity issues are also important and may influence team management. The purpose of the team will be relevant, and the cohesiveness and performance of the team will be affected by these issues. The relative numbers of women in senior teams is often discussed, even though women are not a minority group in society. In some teams there may be an imbalance of representation by profession. For example, a strategic planning team may have two or three accountants but no human resource professionals. Even the age of team members may have an impact because of different attitudes and experiences, or when, for example, one young person feels out of place among much older team members. The following example from New Zealand shows that diversity can have an important impact on company boards.

OB in action

Company boards, as a key managing team in an organisation, have frequently been accused of being too homogeneous in terms of gender, age and ethnic background. A study by Massey University explored board composition and company performance. The study indicated that more diverse boards may perform well in complex environments. Boards in the survey which were homogeneous included Infratil, Wellington Drive Technology and the Strathmore group which had small, all-male boards. Lion Nathan, Michael Hill Investments and TelstraClear were businesses that demonstrated the highest levels of board diversity.[43]

While diversity can improve productivity, faulty processes can undermine diverse teams. Adler provides some common explanations for problems in multicultural teams (and in many cases these may apply equally well to teams with other types of diversity). They include the following:
- Different perspectives and behaviours can prevent people from seeing situations in common ways.
- Dislike and mistrust can occur between members through ignorance, stereotyping or misunderstanding.
- Language and cultural norms (for instance, about punctuality or presenting bad news or different jargons) may cause conflict.
- Communication inaccuracies are common and can cause stress.

Such teams have to spend more time on building cohesion and solidarity than homogeneous teams. However, there is scope for a greater contribution of ideas, more creativity and overall synergy within culturally diverse teams.[44]

This view of diversity presents a challenge for teams in the future. The following 'Counterpoint' provides another perspective on a phenomenon called 'homophily' that may also have an impact on teamwork.

COUNTERPOINT

Too friendly to be effective?

As the old proverb goes, 'Birds of a feather flock together'. Paul Davis has conducted research into the phenomenon of 'homophily' and its impacts in the workplace, including its effect in teams. Homophily, a term coined in 1964 by Lazarfield and Merton, describes the tendency of people to be with others who are similar to themselves in age, social background, ethnicity, gender, interests, geographic location and perhaps in other ways.[45]

Since we often draw attention to the need for diversity or heterogeneity in teams, it can be seen that problems may arise when people cluster in smaller groups within a team. Doing this may undermine the benefits of diversity that might be gained in the team as it might inhibit the range of life experiences, ideas, opinions and attitudes that could be brought to the team process.

(continued)

There is another aspect to this phenomenon. Since team building encourages trust, camaraderie and working closely together, it is possible that team members may become close and homophilic on the basis of their teams. That is, they may tend to cluster in their teams in other contexts, which could inhibit their capacity to gain from networking and/or working with others outside the team to achieve team tasks.

Davis's research showed that managers at a conference who did not know each other tended to sit next to people who were like themselves (based on outward features such as age, gender or cultural background). In another five-day workshop for a company, his research showed that people were six times more likely to arrive and sit with people from their own work area rather than with those from other work areas. They were slow to come back from breaks and on average 25 minutes a day were lost through this. Additionally, work was often rushed, not taken seriously and of low quality. People spent some of their time 'off-task' and sometimes the bare minimum on the task. When Davis intentionally mixed them up on the final day of the workshop, 14 out of 17 people were unhappy with the change and some were openly hostile. Yet they returned from breaks quicker (on average wasting only 12 minutes), spent more of the allotted time completing required tasks, and produced better-quality outcomes. A survey of the participants revealed that they achieved more away from their friends on the last day and were more focused. They networked more, took the workshop more seriously, and put more effort into it. Only two of the 17 said they got nothing out of the change on the fifth day. The participants themselves acknowledged that they behave differently when they work with people that they have a lot in common with.[46]

Questions

1. If homophily can affect team performance as described, should organisations pull back from the trend towards team-based management?
2. How can organisations build diverse but cohesive and effective teams?
3. What role is there for team leadership in managing the phenomenon of homophily?

Team leadership

Contemporary research recommends moving beyond self-managed teams to self-leading teams. Self-leading team members should have more freedom and authority to make decisions, independent of external supervision. Leaders should not compromise team membership processes by imposing control, but rather encourage and facilitate the team's self-managing capacity.[47] This capacity for self-leading is not just anchored in the joint actions of team members but also rests on the development of individuals within the team who are better equipped to self-manage and self-lead. Such an approach appreciates that team members are competent individuals who may be willing and interested in playing a role in the strategic direction of the organisation as well as influencing their own specific work performance. If self-leading teams are also oriented towards the organisation's strategy, they will be able to operate effectively on the organisation's behalf without constant referral to higher-level leaders.

A distinguishing feature of self-leading teams is that workers perform work more for the natural (intrinsic) rewards that are built into the task than to receive externally administered rewards. However, self-leading, team-based work systems can only work under two fundamental conditions:

1. a significant involvement of the workforce in determining the direction of the organisation as well as pursuing that direction
2. an opportunity for the work teams to influence that direction, especially as it relates to their specific work performance.

Summary

Teams and groups

A group is a number of people who interact with one another for a common purpose, whereas a team is a group of people who function as a unit. A team is a small group of people with complementary skills who work together as a unit to achieve a common purpose for which they hold themselves collectively accountable.

Teams and their effectiveness

Teams operate on three levels so that members engaged in team tasks are also concerned with individual needs and the maintenance of the team. Teams can operate to make or do things, or to run things in an organisation. The most effective teams have members with a balance of complementary skills and strengths so that they can achieve synergy.

Team-building approaches

Team building is a series of planned action steps designed to gather and analyse data on the functioning of a team. It is also about implementing changes to increase the team's operating effectiveness. Teamwork occurs when members of a team work together in a way that represents certain core values, all of which promote the use of skills to accomplish common goals. Team building is thus a way of building the capacity for teamwork and high performance. The team-building process is participative and engages all team members in identifying problems and opportunities, planning appropriate actions, making individual commitments to implement these actions, and conducting appropriate evaluation and feedback activities. Team building can involve brainstorming to generate uninhibited ideas, facilitators to raise self-awareness and group awareness, and training to develop team skills. Some specific team-building processes are formal retreats, continual improvement and outdoor experiences.

Team performance and cohesiveness

An important aspect of any team is the set of norms within which it operates. Norms are rules or standards of member behaviour; they are ideas or beliefs about what is appropriate behaviour for team members. Norms identify the way in which 'loyal' members are supposed to behave. As such, they can exert a major influence on teams when members adhere to them. The clarification of roles is important for all members of work teams. Role ambiguities and conflicts create anxieties and stress, and can detract from performance and personal satisfaction. Cohesiveness is a measure of the attractiveness of a team for its members. In a highly cohesive team, members value their place in the team and are very loyal to it. Thus, an important rule of thumb is that members of highly cohesive teams conform to team norms. Consequently, the combination of the team performance norms and level of cohesiveness can reveal a lot about its performance potential. The most favourable situation for any manager or team leader is to be in charge of a highly cohesive team with positive performance norms; the positive norms point behaviour in desired directions, and the high cohesiveness creates desires to live up to the expectations set by these norms. Good managers are able to influence team cohesiveness in ways that support the accomplishment of long-term team effectiveness.

Types of teams

An employee involvement team is any team whose members meet regularly outside of their formal task assignments to address important work-related problems and concerns. Most typically, these teams deal with issues involving total quality management and the quest for continual improvement in operations. Popular types of problem-solving teams are the quality circle, the task force and the autonomous work team. The latter was the precursor to the self-managed work team. A self-managing team is a work group whose members collectively take responsibility for performing the group task and making many of the 'supervisory' decisions relating to task performance on a day-to-day basis. The team members, in the full sense of the word, 'manage' themselves. The traditional level of supervisory management is eliminated, and in its place the work team agrees to accept responsibility for self-management. Members of this team will plan, complete and evaluate their own work; they will collectively train and evaluate one another in task performance; they will share tasks and responsibilities; and they may even determine one another's pay grades. Such teams are based on the concept of empowerment, and offer another creative way to allow people to become more involved in important decisions affecting their work. Under the right circumstances, self-managing teams can contribute to improved productivity for organisations and improved quality of working life for their members. Virtual teams have members who work interdependently towards common goals even though they are not together in the same place at the same time.

Future challenges for work teams

While teams potentially have many advantages, there are some challenges. New technology can enable more empowerment in teams and enhance decision making. However, the lack of face-to-face interaction can undermine levels of trust in virtual teams. Also, team decision making can lead to a diffusion of accountability for decisions. This may be a problem when quality needs to be monitored and improved or corrective action taken. Diversity in teams, especially multicultural teams, may lead to problems such as conflict, misunderstanding, stress and mistrust. This complication is increasing with the growth in global and virtual teams. Finally, there is still debate about whether there should be team leaders or whether team members should be equipped to self-lead in teams.

Chapter 7 study guide

Key terms

autonomous work teams, *p. 245*
brainstorming, *p. 236*
cohesiveness, *p. 240*
employee involvement teams, *p. 244*
groups, *p. 229*
norms, *p. 239*

quality circles, *p. 244*
role, *p. 240*
role ambiguity, *p. 240*
role conflict, *p. 240*
self-managing teams, *p. 245*
task forces, *p. 244*

team building, *p. 230*
teams, *p. 228*
teamwork, *p. 230*
virtual team, *p. 247*

Review questions

1. Explain the key differences between teams and groups and the reasons organisations might wish to instigate teams in their organisations.
2. List and explain the goals of team building.

3. What are the likely performance outcomes for a highly cohesive team and how can team cohesion be increased or decreased?
4. Compare and contrast employee involvement teams and self-managed teams.

Application questions

1. Your team leader is always pushing your work group to work harder, to be more productive, to be the most successful production team in the company. You and your fellow team members just laugh at him and get on with your work. You feel you *are* all productive and there's no need to work any harder. You get your weekly pay and working harder won't change that. What is the likelihood that the team could be more productive and what could the manager do to improve productivity?

2. An external facilitator has been brought in to help in the process of team building for your group. The facilitator is to spend a day a week with the group for the next month, and then one day a month for the following six months. In these sessions, the group will go through a series of team-building activities. The members of your group have been working together for two years and are very familiar with each other. What benefits do you think may come from this facilitation, and why?

3. Your team leader has left the organisation and now your team will be getting a new team leader. After years of being an effective team with this respected and successful team leader, what are the likely challenges the team faces?

4. Your organisation produces linen household goods. In the production of those goods, groups of 15–20 employees typically work in a production unit with a supervisor who gives them frequent directions about what is required. The organisation has decided to go towards a model of self-managing teams after trialling it successfully in the finance and the human resources departments. What are the likely changes that employees will face in changing to this way of working, and how should management introduce the changes?

5. Your team is very close and members of the team will do anything to help each other out, including covering up for each other if there is a crisis or poor performance. What issues are there for the performance of the group?

6. You have a team of seven that operates in several different cities in your country. Your country is

ethnically diverse and the level of knowledge of technological advances in communication and information technology is uneven across different ethnic groups owing to their socioeconomic position in society. Since the success of the team depends on

using new technology to communicate, what can you do to encourage full and equal participation by team members and what will you do to build them into a team?

OB *Research questions*

1. Find two local examples, and/or examples from journal articles, of organisations that have introduced teams. Investigate and compare the organisations in terms of:
   (a) the method of introducing the teams
   (b) the success of the teams
   (c) the perceived differences between team-based management and what existed before.

2. Search for at least two team-building consultants on the Internet. Look for what sorts of team-building processes they offer. What do they promise for organisations that use their services? How do their programs compare with each other?

OB *Running project*

1. Look back at the tasks you completed for chapter 6. Now that you have studied teams, which of the groups you examined in chapter 6 could be described as teams and which could not?

2. Describe the team-building exercises your organisation undertakes.

3. Does the organisation use self-managing teams? Why?

4. Describe a virtual team in your organisation. Be sure to examine why it exists and how the team members work together.

OB *Individual activity*

Identifying norms that influence teams

Objectives

1. To help you determine the norms operating in an organisation
2. To assess the strength of response to particular norms
3. To help clarify the importance of norms as influences on team behaviour

Total time: 60 minutes

Procedure

1. Choose an organisation about which you know quite a bit.

2. Insert each of the statements below into the following question:
   If an employee in your organisation were to [insert statement here], most other employees would, too.

Statements

1. show genuine concern for the problems that face the organisation and make suggestions about solving them (organisational/personal pride)
2. set very high personal standards of performance (performance/excellence)
3. try to make the work group operate more like a team when dealing with issues or problems (teamwork/communication)
4. think of going to a supervisor with a problem (leadership/supervision)
5. evaluate expenditures in terms of the benefits they will provide for the organisation (profitability/cost effectiveness)
6. express concern for the wellbeing of other members of the organisation (colleague/ associate relations)

7. keep a customer or client waiting while looking after matters of personal convenience (customer/client relations)
8. criticise another employee who is trying to improve things in the work situation (innovativeness/creativity)
9. actively look to expand their knowledge to be able to do a better job (training/development)
10. be perfectly honest in answering this questionnaire (candour/openness).

3. For each statement (within the question), indicate your response it terms of A, B, C, D or E.

A Strongly agree or encourage it
B Agree with it or encourage it
C Consider it unimportant
D Disagree with or discourage it
E Strongly disagree with or discourage it

Evaluation
Review your results to decide whether the organisation is likely to provide a suitable environment for effective teams.

Group activity

Brainstorming
Brainstorming really is a fairly simple concept to understand. Most people think they know it quite well, and they probably do. But even though they know it well, people struggle to demonstrate it in a small group. As outlined in the chapter, effective brainstorming is more than just following a simple set of rules and guidelines.

Objective
To practise your brainstorming skills

Time: 20–60 minutes

Process
1. Break into small groups. Discuss the concept of brainstorming, using material from the chapter.
2. Review the following basic rules for brainstorming.
3. Select a topic for brainstorming. Choose a topic that is a problem of real concern — for example, how can we get everyone to come to lectures on time? How can we get class members to participate more in class? What are the best criteria for evaluating students undertaking an organisational behaviour course?
4. Begin the brainstorming period.
5. When no-one has more ideas, formally stop the brainstorming process and begin the closure discussion.

Some basic brainstorming rules
- Each group member is asked to contribute at least one idea.
- No member is allowed to dismiss or criticise the idea or suggestion of another member.
- List each idea, even if the same or similar idea has already been posted.

- Everyone should be asked explicitly to contribute — for example, 'David, do you have any idea to add?'
- Record ideas as quickly as they are stated.
- Encourage group members to contribute more ideas when their contributions slow.
- Encourage funny, silly or seemingly foolish ideas.
- Make sure, before stopping, that all possible ideas are heard and posted. Go around the room and ask everyone.
- Encourage group members to build on or add to ideas already suggested.
- **Important:** do not evaluate the ideas of others while they are being expressed or written down by the brainstorming facilitator or group leader. If this happens, in either a negative or a positive way, the leader should ask the person evaluating to add another idea to the list, thereby channelling such participation into a contribution. Every idea expressed by any member of the group counts. Every idea must therefore be included and added to the list.

Evaluation
At the end of this exercise evaluate how effectively you operated as a team.

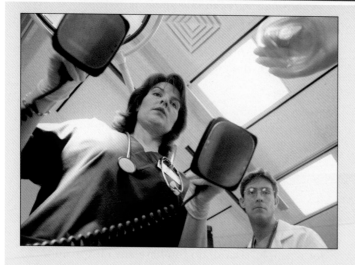

While hospitals are familiar with emergencies, Professor Ken Hillman of Liverpool Hospital in Sydney found that cardiac arrest teams in hospitals were not effectively saving the lives of people who had cardiac arrests *in* hospital, with only about 10 per cent of such patients surviving. He developed the concept of a medical emergency team (MET). Its purpose is to identify risk cases and enable a procedure that gives prompt treatment. While traditionally nurses chart vital signs (pulse and respiratory rates, temperature and blood pressure) there were cultural, hierarchical and status impediments inhibiting their ability to get a doctor to attend to the patient. Usually the doctor was the junior intern or resident, who may have been tied up in some other situation, such as surgery on another patient. The nurses did not feel empowered to insist on their attendance. By the time the doctor came the patient was probably seriously ill, with about 80 per cent of them ending up in the intensive care unit when their arrests could have effectively been prevented by simple manoeuvres such as antibiotics, fluids and oxygen had the patients been treated earlier.

With the introduction of the METs a procedure was put in place whereby the ward nurse could press a cardiac arrest alarm button and a team, with the same qualifications and skills as a cardiac arrest team, would turn up within minutes to look after the patient. Since, in such a cardiac arrest situation, a few minutes or even seconds can be critical in saving a person's life, these response times are vital.

The METs approach has been adopted in many locations, including 2600 US hospitals. One, the Baptist Memphis Hospital calls its MET a 'Medical Response Team'. Two Victorian adopters are Geelong Hospital, which has reduced deaths and cardiac arrests by 20 per cent as a result of introducing its 24-hour on-call MET; and The Austin Hospital, which has dramatically reduced the serious adverse after-effects of surgery by using the approach. There has been a 37 per cent relative reduction in mortality and a 65 per cent drop in cardiac arrests. At Liverpool Hospital the rate of cardiac arrests has been reduced, as has the number of patient deaths and of general ward patients ending up in intensive care. While some other hospitals have failed to demonstrate any differences, Professor Hillman believes the concept has filtered through and has taught many people a lot about how to care about patients in hospitals; the importance of more frequent monitoring of their vital signs; and the importance of a cultural change where nurses can be empowered to call in doctors when they feel it may be necessary. The participants have experienced improved teamwork. Doctors feel more engaged with sick people on the wards, nurses feel they can access doctors when worried about patients, and consultant doctors feel their patients are in a safer medical system. The change involves significant shifts in attitudes for members of the cardiac arrest team, including Professor Hillman, since in the past they would have been likely to have said to a nurse that they were there to deal with people *having* an arrest, not people who *might have* an arrest. Consultant doctors, who were primarily responsible for the patients, would have felt territorial about others intruding on the care of their patients. Professor Hillman believes that, while effective in terms of preventing fatal cardiac arrests in hospitals, the MET concept has also enhanced the way people in the hospital work as a team, and the cooperation between nurses and doctors and between the intensive care and general wards. It has also increased everyone's willingness to question a patient's treatment if he or she is not responding.[48]

Questions

1. What was happening to prevent employees of the hospital working together as a team to help these patients?
2. What features of teamwork does the MET display?
3. How has the MET process assisted teamwork in terms of task performance and team maintenance?

Suggested reading

Deborah L Duarte and Nancy Tennant Snyder, *Mastering virtual teams*, 2nd ed. (San Francisco: Jossey-Bass, 2001).

J Richard Hackman, *Leading teams* (Boston: Harvard Business School Press, 2002).

Judith D Hoover, *Effective small group and team communication*, 2nd ed. (Belmont, CA: Thomson/Wadsworth, 2005).

Sandra Kiffen-Petersen, 'Trust: a neglected variable in team effectiveness', *Journal of the Australian and New Zealand Academy of Management* (JANZAM), vol. 10, no. 1 (2004), pp. 38–53.

Patrick Lencioni, *Overcoming the five dysfunctions of a team: a field guide for leaders, managers, and facilitators* (San Francisco: Jossey-Bass, 2005).

Glenn M Parker, *Cross-functional teams: working with allies, enemies, and other strangers* (San Francisco: John Wiley & Sons, 2003).

David Parkin and Paul Bourke, *What makes teams work* (Melbourne: Macmillan, 2004).

Harold Monty Sacher and Merryl Sacher, *Success through team performance* (Melbourne: Sacher Associates, 2004).

Leigh Thompson, *Making the team*, international/2nd ed. (Upper Saddle River, NJ: Pearson Education, 2004).

Sheila Simsarian Webber and Richard J Klimoski, 'Crews: a distinct type of work team', *Journal of Business and Psychology*, vol. 18, no. 3 (Spring 2004), pp. 261–79.

Mike Woodcock and Dave Francis, *Team metrics: resources for measuring and improving team performance* (Burlington, VT: Gower, 2005).

End notes

1. A Morehead, M Steele, M Alexander, K Stephen and L Duffin, *Changes at work: the 1995 Australian workplace industrial relations survey* (Melbourne: Longman, 1997).

2. Lynette Hoffman, 'What a performance!', *Human Resources* (18 October 2005), pp. 18–19.

3. Lee G Bolman and Terrence E Deal, 'What makes a team work?', *Organizational Dynamics*, vol. 21, no. 2 (Autumn 1992), pp. 34–44.

4. P Ayling and L Thomsen-Moore, '[Tips from two] top achievers', *Management Today* (October 2005), pp. 28–30.

5. B Senior and S Swailes, 'The dimensions of management team performance: a repertory grid study', *Journal of Productivity and Performance Management*, vol. 53, no. 4 (2004), pp. 317–33.

6. 'Should the CEO be one person?', *World Executive's Digest* (February 1993), pp. 22–4.

7. For a good discussion of team building see William D Dyer, *Team building*, 2nd ed. (Reading, MA: Addison-Wesley, 1987).

8. Jon R Katzenbach and Douglas K Smith, 'The discipline of teams', *Harvard Business Review* (March/April 1993), pp. 118–19.

9. Based in part on Katzenbach and Smith, op. cit., p. 113.

10. Based in part on Katzenbach and Smith, op. cit., p. 115.

11. M O'Neill quoted on p. 20 of C Cooper, 'The challenge of management', *Management Today* (July 2005), pp. 18–23.

12. KE Hultman, 'The ten commandments of team leadership', *Training and Development*, vol. 52, no. 2 (February 1998), p. 12.

13. Derived from M Story, 'Ian Morrice: the CEO The Warehouse is bargaining on', *New Zealand Management* (February 2005), pp. 36–9; R Pannett, 'The Warehouse profit slumps 36 per cent', *New Zealand Herald* (9 September 2005); S McMahon and Bloomberg, 'Warehouse writes $30m off its stores', *The Sydney Morning Herald* (12 September 2005).

14. S Rodger, G Woodyatt, J Marinac, J Ziviani and P Watter, 'Teamwork in health and rehabilitation sciences: evaluation of a multiprofessional workshop', *Focus on Health Professional Education: A Multi-Disciplinary Journal*, vol. 6, no. 1 (2004), pp. 8–25.

15. Sivasailam Thiagarajan, 'A game for cooperative learning', *Training and Development*, vol. 46, no. 5 (May 1992), pp. 35–41.

16. Glenn Thompson and Paul F Pearce, 'The team–trust game', *Training and Development*, vol. 46, no. 5 (May 1992), pp. 42–3.

17. 'About turn', *New Zealand Management* (September 2005), pp. 13–14.

18. See Daniel C Feldman, 'The development and enforcement of group norms', *Academy of Management Review*, vol. 9 (1984), pp. 47–53.

19. Developed from Robert F Allen and Saul Pilnick, 'Confronting the shadow organization: how to detect and defeat negative norms', *Organizational Dynamics* (Spring 1973), pp. 6–10.

20. For a good summary of research on group cohesiveness, see Marvin E Shaw, *Group dynamics* (New York: McGraw-Hill, 1971), pp. 110–12, 192.

21. 'Free spirits: volunteering to learn' (interview with Debbie Snelson), *Management Woman* (July 2005), pp. 15–16.

22. RA Guzzo and E Salas (eds), *Team effectiveness and decision making in organizations* (San Francisco: Jossey-Bass, 1995); JR Hackman (ed.), *Groups that work and those that don't* (San Francisco: Jossey-Bass, 1990).

23. Example from 'Time to toss tradition?', *Enterprise* (Autumn 1989), pp. 35–9.

24. K Le Mesurier, 'A healthy alliance', *Business Review Weekly* (23–29 June 2005), p. 50.

25. See Kenichi Ohmae, 'Quality control circles: they work and don't work', *Wall Street Journal* (29 March 1982), p. 16; Robert P Steel, Anthony J Mento, Benjamin L Dilla, Nestor K Ovalle and Russell F Lloyd, 'Factors influencing the success and failure of two quality circles programs', *Journal of Management*, vol. 11, no. 1 (1985), pp. 99–119; Edward E Lawler III and Susan A Mohrman, 'Quality circles: after the honeymoon', *Organizational Dynamics*, vol. 15, no. 4 (1987), pp. 42–54.

26. University of New South Wales School of Medicine, 'Major funding boost to UNSW Medicine research teams' in 'New stories' (2005), http://notes.med.unsw.edu.au/home/newsstories.nsf.

27. AG Dobbelaere and KH Goeppinger, 'The right and wrong way to set up a self-directed work team', *Human Resource Professional*, vol. 5.

28. Katzenbach and Smith, op. cit., p. 112.

29. Richard S Wellins, William C Byham and Jeanne M Wilson, *Empowered teams* (San Francisco: Jossey-Bass, 1993).

30. Spring Singapore, 'Self-managing teams in Becton Dickinson Medical (Singapore)', *Productivity Digest* (December 2000), www.spring.gov.sg/portal/newsroom/epublications/pd/2000_12/index_IP.html (viewed May 2005).

31. Larry Lacy, 'Self-managed work groups step-by-step', *Journal for Quality and Participation*, vol. 15, no. 3 (June 1992), pp. 68–73.

32. Jack Gordon, 'Work teams — how far have they come?', *Training*, vol. 29, no. 10 (October 1992), pp. 59–65.

33. Developed in part from Richard S Wellins, William C Byham and Jeanne M Wilson, 'Proactive teams achieve inspiring results', *World Executive's Digest* (October 1992), pp. 18–24.

34. Jessica Lipnack and Jeffrey Stamps, *Virtual teams*, 2nd ed. (New York: John Wiley & Sons, 2000), p. 18.

35. Glyn Elwyn, Trisha Greenhalgh and Fraser Macfarlane, *Groups: a guide to small group work in healthcare, management, education and research* (Abingdon, UK: Radcliffe Medical Press, 2001), pp. 203–6.

36. Deborah Duarte and Nancy Tennant Snyder, *Mastering virtual teams*, rev. ed. (San Francisco: Jossey-Bass, 2001), pp. 4–23.

37. Elwyn, Greenhalgh and Macfarlane, op. cit., pp. 206–14.

38. J Richard Hackman, *Leading teams: setting the stage for great performances* (Boston: Harvard Business School Press, 2002), pp. 130–2.

39. D Parker, 'Making better chains [strategy and supply]', *Management Today* (June 2005), pp. 28–32.

40. C Handy, 'Trust and the virtual organization', *Harvard Business Review* (May/June 1995).

41. S Jarvenpaa, K Knoll and D Leidner, 'Is anybody out there? The development and implications of trust in global virtual teams', *Journal of Management Information Systems*, vol. 14 (1998).

42. Handy, op. cit.

43. 'Diversity: does it make a better board?', *New Zealand Management* (November 2004), pp. 80–1, describing a study at Massey University by N van der Walt, C Ingley, G Shergill and A Townsend and an emerging paper, 'Board configuration: are diverse boards better boards?'.

44. Nancy Adler, *International dimensions of organizational behavior* (Cincinnati, OH: South-Western, 2002).

45. P Davis, 'Mix to match', *HR Monthly* (September 2005), pp. 42–3.

46. ibid.

47. Greg L Stewart and Murray R Barrick, 'Team structure and performance: assessing the mediating role of intrateamprocess and the moderating role of task type', *Academy of Management Journal* (April 2000), pp. 135–48.

48. 'Medical emergency team (MET)', Norman Swan's interview of Professor Ken Hillman on the Australian Broadcasting Corporation radio program *The health report* (broadcast 20 June 2005), www.abc.net.au/rn/talks/8.30/helthrpt/stories/s1396034.htm; Barwon Health, 'Big team effort saves lives' in *Quality of care*, annual report (Victoria: Barwon Health, 2004), p. 28; IHI.org, 'Building rapid reponse teams' (2005), www.ihi.org/IHI/Topics/Improvement/Move Your Dot/Improvements Stories.

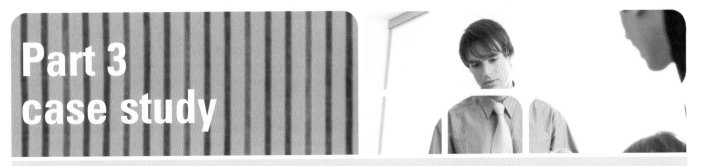

Part 3 case study

TEAMING IN SINGAPORE'S PUBLIC SERVICE FOR THE TWENTY-FIRST CENTURY

Introduction

The idea of working with groups and teams permeates the public sector in Singapore. The Singapore Government's 'Public Service for the 21st Century' (PS21) strategy is built around the ideas of:

- learning
- questioning
- suggesting
- teaming
- sharing.

All the components work together to encourage improvement, responsiveness to citizens' expectations, and a higher quality service. The PS21 strategy also aims to encourage public sector workers to be activists for change who anticipate, welcome and manage it positively. In the PS21 teams, sharing knowledge involves trusting one another and treating people fairly. Team building is an important part of achieving shared knowledge and of achieving all the aims of PS21. The key teams that put PS21 into action across the service are described below.

PS21 teams

Amoebas are groups of junior officers in the service who volunteer to come together to brainstorm issues of interest or to suggest changes. It is thought that these young officers may not be so bound by historical policy interests or entrenched ways of doing things, and that they may also be able to bypass supervisors who may not be open to new ideas. The name 'amoeba' draws links to the single-celled organism that has a short lifespan, and implies working as a single unit. These teams have just 90 days to form, discuss their ideas, submit reports and disband. The proposals help the public (or civil) service to look to the future and have, on hand, ideas and solutions that have been previously thought out.

Work Improvement Teams Scheme (WITS) teams have been around for some time in the Singapore public service. Similar to Six Sigma teams (invented by Motorola and popularised by General Electric), the WITS teams do not necessarily have the same strict focus on measurement and quantitative data analysis. However, like Six Sigma teams, they focus on gaining significant improvements in the organisation, are given considerable resources, and involve top-down identification of projects and team members. In fact, WITS is aimed at empowerment of officers to come together to create continuous improvement and innovative outcomes. Unlike Amoebas, which use only junior officers, WITS teams can use officers from different grades, from different units within the organisations, and even from different agencies within the public sector as a whole. In some cases, such as that of the Singapore Prison Service (SPS) where there were 274 WITS projects in 2002, they sometimes get the clients (prison inmates) to participate. WITS teams consider questions about problems interfering with work; opportunities for improvement to create better outcomes; doing things differently and creating value in their activities; making the organisation ready for changing circumstances; and action to make improvements happen. They are free to use whatever tools they wish to deal with the issue, but the tools must help them to go through a rigorous thinking process so that they can identify the root cause of the problem or the main factor that will allow capitalisation of an opportunity. Project ideas are submitted to supervisors and management prior to being carried out. One of the key problems with WITS teams is that some supervisors lack leadership and interest in the projects and see them as 'just going through the motions' of fulfilling

(continued)

quotas for WITS projects per year. There has also been too much rigidity in adhering to team tools such as 'fishbone diagrams'. Using the quota system for projects works against the aims of the scheme, but does add value because it helps to give an overall picture about whether the scheme is making progress. The head of the civil service Mr Lim Siong Guan believes that WITS is about getting good results out of the teamwork that happens when people get together, grow ideas and learn. It operates in conjunction with another program — the Staff Suggestion Scheme (SSS).

Study teams are another type of PS21 team. These are formed within government agencies (such as ministries and statutory boards) to look into opportunities, or other options, for achieving agency goals. The members of these teams are senior employees with required expertise, not juniors as in the Amoebas. Rather than being restricted to the shorter time frame given to Amoebas, their allocated time is framed around the complexity and nature of the research.

Strategic Issues Group (SIG) teams involve senior officers from different agencies. They come together to examine cross-agency issues at a strategic level, formulating whatever policies or changes to policies are required. They are also expected to question the existing policy approaches during their research process. They report to a steering committee that comprises permanent secretaries (employed heads of the agencies) and ministers (political heads of the agencies).

Zero-In Process (ZIP) action teams find and resolve (zero-in on) difficult and systemic problems (called 'X-files'). These are problems that involve more than one agency or problems that do not fit clearly into one agency or other. X-files also cover problems that recur excessively or that emerge because rules and regulations have become outdated. The ZIP program has been described as a program to smooth out the kinks in projects that straddle different ministries and agencies. In 2003 some 96 X-files had been uncovered and action taken on 68 of them. When such issues emerge, or are found, senior representatives from the relevant agencies are invited, by the ZIP panel, to form a ZIP action team. The ZIP panel is a committee of permanent secretaries. The problems can be found, for example, by an employee such as Nurhana Ismail, who is an executive officer for the Feedback Unit of the Ministry of Community Development and Sports. She reads the content of each mail and email that reaches her department, and if it does not apply to any specific agency, she channels it through the Zero-In Process.

ZIP action teams carry out internal reviews of rules and systems; engage with the community and with the relevant agencies to get their views and involve them in developing solutions; and recommend changes (within a given time frame) and a plan for executing the changes. The ZIP program enables the public service to refresh its rules and regulations and its policies and procedures to ensure they are relevant to public needs. The ZIP reforms are not just about continuous improvement in the public sector; they are also aimed at building up the service, managing the flow of talent, and strengthening teamwork and *esprit de corps* among public servants. The ZIP program operates in conjunction with the Pro-Enterprise Panel (PEP) — which ensures that government rules and regulations support a pro-business environment — and the POWER (Public Officers Working on Eliminating Red-tape) initiative — which endeavours to give public officers greater flexibility to do their jobs effectively rather than to adhere to rules and procedures.

There are many ZIP team success stories, such as these three:

- The Land Transport Authority (LTA) was mandated by the Street Works Act to repair and upgrade back lanes belonging to the government. Unfortunately, many of these lanes were dumping grounds for unwanted furniture and the LTA was not empowered to remove the furniture when it obstructed its work. The LTA had to seek approval from the Singapore Land Authority before it could take any action. The ZIP team investigations revealed no reason why the LTA should not be able to remove the obstructions and the Act was amended to allow it.

- When household maids had been abused, the police, as the first point of contact, found themselves having to accommodate the maids while they investigated the charges. The ZIP action team made arrangements with employment agencies, voluntary welfare organisations and embassies (since the maids were from other countries) to house the maids and help them to seek alternative work. A time limit of six months was put on each case, encouraging resolution, so the maids could return to their home countries as soon as possible.

- When experiencing noise pollution, citizens not only had to identify the cause of the noise, but also decide which agency was responsible (there were three possibilities). Now, as a result of the ZIP action team's intervention, citizens are not put in this situation. If uncertain, they can go to the National Environment Agency (NEA), which will redirect their comments to the relevant agencies.

Other ZIP stories relate to helping people comply with legal requirements when they have a family bereavement, and improving the visitation process at Changi Women's Prison (this involved a Six Sigma process that reduced visitor waiting times). While these may seem to be necessary improvements, the complexity of public sector agencies and the laws, rules and regulations that govern them can typically slow down action and solutions. The ZIP teams can cross boundaries, focus on particular issues and bring about improvements in creative and prompt ways.

There are other teams and groups associated with PS21 and the public service in general. For example, because employee involvement is so critical in the strategy, there is a Staff Well-being Committee (SWC) that is concerned with employee physical, mental and emotional fitness; training and development; and benefits and rewards, including challenge and recognition. There is an Excellence Through Continuous Enterprise Learning (ExCEL) committee, an Organisational Review Committee (ORC), a Functional Committee and a Quality Service subcommittee. Thus, different types of groups and teams are used to facilitate PS21 with the whole strategy managed by the PS21 Office and a PS21 Central Steering Committee (comprising permanent secretaries who are the employed heads of agencies). Each ministry, statutory board or department has its own PS21 committee.

Even outside the explicit scope of the teams outlined, it seems that teams and teamwork are an essential part of the public service in Singapore. Zaleha bte Ali is a senior officer with the General Investigation Team (GIT) in the Singapore Immigration and Registration's (SIR) Enforcement Division. Zaleha is proud to be part of a team that won the Minister's Award for Operational Efficiency from the Ministry of Home Affairs. The award is given to teams or officers that perform exceedingly well in their cases. Zaleha's team investigates offences relating to illegal immigrants and over-stayers (of visas). In a different approach, the Economic Development Board (EDB) has shadow CM (Corporate Management) teams in a bid to involve non-management officers in management-level discussions. This enables fresh perspectives and it is hoped that it results in better decisions, more innovations and better young managers. Those involved in the teams appreciate the learning opportunity it provides. As well as lively discussions on their inputs, their ideas are captured in the EDB's 'ideas portal'. Another interesting EDB development is the establishment of Learning Clubs (LC) in 2003. These clubs comprise officers who decide what they want to learn, who they want to learn it from,

and how they want to learn. They can lead their own learning, find an expert, or learn in the community. These clubs emerge from common interests, enabling sharing and learning that enhances the work of the members. In a similar vein, at the Ministry of Manpower, a Photography Learning Circle was formed in 2001 to promote, improve and sustain employees' interest in learning photography. The membership of the learning circle grew after the group held a three-day exhibition of their works. Innovation circles (I-circles) are a development of the Innovation Unit of the Centre for Organisational Excellence. They bring together 'innovation champions' from across the service to encourage learning, knowledge sharing and discussion. At one meeting of the third I-Circle, participants broke into subgroups to consider 'burning questions' about innovation, and expressed their experiences, frustrations and difficulties in getting innovation happening in their agencies.

Sources: PS21, Office of Public Service Division, Prime Minister's Office, 'Public service for the 21st century', 'Sharing', 'PS21 framework', 'Teaming', 'PS network', 'Staff well-being' and 'PS21 office' (August 2005), http://app.ps21.gov.sg/newps21; the following stories and issues of the public sector magazine *Challenge*, 'Organisational review committee' (May 2001), 'ZIP in action: providing peace of mind for bereaved families'(March 2002), 'Keeping illegal immigrants at bay' (October 2002), 'Passionate about photography' (March 2003), 'Speeding up service delivery' (August 2003), 'Tell her what you think' (August 2003), 'Innovators unite!' (January 2004), 'Innovative "Captains of lives"'(July 2004), 'Make a difference — the spirit of ExCEL' (November 2004), 'More EDB officers have a say' (March 2005), 'The hottest club memberships in town!' (May 2005), 'Improving the visitation process at Changi Women's Prison'(July 2005); 'ZIPping up the civil SERVICE, *New Paper* (31 March 2001); Laurel Teo, 'Zip's the way to swifter service at Govt agencies', *Straits Times* (31 March 2001); 'ZIPping through government red tape', *Straits Times* (10 April 2001); Singapore Government, 'About us', Success stories: 'Backlanes'; 'Who takes care of abused maids', 'Zero-in Process (ZIP)' (August 2005), http://www.zip.gov.sg/success_stories.htm.

(continued)

Questions

1. Find two examples in the case study of 'groups' that can not be clearly identified as 'teams'. Explain your reasons.

2. Consider the types of teams discussed at the end of chapter 7 (for example, self-managing teams, problem-solving teams, virtual teams). Using these explanations, categorise at least three of the teams outlined in the case study into these types (it is not necessary to find one for each category). Explain why you have categorised each as you have.

3. The duration of some of the teams in the PS21 project varies. How might this affect group (or team) development stages, and potential team effectiveness?

4. From the case study, describe at least two of the types of teams and explain why the membership is formulated as it is and how this might relate to the team's purpose and effectiveness, including the team's decision-making processes.

PART 4

MANAGING ORGANISATIONAL PROCESSES AND PERFORMANCE

8 Organisational structure and design   *266*

9 Organisational culture   *308*

10 Power, politics and influence in organisations   *342*

11 Leadership   *382*

12 Decision making   *418*

13 Communication, conflict and negotiation in organisations   *452*

14 Organisational change and innovation   *488*

Part 4 case study: The ups and downs of National Mutual/AXA   *521*

CHAPTER 8
Organisational structure and design

Learning objectives

After studying this chapter, you should be able to:

1. define and compare organisational design and structure and discuss the relationship between them

2. explain the basic factors that impact upon designing organisational structures and what organisational designs may emerge

3. describe the different types of organisational goals and different methods of controlling and coordinating the activities of organisational members

4. define vertical specialisation and explain what is meant by chain of command, unity of command and span of control

5. describe and compare different patterns of horizontal specialisation used by organisations

6. describe some of the emerging forms of organisation design and their implications for the individuals within them.

In a *Business Review Weekly* survey of most admired companies, Macquarie Bank was number one, and its chief executive Allan Moss was the most admired chief executive. In 12 years, Moss took the bank from an organisation with a staff of 1400 and a net profit of A$60 million to a global investment bank with a staff of 7000 and a net profit of A$852 million.

A key to Moss's success is a vigilant pursuit of an entrepreneurial spirit within the bank, regardless of how big the organisation has become. The bank is built on the philosophy of 'freedom within boundaries' or a 'loose-tight' approach to managing the business: managers are given freedom to pursue ideas within tight risk-control boundaries. This means central control is kept to a minimum but issues such as credit risk, market risk, reputation risk and operating standards are monitored closely.

Moss likens the bank to a federation of businesses, in which entrepreneurs can thrive. 'We provide the infrastructure, the capital, the brand and a controlled framework, and they provide the ideas.'

The bank is constantly creating new business units and spinning off listed and unlisted vehicles, giving senior executives an opportunity to run a business as well as being well rewarded. The upshot is that there are always a handful of people who could run the bank at a moment's notice. Apart from offering a strong succession framework, it also satisfies the ambitions of senior executives who are itching to run a business. The biggest changes since Moss became chief executive are the exponential growth of the bank, its globalisation, its presence in the management of financial and non-financial assets, and more lately, private equity.

Besides keeping the millionaires' club a cohesive unit, Moss's main contribution to the bank is his risk-management expertise. Macquarie Bank lives and dies by its ability to assess risk. If it buys the wrong asset, expends into the wrong country, or creates the wrong trust or product, the damage to its brand, its reputation and its relationship with clients and shareholders would be catastrophic because of the cross-promotion of deals throughout the bank. Consequently, risk management is paramount to the bank's success.

Source: Excerpts from Adele Ferguson, 'The ringmaster', *Business Review Weekly* (25–31 August 2005), pp. 40, 42.

Introduction

Like the Macquarie Bank, every organisation must decide how to divide its work or activities, how to coordinate all work-related activities and how to control these activities to ensure that goals are achieved. The organisation must consider its external environment and the internal systems and processes used to transform inputs to outputs. These differences help to explain, for example, why a football club is different to a manufacturing company. A manager of any organisation must ensure consistency between the structure of the organisation, the scale of its operations, the tasks at hand, the needs of all stakeholders and the strategic direction of the organisation. This consistency between structure and operations distinguishes successful organisations from less successful ones.

In this chapter we will first explain the difference between organisational structure and organisational design and then consider the various factors that may impinge upon the design; that is, the scale of the organisation, the technology it utilises, its environment and its strategy. Collectively they will all influence how the structural elements are combined into a suitable design for the organisation. While certain emerging forms of organisational design are presented at the end of the chapter, we must remember that every organisation will be unique.

The basic structural attributes of organisations include the different types of goals that organisations develop and implement. They also involve the techniques used to effect control and coordination within organisations. Other structural considerations are how the organisation allocates authority and manages the chain of command, how labour is divided into organisational units. These elements are, in essence, the building blocks of structure. They reflect various choices that can be made when organising how work is to be done and goals are to be achieved. Understanding all these elements is necessary to predict how they affect employee behaviour.

Organisational structure and design

Formal structure and organisational design

LEARNING OBJECTIVE 1

Organisational design is the process of choosing and implementing a structural configuration for an organisation.

The **formal structure** is the intended configuration of positions, job duties and lines of authority among the component parts of an organisation.

Organisation charts are diagrams that depict the formal structures of organisations.

Organisational structure and design are very closely related. The process of choosing and implementing a structural configuration is referred to as organisational design.[1] Organisational executives should adjust the structural configuration of their organisations to best meet the challenges faced at any given point in time.

Formal structure shows the intended configuration of positions, job duties and lines of authority among different parts of the enterprise. This structure emerges from the process of designing the organisation. It reflects the goals of the organisation and also reflects the contingency factors that impact on the organisation design, such as the organisation's size, environment, technology and strategy. The formal structure also involves the decisions that are made about who has authority, how the organisation and its members will be divided up to achieve tasks and how activities will be controlled and coordinated. We emphasise the word 'formal' simply because the intentions of organisational designers are not always fully realised. While no formal structure can provide the detail needed to show all the activities within an organisation, it is still important because it provides the foundations for managerial action; that is, it outlines the jobs to be done, the people (in terms of position) who will perform specific activities, and the ways in which the total task of the organisation will be accomplished.

Organisation charts are diagrams that depict the formal structures of organisations. A typical chart shows the various positions, the position holders and the lines of authority that link them to one another. The top half of figure 8.1 is a partial organisation chart for a small regional university. The chart allows university employees to locate their positions in the structure and to identify the lines of authority linking them with others in the organisation. In this figure, the head of financial services reports to the registrar and secretary, who reports to the vice-chancellor (the chief executive officer of the university).

Such charts predominate in representing organisational structures. However, there has been some criticism that they only show lines of authority and the division of the organisation into different units. An alternative means of mapping organisational activities has been developed by Mintzberg and Van der Heyden. Their organigraphs show how an organisation works, what it does, and how people, products and information interact. This can bring more insight, or at least a different perspective, to explaining the behaviour of people in organisations. The bottom half of figure 8.1 shows a simple 'organigraph' for teaching in a university.

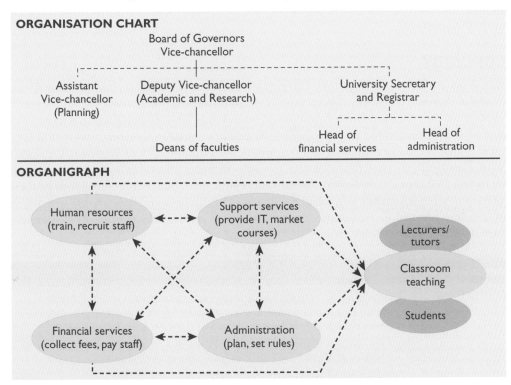

FIGURE 8.1 • A partial organisation chart for a university and an organigraph for university teaching
Source: Organigraph developed from H Mintzberg and L Van der Heyden, 'Organigraphs: drawing how companies really work', *Harvard Business Review* (September/October 1999), pp. 87–94.

In summary, organisational design involves the choices made about how to structure the organisation, and the implementation of those choices. The formal structure explains in more detailed ways how the structural elements are configured. The terms 'organisational structure' and 'organisational design' are sometimes used interchangeably. Since organisational design is a structural configuration, the reasons for this are quite apparent. In the following sections, we will examine basic ways of understanding the design choices and structural features of organisations.

Factors influencing organisational design

OBJECTIVE 2 LEARNING — Factors for organisational design

Some particular factors will have an impact on the choices made when designing the organisation: scale, technology, environment and strategy. This analysis will identify the way in which these factors impact and their implications on design. Some of the possible design outcomes that may emerge are described at the end of the chapter.

Scale

The more individuals in an organisation, the more possible interconnections among them and the less the likelihood of direct interpersonal contact between everyone. Thus, as organisations grow their structure is likely to become more complex. More advanced electronic communication methods and policies, rules and procedures are used as substitutes for direct supervision, both to save money and to ensure consistency. Larger organisations can be more efficient, with potential economies of scale in production and services through repetition, but then there is more need to break tasks down into parts, to allocate authority and to make sure everything and everyone is acting in a coordinated way to achieve the organisation's goals. Larger organisations often have more products, production processes, geographic locations and so on. This additional complexity calls for more sophisticated organisational designs.

Technology

Organisations are said to arrange their internal structures to meet the dictates of their dominant 'technologies' or work flows; this is known as the technological imperative.[2] Technology is the combination of resources, knowledge and techniques that creates a product or service output for an organisation. The match between structure and technology is important for the successful design of organisations. Thompson[3] and Woodward[4] present different classifications that illustrate the possible diversity in technology and these are shown in table 8.1. For example, Woodward's successful small-batch and continuous-process plants have flexible structures with small work groups at the bottom; more rigidly structured plants are less successful. In contrast, successful mass production operations are rigidly structured and have large work groups at the bottom.

The technological imperative is the idea that if an organisation does not adjust its internal structure to the requirements of the technology, it will not be successful.

Technology is the combination of resources, knowledge and techniques that creates a product or service output for an organisation.

TABLE 8.1 • Thompson's and Woodward's classifications of technology

Thompson	
Intensive technology	Involves a team of highly interdependent specialists using a variety, but no certain, techniques to produce the desired outcomes for non-routine problems or situations. Because the problem is unique there are no standard operating procedures and there must be mutual adjustments to deal with it. Examples include the the team in a hospital emergency room and a research development laboratory.
Mediating technology	Links parties that want to become interdependent, such as wholesalers who link producers and retailers. Also, banks link creditors and depositors, and store money and information to facilitate such exchanges. Interdependent depositors and creditors rely on each other through pooled activity of the bank. If one creditor defaults on a loan, no one depositor is injured.
Long-linked technology	The way to produce the desired outcomes is known so the task is broken into sequential, interdependent steps. An example is the high-volume car assembly line.
Woodward	
Small-batch	A variety of custom products, such as tailored suits, are made to fit customer specifications. The machinery and equipment used are generally not elaborate, but considerable craftsmanship is often needed. For example, producing a unique marketing campaign or television movie.
Continuous-process	Producing a few products with considerable automation in an ongoing process. Examples include automated chemical plants and oil refineries.
Mass production	Similar to Thompson's long-linked technology; produces one or a few products using an assembly-line type of system. The work of one group depends on that of another, the equipment is typically sophisticated and the workers are given detailed instructions. Cars and refrigerators are produced in this way.

Sources: Developed from James D Thompson, *Organization in action* (New York: McGraw-Hill, 1967) and Joan Woodward, *Industrial organization: theory and practice* (London: Oxford University Press, 1965).

There are other possible technologies that can be described. For example, with more flexible manufacturing systems there is a trend towards more 'mass customisation', where custom adjustments are possible, even in a mass production process. Such a process would allow an infinite variety of goods and services unique to customer requirements. The following Adidas-Salomon example illustrates this.

Adidas-Salomon utilises a retail concept called Mi Adidas. This process allows customers to visit a footwear store and have their feet measured for width and length. They also choose the colours, design and materials (from a set of options) they want for their shoes and three weeks later they can collect their Adidas Super Nova shoes from the same store (at $40 more than the cost of standard Adidas shoes).[5]

Environment

An effective organisational design reflects powerful external forces as well as the desires of employees and managers. There are two main sets of parameters we can use to explain the environment. First, as open systems, organisations need to receive various inputs from their environment and sell various outputs to their environment. Environments can be labelled as either:

- *General* — that is, the set of cultural, economic, legal–political and educational conditions found in the areas in which the organisation operates. These can include different global economies and markets.
- *Specific* — which involves the mix of owners, suppliers, distributors, government agencies and competitors with which it interacts.

Another basic concern in analysing the environment of the organisation is its complexity. **Environmental complexity** is the estimated magnitude of the problems and opportunities in the organisation's environment, as evidenced by the combination of the following three main factors that emerge uniquely, in the context of each organisation, from the general and specific environments.[6]

> Environmental complexity is the magnitude of the problems and opportunities in the organisation's environment, as evidenced by the degree of richness, interdependence and uncertainty.

1. *Environmental richness.* The environment is *richer* when the economy is growing and improving, customers are spending more and investors investing more; when individuals are improving their education, and others the organisation relies upon are also prospering. Organisational survival is easier, there is more dynamism and there are more opportunities for change. The opposite is *decline*, which occurs in economic recession. Typically, workers may be laid off and the number of working units and managers may be reduced.

2. *Environmental interdependence.* The link between external interdependence and organisational design is often subtle and indirect. The organisation may co-opt powerful outsiders onto its board of directors, and/or adjust its design strategy to absorb or buffer the demands of a more powerful external element. For example, it may include a public relations unit to deal with public pressures or to lobby government for policy change. Because of increasing internationalisation many organisations face a number of 'general environments' and maintain highly complex and diffuse interdependencies with them.

3. *Uncertainty and volatility.* In times of change, investments quickly become outmoded and internal operations no longer work as expected. The obvious organisational design response to uncertainty and volatility is to opt for a more flexible structure. However,

these pressures may run counter to those that arise from large size and technology and the organisation may continue to struggle while adjusting its design a little at a time.

Going global

Businesses are increasingly engaging with global markets. This affects both the markets to which they sell their goods and services and also the labour market they rely on to produce them. The implications for businesses can be significant in terms of opening up new markets, or seeking favourable alliances or outsourcing arrangements. But moving into new countries means moving into new environments too, which can add to the diversity of political, cultural and economic scenarios that the business managers and employees must understand and succeed in.

According to an international survey conducted by PricewaterhouseCoopers (PwC), offshore expansion is an increasing trend among banks and financial services companies, with more than 80 per cent of financial services companies offering some form of offshore operation. Such offshore operations involve setting up a business in a foreign country, setting up a joint venture, or outsourcing their business to another company in the foreign country. India and China are the two most popular countries for such outsourcing, especially in IT functions. Others include Ireland, Romania and the Philippines. Outcomes are not always favourable, however, with more than 15 per cent of the respondents dissatisfied with the cost savings they achieved.[7]

Global markets for produce also have an effect on businesses, both small and large. Michelle Nugan took over her husband's ailing fruit and vegetable wholesaling business in 1986, following his sudden death. She is now managing director of the Nugan Group, based in Griffith, New South Wales. While it began as a growing and wholesaling business it has now diversified and includes different businesses such as Nugan Quality Foods, Nugan Estate Wines and Michelin (a local restaurant). It produces grapes and wine, fruit and fruit juices, and olives. As well as the restaurant business and production of fruit, vegetables and beverages, it also engages in wholesaling and retailing. It operates in a rich environment where there is economic growth and rising consumption of its products. This has allowed the business to keep growing and diversifying over two decades. The company works with another business, CSI Group, which exports its products (including 8000 tonnes of carrot juice each year) to Japan. Nugan has worked hard to develop relationships with her Japanese customers, including travelling to Japan, learning Japanese customs and redecorating her head office with a Japanese flavour. She has kept an inherited (from her husband) Rolls Royce because it gives visiting businessmen the right impression. The manager of CSI Doug Hammond feels like part of the Nugan family. The Nugan Group has supplier contracts with many producers, and has worked on processing and value-adding to its own products, thereby reducing the uncertainty of relying on others in the environment. It must also focus on national and international markets and faces the uncertainty of a predicted 'wine glut' in the next few years.[8]

Strategy

Organisational strategy is the process of positioning the organisation in its competitive environment and implementing actions to compete successfully.[9] The study of linking strategy, organisational design and performance has a long tradition in organisational analysis. While it cannot be covered extensively here, the important point is that the organisation's strategy will be driving its goals and vision, and an organisational design must be established to achieve the vision. For example, an organisation may be endeavouring to become a market leader by having the cheapest or best value-for-money product.

Alternatively, it may be trying to differentiate its product from others. In other words, the degree to which the organisation's strategy is aiming to produce standardised products, and the narrow or broad scope of the organisation's business, may impact on the design choices that are made.

Another issue of strategy involves the organisation building on and refining its unique experience and competencies; that is, competency-based strategies. Business practices that have built up over time and proved a key to the success of a business or the competence of employees may well be factors upon which the business should focus and make design decisions. For example, the design may need to be flexible and allow employees the scope to make decisions, such as where the organisation is trying to capitalise on employee creativity in innovating new products. In other cases, it may be more important to have relatively rigid, formalised structures with more rules and controls.

Organisational goals, control and coordination

OBJECTIVE 3 Goals, control and coordination

The first of the structural *building blocks* are organisational goals. In an organisation, people are organised into a structure in order to work together to achieve organisational goals. This involves breaking people and tasks up into units, allocating authority and making other decisions about how things are done. Two other components of structure are control and coordination, which provide ways of ensuring that these subdivided activities can be brought together to achieve the organisational goals.

Organisational goals

Organisations may be viewed as entities with goals.[10] The goals they pursue are multifaceted and often conflict with, or overlap, one another. These goals are common to individuals within an organisation though their reasons for involvement in the organisation are partly about serving their own individual interests. There are two types of organisational goals. The first centres on how the organisation intends to serve particular groups in society, or with social responsibility, serve society as a whole. The second focuses on organisational survival.

Output goals and serving society

Organisations are inevitably involved in some 'type of business', whether or not it is profit-oriented. They operate to provide products, services, infrastructure or wealth, for example. Output goals define the organisation's type of business, and are the basis of the mission statements that organisations often use to indicate their purposes. These can form the basis for long-term planning and strategies and may help prevent huge organisations from diverting too many resources to peripheral areas.

Output goals are the goals that define the organisation's type of business.

While some organisations may provide benefits to the society as a whole, most target their efforts towards a particular group or groups.[11] The main recipients of the organisation's efforts are the primary beneficiaries. Political organisations serve the common good, while culturally based organisations such as churches may emphasise contributions to their members. Social service organisations such as hospitals are expected to emphasise quality care to patients. In Australia and New Zealand, it is generally expected that the primary beneficiaries of businesses are the shareholders, but this is not the same everywhere. In Japan, long-time workers are typically placed at the centre of the organisation, with an expectation that through them and their secure employment there will be economic growth for the country.

Primary beneficiaries are particular groups expected to benefit from the efforts of specific organisations.

Many larger organisations have found it useful to review, clarify and state carefully their type of business.[12] The following example shows one organisation that has made a considered decision about what business it chooses to be in.

OB in action

Safe Hand Security specialises in close personal protection (CPP). It distinguishes itself from bodyguard services as it not only offers protection but does everything to organise travel, itinerary, transport and entertainment. Its original business was crowd control, but this now comprises only 10 per cent of the business; CPP makes up 70 per cent and investigations the rest. The four principals of the organisation started their business when they began hearing, from their customers, stories about poor quality of service elsewhere. The rapidly growing business now has 150 full- and part-time employees operating in Sydney.[13]

Corporate social responsibility is the obligation of organisations to behave in ethical and moral ways.

In the process of serving society there is an expectation of corporate social responsibility; that is, the organisation or corporation has an obligation to behave in ethical and moral ways. Organisations contributing to societal goals are given broader discretion and may obtain some control over resources, individuals, markets and products at lower costs. Organisations are typically expected to take action to improve society in a socially responsible way, or at least to avoid damaging it. Social responsibility is exhibited towards small and large social beneficiaries for a range of reasons, both altruistic and related to the organisation's reputation. It is important for organisations to maintain society's trust and confidence if they wish to avoid negative impacts on their operations.

Systems goals and organisational survival

Systems goals are goals concerned with conditions within the organisation that are expected to increase its survival potential.

Organisations also face the immediate problem of just making it through the coming years. Systems goals are concerned with the internal conditions that are expected to increase the organisation's survival potential. The list of systems goals is almost endless, because each manager and researcher links today's conditions to tomorrow's existence in a different way. However, for many organisations the list includes *growth, productivity, stability, harmony, flexibility, prestige* and, of course, *human resource maintenance*. For some businesses, analysts consider *market share* and *current profitability* to be important systems goals. Other studies suggest that *innovation* and *quality* also may be considered important.[14]

In a practical sense, systems goals represent short-term organisational characteristics that higher-level managers wish to promote. Systems goals must often be balanced against one another; for instance, a productivity and efficiency drive may cut the flexibility of an organisation. Different parts of the organisation may be asked to pursue different types of systems goal. Higher-level managers, for example, may expect to see their production operations strive for efficiency, while pressing for innovation from their research and development laboratory and promoting stability in their financial affairs. Systems goals provide a 'road map' to assist in linking together various units of an organisation to assure its survival. Well-defined systems goals are practical and easy to understand, focusing the manager's attention on what needs to be done.

Control

Control is the set of mechanisms used to keep actions and outputs within predetermined limits.

Control is one of the basic management functions and is involved with ensuring the organisation achieves what it is intended to achieve. Control is the set of mechanisms used to keep actions and/or outputs (based on pre-determined organisational goals) within predetermined limits.

Control deals with setting standards, measuring results against standards and instituting corrective action.

The control process that is used in activities such as accounting and production is depicted in figure 8.2. Note the iterative nature of the process; in other words, controlling activities within an organisation is an *ongoing* process. Note also that once the actual output is compared with the objective or standard that has been set, the manager may need to decide whether to adjust the standard (if it proves unrealistic or unachievable) or produce a different level of output in step with the standard. For a given project, actual expenditure (output) may be exceeding the budget (standard), so the manager will need to take measures to reduce ongoing costs for the project in some way.

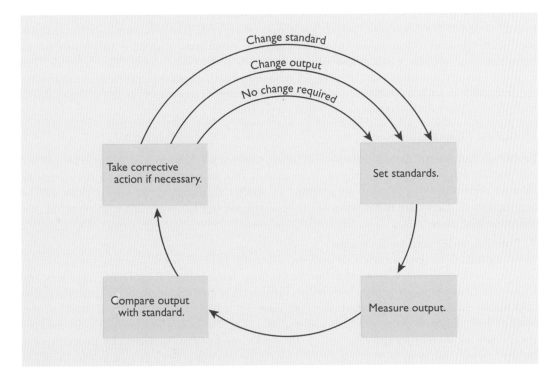

FIGURE 8.2 • The business control process

While controls are needed in all organisations, just a few controls may go a long way. Astute managers need to be aware of the danger of too much control in the organisation, as noted in 'The effective manager 8.1'.

Signs of too much control

Astute managers look for the signs that too much control or inappropriate controls have been placed on their units. They look for:

- too much emphasis on one measured goal to the exclusion of all others
- too much emphasis on the quick fix, and an unwillingness to look for underlying causes of problems or new opportunities
- a tradition of across-the-board cuts rather than reductions linked to demands, constraints and opportunities
- too many vague and unrealistic expectations that breed defeat
- raising of quotas without reward for employees, particularly after employee suggestions for change are implemented.

Output controls

Developing targets or standards, measuring results against these targets and taking corrective action are all steps involved in developing output controls. Output controls focus on desired targets and allow managers to use their own methods for reaching defined targets. Most modern organisations use output controls as a part of an overall method of managing by exception; that is, when identification of a problem triggers corrective actions (see chapter 11). Such controls are popular because they promote flexibility and creativity, as well as facilitating dialogue about corrective action.

There is an important link between controls and goals but it is not necessarily simple or one-way. The links are complex and encompassing. Goals define what is to be achieved and influence the controls set in place to ensure the goals are met. Controls may also have an impact on goals. For example, output goals may be revised if targets cannot be realistically met. Controls over the manner in which tasks are done may also have an impact on an organisation's systems goals, especially if there is little choice over the controls. For example, an organisation may be obliged to comply with certain requirements of government legislation such as workplace safety, or with the requirements of an allied organisation such as a supplier, major customer or alliance partner.

Process controls

Few organisations run on output controls alone. Once a solution to a problem is found and successfully implemented, managers do not want the problem to recur, so they institute process controls. Process controls attempt to specify the manner in which tasks will be accomplished. There are many types of process control, but three groups have received considerable attention.

1. Policies, rules and procedures

Most organisations have a variety of policies, rules and procedures in place at any time. Usually, we think of a policy as a guideline for action that outlines important objectives and broadly indicates how an activity is to be performed. A policy allows for individual discretion and minor adjustments without direct clearance by a higher-level manager. Many organisations have a stated policy towards cultural diversity, for example, that not only outlines their goals for increasing the diversity of the workforce but also specifies the procedures to be used in recruiting staff.

Rules and procedures are more specific, rigid and impersonal than policies. They typically describe *in detail* how a task or series of tasks is to be performed. They are designed to apply to all individuals under specified conditions. Most car dealers, for example, have detailed instruction manuals for repairing a new car under warranty. They must follow strict procedures to obtain reimbursement from the manufacturer for warranty work that they have undertaken.

Other examples of rules and procedures include requirements for employees to:
- have someone countersign approval for payments
- wear certain apparel for certain jobs
- follow particular steps for cleaning equipment (such as coffee machines) or conducting regular maintenance checks (such as of electrical equipment).

Rules, procedures and policies are employed as substitutes for direct managerial supervision, leaving managers to focus on exceptional incidents or unique problems. Under the guidance of written rules and procedures, the organisation can specifically direct the activities of many individuals. It can ensure virtually identical treatment across even distant work locations. The McDonald's hamburgers and fries, for example, taste much the same whether they are purchased in Hong Kong, Kuala Lumpur, Singapore or Sydney, simply because the ingredients and the cooking methods follow standardised written rules and procedures. Employees at St George Bank's call centre also experience process (and output) controls, as the following example illustrates.

Call centres have received much publicity for the degree of control exerted over their workers in terms of reaching certain performance targets and/or having detailed rules about how to carry out their tasks (sometimes called micromanagement). St George Bank's call centre operation was typical; it had an optimum call 'handle time' and an hourly call quota. However, these controls were dropped in 2003 because they were sending the wrong message — workers were aiming to meet their weekly 'statistics' rather than focusing on the quality of assistance they gave customers. However, a senior manager at St George, Antoine Casgrain, believes that some structure and guidelines are still useful because workers do not always have the ability to deliver the work outcomes desired of them.[15]

2. Formalisation and standardisation

Formalisation refers to the written documentation of rules, procedures and policies to guide behaviour and decision making. It is often used to simplify jobs: for example, written instructions allow individuals with less training to perform comparatively sophisticated tasks. Written procedures may also be available to ensure a proper sequence of tasks is executed, even if this sequence is only performed occasionally.

Most organisations have developed additional methods for dealing with recurring problems or situations. Standardisation is the degree to which the range of allowable actions in a job or series of jobs is limited. It involves the creation of guidelines so similar work activities are repeatedly performed in a similar fashion and employees know what they can and cannot do. Remember the example of McDonald's!

Formalisation and standardisation may have variable effects on behaviour, depending on the circumstances and the perceived need for consistency and fairness. In some cases there may be no need for formalisation and standardisation, and rules and regulations may unnecessarily hinder workers' progress in their jobs. In other cases they may be vital for ensuring equity, fair treatment of clients or safety. Typically, a worker's job requirements and limits are clearly defined in a job description, and these often form part of a broad pattern of jobs. However, if you wanted highly creative workers to be innovative in the development of a new product, for example, putting them into straitjacketed jobs might not gain the desired behaviours from them. Sometimes the formalisation of rules and procedures, and/or the clear definition of what a person can do in a job is important for preventing unethical activities in the organisation, as the following 'Ethical perspective' indicates.

> **Formalisation** is the written documentation of work rules, policies and procedures.

> **Standardisation** is the degree to which the range of actions in a job or series of jobs is limited.

Battling fraud

ETHICAL **Perspective**

Organisations that have financial functions (such as banks and accountancy firms) are particularly at risk where it is possible that the funds of their customers, or those of the business itself, could be fraudulently obtained by employees. KPMG released statistics on fraud showing that in Australia and New Zealand, employees instigated 78 per cent of 'big' fraud cases. In 75 per cent of these cases the perpetrator of the fraud acted alone. Warwick Dolman, who is a forensic accountant and a director of a fraud detection firm, and Lisa Bundeson, a former investigative accountant for the Queensland Police major fraud group, both advocate codes of behaviour. These are vital to clarify what employees can and can not do. For example, a code makes clear whether employees can use company software to do private work, and whether taking home

(continued)

company stationery is acceptable or not. Dolman also suggests that budgets are useful control mechanisms because they plan expenditure ahead of time, acting as a basis for looking at any excessive spending in any area. This helps to prevent an employee putting in 'dummy' invoices to obtain money from the firm. While trusting and empowering employees is a popular and valuable strategy, there is sometimes a need to consider the use of some controls to protect customers, fellow employees and the business itself from the fraudulent activity of a few. Clarifying what is required makes the limits of this sort of behaviour very clear.[16]

3. Quality management

Another way to institute process controls is to establish a quality management process. Quality management emerged from the total quality management (TQM) movement founded by W Edwards Deming. The heart of Deming's approach is to institute a process approach to continual improvement based on statistical analyses of the organisation's operations.[17] All levels of management are to be involved in the quality program; managers are to improve supervision, train employees, retrain employees in new skills and create a structure that will push the quality program. The emphasis is on training, learning and consistency of purpose, which appear to be important lessons and all organisations need to be reminded of this constantly.

Coordination

In order to enhance the operation of the organisation, there must be ways to get all the separate activities, people and units working together. Coordination is the set of mechanisms that an organisation uses to link the actions of its units into a consistent pattern. The greater the specialisation in the organisation, the greater the need for effective coordination. Much of the coordination within a unit is handled by its manager. Smaller organisations may rely on their management hierarchy to provide the necessary consistency. But as the organisation grows, managers become overloaded. The organisation then needs to develop more efficient and effective ways of linking work units to one another. Coordination methods can be personal or impersonal.

Coordination is the set of mechanisms used in an organisation to link the actions of its subunits into a consistent pattern.

Personal methods of coordination

Personal methods of coordination produce synergy by promoting dialogue, discussion, innovation, creativity and learning, allowing the organisation to address the particular needs of distinct units and individuals simultaneously. Perhaps the most popular of the wide variety of personal methods is direct contact between and among organisational members. Typically, this involves the development of an effective informal network of contacts within the organisation; for example, direct personal communication and email. Committees, though generally costly and sluggish, are effective for mutual adjustment across unit heads, for communicating complex qualitative information, and for helping managers whose units must work together to adjust schedules, work loads and work assignments to increase productivity. Task forces are typically formed with limited agendas, and involve individuals from different parts of the organisation identifying and solving problems that cut across different departments. Another personal method of coordination involves developing a shared set of values that allows organisational members to predict accurately the responses of others to specific events.

There is no magic involved in selecting the appropriate mix of personal coordination methods and tailoring them to the individual skills, abilities and experience of employees. Managers need to know the individuals involved and their preferences. 'The effective manager 8.2' provides some guidelines for understanding how different personal methods can be tailored to match different individuals.

Selecting personal coordination styles[18]

The astute manager must recognise the following important differences in matching up workers.

1. Individuals and representatives of departments often have their own views of how best to move towards organisational goals.
2. Some individuals emphasise immediate problems and move towards quick solutions; others stress underlying problems and longer-term solutions.
3. Given that each department develops its own unique vocabulary and standard way of communicating, the coordination method chosen should recognise such potential differences and include many opportunities for direct exchange.
4. There are often pronounced departmental and individual preferences for formality.

Impersonal methods of coordination

Impersonal coordination methods are often refinements and extensions of process controls, with an emphasis on formalisation and standardisation. Most larger organisations have written policies and procedures, such as schedules, budgets and plans, that are designed to mesh the operations of several units into a whole.[19] Some other examples of impersonal methods of coordination are:

- cross-departmental work units that coordinate the efforts of diverse functional units
- management information systems (MIS) that coordinate and control the operations of diverse subordinate units. These are computerised substitutes for schedules, budgets and the like. In some firms, MIS still operate as a combined process control and impersonal coordination mechanism. In the hands of astute managers, MIS become an electronic network, linking individuals throughout the organisation. Using decentralised communication systems, supplemented with the telephone, fax machine and email, a manager can greatly improve coordination.

Two broad types of organisational design that reflect the degree of control and coordination in an organisation (as well as the allocation of authority, which is considered in the next section) are mechanistic and organic. A **mechanistic design** is an organisational structure that tends to emphasise authority and control, as well as specialisation in jobs. Organisations of this type stress rules, policies and procedures; specify techniques for decision making; and emphasise well-documented control systems backed by a strong middle management and supported by a centralised staff. In an **organic design** there is more flexibility in how things are done, with fewer rules and procedures; there is even flexibility in how elements of the structure can change quickly in response to changing circumstances. More responsibility is placed in the hands of workers, who are seen as competent and/or expert at what they do.

Mechanistic design emphasises vertical specialisation, hierarchical levels, tight control and coordination through rules, policies and other impersonal methods.

Organic design is an organisational structure that emphasises horizontal specialisation, an extensive use of personal coordination, and loose rules, policies and procedures.

Vertical specialisation

In most larger organisations, there is a clear separation of authority and duties by hierarchical rank. This separation represents **vertical specialisation**, which is a hierarchical division of work that distributes formal authority and establishes where and how critical decisions will be made. This division creates a hierarchy of authority, and a chain of command, that arranges work positions in order of increasing authority. We will also discuss another form of division of labour in the next section on horizontal specialisation.

LEARNING OBJECTIVE 4 ✓ Vertical specialisation

Vertical specialisation is a hierarchical division of labour that distributes formal authority and establishes how critical decisions will be made.

The distribution of formal authority is evident in the responsibilities typically allocated to managers. Top managers or senior executives plan the overall strategy of the organisation and plot its long-term future.[20] Middle managers guide the daily operations of the organisation, help formulate policy, and translate top-management decisions into more specific guidelines for action. Lower-level managers supervise the actions of employees to ensure implementation of the strategies authorised by top management and compliance with the related policies established by middle management.

When allocating authority or specialising vertically, one feature of organisational structure can be explained. That is, those organisations that have many levels in their hierarchies can be described as *tall*. Others that have very few levels can be described as *flat*.

We also consider organisations in terms of how centralised or decentralised they are. The degree of centralisation of decision-making authority is high if discretion to spend money, recruit people and make similar decisions is retained further up the hierarchy of authority. The more such decisions are delegated, or moved down the hierarchy of authority, the greater is the degree of decentralisation.

Applying these characteristics to mechanistic and organic designs we can make the following general (but not the only possible) observations about design. Visually, mechanistic organisations tend to have a tall hierarchy and may resemble a tall, thin pyramid with centralised decision-making senior staff at the top. Taller or more vertically specialised structures have more managers per worker. This may mean closer and tighter control over workers, with formal communication through several layers of hierarchy that can be slow and distorted. People might get frustrated waiting for approval in tall structures and feel unable to take responsibility for their own work.

Organic organisations are more likely to have a flatter structure since more responsibility is delegated down to workers. Flatter organisations with fewer layers of hierarchy and authority, and fewer managers, generally permit sub-managers and employees more discretion; they decentralise decision making and loosen control. Generally speaking, greater decentralisation provides higher subordinate satisfaction and a quicker response to problems, and may give workers a sense of ownership and greater levels of motivation in their work. Decentralisation also assists in the on-the-job training of employees for higher-level positions.

Australia's leading accommodation web site is an example of an organisation that has made decisions about authority allocations.

> **Centralisation** is the degree to which the authority to make decisions is restricted to higher levels of management.

> **Decentralisation** is the degree to which the authority to make decisions is given to lower levels in an organisation's hierarchy.

Wotif.com began in 1999 when its founder and CEO Graeme Wood was asked to help a hotelier fill vacant rooms. He pioneered the selling of last-minute accommodation via the Internet. Now Wotif.com has 6000 hotels (or similar accommodation venues) on its books in 36 global locations and the web site attracts nearly two million user sessions a month (translating into in excess of 100 000 monthly bookings). There are 100 employees internationally in Brisbane, Canada, New Zealand, Singapore and the United Kingdom. Wood has maintained a flat structure in the organisation, with a focus on participation. He believes in keeping lines of communication completely open — a casual and accessible organisation structure where anyone can talk to anyone else whenever they like.[21]

Two other organisational characteristics that emerge from vertical specialisation (though other factors might also contribute) are unity of command and span of control.

Unity of command and span of control

As already indicated, with vertical specialisation, executives, managers and supervisors are hierarchically connected through the 'chain of command'. Individuals are expected to follow their supervisors' decisions in the areas of responsibility outlined in the organisation chart.

Traditional management theory suggests that each individual should have one supervisor and each unit should have one leader. Under these circumstances, there is a unity of command. Unity of command is considered necessary to avoid confusion, to assign accountability to specific individuals, and to provide clear channels of communication up and down the organisation. Unity of command, in a traditional hierarchy, is a readily understood approach for employees. A single boss makes life easier and less ambiguous but it could mean more hierarchical control, impersonality and rigid communication channels.

When vertically specialising the organisation, decisions are made about the number of individuals that each manager directly supervises. To reduce the costs of having many managers, as is the case in flatter organisations, a manager may be given many employees to supervise, though the number any single manager can realistically manage is obviously limited. The concept of the number of individuals reporting to a supervisor is called the span of control. For example, David Liddy, chief executive and managing director of the Bank of Queensland, has nine 'direct reports'. Liddy says he spends 50 per cent of his time looking after staff issues.[22]

Span of control may have a considerable impact on both manager behaviour and employee behaviour. If a supervisor has a *wide* span of control with many subordinates to supervise, it is more likely that the employees will have freedom to do the job their own way (autonomy). This may be suitable if they are highly experienced and/or in a very creative role. Control may be looser and people may have a higher satisfaction level (but not necessarily performance level).

Narrower spans of control are expected when tasks are complex, when employees are inexperienced or poorly trained, and/or when tasks call for team effort.[23] Unfortunately, narrow spans of control yield many levels in the organisational hierarchy. The excessive number of levels is not only expensive (typically requiring more managers), but also makes the organisation unresponsive to necessary change. A research study based on data collected from 74 manufacturing organisations found that differentiating mechanisms such as high job specialisation and narrow spans of control led to poor integration of design manufacturing processes.[24]

Horizontal specialisation

Control, coordination and vertical specialisation are only part of the picture. Managers must divide the total task into separate duties, and group similar people and resources.[25] Different groups or people do different parts of the larger operation. Look again at figure 8.1 and note the two work groups reporting to the university secretary and registrar. Horizontal specialisation is the division of labour that establishes work units or groups within an organisation; it is often referred to as the process of departmentalisation. In the following section we will examine three forms of horizontal specialisation — by function, division and matrix — and also look at some 'mixed' or 'hybrid' forms that can emerge.

Prior to doing this it is valuable to consider the difference between the terms 'line' and 'staff'. In an organisation line personnel conduct the major business that directly affects the organisation. In universities, academic staff, or in factories the workers who make the goods, are line workers. In contrast, staff personnel assist the line units by providing specialised expertise and services, such as accounting, human resources and public relations. The dotted lines on the organisation chart depicted in the top of figure 8.1 denote staff relationships, whereas the solid lines denote line relationships (teaching in the faculties is the major business of the university).

Line personnel are likely to feel more directly involved with the operations of the organisation, especially if they can clearly see their part in achieving the organisation's goals (task significance and task identity from the job characteristics model are particularly relevant). However, a common behavioural consequence is that there tend to be different perspectives between the line and staff groups. Staff personnel are often accused of interfering with line work with their unnecessary forms and procedures (although often they are trying to accomplish important things such as financial audits, legal compliance, payrolls and so on).

Unity of command is the situation in an organisation where each worker has a clear reporting relationship to only one supervisor.

The **span of control** is the number of individuals reporting to a supervisor.

LEARNING OBJECTIVE 5 Horizontal specialisation

Horizontal specialisation is the division of labour through the formation of work units or groups within an organisation.

Line personnel are work groups that conduct the major business of the organisation.

Staff personnel are groups that assist the line units by performing specialised services for the organisation.

Line personnel say they just want to get on with the job, and lower-level managers in particular resent the demands or requirements of staff personnel. Intergroup and interpersonal conflict can be common.

Departmentalisation by function

Functional departmentalisation is the grouping of individuals and resources by skill, knowledge and action.

Grouping individuals by skill, knowledge and action yields a pattern of functional departmentalisation, and represents the most commonly used arrangement.[26] Figure 8.3 shows the organisation chart for a supermarket chain, where each department has a technical specialty considered necessary for efficient operation. The organisation is divided into four main functional groups — financial services, customer and marketing services, distribution and logistics, and company support services — and within each of these groups employees in different sections or departments undertake separate and specialised tasks. In business organisations generally, marketing, finance, production and personnel are important functions. In many small organisations, this functional pattern dominates; for instance, Apple Computer used this pattern early in its development. Functional units or departments are often criticised as encouraging functional 'silos' that stand alone for too much of the time and discourage cooperative and coordinated behaviours. People working in functional departments tend to develop narrow interests, limited perspectives, competitive behaviours, unique language and cultures, and a propensity to pass problems on to other sections.[27]

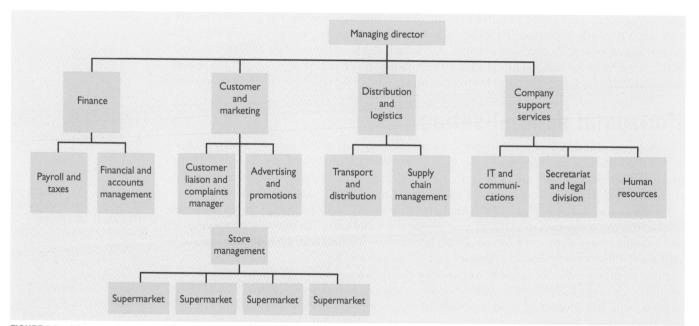

FIGURE 8.3 • A functional pattern of departmentalisation for a supermarket chain

Table 8.2 summarises the advantages (and disadvantages) of a functional pattern. With all these advantages, it is not surprising that the functional form is extremely popular, being used in most organisations, despite some disadvantages. Organisations that rely on functional specialisation may expect the following tendencies to emerge over time:
- an emphasis on quality from a technical standpoint
- rigidity with respect to change, particularly if change within one functional area is needed to help other functional areas
- difficulty in coordinating the actions of different functional areas, particularly if the organisation must continually adjust to changing external conditions.

Advantages	Disadvantages
1. It can yield clear task assignments that are consistent with an individual's training.	1. It may reinforce the narrow training of individuals and lead to boring and routine jobs, e.g. accounts processing. Communication across technical areas is difficult, and conflict between units may increase. Lines of communication across the organisation can become complex.
2. Individuals within a department can easily build on one another's knowledge, training and experience. Facing similar problems and having similar training facilitates communication and technical problem solving.	2. Complex communication channels can lead to 'top management overload'. Top management may spend too much time and effort dealing with cross-functional problems.
3. It provides an excellent training ground for new managers, who must translate their academic training into organisational actions.	3. Individuals may look up the organisational hierarchy for direction and reinforcement rather than focusing on products, services or clients. Guidance is typically sought from functional peers or superiors.
4. It is easy to explain. Most employees can understand the role of each unit, even though many may not know what individuals in a particular function do.	

TABLE 8.2 • Major advantages and disadvantages of functional specialisation

Departmentalisation by division, geography and customer

Alternatively, a **divisional departmentalisation** groups individuals and resources by products, services and/or clients/customers. Figure 8.4 shows a divisional pattern of organisation grouped around products (automotive parts such as transmissions and engines), regions (Asia–Pacific, South American and European) and customers (government accounts, corporate accounts and university/college accounts) for three divisions of a large international organisation. This pattern is often used to meet diverse external threats and opportunities.

Many larger, geographically dispersed organisations that sell to national and international markets use **departmentalisation by geography**. The savings in time, effort and travel can be substantial, and each territory can adjust to regional differences. The National Australia Bank has restructured its retail banking division into 70 geographical regions across Australia.[28] Organisations that rely on a few major customers may organise their people and resources by client. The idea is to focus attention on the needs of the individual customer. To the extent that customer needs are unique, **departmentalisation by customer** can also reduce confusion and increase synergy. Organisations expanding internationally may also divisionalise to meet the demands of complex host-country ownership requirements. NEC, Sony, Nissan and many other Japanese corporations, for example, have developed Australasian divisional subsidiaries to service their customers in the Australasian market. Some huge Europe-based corporations such as Philips and Nestlé have also adopted a divisional structure in their expansion to the Asia–Pacific region. Microsoft Australia illustrates the idea of departmentalisation by customer (see the 'OB in action' on page 284).

The major advantages and disadvantages of divisional specialisation are summarised in table 8.3. In organisations in which satisfying the demands of outsiders is particularly important, the divisional structure may provide the desired capabilities. This pattern can help improve customer responsiveness for organisations that operate in many territories, produce quite different products and services, serve a few major customers or operate internationally.

Divisional departmentalisation is the grouping of individuals and resources by product, service and/or client.

Departmentalisation by geography is the grouping of individuals and resources by geographical territory.

Departmentalisation by customer is the grouping of individuals and resources by client.

Organisations that rely on divisional specialisation can generally expect the following tendencies to occur over time:

- an emphasis on flexibility and adaptability to the needs of important external units
- a lag in the technical quality of products and services compared with that of functionally structured competitors
- difficulty in achieving coordination across divisions, particularly where divisions must work closely or sell to each other.

Steve Vamos took over as director of Microsoft Australia in 2003. He soon realised that he needed to modify the imposed US business structure to suit the Australian market, that is 'aimed at Australian customers in an Australian business environment'. He moved the company from being a sales organisation to having a customer focus. Structurally that meant moving away from a geography-based structure (based on Australian states) to one that was focused on industry groups that the business serviced as customers. These customer divisions service the financial services industry, the telecommunications industry, the public sector and education, and a commercial group (comprising retail, manufacturing and services). This helps the organisation to ask itself who its customers are and to find solutions for them.[29]

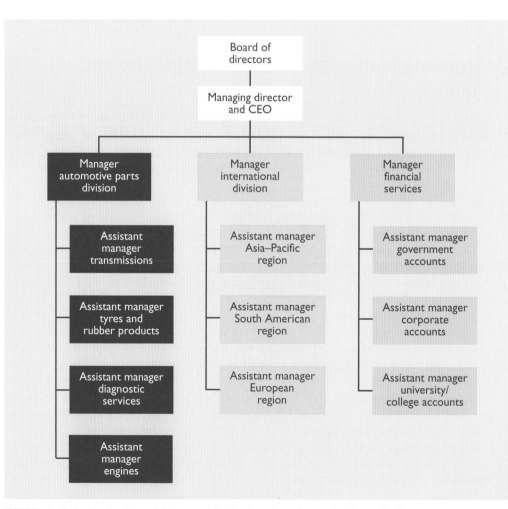

FIGURE 8.4 • A divisional pattern of departmentalisation for a large international organisation

Advantages	Disadvantages
1. It provides adaptability and flexibility in meeting the demands of important external groups.	1. It does not provide a pool of highly trained individuals with similar expertise to solve problems and train new employees.
2. It allows for spotting external changes as they are emerging.	2. It can lead to a duplication of effort as each division attempts to solve similar problems.
3. It provides for the integration of specialised personnel deep within the hierarchy.	3. Divisional goals may be given priority over the health and welfare of the overall organisation; divisional organisations may have difficulty responding to corporation-wide threats.
4. It focuses on the success or failure of particular products, services, clients or territories.	4. Conflict problems may arise when divisions attempt to develop joint projects, exchange resources, share individuals or 'transfer price' one another for goods and services.
5. To the extent that this pattern yields separate 'business units', top management can pit one division against another; for instance, Procter & Gamble has traditionally promoted friendly competition among product groups.	

TABLE 8.3 • Major advantages and disadvantages of divisional specialisation

What Would **You Do?**

Branch offices

Having geographically remote offices or branches can be an important part of doing business in different locations (nationally or internationally). However, there can be problems in keeping connectivity with head office. As Sean Spence (business mentor and consultant) says: 'Mutual contempt is highly corrosive'.[30] He recommends regular visits to the branch offices to maintain face-to-face contact. Such visits can be very effective. One organisation that faces this issue is St George Bank, which has 7400 staff in 400 branches around Australia. Head of Human Resources Brett Wright is aware of the issues and says the bank works to overcome the problems of distance to ensure people in the branches are not forgotten. Not only does the bank want the branch offices to work effectively for the organisation, it does not want to lose talented employees because they are disenchanted with the organisation. HR has a senior management mentoring role in regional areas: Wright has responsibility for the Queensland region and visits the branches regularly.[31]

David Liddy, chief executive of the Bank of Queensland, has a similar practice. Not only does he run a staff hotline between 8.30 and 9.30 every second Friday morning to hear employee comments, he works as a teller in branches on Wednesdays. All executives in the bank are expected to spend one day a month working in a branch so they understand what is happening in the branches and what impact their decisions will have. Liddy says that employees (and customers) are not afraid to say what is wrong.[32]

Julia Ross of Julia Ross Recruitment manages branch offices globally and tries to find a balance between leaving branch offices to operate independently and making sure she knows if something is going wrong. She tries not to over-manage the branches. Information and communication technology can be of particular importance in keeping these vital links between branches and head office. However, there need to be strong human links for real communication and effective performance.

(continued)

Some recommendations include:
- regular communication, including visits and telephone calls (in addition to other electronic communication)
- clear mutual corporate goals and performance indicators against which performance can be monitored and controlled
- flying remote workers in to headquarters to ensure they are involved in important meetings and events
- a balance between focusing on the centre and on the branches
- effective information technology support.[33]

Questions

1. What sort of departmentalisation might lead to remotely located 'branch offices'?
2. There are issues of goals, control and coordination in the management of branch offices. What measures are suggested in relation to these aspects of structure and what other measures would you suggest?
3. You have been receiving performance figures for your branches and find that five of the 15 branch offices are performing poorly. Some of these branches are located in other cities, two in country locations. What could be some likely causes and what would you do to identify the problems and find solutions?

Departmentalisation by matrix

A **matrix structure** is a combination of functional and divisional patterns in which an individual is assigned to more than one type of unit.

From the aerospace industry, a third, unique form of departmentalisation was developed; it is now called a **matrix structure**.[34] In the aerospace industry, projects are technically complex, and they involve hundreds of subcontractors located throughout the world. Precise integration and control is needed across many sophisticated functional specialties and corporations. This is often more than a functional or divisional structure can provide. Thus, departmentalisation by matrix uses both the functional and divisional forms simultaneously. Figure 8.5 shows the basic matrix arrangement for an aerospace program. Note the functional departments (production, marketing and engineering) on one side and the project efforts on the other. Workers and supervisors in the middle of the matrix have two bosses — one functional and one project. For example, if you are one of the people in the marketing function and in the Vulcan project, you would report to the marketing manager, but you would also report to your Vulcan project manager. Thus, the matrix breaks the 'unity of command' principle that is central to bureaucratic hierarchy. Each person in a project team has two bosses. The project manager will be responsible for the person's contribution to the project. The department manager will be responsible for the person's:
- general career development
- pay
- promotion prospects within the organisation
- contributions to the work of the department if/when there are gaps in their project team duties.[35]

It is also possible that some people in such an industry work outside this matrix structure. As you can see from the figure, there may be some people who work in the functional departments (production, marketing and engineering) but who are not necessarily also in a project team.

The major advantages and disadvantages of the matrix form of departmentalisation are summarised in table 8.4. The key disadvantage is the loss of unity of command. Individuals can be unsure as to what their jobs are, who they report to for specific activities, and how various managers are to administer the effort. It can also be an expensive method because it relies on individual managers to coordinate efforts deep within the organisation.

In figure 8.5, note that the number of managers almost doubles compared with the number in either a functional or a divisional structure. Despite these limitations, the matrix structure provides a balance between functional and divisional concerns. Many problems can be resolved at the working level, where the balance between technical, cost, customer and organisational concerns can be rectified.

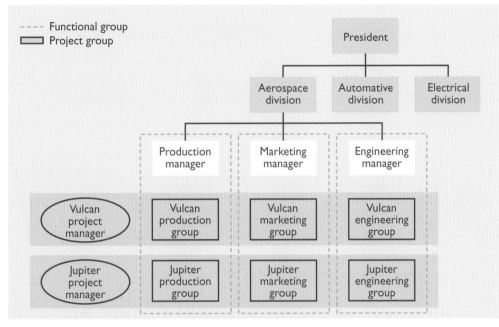

FIGURE 8.5 • A matrix pattern of departmentalisation in an aerospace division

Many organisations also use elements of the matrix structure. Special project teams, coordinating committees and task forces, for example, can be the beginnings of a matrix. A large advertising firm could use project teams for major client contracts. Yet, these temporary structures can be used within a predominantly functional or divisional form without upsetting unity of command or recruiting additional managers.

Advantages	Disadvantages
1. It combines strengths of both functional and divisional departmentalisation.	1. It is expensive.
2. It helps to provide a blending of technical and market emphasis in organisations operating in exceedingly complex environments.	2. Unity of command is lost (because individuals have more than one supervisor).
3. It provides a series of managers able to converse with both technical and marketing personnel.	3. Authority and responsibilities of managers may overlap, causing conflicts and gaps in effort across units and inconsistencies in priorities.
	4. It is difficult to explain to employees.

TABLE 8.4 • Major advantages and disadvantages of a matrix structure

Mixed forms of departmentalisation

As the matrix concept suggests, it is possible to departmentalise by two different methods at the same time, but the matrix form is not the only possibility. Organisations often use a mixture of departmentalisation forms; it may be desirable to divide the effort (group people and resources) by two methods at the same time to balance the advantages and disadvantages of each.

Consider the example in figure 8.6. Notice that this organisation has overall functional units (that is, production, marketing and finance) but that work is divided on a divisional basis (that is, domestic and foreign) within each functional area. Thus, departmentalisation can take different permutations. Another example might be a geographically departmentalised organisation that has functional departments within each major geographical area.

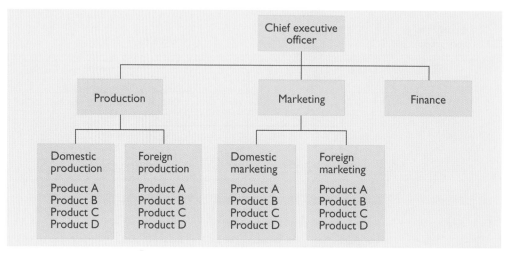

FIGURE 8.6 • Partial organisation chart showing a mixed form of departmentalisation
Source: R Hodgetts and F Luthans, *International management* (New York: McGraw-Hill, 1997).

Implications of emerging forms of work organisation

LEARNING OBJECTIVE 6

Emerging forms of organisational design and workforce implications

Every organisation will develop a unique design in response to its scale, technology, environment and strategic aims, and in terms of the choices it makes about goals, control, coordination, and vertical and horizontal specialisation. Other factors may also have an impact on design, such as the history of the organisation, sudden changes, mergers and acquisitions, and geographical locations.

In this section, we will consider some recognisable types of organisational design in the contemporary world. While they are not necessarily new or unimagined, they do illustrate some generally occurring design trends for organisations. Common forms are the simple design, the bureaucracy, the divisionalised organisation and the conglomerate. However, there are distinctions in the design of organisations even within these categories; for example, variations in the degree of organic or mechanistic design in bureaucracies. Figure 8.7 illustrates these popular basic designs. Other forms of organisation design also emerge, such as alliances, virtual organisations, core–ring designs and adhocracies. These, and their impact on the people working within such organisations, will be briefly examined.

The simple design

A **simple design** is a configuration involving one or two ways of specialising individuals and units.

The **simple design** is a configuration involving the specialisation of individuals and units. That is, vertical specialisation and control typically emphasise levels of supervision without elaborate formal mechanisms (such as rule books and policy manuals), and the majority of the control based with the manager. One or two ways of organising departments are used, and coordination mechanisms are often personal. The organisation visually resembles a 'pyramid' with few staff individuals or units (see the simple design at the top of figure 8.7).

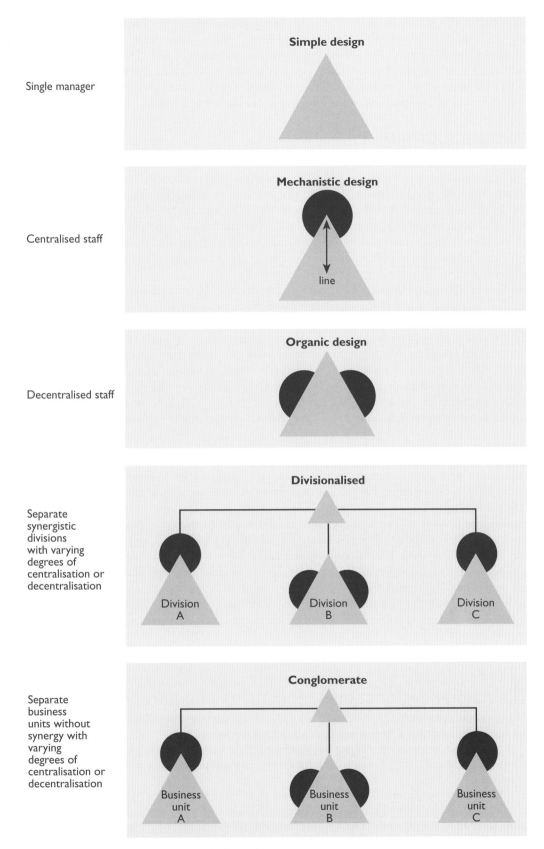

Single manager

Simple design

Centralised staff

Mechanistic design

line

Decentralised staff

Organic design

Separate
synergistic
divisions
with varying
degrees of
centralisation or
decentralisation

Divisionalised

Division
A

Division
B

Division
C

Separate
business
units without
synergy with
varying
degrees of
centralisation or
decentralisation

Conglomerate

Business
unit
A

Business
unit
B

Business
unit
C

FIGURE 8.7 • Visual depiction of different design options

The simple design is appropriate for many small organisations, such as family businesses, retail stores and small manufacturing companies,[36] since these have few people, little necessity for coordination, specialised tasks and hierarchical control. The strengths of the simple design are simplicity, flexibility and responsiveness to the desires of a central manager (in many cases, the owner). A simple design relies on the manager's personal leadership, so this configuration is only as effective as the senior manager.

The bureaucracy

The simple design is a basic building block of all organisations. However, as the organisation grows, additional layers of management and more specialised departments are added. Line and staff functions are separated, and the organisation may begin to expand its territorial scope. In this way, larger organisations become much more structurally complex than small ones.[37] The nature of the organisation changes as layers of management increase, as the division of labour and coordination mechanisms become more elaborate, and as formal controls are established. In addition to the single, senior manager there are other 'levels' of management exercising varying degrees of authority.

The famous German sociologist Max Weber suggested that large organisations would thrive if they relied on legal authority, logic and order.[38] Weber argued that relying on a division of labour, hierarchical control, promotion by merit with career opportunities for employees, and administration by rule was a superior option to the simple design. While Weber knew the bureaucracy he was designing was an ideal type and that it could not always be perfect, he believed that efficiency, fairness and more freedom for individual expression within the organisation would be important outcomes. Bureaucracies are often criticised for being too rule-bound and procedural and some organisations seek to reduce the impact of this, as the following example illustrates. 'The effective manager 8.3' also indicates some of the dysfunctional tendencies of bureaucracies.

A **bureaucracy** is an ideal form of organisation whose characteristics include a division of labour, hierarchical control, promotion by merit with career opportunities for employees, and administration by rule.

David Murray, as chief executive of the Commonwealth Bank, has worked on a transformation strategy to remove bureaucracy. It appears that customer service was hampered by adherence to bureaucratic rules, which were not always enabling a different perspective on a problem. For example, one customer (a small business owner) was denied an overdraft because he did not fulfil the conditions of having an annual business turnover of a particular level. While this rule did help to protect the way in which the bank lent its money, the rules did not allow the bank to take into account the fact that the customer was able to secure the overdraft with a large mortgage over his residential property. He also had an established reputation as a good customer. In the end the customer went elsewhere. Murray is using examples like these to encourage change, particularly by encouraging upward communication from employees at the bottom of the organisation and by simplifying processes.[39]

THE **Effective** Manager 8.3

The natural dysfunctional tendencies of a bureaucracy

All large organisations must systematically work to minimise the dysfunctional characteristics of the modern bureaucracy. Among these dysfunctions are tendencies to:

1. overspecialise and neglect to mitigate the resulting conflicts of interest resulting from specialisation
2. overuse the formal hierarchy and emphasise adherence to official channels rather than problem solving
3. assume senior managers are superior performers on all tasks and rulers of a political system, rather than individuals who should help others reach goals
4. overemphasise insignificant conformity that limits individual growth
5. treat rules as ends in and of themselves rather than as poor mechanisms for control and coordination.

All large organisations are bureaucratic to some extent, though there are variations in the ways they are designed. The following discussion shows some possible variations to bureaucratic design.

Machine bureaucracies (characterised by mechanistic design features, as in figure 8.7) are popular in industries with large-scale operations, such as banks, insurance companies and government offices. However, when the organisation is viewed as too rigid and centralised, employees may feel constrained and the organisation may be hindered in its capacity to adjust to external changes or new technologies. The inherent problems of such mechanistic command-and-control type structures are often overlooked by companies that try to resolve problems by frequent restructuring instead of fundamental changes in design.

On the other hand, a *professional bureaucracy* often relies on organic features in its design.[40] Universities, hospitals, consulting firms, libraries and social services agencies typically adopt this design. A professional bureaucracy looks like a broad, flat pyramid with a bulge in the centre for the professional staff (refer again to figure 8.7, organic design). Power rests with knowledge and the experience of professionals, but control is enhanced by the standardisation of professional skills and the adoption of professional routines, standards and procedures. Given that this design emphasises lateral relations and coordination, centralised direction by senior management is less intense. Although not as efficient as the mechanistic design, this design is better for problem solving, serving individual customer needs and detecting external changes and adjusting to new technologies (but at the sacrifice of responding to central management direction).[41]

The balance of technological and environmental demands can have an impact on the 'mix' of mechanistic and organic features in a bureaucracy. A bureaucracy can have an *organic core with a mechanistic shell*. While the technology of the organisation may call for an organic design to promote flexibility, creativity and innovation, there may be environmental demands that lead to the development of a series of top-level and mechanistic staff units (for example, in response to powerful external groups). This strange design of mechanistic staff units at the top with organic line units towards the middle and bottom of the organisation can protect the organisation externally, while allowing responsible internal operations (see figure 8.8).

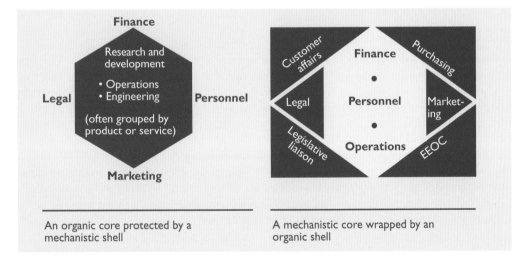

An organic core protected by a mechanistic shell

A mechanistic core wrapped by an organic shell

FIGURE 8.8 • Two design hybrids

A bureaucracy can also have a *mechanistic core with an organic shell*. Very large organisations with technologies that call for mechanistic designs and economies of scale are vulnerable to environmental uncertainty and volatility. A partial solution to the problem is to wrap these inflexible cores within organic staff units. The staff units often attempt to change the external conditions by moderating the volatility in the specific environment and to absorb or buffer as many changes as possible. This latter option is found most often in organisations that must balance efficient production with flexible marketing and design operations. The assembly line is mechanistically structured, yet products may be designed by more organically structured teams.

Divisionalised organisations

Many very large organisations find that neither the mechanistic nor the organic designs are suitable for all their operations. Adopting a machine bureaucracy would overload senior management and yield too many levels of management,[42] but adopting an organic design would mean losing control and becoming too inefficient. Even in the same industry, some business activities may call for an organic structure, while others call for a mechanistic one. The solution is the divisionalised design, by which the organisation establishes a *separate structure for each business or division*. The classic divisional organisation was created for General Motors by Alfred Sloan, who divided the company's operations into divisions for designing and producing Chevys, Oldsmobiles, Pontiacs, Buicks and Cadillacs.[43] Each division was treated as a separate business; each business competed against the others.

In the divisionalised organisation, all the businesses are coordinated by a comparatively small centralised team that provides support such as financial services and legal expertise. Senior line management provides direction and control over the presumably 'autonomous' divisions. In very large organisations, this approach can free top management to establish strategy and concentrate on large, long-term problems. Divisional heads run their own businesses and compete for resources, yet each enjoys the support (financial, personnel, legal and so on) of the larger parent.

While this structure is expensive, because many similar staff and support units must be developed for each division, it allows the organisation greater flexibility to respond to different markets and customers. However, tension between divisional management and senior management is often apparent. It is difficult for corporate executives and corporate staff to allow the divisions to operate as independent businesses. Over time, senior staff may grow in number and force 'assistance' on the divisions. Further, because divisions compete for common resources, coordination across divisions is also often difficult.

Divisionalised design is an organisational structure that establishes a separate structure for each business or division.

The conglomerate

Organisations that own several unrelated businesses are known as conglomerates. The line between the divisionalised form and the conglomerate can often be confusing. For our purposes, the key question is whether there is synergy among the various businesses owned by the corporation. Synergies are potential links, as between computers and information systems, or between financing and vehicle rentals, that create an entity with an output greater than its individual parts. If there is synergy, we would call the organisation divisionalised; if there is little synergy, the organisation is a conglomerate.

Pure conglomerates have not done particularly well in the United States, mainly because substantive knowledge of the various businesses is often needed for them to be successfully managed.[44] While most scholars would argue against conglomerates, and for a more synergistic approach, Wesfarmers has proved to be an exception.

Conglomerates are organisations that own several unrelated businesses.

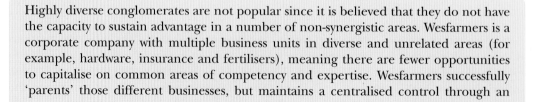

Highly diverse conglomerates are not popular since it is believed that they do not have the capacity to sustain advantage in a number of non-synergistic areas. Wesfarmers is a corporate company with multiple business units in diverse and unrelated areas (for example, hardware, insurance and fertilisers), meaning there are fewer opportunities to capitalise on common areas of competency and expertise. Wesfarmers successfully 'parents' those different businesses, but maintains a centralised control through an integrated system focused on shareholders. Important planning processes, project evaluation, performance measurement and remuneration are all used in this way. In effect, Wesfarmers incubates the businesses until a buyer comes along to buy the business and make use of synergistic opportunities with their own, existing, businesses.[45]

The core–ring organisation

The pressure to enhance productivity in the last decades of the twentieth century encouraged many organisations to 'downsize', or reduce their number of employees. While this trend appears to have slowed, possible large-scale reductions in employee numbers still make headlines, as the following example shows.

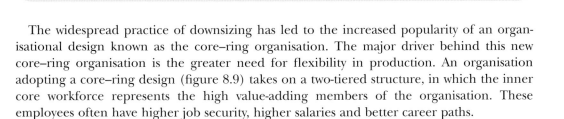

In mid-2005, Kimberly-Clark announced plans to cut 6000 jobs (around 10 per cent of its workforce) and sell 20 plants (17 per cent of its manufacturing facilities). Most of the plant closings were to be in North America and Europe. The move was part of a strategy to strengthen its diaper and healthcare businesses and to expand its presence in emerging markets (such as India and China). The restructuring was designed to achieve economies of scale in existing manufacturing plants.[46]

The widespread practice of downsizing has led to the increased popularity of an organisational design known as the core–ring organisation. The major driver behind this new core–ring organisation is the greater need for flexibility in production. An organisation adopting a core–ring design (figure 8.9) takes on a two-tiered structure, in which the inner core workforce represents the high value-adding members of the organisation. These employees often have higher job security, higher salaries and better career paths.

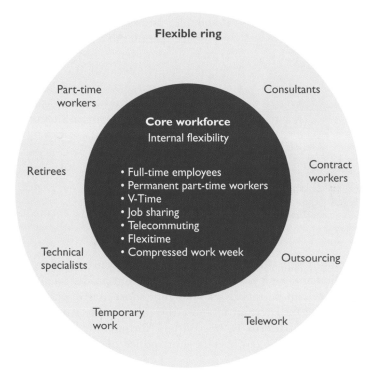

FIGURE 8.9 • Core and peripheral workforce employment options

The second tier of this structure is also known as the flexible ring, and it is made up of a contingent workforce. Contingent workers in this outer ring may supply specialised services to the organisation on an ongoing basis and, as a result, have a relatively stable employment relationship with the core organisation (as least for the duration of their contracts). Traditionally, such services would be contained within the core of a large bureaucratic organisation, but in the core–ring organisation services such as cleaning, information technology and specialist consultants can be more cost-effectively contracted or outsourced.

The largest component of the outer ring consists of lower-skilled, casual employees. Statistics show that approximately 27 per cent of the Australian workforce is casual.[47] Such employees typically experience lower job security, relatively lower pay and a lack of available career paths.[48] Workers in this peripheral category may actually receive a higher hourly rate of pay than that of some core workers in the organisation, but on-costs such as holiday loadings, training costs, sick leave and other fringe benefits do not apply to them because they are employed on a just-in-time basis. From the casual employee's point of view, their employment can be very 'precarious', with little certainty about having a steady income, where the next day's work is coming from, and whether the family can enjoy a holiday together (as they may be called in for work).

Such workers are temporary; fluctuations in the size of this outer ring depend on prevailing levels of demand for the organisation's products. These fluctuations may be due to changes in economic prosperity, market competition or other factors. In some cases, as the Warner Village example shows, the work is seasonal.

OB in action

Warner Village Theme Parks owns Movie World, Sea World and Wet'n'Wild Water World on the Gold Coast in Queensland. There are more than 500 permanent employees at Warner Village ranging from tradespeople and retail, food and service people to entertainers, vets, stuntmen and other performers. Because the business is so seasonal, around 1300 people are hired every year, with about 450 taken on for the Christmas rush. Of these casual workers, around 10 per cent have usually worked for the organisation before.[49]

For the organisation, the core–ring design offers a flexible and cost-effective structure to adapt quickly to such variations in demand for a particular product. When product demand rises, the ring or contingent workforce can be rapidly expanded at short notice, given the high levels of unemployment in most OECD countries over the past decade. Given that organisations no longer expect demand patterns to be constant throughout the year, if demand falls, the contingent workforce can be cut back at short notice depending on the nature and the level of the work required.

Structure for the people — a workers' market?

Organisational designs have often placed more emphasis on getting outcomes for the organisation than considering how the structure benefits the people within it. Designs such as the core–ring model, where workers are seen as human just-in-time inventory to be called upon or dispensed with on demand, reinforce this view. It appears that the main reason for casualised labour is the organisation's bottom line. Casual employees cost less in terms of overheads, rights and benefits (such as leave and superannuation). While there are varying arguments about whether people are dissatisfied or not with being casual, there should perhaps be some concern about whether they are sufficiently productive, committed and motivated. It appears that having casual workers is one of very few ways employers can reduce fixed costs to compete in a global market. But for the workers themselves there is lack of job security, and for the organisations there is potentially high turnover, recruitment and training costs.[50]

While designs do take into account how people might behave, they are less seriously focused on designing the organisation to suit the preferences of its workers. If structural designs benefit the employees and increase their satisfaction and commitment (such as through empowerment and decentralised decision making) it is a bonus, but the key reason for such changes is ultimately productivity and performance. The fact that the increased productivity or performance might be related to job satisfaction in some way helps to justify the designs, but ultimately getting the most out of the workers is the driving aim of organisational design decisions.

However, with ageing populations and increasing labour shortages expected in a number of areas, organisations are now finding that they must respond to the expectations and requirements of valuable workers and potential workers. Other evidence shows that this concern also applies to retaining women in the workforce, and enabling them to reach higher levels in organisations.[51] In any case, the on-call casuals may not always be so readily available.

There is increasing speculation about the ways in which organisations might endeavour to fulfil worker expectations (at least in the areas where they have trouble gaining required workers). With increasing acceptance that many employees are not happy at work, or that they want better work–life balance and/or less stress, organisations must reconsider the needs and satisfactions of workers in relation to the organisational design, just as we do with job design. We need to ask the following types of questions of our workers: Does the functional unit provide you with sufficient development and stimulation? Does the structure impede the way you can effectively relate to customers? Do you fulfil your needs for achievement and power? Can you manage stress and work–life balance in this position? These questions and many others could, in effect, reflect a customer-focus on employees. In recent years, businesses have been conditioned to a 'shortage of jobs' scenario, with a pool of workers keen to get those jobs. Now, there is a trend towards a demand-driven labour market (where good workers are in demand) and organisations must compete for the best of them, just as they would for customers.

Questions

1. How do casual workers experience their work in organisations? What implications are there for their commitment to the organisation and their motivation/satisfaction with it?

2. What features of organisational design and structure, as discussed in this chapter, would act as a motivator to you as a worker?

3. Can organisations design themselves so that they may attract and retain the right sorts of people, who will be satisfied and committed to stay? Why or why not?

The adhocracy

The influence of technological considerations can be clearly seen in small organisations and in specific departments within large ones. In some instances, managers and employees simply do not know the appropriate way in which to service a client or to produce a particular product. This is the extreme of Thompson's intensive type of technology and may be found in some small-batch processes where a team of individuals must develop a unique product for a particular client. Mintzberg suggests that the 'adhocracy' may be an appropriate structure at these technological extremes.[52] An adhocracy is characterised by:

An **adhocracy** is an organisational structure that emphasises shared, decentralised decision making, extreme horizontal specialisation, few levels of management, the virtual absence of formal controls, and few rules, policies and procedures.

- few rules, policies and procedures
- very decentralised, shared decision making among members
- extreme horizontal specialisation, because each member of the unit may be a distinct specialist
- few levels of management
- virtually no formal controls.

The adhocracy is particularly useful when an aspect of the organisation's technology presents two problems: first, the tasks facing the organisation vary considerably and provide many exceptions, as in a hospital; and second, problems are difficult to define and resolve.[53] The adhocracy places a premium on professionalism and coordination in problem solving, especially in solving technical problems. As such, adhocracies are often used as a supplement to other designs to offset their dysfunctional effects.[54] Organisations use temporary task forces, special committees and even contracted consulting firms to provide the creative problem identification and problem solving that the adhocracy promotes. Lotus Development Corporation, for instance, creates autonomous departments to encourage talented employees to develop software programs. Allied Chemical and 3M also set up quasi-autonomous groups to work through new ideas.

Other structural arrangements

Many other forms of organisational design are emerging or exist. They often involve alliances of two or more organisations, or networks of several organisations or of businesses within larger organisations. Some of these are now discussed, and may be useful in describing some organisational or part-organisational designs.

Strategic alliances are announced cooperative agreements or joint ventures between two independent organisations.

Strategic alliances are announced cooperative agreements or joint ventures between two independent organisations. Often these agreements involve corporations that are headquartered in different nations.[55] In high-technology areas, such as robotics, semiconductors, advanced materials (ceramics and carbon fibres) and advanced information systems, a single company often does not have all the knowledge necessary to bring new products to the market. Often the organisations with the knowledge are not even in the same country. In this case, the organisational design must go beyond the boundaries of the organisation into strategic alliances. New Zealand company Comvita is one example of a company that collaborates in alliances. It has signed an agreement with a UK wound-dressing manufacturer to produce its innovative wound dressings (they combine alginate or seaweed fibres with medical-grade manuka honey).[56] Another purpose for alliances is to provide goods in the supply chain, an activity common for major retailers and supermarkets such as Coles Myer.

OB in action

In addition to increasing its shareholdings in a range of retail outlets, such as Country Road and the Just Group, Coles Myer has been increasing its control over supplies to its stores. Like many businesses it is working towards cutting out the middleman and doing the purchasing itself. It has been working on improving its sources in China; between mid-2004 and mid-2005 Coles Myer increased its number of buyers in China from 160 to 200. Five years earlier it barely had a presence in China.[57]

Alliances exist in other forms in other countries. In Europe, for example, they are called informal combines or cartels; competitors work cooperatively to share the market, decrease uncertainty and create more favourable outcomes for all. The legality of such arrangements may vary between countries, depending on trade practices laws and other regulations. For example, in Australia collusion or collaboration in markets is generally illegal (as it is in New Zealand), although in 2003 the Dawson Report suggested that small businesses be given limited rights to join forces for collective negotiations with larger customers or suppliers in order to give them some competitive capacity.[58] In mid-2005 the Australian Competition and Consumer Commission had 32 'serious' cartel investigations on its books,[59] indicating that despite their illegality there are still such alliances operating, though how wittingly is not always clear. In Japan, strategic alliances among well-established organisations in many industries are quite common and linked in a network of relationships called a Keiretsu. For example, organisations may be linked to each other directly via cross-ownership and through historical ties to one bank, such as with the Mitsubishi group. Alternatively, a key manufacturer may be at the hub of a network of supplier organisations, with long-term supply contracts and cross-ownership ties, such as Toyota. Similar arrangements exist elsewhere. The network organisation involves a central organisation that specialises in a core activity, such as design and assembly. It works with a comparatively small number of participating suppliers on a long-term basis for both component development and manufacturing efficiency. Chrysler is a leader in the development of these relationships. More extreme variations of this network design are also emerging to meet apparently conflicting environmental, size and technological demands simultaneously. Organisations are spinning off staff functions to reduce their overall size and concentrate their internal design on technological dictates. Network organisations are de-layered and flexible, with freer and less formal communication, control and coordination. Activities are geared towards alignment with the value chain in the industry, with an array of complementary competencies and resources brought together to achieve the objectives of the network.[60]

> A **network organisation** is a de-layered organisation aligned around the complementary competencies of players in a value chain.

Virtual organisations or virtual alliances emerge from the environment of networks but they are also distinctly dependent on the ready connections gained by information and communications technology. Virtual organisations comprise a range of individuals, groups and businesses who work together in a diversity of working arrangements across space and time. They are characterised by their shared vision; clustering of activities around core competencies; teamwork to implement activities throughout a value chain and to coordinate and make decisions in real time through information technology; and a tendency to empower members at the bottom levels when it serves the needs of the whole group. They tend to be focused on the sharing and processing of knowledge and information through electronic mediums rather than transforming physical resources in physical places. These features enable a high degree of responsiveness to environmental change.[61] Control in virtual organisations occurs through extensive use of videoconferencing and the Internet.[62]

> **Virtual organisations** comprise individuals, groups and businesses that work together across time and space.

Franchises do not fit neatly into a design category but are worth mentioning here. A successful organisation often allows other organisations to buy a franchise to run a 'relatively' independent business using the name, reputation and business product and/or procedure of the parent organisation in return for some payment or fee. While franchises are often thought to be mostly 'imports' (such as KFC, Pizza Hut and McDonald's) there are home-grown franchises as well. In Australia, there are around 850 franchise systems with almost 65 000 outlets and 500 000 employees. Examples include Bakers Delight, Eagle Boys Pizza and Kwik Fix International. An important feature of franchises is that they typically need controls — franchise owners, managers and employees need to operate using the successful system the franchise offers.[63] The following Bank of Queensland and Edmen examples illustrate what may occur in a franchise operation.

The Bank of Queensland has developed a new business model to have franchised branches, thereby enabling more regional branches in Queensland and other states. There is an emphasis in this model on customer service. Owner-managers of the franchises are carefully selected, with only one out of every 14 applicants accepted. They all have experience in retail or commercial banking. The owner-managers put in equity (depending on the size of the branch). The equity is used to fit out bank premises of around 100–110 square metres. The bank provides all the training and takes a share of the net profit margin. The bank also treats its owner-managers in the same way it treats its corporate managers. The Bank of Queensland has 161 branches (including 23 interstate), of which 104 are franchises.[64]

Edmen is an employment agency that began in Wollongong as a small agency for blue-collar workers. The company now has an annual turnover of A$20 million and has expanded its market base to include white-collar and professional workers, as well as servicing the disability support industry. Edmen has been so successful in the disability area that it has been forced to expand interstate (including Brisbane and Adelaide) to service clients such as the Spastic Centre, Mayne, Mission Australia and Wesley Disability. Founder Eddy De Gabriele is now considering ways of dealing with the geographical location of his offices. Two options he is considering are increasing the use of technology to support videoconferencing and other communication systems, and franchising the Edmen concept.[65]

Summary

Formal structure and organisational design

Organisational design is the process of choosing and implementing a formal structural configuration (that is, a formal structure) for an organisation. The structure is typically represented on an organisational chart. Structure defines the configuration of jobs, positions and lines of authority of the various component parts of the organisation.

Factors for organisational design

Four main factors can be said to affect organisational design — scale, technology, environment and strategy. Scale is important since the number of people and the degree of division of labour and authority will have an impact on the complexity of the organisation and the need for compensatory control and coordination mechanisms. Major distinctions in technology are the Thompson (intensive, long-linked, mediating) and Woodward (small batch, mass production, continuous processing) classification systems. The technology of the organisation will have some impact on the chosen structure. Environmental differences have a large impact on the type of organisational design that works best. Both the general environment (background conditions) and specific environment (key actors and organisations) are important, as is the environmental complexity (richness, interdependence, and uncertainty and volatility in the organisation/environment). The organisational design must support the strategy if it is to prove successful. Strategy positions an organisation in its competitive environment. Strategies such as differentiating the business, or leading the market in price and value, or based on competency can have an impact on the organisational design.

Goals, control and coordination

Organisational goals include both output and systems goals. Output goals relate to the type of business the organisation is engaged in; they are concerned with satisfying primary beneficiaries and corporate social responsibility. Systems goals establish a basis for organisational survival and prosperity. Control is the set of mechanisms the organisation uses to keep action and/or outputs within predetermined levels. Output controls focus on desired targets and allow managers to use their own methods for reaching the desired target. Process controls (such as policies, rules, procedures, formalisation and standardisation) attempt to specify the manner in which tasks will be accomplished. Coordination is the set of mechanisms that an organisation uses to link the actions of separate units into a consistent pattern. Coordination methods can be impersonal (such as centralised staff units) or personal (such as network development and task forces). Organisational designs, overall, can be said to be mechanistic (involving many levels of authority, high levels of control and impersonal coordination) or organic (breakup of work horizontally; personal coordination and loose control).

Vertical specialisation

Vertical specialisation is the hierarchical division of labour that specifies formal authority and a chain of command. The organisation's hierarchy can be said to be tall or flat, relating to the number of levels of management or authority in the organisation. Organisational authority can also be centralised (concentrated at the top or centre or the organisation) or decentralised (where decision making is pushed down to lower levels of the organisation). Unity of command defines the situation in which each worker has a clear reporting relationship to only one supervisor. It lessens confusion and provides clear channels of communication. Span of control indicates the number of individuals reporting to a supervisor. Wide spans of control mean the supervisor supervises many people, whereas a supervisor with a narrow span of control will have few employees.

Horizontal specialisation

Horizontal specialisation is the division of labour that results in various work units or groups in the organisation. The distinction between line and staff units can be particularly relevant to horizontal departmentalisation. Line personnel conduct the major business of the organisation while staff personnel assist in performing specialised supportive services. Three main types of 'departmentalisation' are: functional, divisional and matrix departmentalisation. Each structure has advantages and disadvantages. Organisations may successfully use any type, or a mixture, as long as the strengths of the structure match the needs of the organisation's goals.

Implications of emerging forms of work organisation

Each organisation's design will be unique. Smaller organisations often adopt a simple structure; larger organisations often adopt a bureaucratic form. The bureaucracy is an ideal form based on legal authority, logic and order rather than on individual supervision or tradition. While most larger corporations are bureaucracies, they differ in the degree and combination of mechanistic and organic features. Divisionalised organisations establish a separate structure for each business or division in the organisation so that there is emphasis on coping with the particular aspects of that part of the business, but also overall synergy. Conglomerates are organisations that own several unrelated businesses that do not have inherently synergistic advantages. Within divisionalised or conglomerate organisations each business can develop different design features. The core–ring organisation involves an inner core, relatively permanent, workforce with higher job security, higher salaries and better career paths. There is also a flexible outer ring of workers employed on a part-time or casual basis as required. They tend to have lower job security, lower pay and a lack of career paths. This approach enables the organisation to achieve economies by adapting its employment levels to suit the circumstances. The adhocracy is a structural form that emphasises shared, decentralised decision making, extreme horizontal specialisation, few levels of management and few formal controls. Other organisation designs include strategic alliances, networked organisations, virtual organisations and franchises.

Chapter 8 study guide

OB Key terms

adhocracy, *p. 296*
bureaucracy, *p. 290*
centralisation, *p. 280*
conglomerates, *p. 292*
control, *p. 274*
coordination, *p. 278*
corporate social responsibility,
   p. 274
decentralisation, *p. 280*
departmentalisation by customer,
   p. 283
departmentalisation by geography,
   p. 283
divisional departmentalisation,
   p. 283
divisionalised design, *p. 292*

environmental complexity, *p. 271*
formal structure, *p. 268*
formalisation, *p. 277*
functional departmentalisation,
   p. 282
horizontal specialisation, *p. 281*
line personnel, *p. 281*
matrix structure, *p. 286*
mechanistic design, *p. 279*
network organisation, *p. 297*
organic design, *p. 279*
organisation charts, *p. 268*
organisational design, *p. 268*
organisational strategy, *p. 272*
output controls, *p. 276*
output goals, *p. 273*

policy, *p. 276*
primary beneficiaries, *p. 273*
procedure (rule), *p. 276*
process controls, *p. 276*
simple design, *p. 288*
span of control, *p. 281*
staff personnel, *p. 281*
standardisation, *p. 277*
strategic alliances, *p. 296*
systems goals, *p. 274*
technological imperative, *p. 270*
technology, *p. 270*
unity of command, *p. 281*
vertical specialisation, *p. 279*
virtual organisations, *p. 297*

OB Review questions

1. Compare control and coordination and explain two types of each.
2. Explain the difference between mechanistic and organic organisations.
3. Explain and compare the types of technology identified by Thompson and Woodward.
4. What is a core–ring organisation and why does it have an impact on the workforce?

OB Application questions

1. Demonstrate the purpose of an organisational chart in terms of depicting horizontal and vertical specialisation in an organisation.
2. From the perspective of an employee, how might it be to work in the following situations (compare the choices in each of a, b and c):
   (a) a functionally departmentalised organisation compared to a functionally departmentalised organisation with project teams in a matrix structure
   (b) an organisation that is highly decentralised compared with one that is highly centralised
   (c) an organisation that utilises a mass production technology compared to a small batch organisation?
3. In a large organisation employing mostly highly educated professionals, what do you think might be the best approaches to achieving control over those professionals? Explain your answers.

4. Many organisations are becoming flatter, reducing levels of hierarchy and widening the span of control. What advantages and disadvantages would there be in this approach for an organisation that relied on its employees to make judgements on customers' requests (for example, for loans, insurance claims or special consideration of circumstances in social welfare cases)?

5. What form of hybrid design might be necessary for an organisation that is very large and must reach economies of scale, but also needs to adapt to environmental uncertainty? Explain your answer.

6. How would you describe the technology and organisational forms used in the following (it is acceptable to describe a mix of technologies and forms)? Explain your reasons.
   (a) an organisation making a Hollywood movie
   (b) a large company building prefabricated homes and later assembling them on customers' blocks of land
   (c) a firm of solicitors and barristers
   (d) a multinational mining and steel producer

Research questions

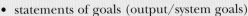

1. Find two local organisations. Try to choose two different-sized organisations that have different processes; for example, retail and service industries. It would be best to avoid organisations that are branches of a bigger organisation, as this would complicate your research. Give a brief overview of these two organisations and what they do and then compare and contrast them in terms of the following criteria: goals, control methods, vertical specialisation, horizontal specialisation and coordination methods. Also assess and compare the scale, environment, technology and strategy of the organisations to consider how this may have affected the design of the organisations.

2. Search the web site of a major retail chain, analysing the chain in terms of the following elements of organisational structure:

- statements of goals (output/system goals)
- explanations or diagrams of the formal structure of the organisation (organisational charts, number of layers in the hierarchy, span of control, apparent centralisation/decentralisation)
- different groups/sections in the organisation (type of specialisation into divisions or departments, line and staff personnel, casual and permanent components of the staff).

Assuming there are different business units within the organisation, analyse the range of businesses or business units in the 'organisation' and draw conclusions based on whether you find them synergistic (or not synergistic) in the design of the entire organisation.

Running project

Complete the following activities for your chosen organisation.

1. Identify the organisation's goals. These might include formal, written goals as well as less obviously stated goals. Try to identify output goals and systems goals.

2. Refer to the organisational chart for your organisation. From this chart, and from everything else you know about how the organisation functions, construct an organigraph for the organisation. Do you think the organisational chart or the organigraph is most useful in understanding the structure of the organisation? Why?

3. How is the organisation departmentalised? Explain how and why this is appropriate (considering types of departmentalisation and issues such as line and staff personnel).

4. How does technology and environment affect the organisational design of your organisation?

5. What are the likely implications of the design and structure of the organisation on the employees?

Vertical and horizontal specialisation: organising XYZ Paper Company

XYZ does not have an organisational chart. The following is a list of its management position titles. Develop an organisational chart by dividing the total task into separate duties, grouping similar people and resources together in a division of labour that establishes specific work units/departments. Draw your organisational chart using both the title and the letter in each box.

A   sales manager
B   accountants
C   engineering department
D   vice-president of personnel
E   president
F   credit manager
G   product A manager (facial tissue, paper towels, napkins, etc.)
H   product B supervisor
I   vice-president of finance
J   advertising manager
K   vice-president of manufacturing
L   quality-control manager
M   product A supervisor
N   product A sales supervisor
O   purchasing manager
P   training manager
Q   data-processing manager
R   vice-president of marketing
S   product B manager (writing paper, envelopes, etc.)
T   sales supervisor product B
U   assistant to the president

After completing the organisational chart, answer the following questions.

1. What is the span of control for the president and each vice-president? Is it broad or narrow?
2. Identify the line and staff units and consider whether XYZ uses standardisation.
3. What type of departmentalisation does your organisational chart have?
4. Use the following criteria to consider whether the organisational design tends towards being organic or mechanistic.

Mechanistic	*Organic*
Stable predictable environment	Innovative unpredictable environment
Strict formal lines of authority	Flexible informal lines of authority
Centralised authority	Decentralised authority
Extensive use of managerial techniques	Minimal use of managerial techniques
Many rules and procedures	Few rules and procedures
Specialist jobs	Generalist jobs
Formal and impersonal coordination and control	Informal and personal coordination and control
Large batch or mass production technology	Made-to-order or long-run process technology
Functional departmentalisation	Divisional departmentalisation

Assessing organisational structure and design

Objectives

To develop and refine your understanding of the basic design and structural characteristics of various organisations

Total time: 60–90 minutes

Procedure

1. In groups of five, choose an organisation with which you are reasonably familiar. Develop a list of its basic structural elements using a chart or table to record all discussion on each of the attributes.
2. Address the following concerns.[66]
   (a) *Product.* What is the core business and the products/services that your organisation provides to customers (or clients, members)? Are its

products of real social value? What technologies are used to produce its products/services?

(b) *Workplace*. Is the workplace safe? Is the business finding ways to involve workers in the decision-making process?

(c) *Environment*. For example, if you have chosen a manufacturer, does the business protect air, water and so on? If you have chosen a financial business, does it use environmental responsibility when investing or underwriting?

(d) *Community*. What kind of commitment does it have to its local and national community? Does it apply some standards to immigrant workers?

3. Suggest an organisational design that best suits your organisation. Discuss why you chose it over other designs (it could be an improved design, or if you think the existing design is best you need to justify it).

Wrap up
Present your team findings to the class.

Case study: *Defence force recruiting*

OB

It has been described as Australia's largest recruiting exercise contract and it is arguably the only recruitment contract of its kind in the world. In 1997, with an eye on costs, the Australian Defence Force (ADF) began a review of its recruitment functions in the army, navy and air force. Its recommendations included investigating and trialling an outsourced recruitment program.

Fast forward to 2005 and ADF recruiting is now a collaboration between the ADF and a civilian recruitment and change management consultancy known as Defence Force Recruiting (DFR), a business unit of Manpower. It is the first time that ADF uniformed staff have worked in collaboration with civilian staff under a civilian organisation's management structure.

This extraordinary partnership evolved from a transition and change management program that took place over two years across the nation.

Talk to the people involved, and they'll say it was one of the most complex organisational and culture change opportunities in the Australian business environment. And so far, the results are promising. As well as reducing costs, the new arrangement has fostered a positive shift in culture. The new business improvement services structure encompassing human resources, learning and development, and quality, has been instrumental in creating an innovative culture where continuous improvement and learning is encouraged and supported throughout the organisation.

Given the spread of the defence forces and the importance of a consistent national approach, DFR was created as an organisation with a 'local–national' approach. The organisation is managed from a central headquarters with each regional office empowered to direct their resources as they see fit. Each area manager is encouraged to manage their business as if it were their own, with support and guidance available from headquarters if needed. Central requirements of the recruitment function such as target allocation, budget allocation and support for systems, processes and people are managed by headquarters.

Continuous improvement is a contractual requirement with ISO 9001/2000 selected as the quality system for DFR. The contract also requires a percentage decrease in the cost of services.

The collaborative nature of DFR means that each group plays to its strengths. Civilian staff perform the majority of the management, planning and administration functions while the ADF staff, and a small number of civilian staff, perform the shared function of candidate attraction, counselling and interviewing.

Each candidate is tested against medical and psychological standards provided by the military. These tests are undertaken by staff from the psychology services function and medical staff from the group's major teaming partner, Health Services Australia.

The final decision on whether a candidate is invited to join the defence force is made by an ADF member from the same service applied for. Enlistment of candidates and the appointment of officer candidates is a function retained by the ADF and is carried out by the senior military recruiting officer at each location.

A key feature of the organisation's structure is that the staff perform their functions in operational cells, not roles.

Culturally, this approach to workplace relations emphasises integrative yet individualistic systems. The manager in DFR is supported by the organisational structure to concentrate on employee participation, HR flow — of candidate and worker, reward systems and work organisation — as opposed to reporting, representation, strategy and other hierarchical structural requirements. The operational worker in DFR can be used in a range of roles and functions to support the manager's mission.

(continued)

The organisation provides coaching, mentoring and flexible working environments, and the cells structure creates the environment where staff become skilled 'all-rounders' who are easily retrained and redeployed. This gives the DFR workforce the operational ability to be flexible and responsive.

Source: Scott Latham, 'On manoeuvres', *HR Monthly* (April 2005), pp. 30–4.

Questions

1. What are the goals of the DFR and how does the structure support the achievement of the goals?

2. What type of horizontal specialisation approach is used in the organisation and how effective is it likely to be?

3. The defence forces are typically considered to have rule-bound, centralised and hierarchical organisations while DFR is said to be flexible and responsive. Discuss the differences between the 'typical' defence force (such as army or navy) and DFR, and the probable impacts on the defence force personnel who now operate in DFR.

OB Suggested reading

Richard M Burton, Børge Obel, *Strategic organizational diagnosis and design — the dynamics of fit*, 3rd ed. (New York: Springer Science + Business Media, 2003).

Graham Hubbard, Delyth Samuel, Simon Heap and Graeme Cocks, *The first XI: winning organisations in Australia* (Brisbane: John Wiley & Sons, 2002).

Harold J Leavitt, *Top down: why hierarchies are here to stay and how to manage them more effectively* (Boston: Harvard Business School Press, 2005).

Tony Lendrum, *The strategic partnering pocketbook* (Sydney: McGraw-Hill, 2004).

W Richard Scott, *Organizations: rational, natural and open systems* (Upper Saddle River, NJ: Prentice Hall, 2003).

Robert Spillane and Lynda Spillane, 'The two faces of authority: a critique', *Journal of the Australian and New Zealand Academy of Management*, vol. 5, no. 1 (1999), pp. 1–11.

Kenichi Ohmae, *The next global stage: challenges and opportunities in our borderless world*, digital ed. (University of Pennsylvania: Wharton School Publishing, 2005).

P Vink, EAP Koningsveld and S Dhondt (eds), *Human factors in organizational design and management - VI* (Oxford: Elsevier Science, 1998).

Robert L Wallace, *Strategic partnerships: an entrepreneur's guide to joint ventures and alliances* (Chicago: Dearborn Trade, 2004).

OB End notes

1. RN Osborn, JG Hunt and LR Jauch, *Organization theory: integrated text and cases* (Melbourne, FL: Krieger, 1984), pp. 123–215.

2. Joan Woodward, *Industrial organization: theory and practice* (London: Oxford University Press, 1965).

3. James D Thompson, *Organization in action* (New York: McGraw-Hill, 1967).

4. Joan Woodward, op. cit.

5. Neil Shoebridge, 'One size fits all', *Business Review Weekly* (7–13 July 2005), p. 63.

6. See RN Osborn and CC Baughn, 'New patterns in the formation of US/Japanese cooperative ventures', *Columbia Journal of World Business*, vol. 22 (1988), pp. 57–65.

7. 'Shifting business offshore growing', *The Sydney Morning Herald* (15 September 2005), www.smh.com.au/news/Business/.

8. Jacqui Walker, 'Second harvest', *Business Review Weekly* (2–8 June 2005), pp. 30–2.

9. LR Jauch and RN Osborn, 'Toward an integrated theory of strategy', *Academy of Management Review*, vol. 6 (1981),

pp. 491–8; Alfred D Chandler, *The visible hand: the managerial revolution in America* (Cambridge, MA: Bellknap, 1977); Karen Bantel and RN Osborn, 'The influence of performance, environment, and size on firm strategic clarity', working paper (Detroit, Michigan: Department of Management, Wayne State University, 1990).

10. See Richard M Cyert and James G March, *A behavioral theory of the firm* (Englewood Cliffs, NJ: Prentice Hall, 1963). A discussion of organisational goals is also found in Charles Perrow, *Organizational analysis: a sociological view* (Belmont, CA: Wadsworth, 1970) and in Richard H Hall, 'Organizational behavior: a sociological perspective' in Jay W Lorsch (ed.), *Handbook of organizational behavior* (Englewood Cliffs, NJ: Prentice Hall, 1987), pp. 84–95.

11. See, for instance, IC MacMillan and A Meshulack, 'Replacement versus expansion: dilemma for mature US businesses', *Academy of Management Journal*, vol. 26 (1983), pp. 708–26.

12. William H Starbuck and Paul C Nystrom, 'Designing and understanding organizations' in PC Nystrom and WH Starbuck (eds), *Handbook of organizational design: adapting organizations to their environments* (New York: Oxford University Press, 1981).

13. Janine Perrett, 'Your safety is what keeps them busy', *The Sydney Morning Herald* (22 July 2005), p. 23.

14. See Paul R Lawrence and Jay W Lorsch, *Organization and environment* (Homewood, IL: Richard D. Irwin, 1969).

15. Peter Vincent, 'Remember who's the boss', *The Sydney Morning Herald*, My Career section (19–20 February 2005), p. 1.

16. Andrew Heathcote, 'To catch a thief', *Business Review Weekly* (3–9 February 2005), pp. 70–71.

17. Adapted from W Edwards Deming, 'Improvement of quality and productivity through action by management', *Productivity Review* (Winter 1982), pp. 12–22; W Edwards Deming, *Quality, productivity and competitive position* (Cambridge, MA: MIT Center for Advanced Engineering, 1982).

18. Adapted from PR Lawrence and JW Lorsch, *Organization and environment: managing differentiation and integration* (Homewood, IL: Richard D. Irwin, 1967).

19. S Lee, 'Organisation in Korean companies: rules and procedures on managerial discretion and employee behaviour', *International Journal of Human Resource Management*, vol. 9, no. 3 (1998), pp. 47–93; I Hau Siu Chow, 'The impact of rules and regulations on work force flexibilities in Hong Kong', *International Journal of Human Resource Management*, vol. 9 (1998), pp. 494–505.

20. For a review see Richard N Osborn, James G Hunt and Lawrence R Jauch, op. cit.

21. P Ayling and L Thomsen-Moore, '[Tips from two] top achievers', *Management Today* (October 2005), pp. 28–30.

22. Amita Tandukar, 'Contrary banker'(interview with David Liddy), *Business Review Weekly* (26 May – 1 June 2005), p. 62.

23. Ralph Davis, *Fundamentals of top management* (New York: Harper & Row, 1951); David Van Fleet and Arthur Bedeian, 'A history of the span of management', *Academy of Management Review* (1977), pp. 356–72.

24. Jeffrey Liker, Paul Collins and Frank Hull, 'Flexibility and standardization: test of a contingency model of product design–manufacturing integration', *Journal of Product Innovation Management*, vol. 16, no. 3 (1999), pp. 248–67.

25. This section is based on Osborn, Hunt and Jauch, op. cit., pp. 273–303.

26. Daniel Twomey, Frederick Scherr and Walter Hunt, 'Configuration of a functional department: a study of contextual and structural variables', *Journal of Organizational Behavior*, vol. 9 (1988), pp. 61–75.

27. John Sullivan, 'Knocking down the silos', *Human Resources* (March 2003), pp. 16–18.

28. 'NAB looking to restore retail business', *The Sydney Morning Herald* (15 September 2005), www.smh.com.au/news/Business/.

29. Lauren Thomsen-Moore, 'Cultural change [Microsoft in Australia]', *Management Today* (August 2005), pp. 7–10.

30. Cameron Cooper, '[Making the outposts feel like] part of the team', *Management Today* (April 2004), pp. 30–2.

31. ibid.

32. Amita Tandukar, op. cit., p. 62.

33. Cameron Cooper, op. cit., pp. 30–2.

34. For a discussion of matrix structures see Stanley Davis, Paul Lawrence, Harvey Kolodny and Michael Beer, *Matrix* (Reading, MA: Addison-Wesley, 1977).

35. Open University, *The effective manager. Unit 9: organisations* (United Kingdom, 1984), p. 19.

36. See Henry Mintzberg, *Structure in fives: designing effective organizations* (Englewood Cliffs, NJ: Prentice Hall, 1983).

37. For a comprehensive review see W Richard Scott, *Organizations: rational, natural, and open systems*, 2nd ed. (Englewood Cliffs, NJ: Prentice Hall, 1987).

38. Max Weber, *The theory of social and economic organization*, AM Henderson and HT Parsons trans (New York: The Free Press, 1947).

39. Tony Boyd, 'Murray's crusade: banish bureaucracy', *The Weekend Australian Financial Review* (14–15 February 2004), p. 10.

40. Mintzberg, op. cit.

41. See Osborn et al., op. cit., for an extended discussion.

42. See Peter Clark and Ken Starkey, *Organization transitions and innovation-design* (London: Pinter Publications, 1988).

43. Osborn et. al., op. cit.

44. ibid.

45. Paul Kerin, 'The gold Wesfarmers', *Business Review Weekly* (1–7 September 2005), p. 32.

46. 'Kimberly-Clark to cut jobs', *The Sydney Morning Herald* (25 July 2005), www.smh.com.au/articles/2005/07/25.

47. Lesley Parker, 'Can you afford casual labour?', *HR Monthly* (February 2004), pp. 20–5.

48. J. Champy, *Reengineering management* (Glasgow: HarperCollins, 1995); Michael Hammer and Steven Stanton, *The reengineering revolution: a handbook* (New York: HarperCollins, 1995); R. Morgan and J. Smith, *Staffing the new workplace* (Chicago, IL: CCH, 1996).

49. Stephen Wisenthal, 'Star system', *Australian Financial Review Boss Magazine* (January 2005), pp. 35–7.

50. Lesley Parker, op. cit., pp. 20–5.

51. Glenda Korporaal, 'Why not jobs for the girls', *The Weekend Australian* (11–12 June 2005), p. 40.

52. Mintzberg, op. cit.

53. Charles Perrow, *Complex organizations: a critical essay*, 3rd ed. (New York: Random House, 1986).

54. Osborn et. al., op. cit.

55. See John Ettlie, 'Technology drives a marriage', *Journal of Commerce* (16 March 1990), p. 6.

56. 'Comvita: healing with honey in the UK', *The National Business Review* (14 July 2005), www.nbr.co.nz.

57. Elizabeth Knight, 'Solly Lew lines up a few more brands', *The Sydney Morning Herald* (27 July 2005), p. 20.

58. Mark Davis and Fiona Buffini, 'Sector "betrayed" by inquiry', *The Weekend Australian*, Financial review section (17–21 April 2003), p. 6.

59. Janine Perrett, 'Cartels don't have to be big', *The Sydney Morning Herald* (22 July 2005), p. 23.

60. Fred Luthans, *Organizational behavior*, 9th ed. (Boston: McGraw-Hill, 2002), pp. 117–19.

61. Derived from Zillur Rahman and SK Bhattachryya, 'Virtual organisation: a strategem', *Singapore Management Review*, vol. 24, no. 2 (2002), pp. 29–45; Christopher Barnatt, 'Virtual organisation in the small business sector: the case of Cavendish Management Resources', *International Small Business Journal*, vol. 15, no. 4 (1997), pp. 36–47.

62. ibid.

63. Jane Cherrington, 'Franchising success', *Management Today* (September 2005), pp. 28–30.

64. Stephen Bartholomeusz, 'The chasm between private and corporate morality', *The Sydney Morning Herald* (14 December 2005), p. 19.

65. Janine Perrett, 'Finding the people who'll look after us', *The Sydney Morning Herald* (1 July 2005), p. 25.

66. Exercise adapted from *Mother Jones Magazine* (June 1985).

CHAPTER 9
Organisational culture

Learning objectives
After studying this chapter,
you should be able to:

1. define the concept of organisational culture and explain its relationship to national culture

2. explain the levels of cultural analysis in organisations and the notions of subcultures and cultural diversity

3. explain the idea of observable aspects of organisational culture and describe stories, rites, rituals and symbols

4. explain how shared values are central in understanding organisational culture and how they relate to organisational action

5. explain how common assumptions comprise the deepest level of organisational culture and how they contribute towards that culture

6. discuss what organisational researchers investigate

7. discuss alternative perspectives on organisational culture and the functions of culture for members of an organisation

8. outline some hints for managing culture

9. summarise the link between ethics and organisational culture.

A survey of 9432 executives in 900 major Australian and New Zealand organisations showed that 90 per cent of executives prefer to create a constructive organisational culture where employees exhibit behaviours such as achievement, self-actualisation, encouragement and affiliation. However, when 132 543 employees at the same organisations were asked to describe the actual culture, the vast majority perceived that they were working in either aggressive or defensive organisational cultures. Predominant behaviours exhibited included avoiding blame, opposing ideas, being critical of others, competing rather than cooperating with coworkers, working long hours to complete tasks, refusing to 'rock the boat' and constantly attempting to make good impressions. In addition, this research showed that organisations with a more constructive culture achieved significantly better earnings/sales ratios and that these were more stable.[1]

So, what is a defensive organisational culture? The State Rail Authority (SRA) in New South Wales, Australia (refer to the part 2 case study on page 184) was found to have a defensive organisational culture. According to the special commission of inquiry into the Waterfall train accident, SRA employees operated within 'an environment of distrust and fear of punishment'[2] when reporting safety concerns. The commission's report outlined the SRA's policies, which placed a heavy emphasis on determining individual culpability for everyone concerned in an incident. This was found to produce avoidance in reporting safety breaches. If safety breaches were reported at all, train drivers were regularly sent for psychological testing, indicating the problem might lie with them rather than within a system. It was reported to the special commission of inquiry that if, on a rare occasion, a driver did raise a safety concern with a controller, the response was to 'stick to time schedules'. If the driver insisted on erring on the side of caution and, as a result, the journey time deviated from the time schedule, there was frequently an investigation into the delay. This indicated that the focus of SRA managers was on the timetable and not necessarily on safety of drivers and passengers.[3] Hence, the defensive nature of the organisational culture at SRA was expressed by staff avoiding blame and having opposing ideas to those of management, especially in the area of safety reporting.

Introduction

Most people have a basic notion of what culture is. The suggestion would probably be that culture studied by anthropologists and sociologists represents the belief systems, values and specific human behaviours that distinguish one society from another. The same can be said of organisations, because they are one significant subsystem within any society. Thus, it is important to have a firm understanding of the elements of organisational culture, what they represent and how some may be used.

Many managers believe that a sound organisational culture is the key to competitive advantage for leading corporations. There is evidence that some successful organisations sustain continued growth and development by 'implanting' a strong culture that is shared and acted on by all members of the organisation.[4] However, others express concerns about striving for a strong organisational culture, because of the difficulties associated with strongly integrated belief systems and the need for creative thinking, innovations and the ability to cope with change.[5] The old methods of command and control are being replaced by methods of participation and involvement, and managers are becoming facilitators, helpers, guides and coaches. These changes require adjustment of individual, group and overall organisational value systems and affect an organisation's culture.

This chapter considers the concept of organisational culture, how it manifests itself within organisations, and its functions. We look at the observable aspects and values of organisational cultures, and common assumptions about organisational culture, and discuss the importance of subcultures, countercultures and the diversity of organisational cultures. Finally, we discuss the link between organisational culture and ethical behaviour.

Organisational
culture and national
culture

Organisational culture is a system of shared beliefs and values that guides behaviour.

The concept of organisational culture

In chapter 1 we examined 'culture' as it applies internationally and ethnically to the various nations and peoples of the world; that is, we looked at national culture. Here, we are concerned with organisational culture. Organisational culture is defined as the system of shared beliefs and values that develops within an organisation and guides the behaviour of its members.[6] Later in this chapter we will add to this definition to make explicit the complexities associated with the notion of organisational culture and cultural research.

Just as no two individual personalities are necessarily the same, no two organisational cultures are identical. Most significantly, management scholars and consultants increasingly believe that cultural differences can have a major impact on the performance of organisations and the quality of work life experienced by their members.

Understanding the connections between organisational and national cultures

It is important to clarify the distinction between organisational culture and national culture. Only then is it possible to understand the connections between the two. The major reason that there is a strong connection is that organisational culture frequently derives from national culture. In other words, many of the shared beliefs and values that develop in organisations can be traced to commonly held assumptions in society.

However, despite being embedded in a national or host culture, organisations will still develop their own individual cultures. Every organisation in Australia, Japan, Ireland, France or Indonesia has a culture that is unique to that organisation. It is influenced by the national culture and frequently mirrors many aspects of it, but it also derives from the particular characteristics and experiences unique to the organisation.

It is important that we do not stereotype organisations in other national cultures as all sharing the same organisational culture; in the same way that not all organisations in our own country share the same organisational culture, neither will all organisations in other countries have similar values and beliefs. Indeed, globalisation makes the distinctions and the connections between national culture and organisational culture even more interesting, as large multinational corporations with an individual organisational culture, bearing some marks of the national culture that spawned them, will have to absorb and consider different national cultures that host their many branches across the world.

Levels of cultural analysis

 **2** Cultural levels, subcultures and diversity

Figure 9.1 graphically depicts three important levels of cultural analysis in organisations: observable culture, shared values and common assumptions. These may be envisioned as layers; the deeper we get, the more difficult it is to discover the phenomenon from the surface.

The first level relates to observable culture, or 'the way we do things around here'.[7] These are the methods that the group has developed and teaches to new members. The observable culture includes the unique stories, ceremonies and corporate rituals that make up the history of a successful work group or the organisation as a whole. It also includes symbols such as physical design, dress codes, logos and badges. Organisational cultural researchers look for patterns *for* behaviour or espoused cultural forms.

Observable culture is behavioural patterns that a group displays and teaches to new members.

The second level of analysis recognises that shared values (for example, 'Quality in this organisation is our cornerstone to success', or 'We value innovative ideas', or 'We will provide the best possible care') can play a critical part in linking people and can provide a powerful motivational mechanism for members of that culture. Organisational values underpin the patterns for behaviour in observable cultural analysis. Many consultants suggest that organisations should develop a 'dominant and coherent set of shared values'.[8] The term 'shared' in cultural analysis implies that the group is a whole. Every member may not agree with the shared values, but they have all been exposed to them and have often been told they are important. Hence, many managers believe that cultivating strong organisational culture will have a positive effect in gaining a competetive advantage.

Shared values are the set of coherent values held by members of the organisation and that link them together.

The corporate uniform is one example of a clearly visible organisational cultural form. Companies are now realising that every member of staff is a potential brand ambassador who can reflect the professional values of the organisation as well as encourage team spirit and productivity.[9] Office & General Cleaning Services, an Auckland-based company, uses a variety of corporate uniforms for its 200 staff, who all display the company logo on their clothing and wear a jade colour scheme to reflect the corporate colours.[10]

Corporate apparel can range from uniform casual wear with a company logo, to specifically designed outfits. Deane Apparel is the largest corporate uniform designer and manufacturer in New Zealand and its clients range from large corporations to small two-person businesses. The company has been in the industry for 70 years and, in the last ten years, the business has grown to over 300 staff, working exclusively on corporate apparel.[11]

A recent trend has been to use designer fashions as uniforms. For example, Korean Air has unvelied its new uniform designed by Italian designer Gianfranco Ferre. Similarly Air France's new 100-piece uniform ensemble was designed by Christian Lacroix. The uniform is very stylish and is meant to reflect the stereotypical French culture.[12]

(continued)

McDonald's in Brazil has just commissioned top Brazilian designer Alexandre Herchovitch to revamp its uniforms,[13] and in the United States the company considered Armani, Tommy Hilfiger, Jay-Z and P.Diddy as designers. McDonald's was hoping that the new designer uniforms would blend in with the 'I'm lovin' it' campaign and appeal to its predominantly young and fashion-conscious workers.[14]

Shared values, such as wearing a uniform with pride, have ties to the important values in society. Unique and shared values can provide a strong identity, enhance collective commitment, provide a stable social system and reduce the need for controls. However, we also need to acknowledge the individual differences within a collective and the value of individuality to the overall organisational culture.

Common assumptions are the collection of truths that organisational members share as a result of their joint experiences and that guide values and behaviours.

At the deepest level of cultural analysis are common assumptions, or the taken-for-granted truths that collections of organisational members share as a result of their joint experience. In most organisational cultures there are a series of common assumptions known to everyone in the organisation. For example, 'we are progressive' or 'we are better at…'. Such assumptions become reflected in the organisation's culture. These common assumptions may surface in an organisational crisis. 'We are different' is a common assumption that permeates the practices of some organisations.

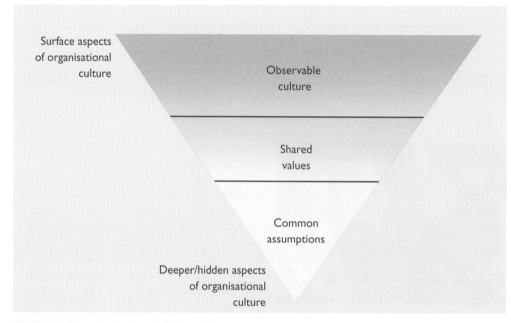

Surface aspects of organisational culture — Observable culture — Shared values — Common assumptions — Deeper/hidden aspects of organisational culture

FIGURE 9.1 • Three levels of analysis in studying organisational culture

Subcultures and countercultures

Subcultures are unique patterns of values and philosophies within a group that are not inconsistent with the dominant culture of the larger organisation or social system.

It is important to recognise distinct groups within a culture. Subcultures represent groups of individuals with a unique pattern of values and philosophy that are not necessarily inconsistent with the organisation's dominant values and philosophy.[15] Strong subcultures are often found in high-performance task forces, teams and special project groups in organisations. In addition, subculture formation has also been linked to educational background, professional identity and distinctive work paradigms.[16] The culture emerges to bind individuals working intensely together: organisational values and assumptions are shared, but actions can be influenced differently by distinct occupational tasks. For example, at a hospital the common assumption of 'doing things better' underpins the common value of providing the best possible care. However, the expressed 'care' is performed diffferently by different occupational groups, each with distinctive interpretations of what 'best care' means. For catering staff this may be providing a meal at the correct temperature, for surgeons this may mean removing the cause of illness, and for the occupational thearapist this may mean helping patients and their relatives to achieve an improved quality of life. Because 'providing the best care' means different things to different individuals and groups, we must expect that conflict arises between occupational subcultures and that this conflict is normal.

In contrast, *countercultures* have a pattern of values and a philosophy that reject the surrounding culture.[17]

Within an organisation, mergers and acquisitions may produce countercultures. Employers and managers of an acquired organisation may hold values and assumptions that are quite inconsistent with those of the acquiring organisation. This is often referred to as the 'clash of corporate cultures'.[18]

Fortunately, not all mergers and acquisitions cause cultural clashes, although this may be a matter of opinion among different subcultures within the new organisation. Understanding the importance of culture can also help a company to absorb or accommodate the cultures within the organisations that are acquired or merge, or to manage the complex interplays in alliances, company formations and employment relations.[19]

Subculture formation may be different according to where the organisation is located in the world. For example, in Japan subcultures may be formed on the basis of date of graduation from university. In Europe, subcultures may exist on the basis of language and in North America on locational similarities. Other subculture formations may be influenced by ethnicity, gender, generational differences, socioeconomic status, place within the organisation, political and religious beliefs, and so forth.

> **Countercultures** are the patterns of values and philosophies that outwardly reject those of the larger organisation or social system.

Imported subcultures and cultural diversity

Every large organisation imports potentially important subcultural groupings when it recruits employees from the larger society. The difficulty with importing groupings from the larger society lies in the relevance these subgroups have to the organisation as a whole. At one extreme, senior managers can merely accept these divisions and work within the confines of the larger culture. However, there are three primary difficulties with this approach. First, subordinated groups, such as members of a specific religion or ethnic group, are likely to form into a counterculture and to work more to change their status than to better the organisation. Second, the organisation may find it extremely difficult to cope with broader cultural changes. Third, organisations that accept and build on natural divisions from the larger culture may find it extremely difficult to develop sound international operations. For example, many Japanese organisations have had substantial difficulty adjusting to the equal treatment of women in their US and European operations.

A recent study found that people from different ethnic and gender groups filter and process information about organisational culture differently. This means that they may interpret the same cultural messages differently. Thus, attempts by management to manipulate cultural elements may need to take account of the fact that they will not be universally and consistently understood. Management efforts to homogenise culture will almost inevitably result in subunit variations in interpretation, and this is likely to contribute to the development of subcultures.[20]

Australia is a multicultural society, with 23 per cent of individuals born overseas, and 43 per cent of Australian-born people having at least one parent born overseas.[21] Therefore, it has become important for organisations to manage this multiculturalism effectively. Robin Ely and David Thomas[22] discuss three paradigms for an organisation's level of openness to multiculturalism.

First, the 'discrimination and fairness' paradigm looks at multiculturalism with respect to equal opportunity, fair treatment, recruitment, and compliance with legislation by ensuring certain numbers of staff from ethnically diverse backgrounds are employed. This paradigm insists that individuals assimilate into the existing organisational culture, and tends to lead to the development of potentially destructive subcultures (as ethnic differences are ignored or suppressed).

Second, the 'access and legitimacy' paradigm for an organisation's level of openess to multiculturalism emphasises gaining access to new and diverse markets by using cultural diversity within the organisation. This may create a feeling of exploitation in staff as they are the 'token representative of their culture'. In addition, this differentiation of individuals from the group can lead to subculture development as differences are highlighted.

Third, the 'learning and effectiveness' paradigm for an organisation's level of openess to multiculturalism incorporates elements of the other two paradigms. Additionally, this paradigm firmly connects diverse ethnicity to diverse approaches to work. According to Ely and Thomas, by creating openess, organisations will find that individuals from different national cultures do not feel devalued by assimilation into the existing organisational culture, nor will subcultures along ethnic lines be created.

Managing cultural diversity in organisations is a skill that contemporary managers must acquire. Many organisations run courses on multiculturalism to ensure knowledge and understanding of national and cultural differences. In addition, many organisations have courses for ethnically different groups and individuals, including English language for the workplace. For example, Medibank Private, Deakin University and the Construction, Forestry, Mining and Energy Union run English language courses that are funded by the Department of Education, Science and Training.[23]

Observable aspects of organisational culture

LEARNING OBJECTIVE 3 ✓

Observable aspects of organisational culture

Look again closely at figure 9.1. Because we are viewing organisational culture from a social constructivist point of view, we assume important aspects of an organisation's culture emerge from the collective experience of its members. These emergent aspects of the culture help make it unique and may well help provide a competitive advantage for the organisation. Some of these features may be directly observed in day-to-day practices. Others may have to be discovered; for example, by asking members to tell stories of important incidents in the history of the organisation. We often learn about the unique aspects of the organisational culture through descriptions of very specific events.[24] By observing organisational symbols and rituals, listening to stories and asking organisational members to interpret what is going on, you can begin to understand the organisation's culture.

Stories, rites, rituals and symbols

The **founding story** is the tale of the lessons learned and efforts of the founder of the organisation.

A **saga** is an embellished heroic account of the story of the founding of an organisation.

Stories indicate the state of an organisation's health. Stories offer evidence of unique qualities and characteristics that an organisation is proud of. A story may be as simple as telling a new employee about the rookie who stood up to the CEO of the company, and progressed quickly through the company because the CEO admired his or her courage (which may be something that is considered to be an important quality of the company in question).[25] Perhaps one of the most important stories concerns the founding of the organisation. The **founding story** often contains the lessons learned from the efforts of an embattled entrepreneur whose vision may still guide the firm. The story of the founding may be so embellished that it becomes a **saga**, a heroic account of accomplishments.[26] Sagas are important because they are used to tell new members the real mission of the organisation, how the organisation operates and how individuals can fit into the company. Rarely is the founding story totally accurate, and it often glosses over some of the more negative outcomes along the way.

If you have job experience, you may well have heard stories concerning the following questions: How will the boss react to a mistake? Can someone move from the bottom to the top of the company? What will get me dismissed? These are common story topics in many organisations.[27] Often the stories will provide valuable hidden information about who is 'more equal' than others, whether jobs are secure and how things are really controlled. The stories suggest how organisational members view the world and live together.

Among the most obvious aspects of organisational culture are rites and rituals. Rites are standardised and recurring activities that are used at special times to influence the behaviours and understanding of organisational members. Rituals are systems of rites. Rituals serve to establish boundaries and relationships between the stakeholders of an organisation through the repetition of events, such as staff meetings or how long people take for lunch. In Japan, for example, it is common for workers and managers to start their work days together with group exercises and singing the 'company song'. Separately, the exercises and song are rites. Collectively, they form part of a ritual.

Rites are standardised and recurring activities used at special times to influence the behaviours and understanding of organisational members.

Rituals are systems of rites.

Rituals and rites may be unique to particular groups within the organisation. Subcultures often arise from the type of technology deployed by the unit, the specific function being performed and the specific collection of specialists in the unit. The boundaries of the subculture may well be maintained by a unique language. Often the language of a subculture, as well as its rituals and rites, emerges from the group as a form of jargon. In some cases, the special language starts to move outside the organisation and enter the larger society. For example, the information technology (IT) industry is renowned for its use of technical language and, slowly, terms such as software, download, floppy, desktop, browser, hyperlink, icon, multimedia and online have become part of mainstream language. On the other hand, many of the IT industry's plentiful jargon terms have yet to find wide acceptance. One such term, used by personnel manning an IT help desk to point to a *user* problem, is 'PEBKAC': Problem Exists Between Keyboard And Chair.

Language is used to convey the meaning of an organisational culture, with particular words and phrases either being unique to an organisation or having a particular meaning in the organisation. It has been suggested that many conversations in organisations are making cultural statements when they convey what the company expects and wants to occur;[28] for example, language can convey meaning about daily routines and habits of employees. It can also be a valuable measure in highlighting possible subcultural differences within an organisation.

Of course, no discussion of corporate culture would be complete without mentioning the symbols found in organisations. A cultural symbol is any object, act or event that serves to transmit cultural meaning. Symbols can include the architecture of a building, the layout of offices and space assigned to employees, the décor of the offices, and the general impression that is communicated to visitors by way of company name and size of the establishment. Although many such symbols are quite visible, their importance and meaning may not be. Other symbols include badges, prizes, organisational branding and stationery.

A cultural symbol is any object, act or event that serves to transmit cultural meaning.

The physical layout of the office is an observable symbol of culture. For example, in an organisation that values knowledge sharing, an open plan may express that value and encourage collegiality and camaraderie. However, a lack of privacy in the workplace can also affect people adversely and have a subliminal effect on what makes them secure and happy. So a culture may express its respect for employees in such an open-plan office if it makes an effort to provide at least acoustical and visual privacy. In a world in which many businesses are failing, physical space can express culture though the permanency and conservatism of its furnishings and decor. The light and fun orientation of many of the fast-growing and fast-falling IT companies has led to a recent trend against this style of work environment. Through their physical work space, organisations are trying to send messages about what they are and what they represent.[29] Many companies spend a lot of money on their office designs to achieve an 'environmental branding', as the following examples illustrate.

OB in action

Staff and managers from all parts and levels of the ING Bank were involved in the design of their Sydney work space. Management's aim in Sydney was to create an open and friendly workplace that reflected the ING Group's commitment to its employees (specifically through its stated principles of teamwork, treating everybody with respect and without discrimination, and employee consultation and participation). They used bold graphics around strong words (for example 'radiate' and 'respect') with natural lighting and a vibrant colour scheme to provide a warm and inviting environment. Open-plan design is conducive to knowledge sharing and better communication flows, as is illustrated by the transparent design of the new and innovative 'spaceship' ING Group headquarters building in Amsterdam. The previous Sydney work space had functional work stations with little energy. Staff members are now proud to go to work, and to bring external associates and clients into their work spaces. A survey run since the changes indicated that there was a positive improvement in morale, with 85 per cent of staff now looking forward to coming to work each day.[30]

HSBC's Discovery Centre at its head office in Sydney aims for a 'hip and groovy, non-corporate workplace'. Colours, furniture and fittings are intended to create a bright and cheerful space for training, learning and knowledge sharing. The HR mission statement of 'attract, retain and motivate' is also promoted in bold cut-out lettering adhered to the floating ceiling.[31]

International SPOTLIGHT

Mary Kay Cosmetics in China

Since its creation in 1963, Mary Kay Cosmetics has become one of the world's largest direct sellers of skin care and colour cosmetics. The company employs 1.3 million beauty consultants in 30 countries around the world.[32] The organisation's mission is to empower women to use their own personal initiative. This is supported by the corporate motto: 'God is first, family second, career third'. Organisational cultural activities at Mary Kay Cosmetics includes regular group hugs, living by the Golden Rule, pink cell phones and pink Cadillacs for successful saleswomen.[33]

In 1995 Mary Kay entered China, a country renowned for being conservative, reserved, collectivist, dedicated and atheist. Due to a government ban on direct selling, the first five months of operation achieved no sales. Despite these initial difficulties, Mary Kay Cosmetics has managed to survive and even thrive in China, by including group hugs and other cultural activities practised in the organisation in Western countries. However, when entering the Chinese market, the corporate motto required modification as 'God is first' was unacceptable. Instead, the Chinese companies altered the motto to 'Principal first, family second, career third'. In an effort to convince its Chinese employees to place themselves and family before their careers, Mary Kay Cosmetics conduct regular educational sessions about the importance of ensuring a balance between family, health and work life as a way to increase sales. The empowerment of women in China remains a challenge as women have a strong sense of loyalty to males, including subordination, which is an integral part of Chinese national culture.[34]

Cultural rules and roles

Organisational culture often specifies when various types of actions are appropriate and where individual members stand in the social system. These cultural rules and roles are part of the normative controls of the organisation and emerge from its daily routines.[35] For instance, the timing, presentation and methods of communicating authoritative directives are often quite specific to each organisation. In one organisation meetings may be forums for dialogue and discussion, where managers set agendas and then let others offer new ideas, critically examine alternatives and fully participate. In another organisation the 'rules' may be quite different. The manager goes into the meeting with fixed expectations. Any new ideas, critical examinations and the like are expected to be worked out in private before the meeting takes place. The meeting is a forum for letting others know what is being done and for passing out instructions on what to do in the future. Cultural rules and roles can become deeply ingrained in organisational behaviour, as they influence 'the way things are done around here', but sometimes they need to be changed.

Dress to express

Decades ago, dress codes were fairly straight-forward; employees wore either a uniform or business attire. These days, an organisation's dress code is one way of defining who and what the organisation stands for. If an organisation is trying to promote a sharp, sleek, professional image then it is likely that individuals will need to dress in a smart manner. On the other hand, if the organisation is trying to foster a relaxed atmosphere of creativity and individualism then it is likely that the dress code will be far more relaxed and casual. Dress codes are a cultural form. For  example, at White Lady Funerals, an Australian all-female funeral parlour, all staff that meet the public are dressed in white suits and carry a white rose to symbolise purity.[36]

The problem may be in defining 'professional dress' and 'casual dress', and whether the same rules apply for men and women. An unfortunate consequence of the new workplace phenomenon, where different organisations require different attire, is that industrial tribunals are increasingly being asked to adjudicate matters that relate to appropriate attire in the workplace. For example, a male console operator at a petrol station was found to have been unfairly dismissed for refusing to take out an earring he was wearing, even though women were allowed to wear such adornments.[37] In another example, a woman at Star City Casino, a 5-star facility in Sydney, Australia, was found to have been unfairly dismissed for refusing to take out a tongue stud which was against the luxury casino's dress policy.[38]

Any workplace dress codes should be reasonable and applicable to men and women and must not breach any antidiscrimination legislation. Further, undesirable items must be clearly stated. For example, if midriff tops or thongs are unacceptable the organisation needs to specifically state this in their policy, along with the reasoning for unacceptability.

Dress codes are best determined in a collaborative effort between managers and their staff, as was the case with the Optus dress code. At the Optus call centre, customer service staff chose a flexible dress code that allows for dress shorts, cargo pants, sneakers and traditional business attire. The list of unacceptable items includes strapless, backless and midriff tops, tracksuit pants, thongs and any clothing embellished with offensive language. In addition, Optus encourages an organisation-wide 'casual Friday'.[39]

(continued)

Shared values and their importance

LEARNING OBJECTIVE 4

Values and organisational culture

Consider figure 9.1 again. In order to describe more fully the culture of an organisation, it is necessary to go deeper than the observable aspects. To many researchers and managers, shared values lie at the heart of organisational culture. Shared values:

- help turn routine activities into valuable, important actions
- tie the corporation to the important values of society
- may provide a very distinctive source of competitive advantage.

OB in action

John Weeks, the author of *Unpopular culture: the ritual of complaint in a British bank*, found that the NatWest Bank in the United Kingdom had a culture of complaining about the culture. This constant complaining about the corporate culture, by employees and managers alike, formed an impenetrable bond between individuals, irrespective of position or status. In addition, John Weeks commented that this deeply entrenched shared value is not too dissimilar to the stereotypical British national pastime of complaining. To prevent a takeover, NatWest leadership attempted to change the culture, but they failed, in part because the employees openly did not support attempts for change. The takeover of NatWest by Royal Bank of Scotland was a success. However, Weeks found that one year after the takeover, old NatWest employees were still complaining.[40]

Linking actions and values

Individuals collectively learn behaviours and concepts to help them deal with problems. In organisations, what works for one person is often taught to new members as the correct way to think and feel. Important values are then attributed to these solutions to everyday problems. By linking values and actions, the organisation taps into some of the strongest and deepest realms of the individual. The tasks a person performs are not only given meaning but value; what one does is not only workable but correct, right and important.

Some successful organisations share some common cultural characteristics. Figure 9.2 provides a list suggested by two well-known US management consultants, Terrence Deal and Allan Kennedy.[41] As you can see from the figure, organisations with 'strong cultures' possess a broadly and deeply shared value system. Increasingly, organisations are adopting values statements that express their commitment to such areas as customer service, product and service quality, creativity and innovation, and social responsibility.

However, a strong culture can be a double-edged sword. Unique, shared values can:

- provide a strong corporate identity
- enhance collective commitment
- provide a stable social system
- reduce the need for formal and bureaucratic controls.

Conversely, a strong culture and value system can reinforce a view of the organisation and its environment. If dramatic changes are needed, it may be very difficult to change the organisation.

A widely shared philosophy. This philosophy is not an abstract notion of the future but a real understanding of what the organisation stands for, often embodied in slogans.

A concern for individuals. This often places individual concerns over rules, policies, procedures and adherence to job duties.

A recognition of heroes. Heroes are individuals whose actions illustrate the shared philosophy and concerns of the company.

A belief in ritual and ceremony. Management understands that rituals and ceremonies are real and important to members and to building a common identity.

A well-understood sense of informal rules and expectations. Employees understand what is expected of them.

A belief that what employees do is important to others. Networking in order to share information and ideas is encouraged.

FIGURE 9.2 • Elements of strong corporate cultures

Common assumptions and organisational culture

OBJECTIVE 5 LEARNING

Common assumptions contributing to culture

At the deepest level of organisational culture (see figure 9.1), there are common understandings known to almost everyone in the corporation: 'we are different', 'we are better at...' and 'we have unrecognised talents'. These shared truths, or common assumptions, often lie dormant until actions violate them.

Common assumptions and management philosophy

If culture is considered a variable that can be changed to affect an organisation's competitive advantage, managers need to recognise what can and what can not be changed in the organisation's culture. The first step is to recognise the group of managers as a subculture in itself. Senior managers often share common assumptions, such as 'we are good stewards', 'we are competent managers' or 'we are practical innovators'. In many organisations, broadly shared common assumptions of senior management go even further. The organisation may have a well-developed management philosophy.

A **management philosophy** links key goal-related issues with key collaboration issues and comes up with a series of general ways in which the organisation will manage its affairs. A well-developed management philosophy is important because it establishes generally understood boundaries for all members of the organisation; it provides a consistent way of approaching novel situations; and it helps hold individuals together by assuring them of a known path towards success. In other words, a well-developed management philosophy is important because it links strategy with how the organisation operates and thus helps an organisation adapt to its environment. For example, Cisco Systems's strategy of growth, profitability and customer service is linked to empowering employees to generate best ideas quickly; hiring the best people, with ideas and intellectual assets that drive success; and disseminating information to compete in an 'ideas world'.

A **management philosophy** links key goal-related issues with key collaboration issues to come up with general ways by which the organisation will manage its affairs.

Elements of the management philosophy may be formally documented in a corporate plan, a statement of business philosophy or a series of goals. Yet it is the unstated but well-understood fundamentals these written documents signify that form the heart of a well-developed management philosophy.

What do organisational culture researchers investigate?

Organisational cultural researchers are interested in researching cultural manifestations while attempting to gather meaning about the patterns that link these manifestations. Studying manifestations includes researching the working environment of a culture; for example, the décor of the office, hierarchal structures and money earned by employees, as well as relationships between organisational members. Joanne Martin identifies four types of cultural manifestations, including cultural forms, formal practices, informal practices and content themes.

Cultural forms are manifestations of organisational culture conveyed to employees. Tools used to convey observable culture include symbols, rituals, stories and language. For example, the 'employee of the month' award or the story of how the company was founded help employees to identify with the organisation's culture as these rituals and stories are all part of 'the way things are done here'. Symbols, such as branding (for example, the golden arches of McDonald's) have meaning. What does your company or university brand symbol on the top of any letterhead convey to you? This is a cultural form!

Formal practices are written down and are, on the surface, easily controllable by management. These can include structure, task and technology, policies and procedures, and financial controls. The formal practices are all expressions of an organisational culture. Therefore, formal practices need to be observed when studying organisational culture.

Informal practices evolve through interaction, are not written down and take the form of *social rules*. Informal practices can include the time used for tea breaks throughout the day and arriving at work a few minutes late or leaving work a few minutes earlier at the end of the day. Such informal practices serve to highlight possible contradictions within the formal practices that are written down and not always adhered to.

Content themes are considered common threads of concern that underlie *interpretations of several organisational cultural manifestations*. Top companies may try to impress certain images on stakeholders and the general public; for example, by promoting respect of the environment in all business pursuits. Companies that include such values in the mission statement or on company web sites are attempting to create positive associations with their brands. Often, the way that managers behave in organisations, such as showing a friendly yet competitive nature to the outside world, will communicate to observers the content themes (or the images the organisation is attempting to create in an audience's mind) of a company being studied.[42]

The majority of cultural studies within organisations take place via information obtained from the views of those members in management. However, it is now widely recognised that organisational cultural researchers must also extract information about how the organisation works by providing members of the organisation who do not hold managerial positions with a tool through which to express their opinions. This ensures the organisational cultural research is conducted from multi-perspectives (see the section on alternative perspectives of culture later in this chapter) and is more complete.

Quantitatively, cultural forms, formal practices and content themes can be measured by way of asking questions about the organisation. This might take the form of an assessment of the general feelings and beliefs participants hold about the organisation, their sense of affiliation with the organisation, and so on.[43] Content themes can be examined by questioning organisational/supervisory characteristics, and by ranking the importance of organisational goals, reputation, engagement with community and service quality. Formal practices are studied by analysing policies and procedures and how these are put into operation. Informal practices are slightly more difficult to measure via questionnaire and are best revealed through interview and observation. Quantitative methods can include survey questionnaires.

Qualitatively, manifestations of organisational culture can be observed by participant observers, who have discussions with organisational members via formal and informal interviews and focus groups. The researcher examines patterns of behaviour, looks at consistencies and inconsistencies in behaviours, and is particularly interested in patterns of behaviours that are more covert. The interviews can include questions about organisational reputation before and after employment. What has changed? This is important as inconsistencies in what is reported to members outside an organisation and what members inside an organisation actually experience may reveal important information about the covert behaviours. Furthermore, the way an employee portrays the organisation to outsiders may differ depending on the position or the occupational group that the organisational member belongs to. This may reveal patterns of inconsistencies between occupational groups, or subcultures. Interview questions can also examine 'accountability' in terms of who sets standards formally and what happens informally. This may highlight the importance of informal practices for the day-to-day functioning of an organisation. Observations can reveal a great deal about the organisation's reliance on formal and informal practices, and organisational content themes. Interpretations help to make sense of interactions between organisational actors and occupational groups, and ultimately the relations between organisational culture and overall organisational performance.

Many organisational cultural researchers use a mix of quantitative and qualitative methods to obtain a complete picture of 'what is going on' in the organisation.

Alternative perspectives on organisational culture

LEARNING OBJECTIVE 7 ✓ Alternative perspectives on organisational culture

Many studies of organisational culture adopt only one perspective of culture: the integrationist perspective, investigating organisational culture in terms of harmony and a supposed organisation-wide consensus.[44] These studies tend either to focus on managers and professionals and/or to present managerial perspectives as representative of organisational culture as a whole. But if a study claims to represent the culture of an entire organisation, then employees of diverse levels and functions should also be studied. This gives us an opportunity to include more than one perspective and to be inclusive of views of members throughout the organisation, rather than presuming that an occupational group, a profession or a functional level represents all organisational voices. Although the integration perspective is most commonly researched and published, there are additional perspectives: the differentiation and ambiguity perspectives.

Integration perspective

Many outlines of organisational culture suggest that it is a single phenomenon in an organisation, or that there is a dominating culture with some subcultures. Dunphy[45] suggests that the way we understand the pattern formed by the elements of organisational culture (the pattern of values, common assumptions, and visible elements or artefacts) can vary. Some who study organisational culture take an integration perspective (or functional perspective or managerial perspective), seeing it as a unified phenomenon in which all the cultural elements are consistent with one another. This perspective is characterised by an organisational state where organisational members, as directed by their leaders, jointly agree on 'the way we do things around here'. This organisational cohesiveness is considered to be a variable that managers can use to adjust organisational culture when change is required. This perspective is characterised by assimilation through unity and harmony among organisational members. They reinforce, integrate and bind people together and core values pervade and characterise the organisation as a whole. Socialisation helps to maintain this consistency.

The integration perspective views organisational culture as a system of shared meanings, unity and harmony.

Differentiation perspective

Some researchers believe that a distinction can be made between corporate culture and organisational culture. *Corporate* culture is devised by management and sold to — or imposed upon — the rest of the organisation. Rituals, stories and values are offered to organisational members as part of seducing them into membership of and identification with the organisation, and of gaining their commitment and behavioural compliance. *Organisational* culture is that which grows or emerges from within the organisation and emphasises members as culture makers, perhaps resisting the dominant culture. Organisational culture takes into account the beliefs and values of organisational members. The overall organisational culture is shared and unique as a result of the patterns of interaction between and within groups. *Organisational* culture can be viewed from additional perspectives to the integration perspective: the differentiation perspective and the ambiguity/fragmentation perspective.

In contrast to the integration perspective, which is seen from a managerial functional point of view, the differentiation perspective views organisational culture as a system of shared beliefs in different groups (often differentiated by location, division, gender, ethnicity and so on). These group values are sometimes in tune with the dominant culture, and sometimes not. Some researchers believe the differentiation perspective is similar to integration, but at lower organisational levels. This perspective is not only characterised by harmony, but also by diversity and inconsistency.

Organisational anthropologists and social researchers believe organisational cultures, even if they represent a system of shared meaning, are not uniform cultures, but rather have sets of subcultures, typically defined by department designations and geographical separation. Rather than finding harmony and unity, these researchers see diversity and inconsistency. Subcultures are not necessarily abnormal or deviant; they are natural outcomes of the different groups, departments and occupational cohorts within the organisation. Such subcultures can enhance the dominant subculture: they accept its core values but bring in other non-conflicting values or countercultural values that directly challenge the values of the dominant subculture. The tension between subcultures shapes the organisational culture itself. The formation of subcultures is sometimes called 'multiculturalism' in organisations.

Individuals develop differences in perception and opinion because of social bondings. Some of these relationships can span organisations. For example, plumbers in a large engineering factory can develop a shared relationship through their membership of a plumbing staff association.

In contrast to the integration perspective, the differentiation perspective sees organisations as characterised not just by harmony and unity, but also by diversity and inconsistency. It accepts the possibility and value of internal conflict and suggests that this normally occurs due to the processes of differentiation and specialisation common in modern organisations.

The **differentiation perspective** views an organisation's culture as a compilation of diverse and inconsistent beliefs that are shared at group level.

Ambiguity/fragmentation perspective

The ambiguity or **fragmentation perspective** does not see clear-cut cultural groupings within organisations as the normal state; rather it sees a normal state in organisations as one of ambiguity, because meanings differ between individuals and within individuals over time. The normal state for meanings, values and behavioural norms is diverse because each individual independently assesses his or her environment. If consensus is observed then it is only momentary and such groupings soon dissolve. The ambiguity lies in the formation of associations between identities that are in a constant state of instability, lacking any form or pattern.[46]

The **fragmentation perspective** views organisational culture as lacking any form of pattern as a result of differing meanings between individuals and within individuals over time.

An ambiguity/fragmentation perspective suggests that there are no clearly identified patterns of culture. Instead there is an ever-changing flow of consensus, divergent views and confusion. This view rejects the idea of 'shared meanings' in favour of the idea that people attribute meanings to phenomena in organisations. They interpret them in random, ambiguous ways, and sometimes the interpretations are shared or partially shared. This perspective further brings into question whether the attribution of meaning in organisations really falls neatly into categories, as suggested by typical organisational culture theory.

The fragmentation perspective sees attempts at cultural change along normative lines as having no effect, because the impact of any change will be absorbed. You cannot change the culture, because change is continual.

However, current followers of alternative perspectives on organisational culture acknowledge that these patterns of culture can be found at any given time within the organisation.[47]

Hence, understanding multiple perspectives of culture goes beyond instilling shared values and beliefs in organisational members, as proposed by integration; it is having an in-depth insight into patterns of overt and covert behaviour that link patterns of integration, differentiation and ambiguity perspectives. Each of these perspectives can operate at any one time or at the same time.[48] Thus, by adding alternative perspectives, organisational culture can be more comprehensively defined as 'the socially constructed patterns of behaviours that link expressions of organisational integration, group differentiation and individual ambiguities together. These patterns of behaviour reflect individual, group and organisational values and beliefs.'[49]

COUNTER**POINT**

Harmony and unity in culture — reality or myth?

Current research into the commercialisation of innovative products and/or services confirms the notion of subcultural differences between occupational groupings. In Australia, Commonwealth Research Centres (CRCs) are organisations with a unique fingerprint, distinguished by the mix of personalities, skills and resources that are drawn together for a particular project, for a fixed period. CRCs are made up of scientists, engineers and commercial managers who are on secondment from universities and other public sector research organisations, such as the Commonwealth Scientific and Industrial Research Organisation (CSIRO), or are contracted for the specific purpose of bringing the product to market. Awareness of the impermanence of employee involvement, and likely return to their previous employer, further increase occupational segregation and, consequently, may jeopardise harmony and unity within the CRC.

Interviews with a manager, scientist and engineer confirm subcultural differences between occupational groups engaged in commercialisation. The scientific group was viewed as very distinct, with comments about scientific culture and practice occurring frequently. Inferred values, such as the high value placed on academic qualifications and publication record, were consistent with existing literature regarding scientific subcultures. The identification of a *scientific* subculture supports the differentiation perspective of organisational culture theory.

In addition, researchers found that occupational subcultures have the potential to act as barriers to, or facilitators of, the outcomes of commercialisation efforts. The emphasis placed upon the reliability, predictability and viability of a product by the engineer and manager are at odds with the scientist's attraction to creativity and novelty. This suggests that different norms affect the value placed on scientific exploration, compared to the production of an on-time end product, according to occupational membership. The research suggests that occupational subcultures, broadly based on membership of scientific or commercial groups, can be made explicit. Further research in this context is being conducted.[50]

(continued)

People tend to cluster in groups with others who share their own value systems. This helps with cooperation and achieving social balance and harmony. Although commitment to the company vision is important, we should accept that within organisations groups, and individuals, can have their own, differing value systems.

Questions

1. What are some of the problems encountered when management tries to maintain a single, integrated culture to control and manage employees towards high-performing outcomes? Explain your answers.

2. Do you think it is possible for employees to work successfully in an organisation whose values do not align with their own personal values? What criteria would you use to decide this?

The functions of organisational culture for its members

Our discussion pointed to the importance of acknowledging multiple perspectives of organisational culture. However, it is undeniable that organisational cultures have an element of functionality. In other words, organisational culture may be influenced by top management in order to achieve a competitive advantage. For example, ideally in your first managerial job, one of the old hands on the job will sit down with you and explain exactly what is to be done, and how and why it is to be done. Experienced individuals know what to do and are aware of all the informal rules surrounding their roles in the organisation.

Through their collective experience, members of an organisation resolve two types of extremely important survival issues. The first is the question of external adaptation: what precisely needs to be accomplished and how can it be done? The second survival issue is the question of internal integration: how do members solve the daily problems associated with living and working together?

External adaptation

External adaptation is the process of reaching goals and dealing with outsiders.

External adaptation involves reaching goals and dealing with outsiders. These issues involve the tasks to be accomplished, the methods used to achieve the goals, and the methods of coping with success and failure.

Through their shared experiences, members develop common views that help guide their day-to-day activities. Organisational members need to know the real mission of the organisation, not just the pronouncements to key constituencies such as shareholders. Members will naturally develop an understanding of how they contribute to the mission via interaction. This view may emphasise the importance of human resources, or it may emphasise the role of employees as cogs in a machine or a cost to be reduced.

Closely related to the organisation's mission and its view of staff contribution are the questions of responsibility, goals and methods. These need to be translated into specific contributions, identifying clearly what the organisation is endeavouring to achieve in its external environment. Organisations often present numerous goals; for example, in relation to strategy or corporate social responsibility and establishing procedures and methods, including the selection of the 'right people' to achieve their aims. They will also define jobs and procedures that reflect their approaches to external adaptation.

The final issues in external adaptation deal with two important, but often neglected, aspects of coping with external reality. First, individuals need to develop acceptable ways of telling outsiders just how good they really are. For example, at 3M, the company most famous for its Post-it Notes, employees talk about the quality of their products and the many new and useful products they have brought to the market. Second, employees must know collectively when to admit defeat. The answer is easy for new projects: for example, at the beginning of the development process, 3M members establish 'drop' points at which to abandon the development effort and redirect it.

In summary, external adaptation involves answering important instrumental or goal-related questions concerning coping with reality, such as: What is the real mission? How do we contribute? What are our goals? How do we reach our goals? What external forces are important? How do we measure results? What do we do if specific targets are not met? How do we tell others how good we are? When do we abandon and move on to something else?

Internal integration

While the questions of external adaptation help a collection of individuals cope with a changing environment, the organisational culture also provides answers to the problems of internal integration. Internal integration deals with the creation of a collective identity and with finding ways of matching methods of working and living together.

Through dialogue and interaction, organisation members begin to characterise their world. They may see it as malleable or fixed, filled with opportunity or threatening. For instance, real progress towards innovation can begin when group members collectively believe that they can change important parts of the world around them and that what appears to be a threat is actually an opportunity for change.

Three important aspects of working together are:
1. deciding who is a member and who is not
2. developing an informal understanding of acceptable and unacceptable behaviour
3. separating friends from enemies.

To work together effectively, individuals need to decide collectively how to allocate power, status and authority, and to establish a shared understanding of who will get rewards and sanctions for specific types of actions.

Managers often fail to recognise these important aspects of internal integration. For example, a manager may fail to explain the basis for a promotion and to show why this reward, the status associated with it and the power given to the newly promoted individual are consistent with commonly shared beliefs. For example, at AstraZenica, a pharmaceutical company, the human resource managers surveyed employees' values in regard to affiliation with the company. They found that important items to the employees include: learning and development opportunities, competitive rewards, an energising work environment and a successful business. So the HR department works in accord with building a capable, talented team with the potential for growth; building credibility by getting the fundamentals right; aligning the HR strategy with the business strategy; and understanding, communicating and measuring the return on investment (ROI) for HR initiatives. HR is committed to constantly reviewing and changing in response to business needs.[51] Although these don't seem to be unusual features they are applied in the organisation in a way that reveals real commitment to the values and principles that underpin them.

We have seen how organisational culture helps members by providing answers to important questions of external adaptation and internal integration. However, there is often an important difference in the answers to these questions between executives towards the top of the organisation and members at the bottom. This may be because senior executives may owe their primary allegiance to their position in the organisation. They may identify with the organisation as a whole and may equate organisational and individual success; and they may want all others in the organisation to believe much the same. Naturally, they expect to be very handsomely rewarded. On the other hand, employees may see themselves as part of a larger, more varied and complex network of relationships. The job may be just an instrumental mechanism, such as a means of getting the financial rewards necessary to live. The distance between the values and beliefs of employees and those of their managers, expressed in the formation of distinct subcultures, may in itself be a cultural construct of an organisation.

Internal integration is the creation of a collective identity and the means of matching methods of working and living together.

Some organisations encourage their middle and senior managers to 'stay in touch with their floor workers' by taking on tasks usually done by employees. This is in an effort to facilitate integration between managers and their employees. However, in practice, employees express a level of discomfort working closely with their managers on their own routine tasks. For example, research found that employees were reluctant to share a task or convey criticism directly to the manager when needed. In addition, managers felt isolated in performing their tasks and expressed discomfort changing roles. The research concluded that in this organisation efforts to facilitate boundary crossing were not very succesful and may even reinforce occupational boundaries between managers and their employees.[52]

This finding signifies that, when attempting to manage organisational culture, different perspectives need to be considered. Approaching organisational culture from a multicultural perspective will be more complex, but that is the true nature of organisational cultural research. Nevertheless, we cannot deny that most research accounts for the integration perspective, giving direction and prescriptions on how to manage an organisation's culture. The next section deals with how a manager might want to manage, reinforce and change culture.

Managing culture LEARNING OBJECTIVE 8

Managing organisational culture: building, reinforcing and changing culture

Managers and researchers agree that strong cultures and shared values and beliefs characterise an organisational setting in which people are committed to one another and to an overriding sense of mission. This commitment can be a source of competitive advantage over such an organisation's rivals. Other organisations, however, resemble a collection of separate units and people who don't seem to have much in common. The organisation may also have a strong culture that does not meet the needs of a changing environment. It is important that managers are able to analyse the nature of an organisation's culture if they seek to manage it. If the culture cannot meet the needs of a changing environment, its very strength becomes a liability; any change program that seeks to develop a different set of shared values and assumptions will constantly be opposed from within the organisation. An organisation may be a mix of subcultures and countercultures. Here, rivalries and value differences may create harmful conflicts.

OB in action

Many organisations attempt to make fundamental changes, adopting new ideas and technology. For example, since the mid-1990s many organisations have tried to adopt the methods of customer relationship marketing (CRM) to help improve revenue through better links with customers. Many have not succeeded, and it seems that failure to deal with deeper cultural issues is one of the reasons. Siebel Systems is a major provider of CRM knowledge and methods. Tom Siebel, who owns 71 per cent of Siebel Systems, claims virtually 100 per cent successful implementation, with customers reporting a return on investment (ROI) in less than 12 months. He blames the failure to fix 'deep problems' in the way the organisation relates to customers for a lack of comparable success among other providers. CRM is not a quick fix; rather, it is part of a large-scale business transformation, according to Gartner's Massachusetts-based vice-president Michael Maez (Gartner is a leading world research company). CRM can not be introduced without adapting a company's culture to accept it. Peter Lalor, a management services executive at AMP in Australia, says the 'major issues are the cultural changes necessary to actually bring about the benefits through the better use of the technology'.[53]

For managers, especially top managers, managing organisational culture is a pressing issue. Many managers believe culture should be considered to be as critical as structure and strategy in establishing the organisational foundations of high performance. For example, Air New Zealand has put several thousand staff members through a leadership cultural change program. According to Charles Goode, one of the company's directors, 'the culture of an organisation and the way people interrelate is the next area of us making a quantum leap in our performance'.[54] Good managers are able to reinforce and support an existing strong culture; good managers are also able to help build resilient cultures in situations where they are absent.[55]

Managers can help foster a culture that provides answers to important questions concerning external adaptation and internal integration. Recent work on the links between corporate culture and financial performance reaffirms the importance of an emphasis on helping employees to adjust to the environment. It also suggests that this emphasis alone is not sufficient. Nor is an emphasis solely on shareholders or customers associated with long-term economic performance. Instead, managers must work to emphasise all three issues simultaneously. Managers are also challenged to consider whether it is possible to manage culture in the same ways for both core and peripheral workforces. Peripheral workers often spend too little time in the company to be socialised into the culture, and core workers may resent peripheral workers experiencing the same positive treatments that they receive. Sometimes managers adopt a two-tier approach to managing culture to deal with these differences.[56] Sometimes, however, managers attempt to revitalise an organisation by dictating major changes rather than by building on shared values. While things may change a bit on the surface, a deeper look often shows whole departments resisting change and many key people who do not want to learn new ways. Such responses may indicate that the responsible managers are insensitive to the effects of their proposed changes on shared values. They fail to ask if the changes are:

• contrary to important values held by participants within the organisation
• a challenge to historically important organisation-wide assumptions
• inconsistent with important common assumptions derived from the national culture outside the organisation.

All too often, executives are unable to realise that they too can be captured by the broadly held common assumptions within their organisations (see 'The effective manager 9.1').[57] Top management may, for example, take a decision to introduce autonomous working teams to improve productivity and innovation, yet not face the reality that the organisational culture invests all authority in the executive management team. In such circumstances, the introduction of autonomous working teams will be disastrous, as decision-making responsibility will not be devolved to the team. Culture influences managerial behaviour as much as that of everyone else in the organisation and astute managers who seek to manage culture will seek to understand it first.

OB in action

John Leonard reported that in 1989 authority holders at the Australian Defence Force Academy (ADFA) routinely abused their authority. The dominance of legal authority that was expected in such an organisation was often replaced by gratuitous or illegal use of power. By 1998, Leonard reported, there remained authoritarian methods but these were allied with a concern for the welfare of subordinates. There was no dominating disparity between civilian and academy values; female cadets seemed to have achieved greater equality; and discrimination and harassment were not noted as before. The relationship between senior and junior cadets was based on a model of leadership and mutual respect, rather than one of fear and intimidation. Leonard indicated that the source of these changes was a deliberate and comprehensive program of change that was carefully sequenced over time. Those responsible for implementing the program were trained, and 'backsliders' who were found to work against the new approach were stripped of their power and privileges. The structure was also drastically altered to avoid power acquisition through control of substantial aspects of the culture.[58]

(continued)

Despite Leonard's report on apparent cultural change between 1989 and 1998, there is evidence that the ADF (Australian Defence Force) continues to foster a culture of illegal power. The last ten years have seen a series of rolling inquiries (six being major parliamentary ones). A 20-month Senate inquiry found that there was still widespread abuse in the ADF, and it had a defective military justice system that was incapable of performing adequately. This enquiry recommended that parts of the military justice system be handed over to the civilian authorities.[59]

Over 150 submissions were made to the inquiry about 'recent events including suicides, deaths through accident, major illicit drug use, serious abuses of power in training schools and cadet units, flawed prosecutions and failed, poor investigations' and included complaints from all ranks.[60]

Air Marshal Angus Houston, the newly appointed Chief of the Australian Defence Force, has promised to do whatever it takes to eradicate bastardisation and to repair the military justice system. However, it is unclear whether Houston will be able to succeed where his predecessors have failed. There is a looming shortage of labour within the defence force, and unless the dominance of illegal authority changes, it is unlikely that the defence force can attract new members to its ranks.[61]

THE **Effective**Manager 9.1

Using organisational culture to help the organisation compete

As more organisations are moving into volatile industries using advanced technology and confronting international competitors, managers may need to help their corporate culture adjust. Here are some pitfalls to avoid and some factors to emphasise when entering and competing in highly volatile, high-technology markets such as computing and biotechnology.

1. When entering the market early, do not allow employees to become disenchanted when facing initial technical barriers and skill development challenges.
2. When entering slowly, do not give competitors too big a lead; keep stressing to all employees the necessity of building technical and market skills.
3. When adding new products to an existing market, take the opportunity to reassess approaches to decision making and management for both new products and old ones; challenge old routines.
4. When adjusting to new markets with new products, avoid using 'conventional wisdom' and stress the development of new ways to compete.
5. When entering the market, foster the Internet culture by embracing all forms of open communication in all possible media.

Ethics and organisational culture

We have already talked quite a lot about ethics in this book and we'll continue to do so. For now, the issue is framed in a question: 'Do organisations vary in the "ethical climates" they establish for their members?' The answer to this question is yes. To many researchers it is clear that the ethical tone or climate of an organisation is set at the top; that is, what top managers do, and the culture they establish and reinforce, makes a big difference to the way lower-level personnel act and to the way the organisation as a whole acts when faced with ethical dilemmas. What is needed in today's complicated times is for more organisations to step forward and operate with strong, positive and ethical cultures.[62] However, instilling ethical behaviour is not just a manager's responsibility; the behaviour of employees can resonate throughout the organisation to set an ethical culture organisation-wide. The ethical climate of an organisation is the shared set of understandings about what is correct behaviour and how ethical issues will be handled. This climate sets the tone for decision making at all levels and in all circumstances.

The **ethical climate** is the shared set of understandings in an organisation about what is correct behaviour and how ethical issues will be handled.

In some organisations today, the ethical climate supports doing the right thing, though often in other organisations — perhaps too many — concerns for operating efficiency may outweigh social considerations when they face difficult decisions. Along with other aspects of organisational culture, therefore, the ethical climate will be an important influence on the behaviour of individual members and the organisation as a whole. When the ethical climate is clear and positive, people know what is expected of them when the inevitable ethical dilemmas occur. They can then act confidently, knowing they will be supported by top management and the entire organisation. The following 'Ethical perspective' illustrates some aspects of the perception of morality, and also the ethics of management invading personal space.

Censorship at work

ETHICAL
Perspective

Certain activities of employees can involve legal liability to an organisation. For example, viewing pornographic images via a work computer could be classed as sexual harassment in certain situations.[63] As a result many organisations can and do monitor their employees' computer usage. Detailed records are kept of what person is on what specific computer accessing web sites and what information they are downloading. In addition, duplicate copies of all emails sent and received are kept, despite many users deleting them. So, to what extent can employers dictate what their employees do?

Open and transparent policies need to be implemented so that all employees know and understand what is expected of them in relation to their organisation's computer usage policies. The policy should be very clear about what is and what is not acceptable; stating that computer usage must be work-related is arguably not explicit enough. The policy must also be adhered to so there is no ambiguity about the cultural expectations of the organisation.[64]

At its heart, the issue is one of consistency. For example, an employee at Bankwest was sacked for sending an email that contained an adult joke. However, when the case went to court it was found that he was discriminated against because there had been another worker at the same organisation who had only been demoted for accessing, storing and emailing soft pornographic images.[65] There have been similar cases at Centrelink,[66] Holden,[67] Toyota[68] and the Department of Family and Community Services.[69]

(continued)

According to a recent survey, employees most likely to view pornographic images on work computers were construction bosses, advertising executives and IT employees, and yet these occupational groups have not been represented in the court cases that refer to Internet or email pornography.[70]

How often do you receive adult material on your computer? What is your opinion on the ethical implications of receiving and sending adult jokes via email. Do you believe this should be monitored and for what reason?

In summary, this chapter has introduced you to the elements of organisational culture, organisational subcultures and how an organisation's culture is formed and researched. It also dealt with how culture is often seen as a function to improve competitive advantage and how it may be managed. In addition, this chapter emphasised the complex nature of an organisation's culture, as organisations are socially constructed by the people in them.

Summary

Organisational culture and national culture

The concept of organisational culture is as important to the management of an organisation as are strategy and structure. As the system of shared beliefs and values that guide and direct the behaviour of members, culture can have a strong influence on day-to-day organisational behaviour and performance. There are connections between organisational culture and national culture, but each organisational culture is unique despite being embedded in a national culture.

Cultural levels, subcultures and diversity

Culture can be analysed through its three components: observable culture — the behaviours that can be seen within an organisation; shared values held by members of an organisation; and, at the deepest level, common assumptions or truths developed and shared by members through their joint experiences in the organisation. Organisations can also experience the strains of dealing with subcultures among various work units and subsystems, as well as possible countercultures, which can be the source of potentially harmful conflicts. There are also challenges for managing different national groupings within the organisation.

Observable aspects of organisational culture

Observable aspects of organisational culture include the stories, rites, rituals and symbols that are shared by organisational members. These are powerful aspects that can be important in helping to establish and maintain a certain culture. Shared meanings and understandings help everyone in a strong culture know how to act and to expect others to act in various circumstances. They provide a common orientation to decision making and action that can facilitate performance. Cultural rules and roles similarly define expectations for behaviour within an organisation and lend consistency to the behaviour of its members.

Shared values and their importance

Values and organisational culture are highly intertwined. Clearly articulated organisational values — such as quality, customer service and innovation — help guide and direct action. When in place and understood, clear and positive values can create a competitive advantage for organisations. They can be a unifying force that brings efforts to bear on highly desirable outcomes.

Common assumptions contributing to culture

Common assumptions and organisational culture are also highly interrelated. Common assumptions are the taken-for-granted truths that are shared by collections of organisational members. Some organisations express these truths in a management philosophy that links key goal-related issues with key collaboration issues into a series of general ways the organisation will manage its affairs. In many cases, the management philosophy is supported by a series of corporate myths.

Organisational culture research

Organsational culture researchers investigate cultural forms, formal and informal practices and content themes. These manifestations can be measured quantitatively and/or qualitatively.

Alternative perspectives on organisational culture

Considering multiple perspectives of culture gives a more complete picture of what is going on in the organisation. A combined view of the integration, differentiation and fragmentation perspective is needed. A well-developed culture can assist in responding to internal and external problems. Through common shared behaviours, values and assumptions, organisational members will clearly understand the organisation's mission, strategies and goals in relation to the external environment. Culture also helps to achieve internal integration — the ability of members to work together effectively on organisational activities. A third function of culture is to help bring management and employees much closer together in their respective goals.

Managing culture

Managing organisational culture is considered a top management task in organisations. A strong culture can be a competitive advantage, and managers can try to create such cultures where none previously existed and/or change existing cultures to become more productive ones. In order to manage organisational culture effectively, the foundations must be established in the management of culture's observable aspects and in the belief systems that are sponsored from the top. Managers need to understand the culture in order to manage it.

Ethics and organisational culture

Ethics and organisational culture must be considered in today's demanding times. The ethical climate of an organisation is the shared set of understandings about what is correct behaviour and how ethical issues will be handled. When properly established, a positive and clear ethical climate can help all organisation members make good choices when faced with ethical dilemmas. It can give them the confidence to act with the understanding that what they are doing is considered correct and will be supported by the organisation.

Chapter 9 study guide

 OB | Key terms

common assumptions, *p. 312*
countercultures, *p. 313*
cultural symbol, *p. 315*
differentiation perspective, *p. 322*
ethical climate, *p. 329*
external adaptation, *p. 324*
founding story, *p. 314*

fragmentation perspective, *p. 322*
integration perspective, *p. 321*
internal integration, *p. 325*
management philosophy, *p. 319*
observable culture, *p. 311*
organisational culture, *p. 310*
rites, *p. 315*

rituals, *p. 315*
saga, *p. 314*
shared values, *p. 311*
subcultures, *p. 312*

OB | Review questions

1. What is organisational culture and what are the levels of analysing culture in organisations?

2. What functions do organisational cultures serve, and how do subcultures and cultural diversity help in this?

3. What are some alternative perspectives of culture? Why is it important to view organisational culture from more than one perspective?

4. What are some ethical issues when managing organisational culture?

OB | Application questions

1. You are a manager who wishes to encourage employees to make suggestions and contribute to new ideas. What aspects of culture could be manipulated to try to encourage this?

2. What observable elements of organisational culture can you identify from your own organisation or an organisation with which you are familiar?

3. Give examples of both formal and informal processes that occur in your organisation or at your university. What can you say about the non-observable culture in your organisation?

4. In a small organisation with 50 employees, senior management has espoused values of equality, respect and high performance for employees and customers. When the latest performance figures for the company are released, management's response is to call the staff to a general meeting and tell them they all have to 'lift their game' if they expect to retain their jobs. What comments can you make on the cultural features of the organisation?

5. Your company has just merged with another that provides a similar service. What issues will emerge in relation to the merging of two organisational cultures and what can managers do to deal with them?

6. Examine the following values and visible elements of culture. What underlying assumptions do you think might exist 'beneath' these aspects of culture?
   - Organisation A values new ideas and selects its highest-performing employees for special monthly creative workshops. Organisation B values new ideas and promises a prize of $4000 to any employee whose idea contributes clearly to increasing profits. Organisation C values new ideas and encourages employees, as owners of shares in the company, to contribute ideas in their day-to-day work.
   - Organisations D, E and F express the importance of high-performing employees. Organisation D conducts annual performance reviews between supervisor and worker, and if workers perform according to requirements they are given an incremental increase in wages. Organisation E conducts

six-monthly reviews and more regular 'chats' between supervisor and worker. If the workers are not performing according to requirements, they are asked to account for their low performance. In Organisation F no reviews are conducted but workers and supervisors work closely together. If employees are demonstrating outstanding performance, their work is commended and publicised in the company newsletter. They also receive a bonus.

- In Organisations G and H an employee makes a significant mistake. In Organisation G the manager speaks to the employee and tries to analyse the problem and find ways to overcome it. In Organisation H the manager discusses the employee's mistake at a team meeting in front of all members of the group and expresses disappointment at his poor behaviour. The incident is also reported to senior management and recorded on the employee's file.

Research questions

1. Search the newspapers and business magazines for news of an impending business merger or takeover. Find out what you can about both organisations' existing cultures.
   (a) From what you have learned about the organisations, what differences do you think there are between the cultures of the two organisations?
   (b) How do you think these differences in culture will affect the merger process, and what issues will management have to deal with to develop a new combined culture?

2. Search the Internet for two different organisations in the same industry — for example, two insurance companies, two major retail chains or two universities. It is especially valuable if you understand the type of activity the organisation carries out and/or if you have had some experience with at least one of them as a customer. Set yourself a purpose for your inquiry to give it some focus. For example, look at the web site and ask questions such as:
   (a) As one of your customers, will I expect customer-focused service?
   (b) Will your employees be helpful?
   (c) Will it be easy for me to do business with your organisation?

   (d) Will you have up-to-date technological interfaces for customers?

Try to assess the answers to these questions at three levels, in the following order (remember you are looking for information about underlying assumptions, shared values and observable symbols of the culture):
- by looking at the images
- by looking at the structure and layout of the web site
- by looking at the information available to answer these questions.

The order is important since you will be looking to see how compatible different aspects of the culture are and how they may vary or conflict with each other.

An example of conflict might be an organisation's claim that 'we put our customers first', while its web site is very difficult for a customer to navigate. An example of compatibility might be if an organisation using the same slogan has a web site that is extremely easy to navigate, with clear, simple, easy-to-understand navigation tools.

Evaluate both web sites and compare the two in the context of your focus question. What observations can you make from this study of the two organisations about the nature of their particular organisational cultures? Does the exercise give you any insights into how easy or difficult it might be to investigate organisational culture?

Running project

Complete the following activities for your chosen organisation.
1. Outline what you consider the key parts of your organisation's observable and non-observable culture (shared values and common assumptions) and give examples.

2. What does your organisation do to manage the organisational culture?
3. To what extent do management's preferred culture and the observable culture correlate? Do any countercultures exist within the organisation?

Assessing your organisation's culture[71]

Choose an organisation you are familiar with.

This 15-question survey has been developed to serve as a starting point for the analysis of organisational culture.

Answer each true/false question according to what is true most of the time. And answer based on how your organisation actually acts — not how you would like it to be.

True/false questions

1. I know how my projects contribute to the success or failure of our organisation.
2. Management here makes lots of announcements to employees.
3. I have colleagues from a wide variety of professional and personal backgrounds.
4. In this organisation, people who are not ready to be promoted after a certain length of time at their level are generally encouraged to leave.
5. Departments or teams compete with each other for our organisation's resources.
6. When people are not getting along here, it is a long time before we directly address the issue.
7. When it is time for me to learn a new skill, training is readily available at no cost to me.
8. When the boss tells us to 'jump!', we ask 'how high?'
9. It takes a long time for this organisation to address customer concerns.
10. Many employees expect to work at this organisation for their whole careers.
11. Senior management says the door is always open — and they mean it.
12. It is fun to work here.
13. We have three or fewer layers of management.
14. We have performance reviews less often than once a year.
15. Compensation and benefits are relatively low here.

Count your 'True' responses in each third of the quiz (questions 1–5, 6–10, 11–15). The section in which you have answered 'True' the most times corresponds to the culture type your organisation most closely matches. If you have the same number of 'True' responses in more than one section, your culture matches this combination of types. Here is a list of primary advantages and potential pitfalls of each one.

For questions 1–5

If you had the most 'True' responses in this set of questions, your company has a *Deliberative/traditional culture*.

Advantages
- This culture tends to be intellectual and thoughtful.
- People in this type of organisation often consider issues carefully prior to making a change.
- The organisation likely has many formal systems, yet flexibly forms and reforms teams in accordance with immediate client needs.
- This cultural type regularly hires groups of new employees, generating a valuable flow of diverse talent with fresh perspectives.
- Senior management communicates frequently to employees.

Pitfalls
- Although plenty of communication usually flows from the top of this organisational type, management often does not indicate interest in feedback from all levels. Beyond making announcements from management, ask for regular feedback so you don't miss critical information and/or valuable innovations from your staff.
- Be careful that your organisation does not discuss change for so long that you miss important opportunities to change for the better.
- Be aware of the cultural implications of fostering competition within a company. Internal competition may create resentment that drives costly turnover.

For questions 6–10

If you had the most 'True' responses in this set of questions, your company has an *Established/stable culture*.

Advantages
- This organisation has most likely been around for a long time and/or is a family business. These organisations tend to have solid institutional memories, so they are not likely to waste resources by repeatedly 'reinventing the wheel'.
- This type of company has processes in place to address most situations.
- Organisations of this type tend to cultivate employees by encouraging development through mentoring programs and/or formal training opportunities.
- This culture type is known for compensating its people relatively well.

Pitfalls

- Typically this type of organisation struggles to handle conflict well, often becoming either conflict avoidant or 'command and control'. If your organisation tends to be conflict avoidant, it may be time to address those problems that are out of hand, or that have been out of hand in the past.
- 'Command and control' style leadership may yield feelings of disconnectedness among employees. Consider assessing employee morale immediately.
- Overall, this culture type tends to be wary of turnover, so take a careful look at your organisation and consider whether it is holding on to people who might best be let go.
- While established systems can be a positive sign of organisational health, make sure your processes are focused toward addressing customer needs in a timely matter. If your processes impede rapid resolution of customer problems, rework them right away.

For questions 11–15

If you had the most 'True' responses in this set of questions, your company has an *Urgent/seat of the pants culture.*

Advantages

- This culture type features a positive work environment, with tight bonds among employees.
- It is likely that an aspect of your organisation's mission includes responding to crisis. People care deeply about the organisation's mission and work hard to achieve the organisation's goals.
- Employees who frequently hurry to beat the clock can create great results in a short time, provided that quality is a strong value in your organisation.
- These organisations tend to have a flat structure that fosters communication and collaboration among employees and speeds the decision-making process.

Pitfalls

- Caution: minimum rewards (both tangible and intangible) and minimum feedback are common to this culture type. Rewards and recognition are important not only to generate loyalty but also to foster collaboration.
- The constant rush to get things done quickly can lead to burnout and increase the ever-present danger of losing talent.
- Although this type of culture generally features frequent upward communication and grassroots change, top-down communication tends to be inadequate. Beyond staying accessible, take time to share important messages and expectations with your entire staff to keep them motivated and moving in the right direction.
- Making decisions under intense time pressure may lead to a reduction in the quality of your products or services.

Is your type different from what you thought it would be? If so, you might have an unrealistic perception of your organisation's character and values.

Group activity

OB

Your university culture

Preparation

Select a university or college, or a department within this institution, to analyse its culture. Answer the following questions.

1. How many stories do you know about it?
2. How many sagas do you know about it?
3. How many myths do you know about it?
4. Identify as many rites and rituals that are used as you can.
5. Identify as many cultural symbols that are used as you can.
6. Identify as many shared meanings that are used as you can.
7. Identify as many rules and roles that are used as you can.
8. Identify as many shared values that are used as you can. Do these values give the organisation or department a competitive advantage?

Objectives

1. To understand the elements of organisational culture
2. To understand how to analyse and manage organisational culture

Total time: 15–45 minutes

Procedure

1. The lecturer or tutor calls on students to give their answers to the eight preparation questions.
2. The more information you have for each question, the stronger is the culture at your university/college or its department. Based on your answers, do you believe the organisation or its unit has a strong or a weak culture?
3. How could the organisational culture be managed to make it stronger?
4. What is the down side of having a strong culture?

Case study: J&J's credo

The Johnson & Johnson organisation comprises 200 companies that operate in 57 countries and employ more than 115 600 individuals worldwide. There is a strong culture that forces employees to view themselves as part of a 'family of companies' that all operate under one credo. 'Our Credo', as it is known, is a one-page document that guides all actions across the family of companies in relation to fulfilling the responsibilities to customers, employees, the community and shareholders.[72]

Our Credo

We believe our first responsibility is to the doctors, nurses and patients,
to mothers and fathers and all others who use our products and services.
In meeting their needs everything we do must be of high quality.
We must constantly strive to reduce our costs
in order to maintain reasonable prices.
Customers' orders must be serviced promptly and accurately.
Our suppliers and distributors must have an opportunity
to make a fair profit.

We are responsible to our employees,
the men and women who work with us throughout the world.
Everyone must be considered as an individual.
We must respect their dignity and recognize their merit.
They must have a sense of security in their jobs.
Compensation must be fair and adequate,
and working conditions clean, orderly and safe.
We must be mindful of ways to help our employees fulfill
their family responsibilities.
Employees must feel free to make suggestions and complaints.
There must be equal opportunity for employment, development
and advancement for those qualified.
We must provide competent management,
and their actions must be just and ethical.

We are responsible to the communities in which we live and work
and to the world community as well.
We must be good citizens — support good works and charities
and bear our fair share of taxes.
We must encourage civic improvements and better health and education.
We must maintain in good order
the property we are privileged to use,
protecting the environment and natural resources.

Our final responsibility is to our stockholders.
Business must make a sound profit.
We must experiment with new ideas.
Research must be carried on, innovative programs developed
and mistakes paid for.
New equipment must be purchased, new facilities provided
and new products launched.
Reserves must be created to provide for adverse times.
When we operate according to these principles,
the stockholders should realize a fair return.

Johnson & Johnson

'Our Credo' reflects the values that all employees share; it enables them to work together for the good of all stakeholders. Although the credo has been updated since it was first written in 1943 to reflect more modern concerns such as work–life balance and the environment, the document still has the same spirit it always had.

Work is organised by unique, small cross-functional integrated teams that rely heavily on each other. Employees are encouraged to grow professionally and personally. Professional development includes opportunities to move to a variety of business units and operating segments, and personal development opportunities include tuition reimbursement, leadership courses and free lunchtime seminars on a variety of non-work-related topics. Employee rewards are based on performance and include salary, annual team and individual bonuses, stock, stock options and award programs. Benefits include medical, dental, life and disability insurance, fitness centres, employee assistance programs, child-care and elder-care assistance, estate planning, a lifeworks program, education and counselling.

Johnson & Johnson encourages individuals to belong to voluntary groups that are organised around a shared interest or characterstic such as race, gender and sexual orientation. The aim is to offer an open forum for exchanging ideas, airing concerns and lobbying for change.

As a result of the credo, the Johnson & Johnson family has won a multitude of annual awards from many of the countries in which it operates. Awards acknowledge having an outstanding reputation, being an admired company, being one of the best organisations to work for, being one of the best organisations for diversity (hispanic, African-American, women and for people with disabilities), encouraging work–life balance and having one of the world's biggest brands.[73]

Questions

1. What observations can you make about employees' values and common assumptions? Is there any link between them?

2. Read 'Our Credo', view the Johnson & Johnson web site on www.jnj.com and view the video 'Our Credo — Worldwide'. Do you think the credo is part of the actual culture at Johnson & Johnson or is it simply another example of corporate rhetoric? Give reasons and examples to back up your answer.

3. If you were a manager in this organisation, what would you do to sustain the current culture?

Suggested reading

Mats Alversson, *Understanding organisational culture* (London: Sage, 2002).

Andrew D Brown, *Organisational culture* (London: Pitman, 1998).

Kim S Cameron and Robert E Quinn, *Diagnosing and changing organisational culture: based on the competing values framework* (Reading, MA: Addison-Wesley, 1999).

David Cray and Geoffrey R Mallory, *Making Sense of managing culture* (London: International Thomson Business Press, 1998).

Terrence D Deal and Allen A Kennedy, *Corporate cultures* (Reading, MA: Addison-Wesley, 1982).

G Hofstede, 'Identifying organisational subcultures: an empirical approach', *Journal of Management Studies*, vol. 35, no. 1 (1998), pp. 1–12.

J Kotter, 'Culture and coalitions', *Executive Excellence*, Australian ed., vol. 15, no. 3 (1998), p. 14.

J Kotter and J Heskett, *Corporate culture and performance* (New York: The Free Press, 1992).

Joanne Martin, *Cultures in organisations* (New York: Oxford University Press, 1992).

Martin Parker, *Organisational culture and identity* (London: Sage, 2000).

M Schultz, *On studying organisational cultures* (Berlin: Walter de Gruyter, 1995).

Steve Simpson, *Cracking the corporate culture code: unwritten ground rules* (Perth: Narnia House, 2001).

W Van Buskrirk and D McGrath, 'Organisational cultures as holding environments: a psychodynamic look at organisational symbolism', *Human Relations*, vol. 52, no. 6 (1999), pp. 805–32.

Elisabeth Wilson, 'Inclusion, exclusion and ambiguity: the role of organisational culture', *Personnel Review*, vol. 29, no. 3 (2000), pp. 274–92.

1. Human Synergistics Corporate web site, http:// www.human-synergistics.com.au/content/articles/papers/ zb-campaign-michael-gourley-apr-04/organisational- culture.asp (viewed 10 July 2005).

2. Special Commission of Inquiry into the Waterfall Rail Accident, 'Final report', ch. 17, p. 219, http:// www.waterfallinquiry.com.au/finalreport/Chapter17.htm (viewed 10 July 2005).

3. Special Commission of Inquiry into the Waterfall Rail Accident, 'Final report', ch. 17, http:// www.waterfallinquiry.com.au/finalreport/Chapter17.htm (viewed 10 July 2005).

4. D Den Hartog and RM Verburg, 'High performance work systems, organisational culture and firm effectiveness', *Human Resource Management Journal*, vol. 14, no. 1 (London, 2004), pp. 55–78.

5. ibid.

6. E Schein, 'Organisational culture', *American Psychologist*, vol. 45, no. 2 (1990), pp. 109–19.

7. T Deal and A Kennedy, *Corporate culture* (Reading, MA: Addison-Wesley, 1982).

8. T Peters and R Waterman, *In search of excellence* (New York: Harper & Row, 1982).

9. P Moore, 'A uniform approach to business', *NZ Business*, vol. 18, no. 1 (2004), pp. 33–5.

10. ibid.

11. Deane Apparel corporate web site, http://www.deane- apparel.co.nz/default.asp (viewed 2 October 2005).

12. B De Lollis, 'Airline hopes new fashions make financial statement: carriers turn to popular designers for uniforms', *USA Today* (7 July 2005), p. B1.

13. M Kepp, 'McDonald's is his kind of place: Herchovitch to redo uniform', *WWD*, vol. 190, no. 42 (2005), p. 12.

14. D Campbell, '"Styling" it?', *Knight Ridder Tribune Business News* (10 August 2005), p. 1.

15. G Hofstede and MH Bond, 'The Confucius connection: from cultural roots to economic growth', *Organisational Dynamics*, vol. 16, no. 4, pp. 4–21.

16. Janna Anneke Fitzgerald and Gregory Teal, 'Health reform and occupational sub-cultures: the changing roles of professional identities', *Contemporary Nurse*, vol. 16, nos 1–2 (2004), pp. 9–19; Janna Anneke Fitzgerald and Alfons Van Marrewijk, 'Redefining organisational control in changing organisations: Two cases of social construction of professional identity in organisations — engineering and medicine', paper presented to 6th international conference on organisational discourse: Arte*facts*, Arche*types* and Archi*texts*, Amsterdam, 28–30 July 2004); Kate Hayes and Janna Anneke Fitzgerald, 'Preliminary findings of an investigation into interactions between commercial and scientific occupational cultures', paper presented to the 6th international CINet conference, Brighton, United Kingdom, 4–7 September 2005.

17. R Jones, B Lasky, H Russell-Gale and M le Fevre, 'Leadership and the development of dominant and countercultures: a narcissistic perspective', *Leadership & Organisation Development Journal*, vol. 25, no. 1/2 (2004), p. 216.

18. J Martin and C Siehl, 'Organisation culture and counterculture', *Organisational Dynamics*, vol. 12 (1983), pp. 52–64.

19. Gina McColl, 'Toll's takeover touch', *Business Review Weekly* (12–18 December 2002), pp. 40–1; Nicholas Way and Jacqui Walker, 'Railway gamble', *Business Review Weekly* (17–23 December 2002), pp. 60–3.

20. Marilyn M Helms and Rick Stern, 'Exploring the factors that influence employees' perceptions of their organisation's culture', *Journal of Management in Medicine*, vol. 15, issue 6 (Hong Kong, 2001), pp. 415–25.

21. Australian Bureau of Statistics, 'Yearbook Australia, population 21/1/2005', http://www.abs.gov.au/ausstats/ abs@.nsf/94713ad445ff1425ca25682000192af2/ 2d7a4bf79f53d825ca256f7200832f90!OpenDocument (viewed 5 July 2005).

22. R Ely and D Thomas, 'Cultural diversity at work: the effects of diversity perspectives on group processes and outcomes', *Administrative and Science Quarterly*, vol. 46, no. 2 (Ithaca, 2001), pp. 229–74.

23. Workplace Diversity Corporate web site, http:// diversityatwork.com.au/recognition_programs/awards/ 2004/ winners.cfm?category=3&showWinner=1,2,3,4,5,6#category 3 (viewed 17 July 2005); Department of Education Science and Training Corporate web site, http://www.dest.gov.au/ NR/rdonlyres/FE5A5102-ED93-4DF7-A0BB- A07F974BABDC/5152/BW_CFMEU.pdf (viewed 17 July 2005).

24. E Schein, 'Organisational culture', *American Psychologist*, vol. 45, no. 2 (1990), pp. 109–19; E Schein, *Organisational culture and leadership* (San Francisco: Jossey-Bass, 1985), pp. 52–7.

25. Joanne Martin, *Cultures in organisations* (New York: Oxford University Press, 1992); Joanne Martin, *Organisational culture: mapping the terrain* (Thousand Oaks, CA: Sage, 2002).

26. C Geertz, *The interpretation of culture* (New York: Basic Books, 1973).

27. JM Byer and HM Trice, 'How an organisation's rites reveal its culture', *Organisational Dynamics* (Spring 1987), pp. 27–41.

28. Kevin McManus, 'The challenge of changing culture', *Industrial Engineer*, vol. 35, no. 1 (2003), pp. 18–19.

29. David Meagher, 'Deep space', *Australian Financial Review BOSS Magazine* (May 2002), pp. 14–15.

30. Amanda Houlihan, 'Essence of beING', *HR Monthly* (June 2002), pp. 36–7; ING Bank web site, www.ing.com; ING Group, *Annual report* 2002 (2002), pp. 8–17; ING Group, *ING in society report* (2001) — both reports online at www.ing.com/ing/contentm.nsf/home_en!readform.

31. Sue Wilde, 'Colour central', *HR Monthly* (April 2002), pp. 42–3.

32. Mary Kay corporate web site, www.marykay.com (viewed 17 July 2005).

33. M Booe, 'Sales force at Mary Kay China embraces the American way', *Workforce Management*, vol. 84, no. 4 (April 2005), pp. 24–5.

34. ibid.

35. Deanne N Den Hartog and Robert M Verburg, 'High performance work systems, organisational culture and firm effectiveness', *Human Resource Management Journal*, vol. 14, no. 1 (London, 2004), pp. 55–79.

36. White Lady Funerals corporate web site, www.whiteladyfunerals.com.au (viewed 7 July 2005).

37. *Bree v Lupevo Pty Ltd* [2003] NSWADT 47 (11 March 2003).

38. *Fairburn v Star City Pty Ltd*, PR931032 (6 May 2003).

39. F Cameron, 'Dressing business down', *HR Manager*, http://www.hrmanager.com.au/index.cfm?wUPub_Id=38&wUIss_Id=148&wUArt_Id=320 (viewed 6 July 2005).

40. J Weeks, *Unpopular culture: the ritual of complaint in a British bank* (Chicago: University of Chicago Press, 2004).

41. Developed from Terrence Deal and Allan Kennedy, *Corporate cultures: the rites and rituals of corporate life* (Reading, MA: Addison-Wesley, 1982).

42. Joanne Martin, *Organisational culture: mapping the terrain* (Thousand Oaks, CA: Sage, 2002), pp. 87, 88.

43. P Degeling, J Kennedy, M Hill, M Carnegie and J Holt, *Professional sub-cultures and hospital reform* (Sydney: Centre for hospital management and information systems research, University of New South Wales, 1998).

44. Joanne Martin, *Organisational culture: mapping the terrain* (Thousand Oaks, CA: Sage, 2002).

45. Richard W Dunphy, 'Organisational culture', *Organisational behaviour: an organisational analysis perspective* (Sydney: Addison-Wesley, 1992), pp. 163–91.

46. Joanne Martin, op. cit.

47. Janna Anneke Fitzgerald, Managing health reform: a mixed method study into the construction and changing of professional identities, unpublished PhD thesis (2002); Joanne Martin, op. cit.; J Martin, *Cultures in organisations: three perspectives* (New York: Oxford University Press, 1992); D Meyerson and J Martin, 'Cultural change: an integration of three different views', *Journal of Management Studies*, vol. 24, no. 6 (1987), pp. 623–47.

48. Joanne Martin, op. cit.

49. Janna Anneke Fitzgerald, Managing health reform: a mixed method study into the construction and changing of professional identities, unpublished PhD thesis (2002).

50. Kate Hayes and Janna Anneke Fitzgerald, 'Preliminary findings of an investigation into interactions between commercial and scientific occupational cultures', paper presented to the 6th international CINet conference, Brighton, United Kingdom, 4–7 September 2005.

51. Craig Donaldson, 'AstraZenica HR: a study in strategic people management', *Human Resources* (November 2002), pp. 12–14.

52. Janna Anneke Fitzgerald and Bob Hinings, 'Changing professional identities: adjusting professional delineations in health', paper presented at the International Federation of Scholarly Associations of Management (IFSAM) VIIth world congress, Goteburg, Sweden, 2004.

53. Brad Howarth, 'The CRM backlash', *Business Review Weekly* (8–14 August 2002), pp. 66–9.

54. Jan McCallum, 'The company champion', *Business Review Weekly* (21–27 February 2002), pp. 46–7.

55. E Ogbonna, LC Harris, 'Managing organisational culture: compliance or genuine change?', *British Journal of Management*, vol. 9, no. 4 (December 1998), pp. 273–88.

56. Emmanuel Ogbonna and Lloyd C Harris, 'Managing organisational culture: insights from the hospitality industry', *Human Resource Management Journal*, vol. 12, no. 1 (2002), pp. 33–53.

57. AC Cooper and CG Smith, 'How established firms respond to threatening technologies', *Academy of Management Executive*, vol. 6, no. 2 (1992), pp. 56–69.

58. From John Leonard, based on his personal studies and written in 'From transformation to transcendence', *Management Today* (April 2001), pp. 20–3.

59. T Harris, 'Military justice missing in action', *The Australian* (17 June 2005), p. 1.

60. Senate Standing Committees on Foreign Affairs, Defence and Trade, 'Inquiry into the effectiveness of Australia's military justice system' executive summary, para 10 (16 June 2005), http://www.aph.gov.au/Senate/committee/fadt_ctte/miljustice/report/index.htm (viewed 15 July 2005).

61. T Allard, 'New defence chief vows to treat his people right', *The Sydney Morning Herald* (5 July 2005) p. 4.

62. SLS Nwachukwu and SJ Vitell, Jr, 'The influence of corporate culture on managerial ethical judgements', *Journal of Business Ethics*, vol. 16, no. 8 (June 1997), pp. 757–76.

63. *Sex Discrimination Act 1984* (Cth), division 3.

64. Federal Privacy Commissioner, 'Guidelines on workplace email, web-browsing and privacy' (March 2000), http://www.privacy.gov.au/internet/email/index.html (viewed 10 July 2005).

65. *Wilmont v Bankwest* WAIRC (13 June 2001).

66. *Williams v Centrelink* AITC (15 January 2004).

67. *Micallef v Holden Ltd* PN 900664 (25 January 2001).
68. *Toyota Motor Corp v AMWU* Print T4675 (18 December 2000).
69. *Murray v Department of Family and Community Services* PR 913897 (1 February 2002).
70. 'Porn viewed at work survey', *The Australian* (4 July 2005), http://www.theaustralian.news.com.au/common/story_page/0,5744,3871981%255E1702,00.html (viewed 8 July 2005).
71. Reproduced from Connect2, http://www.connecttwo.com/article_mirrors/corporate_culture.html (viewed 17 July 2005).
72. Johnson & Johnson corporate web site, 'Our credo', http://www.jnj.com/our_company/our_credo/index.htm;jsessionid=BPQRMADJSHEE4CQPCCFWU2YKB2IIWTT1 (viewed 8 July 2005).
73. Johnson & Johnson corporate web site, http://www.jnj.com (viewed 8 July 2005).

CHAPTER 10
Power, politics and influence in organisations

Learning objectives

After studying this chapter, you should be able to:

1. discuss the meaning of power and explain the sources of power available to managers and employees

2. explain the relationship between power, authority and obedience

3. explain how managers acquire power

4. discuss the meaning and importance of empowerment in organisations

5. explain organisational politics and its dual faces in organisations

6. explain various kinds of political behaviours in organisations

7. discuss the ethical implications of politics in organisations.

With globalisation, global competition and a rapidly changing business environment, the demands on leaders and managers have multiplied. Managers need sufficient influence on others (including, but not limited to, their staff) to be able to convince them of the need for change, flexibility and learning. They need to be able to create alliances and make the most of relationships. They need to devise ways of achieving power through cooperation.

Dick Smith is an interesting case. Smith's business achievements include founding electronics retailer Dick Smith Electronics in 1968 (and selling it to Woolworths in 1982); founding the *Australian Geographic* magazine; and founding Dick Smith Foods in response to the predominance of foreign owned companies in Australia and the increasingly frequent takeovers of previously Australian-owned companies. Smith has created several successful organisations and won public admiration and support (he was even named Australian of the Year). In addition to his achievements in business, Smith is a philanthropist and adventurer. Smith's company gives some of its profits to charities, individuals and families. His adventures include a helicopter flight to the North Pole, and he was part of the first manned balloon flight across Australia.[1] Through such activities and his business pursuits, Smith developed a high public profile. He used this profile and his experience in aviation to become a member and then chairman of the Civil Aviation Safety Authority (CASA). During his time there, he began to introduce a program of substantial changes that would have a significant impact on the safety regulations governing Australian aviators. The Australian aviation industry was divided on the changes and various stakeholders brought considerable pressure on Smith. He resigned from CASA in 1999, with some saying he wanted to leave and others saying he was forced out. Many of Smith's critics suggested his management style, rather than the detail of his air safety reforms, was responsible for the divisions in the industry.

CASA employee John Wood said: 'Dick was totally isolated because of his personality style, his management style ... Dick simply didn't want to seem to listen to any other voices ... You may remember that on the Monday, after three days of intense negotiations, Dick launched his attack against Qantas. He said "Qantas is putting profits before safety". Then he attacked Ansett, he attacked the airforce, he attacked his own staff, he attacked what he describes as the unions — by which I think he means the air traffic controllers, flight service operators, the pilots represented by AFAP and then, when the trial was finally cancelled, he attacked BASI. That's his style and the tragedy of that is that he's isolated himself from all the people he needed to do his job.'[2]

Mark Barnett of the Aircrafts Owners' and Pilots' Association said: 'I understand that Dick can be a difficult man to work with ... the bureaucrats within CASA — many of them have been there a long time — they may feel they can't work with a man like Dick Smith so they entrench themselves.'[3]

After leaving CASA, Smith gained membership of the Australian Government's airspace reform group, where he continued to campaign on air safety standards.[4] He continues his campaign for air safety changes through his web site www.dicksmithflyer.com.au.

As students of organisations, we need to understand that power and politics are very much part of daily business life, both within and across organisational boundaries. Managers and businessmen alike often find themselves in situations where they need to acquire influence over others or ascertain that they have it. There are many ways they can do that. However, as the case of Dick Smith shows, in organisations of the twenty-first century, success or otherwise rests to a great extent on managers' abilities to influence both within their organisations and in wider spheres.[5] Money and resources are not the sole vehicles of power. The ability to network, coupled with concerns for the wider social issues, can also be an important generator of influence in the modern organisation.[6] The power of partnerships and alliances is indisputable.

Introduction

No discussion of organisations would be complete without a study of power and politics. To succeed, managers and entrepreneurs need to acquire many skills. In particular, they need to understand the meaning of power and how it is acquired. Furthermore, their long-term success and the survival of their organisations depend on their ability to network with external economic, social and political players. In addition to their involvement in the business life of their organisation, they are increasingly required to show concerns for social issues as they emerge in their social sphere. This means that the acquisition and maintenance of power within organisations is not a simple process. It depends on a range of internal and external factors.

By virtue of their social dynamics, organisations are the arenas in which power and politics are most frequently found. Every day, in every kind of situation, managers and employees alike use power and politics to achieve their personal goals and do their jobs. A manager hires a personal assistant, a finance manager audits an entire department, a senior manager sacks his personal adviser, a board of directors forces a subsidiary into liquidation, shareholders sack a chief executive officer, a political leader is forced out of office for fraud or sexual misbehaviour — all of these are instances of the use of power, and they often entail politics. Power and politics may be the source of solutions as well as problems in organisations. They are important but remain quite elusive as concepts in organisational behaviour. This is because managers' actions often take place with varying and sometimes contradictory objectives in mind. For instance, a manager may be seeking to maximise profits and dividends to please shareholders, while at the same time attempting to fulfil requests for cost adjustments made by employees, unions and other stakeholders. To be effective, managers need to know how power is acquired and exercised. They also need to know why political behaviours are common in organisations and what may prompt such behaviours.

In this chapter we examine the meaning of power and politics, as well as their effects at both the interpersonal and organisational levels. We outline and discuss some fundamental theoretical contributions to the field. We also investigate practical and contemporary issues that are relevant to managers.

Some of the management activities most commonly affected by politics, power and influence are budget allocations; facilities/equipment allocations; changes to rules and procedures; reorganisation changes; delegation of authority; personnel changes such as promotions and transfers, recruitment and selection, pay and work appraisals; and interdepartmental coordination.[7]

On the one hand, power and politics represent the less desirable side of management. On the other, they can be the essence of what happens in organisations on a daily basis. This is because organisations are not democracies composed of individuals with equal influence. Some organisations are more akin to medieval feudal states, in which managers believe they can rule because they have some divine right. Any attempt to undermine the role of politics in the daily life of managers and employees would be erroneous. In essence, people are political animals. Some organisations have become so political that organisational interests are completely subordinated to individual interests.

Clearly, power and politics are important organisational tools that managers use to get the job done. In effective organisations, astute individuals delicately develop, nurture and manage power and politics. Power is usually a self-centred and individualistic endeavour. Yet there are instances where individual and organisational interests are compatible. The astute manager knows how to find such instances and capitalise on the opportunities. In other words, power and politics may be unsavoury notions to some, but when used with care, they can bring together individual desires for joint accomplishment.[8] They may be the source of solutions as well as problems in organisations.

Power and influence

Power may be defined as 'the potential ability to influence behavior, to change the course of events, to overcome resistance, and to get people to do things that they would not otherwise do. Politics and influence are the processes, the actions, the behaviors through which this potential power is utilized and realized.'[9] In simpler terms, **power** may be defined as the ability to get someone to do something you want done or the ability to make things happen in the way you want. The essence of power is control over the behaviour of others.[10] Power is the force that makes things happen in an intended way; **influence** is a behavioural response to the exercise of power — that is, influence is an outcome achieved through the use of power. Managers use power to achieve influence over other people in the work setting.

Figure 10.1 summarises the link between power and influence. It also identifies the key bases of power that managers can use to influence the behaviour of other people at work. Managers derive power from both organisational and individual sources. We call these sources position power and personal power, respectively.[11] French and Raven first raised this distinction in their landmark study, and it underpins our discussion on the subject.

Power is the ability to get someone else to do something you want done, or the ability to make things happen or get things done in the way you want.

Influence is a behavioural response to the exercise of power.

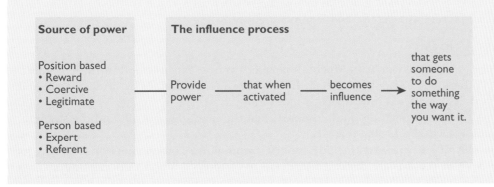

FIGURE 10.1 • Power sources and the influence process

The late Kerry Packer was an influential figure in business, both in Australia and worldwide. On 26 December 2005, when he inherited the Packer business empire upon his father Kerry's death, James Packer faced considerable challenges. He was just 38 years old and bore the stigma of having lost hundreds of millions of dollars in his first big business deal — an investment in the failed One.Tel telecommunications company. Some questioned James's ability to wield the same power and influence within the business and in the wider business world, society and politics. Lachlan Murdoch, who also lost millions in One.Tel, had suggested that James was so upset he was in tears over the One.Tel blunder. It was a strong contrast to the tough business persona of his father. However, James returned to work just 36 hours after Kerry's death, assuming control of the Publishing and Broadcasting Limited (PBL) business empire, which includes Channel Nine TV, ACP Magazines — and through it more than half of Australia's magazines — casinos, coalmines and ski resorts. James had served a ten-year 'apprenticeship', was extremely confident and had a successful record in gaming businesses.

(continued)

Media analyst Roger Colman suggested Kerry had put in place controls to help James avoid making mistakes, including appointing a strong board and senior management team.[12] He made the point that there would be several top people running the business, limiting the ability of James to make and implement unilateral decisions. However, soon after taking the reins, James implemented a number of big decisions, including scrapping plans for a A$4 billion joint venture in a Singapore casino. PBL chief executive officer John Alexander said James had a clear vision for the company's future and that he had the enthusiastic support of the board and the senior management. In a vote of confidence in James, the PBL share price suffered little from the news of Kerry's death. The question over whether James can continue his father's business success and wield the same power and influence within the Packer empire and outside it will be answered over the coming years.[13]

Position power

Three bases of power are available to managers solely as a result of their position in the organisation: reward, coercive and legitimate power.

Reward power

Reward power is the extent to which a manager can use extrinsic and intrinsic rewards to control other people. Managers usually hold power in organisations by virtue of their ability to reward. This power is one aspect of motivation, as we saw in chapter 3. The strength of the power differs depending on the rewards that the manager controls and the strength of the employee's desire for the rewards.

Examples of such rewards include money, promotions, compliments or enriched jobs. These types of rewards are discussed in detail in chapters 3 and 4. Although all managers have some access to rewards, success in accessing and using rewards to achieve influence varies according to the skills of the manager.

Coercive power

Power can also be founded on punishment rather than reward. Managers can cause others to have unpleasant experiences. In such circumstances coercive power is thought of as a form of punishment for failing to complying with the wishes of the power holder. A manager may threaten, for example, to withhold a pay raise, or to transfer, demote or even recommend the firing of an employee who does not act as desired. The manager could also allocate the least desirable task to a person as a form of punishment, or deliberately overlook the employee's good performance. Such coercive power is based on the extent to which a manager can deny desired rewards or administer punishments to control other people.

The availability of coercive power also varies from one organisation and manager to another. It should be noted that this type of power may have negative effects and should be used with caution. For this reason, most organisations devise rules and principles to guide rewards and punishment. Rules may be established to govern, for example, how supervisors may use coercive power to prevent them from using their formal authority arbitrarily to benefit some employees at the expense of others. Most organisations also have a system of 'appeal' to protect employees against coercion and various illegitimate acts, such as harassment in the workplace. Such organisational policies on employee treatment, and the presence of unions, for example, can weaken this power base considerably. Unions point out that when unemployment is high and job insecurity is rampant, employees may feel less able to confront coercive power; further, employees may not seek the assistance of unions for fear of further unpleasant consequences.

Bullying and management competence

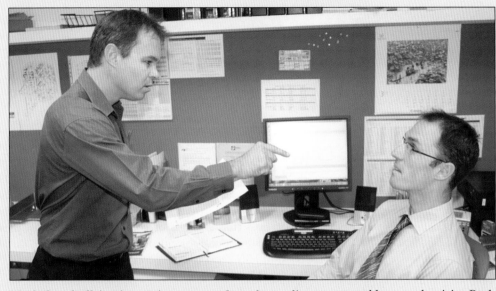

Workplace bullying is a major source of employee discontent and lost productivity. Both employers and employees are threatened by its presence and have an equal interest in its eradication. As a form of employee abuse it has unfortunately become commonplace in organisations.[14] The power to bully can be derived from various sources.

In some cases, position power, such as that of a manager, can be used to bully employees. Such bullying is often made worse by incompetence. Good managers understand that if they have competent employees and treat them well, their organisations will operate smoothly. In contrast, some managers see their employees as threats and endeavour to maintain their power by controlling everyone. Bully managers can intimidate employees with their power to fire or give raises and bonuses.[15] In other cases, people who control the supply of things that other people want use that control to bully those people.[16]

Unfortunately, bullying is on the rise in workplaces around the world. A TMP Worldwide survey to which 5000 employees responded showed that around 18 per cent of them thought their boss bullied them and others; 29 per cent of the employees also believed employers are more hostile towards workers than they were ten years ago. In Australia, the problem has been recognised by the Queensland Government, which has set up Australia's first Workplace Bullying Taskforce. The state of Victoria has also proposed a code of practice for dealing with the problem. While the typical bully can be characterised as a male manager about 40–55 years old, with a results-focused personality and a lack of personnel skills, bullies can cross all classes and occupations and both genders.[17]

A study by the Chartered Management Institute found that more than 30 per cent of IT managers had been bullied at some time in the three years leading up to the study. Some 6 per cent of IT managers admitted behaving in a bullying way. Four in ten of those bullied said no action had been taken by their employer. The most frequent type of bullying in the IT sector occurs when people are undermined by criticism or overloaded with work (78 per cent), followed by verbal insults, unfair treatment and misuse of power or position (72 per cent). Three-quarters of those surveyed said bullying was prompted by a lack of management skills. Personality factors were mentioned by 69 per cent and failure to address previous incidents of bullying by 55 per cent.[18]

(continued)

In Australia, bullying has been so prevalent that several authors have attempted to expose it from both theoretical and practical perspectives.[19] Researchers are not yet sure how to categorise the practice, with some fitting it into the equal opportunity or harassment areas, and others preferring to tie it in with occupational health and stress.[20] No matter how it is labelled, it does appear that there are likely to be many negative outcomes, such as increasing levels of absenteeism, turnover and sick leave, as well as reduced productivity.[21] As a method of pursuing organisational interests it seems that bullying is not a good use of power or influence.

Legitimate power and formal authority

The capacity to command does not always mean the right to command. They should not be equated. Legitimate power relates to the right (rather than capacity) to command. As the third base of power, legitimate power stems from the extent to which a manager can use the internalised belief of employees that the 'boss' has a 'right of command' to control their behaviour. Legitimate power provides an organisationally or culturally afforded right to direct the actions of others, and it is based on a mutually accepted perception that the power holder (in this case, the manager) has the right to influence the employee. In this context, managers are the bosses, their employees are the subordinates, and many routine instructions and requests are accepted simply because everyone agrees that employees should do what managers say. Legitimate power allows a manager to approve or deny employee requests for such things as job transfers, equipment purchases, personal time off or overtime work.

Legitimate power is often used interchangeably with the term *formal authority*. The two terms represent a special kind of managerial power that exists because employees believe it is legitimate for a person occupying the managerial role to have the right to command. Companies as entities need to consider that they hold considerable position power.

Legitimate power confers on an individual the legal authority to control and use organisational resources to accomplish organisational goals. For example, the organisation's board of directors grants the legitimate power of a chief executive officer, which gives him or her authority over all organisational resources. In turn, the chief executive officer has the right to confer legitimate power upon managers lower down in the organisation's hierarchy. Supervisors, too, have legitimate power over their employees.

An important part of legitimate power is process power. Process power is acquired when individuals are put in positions that allow them to influence how inputs are transformed into outputs. In their endeavour to meet production targets, organisations often establish positions for process specialists, who work with managers to ensure production targets are met. The specialists may sometimes turn into analysts or have to work with analysts. The analysts are individuals who are given control over the analytical process used to make decisions. For instance, an organisation may nominate a financial controller to monitor the efficiency of a production process. Another example is where an organisation uses business process re-engineering systems. Such systems are typically designed to empower workers and supervisory staff by giving them responsibility for entire processes. Hence, they overturn traditional management techniques that call for processes to be dissected and managed from the top, with workers trained to complete localised, repetitive tasks.

Information is also an important source of power. Managers with legitimate authority who do not have control over information they need in their role, would most likely be dependent on those who hold such information. Hence, in order for managers to effectively exercise their legitimate power, they need to secure control over information that is vital to their day-to-day managerial activities. Without such control, they are dependent on others who may manipulate such information to suit their own personal interests and agendas.

Legitimate power is the extent to which a manager can use the internalised belief of an employee that the 'boss' has a 'right of command' to control other people.

Process power is the control over methods of production and analysis.

This is often referred to as 'restrictive control', which is 'a form of power exertion in which one actor pushes his wishes through against the interests of another actor'.[22] In essence, **information power** constitutes an important part of legitimate power.

Information power is the extent to which individuals have control over information needed by others.

International **SPOTLIGHT**

The end of the empire?

In July 2005, media mogul Rupert Murdoch's 33-year-old son Lachlan, long expected to succeed his father as the head of News Corp, resigned from his job as deputy chief operating officer. Lachlan was the second potential successor to leave the company. His older sister Elisabeth had left UK satellite broadcaster BSkyB in 1996.

For 15 years, it had seemed Lachlan was being groomed to take over the company — considered one of the most powerful media companies in the world. Industry commentators were shocked by Lachlan's departure and Rupert himself issued a media release expressing his 'sadness' at Lachlan's decision. There was speculation that Lachlan could not cope with his father's involvement in Lachlan's areas of the business. Lachlan's departure threatens the Murdoch family's control over what is, after all, a public company; the Murdoch family holds 30 per cent of the shares. James Murdoch, chief executive of BSkyB, is not considered an automatic replacement for Lachlan as he lacks experience in the US aspects of the company. Murdoch's other children are still infants.

Sources: Jon Ashworth, 'The corridors of power', *Accounting Age*, http://www.accountancyage.com/accountancyage/comment/2141853/corridors-power (viewed 19 December 2005); 'End of a dynasty', *7 Days* (2 August 2005), http://www.7days.ae/special-reports/end-of-a-dynasty.html (viewed 19 December 2005); Tom Scocca and Observer staff, 'Why Lachlan flew the coop: it was Rupe', Mediachannel.org, http://mediachannel.org/blog/node/456?PHPSESSID=6f8ac73d86337a88910e5dfd18ffabc3 (viewed 19 December 2005); 'What next for the Murdoch dynasty?', *Money Weekly* (5 August 2005), http://www.moneyweek.com/article/1086/investing/other-viewpoints/mwk-murdoch.html (viewed 19 December 2005).

Personal power

Personal power resides in the individual and is independent of the position the individual holds. However, the management literature considers that, in essence, the two main bases of personal power are expertise and reference.

Expert power

Expert power is the ability to control another person's behaviour through the possession of knowledge, experience or judgement that the other person does not have but needs. Employees would obey a supervisor possessing expert power because they feel the boss knows more about what is to be done or how it is to be done. Similarly, patients would typically listen to their doctor's recommendation because the doctor is more knowledgeable about medicine than they are. Computer specialists can influence non-technical staff behaviour because they have special knowledge that may be critical to the rest of the staff.

Expert power is the ability to control another's behaviour through the possession of knowledge, experience or judgement that the other person does not have but needs.

Access to or control over information is an important element in this particular power base. However, the proliferation of information technology means expert power is more likely to be challenged as individuals gain access to specialist knowledge. Patients, for example, are increasingly seeking medical information on the Internet and challenging decisive expert decisions by their doctors.

'Expertise' is potentially a multifaceted concept that may include many areas of knowledge and information. Even those who know how to manage knowledge or know what knowledge is needed may be called 'experts'. Chapters 1 and 2 referred to the importance of knowledge management in our organisations and how it is necessary to gain knowledge, share it and use it for the benefit of the organisation. In that context, we should see experts as those who have any knowledge, judgement or experience that is required. For this reason a low-level employee without specialist training who has been in the organisation a considerable period may have experience or knowledge that is needed and that therefore may potentially influence the behaviour of others. Other sorts of knowledge also fit into this category. Gossip, for example, can be a form of knowledge or expertise with which a person may potentially influence the behaviour of others.

Access to key organisational decision makers is another element in expert power. A person's ability to contact key people informally can allow for special participation in the definition of a problem or issue, alteration in the flow of information to decision makers, and lobbying for use of special criteria in decision making. However, individuals with expert power do not always have the desire to exercise influence over others. In this case, managers with legitimate power have to develop good working relationships with employees who hold expert power.

WhatWould YouDo?

Working in a detention centre

The following is an extract of Margot O'Neill's interview with Dr Simon Lockwood on the ABC's *Lateline* program. Lockwood was the longest-serving medical officer at the Woomera detention centre, which was closed in 2003.

'7th April 2002, a 12-year-old boy tried to kill himself today.'

'6th June 2002, a female detainee signed a suicide note in blood.'

MARGOT O'NEILL: Dr Lockwood watched Woomera descend into a living hell, and it wasn't just detainees who were broken.

The trauma of the families locked inside spread to the Australian officers paid to guard them.

DR SIMON LOCKWOOD: A lot of the officers would cope with the stress by going to the pub and drinking themselves into oblivion or gambling on the pokies, so there was a lot of social problems in the town.

MARGOT O'NEILL: But did the Government know that it had a mass psychiatric disaster on its hands inside the detention centre?

DR SIMON LOCKWOOD: They did know.

They definitely knew that a major amount of the population were very sick.

MARGOT O'NEILL: And they just decided not to do anything about it?

DR SIMON LOCKWOOD: Well, they must have, because they didn't do anything about it.

MARGOT O'NEILL: Unlike many of his medical colleagues, Dr Lockwood decided not to go public.

Instead, Simon Lockwood took his case directly to Canberra, addressing a meeting of officials from the Immigration Department, or DIMIA.

For more than two hours Dr Lockwood told a room full of bureaucrats about the detention centre's catastrophic impact on families, on children.

DR SIMON LOCKWOOD: And then towards the end of the meeting one of the bureaucrats said to me, in front of everyone there, 'That sounds all well and good to us, Simon, but we don't want to make it so nice for them in detention that they won't want to leave.'

I knew that I'd spoken for two hours probably for nothing.

MARGOT O'NEILL: By now Woomera was the country's most controversial detention centre, attracting violent protests, which Simon Lockwood says only made camp life even more difficult.

DR SIMON LOCKWOOD: They never helped, because I always thought that it would be better for those protesters to go to Philip Ruddock's office and protest there, because the amount of distress and tension in the camp that was brought on by those protests lingered for months.

MARGOT O'NEILL: Dr Lockwood tried to get the worst-affected people, including children, out of the detention centre.

But he was often blocked by DIMIA.

DR SIMON LOCKWOOD: The problem that I had with DIMIA was that they're not doctors, they're not nurses, they're not psychologists, and yet they would do the opposite of what was recommended by an expert in child psychiatry, for example.

On what basis?

Because no-one died, DIMIA or the bureaucrats believed that no-one made genuine attempts, but I can tell you being the doctor that was looking after those people and saving their lives, that that wasn't the case.

I look back on it now and I find it hard to believe that it was in Australia that we had a place like that, that it couldn't have been better designed to break people down, detainees and staff.

Source: 'Woomera detention centre doctor speaks out', transcript of Australian Broadcasting Corporation television program *Lateline*, 27 October 2004, http://www.abc.net.au/lateline/content/2004/s1229335.htm.

(continued)

Referent power

Referent power is the ability to control another's behaviour because that person wants to identify with the power source. In this case, employees would obey the boss because they want to behave, perceive or believe as the boss does. This might occur, for example, because the employee likes the boss personally and therefore tries to do things in the way the boss wants them done. In a sense, the employee behaves to avoid doing anything that would interfere with the pleasing boss–employee relationship.

Individuals may have one or more such sources of power, to varying degrees and in varying combinations. It is important that managers do not rely on a single source of power, as this may limit their effectiveness. For example, managers who rely only on legitimate power may have very limited ability to influence the behaviour of others, and their efforts may be undermined by the referent power of informal leaders.

The relationship between power, authority and obedience

LEARNING OBJECTIVE 2

Power, authority and obedience

Power is the potential to control the behaviour of others; formal authority is the potential to exert such control through the legitimacy of a managerial position. Yet we also know that people who seem to have power do not always get their way. This leads us to the subject of obedience. Why do some people obey directives while others do not? More specifically, why should employees respond to a manager's authority, or 'right to command', in the first place? Further, given that employees are willing to obey, what determines the limits of obedience?

The Milgram experiments

These last questions point to Stanley Milgram's seminal research on obedience.[23] Milgram designed an experiment to determine the extent to which people obey the commands of an authority figure, even if they believe they are endangering the life of another person. The subjects were 40 males, ranging in age from 20 to 50 years and representing a diverse set of occupations (engineers, salespeople, school teachers, labourers and others). They were paid a nominal fee for participation in the project, which was conducted in a laboratory at Yale University.

The subjects were told (falsely) that the purpose of the study was to determine the effects of punishment on learning. The subjects were to be the 'teachers'. The 'learner', an associate of Milgram's, was strapped to a chair in an adjoining room with an electrode attached to his wrist. The 'experimenter', another confederate of Milgram's, was dressed in a grey laboratory coat. Appearing impassive and somewhat stern, the experimenter instructed the teacher to read a series of word pairs to the learner and then to re-read the first word along with four other terms. The learner was supposed to indicate which of the four terms was in the original pair by pressing a switch that caused a light to flash on a response panel in front of the teacher.

The teacher was instructed to administer a shock to the learner each time a wrong answer was given. This shock was to be increased by one level of intensity each time the learner made a mistake. The teacher controlled switches that ostensibly administered shocks ranging from 15 to 450 volts. In reality, there was no electric current in the apparatus, but the learner purposely and very frequently 'erred', responding to each level of 'shock' in progressively distressed ways. A summary of the switch markings and the learner's fake responses to the various levels of shock is shown in figure 10.2.

Switch voltage marking	Switch description	'Learner's' responses
15–60	Slight	No sound
75–120	Moderate	Grunts and moans
135–180	Strong	Asks to leave
195–240	Very strong	Cannot stand the pain
255–300	Intense	Pounds on wall
315–360	Extreme intensity	No sound
375–420	Danger: severe shock	No sound
435–450	XXX	No sound

FIGURE 10.2 • Shock levels and set learner responses in the Milgram experiment

If a teacher proved unwilling to administer a shock, the experimenter used the following sequential prods to get him to perform as requested.

1. 'Please continue' or 'Please go on'.
2. 'The experiment requires that you continue.'
3. 'It is absolutely essential that you continue.'
4. 'You have no choice, you must go on.'

Only when the teacher refused to go on after the fourth prod would the experiment be stopped. When would you expect that the 'teachers' would refuse to continue?

Milgram asked some of his students and colleagues the same question. Most felt that few, if any, of the subjects would go beyond the 'Very strong shock' level. But 26 subjects (65 per cent) continued to the end of the experiment and shocked the 'learner' to the XXX level! None stopped before 300 volts — the point at which the learner pounds on the wall. The remaining 14 subjects refused to obey the experimenter at various intermediate points.

Most people are surprised by these results, as was Milgram. The question is why other people would have a tendency to accept or comply with authoritative commands under such extreme conditions. Milgram conducted further experiments to try to answer this question. The subjects' tendencies towards compliance were somewhat reduced when:

• experimentation took place in a rundown office (rather than a university lab)
• the victim was closer
• the experimenter was farther away
• the subject could observe other subjects.

The level of compliance was still much higher than most of us would expect. The results of this experiment are useful and informative. However, the conduct of this type of experiment would probably not be permitted under today's more demanding guidelines for research. Social scientists now abide by increasingly stringent rules on research ethics.

Obedience and the acceptance of authority

As the Milgram experiments suggest, there are strong tendencies among individuals to follow the instructions of the boss. Direct defiance within organisational settings is quite rare. If the tendency to follow instructions is great and defiance is rare, then why do so many organisations appear to drift into apparent chaos? The answer to this question lies at the heart of the contribution made by the well-known management writer Chester Barnard.[24] Essentially, Barnard's argument focused on the 'consent of the governed' rather than on the rights derived from ownership. He argued that employees will accept or follow a directive from the boss only under special circumstances, and all four must be met.

1. The employee can and must understand the directive.
2. The employee must feel mentally and physically capable of carrying out the directive.

3. The employee must believe the directive is not inconsistent with the purpose of the organisation.

4. The employee must believe the directive is not inconsistent with his or her personal interests.

These four conditions are carefully stated. To accept and follow an order, employees do not need, for instance, to understand how the proposed action will help the organisation; they only need to believe the requested action is not inconsistent with the purpose of the organisation. The astute manager will not take these guidelines for granted. In giving directives, the astute manager recognises that the acceptance of the request is not assured. If the directive is routine, then it is not surprising that the employee may merely comply without enthusiasm. The manager needs to understand what employees consider acceptable or unacceptable actions.

Obedience and the zone of indifference

Most people seek a balance between what they put into an organisation (contributions) and what they get from an organisation in return (inducements). Within the boundaries of the psychological contract (see chapter 1), therefore, employees will agree to do many things in and for the organisation because they think they should; that is, in exchange for certain inducements, employees recognise the authority of the organisation and its managers to direct their behaviour in certain ways. Based on his acceptance view of authority, Chester Barnard calls this area in which directions are obeyed the 'zone of indifference'.

A **zone of indifference** is the range of authoritative requests to which employees are willing to respond without subjecting the directives to critical evaluation or judgement — that is, the range in which they are indifferent. Directives falling within the zone are obeyed; requests or orders falling outside the zone of indifference are not considered legitimate under terms of the psychological contract. The latter directives may or may not be obeyed. This link between the zone of indifference and the psychological contract is shown in figure 10.3.

The **zone of indifference** is the range of authoritative requests to which an employee is willing to respond without subjecting the directives to critical evaluation or judgement — that is, the requests to which the employee is indifferent.

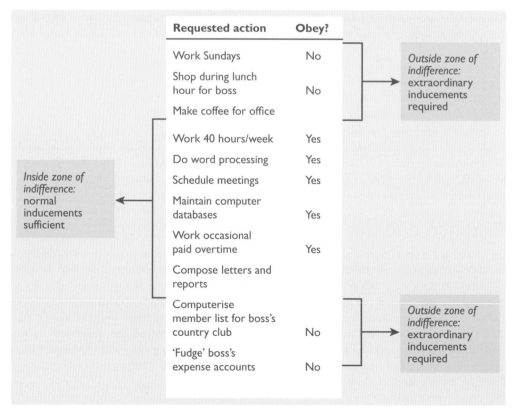

Requested action	Obey?
Work Sundays	No
Shop during lunch hour for boss	No
Make coffee for office	
Work 40 hours/week	Yes
Do word processing	Yes
Schedule meetings	Yes
Maintain computer databases	Yes
Work occasional paid overtime	Yes
Compose letters and reports	
Computerise member list for boss's country club	No
'Fudge' boss's expense accounts	No

Outside zone of indifference: extraordinary inducements required

Inside zone of indifference: normal inducements sufficient

Outside zone of indifference: extraordinary inducements required

FIGURE 10.3 • Hypothetical psychological contract with a secretary showing zone of indifference

The secretary whose psychological contract is shown in figure 10.3 may be expected to perform a number of activities falling within the zone of indifference with no questions asked. Examples include scheduling meetings and maintaining computer databases. But there may be times when the boss would like the secretary to do things falling outside the zone, such as running personal errands for the boss on the secretary's lunch hour. This requires efforts to enlarge the zone to accommodate additional behaviours. In these attempts, the boss will most likely have to use more incentives than pure position power. In some instances, such as Sunday work and 'fudging' of expense accounts, no power base may be capable of accomplishing the desired result. Before leaving this discussion, there is another side to power, authority and obedience with which you should be familiar as a manager. That side is your own zone of indifference and tendency to obey. When will you say 'no' to your boss? When should you be willing to say 'no'? At times, the situation may involve ethical dilemmas, where you may be asked to do things that are illegal, unethical or both. Research on ethical managerial behaviour shows that supervisors are singled out by their employees as sources of pressure to do such things as support incorrect viewpoints, sign false documents, overlook the supervisor's wrongdoing and do business with the supervisor's friends.[25]

Most of us will occasionally face ethical dilemmas during our careers. Saying 'no' or 'refusing to keep quiet' can be difficult and potentially costly, as many whistleblowers discover. But it may still be the right thing to do.

It is possible to say 'no' and to air issues, however, without going as far as whistleblowing the whole issue in the courts, the media or elsewhere. In such cases, other measures can be tried. Employees may have recourse to the law, for example, in cases of occupational health or safety, workers compensation, unfair dismissal or discrimination. The 'legitimate power' of managers may be countered by the employees' knowledge of their rights. However, contesting the power of a manager may not always be easy. It is also important to question how much power employees have when establishing some of their rights through the enterprise bargaining process that sets up working agreements between workers and employers.

When resources are scarce and differences endure, politics and power become central features of organisational life. In this situation, goals, structure and policy tend to emerge from bargaining and negotiation among the major interest groups. The pursuit of self-interest and power is the basic process in organisations. Organisational change is always political and occurs whenever a particular individual or group is able to impose an agenda on the organisation.

Dealing with insubordinate employees

THE **Effective** Manager   10.1

1. Explore the reasons for the unacceptable behaviour.
2. Inform the employee that he or she has engaged in unacceptable conduct and that certain conducts are strongly expected of all employees. Refer to the specific rules or policies in that respect.
3. Discuss the negative consequences that will occur if the employee fails to change unacceptable behaviours.
4. Clearly outline the positive consequences of changing the improper behaviour.
5. Develop an action plan that you and the employee agree on to change the unacceptable behaviour.

Managing with power and influence

LEARNING OBJECTIVE **3**   Managerial power and influence

Managing with power means recognising that there are varying interests in almost every organisation. It also means determining how various individuals and groups perceive issues.

Further, it means understanding that power is needed to get things done, and that sources of power must be developed. Managing with power also requires an understanding of the strategies and tactics through which power is developed and used in organisations. By learning to manage with power, managers are able to achieve both their own goals and the goals of their organisation.

A considerable part of any manager's time will be directed towards what is called 'power-oriented' behaviour — that is, behaviour directed primarily at developing or using relationships in which other people are to some degree willing to defer to your wishes.[26] Figure 10.4 shows three basic dimensions of power and influence with which a manager will become involved in this regard: downward, upward and lateral. Also shown in the figure are some preliminary ideas for achieving success along each of these dimensions.

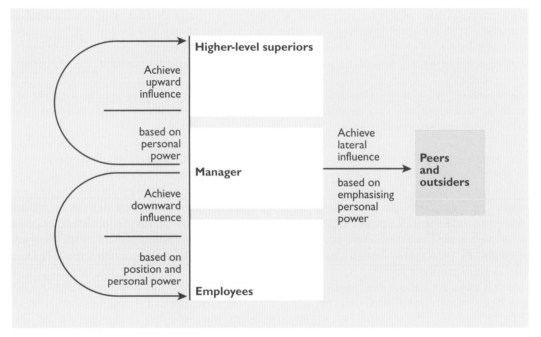

FIGURE 10.4 • Three dimensions of managerial power and influence

When 'facing upwards', managers must rely on the use of personal power to achieve influence over higher-level superiors. In contrast, when 'facing downwards', managers can mobilise both position and personal power in dealing with employees. In lateral relations with peers and outsiders, the manager must again emphasise personal power to achieve the desired influence.

Acquiring managerial power

The effective manager is one who, over time, succeeds in building and maintaining high levels of both position and personal power. Only then will sufficient power of the right types be available when the manager needs to exercise influence on downward, lateral and upward dimensions.

Enhancing position power

As we mentioned earlier, position power is based on formal authority and the legitimacy of a manager's location in the organisation's hierarchy of authority. Position power can be enhanced when managers are able to demonstrate to others that their work units are highly relevant to organisational goals, and are able to respond to urgent organisational needs. In addition, there are five general guidelines for enhancing position power.[27]

1. *Increase your centrality and critical role in the organisation* by acquiring a more central role in the work flow, having information filtered through you, making at least part of your job responsibilities unique, expanding your network of communication contacts, and occupying an office convenient to main traffic flows.

2. *Increase the personal discretion and flexibility of your job* by removing routine activities, expanding task variety and novelty, initiating new ideas, getting involved in new projects, participating in the early stages of the decision-making process, and avoiding 'reliable performance criteria' for judging your success on the job.

3. *Build tasks into your job that are difficult to evaluate* by creating an ambiguous job description, developing a unique language or set of labels in your work, obtaining advanced training, becoming more involved in professional associations, and exercising your own judgement.

4. *Increase the visibility of your job performance* by expanding the number of contacts you have with senior people, making oral presentations of written work, participating in problem-solving task forces, sending out notices of accomplishment that are of interest to the organisation, and seeking additional opportunities to increase personal name recognition.

5. *Increase the relevance of your tasks to the organisation* by becoming an internal coordinator or external representative, providing services and information to other units, monitoring and evaluating activities within your own unit, expanding the domain of your work activities, becoming involved in decisions central to the organisation's top-priority goals, and becoming a trainer or mentor for new members.

Enhancing personal power

Personal power arises from personal characteristics of the manager rather than from the location and other characteristics of the position in the organisation's hierarchy of authority. Two primary bases of personal power rest in expertise and reference. Therefore, three personal characteristics have special potential to enhance personal power in an organisation.[28]

1. *Knowledge and information.* Managers can enhance their personal power through the expertise gained by possessing special knowledge (by education, training and experience) and information (through special access to data and/or people).

2. *Personal attractiveness.* Managers' reference power will be increased by characteristics that enhance their 'likeability' and create personal attraction in their relationships with other people. These include pleasant personality characteristics, agreeable behaviour patterns and attractive personal appearance.

3. *Effort.* The demonstration of sincere hard work in task performance can also increase personal power by enhancing both expertise and reference. A person who is perceived to try hard may be expected to know more about the job and thus be sought out for advice. Managers who try hard are also likely to be respected for the attempt, and others may even come to depend on them to maintain that effort.

While all of these methods may have merit in some contexts, and may increase the power of individuals, there is no guarantee that such approaches will not be utilised unethically — this is something that will be a matter of judgement and/or analysis in each case. It is also possible that some of these approaches may work against the principles of empowerment to a greater or lesser extent. Empowerment is discussed later in the chapter.

Turning power into influence

The acquisition of power is certainly an important task for any manager. Actually using this power well to achieve the desired influence over other people is another challenge.

Consider the following examples of how some managers attempt to exercise influence:

'I voice my wishes loudly.'

'I offer a *quid pro quo* — that is, I offer to do for them if they do for me.'

'I keep at it and reiterate my point over and over again until I get my way.'

'I have all the facts and figures ready, and I use them as necessary.'

'I go over the boss's head to higher levels when I get turned down.'

Practically speaking, there are many useful ways of exercising influence. The most common strategies involve:[29]
- *reason* — using facts and data to support a logical argument
- *friendliness* — using flattery, goodwill and favourable impressions
- *coalition* — using relationships with other people for support
- *bargaining* — using the exchange of benefits as a basis for negotiation
- *assertiveness* — using a direct and forceful personal approach
- *higher authority* — gaining higher-level support for requests
- *sanctions* — using organisationally derived rewards and punishments.

Research on this particular set of strategies for achieving managerial influence suggests that reason is the most popular strategy overall.[30] In addition, friendliness, assertiveness, bargaining and higher authority are used more frequently to influence employees than to influence supervisors. This pattern of influence attempts is consistent with our earlier contention that downward influence generally includes the mobilisation of both position and personal power sources, while upward influence will more likely draw on personal power. Other influence tactics have also been studied. The following list is drawn from the work of Gary Yukl and his colleagues. The tactics are:
- *rational persuasion* — using logical arguments and factual evidence
- *consultation* — seeking a person's involvement in an activity in which you require their support or assistance
- *inspirational appeals* — appealing to a person's values, ideals or aspirations to arouse enthusiasm and confidence to carry out the task
- *personal appeals* — appealing to a person's feelings of loyalty and friendship
- *ingratiation* — trying to get a person in a good mood or thinking of you favourably before making a request
- *exchange* — offering an exchange of favours, or a willingness to exchange favours, or a share in the benefits of an action
- *pressure* — using demands, threats, frequent checking or constant reminders
- *legitimating tactics* — claiming the authority or right to make your request by showing how it links with organisational rules, policies, practices or traditions
- *coalition tactics* — seeking the aid of others to help persuade a target person to do what you request.[31]

The researchers found, consistent with earlier studies of the same set, that consultation, inspirational appeals and strong rational persuasion are the most effective tactics. However, variation could be expected based on the context, the direction of the influence attempt and the objectives of the influence attempt. They suggest that managers diagnose their power relationships carefully in order to be able to use the tactics effectively.[32]

Little research is available on the specific subject of upward influence in organisations. This is unfortunate because truly effective managers are able to influence their boss as well as their employees. One study reports that both supervisors and employees view reason, or the logical presentation of ideas, as the most frequently used strategy of upward influence.[33]

However, when queried on reasons for success and failure, both groups exhibit similarities and differences in their viewpoints. Table 10.1 shows that the perceived causes of success in upward influence are similar for both supervisors and employees, and involve the favourable content of the influence attempt, the favourable manner of its presentation, and the competence of the employee.[34] The two groups disagree on the causes of failure, however. Employees attribute failure in upward influence to the closed-mindedness of the supervisor, the unfavourable content of the influence attempt, and unfavourable interpersonal relationships with the supervisor. In contrast, supervisors attribute failure to the unfavourable content of the attempt, the unfavourable manner in which it was presented, and the lack of competence of the employee.

Supervisor's views	Employee's views
Favourable content of influence attempt; favourable manner in which attempt was made; competency of employee	Agreement with supervisor's views
Unfavourable content of influence attempt; lack of competence of employee; poor manner in which attempt was made	Unfavourable content of influence attempt; closed-mindedness of supervisor; poor interpersonal relations with supervisor

TABLE 10.1 • Perceived causes of success and failure in upward influence attempts

However, power and influence do not just work up and down within the organisation; customers also have the opportunity to exert influence over various processes and decisions in the organisation, They do so through increasing consumer demands, greater concern for and response to consumer feedback, and the increasing availability of information on-line. Shareholders, and people in wider society, may also have some potential to influence decisions and behaviours in organisations. Such influence is not necessarily intentional, and typically not as strong as power sources inside the organisation. This shows that power and influence do not just emerge and function within the organisation, but come from outside as well.

Exercising upward influence

Power and influence may also be exercised upward. Research indicates that a number of upward influence tactics may be used.[35] The most common tactics are:

- *rationality* — refers to the use of facts and data to support a logical argument or to alter the thinking of a supervisor or manager
- *coalition* — involves making claims about support for your position from others in the organisation
- *ingratiation* — use of impression management, flattery and goodwill, and the promotion of a pleasant relationship when making a request
- *exchange of benefits* — pertains to negotiating by means of bargaining or favours
- *assertiveness* — a direct and forceful approach
- *upward appeal* — involves gaining the support of those higher up in the organisation to back your requests.

Empowerment

Empowerment is the process by which managers help others acquire and use the power needed to make decisions affecting themselves and their work (chapter 3). More than ever before, managers in progressive organisations are expected to be good at — and highly comfortable with — empowering the people with whom they work. Rather than considering power as something to be held only at higher levels in the traditional 'pyramid' of an organisation, this view considers power to be something that everyone working in flatter and more

LEARNING OBJECTIVE 4 — Empowerment

Empowerment is the process by which managers help others acquire and use the power needed to make decisions in their work.

collegial structures can share. Empowerment is a key foundation of the increasingly popular self-managing work teams and other creative worker involvement groups. Despite this, there are limits to the process of empowerment, which we discuss in some detail on pages 361–2.

Power keys to empowerment

One base for empowerment is a radically different view of power itself. Our discussion so far has focused on power exerted over other individuals. In contrast to this, the concept of empowerment emphasises the ability to make things happen. Cutting through all the corporate rhetoric on empowerment is difficult because the term has become fashionable in management circles. However, each individual empowerment attempt needs to be examined in the light of how power in the organisation will be changed.

Expanding the zone of indifference

When embarking on an empowerment program, management needs to recognise the current zone of indifference and systematically move to expand it. All too often, management assumes that its directive for empowerment will be followed; however, managers often fail to show precisely how empowerment will benefit the individuals involved.

Power as an expanding pie

Along with empowerment, employees need to be trained to expand their power and their new influence potential. This is the most difficult task for managers and a difficult challenge for employees, because it often changes the dynamic between supervisors and employees. The key is to change the concept of power within the organisation — from a view that stresses power over others to one that emphasises the use of power to get things done. Under the new definition of power, all employees can be more powerful.

In practical terms, empowerment means that all managers will need to emphasise different ways of exercising influence. Appeals to higher authority and sanctions will need to be replaced by appeals to reason, friendliness and bargaining. More than a few employees will be uncomfortable when asked to be assertive or to engage in bargaining. Yet these influence techniques are likely to become more important with the spread of empowerment. Special support may be needed for these individuals so that they can become comfortable in developing their own power.

Empowering others

When an organisation attempts to move power down the hierarchy, it also needs to alter the existing pattern of position power. Changing this pattern raises important questions. Can 'empowered' individuals give rewards and sanctions? Has their new right to act been legitimised with formal authority? All too often, attempts at empowerment disrupt well-established patterns of position power, and threaten middle and lower-level managers. As one supervisor said, 'All this empowerment stuff sounds great for top management. They don't have to run around trying to get the necessary clearances to implement the suggestions from my group. They never gave me authority to make the changes, only the new job of asking for permission.'

When all goes well, everyone can gain from empowerment. To keep the organisation competitive, top management must attend to a variety of challenging and strategic forces in the external environment. While top management tends to concentrate on decisions about strategy and dynamic change, others throughout the organisation must be ready and willing to make critical operating decisions. By providing these opportunities, empowerment increases the total power available in an organisation. In other words, the top levels do not have to give up power for the lower levels to gain it. The same basic argument holds true in any manager–employee relationship.

'The effective manager 10.2' lists a few emerging guidelines for managing the empowerment of others.

Empowerment varies in the degree to which it is applied and accepted in any organisation. Empowerment can range from the addition of extra small tasks to full involvement and responsibility for important decision making or project completion. Clearly, quantifying the degree of empowerment is a difficult and complex task. In the United Kingdom an empowerment audit (EA) was developed to try to measure the degree of empowerment, resulting in a matrix of 15 major indicators, each with a five-point scale of traditional, participative, involved, early self-directed and mature self-directed.[36] Empowerment involves the development of all employees, including managers. There is a significant risk that trying to introduce the highest degrees of empowerment too quickly will fail to give people time to develop and adjust to new demands. The result may be that they conclude that empowerment can not or did not work, when a slower, steadier program of introduction may have allowed individuals to adapt to empowerment over time.

The limits of empowering others

Empowerment programs can transform a stagnant organisation into a vital one by creating a shared purpose among employees, encouraging greater cooperation and, most importantly, delivering enhanced value to customers. Despite that potential, empowerment programs often fall victim to the same structural and cultural problems that made them desirable in the first place. On the one hand, many managers may view empowerment as a threat, and may continue to measure their personal status and value in terms of the hierarchical authority they wield. These managers perceive the shift of responsibility for work assignments and output evaluation to employees as a loss of authority and a change to a less satisfying role. As a result, they may resist empowerment efforts. On the other hand, some employees mistake empowerment for discretionary authority — that is, the power to decide things unilaterally — and lack the necessary cooperative skills, in which managers neglect or refuse to train them. Most employees define power in terms of discretion — that is, the ability to make unilateral decisions — and therefore expect an empowerment program to increase their personal decision-making ability. This expectation can lead to conflicts between employees and managers about the limits of power and the actions that violate accepted practice. Employees need to be coached that being empowered does not mean having more personal discretion. It means having an increased ability to create value for customers. A key element of this concept is the belief that effective value creation depends on interdependence and cooperation, with corresponding limits on personal discretion.

Dual faces of politics

LEARNING
5
OBJECTIVE

Organisational politics

Any study of power and influence inevitably leads to the subject of 'politics'. Political processes form the dynamic that enables the formal organisation to function. In a sense, power and politics act as the lubricant that enables the interdependent parts of the organisation to operate smoothly together.

The word 'politics' may conjure up thoughts of illicit deals, favours and special personal relationships. Politics is a common game played in business organisations. How well the game is played depends on the skill of the political players and how well they choose and use the organisation. This image of organisational politics whereby shrewd, often dishonest, practices are used to obtain influence is reflected in Machiavelli's classic sixteenth-century work, *The prince*, which outlines how to obtain and hold power via political action. For that reason, political actions are also referred to in terms of 'Machiavellianism' (chapter 2).

Politics may also be described as the art of using influence, authority and power to achieve goals. These goals may be self-interested for an individual, group or department, for example. Political skills, like technical skills, are a tool for getting things done. Managers must develop an understanding of the concepts of influence, power and authority before they can use politics effectively. If managers have an understanding of these concepts, along with an awareness of the self-interest barriers (departmental, personal, corporate and group self-interest), then they are able to present views or decisions to the self-interest group in the least threatening manner possible. Managers should frequently and openly discuss the political ramifications of all decisions confronting a department. They can use this to illustrate political realities, and to explain the many nuances of good political planning.

The two traditions of organisational politics

To survive in a highly political environment requires particular skills, including the ability to recognise those who are playing political games despite surface appearances of openness and cooperation. It also requires the ability to identify the power sources of the key players, and to build your own alliances and connections.

There are two quite different traditions in the analysis of organisational politics.

Politics as unsanctioned and self-interested

Organisational politics is the management of influence to obtain ends not sanctioned by the organisation, or to obtain sanctioned ends through non-sanctioned means of influence.

This first tradition builds on Machiavelli's philosophy and defines politics in terms of self-interest and the use of non-sanctioned means. In this tradition, organisational politics may be formally defined as the management of influence to obtain ends not sanctioned by the organisation, or to obtain sanctioned ends through non-sanctioned means of influence.[37] Managers are often considered political when they seek their own goals or use means not currently authorised by the organisation. It is also important to recognise that where there is uncertainty or ambiguity it is often extremely difficult to tell whether a manager is being political in this self-serving sense.[38]

In politics, contesting forces compete for favourable outcomes on decisions involving who gets what and how. Political activity is usually stronger where there are no prescribed routine answers or no stated policy. It also centres around the interpretation of existing policies and those situations involving value judgements. Any organisation that attempts to totally reduce these arenas of political activity by instituting rules, regulations and policies from the top would quickly strangle in its own red tape.

Politics as a compromise between competing interests

The second tradition treats politics as a necessary function resulting from differences in the perceived self-interest of individuals. Organisational politics is viewed as the art of compromise among competing interests. In a heterogeneous society, individuals will disagree on whose self-interest is most valuable and whose concerns should be bounded by collective interests. Politics arise because individuals need to develop compromises, avoid confrontation and live together. The same holds true in organisations, where individuals join, work and stay together because their self-interest is served. Further, it is important to remember that the goals of the organisation are established by organisationally powerful individuals in negotiation with others. Thus, organisational politics is also about the use of power to develop socially acceptable ends and means that balance individual and collective interests.

The belief that everything that happens in the organisation is the result of human beings pursuing their rational self-interest implies that ideas do not matter at all. People are often taught that arguments and theories will have no impact on them because they will just do whatever is in their rational self-interest. Within the liberal tradition, the fundamental power of ideas is often denied. This thesis, which has become especially prominent in public sector organisations, holds that starting with standard economic assumptions, it is possible to explain behaviours within public sector organisations. Of course the behaviour of all public officials is guided by ideas. The difference is that some keep tabs on their ideas, others do not, and others do it in a perverse way. Therefore, one cannot deny that people are motivated by ideas — small ones, borrowed ones, scrutinised ones. This is indeed paradoxical.

The important point here is that if you go to work expecting other people in the organisation to behave rationally and logically at all times, then you will be surprised. Self-interest, or the pursuit of ideas, will be present.

The perception of political behaviour

The study of power and political behaviour has been described as consistent and finite in many books over many years. However, there are some arguments to suggest that this approach is misleading us, or limiting us, in our understanding of how power and politics might actually work in organisations. Power is usually studied in terms of 'sources' of power and the idea of political behaviour often presents negative impressions of self-interested people disrupting organisational effectiveness. Such an approach implies that some people have power simply because of personal characteristics or because of their position in the organisation. However, there are arguments against a 'sources of power' approach, with power being defined instead as *a force created by differences*. Power can be seen as a far more *social* and *cultural* phenomenon by which those who have power are distinguished from those who do not through *perceived differences*. These differences are perceived within a socially constructed reality developed through the shared meanings of culture. Thus, you may have power in relation to another person because that person perceives that you have something they do not. This approach is useful in helping to explain not just individual power relations but also power that occurs in groups and organisational structures.[39] These perceived differences emerge, in part, from the wider social distinctions in society such as class, gender, law and education.[40]

If we take a cultural approach to power and politics, with interaction between social actors whose differences result in the forces of power, then we widen our understanding of political behaviour as being about social change. Different male and female management styles, as well as a range of different ethnic and other

(continued)

aspects of diversity in organisations may increase differences, or perceived differences, in organisations and challenge the existing way that problems are framed in the organisation.[41] Political behaviour is not necessarily about self-interest, with people stepping outside the accepted rules. It can be about the behaviour that continuously shapes and modifies those 'rules'. It is idealistic to imagine that there can be rules and regulations to cover every contingency, that authority can be assigned to a manager to the extent that the person does not have to find his or her own ways of solving problems. Similarly, it is unlikely that we will always know who has expertise to solve problems, or even what expertise is needed. Even personal power cannot dictate behaviour in consistent ways. It does seem that the study of power and political behaviour is usually linked to focusing on the purposes of behaviour (outcomes or ends), how the behaviour occurs (means used), and the context in which the behaviour occurs. Political behaviour does not have to be about advancing *self*-interest, though it may be about advancing *specific* interests within organisations. While we understand position power as being linked to authority, rewards and coercion, in this alternative understanding political behaviour can imply non-coercive forms of social order.[42]

Questions

1. If organisations are becoming increasingly diverse in terms of demographics, what are the implications for the level of political behaviour in organisations?
2. In the context of this article, what differences do you think exist between power and political behaviour?

Types and levels of political behaviour

LEARNING OBJECTIVE 6

Organisational politics in action

Political action is a part of organisational life; it is best to view organisational politics for its potential to contribute to managerial and organisational effectiveness. It is in this spirit that we now examine political action in organisations from the perspectives of managers, subunits and chief executives. Organisational politics occurs in different ways and across different levels in the organisation.

Office politics and the informal network

An organisational chart can show who is the boss and who reports to whom. However, this formal chart will not reveal which people confer on technical matters or discuss office politics over lunch. Much of the real work of an organisation is achieved through this informal organisation with its complex network of relationships that cross functions and divisions.

As companies in Australasia continue to flatten their structures and rely on teams, managers tend to rely less on their authority and more on understanding these informal networks. However, whether the organisation is flat or tall, one aspect of politics will always prevail — 'office politics'.

Office politics is as prevalent today as it ever was. The person who knows just when and whom to flatter, or the person who can befriend the boss, or the one who knows everyone's business — they all carry considerable clout and they know it. Most people who fall victim to the ravages of office politics fall into one of two basic categories — the innocents who unwittingly offend the wrong people, and the savvy players who let their defences down too soon. To thrive in the political landscape of the office, it is a good idea to become allied with admirable people, to be concerned primarily with your own business, not to overdo politics and to strive for trust.

Political action and the manager

Managers may gain a better understanding of political behaviour by placing themselves in the positions of other people involved in critical decisions or events. Each action and decision can be seen as having benefits and costs to all parties concerned. Where the costs exceed the benefits, the manager may act to protect their position.

Figure 10.5 shows a sample payoff table for two managers, Lee and Leslie, in a problem situation involving a decision about whether to allocate resources to a special project. If both managers authorise the resources, the project gets completed on time, and their company keeps a valuable client. Unfortunately, by doing so, both Lee and Leslie will over-spend their budgets. Taken on its own, a budget overrun would be bad for the managers' performance records. Assume that the overruns will be acceptable only if the client is retained. Thus, if both managers act, both they and the company win, as depicted in the upper left block of the figure. Obviously, this is the most desirable outcome for all parties concerned.

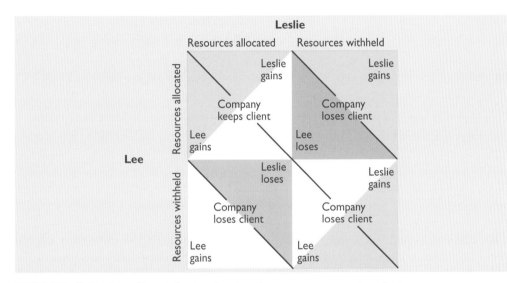

FIGURE 10.5 • Political payoff matrix for the allocation of resources on a sample project

Assume that Leslie acts, but Lee does not. In this case, the company loses the client, Leslie overspends the budget in a futile effort, but Lee ends up within budget. While the company and Leslie lose, Lee wins. This scenario is illustrated in the lower left block of the figure. The upper right block shows the reverse situation, in which Lee acts but Leslie does not; in this case, Leslie wins, while the company and Lee lose. Finally, if both Lee and Leslie fail to act, they each stay within the budget and therefore gain, but the company loses the client.

The company clearly wants both Lee and Leslie to act. But will they? Would you take the risk of overspending the budget, knowing that your colleague might refuse? The question of trust is critical here, but building trust among comanagers and other workers takes time and can be difficult. The involvement of higher-level managers may be needed to set the stage better. Yet we would predict that both Lee and Leslie would fail to act because the 'climate' or 'culture' in many organisations too often encourages people to maximise their self-interest at minimal risks. What we need are more settings in which people are willing to take a chance and are rewarded for doing so.

Power, or the ability to obtain, retain and move resources, requires two sets of attributes: competence and political intelligence. The first, and probably most important, strategy for improving an individual's political intelligence is to be able to read the work climate, prefer-ably before beginning work.

Political action and subunit power

Political action links managers more formally to one another as representatives of their work units. In chapter 7 we examined the group dynamics associated with such intergroup relationships. Table 10.2 highlights five typical lateral and intergroup relationships in which you may engage as a manager: work flow, service, advisory, auditing and approval relationships.[43] The table also shows how lateral relationships further challenge the political skills of a manager; each example requires the manager to achieve influence through some means other than formal authority.

TABLE 10.2 • Relationships of managers and associated influence requirements

Type of relationship	Sample influence requirements
Work flow — contacts with units that precede or follow in a sequential production chain	An assembly-line manager informs another line manager responsible for a later stage in the production process about a delay.
Service — contacts with units established to help with problems	An assembly-line manager asks the maintenance manager to fix an important piece of equipment as a priority.
Advisory — contacts with formal staff units that have special expertise	A marketing manager consults with the personnel manager to obtain special assistance in recruiting a new salesperson.
Auditing — contacts with units that have the right to evaluate the actions of others	A marketing manager tries to get the credit manager to retract a report criticising marketing's tendency to open bad-credit accounts.
Approval — contacts with units whose approval must be obtained before action may be taken	A marketing manager submits a job description to the company affirmative action officer for approval before recruiting for a new salesperson can begin.

To be effective in political action, managers should understand the politics of subunit relations. Line units are typically more powerful than are staff groups, and units towards the top of the hierarchy are often more powerful than are those towards the bottom. In general, units gain power as more of their relations with others are of the approval and auditing types. Work flow relations are more powerful than advisory associations, and both are more powerful than service relations. Units can also increase power by incorporating new actions that tackle and resolve difficult problems. Certain strategic contingencies can often govern the relative power of subunits. For a subunit to gain power, it must increase its control over:[44]

* *access to scarce resources*. Subunits gain in power when they obtain access to, or control, scarce resources needed by others.
* *the ability to cope with uncertainty*. Subunits gain in power when they are able to cope with uncertainty and help solve problems that uncertainty causes for others.
* *centrality in the flow of work*. Subunits gain in power when their position in the work flow allows them to influence the work of others.
* *substitutability of activities*. Subunits gain in power when they perform tasks or activities that are non-substitutable — that is, when they perform essential functions that others cannot complete.

Political action in the chief executive suite

From the Holmes à Courts to the Murdochs to the Packers, Australians have been fascinated by the politics of the chief executive suite. An analytical view of executive suite dynamics may lift some of the mystery behind the political veil at the top levels in organisations.

Resource dependencies

Executive behaviour can sometimes be explained in terms of **resource dependencies** — that is, the organisation's need for resources that others control.[45] Essentially, the resource dependence of an organisation increases as:

- needed resources become more scarce
- outsiders have more control over needed resources
- there are fewer substitutes for a particular type of resource controlled by a limited number of outsiders.

Thus, one political role of chief executives is to develop workable compromises among the competing resource dependencies facing the organisation — compromises that enhance the executive's power. To create such compromises, executives need to diagnose the relative power of outsiders and to craft strategies that respond differently to various external resource suppliers.

For larger organisations, many strategies may centre on altering the organisation's degree of resource dependence. Through mergers and acquisitions, an organisation may bring key resources within its control. By changing the 'rules of the game', an organisation may also find protection from particularly powerful outsiders; for instance, trade barriers may protect markets, or labour unions' 'right to work' laws may check union activity. Yet, there are limits on the ability of even our largest and most powerful organisations to control all important external contingencies. International competition has narrowed the range of options for chief executives; they can no longer ignore the rest of the world. Some may need to redefine fundamentally how they expect to conduct business. Once, many large firms in the Asia–Pacific region could go it alone without the assistance of foreign corporations, for example. Now chief executives are increasingly leading them in the direction of joint ventures and strategic alliances with foreign partners from around the globe. Such 'combinations' provide access to scarce resources and technologies among partners, as well as new markets and shared production costs.

> **Resource dependencies** occur when the organisation needs resources that others control.

Organisational governance

Organisational governance refers to the pattern of authority, influence and acceptable managerial behaviour established at the top of the organisation. This system establishes what is important, how issues will be defined, who should and should not be involved in key choices, and the boundaries for acceptable implementation. Those studying organisational governance suggest that a 'dominant coalition' comprising powerful organisational actors is a key to its understanding.[46] While you might expect many top officers within the organisation to be members of this coalition, the dominant coalition occasionally includes outsiders with access to key resources. Thus, analysis of organisational governance builds on the resource dependence perspective by highlighting the effective control of key resources by members of a dominant coalition.

> **Organisational governance** is the pattern of authority, influence and acceptable managerial behaviour established at the top of the organisation.

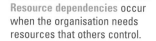

The issue of the governance and accountability of corporations has recently come to the fore following a wave of high-profile corporate scandals and collapses.[47] Undoubtedly the highest profile examples are US companies Enron and WorldCom, but Australia has its own cases in HIH and One.Tel. Corporate governance is concerned with the accountability of management to act in the interests of all stakeholders.[48]

This view of the executive suite recognises that the daily practice of organisational governance is the development and resolution of issues. Via the governance system, the dominant coalition attempts to define reality. By accepting or rejecting proposals from employees, by directing questions towards the interests of powerful outsiders, and by selecting individuals who appear to espouse particular values and qualities, the pattern of governance is slowly established within the organisation. Further, this pattern rests, at least in part, on very political foundations.

Whereas organisational governance was an internal and rather private matter in the past, it is becoming more public and openly controversial in many instances. While some argue that senior managers do not represent shareholder interests well enough, others are concerned that too little attention is given to public concerns — especially among those running organisations with high-risk technologies such as chemical processing, integrated oil refining and nuclear power. Even the ability to compete on a global scale can be controversial. While senior managers may blame such external factors as unfavourable trade laws and a 'weak' dollar, their critics suggest that a lack of global operating knowledge limits the corporations these managers are supposed to be leading.[49]

OB in action

An episode of boardroom turmoil at the National Australia Bank illustrates the extent to which power and politics operate at the highest levels of organisations. The NAB board was thrown into disarray after the bank lost A\$360 million due to weakness in its control of foreign exchange trading staff. The board adopted a report that placed the blame on board and audit committee member Catherine Walter. When Walter refused to resign, the board asked shareholders to remove her. Walter fought back, claiming she was being harassed and pointing out that the chairman was on the same committee overseeing foreign exchange trading as she had been. Some commentators said the chairman's decision to call for Walter's resignation at an extraordinary general meeting was absurd and reflected a lapse of management skill. Walter said effective boards should promote independence of thought and that leaders should work for what is right, not what is popular.

There is another new wrinkle in the discussions of organisational governance and executive pay. When corporations downsize, when they ask employees to take on new responsibilities in the form of empowerment initiatives, and when they start cutting such benefits as health care, employees begin to ask some serious questions about excessive executive compensation.

The politics of empire building

Executives are increasingly thinking in terms of kinship, paying more attention to personal networks to enhance their individual value, power and influence. It is a logical reaction to the rapid increase in the pace of business that can encourage an executive to focus on short-term results: many executives see their career prospects in terms of 'success today or gone tomorrow'.

Under such circumstances, executives may be inclined to recruit a 'mate' (someone they know well) as the best candidate for a position. When executives are judged on short-term achievements, their success depends on assembling an effective team quickly. It often can seem a rational choice for managers to bring in people they know, but the downside is that the lack of formal recruitment processes may mean the wrong people are hired. Morale may also suffer as existing staff see the boss's 'mates' moved into managerial positions ahead of them. Another risk is that people may start to believe the new executive is building a protective power base rather than developing a high-performance team. It is important for managers to realise that a good working relationship is only one element in achieving high performance. They also need to ensure any new employees are adding value to the organisation.

Another important consideration is that focusing on short-term financial results alone means a loss of focus on the deeper values of an organisation, such as its long-term relationship with the community or its distinctive values that attract both employees and customers. A perception of nepotism can be harmful to an executive.

The forces of extreme competition and globalisation are leading to the formation of executive teams — teams of managers that move as units to set up new businesses or turn around poorly performing ones. When large executive salaries are involved, and the time frames of organisational commitment are shortened, such teams may be seen as executive mercenaries. Such team movements can be a natural progression from forming good alliances, and introducing a team with good working relationships already in place can enhance performance. However, a lack of conflict in an executive team does not always guarantee high performance. Conflict is part of working in a team, and if managed well can add to its creativity and problem-solving skills (see chapter 7). Thus, there are benefits from hiring and sustaining diversity in executive teams as well as in organisations overall.

Many organisations believe they are reducing risk by hiring a complete executive team comprising individuals who have previously worked together. However, existing employees may perceive such a hiring policy as an exercise in empire building, and it may be difficult to attract employee commitment to the new team when employees question the organisational equity and fairness of such a team. Mistrust can result in a severe loss of morale in the company, and it may be difficult to convince employees that the organisation still rewards according to merit, and that promotions are earned through high performance. If the organisation introduces an empowerment program, employees may see the potential benefits but feel apprehensive about the likelihood of added opportunities if they no longer believe that merit will secure advancement. Under such circumstances, employees' immediate reaction to any change program may be one of guarded optimism, cynicism or mistrust. These reactions will inhibit the change process.

The consequences of power and politics

Whether or not organisational politics is good or bad may be a matter of perspective and depend on each situation. It may be good for an individual but not for the organisation, or individuals might suffer but the organisation might be better off.

The double-edged sword of organisational politics

The two different traditions of organisational politics (described on pages 362–3) are reflected in the ways in which executives describe their effects on managers and their organisations. In one survey, 53 per cent of those interviewed indicated that organisational politics enhanced the achievement of organisational goals and survival.[50] Yet 44 per cent suggested that it distracted individuals from organisational goals. In this survey, 60 per cent of respondents suggested that organisational politics was good for career advancement; 39 per cent reported that it led to a loss of power, position and credibility.

Organisational politics is not automatically good or bad. It can serve a number of important functions, including helping managers to:

- *overcome personnel inadequacies.* As a manager, you should expect some mismatches between people and positions in organisations. Even in the best-managed organisations, mismatches arise among managers who are learning, burned out, lacking in needed training and skills, overqualified, or lacking the resources needed to accomplish their assigned duties. Organisational politics provides a mechanism for circumventing these inadequacies and getting the job done.

- *cope with change.* Changes in the environment and technology of an organisation often come more quickly than an organisation can restructure. Even in organisations that are known for detailed planning, unanticipated events may occur. To meet unanticipated problems, people and resources must be moved into place quickly before small headaches become major problems. Organisational politics can help to identify such problems, and to move ambitious, problem-solving managers into the breach.
- *substitute for formal authority.* When a person's formal authority breaks down or fails to apply to a particular situation, political actions can be used to prevent a loss of influence. Managers may use political behaviour to maintain operations and to achieve task continuity in circumstances in which the failure of formal authority may otherwise cause problems.

Politics pervades most commercial and industrial organisations, and the organisation is frequently the loser. The varying political tactics can be highly counterproductive because they may be used to discredit and disable often more able colleagues.[51]

If political behaviour is effective in achieving organisational goals and overcoming the weaknesses of managers or of the system and processes in the organisation, then it *may* be highly beneficial. There may be cases in which politics dominates organisational activity to an extent that the activity is dysfunctional. Alternatively, it is unlikely that political behaviour never occurs, and if such a case existed it might be equally dysfunctional. The following sections on ethics and trust give further insight into political behaviour.

The ethics of power and politics in an organisation

LEARNING 7 OBJECTIVE

The ethics of power and politics

All managers use power and politics to get their work done, but every manager also bears a responsibility to do so in an ethical and socially responsible fashion. By recognising and confronting ethical considerations, each of us should be better prepared to meet this important challenge. No treatment of power and politics in organisations is complete without considering the related ethical issues. We can begin this task by clarifying the distinction between the non-political and political uses of power.[52] Power is non-political when it remains within the boundaries of usually formal authority, organisational policies and procedures, and job descriptions, and when it is directed towards ends sanctioned by the organisation. When the use of power moves outside the realm of authority, policies, procedures and job descriptions, or when it is directed towards ends not sanctioned by the organisation, that use of power is said to be political.

When the use of power moves into the realm of political behaviour, important ethical issues emerge. It is in this context that a manager must stop and consider more than a pure 'ends justify the means' logic. These issues are broader and involve distinctly ethical questions, as the following example shows.[53] When the role and importance of political actions is overemphasised and upheld, employees may be discouraged and may be led to slacken or underperform. This is because they come to realise that their effectiveness is limited not by knowledge of their own technical field, but by organisational and political factors, in the settings in which they operate. When prolonged, the situation will lead them to think that they have little direct control over events and must make progress by influencing others.

Chan is the production manager of a work group responsible for meeting a deadline that will require coordinated effort among her employees. Believing that the members of the work group will pull together and meet the deadline if they have a little competition, Chan decides to create the impression that members of the sales department want the group to fail to meet the deadline so sales can gain an edge over production in upcoming budgetary negotiations.

Think about what Chan's decision means. On the one hand, the action may seem justifiable if it works and the group gets its assigned job done on time. On the other hand, there may be negative side effects. What about the possibility that the sales and production departments will lose trust in one another and thus find it difficult to work together in the future? Also, consider the fact that Chan was 'creating an impression' to achieve her goal. Isn't this really 'lying'? And, if it is, can we accept lying as an ethical way for a manager to get a job done?

Work in the area of ethical issues in power and politics suggests the usefulness of the integrated structure for analysing political behaviour depicted in figure 10.6. This structure suggests that a person's behaviour must satisfy the following criteria to be considered ethical.[54]

1. *Utilitarian outcomes.* The behaviour results in optimisation of satisfactions of people both inside and outside the organisation; that is, it produces the greatest good for the greatest number of people.
2. *Individual rights.* The behaviour respects the rights of all affected parties; that is, it respects basic human rights of free consent, free speech, freedom of conscience, privacy and due process.
3. *Distributive justice.* The behaviour respects the rules of justice; that is, it treats people equitably and fairly, as opposed to arbitrarily.

The figure also indicates that there may be times when a behaviour is unable to pass these criteria but can still be considered ethical in the given situation. This special case must satisfy the criterion of overwhelming factors, in which the special nature of the situation results in:

- conflicts among criteria (for example, a behaviour results in some good and some bad)
- conflicts within criteria (for example, a behaviour uses questionable means to achieve a positive end)
- an incapacity to employ the criteria (for example, a person's behaviour is based on inaccurate or incomplete information).

Choosing to be ethical often involves considerable personal sacrifice. Four rationalisations are often used to justify unethical choices.

1. Individuals feel the behaviour is not really illegal and thus could be moral.
2. The action appears to be in the organisation's best interests.
3. It is unlikely the action will ever be detected.
4. The action appears to demonstrate loyalty to the boss or the organisation.

While these rationalisations may appear compelling at the moment of action, each deserves close scrutiny. The individual must ask: 'How far is too far?', 'What are the long-term interests of the organisation?', 'What will happen when (not if) the action is discovered?', and 'Do individuals, groups or organisations that ask for unethical behaviour deserve my loyalty?'[55]

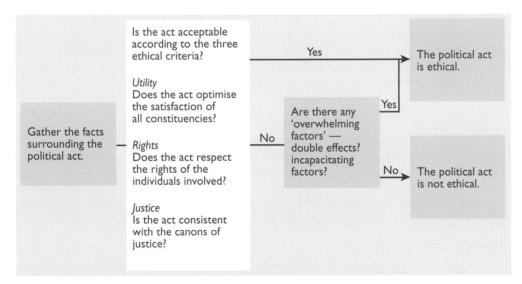

FIGURE 10.6 • An integrated structure for analysing political behaviour in organisations

Source: Manuel Velasquez, Dennis J Moberg and Gerald F Cavanagh, 'Organizational statesmanship and dirty politics: ethical guidelines for the organizational politician', *Organizational Dynamics*, vol. 11 (August 1983), p. 73. Used by permission.

Trust and managerial influence

Earlier in the chapter we looked at how critical trust is to managerial influence.[56] Generating trust in relationships involves taking an ethical stance. In a general sense, trust is the level of confidence you feel when you think about a relationship. Managers increase their influence when they build high-trust relationships with their employees. This influence does not operate through the manager, but through the common principles and values on which both parties have agreed, and through the past experience of keeping promises.

Any relationship in which employees find it difficult to trust their managers is troublesome. Managers experiencing a low-trust relationship with their employees are more likely to experience problems of harmonious and effective control in their day-to-day management. Managers vary in their predisposition to trust their employees. As we saw in chapter 2, individuals have personality differences. Distrustful managers tend to perceive their employees as self-centred, uncaring, intolerant, unmotivated and unresponsive. Their perceptions of employee behaviours and motives are biased by their initial suspicion.

Once trust has been violated it is doubly difficult to re-establish it. Even if a manager introduces change and tries to improve workplace relations, employees will tend to perceive positive actions in a negative light. This occurs, for example, when employees have undergone a series of downsizing decisions in a betrayal of earlier promises and yet are asked to retain faith in managerial promises for the future. In this situation, most employees would be unwilling to accept the promises in good faith because their trust has been violated. Further, every error, however unintentional, becomes one more piece of evidence that the new promise will also be betrayed and that nothing in workplace relations will change. It is not impossible to begin to repair the damage inherent in such a cycle, but the potential for rebuilding a relationship is fragile, especially when uncertainty and job insecurity continue to be part of organisational life. For these reasons, trustworthiness is a distinctive trait of an effective manager, and essential for effective influence. Managers who are considered untrustworthy will find it difficult to influence employees from either a position or personal power base.[57]

Summary

Power and its sources

Power is an essential managerial resource. It is demonstrated by the ability to get someone else to do what you want them to do. Power vested in managerial positions derives from three sources: rewards, punishments and legitimacy. Legitimacy, which is the same as formal authority, is based on the manager's position in the hierarchy of authority. Personal power is based on a person's expertise and reference; it allows managers to extend their power beyond that which is available in their position alone.

The relationship between power, authority and obedience

Power, authority and obedience are interrelated. Obedience occurs when one individual responds to the request or directive of another person. In the Milgram experiments, it was shown that people may have a tendency to obey directives coming from others who appear powerful and authoritative, even if these directives seem contrary to what the individual would normally consider to be 'right'. A zone of indifference defines the boundaries within which people in organisations will let others influence their behaviour without questioning it. Ultimately, power and authority work only if the individual 'accepts' them.

Managerial power and influence

Managerial perspectives on power and influence must include the practical considerations of how to obtain the power needed to get the job done. Managers can pursue various ways of acquiring both position and personal power. They can also become skilled at using various tactics, such as reason, friendliness, ingratiation and bargaining, to influence superiors, peers and employees.

Empowerment

Empowerment is the process through which managers help others acquire and use the power needed to make decisions that affect themselves and their work. Clear delegation of authority, integrated planning and the involvement of senior management are all important to implementing empowerment. However, the key to success lies in redefining power so everyone can gain. The redefinition emphasises power as the ability to get things done rather than to get others to do what you want.

Dual faces of politics

Organisational politics are inevitable. Managers must become comfortable with political behaviour in organisations and then use that behaviour responsibly and to good advantage. Politics involve the use of power to obtain ends not officially sanctioned, or to achieve sanctioned ends through unsanctioned means. Organisational politics is also use of power to find ways of balancing individual and collective interests in otherwise difficult circumstances.

Types and levels of political behaviour

Political action in organisations can be examined at the managerial, subunit and chief executive levels. It may also occur widely throughout the organisation's informal networks. For the manager, politics often occur in decision situations in which the interests of another manager or individual must be reconciled with their own. Politics also involve subunits that jockey for power and advantageous positions. For chief executives, politics come into play as resource dependencies with external environmental elements must be strategically managed, and as organisational governance is transacted among the members of a 'dominant coalition'. To minimise their risks when assembling teams to meet short-term objectives, managers may resort to hiring people with whom they have previously worked. This may be perceived as nepotism or an attempt at empire building. Managers need to be aware of the challenges of using teams of people they know well, who may be seen as 'mates' rather than the best people for the job.

The ethics of power and politics in an organisation

Organisational politics can be effective in getting things done in an organisation. It is not necessarily good or bad. Political behaviour can be especially useful in overcoming personnel inadequacies, in coping with change and in substituting for formal authority when it breaks down or does not cover a particular situation.

The ethics of power and politics are common to those found in any decision situation. Managers can easily slip into questionable territory as they resort to power plays and politics to get their way in situations where resistance exists. While this behaviour may be 'rationalised' as acceptable, it may not meet the personal test of ethical behaviour established in chapter 1. When political behaviour is ethical, it will satisfy the criteria of utilitarian outcomes, individual rights, distributive justice and/or overwhelming factors. Managers need to develop high-trust relationships and understand that trust involves taking an ethical stance. If they do not keep promises, or if they betray trust, then employees will be less likely to accept managerial influence from either a position or a personal power base.

Chapter 10 study guide

OB ## Key terms

coercive power, *p. 346*
empowerment, *p. 359*
expert power, *p. 349*
influence, *p. 345*
information power, *p. 349*

legitimate power, *p. 348*
organisational governance, *p. 367*
organisational politics, *p. 362*
power, *p. 345*
process power, *p. 348*

referent power, *p. 352*
resource dependencies, *p. 367*
reward power, *p. 346*
zone of indifference, *p. 354*

OB ## Review questions

1. Explain how power is acquired.
2. Explain some of the the ethical implications of power and politics.

3. How might personal power differ from authority?
4. Explain the meaning and importance of empowerment in an organisational context.

OB ## Application questions

1. Under what circumstances would managers increase their power and influence over other managers?
2. Why would organisations wish to empower their employees? Describe some of the risks associated with excessive empowerment?
3. How would a manager work to acquire greater levels of power, and is it ethical to do so? Explain your response, giving reasons and examples to support your point of view.

4. Describe some of the political tactics and tricks that an employee may use to gain influence and some power advantage over his or her manager.
5. Personal assistants and secretaries of people in power tend to have much influence in organisations. Explain the reasons and rationales for such influence.
6. Your lecturer asks you to complete and submit an assignment. Explain the various bases of power that she or he would be utilising to influence you and ensure your compliance.

OB ## Research questions

1. Find out what you can about 'emotional intelligence' and use that information to address the following questions. You may like to add specific examples to support your answers.
   (a) What is emotional intelligence, and how might it be used as a source of power for managers in an organisation?
   (b) Explain ways in which emotional intelligence might help managers engage in successful political behaviours?

   (c) What are the likely implications for ethics, trust and organisational effectiveness if managers are able to draw upon their emotional intelligence for political behaviours?

2. Search the Internet for information about a major company that you are familiar with. Try to find profiles of the directors either on the company web site or by conducting name searches. You may find information about their personal lives, their business activities, what other boards they serve on or what

other companies they are involved in. Report on the kind(s) of people who hold power on the board of the particular company you are investigating and where else they might have wealth, power and interests. What are the possible implications for the board of your company in terms of power and influence and relationships with other companies?

Running project

Complete the following activities for your chosen organisation.

1. Choose a manager in your organisation and explain the various types of power that he or she holds.

2. Try to identify others who hold various types of power (for example, referent power or expert power).

3. Assess the level to which your organisation empowers its employees. What has motivated this level of empowerment? What are the outcomes?

4. Identify recent examples of political behaviour in your organisation. Briefly assess them against figure 10.6 to determine whether they were ethical or unethical according to the model offered by Velasquez, Moberg and Cavanagh.

5. Try to identify an example of misuse of power in your organisation.

If you are studying an organisation to which you have direct access, exercise careful discretion in finding information for and answering questions 4 and 5.

Individual activity

Influence tactics

Objective
To check your understanding of influence tactics and when they may be most useful

Procedure
Read each of the following 11 statements made by Jackie to Lee and, by applying them to the given scenario:
(a) decide which influence tactic is being used and briefly explain your reasoning
(b) rank each statement from 1 to 11 in terms of how effective it might be in influencing Lee (although you have limited information, consider how you might feel and react if you were Lee)
(c) decide whether and why you think the approach is ethical and briefly explain your reasoning.

Scenario
The senior management of the organisation is developing a new proposal to introduce performance pay into the organisation. Jackie and Lee are managers at the same level in the organisation but in different sections. Jackie is seeking Lee's support to fight the proposal.

1. Come on, Lee. You've got to accept that this is the worst thing the company can do — look at the figures and how they show it won't work.

2. Lee, you've got to join me in fighting this proposal. I have to have your help.

3. I know you've always believed that performance pay will only ever advantage senior management while the rest of us are left carrying the workload. This is the only way our department is going to get ahead, and you're so good at speaking in public.

4. Lee, you need to help me fight this. If you don't, I'll have to reconsider the special arrangements I have for your staff when they want something from my department.

5. We need to get together to fight this proposal before it gets approved and ruins our operations.

6. Come on, Lee. The manager of Finance agrees with me that this proposal won't work.

7. I'd like you to help me fight this proposal. I'd help you out in the same situation, just as I did last year when you needed help with your upgrading application.

8. An intelligent person like you will immediately see that this proposal won't work.

9. Hi, Lee, you're looking bright and healthy today. That was a great job you did on last month's report.

10. If you support me on fighting this, I'll support you in your promotion application.

(continued)

11. Lee, would you look at this memo I've prepared to present a counter-argument to the performance pay proposal. I'd value your opinion.

Evaluation

Once you have ranked your responses, compare them to the information in the chapter that explains which influence tactics are likely to be most effective.

OB Group activity

Machiavellianism

Objectives

1. To assess individual Machiavellianism (Mach) scores
2. To explore the dynamics of power in a group environment
3. To develop an understanding of the rewards and frustrations of held power
4. To analyse behaviours of various Mach personality types

Total time: 45–60 minutes

Procedure

1. Complete the following ten-item Mach assessment instrument.[58] Follow directions for scoring your instrument individually.
2. Form a group of five to seven persons, and designate one individual as the official group 'observer'.
3. The observer will not participate in any of the discussion but will take notes on the activities of the group and later report to the class.

4. Your lecturer will announce the topic to be discussed. The topic should be highly controversial and stimulating, and one that encourages different viewpoints.
5. The observer will begin by handing a specific textbook or magazine to one member of the group. Only that member of the group may speak. The textbook or magazine will be held by that person until another member of the group signals, nonverbally, that they wish to have it. The person with the textbook or magazine may refuse to relinquish it, even when signalled. The group discussion has a time limit of 15 minutes.
6. Following the controversial discussion period, the group observer leads a group discussion on what they observed and learned about power phenomena, frustrations, feedback and so on.
7. Each group observer then presents what the group has learned to the entire class.

Mach assessment instrument

For each of the following statements, circle the number that most closely resembles your attitude.

	DISAGREE			AGREE	
Statement	A lot	A little	Neutral	A little	A lot
1. The best way to handle people is to tell them what they want to hear.	1	2	3	4	5
2. When you ask someone to do something for you, it is best to give the real reason for wanting it rather than reasons that may carry more weight.	1	2	3	4	5
3. Anyone who completely trusts someone else is asking for trouble.	1	2	3	4	5
4. It is hard to get ahead without cutting corners here and there.	1	2	3	4	5
5. It is safest to assume that all people have a vicious streak, and that it will emerge when they are given a chance.	1	2	3	4	5
6. You should take action only when it is morally right.	1	2	3	4	5

	DISAGREE			AGREE	
	A lot	A little	Neutral	A little	A lot
7. Most people are basically good and kind.	1	2	3	4	5
8. There is no excuse for lying to someone.	1	2	3	4	5
9. Most people forget more easily the death of their father than the loss of their property.	1	2	3	4	5
10. Generally speaking, people will not work hard unless forced to do so.	1	2	3	4	5

Scoring key and interpretation

This assessment is designed to compute your Machiavellianism (Mach) score. Mach is a personality characteristic that taps people's power orientation. The high-Mach personality is pragmatic, maintains emotional distance from others, and believes that ends can justify means. To obtain your Mach score, add up the numbers you circled for questions 1, 3, 4, 5, 9 and 10. For the other four questions, reverse the number you have circled, so 5 becomes 1, 4 is 2, and 1 is 5. Then total both sets of numbers to find your score. A random sample of adults found the national average to be 25. Students in business and management typically score higher.

Research using the Mach tests has found the following results.

- Men are generally more Machiavellian than women.
- Older adults tend to have lower Mach scores than those of younger adults.
- There is no significant difference between high Machs and low Machs on measures of intelligence or ability.
- Machiavellianism is not significantly related to demographic characteristics such as educational level or marital status.
- High Machs tend to be in professions that emphasise the control and manipulation of people — for example, managers, lawyers, psychiatrists and behavioural scientists.

Case study: Making Memories

OB

Scott stormed into his office. After he had spent four months developing a new system to track and quickly resolve consumer complaints at Making Memories, the management committee had decided that a commercially developed product was to be brought in to do the job. Scott had been in charge of handling customer complaints since he began his term in the business six months ago, and this was a key task in his job. He was proud of his proposal. He felt sure it would impress the owner-manager, Larry, and he was keen to do so since he was hoping his job would be made permanent.

Making Memories had been so successful that it had established outlets in all of Australia's capital cities, although only the consultants operated in these locations, with the small team of functional managers remaining in the Brisbane headquarters. The company produced personalised cards, albums, speeches and stories for significant occasions such as family reunions and special anniversaries. It was a unique business, with little competition and a wealthy clientele, but recent errors had led to angry customers and disputed accounts. Customer consultants, such as Trudy, interviewed customers and developed products to suit each customer's specific requirements. They had to pay a lot of attention to the stories, photos and other information given to them by customers to ensure they did a good job. Since the complaints had begun they were feeling very vulnerable to criticism.

Afterwards Scott thought about the meeting. When the issue came up for discussion he had risen confidently to present his report, but as he stood, Trudy had sent a buzz around the table: 'Hey everyone, CustomerFix have just brought out a new system that does this job for us.

(continued)

It's got all the bells and whistles so we can produce the right reports.' She handed around some brochures. After that Scott's presentation did not seem to go well, although everyone listened politely. Kerry, who had been fiddling with her calculator, said that as manager of finance (she handled the accounts of the business without support staff) she felt that Scott's figures were just too costly compared with the prices suggested in the brochure. Jim, in charge of IT (with two support staff), smiled at the others around the table and said, 'Great work, Scott, but I don't think we really need to go to all the trouble of setting up our own system. My staff are busy as it is, and this system is ready-made.' Scott argued that the system needed to be tailor-made in view of the very special nature of their work, but Trudy disputed this.

'You don't seem to trust us, Scott. With a product like this, our consultant staff will have a system to help them do what they already do well. They'll be able to identify and correct their own mistakes, preventing them if at all possible.'

'But you don't even know how it works,' Scott began. Kerry, who had encouraged Scott to undertake this investigation, interrupted, saying that if there was already an answer out there for their business they should run with it. 'I had Kim, the head of the customer consultants, investigate its suitability after Trudy mentioned it to me last week, and Kim reported that it's ideal.'

Kerry put it to the vote that, assuming the figures were right, they adopt the CustomerFix system as soon as possible.

Questions

1. What sources of power do the various staff members on the committee have in relation to one another? In what directions might influence be exerted in this committee, and how much influence might have already been used before the meeting?

2. What sort of political or power tactics are being used by the members of this committee, and what interests might they have in using them?

3. Do you think that the best outcome has resulted? Explain your answer.

OB Suggested reading

Peter Block, *The empowerment manager* (San Francisco: Jossey-Bass, 1987).

Lee G Bolman and Terrence E Deal, *Escape from cluelessness: a guide for the organizationally challenged* (New York: AMACOM, 2000).

Kenneth E Boulding, *Three faces of power* (Newbury Park, CA: Sage, 1989).

Dave Buchanan and Richard Badham, *Power, politics and organisational change: winning the turf game* (London: Sage, 1999).

David Butcher and Martin Clarke, *Smart management: using politics in organizations* (New York: Palgrave, 2001).

Ernest Alan Buttery and Ewa Maria Richter, 'On Machiavellian management', *Leadership and Organization Development Journal*, vol. 24, no. 8 (2003), pp. 426–35.

Allan R Cohen and David L Bradford, *Influence without authority* (New York: John Wiley & Sons, 1990).

Phillipe Daudi, P*ower in the organization: the discourse of power in managerial p*raxis (New York: Basil Blackwell, 1986).

Kyle Dover, 'Avoiding empowerment traps', *Management Review*, vol. 88, no. 1 (1999), pp. 51–5.

Mary Ann Hazen, 'Response to "The revolt against cultural authority: power/knowledge as an assumption in organization theory"', *Human Relations*, vol. 50, no. 9 (1997), pp. 1079–84.

Will Kalkhof and Christopher Barnum, 'The effects of status-organizing and social identity processes on patterns of social influence', *Social Psychology Quarterly*, vol. 63, issue 2 (June 2000), p. 95(21).

Michael Korda, *Power: how to get it, how to use it* (New York: Random House, 1975).

Meni Koslowsky and Shmuel Stashevsky, 'Organizational values and social power', *International Journal of Manpower*, vol. 26, no. 1 (2005), pp. 23–34.

John P Kotter, *A force for change: how leadership differs from management* (New York: The Free Press, 1990).

Mark McCutcheon, 'Pulling punches', (April 2002), p. 39.

Stanley B Petzall, Christopher T Selvarajah and Quentin F Willis, *Management: a behavioural approach* (Melbourne: Longman, 1991), ch. 8.

Jeffrey Pfeffer, *Managing with power: politics and influence in organizations* (Boston: Harvard Business School Press, 1994).

James T Scarnati, 'The Godfather theory of management: an exercise in power and control' *Management Decision*, vol. 40, no. 9 (2003), pp. 834–41.

D Sims, S Fineman and Y Gabriel, *Organizing and organizations* (London: Sage, 1993), ch. 8.

Theresa Vescio, K Mark Snyder and David A Butz, 'Power in stereotypically masculine domains: a social influence strategy X stereotype match model, *Journal of Personality and*

Social Psychology, vol. 85, issue 6 (December 2003), p. 1062(17).

Rachid Zeffane and David E Morgan, 'The implication of change strategies on organisational trust: evidence from Australia' in T Taillieu (ed.), *Organisational partnerships and cooperative strategies* (Leuven: Garant, 2001).

Rachid Zeffane and David E Morgan, 'Organisational change and trust: can management be trusted to change', *International Journal of Human Resource Management*, special Issue on Trust in the Workplace, vol. 14, no. 1 (2003), pp. 55–75.

End notes

1. Amazing Australian Entrepreneurs, http://www.amazingaustralia.com.au/entrepeneurs.htm.
2. Australian Broadcasting Corporation, 'A turbulent career', *7.30 Report* transcript, www.abc.net.au/7.30/stories/s20315.htm (viewed 19 December 2005).
3. ibid.
4. 'Dick Smith should be heeded', *The Age* (9 August 2004), http://www.theage.com.au/articles/2004/08/08/1091903443347.html?from=storylhs&oneclick=true#top.
5. Will Kalkhoff and Christopher Barnum, 'The effects of status-organizing and social identity processes on patterns of social influence', *Social Psychology Quarterly*, vol. 63, issue 2 (June 2000), p. 95(21).
6. ibid.
7. WN Shaw, 'Politics and management services', *Management Services*, vol. 30, issue 12 (December 1986), pp. 8–12.
8. Rosabeth Moss Kanter, 'Power failure in management circuit', *Harvard Business Review* (July/August 1979), pp. 65–75.
9. Jeffrey Pfeffer, 'Understanding power in organizations', *California Management Review*, vol. 34, no. 2 (1992), p. 45.
10. John RP French and Bertram Raven, 'The bases of social power' in Dorwin Cartwright (ed.), *Group dynamics: research and theory* (Evanston, IL: Row, Peterson, 1962), pp. 607–23.
11. See French and Raven, op. cit.
12. 'James Packer to take over family reigns', transcript of Australian Broadcasting Corporation radio program *AM*, 28 December 2005, www.abc.net.au/am/content/2005/s1538639.htm (viewed 19 January 2006).
13. Chris Jones, 'James Packer takes the reins', *The Herald Sun* (29 December 2005), www.heraldsun.news.com.au/common/story_page/0,5478,17679473%255E664,00.html (viewed 19 January 2006).
14. Office of the Ombudsman web site, http://www.employeeombudsman.sa.gov.au/info/Bullies_not_wanted.asp.
15. 'Does your boss make you sick?', http://www.geocities.com/sonnisc/bully1.html.
16. Office of the Ombudsman web site, http://www.employeeombudsman.sa.gov.au/info/Bullies_not_wanted.asp.
17. Julie-Anne O'Hagan, 'Bully for you', *The Sydney Morning Herald*, My Career section (18–19 May 2002), p. 1.
18. Tash Shifrin, 'Workplace bullying is widespread, survey shows', *Computer Weekly* (27 September 2005), p. 55.
19. See for example Charlotte Rayner, Michael Sheehan and Michelle Barker, 'Theoretical approaches to the study of bullying at work', *International Journal of Manpower*, vol. 20, no. 1 (1999); Michael Sheehan, Michelle Barker and Charlotte Rayner, 'Applying strategies for dealing with workplace bullying', *International Journal of Manpower*, vol. 20, no. 1 (1999); Michael Sheehan, 'Workplace bullying: responding with some emotional intelligence', *International Journal of Manpower*, vol. 20, no. 1 (1999).
20. 'Workplace bullying: a new angle on an old problem', *HR Monthly* (April 2002), p. 44.
21. O'Hagan, op. cit.
22. Wolfgang Scholl, 'Restrictive control and information pathologies in organizations. Social influence and social power: using theory for understanding social issues', *Journal of Social Issues*, vol. 55, issue 1 (Spring 1999), p. 101(1).
23. Stanley Milgram, 'Behavioral study of obedience' in Dennis W Organ (ed.), *The applied psychology of work behavior* (Dallas: Business Publications, 1978), pp. 384–98. Also see the following works by Stanley Milgram: 'Behavioral study of obedience', *Journal of Abnormal and Social Psychology*, vol. 67 (1963), pp. 371–8; 'Group pressure and action against a person', *Journal of Abnormal and Social Psychology*, vol. 69 (1964), pp. 137–43; 'Some conditions of obedience and disobedience to authority', *Human Relations*, vol. 1 (1965), pp. 57–76; *Obedience to authority* (New York: Harper & Row, 1974).
24. Chester Barnard, *The functions of the executive* (Cambridge, MA: Harvard University Press, 1938).
25. See Steven N Brenner and Earl A Mollander, 'Is the ethics of business changing?', *Harvard Business Review*, vol. 55 (February 1977), pp. 57–71; Barry Z Posner and Warren H Schmidt, 'Values and the American manager: an update', *California Management Review*, vol. 26 (Spring 1984), pp. 202–16.
26. John P Kotter, 'Power, success, and organizational effectiveness', *Organizational Dynamics*, vol. 6 (Winter 1978), p. 27.
27. David A Whetten and Kim S Cameron, *Developing managerial skills* (Glenview, IL: Scott, Foresman, 1984), pp. 250–9.
28. Whetten and Cameron, op. cit., pp. 260–6.
29. David Kipinis, Stuart M Schmidt, Chris Swaffin-Smith and Ian Wilkinson, 'Patterns of managerial influence: shotgun

managers, tacticians, and bystanders', *Organizational Dynamics*, vol. 12 (Winter 1984), pp. 60, 61.

30. ibid., pp. 58–67; David Kipinis, Stuart M Schmidt and Ian Wilkinson, 'Intraorganizational influence tactics: explorations in getting one's way', *Journal of Applied Psychology*, vol. 65 (1980), pp. 440–52.

31. Adapted from Gary Yukl, Patricia J Guinan and Debra Sottolano, 'Influence tactics used for different objectives with subordinates, peers, and superiors', *Groups & Organization Management*, vol. 20, no. 3 (September 1995), p. 275.

32. ibid, pp. 294–5.

33. Warren K Schilit and Edwin A Locke, 'A study of upward influence in organizations', *Administrative Science Quarterly*, vol. 27 (1982), pp. 304–16.

34. ibid.

35. David Kipinis, Stuart M Schmidt, Chris Swaffin-Smith and Ian Wilkinson, 'Patterns of managerial influence: shotgun managers, tacticians, and bystanders', *Organizational Dynamics*, vol. 12 (Winter 1984), pp. 58–67; David Kipinis, Stuart M Schmidt and Ian Wilkinson, 'Intraorganizational influence tactics: explorations in getting one's way', *Journal of Applied Psychology*, vol. 65 (1980), pp. 440–52.

36. Martin Dufficy, 'The empowerment audit-measured improvement', *Industrial and Commercial Training*, vol. 30, issue 4 (1998), pp. 142–6.

37. Bronston T Mayes and Robert W Allen, 'Toward a definition of organizational politics', *Academy of Management Review*, vol. 3, no. 4 (1977), p. 675.

38. Jeffrey Pfeffer, *Power in organizations* (Marshfield, MA: Pitman, 1981), p. 7.

39. Terry. F Waters-Marsh, 'Exploiting differences: the exercise of power and politics in organisations' in R Wiesner and B Millett (eds), *Management and Organisational Behaviour* (Brisbane: John Wiley & Sons, 2001), pp. 153–60.

40. Gareth Morgan, *Images of organization* (London: Sage, 1986), pp. 141–98.

41. Jarek Czechowicz, 'The winning ways of men and women', *Management Today* (January/February 2001), pp. 14–19.

42. Morgan, op. cit.

43. Developed from James L Hall and Joel L Leldecker, 'A review of vertical and lateral relations: a new perspective for managers' in Patrick Connor (ed.), *Dimensions in modern management*, 3rd ed. (Boston: Houghton Mifflin, 1982), pp. 138–46, which was based in part on Leonard Sayles, *Managerial behavior* (New York: McGraw-Hill, 1964).

44. See Jeffrey Pfeffer, *Organizations and organization theory* (Boston: Pitman, 1983); Jeffrey Pfeffer and Gerald R Salancik, *The external control of organizations* (Englewood Cliffs, NJ: Prentice Hall, 1978).

45. ibid.

46. James D Thompson, *Organizations in action* (New York: McGraw-Hill, 1967).

47. Michelle Hannen, 'What a bottler', *Business Review Weekly* (17–23 January 2002), p. 36.

48. Global Union Research Network (GURN), 'Corporate governance', http://www.gurn.info/topic/corpgov/.

49. RN Osborn and DH Jackson, 'Leaders, riverboat gamblers, or purposeful unintended consequences in management of complex technologies', *Academy of Management Journal*, vol. 31 (1988), pp. 924–47; M Hector, 'When actors comply: monitoring costs and the production of social order', *Acta Sociologica*, vol. 27 (1984), pp. 161–83; T Mitchell and WG Scott, 'Leadership failures, the distrusting public and prospects for the administrative state', *Public Administration Review*, vol. 47 (1987), pp. 445–52.

50. BE Ashforth and RT Lee, 'Defensive behavior in organizations: a preliminary model', *Human Relations* (July 1990), pp. 621–48; personal communication with Blake Ashforth, December 1992.

51. Amos Drory and Tsilia Romm, 'The definition of organizational politics: a review', *Human Relations*, vol. 43, no. 11 (1990), pp. 1133–54.

52. This discussion is based on G Cavanagh, D Moberg and M Velasquez, 'The ethics of organizational politics', *Academy of Management Review*, vol. 6 (1981), pp. 363–74 and Manuel Velasquez, Dennis J Moberg and Gerald Cavanagh, 'Organizational statesmanship and dirty politics: ethical guidelines for the organizational politician', *Organizational Dynamics*, vol. 11 (1983), pp. 65–79, both of which offer a fine treatment of the ethics of power and politics.

53. Adapted from G Cavanagh, D Moberg and M Velasquez, 'The ethics of organizational politics', *Academy of Management Review*, vol. 6 (1981), pp. 363–74.

54. These criteria are developed from Cavanagh, Moberg and Velasquez.

55. Saul W Gellerman, 'Why "good" managers make bad ethical choices', *Harvard Business Review*, vol. 64 (July/August 1986), pp. 85–97.

56. Rachid M Zeffane and David E Morgan, 'The implication of change strategies on organisational trust: evidence from Australia' in T Taillieu (ed.), *Organisational partnerships and cooperative strategies* (Leuven: Garant, 2001); Rachid M Zeffane and David E Morgan, 'Organisational change and trust: can management be trusted to change', *International Journal of Human Resource Management*, special issue on Trust in the Workplace, vol. 14, no. 1 (2003), pp. 55–75.

57. Fernando L Flores and Robert C Solomon, 'Rethinking trust', *Business and Professional Ethics Journal*, vol. 16, no. 1 (Spring 1997), p. 47; BF Meeker, 'Cooperative orientation, trust and reciprocity', *Human Relations* (March 1984), pp. 225–43; Dennis J Moberg, 'Trustworthiness and concientiousness as managerial virtues', *Business and Professional Ethics Journal*, vol. 16, no. 1 (Spring 1997), p. 171; Edward Soule, 'Trust and managerial responsibility', *Business Ethics Quarterly*, vol. 8, no. 2 (April 1998), p. 249.

58. Exercise adapted from R Christie and FL Geis, *Studies in Machiavellianism* (New York: Academic Press, 1970). Reproduced by permission.

CHAPTER 11
Leadership

OBJECTIVE **LEARNING**

Learning objectives
After studying this chapter,
you should be able to:

1. explain the difference between leadership and management

2. understand and evaluate trait and behavioural theories of leadership

3. understand and evaluate situational contingency theories of leadership

4. discuss charismatic leadership and transformational leadership

5. outline some of the current issues in diversity in leadership.

David Moffatt is Telstra's Group Managing Director, Consumer and Marketing, and prior to that he was Telstra's chief financial officer. Before joining Telstra, Moffatt had held positions as chief executive officer (CEO) of General Electric – Australia and New Zealand and CEO of GE Capital – Australia and New Zealand. Earlier in his career, he had held leadership roles with Palmer Tube Mills, Citibank and Bain & Company.

His career has given him a unique insight into leadership and management — their similarities and differences, and how the requirements of leaders vary across roles and organisations. Moffatt believes the CEO role and other senior management roles have a lot in common in terms of fundamental leadership skills, but that the emphasis is different. Moffatt says CEOs must be visionaries. They need to drive growth, be responsible for shaping and nurturing a company's culture, ensure the company is focused on the customer, promote values, and serve as the public face of the organisation. Other senior management roles, such as the chief financial officer, require more analysis and problem solving, and focus on enabling others in the organisation.

Leadership skills are still important: Moffat is responsible for the performance of thousands of people across various functions in the company. All of those people require leadership; a leader with strong people leadership skills. His staff want to be kept informed about where the organisation is going and what opportunities are available to be part of that process.

On final analysis, Moffat believes that the challenge facing a leader depends on the type of business she or he is in. 'In an organisation that is growing rapidly, a lot of the people issues almost resolve themselves, due to the inherent excitement of growth in the organisation. In an established organisation where the emphasis is on getting more productive, the issue is more difficult. You have to spend a lot more time working with people, being transparent, on getting more done with less, and linking back all the time to customer imperatives.'[1]

Introduction

As the chapter opening shows, regardless of their rank, senior managers are expected to play a leadership role. As leaders, they are expected to foster work environments conducive to learning and self-renewal. They need to develop a capability to create an appetite and agility for continuous change. They must encourage relationships and be able to build trust across the organisation. In fact, for most organisations to prosper and perform nationally and internationally, their managers need strong leadership skills. While the importance of leadership is indisputable, there is no singular type or style of leadership that works in all situations. Yet, the kind of leadership that is vital for organisational success is not a phenomenon that develops magically on its own.[2]

Continuing the discussions of power and influence, this chapter focuses on the topical issue of leadership — a special form of influence and the subject of enduring interest in organisational behaviour. Most attention has been focused on answering the central question — what makes a good leader? Is it personality characteristics, a set of behaviours, or the ability to adapt leadership style to different followers and situations? Can effective leadership be taught or is it something a person is born with?

Some people have posed an even more fundamental question — are leaders always accountable for failures or lack of achievement of their group or organisation? Let us think of a professional sports team that has had a bad season and the likelihood of the coaches taking the blame for the bad performance. This is a recurrent phenomenon. Yet it is hard to believe that coaches are always to blame for the failure of a team.

In this chapter we first examine the traditional approaches to leadership.[3] We will differentiate between notions of leadership and management, and summarise and evaluate the major theories of leadership. The essential elements of 'new leadership theory', particularly charismatic and transformational ideas, will then be identified. We will also discuss the issue of diversity as it poses a challenge to leadership.

Until recent years, little leadership research had been undertaken in Australia and New Zealand. More recently, a few projects on leadership were initiated which include data from Australia and New Zealand. Among others, the works of Ken Parry and Neal Ashkanasy are to be noted.[4] The more recent empirical research on leadership in the Australian context, co-led by James Sarros from Monash University, reinforced the importance of this topic both in theory and in practice. In particular, the Australian Business Leaders Survey (ABLS) identified dominant leadership styles of Australian executives, their perceptions of organisational culture and their responses to current issues related to leadership performance. We will look at some of the survey findings in this chapter.[5]

Leadership and management

Differences between leadership and management

LEARNING OBJECTIVE 1

In earlier chapters of this book we often referred to 'managers' and to 'management functions'. A fundamental question is whether leadership and management are (or can be) separated. There is often heated controversy over whether leaders are different from managers, and whether management is different from leadership.

A simple distinction would be to say that leadership is more concerned about doing the right thing while management is about doing things right Another way to make the same distinction is to argue that management is more concerned with promoting stability and enabling the organisation to run smoothly, while the role of leadership is to promote adaptive and long-term change. Managers see and solve problems, while leaders see possibilities to overcome these by going beyond them.

Hence leaders' roles are distinguishable from those of managers:

Managers are concerned with making things happen and keeping work on schedule, engaging in routine interactions to fulfil planned actions.

Leaders provide inspiration, create opportunities, coach and motivate people to gain their support on fundamental long-term choices.

- **Managers** are concerned with making things happen and keeping work on schedule, engaging in routine interactions to fulfil planned actions.
- **Leaders** provide inspiration, create opportunities, coach and motivate people to gain their support on fundamental long-term choices.

Leadership is all about using appropriate interpersonal styles and methods in guiding individuals and groups towards task accomplishment.

In practice, however, most managers are expected to be leaders or to play leadership roles as well. They are expected to be able to influence and inspire the people in their organisation to work willingly towards organisational goals, and to encourage high-quality results. What is often required of them, in the same way as it is for leaders, is a balanced and strong concern for both people and task.

In the main, leadership is a special case of interpersonal influence that gets an individual or group to do what the leader wants them to do.

Leadership may take two forms:

1. formal leadership, which is exerted by individuals appointed to or elected to positions of formal authority in organisations
2. informal leadership, which is exerted by individuals who become influential because they have special skills that meet the needs and resources of others.

Both types of leadership are important in organisations.

Leadership is a special case of interpersonal influence that gets an individual or group to do what the leader wants done.

Formal leadership is the process of exercising influence from a position of formal authority in an organisation.

Informal leadership is the process of exercising influence through special skills or resources that meet the needs of other people.

Development of theories on leadership

The leadership literature is vast and consists of numerous approaches. In figure 11.1 these approaches are arranged to help you understand and use them. The theories are divided into two categories: traditional leadership and new leadership.[6] As you will see, both are important for a leader. The traditional perspectives go back many years and vary in the emphasis they place on the role of leadership.

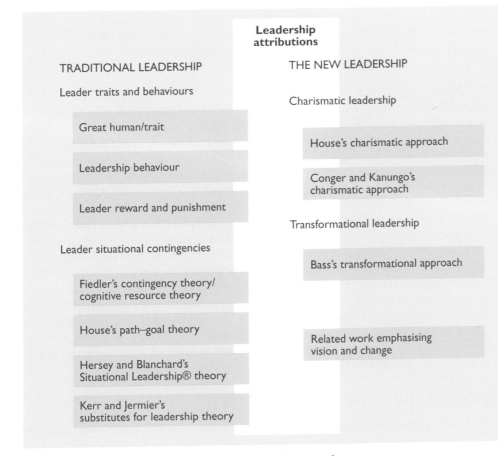

FIGURE 11.1 • Representative traditional and new leadership perspectives

The trait and behaviour approaches on the top left of figure 11.1 conceptualise leadership as central to the various task performance and human resource maintenance outputs emphasised in our individual performance equation. Most of the situational contingency approaches also conceive of leadership as central but only in combination with various other situational aspects called 'situational contingencies'. The last of these approaches — Kerr and Jermier's substitutes for leadership theory — raises the question of whether such factors as employee experience and detailed company policies and procedures may provide so much structure (that is, act as leadership substitutes) that hierarchical leadership is not needed. For example, think of how little leadership guidance or structure you need to do something at which you are experienced.

Figure 11.1 depicts attribution theory as overlapping both the traditional and new leadership perspectives (the new more than the traditional). The new leadership shows a range of theories emphasising some combination of charisma (that is, attribution of exceptional abilities to the leader), vision or change.

Leadership development is crucial in Australian organisations, according to Glenn Bates.[7]

The quality and performance of our present and future leaders are [the] key to building longer-term capability. The impact of leaders at all levels is so great — both on the future of the organisation and on the wellbeing and effectiveness of the people within it — that we must get this aspect right.

Trait and behavioural theories of leadership

LEARNING OBJECTIVE 2

Traditional leadership approaches: trait and behavioural theories

All the trait and behavioural approaches assume, in one way or another, that selected personal traits or behaviours have a major impact on leadership outputs; that is, according to these theories, leadership is central and other variables are relatively less important. However, the various approaches offer different explanations for leadership results.

Trait theory

Trait theory is the earliest approach used to study leadership and dates back to as early as the turn of the twentieth century. The early studies attempted to identify those traits that differentiated the 'great person' in history from the masses (for example, how did Peter the Great differ from his followers?).[8] This approach led to a research emphasis that tried to separate leaders from non-leaders, or more effective leaders from less effective leaders. The argument was that certain traits are related to success and that these traits, once identified, could be used to select leaders. This argument is made in chapter 2, concerning individual attributes, except that this earlier research concentrated on leaders and looked for general traits, cutting across groups and organisations. Thus, researchers looked at traits such as height, integrity, intelligence and the like. Proof of this theory lies in predicting and finding a set of traits (charisma, intelligence and so on) that differentiates effective leaders from ineffective ones — that is, it is derived from whether a set of traits distinguishes leaders from non-leaders (followers).

For various reasons, including inadequate theorising, inadequate measurement of many traits and failure to recognise possible differences in organisations and situations, the studies were not successful enough to provide a general trait theory.[9] But they laid the groundwork for considering certain traits, in combination with other leadership aspects (such as behaviours), that forms the basis for some of the more current theories.

Behavioural theories

By the 1940s attention had turned towards a behavioural position about leadership. In essence, the focus changed from attempting to identify the inner traits of leaders to one of examining their behaviour.

Like the trait approach, the behavioural theories approach assumes that leadership is central to performance and human resource maintenance. However, instead of dealing with underlying traits, it considers behaviours or actions. Two classic research programs at the University of Michigan and Ohio State University provide useful insights into leadership behaviours.

The Michigan studies

In the late 1940s researchers at the University of Michigan introduced a program of research on leadership behaviour. The researchers were concerned with identifying the leadership pattern that results in effective performance. From interviews of high- and low-performing groups in different organisations, the researchers derived two basic forms of leader behaviours: employee-centred and production-centred. *Employee-centred supervisors* are those who place strong emphasis on the welfare of their employees. In contrast, *production-centred supervisors* tend to place a stronger emphasis on getting the work done than on the welfare of the employees. In general, employee-centred supervisors were found to have more productive work groups than those of the production-centred supervisors.[10]

These behaviours may be viewed on a continuum, with employee-centred supervisors at one end and production-centred supervisors at the other. Sometimes, the more general terms 'human relations oriented' and 'task oriented' are used to describe these alternative leader behaviours.

The Ohio State studies

An important leadership research program was started at Ohio State University at about the same time as the Michigan studies. A questionnaire was administered in both industrial and military settings to measure subordinates' perceptions of their superiors' leadership behaviour. The researchers identified two dimensions similar to those found in the Michigan studies: *consideration* and *initiating structure*.[11] Highly considerate leaders are sensitive to people's feelings and, much like employee-centred leaders, try to make things pleasant for their followers. In contrast, leaders high in initiating structure are more concerned with spelling out task requirements and clarifying other aspects of the work agenda; they may be seen as similar to production-centred supervisors. These dimensions are related to what people sometimes refer to as socioemotional and task leadership, respectively. They also encompass what we discussed in chapter 8 as group maintenance and task activities.

At first, the Ohio State researchers thought that a leader high on consideration, or socioemotional warmth, would have more highly satisfied and/or better performing employees. Later results indicated that leaders should be high on both consideration and initiating structure behaviours. This dual emphasis is reflected in the Leadership Grid® approach.

The Leadership Grid®

Robert Blake and Jane Mouton developed the Leadership Grid® perspective.[12] It measures a manager's:
- *concern for people* and
- *concern for production*.

The results are then plotted on a nine-position grid that places these concerns on the vertical axis and horizontal axis, respectively (figure 11.2). A person with a 9/1 score is a 'country club manager' (9 on concern for people; 1 on concern for production). Some other positions are 1/1 — impoverished management style — and 1/9 — task management style. A 5/5 style, in the middle of the grid, is a middle-of-the-road management style. The ideal position is a 9/9 'team manager' (high on both dimensions).

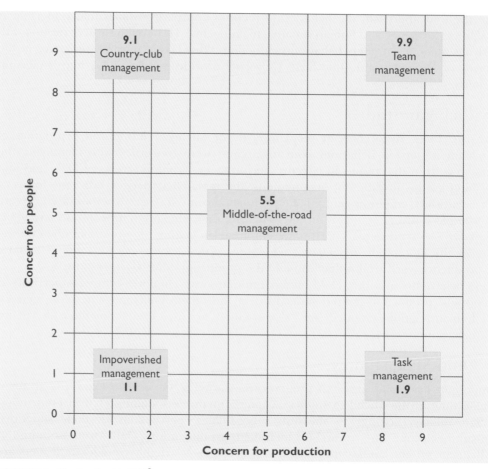

FIGURE 11.2 • The Leadership Grid®

The behavioural approaches discussed share a common emphasis on the importance of people-oriented and production- or task-oriented behaviours in determining outputs. But how well do these behaviours transfer internationally? Research in the United States, the United Kingdom, Hong Kong and Japan shows that the behaviours, although they seem to be generally important in all these countries, must be carried out in different ways in different cultures. UK leaders, for instance, are seen as considerate if they show employees how to use equipment, whereas in Japan the highly considerate manager helps employees with personal problems.[13]

Situational contingency theories of leadership

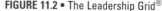

LEARNING **3** OBJECTIVE

Situational contingency theories of leadership

Despite their usefulness, behavioural theories of leadership proved difficult to justify. Leaders with the same behavioural tendencies could find success in one situation and not in another. This led researchers to propose that perhaps the leader's situation is a critical contributor to the likelihood of success. Adding situational characteristics underlined the fact that leadership is more complex than isolating a set of unique traits or behaviours. This led to the emergence of the contingency approach to leadership, which encompasses a number of theories.

Some of the main contributions of these theories include the work of Fred Fiedler, Robert House, Paul Hersey and Kenneth Blanchard, and Steven Kerr and John Jermier.

Fiedler's leadership contingency theory

The first situational contingency approach we consider is Fred Fiedler's, because his work essentially started the situational contingency era in the mid-1960s.[14] Fiedler's approach predicts work group effectiveness. His theory holds that group effectiveness depends on an appropriate match between a leader's style and the demands of the situation. Specifically, Fiedler considers the amount of control the situation allows the leader. Situational control is the extent to which leaders can determine what their group is going to do, and what will be the outcomes of the group's actions and decisions. Where control is high, leaders can predict with a good deal of certainty what will happen when they want something done.

Fiedler uses an instrument called the least preferred coworker (LPC) scale to measure a person's leadership style. Respondents are asked to describe the person with whom they are able to work least well (their least preferred coworker, or LPC), using a series of adjectives such as these:

Unfriendly   ....   Friendly

            1   2   3   4   5   6   7   8

Pleasant   ....   Unpleasant

            1   2   3   4   5   6   7   8

Fiedler argues that high LPC leaders (those describing their LPC very positively) have a relationship-motivated style, while low LPC leaders have a task-oriented style. In other words, relationship-oriented leaders describe more favourably the person with whom they are least able to work than do task-oriented leaders.

Fiedler considers this task or relationship motivation to be a trait that leads to either directive or nondirective behaviour, depending on whether the leader has high, moderate or low situational control (as already described).

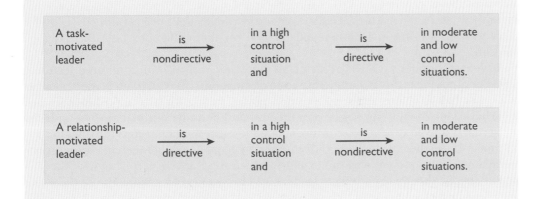

Let us now elaborate on Fiedler's situational control concept and its match with task- and relationship-oriented styles. Figure 11.3 shows the task-oriented leader as having greater group effectiveness under high and low situational control, while the relationship-oriented leader has a more effective group under a moderate control situation.

The figure also shows that Fiedler measures high, moderate and low control with the following three variables arranged in the situational combinations indicated:

- *leader–member relations* (good/poor) — member support for the leader
- *task structure* (high/low) — spelling out of the leader's task goals, procedures and guidelines in the group
- *position power* (strong/weak) — the leader's task expertise and reward/punishment authority.

Situational control is the extent to which leaders can determine what their group is going to do and what the outcomes of their actions and decisions are going to be.

Least preferred coworker (LPC) scale is a measure of a person's leadership style based on a description of the person with whom respondents have been able to work least well.

Following are some examples showing how different combinations of these variables provide differing amounts of situational control. First, consider the experienced and well-trained supervisor of a group that manufactures a part for a car engine. The leader is highly supported by his group members and can grant raises and make hiring and firing decisions. This supervisor would have high situational control and would be operating in situation I in figure 11.3. Likewise, those leaders operating in situations II and III would have high situational control, although not as high as that of our production supervisor. In any of these three high-control situations, a task-oriented leader behaving nondirectively would have the most effective group.

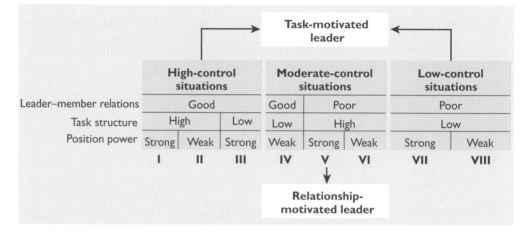

FIGURE 11.3 • Predictions from Fiedler's contingency theory of leadership

Contrast the previous example with the chair of a student council committee of volunteers who are not happy about this person being the chair and who have the low-structured task of organising a Parents' Day program to improve school–parent relations. Here we have a low-control situation (situation VIII) calling for a task-motivated leader who would need to behave directively. In other words, Fiedler argues that the leader must act directively in this situation to keep the group together and focused on the ambiguous task; the situation demands it.

Finally, let us consider a well-liked academic department head with a tenured lecturing staff. Fiedler argues that this is a moderate-control situation (IV) with good leader–member relations, low task structure and weak position power, calling for a relationship-motivated leader. The leader should emphasise nondirective and considerate relationships with the lecturing staff. Can you develop one or two moderate-control relationships for situation V?

To summarise, Fiedler's model links effectiveness with the match between the leader's style of interacting with employees and the extent to which the leader has control over the situation. Put simply, this theory predicts leadership effectiveness as a function of these two factors. Using Fiedler's developed LPC (least preferred coworker) questionnaire, it is possible to identify a person's style (person or task oriented) and then assess the situational component through three criteria — leader–member relations, task structure and position power.

Fiedler's cognitive resource theory[15]

Fiedler has since moved beyond his contingency theory by developing the cognitive resource theory. Cognitive resources are abilities or competencies. According to this approach, whether a leader should use directive or nondirective behaviour depends on the following situational contingencies: the leader's or subordinate group member's ability/competency; stress; experience; and group support of the leader. Basically, cognitive resource theory is most useful because it directs us to leader or subordinate group member ability, which other leadership approaches typically do not consider.

The theory views directiveness as most helpful for performance when the leader is competent, relaxed and supported. In this case, the group is ready and directiveness is the clearest means of communication. When the leader feels stressed, they are diverted. In this case, experience is more important than ability. If group support is low, then the group is less receptive and the leader has less impact. Group member ability becomes most important when the leader is nondirective and there is strong support from group members. If group support is weak, then task difficulty or other factors have more impact than do either the leader or the followers.

More recent studies have verified and extended Fiedler's contingency model of leadership effectiveness to followers' behaviour. For instance, a recent study of personnel serving with the US army in Europe re-examined the relationship between followers' motivational disposition, situational favourability and followers' performance. That study found that, in accordance with Fiedler, relations-oriented followers performed better in moderately favourable situations while task-oriented followers performed better in highly unfavourable situations.[16]

Although there are still unanswered questions concerning Fiedler's contingency theory (especially concerning the meaning of LPC), the theory continues to receive relatively strong support both in academia and in practice.

House's path–goal theory of leadership

Another well-known approach to situational contingencies is one developed by Robert House based on the earlier work of others.[17] This theory has its roots in the expectancy model of motivation (chapter 3). The term 'path–goal' is used because it emphasises how a leader influences employees' perceptions of both work goals and personal goals and the links or paths found between these two sets of goals.

The theory assumes that a leader's key function is to adjust his or her behaviours to complement situational contingencies, such as those found in the work setting. House argues that when the leader is able to compensate for things lacking in the setting, employees are likely to be satisfied with the leader. The leader could, for example, help remove job ambiguity or show how good performance could lead to more pay. Performance should improve as leaders clarify the paths by which effort leads to performance (expectancy) and performance leads to valued rewards (instrumentality). Redundant behaviour by the leader will not help, and may even hinder, performance. People do not need a boss telling them how to do something that they already know how to do!

House's model represents a process approach to leadership that takes into account three interrelated variables. The overall process in sequential order is:

Details of House's approach are summarised in figure 11.4. The figure shows four types of leader behaviours — directive, supportive, achievement-oriented and participative —and two categories of situational contingency variables — employee attributes and work-setting attributes. The leader behaviours are adjusted to complement the situational contingency variables to influence employee satisfaction, acceptance of the leader and motivation for task performance.

- **Directive leadership** has to do with spelling out the what and how of employees' tasks; it is much like the initiating structure mentioned earlier.
- **Supportive leadership** focuses on employee needs and wellbeing, and promotes a friendly work climate; it is similar to consideration.

Directive leadership is leadership behaviour that spells out the what and how of employees' tasks.

Supportive leadership is a leadership style that focuses on employee needs and wellbeing, and promotes a friendly work climate; it is similar to consideration.

Achievement-oriented leadership is leadership behaviour that emphasises setting challenging goals, stressing excellence in performance and showing confidence in the group members' abilities to achieve high standards of performance.

Participative leadership is a leadership style that focuses on consulting with employees, and seeking and accounting for their suggestions before making decisions.

- **Achievement-oriented leadership** emphasises setting challenging goals, stressing excellence in performance and showing confidence in the group members' abilities to achieve high standards of performance.
- **Participative leadership** focuses on consulting with employees and seeking and accounting for their suggestions before making decisions.

The contingency variables include employee attributes and work-setting or environmental attributes. Important employee characteristics are authoritarianism (closed-mindedness, rigidity), internal–external orientation (for example, locus of control) and ability. The key work-setting factors are the nature of the employees' tasks (task structure), the formal authority system and the primary work group.

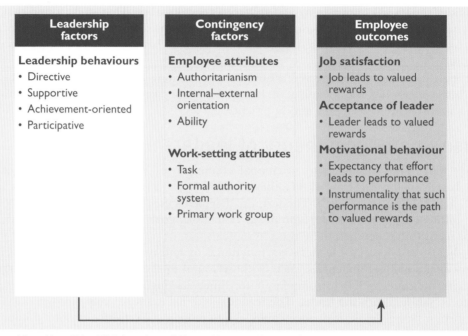

FIGURE 11.4 • Summary of major path–goal relationships in House's leadership approach

Source: Adapted from Richard N Osborn, James G Hunt and Lawrence R Jauch, *Organizational theory: an integrated approach* (New York: John Wiley & Sons, 1980), p. 464. Reprinted with permission.

House's path–goal approach has attracted considerable research, and there is support for the theory in general as well as for the particular predictions discussed earlier.[18] Not all aspects shown in figure 11.4 have been tested, and few applications have been reported in the literature. The path–goal approach lends itself to at least a couple of possibilities, however. First, training could be used to change leadership behaviour to fit the situational contingencies. Second, the leader could be taught to diagnose the situation and to learn how to change the contingencies (employee attributes and work-setting attributes).

Hersey and Blanchard's Situational Leadership® model

The Situational Leadership® model developed by Paul Hersey and Kenneth Blanchard is similar to the other situational approaches in its view that there is no single best way to lead.[19] Like the approaches discussed earlier, Situational Leadership® emphasises situational contingencies. Hersey and Blanchard focus on the readiness of followers, in particular. Readiness is the extent to which people have the ability and willingness to accomplish a specific task. Hersey and Blanchard argue that 'situational' leadership requires adjusting the leader's emphasis on task behaviours (for example, giving guidance and direction) and relationship behaviours (for example, providing socioemotional support) according to the readiness of followers to perform their tasks.

The model identifies four leadership styles:

- delegating
- participating
- selling
- telling.

Each emphasises a different combination of task and relationship behaviours by the leader. The model suggests a particular leadership style for followers at each of four readiness levels.

A telling style is best for low follower readiness. The direction provided by this style defines roles for people who are unable and unwilling to take responsibility themselves; it eliminates any insecurity about the task that must be done.

A selling style is best for low to moderate follower readiness. This style offers both task direction and support for people who are unable but willing to take task responsibility; it involves combining a directive approach with explanation and reinforcement to maintain enthusiasm.

A participating style is best for moderate to high follower readiness. Able but unwilling followers require supportive behaviour to increase their motivation; by allowing followers to share in decision making, this style helps enhance the desire to perform a task.

A delegating style is best for high readiness. This style provides little in terms of direction and support for the task at hand; it allows able and willing followers to take responsibility for what needs to be done.

This Situational Leadership® approach requires the leader to develop the capability to diagnose the demands of situations and then to choose and implement the appropriate leadership response. The theory gives specific attention to followers and their feelings about the task at hand. It also suggests that an effective leader reassess situations over time, giving special attention to emerging changes in the level of readiness of the people involved in the work. Again, Hersey and Blanchard advise that leadership style should be adjusted as necessary to remain consistent with actual levels of follower readiness. They further suggest that effectiveness should improve as a result.[20]

The Situational Leadership® approach has a great deal of intuitive appeal for managers but little systematic research support. What support is available is not very strong, and the theory still needs systematic empirical evaluation.[21]

The approach does include an elaborate training program that has been developed to train leaders to diagnose and emphasise appropriate behaviours. Internationally, this program is particularly popular in Europe, where an organisation headquartered in Amsterdam provides Situational Leadership® training for leaders in many countries.

Substitutes for leadership

In contrast to the previous approaches listed in figure 11.1, the 'substitutes for leadership' perspective argues that sometimes hierarchical leadership makes essentially no difference. John Jermier and others contend that certain individual, job and organisational variables can either serve as substitutes for leadership or neutralise a leader's impact on employees.[22] Examples of these variables are shown in figure 11.5. Experience, ability and training, for example, can serve as individual characteristics; a highly structured or routine job can serve as a job characteristic; and a cohesive work group can serve as an organisational characteristic.

Substitutes for leadership make a leader's influence both impossible and unnecessary. *Neutralisers* make a leader's influence impossible but not unnecessary; substitutes replace a leader's influence. As you can see in figure 11.5 it will be difficult, if not impossible, for a leader to provide the kind of task-oriented direction already available to an experienced, talented and well-trained employee. Further, such direction will be unnecessary, given the employee's characteristics. The figure shows a similar argument for a highly structured task.

Substitutes for leadership are organisation, individual, or task-situational variables that substitute for leadership in causing performance/human resource maintenance.

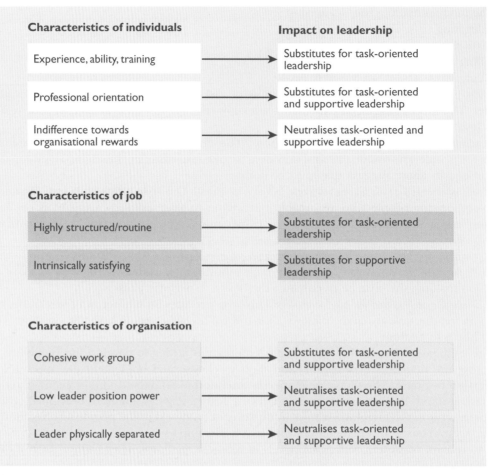

FIGURE 11.5 • Example leadership substitutes and neutralisers

Source: Based on Steven Kerr and John Jermier, 'Substitutes for leadership: their meaning and measurement', *Organizational Behavior and Human Performance*, vol. 22 (1978), p. 387; and Fred Luthans, *Organizational behavior*, 6th ed. (New York: McGraw-Hill, 1992), ch. 10.

Now let us look at a couple of neutralising examples in the figure. If leaders have low position power or formal authority, their leadership may be negated, even though task structuring and supportiveness are still needed. If leaders are physically separated from employees, their task-oriented and supportive leadership may be negated but still necessary.

The substitutes for leadership perspective is a more generalised version of the situational contingency approaches mentioned earlier, particularly House's path–goal theory. However, the substitutes perspective goes further by assuming that leadership in some cases has no impact on outputs because it is replaced by other factors. The earlier situational approaches argued that both leadership and other factors are needed.

Research on the substitutes theory has shown mixed results. Some work comparing Mexican and US workers suggests both similarities and differences between various substitutes in the two countries.[23] Within the United States, some early work appeared to support the theory, but two later, comprehensive studies (covering 13 different organisations) provided little support.[24]

Despite this last finding, given the emerging importance and popularity of work teams, leadership substitutes are likely to be important and need to be tailored to the team-oriented workplace. Thus, in place of a leader specifying standards and ways of achieving goals (task-oriented behaviours), the team will set its own standards and substitute these for the leader's.

Emerging leadership perspectives

So far, we have taken a well-trodden path in presenting theories of leadership from a historical perspective. However, no building-block progression of knowledge is assumed, and you should be careful not to jump to the conclusion, for example, that most recent is necessarily best!

More recent ideas are attribution theory of leadership, charismatic leadership, transaction versus transformational leadership, and leading through empowerment.

The more recent approaches to leadership have tended to move right away from traditional leadership characteristics and endorse charisma, vision and transformation as catalysts to effective leadership.

OBJECTIVE 4 LEARNING

Charismatic leadership and transformational leadership

OB in action

> In his introduction to *Hitler and Churchill: secrets of leadership*,[25] Andrew Roberts suggests Adolf Hitler was a 'charismatic' leader while Winston Churchill was an 'inspirational' leader. Hitler rose to power by recognising and capitalising on the German resentment towards the Treaty of Versailles. He sustained his power using the convenient scapegoat of the Jewish people. He promoted a vision of a new and glorious German empire. Churchill's vision was to create a powerful alliance to defend freedom. He created a popular mood and sustained it with courage and persistence. In the light of history the inspirational leader prevailed over the charismatic one. Roberts suggests that leaders, be they like Churchill or Hitler, create a common goal with which people can wholeheartedly identify, but that *managers* lack that guiding vision.[26]

The general notion that leadership is largely symbolic or 'in the eye of the beholder' has carried over to a related set of research directions. Ironically, the first of these argues that leadership makes little or no real difference to organisational effectiveness. The second tends to attribute greatly exaggerated importance to leadership and leads us into charisma and other aspects of the new leadership. Let us briefly examine each of these two directions.

Charismatic approaches[27]

Charismatic leadership uses attribution theory to suggest that we make attributions of heroic leadership competencies or personal characteristics when we see good leaders in action. Conger and Kanungo, for example, assert that charismatic leaders are self-confident, display an articulate vision and have strong conviction of their vision.[28]

Robert House and his associates have produced some work based on extensions of an earlier charismatic theory that House developed (not to be confused with House's path–goal theory, discussed earlier in the chapter). Especially interesting is the fact that House's theory uses both *trait* and *behaviour* combinations.

House sees charismatic leaders as those 'who by force of their personalities are capable of having a profound and extraordinary effect on followers'. Essentially, these leaders are high in need for power and have high feelings of self-efficacy and conviction in the moral rightness of their beliefs; that is, the need for power motivates these people to want to be leaders and this need is then reinforced by their conviction of the moral rightness of their beliefs. The feeling of self-efficacy, in turn, makes people feel that they are capable of being leaders. These traits then influence such charismatic behaviours as role modelling, image building, articulating goals (focusing on simple and dramatic goals), emphasising high expectations, showing confidence and arousing follower motives.

Charismatic leaders are those leaders who, by force of their personal abilities, are capable of having a profound and extraordinary effect on followers.

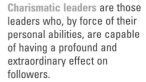

House and his colleagues also summarise several other studies that support aspects of the theory. Some of the more interesting related work has shown that negative, or 'dark-side', charismatic leaders emphasise personalised power (focus on themselves), while positive, or 'bright-side', charismatics emphasise socialised power that tends to empower their followers. This helps explain differences between such dark-side leaders as Adolf Hitler, David Koresh and Reverend Jim Jones and bright-side leaders such as Martin Luther King Junior,[29] Nelson Mandela or Gandhi.

Jay Conger has developed a four-stage charismatic leadership theory based on his work with Rabindra Kanungo.[30] In the first stage, the leader develops a vision of idealised change that moves beyond the status quo; for example, US President John F Kennedy had a vision of putting a man on the moon by the end of the 1960s. In the second stage, the leader communicates the vision and motivates the followers to go beyond the status quo. In stage three, the leader builds trust by exhibiting qualities such as expertise, success, risk taking and unconventional actions. In the final stage, the leader demonstrates ways to achieve the vision by means of empowerment, behaviour modelling for followers and so forth. Conger and Kanungo have argued that if leaders use behaviours such as vision and articulation, environmental sensitivity and unconventional behaviour, rather than maintaining the status quo, followers will attribute charismatic leadership to them. Such leaders are also seen as behaving quite differently from those labelled 'noncharismatic'.[31]

Recent research on leadership involving three countries in Asia (Singapore, New Zealand and India) showed that charisma and vision were made up of two charismatic factors (social sensitivity and persuasive personality traits) and two visionary factors ('expert and analytical' and 'visionary and futuristic'). Tests across the three countries showed that the two visionary factors influenced reported performance and the two charismatic factors influenced employee commitment. Only social sensitivity predicted both performance and commitment of employees.[32]

Another important leadership researcher, Gary Yukl, has addressed the issue of whether charismatic and transformational leadership (see the following section) are compatible — can a leader be both highly transformational and highly charismatic at the same time? This issue concerns the role of followers. Transformational leadership usually involves empowering followers and making them partners in the change process, whereas charismatic leadership is more likely to require followers to place their trust in the leader's special expertise to achieve radical change. While these leadership approaches are often grouped together, Yukl's work directs us to consider this aspect of leadership behaviour more closely.[33]

Another recent empirical study involving 180 participants (51 managers and 129 employees) from 37 large-scale companies in Taiwan examined the interface between value and charisma and the inherent value intervening mechanism: the fit between the person's and organisation's values. One of its main findings was that CEO charismatic leadership had both direct and indirect effects on employees' extra effort to work, and satisfaction with the CEO, as well as their commitment to the organisation. However, that study also found that these relationships were mediated by employees' perceived person–organisation values fit.[34]

Transactional and transformational leadership approaches

We made the point earlier that transformational leadership has many similarities to charismatic leadership but involves the followers as partners. Building on notions originated by James MacGregor Burns, as well as ideas from House's work, Bernard Bass has developed an approach that focuses on both transformational and transactional leadership. The high points are summarised in figure 11.6.

Let us start by discussing Bass's transactional category. **Transactional leadership** involves daily exchanges between leaders and employees, and is necessary for achieving routine performance on which leaders and employees agree. It is based on transactions that occur between leaders and followers. These transactions may include agreements, contingent rewards, communications or exchanges between leaders and followers. There are many dimensions of transactional leadership:

- **Contingent rewards** involve providing various kinds of reward in exchange for accomplishing mutually agreed goals (for example, your boss pays you a $500 bonus for completing an acceptable article by a certain date). Conversely, you could be subject to disciplinary action for failing to achieve the goals.
- **Active management by exception** involves concentrating on occurrences which deviate from expected norms, such as irregularities, mistakes, exceptions and failures to meet standards. This means watching for deviations from rules and standards, and taking corrective action (for example, your boss notices that you have an increasing number of defects in your work and helps you adjust your machine to correct these).
- **Passive management by exception** involves intervening only if standards are not met (for example, your boss comes to see you after noticing your high percentage of rejects in the weekly production report).
- **Laissez faire leadership** involves abdicating responsibilities and avoiding decisions (for example, your boss is seldom around and does not follow through on decisions that need action).

Transactional leadership involves daily exchanges between leaders and followers, and is necessary for achieving routine performance on which leaders and followers agree.

Contingent rewards are rewards that are given in exchange for mutually agreed goal accomplishments.

Active management by exception involves watching for deviations from rules and standards and taking corrective action.

Passive management by exception involves intervening with employees only if standards are not met.

Laissez faire leadership involves abdicating responsibilities and avoiding decisions.

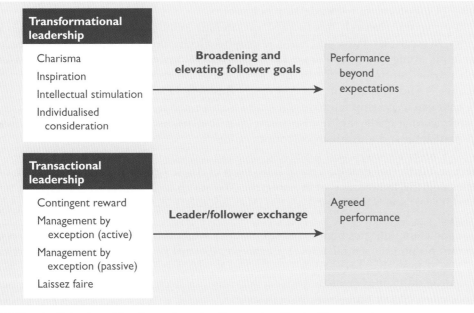

FIGURE 11.6 • High points of Bass's transformational/transactional leadership approach

Transformational leadership might go beyond this routine accomplishment, however. For Bass, transformational leadership occurs when leaders broaden and elevate the interests of their followers; when they generate awareness and acceptance of the purposes and mission of the group; and when they stir their followers to look beyond their own self-interest for the good of others.

Transformational leadership is a leadership style by which the followers' goals are broadened and elevated, and confidence is gained to go beyond expectations. This approach to leadership is based on motivating followers to do more than they originally intended, and often more than they thought possible. It involves guiding, influencing and inspiring people to excel and to contribute towards the achievement of organisational goals.

Transformational leadership is a leadership style by which the followers' goals are broadened and elevated, and confidence is gained to go beyond expectations.

When Ralph Norris took over as head of Air New Zealand he set out to replace the company's earlier dictatorial leadership model with a model that emphasises the power of the people working for the company. In his words, 'Companies can no longer get away with telling staff to check in their brain in the morning and then proceed to tell them what to do'.

In recent times, the ethical nature of transformational leadership has been the subject of much debate and controversy. Parry and Proctor-Thomson[35] argued that such debate has been demonstrated through the ways transformational leaders have been described. Labels and descriptors have included 'narcissistic', 'manipulative' and 'self-centred', but also 'ethical', 'just' and 'effective'. Using the Perceived Leader Integrity Scale (PLIS) and the Multi-Factor Leadership Questionnaire (MLQ) in a national sample of 1354 managers, they found a moderate to strong positive relationship between perceived integrity and the demonstration of transformational leadership behaviours.

The more recent research has focused on training requirements for transformational leadership. In particular, Parry and Sinha tested the effectiveness of transformational leadership training, using the Full Range Leadership Development (FRLD) program. Their research revealed an increase in the display of transformational leadership factors by the participants.[36] The findings of the Australian Business Leadership Survey revealed that transformational leadership tended to be more highly rated by Australian executives.[37]

Transformational leadership tends to have four dimensions: charisma, inspiration, intellectual stimulation and individualised consideration.[38]

Charisma is a dimension of leadership that provides vision and a sense of mission, and instils pride, respect and trust.

- Charisma provides vision and a sense of mission, and instils pride, along with follower respect and trust (for example, Steve Jobs, head of Apple Computer, showed charisma by emphasising the importance of creating the Macintosh as a radical new computer, and showed it again when he focused on the iMac, another radical departure from computer standards).

Inspiration is the communication of high expectations, the use of symbols to focus efforts, and the expression of important purposes in simple ways.

- Inspiration communicates high expectations, uses symbols to focus efforts, and expresses important purposes in simple ways (for example, Richard Branson, chief executive officer of Virgin Airlines, has been known to personally greet passengers on flights that have experienced difficulties or been delayed, and when in Australia he actually travels alongside passengers commuting from state to state).[39]

- Intellectual stimulation promotes intelligence, rationality and careful problem solving (for example, your boss encourages you to look at a difficult problem in a new way).

Intellectual stimulation promotes intelligence, rationality and careful problem solving.

- Individualised consideration provides personal attention, treats each employee individually, and coaches and advises (for example, your boss drops by and makes remarks reinforcing your worth as a person).

Individualised consideration is a leadership dimension by which the leader provides personal attention, treats each employee individually, and coaches and advises employees.

Together, charisma and inspiration transform follower expectations, but intellectual stimulation and individualised consideration are also needed to provide the necessary follow-through.

Bass concludes that transformational leadership is likely to be strongest at the top management level, where there is the greatest opportunity for proposing and communicating a vision. But it is by no means restricted to the top level; it is found throughout the organisation. Further, transformational leadership operates in combination with transactional leadership.

Transactional leadership is similar to most of the traditional leadership approaches mentioned earlier, and leaders need both transformational and transactional leadership to be successful, just as they need both leadership and management.

The four 'I's of transformational leadership

The following useful pointers about transformational leadership are given by Bruce Avolio and his associates:[40]

- *Individualised consideration* — pay attention to individual employees
- *Intellectual stimulation* — be concerned with helping people to think through new ways
- *Inspirational motivation* —inspire people to give their best
- *Idealised influence* — engender respect and trust that gives power and influence over people

Recent research has highlighted the importance of emotional awareness and emotional intelligence in organisations. A study involving Australian leadership and management students indicated that emotions play an important role in understanding organisational behaviours. The findings suggested that those teaching leadership must pay greater attention to emotional intelligence.[41]

To summarise, transactional leaders guide employees in their tasks towards the achievement of pre-stated goals, whereas transformational leaders inspire their employees to transcend individual interest for the sake of their organisation.

Bryman has summarised a large number of studies using Bass's approach, ranging from six studies on the extra effort of followers to 16 studies on performance or effectiveness, to nearly a dozen covering various aspects of satisfaction. Still other studies cover such outcomes as burnout and stress and the predisposition to act as innovation champions. The strongest relationships tend to be associated with charisma or inspirational leadership, although in most cases the other dimensions are also important. These findings are impressive and broaden leadership outcomes beyond those used in the traditional leadership studies.[42]

Bernard Bass has also recently reviewed the two decades of research into transformational leadership. Recent findings in the field include evidence of why transformational leadership is more effective than transactional leadership, and of why female leaders may be more transformational than their male counterparts. Bass concluded, despite an abundance of applied research, that more basic research and theory development is needed. More work needs to be done, for example, on how context affects transactional and transformational leadership, and on how transformational leadership moves followers from compliance to the identification and internalisation of values and beliefs beyond their own self-interest.[43]

Lessons from Jack Welch

International SPOTLIGHT

Jack Welch's goal was to make General Electric (GE) 'the world's most competitive enterprise'. He knew that it would take nothing less than a 'revolution' to transform that dream into a reality. 'The model of business in corporate America in 1980 had not changed in decades. Workers worked, managers managed, and everyone knew their place. Forms and approvals and bureaucracy ruled the day.' Welch's self-proclaimed revolution meant waging war on GE's old ways of doing things and reinventing the company from top to bottom.

(continued)

Jack Welch is all about leadership, not management. Actually, he wanted to discard the term 'manager' altogether because it had come to mean someone who 'controls rather than facilitates, complicates rather than simplifies, acts more like a governor than an accelerator'. Welch has given a great deal of thought to how to manage employees effectively so that they are as productive as possible. And he has come to a seemingly paradoxical view. The less managing you do, the better off your company. Manage less to manage more.

Welch decided that GE's leaders, who did too much controlling and monitoring, had to change their management styles. 'Managers slow things down. Leaders spark the business to run smoothly, quickly. Managers talk to one another, write memos to one another. Leaders talk to their employees, talk *with* their employees, filling them with vision, getting them to perform at levels the employees themselves didn't think possible. Then (and to Welch this is a critical ingredient) they simply get out of the way.'

Source: Vadim Kotelnikov, '25 lessons from Jack Welch', 1000ventures.com, http://www.1000ventures.com/business_guide/crosscuttings/leadership_vs_mgmt.html (viewed 10 August 2005).

The new leadership revisited

Thus far we have covered representative approaches to the new leadership, as summarised in figure 11.1. These approaches have cut across the concepts of attribution, charisma and transformation. Other related work differs from traditional leadership but does not include charisma and treats transformation differently from Bass's approach. However, all this work includes vision in one way or another. Table 11.1 summarises the core themes of this work and the charismatic and transformational approaches discussed earlier, in contrast to traditional leadership.[44]

In addition to contrasting the core themes of traditional and new leadership, it is important to answer questions concerning the role of new leadership in the workplace.

Questions and answers concerning the new leadership

Can people be trained in new leadership? Research in this area argues that training in new leadership is possible. Bass and his colleagues have put a lot of work into such training efforts. They have created one workshop that lasts from three to five days, with later follow-up. Initially, leaders are given feedback on their scores on Bass's measures. Then the leaders devise improvement programs to strengthen their weaknesses and work with the trainers to develop their leadership skills. Bass and Avolio report findings that demonstrate beneficial effects from this training. They also report on team training and programs tailored to individual organisations' needs.[45] Similarly, Conger and Kanungo propose training to develop the kinds of behaviour summarised in their model.[46]

The National Australia Bank has implemented tailored leadership programs to build leadership capabilities throughout the organisation. It sees leadership, combined with a high-performance culture and people policies that align with business goals, as crucial to success. NAB's leaders pride themselves on being the champions of transformation. The NAB has a National Leadership Standard (NLS) to serve as a benchmark for behaviours that will enable it to achieve its vision and goals. The Corporate Leadership Council has described the NAB's executive coaching program as one of the most innovative and effective coaching methods it has seen.[47]

Finally, a couple of approaches with a special emphasis on vision emphasise training. Kouzes and Posner report the results of a week-long training program. The program involved training of leaders on five dimensions oriented around developing, communicating and reinforcing a shared vision. According to Kouzes and Posner, leaders showed an average 15 per cent increase in these visionary behaviours ten months after participating in the program.[48] Similarly, Sashkin has developed a leadership approach that emphasises various aspects of vision and organisational culture change. Sashkin discusses ways to go about training leaders to be more visionary and to enhance the culture change.[49] Many of the new leadership training programs involve a heavy, hands-on workshop emphasis so leaders do more than just read about vision.

Is new leadership always good? No. As we pointed out earlier, dark-side charismatics, such as Adolf Hitler, can have negative effects on the population of followers.

Is new leadership always needed? No. Sometimes emphasis on a vision diverts energy from more important day-to-day activities.

Is new leadership by itself sufficient? No. New leadership needs to be used in conjunction with traditional leadership.

Is new leadership important only at the top? Probably not. While generally considered most important at the top levels, new leadership is considered by some experts to apply at all organisational levels.

Less emphasis needed on	Greater emphasis needed on
Planning	Having a vision/mission
Allocating responsibility	Infusing vision
Controlling and problem solving	Motivating and inspiring
Creating routine and equilibrium	Creating change and innovation
Retaining power	Empowering others
Creating compliance	Creating commitment
Emphasising contractual obligations	Stimulating extra effort
Exhibiting leader detachment and rationality	Exhibiting interest in others and intuition
Taking a reactive environmental approach	Taking a proactive environmental approach

TABLE 11.1 • Themes in the new leadership literature

20 characteristics of a strong leader

THE **Effective** Manager 11.2

1. *A sense of mission.* They have clarity of vision and mission which provides the foundation to excite and inspire others in the team and organisation.
2. *Values-based measurable goals.* They have clear understanding of the values of both the organisation and individuals and these form the foundations enabling them to meet clear objectives. At their instigation the concept of ownership of goals unifies members of the team and organisation and continues to provide everyone involved with a clear sense of direction towards a common cause.
3. *Action orientation.* They are entrepreneurial, innovative and forward in their thinking, and they launch quickly. An attitude of 'we can do it!' prevails.
4. *Courage.* They are initiators of action and attack, they persistently stay the course, believing that the future belongs to the risk-taker.
5. *Planners and strategists.* They are big-picture thinkers, taking the long view, looking at all options and outcomes. Concentrating on personal strengths and weaknesses, always aware of what could be the worst possible outcome, in order to avoid it.

(continued)

6. *Inspiring and motivational.* They have an ability to draw out additional capacity within others, to arouse enthusiasm with total commitment. High levels of regular encouragement establish trust, confidence and loyalty.

7. *Committed to success.* They are future oriented, never thinking of failure, always learning from mistakes. They display a commitment to excellence and quality performances from products, services and people within the organisation.

8. *Communicators.* They have the ability to delegate with agreed clear responsibilities. Everyone in the team knows what is expected of him/her, consequently instilling meaning and purpose into a task.

9. *Low pressure salespeople.* They possess a sound knowledge of the 'relationship' selling process and how to apply it in daily interactions with customers and members of the organisation to make them feel significant. They have excellent presentation and negotiation skills, and are prepared to compromise, always looking for a win–win solution.

10. *Visibility.* Never hiding behind a desk, they are always available to meet and talk with customers and team members. They actively seek responses to improve products, services and leadership style and achieve targets.

11. *Team builder.* They demonstrate clear coaching skills which enables them to determine ineffective team members. Only quality people are hired and continually developed via appropriate training strategies. Tasks are distributed to most suited individuals where they can make a major contribution. Open communication abounds.

12. *Prioritising.* They ensure measurable and prioritised key result areas are known by all.

13. *Love of leadership.* They are self-reliant with a strong desire to be in charge. If asked, they like to make their own decisions and to be in control; however, they also recognise that in order to lead, an individual must first be a good follower.

14. *High self-esteem and positive self-image.* They gain self-knowledge via introspection and this provides sensitivity towards the feelings of others in the team and organisation. Strong leaders know their limitations and honestly evaluate themselves.

15. *Self-motivated.* They have a strong vision which provides them with the ability to continually set higher goals and gain commitment from others.

16. *Ask advice.* They are able to build upon their known strengths. They are prepared to seek advice from others in order to discover and compensate for any weaknesses.

17. *Power through cooperation.* They are always seeking talented people and developing relationships with key people. They understand and appreciate that if others are first helped to achieve their goals, they will in return assist you towards achieving your goals.

18. *Listening.* They learn to listen without interrupting, understanding that the more people are allowed to discuss an idea the more likely they will be committed towards its implementation.

19. *Integrity.* They understand that trust and credibility are the foundation of strong leadership. They always keep promises and are prepared to stand up for their beliefs, knowing that those beliefs are based upon sound personally-owned values.

20. *Continual personal growth.* They have a strong commitment towards life-learning and ensure their own self-improvement through reading, study and personal development courses.

Source : Australian Business Limited, 'Leadership — do you have what it takes?', http://www.australianbusiness.com.au (viewed 20 December 2005).

COUNTER**POINT**

Servant leadership

In recent times, some researchers have attempted to rejuvenate a relatively old concept of leadership: 'servant leadership'. Servant leaders are those who make a deliberate choice to serve others and to put other people's needs, aspirations and interests above their own.[50] The servant leader operates on the assumption that 'I am the leader, therefore I serve' rather than 'I am the leader, therefore I lead', which could be seen as more characteristic of most of the other perspectives on leadership.[51]

People follow servant leaders freely because they trust them. One of the tests of servant leadership is how those served (led) benefit.

Spears[52] identified ten critical characteristics of the servant leader. Many are similar to the characteristics identified in other models but with a very strong focus on the followers.

1. Servant leaders must reinforce their communication skills by *listening* to others.
2. Servant leaders strive to understand and *empathise* with others.
3. Learning to *heal* oneself and others is a unique characteristic.
4. Self-*awareness* strengthens the servant leader — as it does all leaders.
5. Servant leaders rely on *persuasion* rather than positional authority.
6. Servant leaders are able to *conceptualise*, to see beyond the day-to-day and to dream great dreams.
7. *Foresight* is the characteristic that enables servant leaders to understand the lessons of the past, the realities of the present, and the likely consequences of a decision for the future.
8. In these days of corporate distrust, *stewardship* is a most attractive element of servant leadership, particularly if it can be combined with foresight.
9. Servant leaders are *committed* to the personal, professional and spiritual growth of each individual in the organisation.
10. Servant leaders seek to identify means for *building community* among those who work within any given institution.

Questions

1. Have you experienced servant leadership?
2. What do you think are the strengths and weaknesses of the servant leadership perspective on leadership?

The accountability of company leaders

While many memorable business moments that occurred at the beginning of the twenty-first century have been recorded and will be replayed, surely the greatest focus will be on those organisations whose leaders, either through unethical behaviour or through bad management decisions, led their companies to ultimate demise: companies such as Australian airline Ansett, whose problems stemmed from airline safety lapses, loss of market share and a run of poor managers; and insurance giant HIH, whose executives were accused of insider trading and misleading behaviour. All will make interesting topics for case studies and business reports that the next generation of junior managers will produce during their years in the higher education system. They will be the topic of research on leaders who crossed the ethical line yet were arrogant enough to think that they would not be caught out.

Consider disgraced businessman Steve Vizard, who made a series of secret share deals, ultimately leading to his prosecution. Vizard, as a Telstra director, had been privy to a series of emails in which then Telstra boss Ziggy Switkowski outlined plans to increase its stake in dot-com company Sausage Software. Shortly thereafter Vizard purchased $500 000 worth of shares in Sausage, earning a $140 000 windfall (on paper at least) within 10 days of his first illegal transaction.[53] When convicted, Vizard was banned from being a company director for ten years and was fined almost $400 000.[54]

And what of those who continue to practise unethically? Since the recent exposure of so many unethical practices, much has been written about the need for more stringent corporate governance. Surely the ultimate onus should be on the organisations, their boards of directors and even the shareholders to exert pressure to ensure that those in a position of power are not given the opportunity to abuse that power. The question is 'how?'.

Maybe one good starting point is back in the classroom. What a good opportunity for academics, mentors and managers to introduce a more wholistic ethical approach into their teaching and training processes. Rather than focus only on the legal consequences or impact on a company's bottom line of accounting malpractice, misrepresentation and incompetence, teachers should discuss some of the greater effects that such misdemeanors can have on our society.

Gender, age and cultural diversity — current issues in leadership

Diversity in leadership

Much of the leadership theory and research has been conducted within a North American context and has focused primarily on masculine models of leadership. Given the globalisation of business, the increasing cultural diversity of domestic societies, the ageing of the workforce, and the importance of women in the workforce and the community, this is a significant gap in leadership studies.

Gender and leadership

Women are increasingly accessing leadership roles that have traditionally been occupied by men. In reviewing recent research on transformational leadership, we mentioned that Bass indicates that women are more disposed towards transformational leadership than are men. This tendency is illustrated by female leaders who are vision driven, and who emphasise both the importance of empowering employees and participative forms of leadership, and the links between business and the community.

OB in action

Gail Kelly is one of Australia's highest-profile female leaders. Kelly was appointed as the managing director and chief executive officer of the St George Group in 2002, having previously been head of customer service at the Commonwealth Bank of Australia. Before her appointment, speculation was rife that St George would be acquired by one of Australia's big four banks, but the bank has remained independent and has recorded strong performances under Kelly's leadership. She now has an open-ended contract with St George — an invitation to stay indefinitely.

Gary Yukl has reviewed the research on leadership and gender differences, and concludes that it is 'inconclusive'.[55] Others argue that, rather than a focus on gender differences, the gender blindness of leadership models needs a fundamental re-examination. Sinclair argues that we need to review the relationship between heroic masculinity and corporate leadership, and that if this is not done, leadership will remain the privilege of a homogeneous elite. Such homogeneity in leadership, in the face of dramatic changes in workforce and customer diversity, is a potential liability.[56]

In Australia, recent findings from the Australian Business Leadership Survey revealed that female executives tended to record significantly higher mean scores on all aspects of transformational leadership. They also tended to score higher on effectiveness and satisfaction in their leadership approach, compared to male executives.[57]

The difficulties women still face in progressing up the corporate hierarchy (referred to as the 'glass ceiling') may have led to the unique and diverse paths women have taken to leadership positions. Some transfer into leadership positions from other fields (rather than rising within a corporate structure); others become leaders of organisations through succession in family business. Still others start their own small businesses, which may then grow into substantial corporations.[58]

Despite the persistent impact of the 'glass ceiling', some women have succeeded in penetrating it, as the following examples indicate. Julie Dill, managing director Asia–Pacific, Duke Energy International; Christine O'Reilly, chief executive officer, GasNet Australia Trust; and Sue Ortenstone, chief executive, Epic Energy, each led one of Australia's key gas pipeline operating companies in an industry that would once have been described as stereotypically male dominated.

On a wider international scale, a recent study on Arab women's conceptions of leadership compared women's leadership authority values in Oman, the United Arab Emirates and Lebanon. It found evidence of common leadership authority values in the Gulf countries (Oman and the UAE). Lebanon, meanwhile, was distinguished by relatively low levels of 'traditional' authority, and very high levels of 'charismatic' authority. The findings demonstrate important regional similarities and difference in leadership authority values in the 'Arab world'.[59]

Leadership and age

Age of leadership is another important current diversity issue. While the average age of leaders in large corporations is probably over 55, there are many examples of leaders who are much younger, such as Brett Godfrey, CEO of Virgin Blue Australia, and Maureen Plavsic, managing director of the Seven Network. Also, many younger entrepreneurs are running their own small, successful companies. A survey of more than 500 senior executives and human resources managers revealed that almost 62 per cent of organisations sought applicants for executive positions from the 31–40 age group, while nearly 23 per cent preferred those in their forties. None said they would choose managers and executives in their fifties. About 70 per cent said they would retrench executives over 50 ahead of others because they perceived them as inflexible and unwilling to change.[60] The question to ask therefore is: 'Does maturity in years in a leader represent valuable experience or does it suggest it's time to make way for someone younger with fresh ideas?' A fair answer would be to judge each individual on his or her merits, rather than fall into the trap of stereotyping. Interestingly, however, some executives do choose to move out of the corporate spotlight early — not to retire but simply to change direction, sometimes into an even more challenging career. For example, Keith Gregory, 63, left a 90-hours-a-week job at BP and bought a grazing property in Victoria. Malcolm Richmond, 58, former Rio Tinto research and development managing director, became a full professor in business and engineering at Curtin University.[61] The issue of age and experience versus youth and energy will always be a challenge in leadership, yet surely the collaboration of executives at both ends of the age spectrum can bring a variety of qualities and perspectives to the organisation.

WhatWould You**Do?**

Succession planning

ComCo is a privately owned software company based in Auckland, New Zealand. Since its inception almost 30 years ago, ComCo has prided itself on successful staff retention strategies and employee loyalty, and because of this ComCo has been the focus of many business press reports. ComCo's distribution channels are worldwide and the company continues to enjoy growth. Frank Barker is the founder and CEO of the company and is highly respected among his peers. A charismatic man, Frank displays many of the 'new leadership' qualities. Frank's senior management team are long-time employees and very experienced in their roles.

Recently Frank has become concerned about the future and succession strategy of ComCo. He is aware that most of the senior managers are approaching the last years of their working lives, yet no-one has ever consulted Frank about retirement. Typical of many baby boomers, the senior managers are not seriously thinking about retirement and, although they have sound superannuation plans through ComCo, the issue of being replaced or succeeded by someone else is never discussed. However, Frank is also aware of potential health issues associated with age and the way these might affect ComCo's managers over the next few years.

A senior management team meeting is scheduled for the end of the week, and Frank is keen to focus the meeting on retirement planning and succession. He is not sure how to tackle the problem but has done some research to source facts and figures to present to the team. On a positive note, he found one study, conducted by the Australian Bureau of Statistics, indicating that older does not necessarily mean less productive and that workers over 55 have the lowest level of absenteeism of all age groups.[62] On a less positive note, he noted that the generation that will replace them, the so-called baby busters, is smaller than the boomer generation,[63] which might inhibit his succession plans. Of course, Frank's senior managers know the business inside out and have extremely strong relationships with ComCo's customers, suppliers and other important stakeholders, so any succession planning must be carried out carefully and slowly.

Nonetheless Frank knows it is his responsibility as head of the company to see that he develops the junior managers at ComCo and coaches them to become more involved in the major decision-making processes so they are prepared to succeed as the new senior management team.

Questions

1. If you were Frank, what steps would you take to lead the junior managers towards succession at ComCo over the next few years?

2. How could you maintain loyalty and productivity from the current senior management team once you have discussed your concerns about lack of retirement planning among the group?

Leadership and culture

Using a similar approach to that of Geert Hofstede,[64] Robert House and his colleagues embarked on an ambitious research project involving 62 countries. The GLOBE project investigated how cultural values are related to organisational practices, conceptions of leadership, the economic competitiveness of societies, and the human condition of an organisation's members. More than 17 000 managers participated worldwide. Some of the main results of the project indicated that cultural values contributed either positively or negatively to the leadership profiles. For example, power-distance values were found to be a negative predictor of charismatic/value-based and participative leadership, but gender egalitarianism proved to be a positive predictor of the same. One of the key recommendations of the project was that leaders need to be aware of the links between cultural values and leadership practices.[65] Other recent cross-national comparative studies have also reinforced the relevance of culture in leadership.[66]

Summary

Differences between leadership and management

Leadership and management differ in that management is designed to promote stability or to make the organisation run smoothly, while the role of leadership is to promote adaptive change. A leadership function corresponds to each of the management functions but is carried out differently.

Traditional and new leadership differ. Traditional leadership approaches range from trait and behaviour approaches that give leadership a central role in performance and human resource maintenance outputs to various approaches that combine leadership with situational contingencies to predict outputs. The new leadership differs from traditional leadership primarily in that it emphasises vision and change, and focuses on attribution, charisma, transformation and related concepts.

Trait and behavioural theories of leadership

Trait and behavioural leadership approaches argue that leader traits or behaviours have a major impact on leadership outcomes. Traits are more innate and harder to change than behaviours. They are also often used with behaviours in a situational contingency or new leadership approach.

Situational contingency theories of leadership

Leader situational contingency approaches argue that leadership, in combination with various situational variables, has a major impact on outcomes. Sometimes, as in the case of the substitutes for leadership approach, the role of the situational variables replaces that of leadership to the point that leadership has little or no impact in itself. Fiedler's contingency theory, House's path–goal theory, and Hersey and Blanchard's Situational Leadership® theory are other approaches that consider the impact not just of leadership but of various situational contingencies.

Charismatic leadership and transformational leadership

Attribution theory overlaps traditional and new leadership by emphasising the symbolic aspects of leadership. These aspects are an especially important part of the new leadership, charismatic, transformational and related perspectives, according to which followers tend to attribute heroic or extraordinary leadership abilities to a leader when they observe certain behaviours from that leader. These attributions can then help transform followers to achieve goals that go beyond their own self-interest and, in turn, help transform the organisation.

Charismatic leadership approaches emphasise the kind of leader–follower social relationship summarised above. Two of these approaches emphasised earlier are House and associates' approach and the work of Conger and Kanungo.

Transformational leadership approaches are typically broader than charismatic ones. Bass and associates' transformational approach is a particularly well-known theory that includes charisma as one of its dimensions. It separates vision-oriented transformational leadership from day-to-day transactional leadership, and argues that the two work in combination. Transformational and charismatic leadership, and the new leadership in general are important because they facilitate change in our increasingly fast-moving world.

Diversity in leadership

Western, masculine models have dominated leadership theory and research. Such a limitation is significant given the increasing diversity of the workforce and society in general. In Australia the progress of women's representation in organisational leadership positions at executive and board level has been slow, but recently women have gained a greater presence in leadership roles across many industries, some of which were traditionally male dominated. We are also seeing much younger company leaders, both male and female, who are excelling in their field. Recent research has explored the need to recognise the impact of culture on leadership styles and the appropriateness of approaches across different cultures.

Chapter 11 study guide

Key terms   OB

achievement-oriented leadership, *p. 392*

active management by exception, *p. 397*

charisma, *p. 398*

charismatic leaders, *p. 395*

contingent rewards, *p. 397*

directive leadership, *p. 391*

formal leadership, *p. 385*

individualised consideration, *p. 398*

informal leadership, *p. 385*

inspiration, *p. 398*

intellectual stimulation, *p. 398*

laissez faire leadership, *p. 397*

leaders, *p. 384*

leadership, *p. 385*

least preferred coworker (LPC) scale, *p. 389*

managers, *p. 384*

participative leadership, *p. 392*

passive management by exception, *p. 397*

situational control, *p. 389*

substitutes for leadership, *p. 393*

supportive leadership, *p. 391*

transactional leadership, *p. 397*

transformational leadership, *p. 397*

Review questions   OB

1. Review and discuss the pros and cons of the trait and behavioural approaches to leadership.

2. Discuss the reasons for the popularity of the contingency approach to leadership.

3. Explain how leadership and trust may be related.

4. What can managers do to help develop some of the new leadership characteristics?

Application questions   OB

1. You will recall that we discussed that leadership appears in two forms, *formal leadership* and *informal leadership*. Think of a situation in which you have been part of a group or a team, maybe at work or in your recreational time. Reflect on that situation — its actual dynamics and the outcome. Identify the *formal* and *informal leadership* roles and how they played out in your example. How did each of the leaders contribute to the outcome? Who was the most effective? What did you learn from that?

2. You have recently formed a new consulting business with three colleagues whom you met while studying at university. Explain the process you will go through to establish the leadership role for the business. For example, would the role of leader automatically be given to the person who initiated the consulting idea or would you consider another method of selection?

3. Using an example of a situation you are familiar with, ideally in the workplace, identify and explain the different dynamics between *leadership* and *management*.

4. Your company has offered you a promotion as head of a division in a country that has a very different culture from that of your native country. While you are excited by the new challenge, you are also aware that you need to consider whether your leadership style will be effective or appropriate for the new location. Using two countries of your choice (your native country and one with a different culture), outline four of the most important factors relating to the style of leadership you should adopt when considering the offer of promotion into the new culture.

5. In this chapter we discussed the concept of new leadership training. Prepare a two-page case either for or against the following statement:

   People can be trained in new leadership.

(continued)

This exercise could provide an opportunity for an interesting debate among several groups in your organisational behaviour class.

6. Imagine you have been asked to address a class of high-school students who are in their final year and looking forward to graduating. Their social studies teacher did not provide you with much information other than that she wanted you to deliver a ten-minute speech on how the students can develop their leadership potential. Prepare a list of the things you would include in your speech. Be sure to make the content relevant for the group you are speaking to — that is, young adults who are about to embark on their individual career journeys. Rather than past or current leaders, you may want to consider what the future might demand of leaders and what attributes they will need to cater to that demand. You should consider issues at a macro as well as micro level. This exercise will be interesting as a class discussion, and your lecturer may want to expand the topic into an assignment.

OB Research questions

1. Some scholars have argued that the new leadership style in its various forms involves mystical qualities that few people possess. Others have argued that it can be readily identified and that people can be trained to display it.

   You are required to prepare two scripts. The first is a script for the CEO of a major telecommunications company to present to a small group of junior managers who show great leadership potential. In this case, the CEO is emphasising the need for new leadership approaches to be adopted by the junior managers. The second is a script for a leader supporting the case for a more traditional leadership approach to a particular situation. This might be a one-off situation in which a more directive leadership style is appropriate.

   Following are several questions you may want to consider, but you may prepare your own topics if you wish.

   (a) How mystical is the new leadership? How desirable is it?

   (b) How successful do you think leaders who use your new leadership script might be in convincing followers that they are charismatic or transformational?

   (c) Do you think one particular leadership style is more appropriate than another when considering the gender of a particular group — for example, men leading women or women leading men?

   (d) Do you think leadership approaches should change depending on the circumstances, the industry or the current environment?

2. Leadership is a topical and controversial subject in the global business arena. Using the Internet, search through leadership links on sites such as the Australian Institute of Management, www.ceoforum.com.au; the Australian Institute of Company Directors; the *New Zealand Management* journal; or *The British Journal of Administrative Management*. When your search is complete, and as a result of the information you have compiled from your search, compose a list of five common characteristics that successful leaders are currently perceived to display.

OB Running project

Complete the following activities for your chosen organisation.

1. Choose a few of the most senior people in the organisation and assess whether they are leaders, managers or both, according to the descriptions given in this chapter. Do you think there is a genuine difference?

2. Try to identify the leadership traits of the leaders in the organisation. Do the traits vary between the top managers of the organisation and lower-level managers? Plot each on the Leadership Grid® (figure 11.2).

3. Choose one of the leadership models discussed in this chapter and use it to analyse the leadership of one of the leaders in your organisation.

4. How important is the top manager or other top leader in your organisation? Do they individually make a difference? Would you expect the overall performance of the organisation to change if a new leader took over? Why or why not?

5. What degree of diversity is there among the leaders in your organisation? Explain, specifically for your organisation, why the diversity or lack of diversity has occurred.

Individual activity

Survey of leadership

Objective

To develop your ability to assess leadership styles

Total time: 15 *minutes*

SURVEY OF LEADERSHIP[67]

The following ten questions ask about your supervisor's leadership behaviour and practices. Try to respond on the basis of your actual observations of your supervisor's actions; tick the box that corresponds to your observations.

To a great extent
To a considerable extent
To a moderate extent
To a slight extent
To almost no extent

To what extent:

	To a great extent	To a considerable extent	To a moderate extent	To a slight extent	To almost no extent
1. is your supervisor easy to approach?	☐	☐	☐	☐	☐
2. does your supervisor encourage people to give their best effort?	☐	☐	☐	☐	☐
3. does your supervisor show you how to improve your performance?	☐	☐	☐	☐	☐
4. does your supervisor encourage people to work as a team?	☐	☐	☐	☐	☐
5. does your supervisor pay attention to what you say?	☐	☐	☐	☐	☐
6. does your supervisor maintain high standards of performance?	☐	☐	☐	☐	☐
7. does your supervisor provide the help you need so you can schedule work ahead of time?	☐	☐	☐	☐	☐
8. does your supervisor encourage people to exchange opinions and ideas?	☐	☐	☐	☐	☐
9. is your supervisor willing to listen to your problems?	☐	☐	☐	☐	☐
10. does your supervisor offer new ideas for solving job-related problems?	☐	☐	☐	☐	☐

Scoring

Score 1 for almost no extent, 2 for slight, 3 for moderate, 4 for considerable and 5 for great. Now fill in the following boxes.

(continued)

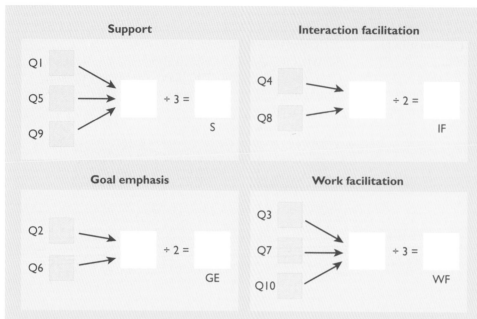

Interpretation

Support (S) and *interaction facilitation (IF)* are the two dimensions that define interpersonal or relationship-centred leadership behaviours. Support refers to the leader's personal concern for employees, while interaction facilitation measures how the leader encourages teamwork among employees. The two scores, S and IF, can be added to yield an overall interpersonal relationship score.

Goal emphasis (GE) and *work facilitation (WF)* both centre on task-oriented leader behaviour. Goal emphasis simply refers to the degree to which the leader emphasises the importance of achieving high goals, while work facilitation measures the degree to which the leader engages in behaviour that helps employees to get their jobs done effectively. The two scores, GE and WF, can be added to yield an overall task orientation score.

OB | *Group activity*

Leadership in action

Objectives

1. To provide an opportunity to observe different types of leadership
2. To examine the link between leadership and situational contingencies
3. To develop your understanding of your own leadership behaviour
4. To develop your ability to analyse leadership in action

Total time: 90 minutes

Procedure

1. Form a circle of 8–18 people in a large area of empty space where you can spread out without running into chairs or walls.

2. Ask for a volunteer(s) to be an observer: if your group is small, one observer will do; if your group has 18 people, you can have three observers. The observers should withdraw from the circle and read the observer instructions.

3. Everyone in the circle should put on a blindfold. (If you wear glasses, place them in your pocket or give them to an observer to hold.)

4. The instructor will read you the instructions for the exercise. You have 20 minutes to complete the assigned task.

5. Please answer the following questions individually in the next ten minutes.
   (a) What types of leadership emerged in this exercise? In your opinion, who were the leaders? Why? What leader behaviours did they exhibit?

(b) What occurred in the group to help you solve the problem?

(c) What occurred in the group that hindered you from solving the problem or from solving it quickly?

(d) What did you learn about leadership from this exercise?

(e) What did you learn about yourself as a leader in this exercise?

6. Discuss the questions in step 5 in smaller groups (four to six people). Ask the observers what they observed. Choose a representative to report to the entire class a summary of your observations.

7. Undertake a plenary debriefing session.

(a) The observer(s) briefly and objectively describe what happened when their group did the blindfold exercise. Next, the group representatives present their report.

(b) Can you see any relationships between this exercise and the 'real world' you experience at work or in other organisational settings?

(c) What are the important contingencies in this particular situation? What type of leadership works best in a situation like this? What leader behaviours are needed?

(d) There are no leaders without followers. In this exercise, what were the characteristics of a good follower?

(e) If you were to repeat this exercise, what would you do differently to be a better leader?

Observer instructions

Do not talk, laugh or make any noises at all during the exercise. Do keep an eye out for the group members' safety; move any items that could trip them and warn them if they are approaching the edge of a cliff (see the following instructions). Otherwise, do not talk to them or to the other observers.

Please undertake the following tasks based on your observations.

1. Look for leadership behaviour in the group. Who emerged as leaders? What did they do to become leaders?

2. Please observe and describe the group's communication patterns and nonverbal language.

3. Describe how the group made decisions. Be prepared to share these observations in the group discussion of the exercise.[68]

Instructions for exercise (to be read to the group after they are blindfolded)

You are the last survivors of a secret intelligence unit that has just escaped from an ambush at the local airport. You were on a mission to a small country to rescue a high-ranking official of great strategic importance to your own country, who was being held as a political prisoner. The operation was successful and the official made it onto the last plane, but your unit was left behind; you were all occupied defending the airport against local militia. Unfortunately, you sustained a number of minor casualties and one fatality, your commander. However, there is a backup plan. You know that if your unit does not make the plane you are to assemble at the top of a cliff where military helicopters will ferry you back to a waiting ship. You have made it to the vicinity of the cliff, but it is pitch black. The helicopters will attempt a rescue only if they can identify you as the stranded unit.

Before the mission it was agreed that the signal would be established by your unit forming a square on the top of the cliff; if at night, special heat-detecting radar would be used to locate you. Somehow you have to form this square in the dark, on the edge of a cliff with a 50-metre drop to rocks and the ocean. Time is not on your side. Your unit succeeded in destroying five local militia vehicles back at the airport, but this delaying tactic will not hold the enemy for more than 20 minutes.

Case study: Leadership challenge

ABC Accounting Associates is a small organisation with a total of eight employees, including management. The organisation has been in operation for 15 years and most of the employees have been there since the beginning. It has a traditional management structure — a managing director, Harry, and two other directors, Stephen and Margaret. The three senior managers — Lou, Mark and Maria — are responsible for most of the

clients' basic accounting and bookkeeping needs, and two administration staff — Franco and Betty — are responsible for ABC's day-to-day office duties.

ABC has very few clients; however, they are profitable for the organisation and very loyal. Most have been with ABC for more than ten years and it is highly unlikely that they will move to another accounting firm, as they are completely satisfied.

(continued)

Internally, however, things are not so good. For many years, ABC functioned well under the leadership of Harry. Harry is now in his late 60s and is getting a little tired and bored with the day-to-day operations. He also suffers from poor health, but without ABC his health would probably decline even more. Harry's boredom is reflected in his attitude to work and his motivation to expand the business. Stephen and Margaret are much younger and keen to expand ABC, although Stephen tends to let his outside interests get in the way of work and often disappears for several hours at a time.

Over the past 18 months there has been a large inequity of commitment and productivity between the three directors. Harry shows no interest in the business at all. Stephen is keen to build the business, but spends only half the amount of time at the office that Margaret spends. Margaret has the most experience and works extremely long hours, so does not have much time to socialise with the other employees.

More than 80 per cent of the clients on ABC's books are there because of Margaret. If Margaret decided to leave ABC, the business would probably not survive, as the clients would no doubt ultimately follow her. The employees at ABC are not aware of this and think that it is Harry's efforts and experience that keep the clients loyal to the organisation. Margaret has so far tolerated the situation in the hope that one day she will succeed Harry as managing director — she is, after all, Harry's daughter!

Margaret is getting to the point where her frustrations can no longer be tempered. Although she gets some degree of support from the other employees at ABC, she feels that Stephen and Harry are taking advantage of her. Margaret is a very loyal person, but things are quickly coming to a head.

There is a directors' meeting this afternoon at 4 pm, and Margaret has been asked to prepare the agenda — the other two directors are out to lunch. This is the last straw for Margaret so she decides to prepare an agenda, but not with the usual topics that Stephen and Harry expect. This time Margaret challenges the leadership issue at ABC.

Questions

1. Briefly explain how Margaret should approach the leadership issue with Harry and Stephen during the meeting.
2. What leadership style do you think would be appropriate for ABC Accounting?
3. Given that the employees are quite satisfied under Harry's directorship, how should they be approached regarding a potential leadership change at ABC?

OB | *Suggested reading*

Bernard M Bass, *Bass and Stogdill's handbook of leadership* (New York: The Free Press, 1990).

Alan Bryman, *Charisma and leadership in organizations* (London: Sage, 1992).

John W Gardner, *On leadership* (New York: The Free Press, 1989).

Robert Goffee and Gareth Jones, 'Why should anyone be led by you?', *Harvard Business Review*, vol. 78, no. 5 (September/October 2000), pp. 62–70.

James M Kouzes and Barry Z Posner, *The leadership challenge* (San Francisco: Jossey-Bass, 1989).

EA Locke, S Kirkpatrick, JK Wheeler, J Schneider, K Niles, H Goldstein, Welsh and DO Chah, *The essence of leadership* (New York: Lexington/Macmillan, 1991).

David J Pauleen, 'Leadership in a global virtual team: an action learning approach', *Leadership and Organization Development Journal*, vol. 24, no. 3 (2003), pp. 153–62.

Frederick F Reichheld, 'Lead for loyalty', *Harvard Business Review*, vol. 79, no. 7 (July/August 2001), pp. 76–84.

Robert W Rowden, 'The relationship between charismatic leadership behaviors and organizational commitment', *Leadership and Organization Development Journal*, vol. 21, no. 1 (2000), pp. 30–5.

Charlotte D Shelton, Mindi K McKenna and John R Darling, 'Leading in the age of paradox: optimizing behavioral style, job fit and cultural cohesion', *Leadership and Organization Development Journal*, vol. 23, no. 7 (2002), pp. 372–9.

Amanda Sinclair, *Doing leadership differently* (Melbourne: Melbourne University Press, 1998).

Amanda Sinclair, 'Race around the office', *Australian Financial Review BOSS Magazine* (April 2001), pp. 51–3.

Graham Turner, 'Flying high', *Australian Financial Review BOSS Magazine* (2002 annual), pp. 52–5.

Michael Useem, 'The leadership lessons of Mount Everest', *Harvard Business Review*, vol. 79, no. 9 (October 2001), pp. 51–8.

Gary Yukl, *Leadership in organizations* (New Jersey: Prentice Hall, 1998).

End notes

1. CEO Dialogue, 'Visionaries and enablers: CEO and CFO leadership styles', http://www.ceoforum.com.au/200304_ceodialogue.cfm (viewed 20 December 2005); Telstra, 'Telstra executives & directors', www.telstra.com.au (viewed 20 December 2005).

2. Karen Kahler, 'Leadership: different venues, common themes', *Financial Executive International* (July/August 2001), http://www.fei.org/magazine/articles/7-8-2001_CoverStory.cfm.

3. See Alan Bryman, *Charisma and leadership in organizations* (London: Sage, 1992), ch. 5.

4. Neal M Ashkanasy and Marie T Dasborough, 'Emotional awareness and emotional intelligence in leadership teaching', *Journal of Education for Business*, vol. 79, no. 1 (September–October 2003), p. 18(5); Ken W Parry, 'The new leader: a synthesis of leadership research in Australia and New Zealand', *Journal of Leadership Studies*, vol. 5, no. 4 (Fall 1998), p. 82.

5. Australian Institute of Management–Monash University, 'Key findings, Australian Business Leadership Survey', http//www.aim.com.au/research/AIM_abls_keyfindings.pdf (viewed 20 December 2005).

6. Bryman, op. cit., p. 1.

7. G Bates, 'Taking the lead on leadership', *HR Monthly* (February 1996).

8. Ralph M Stogdill, *Handbook of leadership* (New York: The Free Press, 1974).

9. ibid.; Bernard M Bass, *Bass and Stogdill's handbook of leadership* (New York: The Free Press, 1990).

10. Rensis Likert, *New patterns of management* (New York: McGraw-Hill, 1961).

11. Bass, op. cit., ch. 24.

12. Robert R Blake and Jane S Mouton, *The new managerial grid* (Houston: Gulf, 1978).

13. See MF Peterson, 'PM theory in Japan and China: what's in it for the United States?', *Organizational Dynamics* (Spring 1988), pp. 22–39; J Misumi and MF Peterson, 'The performance-maintenance theory of leadership: review of a Japanese research program', *Administrative Science Quarterly*, vol. 30 (1985), pp. 198–223; PB Smith, J Misumi, M Tayeb, MF Peterson and M Bond, 'On the generality of leadership style measures across cultures', paper presented at the International Congress of Applied Psychology, Jerusalem, July 1986.

14. This section is based on Fred E Fiedler and Martin M Chemers, *The leader match concept*, 2nd ed. (New York: John Wiley & Sons, 1984).

15. This section is based on Fred. E Fiedler and Joseph E Garcia, *New approaches to effective leadership* (New York: John Wiley & Sons, 1987).

16. Richard L Miller; Jeanne Butler and Charles J Cosentino, 'Followership effectiveness: an extension of Fiedler's contingency model', *Leadership and Organization Development Journal*, vol. 25, no. 4 (2004), pp. 362–8.

17. This section is based on Robert J House and Terence R Mitchell, 'Path–goal theory of leadership', *Journal of Contemporary Business* (Autumn 1977), pp. 81–97.

18. House and Mitchell, op. cit.

19. See the discussion of this approach in Paul Hersey and Kenneth H Blanchard, *Management of organizational behavior* (Englewood Cliffs, NJ: Prentice Hall, 1988).

20. ibid.

21. For some criticisms see Claude L Graeff, 'The situational leadership theory: a critical view', *Academy of Management Review*, vol. 8 (1983), pp. 285–91.

22. The discussion in this section is based on Steven Kerr and John Jermier, 'Substitutes for leadership: their meaning and measurement', *Organizational Behavior and Human Performance*, vol. 22 (1978), pp. 375–403; Jon P Howell, David E Bowen, Peter W Dorfman, Steven Kerr and Phillip M Podsakoff, 'Substitutes for leadership: effective alternatives to ineffective leadership', *Organizational Dynamics* (Summer 1990), pp. 21–38.

23. Phillip M Posakoff, Peter W Dorfman, Jon P Howell and William D Todor, 'Leader reward and punishment behaviors: a preliminary test of a culture-free style of leadership effectivess', *Advances in Comparative Management*, vol. 2 (1989), pp. 95–138; T.K Peng, 'Substitutes for leadership in an international setting', unpublished manuscript (Texas: College of Business Administration, Texas Tech University, 1990).

24. Based on 'The Columbus effect: unexpected findings and new directions in leadership research', presentation made at annual meeting, Academy of Management, Las Vegas, August 1992.

25. Andrew Roberts, *Hitler and Churchill: secrets of leadership*, (London: Weidenfeld and Nicolson, 2003).

26. 'Why good leaders are hard to find', *The Age* (2 August 2003), http://www.theage.com.au/articles/2003/08/01/1059480538838.html?oneclick=true.

27. Bass, op. cit., ch. 12.

28. JA Conger and RN Kanungo, *Charismatic leadership, the elusive factor in organizational effectiveness* (San Francisco: Jossey-Bass, 1988).

29. See Jane M Howell and Bruce J Avolio, 'The ethics of charismatic leadership: submission or liberation', *The Academy of Management Executive*, vol. 6, no. 2 (May 1992), pp. 43–54.

30. Conger and Kanungo, op. cit.

31. ibid.; JA Halpert, 'The dimensionality of charisma', *Journal of Business and Psychology*, vol. 4, no. 4 (Summer 1990).

32. See Alvin Hwang, Naresh Khatri and ES Srinivas, 'Organizational charisma and vision across three countries', *Management Decision*, vol. 43, issue 7/8 (2005), pp. 960–74.

33. Gary Yukl, 'An evaluation of conceptual weaknesses in transformational and charismatic leadership theories', *Leadership Quarterly*, vol. 10, no. 2 (1999), pp. 285–305.

34. See Min-Ping Huang, Bor-Shiuan Cheng, Li-Fong Chou, 'Fitting in organizational values: the mediating role of person-organization fit between CEO charismatic leadership and employee outcomes', *International Journal of Manpower*, vol. 26, issue 1 (January 2005), pp. 35–49.

35. Ken W Parry and Sarah B Proctor-Thomson, 'Perceived integrity of transformational leaders in organisational settings', *Journal of Business Ethics*, vol. 35, no. 2 (15 January 2002), p. 75(22).

36. Ken Parry and Paresha Sinha, 'Researching the trainability of transformational organizational leadership', *Human Resource Development International*, vol. 8, no. 2 (June 2005), p. 165(19).

37. Australian Institute of Management–Monash University, 'Key findings, Australian Business Leadership Survey', http//www.aim.com.au/research/AIM_abls_keyfindings.pdf ,viewed on 20 December 2005.

38. See BM Bass, *Leadership and performance beyond expectations* (New York: The Free Press, 1985); A Bryman, *Charisma and leadership in organizations* (London: Sage, 1992), pp. 98–9.

39. Kets de Vries, 'Charisma in action: the transformational abilities of Virgin's Richard Branson and AAB's Percy Barnevik', *Organizational Dynamics* (Winter 1998), p. 18.

40. B Avolio, D Waldman and F Yammarino, 'Leading in the 1990s: the four Is of transformational leadership', *Journal of European Industrial Training*, vol. 15, no. 4 (1991), pp. 9–16.

41. See Neal M Ashkanasy and Marie T Dasborough, 'Emotional awareness and emotional intelligence in leadership teaching', *Journal of Education for Business*, vol. 79, no. 1 (September–Ocober 2003), p. 18(5).

42. Bryman, op. cit., ch. 6; K Inkson and AT Moss, 'Transformational leadership — is it universally applicable?', *Leadership and Organizational Development*, vol. 14, no. 4 (1993), pp. 1–11; MS Frank, 'The essence of leadership', *Public Personnel Management*, vol. 22, no. 3 (Fall 1993).

43. Bernard M Bass, 'Two decades of research and development in transformational leadership', *European Journal of Work and Organizational Psychology*, vol. 8, no. 1 (1999), pp. 9–32.

44. Adapted from Bryman, op. cit., p. 111.

45. See BM Bass and BJ Avolio, 'The implications of transactional and transformational leadership for individual team, and organizational development', *Research in Organizational Change and Development*, vol. 4 (1990), pp. 231–72.

46. See Jay A Conger and Rabindra N Kanungo, 'Training charismatic leadership: a risky and critical task' in Conger and Kanungo, op. cit., ch. 11.

47. National Australia Bank corporate web site, 'People, leadership and culture', http://www.nabgroup.com/0,,38458,00.html (viewed 20 December 2005).

48. See JR Kouzes and BF Posner, *The leadership challenge: how to get extraordinary things done in organizations* (San Francisco: Jossey-Bass, 1991).

49. Marshall Sashkin, 'The visionary leader' in Conger and Kanungo, op. cit., ch. 5.

50. RK Greenleaf, *Servant leadership: a journey into the nature of legitimate power and greatness* (New York: Paulist Press, 1977).

51. Sen Sendjaya and James C Sarros, 'Servant leadership: its origin, development, and application in organizations', *Journal of Leadership & Organizational Studies*, vol. 9, no. 2 (Fall 2002), p. 57.

52. Larry C Spears (ed.), *Reflections on leadership* (New York: John Wiley & Sons, 1997).

53. Mathew Charles, 'Sausage shares delivered Vizard a $140,000 windfall', *Courier Mail* (22 July 2005), p. 29.

54. Jesse Hogan and Leonie Wood, 'Vizard banned 10 years, fined $390,000', *The Sydney Morning Herald* (28 July 2005).

55. Gary Yukl, *Leadership in organizations*, 4th ed. (Englewood Cliffs, NJ: Prentice Hall, 1998).

56. Amanda Sinclair, *Doing leadership differently* (Melbourne: Melbourne University Press, 1998), p. 13.

57. Australian Institute of Management–Monash University, 'Key findings, Australian Business Leadership Survey', http//www.aim.com.au/research/AIM_abls_keyfindings.pdf (viewed 20 December 2005).

58. Nancy J Adler, 'Global women leaders: a dialogue with future history' in David L Cooperrider and Jane E Dutton (eds), *Organizational dimensions of global change* (Thousand Oaks, CA: Sage, 1999), p. 327; Sinclair, op. cit., p. 7.

59. See Mark Neal, Jim Finlay and Richard Tansey, 'My father knows the minister: a comparative study of Arab women's attitudes towards leadership authority', *Women in Management Review*, vol. 20, issue 7 (October 2005), pp. 478–97.

60. Adrienne Jones, 'The rock of the ages', *Australian Financial Review BOSS Magazine* (August 2001), pp. 24–8.

61. Nick Tabakoff and Robert Skeffington, 'At last, experience pays', *Business Review Weekly* (3 November 2000), pp. 66–7.
62. Nick Tabakoff and Robert Skeffington, 'The wise old heads are back', *Business Review Weekly* (3 November 2000), pp. 61–4.
63. HBR/NY Times Syndicate, 'When they're 64', *Australian Financial Review BOSS Magazine* (August 2001), p. 29.
64. See G Hofstede, *Culture's consequences: international differences in work-related values* (Beverly Hills, CA: Sage, 1980).
65. Robert House, Mansour Javidan, Paul Hanges and Peter Dorfman, 'Understanding cultures and implicit leadership theories across the globe: an introduction to project GLOBE (global leadership and organizational behavior effectiveness)', *Journal of World Business*, vol. 37, no. 1 (Spring 2002), p. 3(8).
— Robert J House, Paul J Hanges, Mansour Javidan, Peter W Dorfman and Vipin Gupta (eds), *Culture, leadership and organizations: the GLOBE study of 62 societies* (Thousand Oaks, CA: Sage, 2004).
66. See for example Hugo Zagorsek, Marko Jaklic, Stanley J Stough, 'Comparing leadership practices between the United States, Nigeria, and Slovenia: does culture matter?', *Cross Cultural Management: An International Journal*, vol. 11, issue 2 (June 2004), pp. 16–34.
67. Adapted from *The survey of organizations*, © 1980 by the University of Michigan and Rensis Likert Associates. Reprinted by permission of the Institute for Social Research.
68. Group procedure/process adapted from David A Kolb, Joyce S Osland and Irwin M Rubin, *Organizational behavior: an experiential approach*, 6th ed. (Englewood Cliffs, NJ: Prentice Hall, 1995). Adapted with permission of Prentice Hall, Inc.

CHAPTER 12
Decision making

Learning objectives

After studying this chapter, you should be able to:

1. define decision making

2. list the two types of decisions and discuss the decision environments found in today's organisations

3. outline the sequential steps in the decision-making process

4. summarise and contrast the classical and behavioural decision-making models

5. explain why intuition, judgement and creativity are essential aspects of quality decision making

6. state the conditions under which individuals or groups are best placed to make and take decisions in organisations

7. discuss some of the issues facing managers who have to make decisions in today's highly competitive and global organisations.

In chapter 9 we discussed organisational culture. Organisational values and beliefs (espoused and embedded) are shared and unique to that organisation and, consequently, affect decision making in an organisation. A normative organisational culture implies that decision making practice at all levels of the organisation takes place from similar perspectives. However, evidence given at the Waterfall inquiry (see the opening of chapter 9) suggests that operational and managerial staff at the State Rail Authority work within different cultural frames. Operational staff employ a culture of safety, whereas managerial staff are concerned with ensuring trains run according to the timetable. This can lead to tensions when making non-routine decisions. For example, when a choice needs to be made between safety and the economic and political consequences of running late, it is interesting to see two perspectives at work. The following conversation took place when a driver was notified of the presence of a suicidal trespasser on the train tracks ahead.

Controller:	. . . you can reduce your speed through the area there and keep running. Over.
Driver:	No, it's quite obvious this person has no respect for their wellbeing, their safety, they are wandering onto the line.
Controller:	What assessment is that driver?
Driver:	A risk assessment.
Controller:	You can run at restricted speed.
Driver:	I'm not going to run at restricted speed.
Controller:	You're not going to run at restricted speed?
Driver:	They're around out there.
Controller:	The person is on the up Illawarra local.
Driver:	They're crossing from up and down Illawarra.
Controller:	Driver you can proceed down at walking pace.
Driver:	Excuse me, and what happens if the person takes a dive under the train?
Controller:	Walking pace driver.
Driver:	No, I'm not going out there sorry.
Controller:	On what grounds driver?
Driver:	A risk assessment.
Controller:	A risk assessment?
Driver:	And they're walking around, it's quite obvious . . .
Controller:	I've sent the duty manager, Arncliffe to go up and apprehend the person. Over.
Driver:	The person is still out there.
Controller:	I've asked the duty manager, the police are nearly there, the duty manager is going out to apprehend the person, thank you.
Driver:	And I'll wait till they remove the person.
Controller:	No, driver you'll remove your train now!
Driver:	This is 11 bravo out.
Controller:	An inspector will meet you at Hurstville. Operations out.[1]

In this case the train was late as the driver refused to move it until the risk had been removed. It is evident that the objective of having both a reliable *and* safe rail system is somewhat difficult when making decisions that are not routine. From this conversation it is clear that tensions exist between operational and managerial decision makers. Managers need to be aware of all consequences when making decisions, including those beyond their own immediate goals. In this case, the driver was punished for his insubordination when he decided to delay the train. However, what would have transpired if the driver had been found to have contributed to a person's death by proceeding? This chapter evaluates some decision-making models, processes and ethical considerations.

Introduction

In today's global and highly competitive markets, organisations live and die on the choices made by their members (managers and others) and the extent to which these members can effectively learn to define and make better choices. Decision making really does lie at the heart of successful organisations.

We start the chapter with a formal definition of decision making, linking it to the nature of problem solving. This is followed by a short discussion on the kind of decisions and decision environments that managers typically face in modern organisations. We then contrast models of decision making, together with their sequential steps. Some important ingredients of quality decision making, including the skilful use of intuition, judgement and creativity, are also presented. The chapter concludes with a short discussion on current issues that are influencing decision making in today's organisations, and presents a model for ethical decision making.

Define decision making — LEARNING OBJECTIVE 1

Decision making in organisations

Henry Mintzberg is famous for his work on managerial roles. His research — based on recording the work of senior managers — suggests that in performing their tasks, they fulfil ten distinct roles broadly classified into interpersonal roles, informational roles and decision roles.

Mintzberg defined decision making as the process of choosing a course of action for solving a problem or seizing an opportunity.[2] The choice usually involves two or more possible alternatives. Considered diagramatically, it looks like figure 12.1.

> **Decision making** is the process of identifying a problem or opportunity and choosing among alternative courses of action.

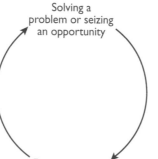

> **Routine problems** are problems that arise routinely and that can be addressed through standard responses.

FIGURE 12.1 • Defining decision making — getting things done

Types of decisions and decision environments — LEARNING OBJECTIVE 2

Types of decisions made by managers

Two basic types of managerial decisions relate to the presence of both routine and non-routine problems in the work situation. Routine problems arise regularly and can be addressed through standard responses, called programmed decisions. These responses simply implement solutions that have already been determined by past experience as appropriate for the problem at hand. Examples of programmed decisions are reordering inventory automatically when stock falls below a predetermined level, and issuing a written reprimand to someone who violates a personnel procedure.

> **Programmed decisions** are decisions that implement specific solutions determined by past experience as appropriate for the problems at hand.

Non-routine problems are unique and new. When standard responses are not available, creative problem solving is called for. These crafted decisions are specifically tailored to a situation. Senior managers generally spend a greater proportion of their decision-making time on non-routine problems. An example is the marketing manager faced with countering a competitor's introduction of a new product from abroad. Although past experience may help, the immediate decision requires a solution based on the unique characteristics of the present market situation.

> **Non-routine problems** are unique and new problems that call for creative problem solving.

> **Crafted decisions** are decisions created to deal specifically with a situation at hand.

The types of problems and decisions can be summarised as:

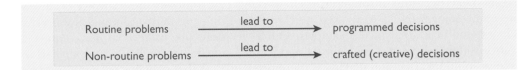

Routine problems ————lead to————→ programmed decisions

Non-routine problems ————lead to————→ crafted (creative) decisions

Decision environments of managers

When making either programmed or crafted decisions, managers confront decision environments that affect the kinds of decisions made. Problem-solving decisions in organisations are typically made under three different conditions or environments: certain, risk and uncertain.[3]

Certain environments exist when information is sufficient to predict the results of each alternative in advance of implementation. When a person invests money in a savings account, for example, absolute certainty exists about the interest that the money will earn in a given period of time. Certainty is an ideal condition for managerial problem solving and decision making. The challenge is simply to locate the alternative offering a satisfactory or even ideal solution. Unfortunately, certainty is the exception rather than the rule in managerial decision environments.

Risk environments involve a lack of complete certainty regarding the outcomes of various courses of action, but some awareness of the probabilities associated with their occurrence. A *probability*, in turn, is the degree of likelihood that an event will occur. Probabilities can be assigned through objective statistical procedures or through managerial intuition. For example, statistical estimates of quality rejects in production runs can be made, or a senior production manager can make similar estimates based on past experience. Risk is a fairly common decision environment faced by managers. Managers often need to weigh up *likelihood* of an event versus the *consequence* of the event. Risks can then be assessed to be high, medium or low. Refer to the scenario at the beginning of this chapter. If you were the controller, how would you have assessed the risk in that particular situation?

Uncertain environments exist when managers are unable to assign probabilities to the outcomes of various problem-solving alternatives. This is the most difficult of the three decision environments. Uncertainty forces managers to rely on individual and group creativity to succeed in problem solving. It requires unique, novel and often totally innovative alternatives to existing patterns of behaviour. Responses to uncertainty are often heavily influenced by intuition, educated guesses and hunches, which in turn are heavily influenced by perception.

Certain environments are decision environments in which information is sufficient to predict the results of each alternative in advance of implementation.

Risk environments are decision environments that involve a lack of complete certainty but that include an awareness of probabilities associated with the possible outcomes of various courses of action.

Uncertain environments are decision environments in which managers are unable to assign probabilities to the possible outcomes of various courses of action.

OB in action

Govplace is a North American-based value-added reseller (VAR) of computer solutions and has been in operation since 1995. Several years ago, as the IT bubble burst, Sean Burke (founder and president) and Adam Robinson (CEO) faced a tough decision in an uncertain environment. After assessing their environment, the pair took the brave step of closing their commercial operations to focus solely on public sector business. At the time the public sector arguably offered more certainty and less risk than commercial business. The decision was successful and became a turning point for the company, with Govplace positioned as one of the faster-growing solutions providers in North America.[4]

Steps in the decision-making process

Managers make decisions throughout their working day. Many of these involve relatively unimportant matters that are resolved quickly. Prioritising the daily tasks and authorising project expenditure are typical examples. Other decisions are more complex, requiring careful consideration of the problem or opportunity, and the formulation and analysis of alternative solutions. Decision making is therefore a process that contains several important steps; the final choice is simply one step along the way.

The four basic steps in systematic decision making are shown in figure 12.2. The first step is to recognise that a problem or opportunity exists and that something must be done about it. But, more than this, the real nature of the problem or opportunity has to be defined and assessed. A human resource manager investigating the low levels of job satisfaction indicated in an employee survey must first determine the root cause of the problem (low wages, poor physical conditions and so on) before making any attempt to solve the problem. The key is accurate information that is carefully evaluated.

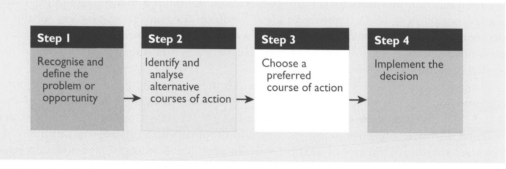

FIGURE 12.2 • The decision-making process

The next step is to pose alternative courses of action to remedy the situation. The criteria to be used when assessing the relative merits of these alternatives are also selected. Relevant criteria might include ceilings on costs, industry specifications, work experience, ease of use, maintenance requirements and so on. Usually, two or more alternatives are available, and they measure up against the assessment criteria in different ways. If poor physical conditions are found to be the root cause of the problem just mentioned, then the alternative solutions might include moving to a new factory site or refitting the existing facility. Minimising the cost and production time lost is among the criteria important to management in their search for a solution.

The choice is made during step 3, after analysing the various alternatives. Here the manager has to assess the consequences of choosing one option over another. But, as you now know, there is usually an element of risk or uncertainty in making any choice. Implementation of the decision occurs during step 4. Let us assume that the manager chooses to refit the existing facility because this appears to be the least costly and inconvenient alternative. Unfortunately, an unforeseen shortage of precision instruments needed for production is identified, increasing costs and extending the period of lost production. This is an often-repeated story in the complex world of managers. One reason decision making is often complex is because managers are faced with an ever-expanding amount of available knowledge.

Approaches to decision making

Organisational behaviour theorists maintain that there are two alternative approaches to decision making (figure 12.3) — classical and behavioural. A discussion of each will help you further understand the processes through which managers can and do make decisions.[5]

Classical decision theory views the manager as acting in a world of complete certainty. The manager faces a clearly defined problem, knows all possible action alternatives and their consequences, then chooses the alternative that offers the best, or 'optimum', resolution of the problem. Clearly, this is an ideal way to make decisions. Classical theory is often used as a model for how managers should make decisions.

Classical decision theory views the manager as acting in a world of complete certainty.

Behavioural scientists are cautious about classical decision theory. They recognise that the human mind is a wonderful creation, capable of infinite achievements, but they also recognise that human beings have cognitive limitations. The human mind is limited in its information-processing capabilities. Information deficiencies and overload compromise the ability of managers to make decisions according to the classical model. As a result, behavioural decision theory gives a more accurate description of how people *actually* make decisions in work situations.

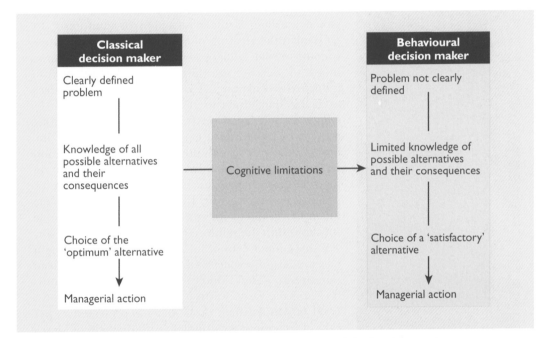

FIGURE 12.3 • Managerial decision making viewed from the classical and behavioural perspectives

Behavioural decision theory states that people act only in terms of what they perceive about a given situation. Rather than facing a world of complete certainty, the behavioural decision maker is seen as acting under uncertainty and with limited information. Managers make decisions about problems that are often ambiguous; they have only a partial knowledge about the available action alternatives and their consequences; and they choose the first alternative that appears to give a satisfactory resolution of the problem. This model is referred to by Herbert Simon as a satisficing style of decision making.[6] Simon and a colleague state:

Behavioural decision theory refers to the idea that people act only in terms of what they perceive about a given situation.

> Most human decision making, whether individual or organisational, is concerned with the discovery and selection of satisfactory alternatives; only in exceptional cases is it concerned with the discovery and selection of optimal decisions.

Satisficing means choosing the first satisfactory alternative rather than the optimal decision.

The key difference between a manager's ability to make an optimum decision in the classical style and the tendency to make a satisfying (or good enough) decision in the behavioural style is the presence of cognitive limitations and their impact on our perceptions. Cognitive limitations impair our abilities to define problems, identify action alternatives and choose alternatives — the key steps in the decision-making process.

The precautionary principle

The precautionary principle works on the basis that it is better to be safe than sorry. In a way, the principle limits personal perception of scientific data, and directs decision makers to err on the side of caution if the consequences of making the wrong decision are serious or irreversible.[7] For example, lack of scientific certainty should not be used as a reason for failing to take measures to prevent degradation of the environment when there are threats of serious or irreversible damage.

According to many scientists, one of the causes of global warming is the destruction of rainforests. In particular, the clearing of South American rainforests is controversial; while governments allow for communities to destroy the forests in order to survive, industrialised nations are condemning these practices as being dangerous to the global environment. In response, and based on the precautionary principle, the US pharmaceutical giant Merck & Company Inc has found a creative solution to the commercialisation of the rainforest much desired by locals — a solution that does not include the destruction of trees. Merck has an agreement worth US$1 million with the Costa Rican Government for the right to search for usable species within the rainforest. In addition, the company will share 5 per cent of future royalties on any drug it develops from a species obtained in the Costa Rican rainforests. The Merck venture is significantly boosting the Costa Rican national budget of just over US$1 billion. Further, Costa Rica has preserved 25 per cent of its natural environment with the help of Merck and other corporate venturers who have made the areas productive. As any royalties begin to filter into the Costa Rican Government they will allow it to preserve even more of the natural environment.[8]

Intuition, judgement and creativity

LEARNING OBJECTIVE 5

Intuition is the ability to know or recognise quickly and readily the possibilities of a given situation.

The role of intuition

A key element in successfully making non-programmed decisions is intuition. Intuition is the ability to know or recognise quickly and readily the possibilities of a given situation.[9] Intuition adds an element of spontaneity to managerial decision making and, as a result, it offers the potential for greater creativity and innovation. Especially in risk and uncertain environments, successful managers are probably using a good deal of intuition in problem solving. It is a way of dealing with situations in which precedents are unclear, 'facts' are limited or tenuous, and time is of the essence.

A debate among scholars regarding how managers really plan highlights the importance of intuition for the practising manager. On one side of the issue are those who believe that planning can be taught and carried out in a systematic step-by-step fashion. On the other side are those who believe that the nature of managerial work makes this hard to do in practice. The ideas of Henry Mintzberg illustrate this.[10]

- *Managers favour verbal communications.* Thus, they are more likely to gather data and to make decisions in a relational or interactive way than in a systematic step-by-step fashion.
- *Managers often deal with impressions.* Thus, they are more likely to synthesise than analyse data as they search for the 'big picture' to make decisions.
- *Managers work fast, do a variety of things and are frequently interrupted.* Thus, they do not have a lot of quiet time alone to think, plan or make decisions systematically.

Indeed, managers should systematically plan in a step-by-step manner, but they should also recognise the job demands noted by Mintzberg and others, and hone their intuitive skills.

COUNTER**POINT**

Intuitive decision making

There will always be instances, mostly recognised in hindsight, where capable and successful managers make poor decisions. Bob Hoel, executive director of the Filene Institute, believes that mistakes are often a result of over-reliance on intuition rather than objective facts.[11] This can occur because experience combined with intuition can lead to snap judgements that are made before all objective evidence is available for evaluation. In addition, conclusions made by different individuals on the same evidence can vary greatly. Leaf Van Boven, a University of Colorado psychology professor who studies the role of emotions in decision making, states that polarised opinions occur because decision makers are largely seeking confirmation of their initial hunches or suspicions when exposed to the same body of information.[12] This would suggest that decisions are not made solely on the basis of rationality; rather, individual intuition, feelings, emotions and experience influence the decision-making process.

On the other hand, it would be naive to suggest that decisions are best made by ignoring your intuition.[13] In fact there are some individuals who are routinely required to make intuitive decisions, especially those who work in the emergency services (police, paramedics, hospital staff and firefighters). Intuition is said to be an instantaneous, emotional and often irrational reaction to a situation that can be risky. However, it is also said to be a fast analytical reasoning that is clearly based on experience and practice drills, where judgement is simply analysis 'frozen into habit'.[14]

Nevertheless, there are limitations when making decisions solely on intuition. 'Gut instinct' can be wrong, particularly if a reaction is based on emotions that bear no correlation to any previous learning or experience. Hence, confident decision makers will generally use a combination of logic and intuition to arrive at a sound decision.[15]

Questions

1. Give three examples of instances in the workplace where use of intuition should be limited when making decisions.
2. Many business leaders openly profess to use intuition to guide their decisions. Search the Internet to discover what part intuition has played in the success of a business leader of your choosing.

The use of judgement heuristics

Judgement, or the use of the intellect, is important in all aspects of decision making. Analysing alternative courses of action and choosing one course (steps 2 and 3 in the decision-making process) involve making judgements.

Research shows that managers and others use heuristics — simplifying strategies or 'rules of thumb' — when making decisions. Heuristics can make it easier for managers to deal with uncertainty and limited information, and can prove helpful on certain occasions. But they can also lead to systematic errors that affect the quality of any decisions made.[16]

Judgement is the use of the intellect in making decisions.

Heuristics are simplifying strategies or 'rules of thumb' that people use when making decisions.

Managers often use heuristics when making decisions about expenditures. For example, many organisations, such as the Australian Government, use budget forecasting based on events that happened in the past few years.[17] Another example can be found in the recent pay increases for City Rail staff in Sydney. The negotiations started from an initial value that represented the responsibility of rail workers in the past; this led to vast pay increases for rail workers, influenced by their increased responsibilities and the consumer demands of rail users.[18] The problem is that, regardless of the basis of the initial value, adjustments from the initial value tend to be insufficient. In other words, if the initial value of the pay is deemed too low, the adjustment from that value is also likely to be too low. The result is that rail workers, despite having received a pay rise, are still underpaid considering the increase in responsibility they now carry. Thus as a result of using heuristics, different *initial* values can yield a different decision for similar problems.[19]

It is inevitable that people will adopt some way of simplifying decisions, usually producing correct or partially correct judgements. A decision maker should be aware of the following common judgemental heuristics.[20] One involves assessing an event based on past occurrences that are easily available in your memory; for example, the product manager who bases a decision not to fund a new product on his or her recollection of the recent failure of a similar product. In this case, the existence of a past product failure has negatively, and perhaps inappropriately, biased the manager's judgement of the new product.

What about a situation in which you assess the likelihood of an event occurring based on the similarity of that event to your stereotypes of such occurrences? An example is the supervisor who takes on a new employee not because that person has any special personal qualities but because they have a degree from a university known to have produced high performers in the past. In this case, the individual's alma mater — and not their job qualifications — is the basis for the decision to recruit.

In addition to using these judgemental heuristics, managers are prone to two more general biases in decision making:

- the confirmation trap, whereby managers seek confirmation for what is already thought to be true and neglect opportunities to look for disconfirming information
- the hindsight trap, whereby managers overestimate the degree to which they could have predicted an event that has already taken place.

Creativity

Creativity is the development of unique and novel responses to problems and opportunities.

Creativity in decision making involves the development of unique and novel responses to problems and opportunities. In a complex and dynamic environment, creativity in making 'crafted decisions' often determines how well organisations and their members respond to important challenges.

OB in action

New Zealand's Kevin Roberts, the chief executive of leading ideas company Saatchi & Saatchi and a well-regarded management commentator, believes that creativity and emotion are critical to successful organisational change, innovation and competitive advantage. According to Roberts, 'peak performing organisations' enthuse workers by deliberately connecting their mission and goals with employees' emotional realities. Roberts states: 'If the emotion centres of our brain are damaged in some way, we don't just lose the ability to laugh or cry. We lose the ability to make decisions. Without emotion, rational thought slows and disintegrates. Our reason must have emotion to engage it.'[21] Roberts advocates that creativity within individuals is inspired by passion. Hence, emotion is necessary to develop novel responses. For more information on Kevin Roberts's perspectives on creativity, visit www.saatchikevin.com.

In chapter 6 we pointed out that the group is an important resource for improving creativity in decision making. Indeed, managers who make good use of techniques such as brainstorming, nominal groups and the Delphi method (discussed later in this chapter) can greatly expand their creative potential. Here we look more specifically at the decision-making implications of these four stages of creative thinking:[22]

1. *preparation and problem definition* — choosing good problems to solve and then framing them broadly to consider as many alternatives as possible
2. *incubation* — looking at problems in diverse ways that allow for the consideration of unusual alternatives; avoiding tendencies towards purely linear and systematic problem solving
3. *illumination* — responding to flashes of insight and recognising when all pieces to the puzzle suddenly fit into place
4. *verification* — avoiding the tendency to relax after illumination occurs and, instead, proceeding with logical analysis to confirm that good problem-solving decisions have really been made.

To sum up, many academics and management practitioners argue that there is a clear relationship between creative thinking and organisational effectiveness or business excellence.[23]

Making a choice and implementing a decision

Now we turn our attention to steps 3 and 4 in our model. Look back again at figure 12.2. Once alternative solutions to a problem or opportunity have been developed, a preferred course of action must be chosen and that decision needs to be implemented, because management is about action! The overall aim is to achieve the best result using the least resources, and creating the least amount of risk and uncertainty (if that is possible).

However, managers working at all levels, in all areas and in all types and sizes of organisation are not supposed to just make decisions. They are supposed to make good decisions. Sometimes this means being willing to override previous commitments and to discontinue a course of action that is not working out the way it should. Frequently, it means crafting a creative solution to a non-routine problem. In all cases, successful managers make the right decisions in the right way at the right time. When it comes to managing the decision-making process, we can say that an effective manager is one who is able to pick precisely which problems are amenable to managerial decision making.

There are two important aspects of deciding to decide. The first step is selecting the problems and opportunities that deserve managerial attention. We talked about this earlier (step 1 in the model), but it requires more comment at this point. The second step is choosing a strategy for involvement.

Selecting problems carefully

OBJECTIVE 6 LEARNING Conditions for decision making

Managers are too busy and have too many things to do with their valuable time to respond personally by making decisions on every problem or opportunity that comes their way. The effective manager knows when to delegate decisions to others, how to set priorities and when to abstain from acting altogether. When confronted with a problem, therefore, they ask themselves the following questions:[24]

• *Is the problem easy to deal with?* Small and less significant problems should not get as much time and attention as bigger ones. Even if a mistake is made, the cost of decision error on small problems is also small.
• *Might the problem resolve itself?* Putting problems in rank order leaves the less significant for last. Surprisingly, many of these less important problems will resolve themselves or will be solved by others before the manager gets to them. One less problem to solve leaves decision-making time and energy for other purposes.

- *Is this my decision to make?* Many problems can be handled by people at lower levels in the hierarchy. These decisions should be delegated. Other problems can and should be referred to higher levels. This is especially true for decisions that have consequences for a larger part of the organisation, more so than for those under a manager's immediate control.

To these three questions we add one of our own:

- *Is this a solvable problem within the context of the organisation?* The astute manager recognises the difference between problems that are amenable to solutions within the context of the organisation and those that are simply not solvable on a practical level.

Strategies for involvement — who decides?

One mistake made by many new managers is to presume that they must solve the problems and make the decisions themselves. In practice, managers end up making decisions in any or all of the following ways:

- **Individual decisions.** Managers make the final choice alone based on information that they possess and without the participation of others. Sometimes called an authority decision, this approach often reflects the manager's position of formal authority in the organisation.
- **Consultative decisions.** The manager solicits inputs on the problem from other people. Based on this information and its interpretation, the manager then makes a final choice.
- **Group decisions.** The manager not only consults with others for information inputs but asks them also to participate in problem-solving discussions and in making the actual choice. Although sometimes difficult, the group decision is the most participative of the three methods of final choice and the one that seeks true group consensus.

Good managers know when and how to use each of these methods. The basic goal, of course, is always to make a 'good' decision — that is, one that is high quality, timely and both understandable and acceptable to those whose support is needed for implementation. Further, good decisions can be made by each method — individual, consultative or group — if the method fits the needs of the situation (see 'The effective manager 12.1').

Individual decisions are decisions made by one individual on behalf of the group.

Consultative decisions are decisions made by an individual after seeking input from or consulting with members of a group.

Group decisions are decisions made by all members of the group, ideally with consensus being achieved.

Generally, good decisions are consultative decisions, but when is consultation finite, and who decides that? For example, since the 1940s governments have been discussing the supposedly urgent need to upgrade Sydney's Kingsford Smith Airport (KSA) runway facilities to cope with increasing demand for landing rights from national and international carriers.

Options were to first build a third runway and then build an additional airport. Since 1946, 19 potential sites for a second Sydney Airport have been identified, including the suburbs of Holsworthy and Badgery's Creek, and Goulburn, a town located in the outer south-west of Sydney. An airport 200 km from Sydney was proposed in conjunction with the development of a very fast train (VFT) network between Sydney, Canberra and Melbourne.

In 1989, after extensive consultation, then Prime Minister Bob Hawke announced that a third runway would be built at the current airport and an additional airport would be built at Badgery's Creek. Local communities around KSA and in Sydney's west were extremely vocal in their opposition. By 1994, the third runway was opened amid a wave of protests about excessive noise, but work was yet to commence at Badgery's Creek. In 1996, the previously firm decision to build a second airport at Badgery's Creek was beginning to waver, and Holsworthy was once again suggested as an alternative building site. In 2004, the government proposed an investigation of the possibility of building an airport at Wells Creek, located in the Southern Highlands of New South Wales. This suggestion has also resurrected the proposal for a VFT network.

At time of writing, there is still no firm decision about building an additional airport in Sydney to cope with increasing demands. One reason for indecision is the community participation model used, including consultation about infrastructure, environmental impacts, noise, danger and the like. Although seemingly economically attractive, few communities choose to have an airport in their vicinity. In addition, governments are not in power long enough to endorse such a large decision and take responsibility for it to be carried out.[25]

Improving organisational problem-solving skills

THE **Effective** Manager 12.1

- Believe that most problems can be solved.
- Ensure there is organisational commitment to solving problems. If top management is committed to continual improvement, then a strong message is sent to the rest of the organisation.
- Let people know that solving problems is part of their jobs, and that they are accountable for solving their day-to-day problems.
- Ensure employees receive training in problem solving.
- Recognise when problems have been solved and praise successful problem solving.
- Ensure teams communicate their successful problem solving so other teams benefit from their experience.
- Work towards problem solving becoming a habit of every employee.[26]

Managing participation in decision making

Victor Vroom, Philip Yetton and Arthur Jago have developed a framework for helping managers to choose which of the three decision-making methods is most appropriate for the various problem situations encountered in their daily work efforts.[27] Their framework begins by expanding the three basic decision-making methods just discussed into the following five forms.

- AI (*first variant on the authority decision*). The manager solves the problem or makes the decision alone, using information available at that time.
- AII (*second variant on the authority decision*). The manager obtains the necessary information from employees or other group members, then decides on the solution to the problem. The manager may or may not tell employees what the problem is before obtaining the information from them. The employees provide the necessary information but do not generate or evaluate alternatives.

- CI (*first variant on the consultative decision*). The manager shares the problem with relevant employees or other group members individually, collecting their ideas and suggestions without bringing them together as a group. The manager then makes a decision that may or may not reflect the employees' input.
- CII (*second variant on the consultative decision*). The manager shares the problem with employees or other group members, collectively obtaining their ideas and suggestions. The manager then makes a decision that may or may not reflect the employees' input.
- G (*the group or consensus decision*). The manager shares the problem with the employees as a total group and engages the group in consensus seeking to arrive at a final decision.

The central proposition in this model is that the decision-making method used should always be appropriate to the problem being solved. The challenge is to know when and how to implement each of the possible decision methods as the situation requires.

Vroom and Jago use a flow chart to help managers analyse the unique attributes of a situation and use the most appropriate decision method for the problem at hand. Key issues involve the quality requirements of a decision, the availability and location of the relevant information, the commitments needed for follow-through and the amount of time available.

The Vroom and Jago model at first seems complex and cumbersome, yet there is a useful discipline in the model: it helps you recognise how time, quality requirements, information availability and employee acceptance issues can affect decision outcomes. It also helps you to remember that all of the decision methods are important and useful. The key to effectively managing participation in decision making is evident: know how to implement each decision method in situations for which it is most suited, and then do it well.

How groups make decisions

Edgar Schein, a noted scholar and consultant, has worked extensively with groups to analyse and improve their decision-making processes. He observes that groups may make decisions through any of the following six methods:[28]

1. *Decision by lack of response.* A course of action is chosen by default or lack of interest.
2. *Decision by authority rule.* One person dominates and determines the course of action.
3. *Decision by minority rule.* A small subgroup dominates and determines the course of action.
4. *Decision by majority rule.* A vote is taken to choose among alternative courses of action.
5. *Decision by consensus.* Not everyone wants to pursue the same course of action, but everyone agrees to try it.
6. *Decision by unanimity.* Everyone in the group wants to pursue the same course of action.

As you read more about these alternative decision methods, think how often you encounter them in your own group activities. Think, too, about the consequences resulting from each. In *decision by lack of response*, one idea after another is suggested without any discussion taking place. When the group finally accepts an idea, all others have been bypassed and discarded by simple lack of response rather than by critical evaluation. In *decision by authority rule*, the chairperson, manager or some other authority figure makes a decision for the group. This can be done with or without discussion and is time efficient. Whether the decision is a good one or a bad one depends on whether the authority figure has the necessary information, and on how well this approach is accepted by other group members. In a *decision by minority*, two or three people are able to dominate or 'railroad' the group into making a decision with which they agree. This is often done by providing a suggestion and then forcing quick agreement by challenging the group with statements such as: 'Does anyone object? . . . Let's go ahead then'.

One of the most common ways in which groups make decisions, especially when there are early signs of disagreement, is *decision by majority rule*. Here, formal voting may take place, or members may be polled to find the majority viewpoint. This method parallels the democratic political system and is often used without awareness of its potential problems. The very process of voting can create coalitions; that is, some people will be 'winners' and others will be 'losers' when the final vote is tallied. Those in the minority — the 'losers' — may feel left out or discarded without having had a fair say. As a result, they may be less committed to implementing the decision of the 'majority' and may carry lingering resentments that will impair group effectiveness in the future.

Another alternative is *decision by consensus*. Formally defined, a consensus exists after discussion leads to one alternative being favoured by most members and the other members agreeing to support it. When a consensus is reached, even those who may have opposed the chosen course of action know that they have been heard and have had a fair chance to influence the decision outcome. Consensus, therefore, does not require unanimity.

A *decision by unanimity* may be the ideal state of affairs. Here all group members agree totally on the course of action to be taken. This is a 'logically perfect' group decision method that is extremely difficult to attain in practice. Groups sometimes turn to authority decisions, majority voting or even minority decisions because managing the group process to achieve consensus or unanimity is difficult. 'The effective manager 12.2' lists guidelines for members in consensus-seeking groups.[29] Another useful typology of decision making in group situations is that proposed by the US Center for Rural Studies (shown in table 12.1). In this typology, six types of decision-making processes are identified, each with its advantages and disadvantages.

TABLE 12.1 • Decision making in groups

Type of decision process	Meaning of process	Advantages	Disadvantages
1. Individual/ autocratic	Designate a leader to make all the decisions without consulting the group in any way.	Applies to administrative needs; useful for simple, routine decisions; should be used when little time is available to make the decision, or when group members lack the skills and information to make the decision any other way.	One person is not a good resource for every decision; advantages of group interaction are lost; no commitment to implementing the decision is developed among other group members; resentment and disagreement may result in sabotage and deterioration of group effectiveness; resources of other members are not used.
2. Authority/ expert based	Select the most expert member of the group and abide by his or her decision.	Useful when the expertise of one person is so far superior to that of all other group members that little is to be gained by discussion; should be used when the need for membership action in implementing the decision is slight.	It is difficult to determine who the expert is; no commitment to implement the decision is built; advantages of group interaction are lost; resentment and disagreement result in sabotage and deterioration of group effectiveness; resources of other members are not used.
3. Average of members' opinions	Poll members of the group, and then average the results.	Useful when it is difficult for group members to meet, when the decision is so urgent that there is no time for group discussion, when member commitment is not necessary for implementing the decision, or when group members lack the skills and information to make the decision any other way; applicable to simple routine decisions.	There is not enough interaction among group members for them to gain from each other's resources and from the benefits of group discussion; the group does not develop a commitment to implement the decision; unresolved conflict and controversy may damage group effectiveness in the future.

(continued) |

Type of decision process	Meaning of process	Advantages	Disadvantages
4. Majority control	Discuss an issue, then vote when 51 per cent or more accept the course of action.	Can be used when sufficient time is lacking for decision by consensus, when the decision is not so important that consensus needs to be used, or when complete member commitment is not necessary for implementing the decision; closes discussion on issues that are not highly important for the group.	Usually leaves an alienated minority, which damages future group effectiveness; relevant resources of many group members may be lost; full commitment to implement the decision is absent; full benefit of group interaction is not obtained.
5. Minority control	Allow two or more members to serve as an executive, with committee authority to make decisions.	Can be used when everyone cannot meet to make a decision, when the group is under such time pressure that it must delegate responsibility to a committee, when only a few members have any relevant resources, or when broad member commitment is not needed to implement the decision; useful for simple, routine decisions.	Does not use the resources of many group members; does not establish widespread commitment to implement the decision; unresolved conflict and controversy may damage future group effectiveness; not much benefit from group interaction.
6. Consensus	Discuss until the group arrives at a collective opinion acceptable to all members of the group.	Produces an innovative, creative and high-quality decision; elicits commitment by all members to implement the decision; uses the resources of all members; enhances the future decision-making ability of the group; useful in making serious, important and complex decisions to which all members are to be committed.	Takes a great deal of time and psychological energy and a high level of member skill; time pressure must be minimal; not useful in an emergency.

Source: Adapted from Lois Frey, Bob Biagi and Duane Dale, 'Decision making methods: advantages and disadvantages', http://crs.uvm.edu/gopher/nerl/group/b/g/Exercise11.html.

THE **Effective** Manager 12.2

Guidelines for achieving group consensus

1. Avoid blindly arguing your case. Present your position clearly and logically, but listen to others' reactions; consider them carefully before pressing your point.
2. Do not change your mind just to reach agreement and avoid conflict. Yield to or support only those positions you believe have merit and sound foundations.
3. Avoid using 'conflict-reducing' procedures, such as holding a majority vote, tossing a coin, averaging or bargaining in reaching decisions.
4. Try to involve everyone in the decision process. Seek out and respect differences of opinion. Allow disagreements to bring a wide range of information and opinions to the deliberations.
5. Do not assume that someone must win and someone must lose when discussions reach a stalemate. Keep pressing to find an alternative acceptable to all members.
6. Discuss the assumptions underlying positions, listen carefully to one another, and encourage the participation of all members.

Groupthink

Social psychologist Irving Janis defines groupthink as the tendency of members in highly cohesive groups to lose their critical, evaluative capabilities.[30] Janis believes that because highly cohesive groups demand conformity, there is a tendency for their members to become unwilling to criticise one another's ideas and suggestions. Desires to hold the group together and to avoid unpleasant disagreements lead to an overemphasis on concurrence and an underemphasis on realistically appraising alternative courses of action.

Groupthink is a rationalisation process that develops when group members begin to think alike. It can be encouraged by leaders who do not tolerate dissent, and it can develop when employees underestimate potential problems.

Groupthink is also a mode of thinking that people engage in when they are deeply involved in a cohesive in-group, when the quest for unanimity overrides their motivation to realistically appraise alternative courses of action. During groupthink, small groups develop shared illusions and related norms that interfere with critical thinking and reality testing. Some symptoms of groupthink are arrogance, over-commitment and excessive loyalty to the group. Other symptoms of groupthink are found in 'The effective manager 12.3' on page 434. They can be used to help spot this phenomenon in practice.

Groupthink is the tendency of members in highly cohesive groups to lose their critical, evaluative capabilities.

Seventy-three seconds after its launch on 28 January 1986, the *Challenger* space shuttle exploded, killing the seven astronauts aboard. The cause of the explosion was found to be the failure of the O-ring seals on the solid rocket booster joints on the space shuttle. In the year prior to the *Challenger* launch, test launches and numerous investigations had shown that in low temperatures the O-ring seals failed to seal the joints, leaving them vulnerable to the high temperatures created at launch and thus increasing the possibility of explosion.

The day before the *Challenger* launch, managers were made aware of the low temperature forecast for the launch date and a meeting was called between managers and senior engineers. The engineers presented compelling data that a launch with an outside temperature of −7.8°C was dangerous and strongly recommended against launching *Challenger*. NASA managers, burdened by the economic consequences of the delayed launch, argued for continuation of the mission.

Eventually the engineers' concerns were dismissed as the head of the management team, Jerry Mason, turned to Bob Lund, vice-president of engineering, and asked him to 'take off his engineering hat and put on his management hat'. After some discussion, it was unanimously recommended that the *Challenger* mission go ahead as scheduled.[31] Further information and an analysis of groupthink symptoms in this case can be obtained by watching the video *A major malfunction*.[32]

Janis suggests the following action guidelines for best dealing with groupthink.[33]
- Assign the role of critical evaluator to each group member; encourage a sharing of objections.
- Have the leader avoid seeming partial to one course of action.
- Create subgroups operating under different leaders and working on the same problem.
- Have group members discuss issues with employees and report back on their reactions.
- Invite outside experts to observe group activities and to react to group processes and decisions.
- Assign one member of the group to play a 'devil's advocate' role at each meeting.
- Write alternative scenarios for the intentions of competing groups.
- Hold 'second-chance' meetings after consensus is apparently achieved on key issues.

Spotting the symptoms of 'groupthink'

- *Illusions of group invulnerability*. Members believe the group is beyond criticism or attack.
- *Rationalising unpleasant data*. Members refuse to accept or thoroughly consider contradictory data or new information.
- *Belief in inherent group morality*. Members believe the group is 'right' and above reproach by outsiders.
- *Negative stereotyping of outsiders*. Members refuse to look realistically at other groups; they may view competitors as weak, evil or stupid.
- *Applying pressure to deviants*. Members refuse to tolerate anyone who suggests that the group may be wrong; every attempt is made to get conformity to group wishes.
- *Self-censorship by members*. Members are unwilling to communicate personal concerns or alternative points of view to the group as a whole.
- *Illusions of unanimity*. Members are quick to accept consensus; they do so prematurely and without testing its completeness.
- *Mind guarding*. Members of the group keep outsiders away and try to protect the group from hearing disturbing ideas or viewpoints.

Techniques for improving decision making in groups

As you can see, the process of making decisions in any group is a complex and even delicate one. Group dynamics must be well managed to balance individual contributions and group operations. The following equation helps keep this point in mind:[34]

$$\text{Group decision effectiveness} = \text{individual contributions} + \text{group process gains} - \text{group process losses}$$

Over the years, social scientists have studied ways of maximising the assets of the group decision-making process while minimising its liabilities to take full advantage of the group as a decision-making resource. A particular point of concern is with the process losses that are often associated with free-flowing open group meetings, such as a committee deliberation or a staff meeting to address a specific problem.

The advantages in using committees or groups for decision-making or developing recommendations for a decision maker include collective wisdom or combined expertise, motivation, individual development and decision acceptance. The pitfalls that beset group or committee decision making can be roughly classified as human limitations and procedural problems. Among the human limitations are the fatigue factor, dominant personalities in the group and a lack of information. Procedural problems include procedures adopted, the time element and a lack of authority. Understanding the players and the process is the first step in making group decision making more effective.

Free-flowing open group meetings are settings in which the risk of social pressures to conform, domination, time pressures and even highly emotional debates may detract from the purpose at hand. It is precisely in such situations that special group decision techniques may be used to ensure that everyone gets a chance to participate and that the creative potential of the group is tapped to the fullest. Good examples are the brainstorming, nominal group and Delphi techniques, discussed shortly.[35]

When a department is not operating at an acceptable or desired level, the symptoms can often be found in meetings, memoranda and other forms of interaction. Many would say that a quantifiable reduction in trust — writing a memo to confirm a discussion, for instance — shows that people are looking out for themselves and are not at ease.

Experiential techniques, by use of which groups complete physical events and group games and relate their experiences back to the work environment, have become increasingly popular methods of reinvigorating work groups. Once a department is sold on the idea of changing through group dynamics, an assessment can be made of the group's productivity and internal ability to function. The group then decides on the goals it wants to accomplish in the future. By giving groups experiences that encourage them to raise their benchmarks, experiential programs seek to instil new expectations in members.[36] If they are run on a regular basis, experiential programs may also contribute to building and/or reinforcing a 'group culture'.

Another technique for contributing ideas for decision making is brainstorming. In brainstorming, group members actively generate as many ideas and alternatives as possible, and they do so relatively quickly and without inhibitions. Brainstorming is discussed in detail in chapter 7.

The nominal group technique is a group decision technique that uses structured rules for minimising interactions to facilitate decision making on potentially controversial subjects. Participants are given a 'nominal question' and asked to generate ideas in response to it. The ideas are recorded, and group members vote on the best idea.[37] The structured nature of the nominal group and the voting procedure allows ideas to be evaluated without risking the inhibitions, hostilities and distortions that may occur in an open meeting. This makes the nominal group technique very useful in otherwise difficult or unwieldy group decision situations.

A third group decision approach, the Delphi technique, was developed by the Rand Corporation for use in situations in which group members are unable to meet face to face. In this procedure, a series of questionnaires is distributed to a panel of decision makers, and responses are summarised by the decision coordinator. The process is repeated until consensus is reached and a clear decision emerges.

One of the problems with the Delphi technique relates to the complexity and cost of administering this series of questionnaires. However, the technique does make group decision making possible in circumstances in which it is physically impossible to convene a meeting. A natural extension of the technique is the application of group decision software in computer network groups.

The problem of escalating commitment

We mentioned at the beginning of this section that effective managers should be making *good* decisions, and that they should be prepared to override previous commitments and discontinue courses of action that are just not working. Often this means being bold and decisive! However, many managers fall into the trap of escalating commitment. Recognised by social psychologists as common and potentially dysfunctional, it is the tendency to continue with a previously chosen course of action even though feedback indicates that it is not working.[38]

Escalating commitment is encouraged by the popular adage: 'If at first you don't succeed, try, try again'. Current wisdom in organisational behaviour supports an alternative view: good decision makers know when to call it quits. They are willing to reverse previous decisions and commitments, and thereby avoid further investments in unsuccessful courses of action. However, the self-discipline required to admit mistakes and change courses of action is sometimes difficult to achieve. Often the tendency to escalate commitments to previously chosen courses of action outweighs the willingness to disengage from them. This occurs as decision makers:[39]

- rationalise negative feedback as simply a temporary condition
- protect their egos and avoid admitting the original decision was a mistake
- use the decision as a way of managing the impressions of others, such as a boss or peers
- view the negative results as a 'learning experience' that can be overcome with added future effort.

Escalating commitment is the tendency to continue with a previously chosen course of action even when feedback suggests that it is failing.

Escalating commitment is a form of decision entrapment that leads people to do things that are not justified by the facts of the situation. Managers should be proactive in spotting 'failures' and open to reversing decisions or dropping plans that do not appear to be working.

Issues facing today's managers

LEARNING OBJECTIVE 7

Current issues in organisational decision making

In today's environments, the problems facing organisational decision makers seem to get harder and more complex. We face difficult stresses and strains as the quest for higher productivity challenges the needs, talents and opportunities of people at all levels of responsibility. Prominent among the current issues relating to decision making in today's workplace are those dealing with culture and technology.

Culture and decision making

The forces of globalisation and workforce diversity have brought increased attention to how culture may influence decision making.

The cultural dimensions of power-distance and individualism–collectivism have special implications for decision making. Workers from high power-distance cultures may expect their supervisors to make the decisions and may be less inclined than individualists to expect or wish to be involved in decision-making processes. Signs of good managers in cultures emphasising and respecting status differences may include a willingness to act as an expert in problem solving and to be decisive; a manager who seems uncomfortable making decisions without group involvement and consensus may be less favourably viewed.

Values relating to individualism–collectivism also affect cultural tendencies towards participation in decision making. Decision making in collectivist cultures tends to be time consuming, with every effort being made to gain consensus. The results are slower decisions but smooth implementation. Decision making in individualist cultures, by contrast, is oriented more towards being decisive, saving time and using voting to resolve disagreements. The results are often implementation problems and delays.[40] In collectivist Japan, for example, many companies use the *ringi* system — a group decision approach by which workers indicate written approval of proposals prior to their acceptance and implementation.[41] In more individualist France, it is common for decisions made at higher corporate levels to be passed down the hierarchy for implementation.[42]

Culture may even play a role in determining whether a decision is necessary at all — in other words, whether the situation should be changed. North Americans tend to perceive situations as problems to be solved and want to do something about them. Other cultures, such as Thai and Indonesian societies, are more prone to accept the status quo.[43]

Technology and decision making

Artificial intelligence, or AI, studies how computers can be made to think like the human brain.

There is no doubt that today's organisations are becoming more sophisticated in applying computer technologies to facilitate decision making. Developments in the field of artificial intelligence — the study of how computers can be programmed to think like the human brain — are many and growing.[44] Nobel laureate and decision scientist Herbert Simon is convinced that computers will some day be more intelligent that humans. Already the applications of artificial intelligence to organisational decision making are significant. We have access to decision-making support from *expert systems* that reason like a human expert and follow 'either/or' rules or heuristics to make deductions, *fuzzy logic* that reasons beyond either/or choices in more imprecise territory, and *neural networks* that reason inductively by simulating the brain's parallel processing capabilities. Uses for such systems may be found everywhere from banks, where they may help screen loan applications, and hospitals, where they check laboratory results and possible drug interactions, to the factory floor, where they schedule machines and people for maximum production efficiencies.

Computer support for group decision making, including developments with the Internet and intranets, breaks the decision-making meeting out of the confines of face-to-face interactions. With the software now available, people working in geographically dispersed locations can define problems and make decisions together and simultaneously. Research confirms that group decision software can be especially useful for generating ideas, such as in electronic brainstorming, and improving the time efficiency of decision making.[45] People working under electronically mediated conditions tend to stay focused on tasks and avoid the interpersonal conflicts and other problems common in face-to-face deliberations. On the negative side, decisions made by 'electronic groups' carry some risk of being impersonal and perhaps less compelling in terms of commitments to implementation and follow-through. Further, there is evidence that the use of computer technology for decision making is better accepted by today's university or college students than by people who are already advanced in their organisational careers.[46]

Pickberry Vineyard, a Californian winery, uses an automated watering protocol system that is run by a network of remote sensors. The sensors are used to monitor moisture and rain levels and a variety of other weather and soil conditions. Depending on the analysis of the data received, water usage is adjusted automatically. However, when temperature differences are detected, the AI system will only notify human decision makers. Temperature fluctuations are detrimental to wine making as grapes must be protected from large temperature drops. Thus, the decision on how to intervene is still made by individuals, rather than an artificial intelligence.[47]

Ethical decision making

The nature and extent of ethical decision making is subject to ongoing debate. Some scholars profess that ethics has no role to play in organisational decision making: for example, economist Milton Friedman said that making decisions on purely ethical grounds may not be in the interest of organisational profit making and responsibility to shareholders.[48] Despite such views, contemporary managerial attitudes towards ethics and social responsibility suggest that ethics is a relevant and important aspect of management function in contemporary managerial decision making.[49] Organisations constantly influence what we do and have influenced the changes that have taken place within society over time. Therefore, large and complex organisations can be regarded as moral entities in their own right.

Organisational operators solve economic problems by distributing goods and services across society in the best possible way, but the purpose of industry is not just profit making; it is also to serve the general welfare.[50] Therefore, in contemporary organisations, making ethically and socially responsible decisions is considered 'worthy' for both organisations and society as a whole.

To 'be ethical' you needs to determine whether your *actions* are ethical or not. These determinations, according to Gregory Foster, can be based on numerous theoretical underpinnings,[51] such as:

- A *principle, rule, law or regulation.* For example, if the law states it is wrong to discriminate on the basis of race or gender, then it is unethical to break this law. This is known as *deontology.*

- *Behavioural or ethics codes.* For example, it would be unethical for a Christian to break the Ten Commandments, or for a Hindu to break the rules of Dharma. Similarly, it is considered unethical for workers to break a code of ethics that the organisation has in place.

- *The consequences of our proposed actions or utilitarianism.* When making decisions, the ethical choice is the one that has the outcome of the greatest good for the greatest number. It is this theory that states that the end justifies the means. Utilitarianism is commonly used in business in the form of a cost–benefit analysis.

- *The rights of the stakeholders involved and what obligations we owe.* This is also known as Kant's theory of deontology. Kant's work is complex and tests whether something is ethical or not via his 'categorical imperative'. The categorical imperative says that an action is only ethical if it can become universal law, if it treats individuals as an ends not a means, and if it applies to all other individuals.

- *Values, traits, and behaviours or virtues we consider worthy.* Virtue ethics dates back to the Eastern and Western philosophies of Confucius and Aristotle. For example, Aristotle's philosophy indicates that the virtuous path is the middle path between two undesirable attributes; so between recklessness and cowardice is courage. Therefore, to be courageous when making ethical decisions is the virtuous and right thing to do.

It is important to note that all these theories have weaknesses; for example, deontology does not allow for exceptions — it is very black and white. Utilitarianism can result in unjust outcomes because it is dependent on what is good for the majority. Virtue ethics and other self-awareness theories rely heavily on individual perception; for example, what one individual sees as entrepreneurial, another may see as high risk taking.

The dominance of economics, based on the free market; increasing competition; and quests for corporate and organisational survival, nationally and internationally, have had an impact on the extent to which individuals and organisations are prepared to act ethically when making decisions. The simplest way of making decisions would be to use a tool or algorithm that produces a flowchart showing how to come to the most ethical decision. Unfortunately, ethical decision making is extremely complex. Before moving on to an ethical decision-making framework, it is important to reflect on the determinations already mentioned and what it is that influences our judgement about what is right or wrong.

The classical approach to decision making tends to preclude the use of judgement and intuition and determines that decisions are made through *deductive* reasoning. However, the information required to make a rational decision is often not available and therefore judgement has to be exercised. Judgement is effectively dependent on previous experience, and how these experiences have shaped the person's paradigm or 'world view'. This method of learning by experience is also called heurism (as discussed earlier), or one for which no algorithm exists and which therefore depend on *inductive* reasoning — building upon past experiences of similar problems.

Ethical decisions are rarely black and white. This is because ethical decision making generally involves numerous, often conflicting, morals. The difficulty of reconciling these conflicting morals lead to ethical dilemmas.

An **ethical dilemma** occurs when a person must decide between competing values and beliefs, often in complex and value-laden contexts.[52] In organisations, ethical dilemmas occur when a person's behaviour or the behaviour of others conflict with personal beliefs and values. Organisations need to make their ethical principles known to their staff. When organisational and individual values differ it causes stress and this is difficult to remove. An employee suffering an ethical dilemma has only three choices: he or she can change the behaviour, change their personal beliefs or rationalise the behaviour. Most rationalise the behaviour, as this is obviously the simplest option.

An **ethical dilemma** occurs when a person must make a decision that requires a choice among competing sets of principles.

People in organisations tend to use after-the-fact rationalisations to 'excuse' or 'explain' unethical behaviour. The common rationalisations include:[53]

- pretending the decision is not really unethical or illegal
- excusing the intended behaviour by saying it really is in the organisation's or your own best interests
- assuming the decision is acceptable because no-one else would ever find out about it
- expecting your superiors to support and protect the decision if anything should go wrong.

Ethical decision-making framework

It is clear that personal reflection and critical analysis are needed in order to introduce some measure of objectivity into discussions that are essentially subjective due to our own bias (brought about by experience and socialisation).[54] This is where an ethical decision-making model can be useful as it forces us to look beyond our preconceived ideas and judgements.

Making ethical decisions is not easy — this framework is not a 'one best way' solution. Indeed, there is no such thing when discussing ethics; nor is there any clear right or wrong decision. However, applying the framework may improve the prospects of making a sound decision,[55] because a framework allows for eclectic theories to be used and assists in structuring thought processes.

An ethical decision-making framework is a series of steps designed to ensure that ethical theory is applied properly and appropriately. Its aim is to identify important ethical considerations so they can be fully thought through. The steps in the following framework are an adaptation of work done by John Harrison[56] and Simon Longstaff.[57]

1. Identify all the stakeholders that will be affected by the decision.
2. State the facts of the decision to be made without making any statement as to their rightness or wrongness. Many issues create controversy; you need to take the emotion out of the decision and look at the facts.
3. Highlight the principles, values and codes relevant to the decision, in particular those that appear to be in conflict. Occasionally things may appear to be in conflict initially, but upon further investigation can actually be reconciled.
4. Investigate all the possible options available to resolve the decision.
5. Assess all the options identified in step 4, in line with the various ethical theories and while making sure that the duties and/or responsibilities of all parties are recognised; for example:
   - Apply deontology to identify the legal, moral and equitable rights of all affected parties and which option will best protect those rights.
   - Apply utilitarianism to identify all the benefits and harms each option will produce; in particular, identify which option will produce the best outcome.
   - Apply virtue ethics to identify which course of action develops moral virtue.
6. Ask yourself the following questions to 'road test' the decision:
   - If the decision goes on the public record, how would I feel? If you would not be happy then that is your inner-self telling you that you are about to break your own moral code.
   - How would you vindicate the decision to your close family members (also called 'the double check'[58])?
   - What will this proposed course of action do to your character or the character of your organisation? Reputation is a key businesses asset; making a decision that will irreparably damage that reputation is not a sound decision.

- Will everyone around you respond to the decision in the same way? If they cannot, then why should you be able to respond in that way?
- How would you like it if someone did this to you? If you would feel bad, then clearly others would probably not like it either.
- Will the proposed course of action bring about a good result for all involved? If the result is not good for all, then why are you doing it?
- Is the proposed course of action consistent with your espoused values and principles? Individuals make up an organisation. In business life or personal life, individuals should always be true to their own values.

7. Make your decision and implement it, accepting responsibility for the outcome; stand by your decision and be prepared to justify it.

All stakeholders need to be taken into account and they should all be involved with modern business decision making. Often an assumption is made that stakeholder groups are in opposition to each other; for example, tensions between shareholders' interests and community interests. However, stakeholders are often members of more than one group. For example, an employee may also be a shareholder and a member of the community.[59] Therefore, using a decision-making approach that applies several ethical perspectives ensures that the decision taken will be one that is 'ethical' according to the views of all stakeholders, irrespective of the theoretical evaluation.

WhatWould **You**Do?

A sound decision?

You have worked part-time for a well-known accounting firm during the final two years of your university studies, and are almost guaranteed a full-time position on graduation. Most of your experience to date has been in the auditing department, where you have assisted the managers with several large company accounts. The company has an established professional development plan for young graduates like yourself, so you have reasonably clear expectations of your work assignments and promotion prospects for the next few years. On graduation you would expect to be rotated into the taxation group, and would later have the opportunity to take full responsibility for some important clients. You were reasonably content with these prospects until yesterday, when you received a letter from a recruitment consultancy, inviting you to attend an interview for possible employment with a newly established global company. The letter mentioned overseas travel, challenge and the opportunity to broaden into a management consultancy role — things that appeal to you but that you had thought were out of reach. You are flattered, but surprised and unsure of what to do — after all, you thought your future was laid out for you, and so did your family. Now you may be in a position to choose between two alternative career options.

Questions
1. Why does this situation present a difficult dilemma for you?
2. What steps can you take to ensure that the decision you make is a sound one?

Ethical decision-making standards and practices are part of an organisation's culture and often permeate the organisation from the top down. The following 'Ethical perspective' shows that companies can damage their reputational capital when making unethical choices.

ETHICAL
Perspective

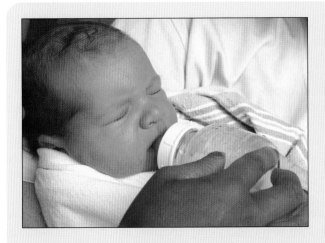

Nestlé baby formula

Nestlé has been a successful producer of baby milk formula since 1867.[60] From 1973 to 1984, when breastfeeding went somewhat out of fashion in the United States and Europe, Nestlé expanded its formula business into Africa. Large billboards showing happy, modern mothers and well-fed babies were placed in communities and new mothers were visited by company representatives — in nurse's uniform — offering free samples of formula. As new mothers took advantage of the free samples of formula, their individual breast milk production fell significantly — a woman's body only continues to produce breast milk as long as the baby continues to suckle. The mother's inability to breastfeed created an economic certainty for Nestlé: once women can not breastfeed, they have no alternative but to bottle feed their babies with formula.[61]

However, many of the African women who used the free samples in hospital found the formula was not available when they returned to their remote villages. Others could not afford it and over-diluted the formula powder to make it last longer. Many new mothers diluted the powder with local unsterilised water, possibly contributing to malnutrition and serious illnesses.[62]

The situation is complex because, legally and ethically, Nestlé's marketing practices were perfectly reasonable and acceptable in Western countries. However, some critics considered that using the same marketing techniques in developing countries may be immoral. In 1977 a US-based coalition instigated a global boycott of all Nestlé products. The boycott lasted for seven years, only ending after Nestlé and many other formula manufacturers agreed to follow the World Health Organisation's (WHO) 'Code of marketing of breast milk substitutes'.[63] Nestlé's reputation again came under scrutiny as allegations surfaced that the company had interpreted the WHO code rather loosely. Once again there were calls from the International Baby Food Action Network (IBFAN) to boycott the company. The allegations are that Nestlé still promotes infant formula, follow-up milks and other breast milk substitutes to the public. In addition, the company allegedly promotes formula to healthcare workers in healthcare facilities, and offers free or low-cost supplies.[64] Nestlé strongly denies these allegations and has stated that it does not promote its products, but simply provides educational material, which is not a violation of the WHO code. In response to the other allegations Nestlé has stated that it cannot answer them as they are too vague to investigate.[65]

Irrespective of who is correct and who is not, the issue is whether Nestlé and other organisations have an ethical obligation to change their well-established legitimate (Western) practices when operating in developing countries.

Summary

Define decision making

Decision making in organisations is a continuing process of identifying problems and opportunities and then choosing among alternative courses of action for dealing with them successfully. According to classical decision theory, managers seek 'optimum' solutions, while behavioural decision theory recognises that managers 'satisfice' and accept the first available satisfactory alternative.

Types of decisions and decision environments

Routine problems arise on a regular basis and can be resolved through standard responses called programmed decisions. Non-routine problems require tailored responses referred to as crafted decisions. Managers make decisions in three different environments: certain, risk and uncertain. Under certainty, everything about the alternative solutions is known and a choice will lead to an outcome that is highly predictable. Under risk, the manager can estimate the probability that particular outcomes will result from the choices made, but there are no guarantees. In uncertain environments the choice is made with little real knowledge of what might eventuate.

Steps in the decision-making process

The decision-making process involves four sequential steps: recognise and define a problem; identify and analyse alternative courses of action; choose a preferred course of action; and implement the decision.

Classical versus behavioural decision-making models

In classical decision theory the manager operates in a world of complete certainty and always knows what will happen if a certain choice is made. Under behavioural decision theory, the manager is normally faced with risk or uncertainty when making decisions because of incomplete knowledge, ambiguity in the situation, lack of time to continue collecting and analysing information, and other constraints.

Intuition, judgement and creativity

Intuition, judgement and creativity are all critical in effective managerial decision making. Intuition — the ability to recognise the possibilities of a situation quickly — is increasingly considered an important managerial asset. Judgement is the use of cognitive skills to make choices among alternatives, but heuristics (or simplifying rules of thumb) can potentially bias decision making. Creativity limitations can be overcome, and decision making improved, through individual awareness and a good use of groups as problem-solving resources.

Conditions for decision making

Managers must know how to involve others in decision making and how to choose among individual, consultative and group decision methods. This is often a complex process. The Vroom–Jago model identifies how decision methods can be varied to meet the unique needs of each problem situation. Key issues involve quality requirements, information availability and time constraints. Groups can make decisions in different ways: decisions by lack of response, authority rule, minority rule, consensus and unanimity. There are potential benefits to making decisions in a group. Typically, a group decision is based on more information and results in better member understanding and commitment. The liabilities include greater time requirement and the dangers of groupthink.

Issues facing today's managers

Globalisation and workforce diversity have brought into play the significance of culture in managerial decision making. Culture can dictate, for example, who should make the decision and the speed of the decision-making process within the organisation.

Computers are being used more and more to facilitate decision making, but it is important to recognise both the benefits and the limitations of these sophisticated artificial intelligence initiatives.

Ethical issues in decision making are extremely relevant in today's organisations. Managers are often faced with critical ethical dilemmas — situations in which a preferred, particular decision may lead to an outcome that could be perceived as unethical or perhaps even illegal by others inside and outside of the organisation. Using a decision-making model can assist managers in this regard.

Chapter 12 study guide

OB | *Key terms*

artificial intelligence, *p. 436*
behavioural decision theory, *p. 423*
certain environments, *p. 421*
classical decision theory, *p. 423*
consultative decisions, *p. 428*
crafted decisions, *p. 420*
creativity, *p. 426*
decision making, *p. 420*

escalating commitment, *p. 435*
ethical dilemma, *p. 439*
group decisions, *p. 428*
groupthink, *p. 433*
heuristics, *p. 425*
individual decisions, *p. 428*
intuition, *p. 424*
judgement, *p. 425*

non-routine problems, *p. 420*
programmed decisions, *p. 420*
risk environments, *p. 421*
routine problems, *p. 420*
satisficing, *p. 423*
uncertain environments, *p. 421*

OB | *Review questions*

1. Explain how three types of environments can have an impact on the decision-making process.
2. Why is identification of the problem (step 1 in the decision-making process) so important and how does this step relate to ethical decision making?
3. How does heurism relate to the general biases that many managers have with respect to decision making?
4. What can an organisation do to improve its creativity?

OB | *Application questions*

1. Often at university, students are required to work in groups with people they have never met before. When choosing potential group members, how do you make the decision on who you are going to work with? In your answer please explain the decision-making environments.
2. A member of your staff has put together a business plan to produce and market a new product. The plan is very comprehensive, and conservative figures estimate that the new product would be highly profitable for your organisation. However, your previous experience with this particular staff member has caused you to not fully trust him. Despite having no tangible reason for your lack of trust, you decide not to go ahead with the project. Your board of directors now wants an explanation for your decision. How do you justify and explain your behaviour? In your answer comment on rational, intuitive, heurisistic and ethical considerations.

3. You have been working within a group on a large project that has taken six months. Unfortunately, a crisis occurs just prior to the project's completion date, signifying a significant delay in finalisation. Redirection decisions must be made immediately to salvage any losses. In your opinion, and considering what you have learned in this chapter, who should make decisions in such a crisis: the manager accountable for project outcomes or the group responsible for the project, or should this be a consultative process for decision making? Explain the reasons for your choice.
4. Decisions on whether or not to grant finance credit to an individual are often made using decision-making software. What are the advantages and disadvantages of using such technology?
5. You have recently been sent to a regional office to help implement much-needed organisational changes. You have been told that some of the day-to-day operating

decisions are to be made collectively by the workers and that you will be informed of their decisions when you get there. Upon arrival you discover that no decisions have been made, and you are working to a deadline to complete implementation of change.

Using what you have learnt in this chapter, explain what you will do from here.

6. What career path have you chosen? How did you arrive at this important decision? Please use what you have learnt in this chapter to explain your answer.

Research questions

1. As corporations move to coordinate operations that are spread across various nations, senior executives are realising that there are often substantial differences in the decision-making styles in different countries. Systematically review the recent scholarly and practitioner literature on decision making to answer the following questions, then write a report that summarises the most recent thinking on the issues raised. You must reference your work. Your lecturer may ask you to present a formal 'executive-style' five-minute summary of your findings.
    (a) What are some of the major decision-making styles typically found in corporations headquartered in Asia and New Zealand?

    (b) How compatible are the styles in Asia and New Zealand with those typically found in Australia?
2. One visible guideline for organisational behaviour is an organisation's code of ethics. Search the Internet and compare and contrast codes of ethics of either two large organisations — one in the private sector (for example, a bank), one in the public sector (for example, a health service) — or the code of one of these organisations and a professional code of ethics (for example, a code of ethics for accountants). How do these codes assist the decision-making practices of staff? How do you interpret these codes and is your interpretation the same as that of other members in your class? What are the implications of the different interpretations, if any?

Running project

Complete the following activities for your chosen organisation.
1. Try to identify several examples of routine problems and programmed decisions and non-routine problems and crafted decisions at your organisation. If you cannot access this information directly, consider the way the organisation works and some of the internal

and external factors affecting the organisation to identify the types of decisions facing the organisation.
2. Compare the extent to which the organisation relies on (a) heuristics and (b) creativity in its approach to decision making.
3. What arrangements does the organisation have in place to ensure ethical decision making?

Individual activity

Decision-making biases

Instructions

How good are you at avoiding potential decision-making biases? Test yourself by answering the following questions:
1. Which is riskier?
    (a) Driving a car on a 1000 km trip
    (b) Flying on a 1000 km commercial airline flight

2. Are there more words in the English language:
    (a) that begin with 'r'?
    (b) that have 'r' as the third letter?
3. Mark is finishing his MBA at a prestigious university. He is very interested in the arts and at one time considered a career as a musician. Is Mark more likely to take a job:
    (a) in the management of the arts?
    (b) with a management consulting firm?

(continued)

4. You are about to hire a new central-region sales director for the fifth time this year. You predict that the next director should work out reasonably well since the last four were poor performers and the odds favour hiring at least one good sales director in five tries. Is this thinking:

(a) correct?

(b) incorrect?

5. A newly hired engineer for a computer company in Perth has four years experience and good all-round qualifications. When asked to estimate the starting salary for this employee, a chemist with very little knowledge about the profession or industry guessed an annual salary of $45 000. What is your estimate?

$_____ per year

Scoring

Your instructor will provide answers and explanations for the assessment questions.

Interpretation

Each of the preceding questions examines your tendency to use a different judgemental heuristic. In the third edition of his book *Judgment in managerial decision making* (New York: Wiley, 1994, pp. 6–7), Max Bazerman calls these heuristics 'simplifying strategies, or rules of thumb' used in making decisions. He states: 'In general, heuristics are helpful, but their use can sometimes lead to severe errors ... If we can make managers aware of the potential adverse impacts of using heuristics, they can then decide when and where to use them.' This assessment offers an initial insight into your use of such heuristics. An informed decision maker understands the heuristics, is able to recognise when they appear, and eliminates any that may inappropriately bias decision making.

Write down a situation that you have experienced in which some decision-making bias may have occurred. Be prepared to share and discuss this incident with the class.

Source: Adapted from Max H. Bazerman, *Judgment in managerial decision making*, 3rd edn (New York: Wiley, 1994), pp. 13–14. This material is used by permission of John Wiley & Sons, Inc.

OB Group activity

The fishing trip

Objectives

1. To help you experience both individual and group work when confronting a non-routine problem situation

2. To show you the advantage of assessing and analysing differences between individual decision-making methods and group decision-making methods; and also to give you some insight into the processes used to make decisions

Total time: *60–75 minutes*

Procedure

1. Read the following story, 'The fishing trip'.[66]

2. Assume you are a member of the group in the story, and rank the items in order of importance under column A on the form provided.

3. Form groups of four to six people and rank the items again, this time placing your group rankings under column B.

4. Obtain the ranking information of an experienced sea captain, record it in column X, and then follow further direction from your lecturer or tutor.

The fishing trip

It was the first week in August when four friends set out on an overnight fishing trip in the Gulf of Carpentaria. Everything went well the first day — the sea was calm, they caught fish and later they camped out on a lovely little island. However, during the night a very strong wind pulled the anchor free and drove their boat ashore, and the pounding waves broke the propeller. Although there were oars in the boat, the motor was useless.

A quick review of the previous day's journey showed that the group was about 100 kilometres from the nearest inhabited land. The small deserted island they were on had a few scrub trees and bushes but no fresh water. They knew from their portable AM–FM radio that the weather would be hot and dry, with daytime temperatures expected to be above 38°C for the rest of the week. They were all dressed in light clothing, but each had a windbreaker for the cool evenings. They agreed that whatever happened they would stick together.

Their families back on shore expected the group to return from their trip that evening and would surely report them missing when they did not return. However, they realised that it might take time for someone to find them because they had gone out further than anyone might have expected.

Although some members of the group were quite concerned about this predicament, there was no panic. To help keep the group calm, one member, Jim, suggested that they take an inventory of the food and equipment available to them, just to be safe. 'It may be several days before we are rescued,' Jim said, 'and I think we should prepare for that'. Kate, Tom and Ann agreed, and their effort produced the list of items that follows.

After the list was completed, Jim suggested that every person independently rank each item according to its importance to the survival of the group. They all agreed to do this.

Items available	A	B	X
Each person has:			
(a) one windbreaker			
(b) one poncho			
(c) one sleeping bag			
(d) one pair of sunglasses.			
The boat contains:			
(e) a cooler with two bottles of soft drink per person and some ice			
(f) one large flashlight			
(g) one first-aid kit			

Items available	A	B	X
(h) fishing equipment			
(i) matches, rope and a few tools			
(j) one compass mounted on the boat			
(k) two rear-view mirrors that can be removed from the boat			
(l) one 'official' navigational map of the gulf area where the friends are			
(m) one salt shaker (full)			
(n) one bottle of liquor.			

Case study: *Child protection*

OB

Many business students will find themselves working for government departments, where outcomes of decisions can have serious consequences for the safety of a child. The issue of child protection has been in the media more frequently in recent years, and there are increasing numbers of stories about child abuse cases that are slipping through the system. For some, this is a clear indication that the decision-making process is flawed. As with any decision, information from all parties involved plays a large part in the process. These parties may include the child, family members, doctors, teachers, case workers (and their supervisors), the police and others. For example, a family member, doctor, teacher, or a concerned citizen may make an allegation.

Once the written reports are completed a risk assessment is undertaken by social workers or case workers. In a government department characterised by bureaucratic processes, other relevant professionals may become involved and, as a result, it is unlikely that any one person knows *all* the facts. This can lead to decisions being made on incomplete information. For example, reports of abuse may be made by three different people

(continued)

about different circumstances relating to one child, but if the allegations are investigated by three different officers (which often happens), there will be three separate investigations. The three incidents combined would raise more concern about a child's welfare than any single incident. So there is a heavy dependence on cooperation and communication within and between government departments in order to identify what may be the most urgent cases.

If the information is shared, it is often communicated from one officer to the other, which can affect how judgements about the case are made. For example, case workers may inadvertently be selective about what information is shared, may pass a determination about the (non)urgency of the situation, or indicate a level of truth to a story. The scenario becomes reminiscent of a game of Chinese whispers and, as happens in the game, often there are errors in communication that can be catastrophic.[67]

Questions

1. Use concepts covered in this chapter to explain the flaws in the current decision-making process.

2. What remedies would you suggest to the government department to ensure 'good' decisions are made?

OB Suggested reading

JA Fitzgerald and K Hamilton, 'Ethics and social responsibility' in P Murray and D Poole (eds), *Contemporary management issues* (Sydney: Thompson Learning, 2006).

E Frank Harrison, 'The essence of management decision', *Management Decision*, vol. 38, no. 7 (2000), pp. 462–9.

Philip F Helle, 'Creativity: the key to breakthrough changes, how teaming can harness collective knowledge', *Hospital Material Management Quarterly*, vol. 21, no. 1 (1999), pp. 7–12.

CV Helliar, DM Power and CD Sinclair, 'Managerial "irrationality" in financial decision making', *Managerial Finance*, vol. 31, no. 4 (2005), pp. 1–11.

Alan Lovell, 'Ethics as a dependent variable in individual and organisational decision making', *Journal of Business Ethics*, vol. 37 (2002), pp. 145–63.

G McCray, R Purvis and C McCray, 'Project management under uncertainty: the impact of heuristics and biases', *Project Management Journal*, vol. 33, no. 1 (2002), pp. 49–57.

Nicholas O'Regan, Martin Sims and Abby Ghobadian, 'High performance: ownership and decision-making in SMEs', *Management Decision*, vol. 43, no. 3 (2005), pp. 382–96.

Vick L Sauter, 'Intuitive decision making', *Communications of the ACM*, vol. 42, no. 6 (1999), pp. 109–15.

Marcus Selart, 'Understanding the role of locus of control in consultative decision-making: a case study', *Management Decision*, vol. 43, no. 3 (2005), pp. 397–412.

OB End notes

1. Special Commission of Inquiry into the Waterfall Rail Accident, 'Final report', ch. 17, pp. 217–18, http://www.waterfallinquiry.com.au/finalreport/Chapter17.htm (viewed 10 July 2005).

2. For an excellent overview see George P Huber, *Managerial decision making* (Glenview, IL: Scott, Foresman, 1980).

3. See also John R Schermerhorn, Jr, *Management for productivity* (New York: John Wiley & Sons, 1989), pp. 70–1.

4. TC Doyle and S Lang, 'The leadership issue: managing your way to the top — insights from top executives and experts on management, decision-making and risk-taking', *VARbusiness*, issue 2116 (25 July 2005), p. 30.

5. This discussion is based on James G March and Herbert A Simon, *Organizations* (New York: John Wiley & Sons, 1958), pp. 137–42.

6. ibid. See also Herbert A Simon, *Administrative behavior* (New York: The Free Press. 1947).

7. N Ashford, 'Incorporating science, technology, fairness, and accountability in environmental, health, and safety decisions', *Human and Ecological Risk Assessment*, vol. 11, no. 1 (2005), pp. 85–96.

8. RT De George, *Business ethics*, 6th ed. (New Jersey: Prentice Hall, 2006).

9. Weston H Agor, *Intuition in organizations* (Newbury Park, CA: Sage, 1989).

10. Henry Mintzberg, 'Planning on the left side and managing on the right', *Harvard Business Review*, vol. 54 (July/August 1976), pp. 51–63; H Minzberg, 'Decision making: it's not what you think', *MIT Sloan Management Review*, vol. 42, no. 3 (2001), pp. 89–93.

11. R Pipoli, 'CEOs & mistakes; study, discussion looks at management miscues', *Credit Union Journal*, vol. 9, no. 7 (21 February 2005), p. 1.

12. D Coffield, 'For most debate viewers, the choice is a snap', *Denver Post* (30 September 2004), p. A.01.

13. R Pipoli, op. cit., p. 1.

14. JR Patton, 'Intuition in decisions', *Management Decision*, vol. 41, no. 10 (2003), p. 989.

15. ibid.

16. The classic work in this area is found in a series of articles by D Kahneman and A Tversky: 'Subjective probability: a judgement of representativeness', *Cognitive Psychology*, vol. 3 (1972), pp. 430–54; 'On the psychology of prediction', *Psychological Review*, vol. 80 (1973), pp. 237–51; 'Prospect theory: an analysis of decision under risk', *Econometrica*, vol. 47 (1979), pp. 263–91; 'Psychology of preferences', *Scientific American* (1982), pp. 161–73; 'Choices, values, frames', *American Psychologist*, vol. 39 (1984), pp. 341–50.

17. Commonwealth Treasury, '2004–2005 Budget paper no 1, statement 11: statement of risks', www.budget.gov.au/2004-05/bp1/html/bst11.htm (viewed 20 July 2005).

18. J Maley, 'Train drivers not to blame, say tetchy commuters', *The Sydney Morning Herald* (9 November 2004), http://www.smh.com.au/news/National/Train-drivers-not-to-blame-say-tetchy-commuters/2004/11/08/1099781324623.html (viewed 20 July 2005).

19. M Bazerman, *Judgement in managerial decision-making*, 5th ed. (New York: Wiley & Sons, 2002).

20. Definition and subsequent discussion based on Max H Bazerman, *Judgement in managerial decision making*, 2nd ed. (New York: John Wiley & Sons, 1990), pp. 11–39.

21. K Roberts, 'A new world', address to ANZAM and IFSAM World Congress, Surfers Paradise, 11 July 2002.

22. G Wallas, *The art of thought* (New York: Harcourt, 1926), cited in Bazerman, op. cit.

23. Jacob K Eskildsen, Jens J Dahlgaard and Anders Norgaard, 'The impact of creativity and learning on business excellence', *Total Quality Management*, vol. 10, nos 4–5 (1999), pp. 523–30. <T/S pls make lc letter o with stroke>

24. James AF Stoner, *Management*, 2nd ed. (Englewood Cliffs, NJ: Prentice Hall, 1982), pp. 167–8.

25. R Webb and R Billing, 'Second Sydney Airport — a C chronology' (Economics, Commerce and Industrial Relations Group, 4 August 2004), http://www.aph.gov.au/library/pubs/chron/2003-04/04chr02.htm (viewed 11 August 2005).

26. CC Harwood, 'Solving problems', *Executive Excellence*, vol. 16 (9 September 1999), p. 17.

27. See Victor H Vroom and Philip W Yetton, *Leadership and decision making* (Pittsburgh: University of Pittsburgh Press, 1973); Victor H Vroom and Arthur G Jago, *The new leadership* (Englewood Cliffs, NJ: Prentice Hall, 1988).

28. This discussion is developed from Edgar H Schein, *Process consultation*, vol. I, 2nd ed. (New York: Addison-Wesley, 1988), pp. 69–75.

29. Developed from guidelines presented in the classic article by Jay Hall, 'Decisions, decisions, decisions', *Psychology Today* (November 1971), pp. 55, 56.

30. Irving L Janis, 'Groupthink', *Psychology Today* (November 1971), pp. 43–6; Irving L Janis, *Groupthink*, 2nd ed. (Boston: Houghton Mifflin, 1982). See also J Longley and DG Pruitt, 'Groupthink: a critique of Janis' theory' in L Wheeler (ed.), *Review of personality and social psychology* (Beverly Hills, CA: Sage, 1980); Carrie R Leana, 'A partial test of Janis's groupthink model: the effects of group cohesiveness and leader behavior on decision processes', *Journal of Management*, vol. 11, no. 1 (1985), pp. 5–18.

31. R Boisjoly, E Curtis and E Mellican, 'Roger Boisjoly and the *Challenger* disaster: the ethical dimensions', cited in T Beauchamp and N Bowie (eds), *Ethical theory and business*, 7th ed. (New Jersey: Prentice Hall, 2004), pp. 123–36 at p. 128; *A major malfunction*, BBC Education & Training videorecording (1998).

32. *A major malfunction*, BBC Education & Training videorecording (1998).

33. Developed from Irving Janis, *Victims of groupthink*, 2nd ed. (Boston: Houghton Mifflin, 1982).

34. See Gayle W Hill, 'Group versus individual performance: are N + 1 heads better than one?', *Psychological Bulletin*, vol. 91 (1982), pp. 517–39.

35. These techniques are well described in George P Huber, *Managerial decision making* (Glenview, IL: Scott, Foresman, 1980); Andre L Delbecq, Andrew L Van de Ven and David H Gustafson, *Group techniques for program planning: a guide to nominal groups and Delphi techniques* (Glenview, IL: Scott, Foresman, 1975); William M Fox, 'Anonymity and other keys to successful problem-solving meetings', *National Productivity Review*, vol. 8 (Spring 1989), pp. 145–56.

36. Robert Carey, 'Is your team tired?', *Successful Meetings*, vol. 41, no. 12 (November 1992), pp. 97–100.

37. See Delbecq et al., op. cit.; Fox, op. cit.

38. Barry M Staw, 'The escalation of commitment to a course of action', *Academy of Management Review*, vol. 6 (1981), pp. 577–87; Barry M Staw and Jerry Ross, 'Knowing when to pull the plug', *Harvard Business Review*, vol. 65 (March/April 1987), pp. 68–74. See also Glen Whyte, 'Escalating commitment to a course of action: a reinterpretation', *Academy of Management Review*, vol. 11 (1986), pp. 311–21.

39. Bazerman, op. cit., pp. 79–83.

40. See Fons Trompenaars, *Riding the waves of culture* (London: Nicholas Brealey, 1993).

41. J Tang, 'Its payback time', *Asia Computer Weekly* (11 April 2005), p. 1.

42. J Schramm-Nielsen, 'Cultural dimensions of decision making: Denmark and France compared', *Journal of Managerial Psychology*, vol. 16, no. 5/6 (2001), pp. 404–24.

43. Nancy J Adler, *International dimensions of organizational behavior*, 2nd ed. (Boston: PWS-Kent, 1991).

44. See 'Computers that think are almost here', *Business Week* (17 July 1995), pp. 68–73.

45. AR Dinnis and JS Valacich, 'Computer brainstorms: two heads are better than one', *Journal of Applied Psychology* (February 1994), pp. 77–86.

46. B Kabanoff and JR Rossiter, 'Recent developments in applied creativity', *International Review of Industrial and Organizational Psychology*, vol. 9 (1994), pp. 283–324.

47. T Davenport and J Harris, 'Automated decision making comes of age', *MIT Sloan Management Review*, vol. 46, no. 4 (2005), pp. 83–9.

48. M Friedman, 'The social responsibility of business is to increase its profits', *New York Times Magazine* (13 September 1970), reprinted in S Collins-Chobanian, *Ethical challenges to business as usual* (New Jersey: Prentice Hall, 2005), pp. 224–9.

49. J Kujala, 'Understanding managers' moral decision-making', *International Journal of Value-Based Management*, vol. 16, no. 1 (2003), pp. 37–52; P Ulrich and U Thielemann, 'How do managers think about market economy and morality? Empirical studies into business-ethical thinking patterns', *Journal of Business Ethics*, vol. 12 (1993), pp. 879–98.

50. D Lee, P Newman and R Price, *Decision making in organisations* (London: Pitman Publishing, 1999).

51. GD Foster, 'Ethics: time to revisit the basics', *The Humanist*, vol. 63, no. 2 (2003), pp. 30–7.

52. L Ehrich, N Cranston and M Kimber, 'Public sector managers and ethical dilemmas', *Journal of The Australian And New Zealand Academy Of Management*, vol.10, no. 1 (2004), pp. 25–37.

53. Saul W Gellerman, 'Why "good" managers make bad ethical choices', *Harvard Business Review*, vol. 64 (July/August 1986), pp. 85–90. See also Barbara Ley Toffler, *Tough choices: managers talk ethics* (New York: John Wiley & Sons, 1986) and Shari Collins-Chobanian, *Ethical challenges to business as usual* (New Jersey: Prentice Hall, 2005).

54. GD Foster, 'Ethics: time to revisit the basics', *The Humanist*, vol. 63, no. 2 (2003), pp. 30–7.

55. GD Foster, op. cit.

56. J Harrison, *Ethics for Australian business* (Sydney: Prentice Hall, 2001).

57. S Longstaff, 'Ethical issues and decision-making', www.ethics.org.au (viewed 20 July 2005).

58. J Schermerhorn, J Campling, D Poole and R Wiesner, *Management: an Asia–Pacific perspective* (Milton, QLD: John Wiley & Sons Australia Ltd, 2004).

59. TJ Radin, 'To propagate and to prosper: a naturalistic foundation for stakeholder theory', *Ruffin Series in Business Ethics*, Business, science and ethics (1 January 2004), pp. 289–310.

60. Nestlé corporate web site, http://www.babymilk.nestle.com/History/ (viewed 11 August 2005).

61. R De George, *Business ethics*, 6th ed. (New Jersey: Prentice Hall, 2006), pp. 324–5.

62. ibid.

63. ibid.

64. International Baby Food Action Network (IBFAN), 'Breaking the rules, stretching the rules' (2004), http://www.ibfan.org/english/pdfs/btr04.pdf (viewed 12 August 2005).

65. Nestlé baby milk web site, http://www.babymilk.nestle.com/News/All+Countries/OtherNestlé+examines+report+on+alleged+WHO+Code+violations.htm (viewed 4 October 2005).

66. Exercise developed from Charles Wales and Robert Stages, 'The fishing trip', under an Exxon Guided Design IMPACT Grant.

67. Information from Arthur Firkins, 'Discourse and decision making in child protection practice', paper presented to ninth Australasian Conference on Child Abuse and Neglect, Sydney Convention Centre, Darling Harbour, 24–27 November 2003.

CHAPTER 13
Communication, conflict and negotiation in organisations

Learning objectives
After studying this chapter,
you should be able to:

1. define communication and discuss its role in organisations

2. define conflict and explain how it may affect organisational effectiveness

3. explain how managers may deal with conflict effectively

4. explain the role of negotiation in organisations

5. discuss managerial issues in negotiation.

Differences, misunderstandings and disagreements are a part of the daily life of individuals and organisations alike. If not dealt with constructively, such problems can be destructive for both the individual and the organisation. Poor communication, or an absence of communication, is often the cause of conflict. Leaving conflict unresolved exposes organisations to greater risk of losing employees: those involved, or those around them who have been drawn in to the conflict, may decide to leave the organisation to escape what has become a negative environment. In addition to the loss of knowledge and experience, the organisation is then faced with the cost of hiring and training a replacement employee.

Communication problems and unresolved conflict cannot be expected simply to disappear of their own accord. While it may seem daunting, it is possible to take constructive steps to improve communication and resolve conflict in organisations. Managers need to strive to improve communication, address conflict and engage in appropriate negotiation processes.

Some types of negotiation can be particularly difficult. The motivation behind a service offered by Comcare is a case in point. Comcare is an Australian statutory authority with responsibility for workplace safety, rehabilitation and compensation in the Commonwealth jurisdiction. It aims to help Commonwealth agencies prevent workplace injury and disease and to manage the human and financial costs of such injury and disease by helping injured employees return to work. As part of its strategy to promote good communication, effective conflict management and appropriate negotiation mechanisms, Comcare introduced a new model to assist in complex claims management — psychological injury claims in particular — designed to streamline the collection and documentation of facts relating to each case. The process requires the agreement of both the injured employee and the employer to participate in the application of the model. Once agreement is obtained, a Comcare consultant contacts each party to arrange separate interviews to discuss, clarify and confirm the claim facts. The consultant documents the claim facts, clarifies any inconsistencies and confirms the accuracy of the report with each party. The report is then provided to Comcare to assist in determining the claim. This approach reduces the period of time that liability is under question, so supporting an early return to work. The process recognises the need for open and cooperative communication between the parties to a claim. A preliminary evaluation of the application of the model suggested the model was effective in achieving its objectives, but it is still too early to determine the extent of the gains from the model. Subject to further evaluation, it is anticipated that the model will be applied more broadly in coming years.

Sources: Roslyn Gaskell, 'How effectively is your organisation managing conflict?', *hrconnection*, vol. 8 (2003), http://www.davidsontrahaire.com.au/upload/HR_Connection_Volume_8.pdf (viewed 12 September 2005); Comcare corporate web site and *Comcare annual report 2002–03*, http://www.comcare.gov.au/ (viewed 12 September 2005).

Introduction

The study of communication encompasses nearly all of the critical topics that are basic to understanding human behaviour in general and human functioning within organisations in particular. In fact, communication and organisational success are directly related. Good communication can have a positive and mobilising effect on employees. Poor communication can produce powerful negative consequences, such as distortion of goals and objectives, conflict, misuse of resources and inefficiency in performance of duties.

The ability to manage good communication and handle conflict effectively is a necessary skill in all management roles. In any situation where people interact, there is potential for disagreement, challenge and conflict. No area of an organisation is devoid of conflict, and in some cases conflict can be a good and healthy thing. Constructive conflict can promote creativity, and make people reassess situations, identify problems and find new solutions. However, when conflict in the workplace becomes chronic or disproportionate, or leads to lost productivity and stress, then managers must deal with the problem. In some instances it can indicate that organisational members are seeking more effective means of communication that will help resolve the conflict. In other instances, organisational members could be challenging normal processes and procedures in an effort to improve productivity or introduce innovative systems. Hence, in order to resolve conflict, managers are increasingly required to possess negotiating skills. Such skills may in turn be used as a vehicle to create change or develop new opportunities.

In this chapter we will cover the basic process of communication and related issues in organisations. Also, because the daily work of people in organisations is based on communication and interpersonal relationships, conflict situations often arise and managers need to understand these and know how to deal with them. Hence, the chapter will also introduce you to conflict and negotiation as key processes of organisational behaviour.

Communication in organisations

Communication and its role in organisations

LEARNING OBJECTIVE 1

Organisational communication is the process by which entities exchange information and establish a common understanding.

We can think of interpersonal communication as a process of sending symbols with attached meanings from one person to another. These interpersonal foundations form the basis for discussing the larger issue of communication within the organisation. Organisational communication is the process by which members exchange information and establish a common understanding.

When we communicate with others, we are usually trying to influence other people's understanding, behaviour or attitudes. We are trying to share meaning in some way. As Mintzberg stresses, we are communicating with others to inform, instruct, motivate or seek information. For example, you may wish to inform your human resource manager that staff turnover is up 5 per cent this month, or instruct your assistants to clean up their desks and work more methodically. Perhaps you want to have an informal chat with Harry to let him 'get things off his chest' in the hope that he will be happier and thus be more motivated to work effectively. Or perhaps you are going to call a staff meeting to gather information on a particular problem.

While the function of interpersonal communication is really to share meaning, effective organisational communication can provide substantial benefits to the organisation's members. Four functions are particularly important: achieving coordinated action, developing information, expressing feelings and emotions, and communicating roles.

From a top-management perspective, a primary function of organisational communication is to achieve coordinated action. The collection of individuals that make up an organisation remains an unfocused group until its members are in effective communication with one another. It is important that managers and individuals are aware of techniques in communication that are appropriate for their organisation's structure.

Interpersonal communication

The key elements in the interpersonal communication process are illustrated in figure 13.1. They include a source (a person who is responsible for encoding an intended meaning into a message) and a receiver (a person who decodes the message into a perceived meaning). While the process may appear to be elementary, it is not quite as simple as it looks. Let us examine the model in some detail to identify the main elements in the process, the sequencing of these elements, and weaknesses in the process that can lead to communication problems or distortions.

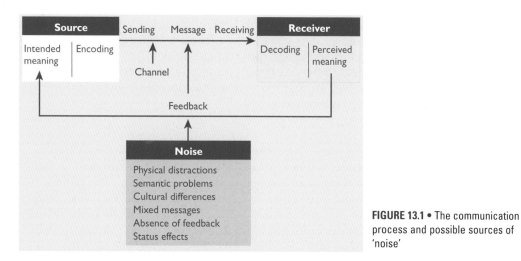

FIGURE 13.1 • The communication process and possible sources of 'noise'

The conventional communication process is made up of the following essential components: the information source, the encoding of a message, the selection of a channel, the transmission of the message, the decoding of the message, feedback from the receiver of the message and any 'noise' (or interference) that may have affected accurate decoding (or interpretation of the message).

The information source is a person or group of persons with a reason to communicate with some other person(s), the receiver(s). The reasons for the source to communicate include changing the attitudes, knowledge or behaviour of the receiver. A manager, for example, may want to communicate with the boss to make him or her understand why the manager's work unit needs more time to finish an assigned project. Of course, the manager will want to do so in such a way that indicates respect for the receiver and an understanding that the job is important, among other factors.

The next step in the process is encoding — the process of translating an idea or thought into meaningful symbols. This translation, or encoding, process results in the transmission of a message via a channel that may consist of verbal, written and/or nonverbal symbols (such as gestures or body language), or some combination of all three. The message is what is communicated. A channel is the medium through which the message may be delivered in organisational communication. The choice of channels may alter the effectiveness of the intended message. For many people, it is easier to communicate verbally and face to face, for example, than in a letter or memo. On the other hand, perhaps our manager would prefer to carefully construct a formal memo to his or her boss to set out the reasons why the work unit needs more time. Our manager should consider whether the boss might interpret the choice of a memo rather than a face-to-face meeting as avoidance. Alternatively, the boss might give the matter more weight if a letter arrives in an envelope in the in-tray than if the issue is briefly mentioned in an email. The manager's message is simple: 'Our work unit needs more time to complete this task', but there are many ways to try to communicate that message.

An **information source** is a person or group of persons with a reason to communicate with some other person(s), the receiver(s).

Encoding is the process of translating an idea or thought into meaningful symbols.

Transmission is the actual communication of a message from one person to another through a chosen channel.

Channels are the media through which the message may be delivered.

The **receiver** is the individual or group of individuals that hear or read or see the message.

Decoding is the interpretation of the symbols sent from the sender to the receiver.

Feedback is the process of telling someone else how you feel about something the person did or said, or about the situation in general.

Noise is anything that interferes with the effectiveness of the communication attempt.

The process of communication does not stop with the sender. The *receiver* is the individual who hears (or reads or sees) the message. The receiver may or may not attempt to decode the message. *Decoding* involves interpreting or translating the symbols sent. This process of translation may or may not result in the assignment of the same meaning intended by the source. Frequently, the intended meaning of the source and the meaning perceived by the receiver differ, or the receiver may have difficulty interpreting the message. Our manager wants the boss to understand that the work unit needs more time to complete a task. Will the boss interpret the message this way? Alternative interpretations could be that the work unit is underperforming, that the manager is underperforming, or that the manager is seeking the appointment of more staff.

Most receivers are well aware of the potential gap between an intended message that was sent and the message that is received. *Feedback* is the process by which receivers acknowledge the communication and return a message concerning how they feel about the original message. Throughout the process, there may be any number of disturbances. *Noise* is the term used to indicate any disturbance within the communication process that disrupts the matching process between sender and receiver.

OB in action

Consider a simple example of noise. A professor is delivering a lecture in a lecture theatre filled with attentive students. The students' attention to the lecture means that only the professor speaks and there is no interference. The fact that only the professor speaks creates a 'silent' channel that allows the sound of the professor's voice and spoken words to flow freely to the ears of the students. However, if in the midst of an uninteresting lecture topic, some students begin to whisper among themselves or giggle, their sounds would creep into the 'silent' channel and combine with the professor's sound waves. This would make the lecture 'noisy' to dedicated students who wish to listen to the professor.

It is a challenging task to communicate accurately. Managers and employees alike can make mistakes. As a study by Thomas Dahle[1] clearly indicates, some forms of exchange between superiors and employees must be handled with great care.

Effective and efficient communication

Effective communication occurs when the intended meaning of the source and the perceived meaning of the receiver are the same. This should be the manager's goal in any interpersonal communication attempt. However, it is not always achieved. Even now, we worry whether you are interpreting our written words as we intend. Our confidence would be higher if we were face to face in class together and you could ask clarifying questions. This opportunity to offer feedback and ask questions is one way of increasing the effectiveness of communication.

Efficient communication occurs at minimum cost in terms of resources expended. Time is an important resource in the communication process. Picture your lecturer taking the time to communicate individually with each student in your class. It would be virtually impossible to do so. And even if it were possible, it would be costly in terms of time. Managers often choose not to visit employees personally to communicate messages. Instead, they rely on the efficiency of telephone conversations, memos, posted bulletins, group meetings, email, teleconferencing or videos. However, efficient (economical) communications are not always effective. A low-cost communication, such as email, may save time for the sender, but it does not always achieve the desired results in terms of the receiver's perceived meaning. Similarly, an effective communication may not be efficient. For a manager to visit each employee and explain a new change in procedures may guarantee that everyone truly understands the change, but it may also be prohibitively expensive in terms of the required time expenditure.

Managers are busy people who depend on their communication skills to remain successful in their work. You need to learn how to maximise the effectiveness of your communications with others and to achieve reasonable efficiency in the process. These goals require the ability to overcome a number of communication barriers that commonly operate in the workplace. Such barriers may include cultural differences, defensiveness, misreading of non-verbal communication, and stereotyping.[2]

Communication channels

In a very important sense the organisation is a network of information and communication channels. Traditionally, there were formal and informal channels, but the electronic age has added a third category — quasiformal channels. While comparatively few managers are in a position to establish organisation-wide communication channels, all managers should understand and be able to use each of the multiple channels for communication within their organisation.

Formal communication channels follow the chain of command established by an organisation's hierarchy of authority. An organisation chart, for example, indicates the proper routing for official messages passing from one level or part of the hierarchy to another. Because formal communication channels are recognised as official and authoritative, written communication in the form of letters, memos, policy statements and other announcements typically adheres to these channels.

Although necessary and important, formal channels constitute only one part of a manager's overall communication responsibilities. Interpersonal networks represent the use of the formal channels just described as well as a wide variety of informal communication channels that do not adhere to the organisation's hierarchy of authority. These informal channels coexist with the formal channels but frequently diverge from them by skipping levels in the hierarchy and/or cutting across vertical chains of command.

In addition, there are many instances of chief executive officers and chairpersons of contemporary organisations who go to great lengths to improve communication with the entire staff. In some organisations managers may prefer to walk around to meet with and talk to floor employees as they do their jobs. 'Management by wandering around' can help develop trust in working relationships with employees and can avoid barriers caused by status effects.

Effective communication is communication in which the intended meaning of the source and the perceived meaning of the receiver are one and the same.

Efficient communication is communication at minimum cost in terms of resources expended.

Formal communication channels are communication channels that follow the chain of command established by the organisation's hierarchy.

Informal communication channels are communication channels that do not adhere to the organisation's hierarchy.

Managers who spend time walking around can greatly reduce the perceived 'distance' between themselves and their employees. Management by wandering around can also reduce selective perception biases by reducing the gap between what individuals want to hear and see and what is actually occurring. Managers can also create an atmosphere of open and free-flowing communication. As a result, more and better information is available for decision making, and the relevance of decisions to the needs of lower-level personnel increases. Of course, the wandering around must be a genuine attempt to communicate; it should not be perceived as just another way to 'check up' on employees.

While formal channels conform to the organisation's chain of command and informal channels emerge from day-to-day activities, a set of quasiformal channels also exists in most corporations today. Quasiformal channels are planned communication connections between holders of various positions within the organisation. They are part of the organisation's overall management information system.

OB in action

In some organisations, the management information system is highly centralised through a central computer. Here, the organisation protects information and distributes it only on an authorised basis. Conversely, some organisations, such as 3M, encourage the development of informal networks and open communication channels throughout the organisations. Most corporations do not go to either extreme. Instead, they develop information systems with different levels of access and specified contact points linking individuals in specific positions. As a salesperson, for instance, you would not have access to the confidential credit report on a key client, but you would have direct access to the production chief in charge of developing the order for the client.

An organisation exists and must be managed as a system of interdependent parts performing distinct but coordinated functions. When work flow interdependence is such that a person or group must rely on task contributions from one or more others to achieve its goals, the circumstances are ripe for developing a quasiformal communication link. In small organisations, these work flow relationships often evolve into important informal communication links. However, in large organisations, management must often plan quasiformal links to connect individuals and groups. With the aid of computers and electronic mail systems, it is now possible to connect work flow related units across the globe.

ETHICAL
Perspective

How much information to share

If knowledge is power, it is reasonable to propose that knowledge should be continually channelled to employees to give them the power to develop the organisation. In fact, many modern managers no longer believe in the old concept that there is power in senior management holding onto information. Managers need to share information with employees to stimulate feedback from them on what is working, what isn't and why. It can, however, be difficult to know how much information and what sort of information to share. For example, employees need to be kept well informed about a company's strategic direction so they are able to make the right decisions in their individual and team capacities, yet there are many cases in which information is considered commercially confidential or private to certain individuals.[3] Could this lead to an ethical dilemma for senior managers over what information to share and what to protect? The decision often remains at the discretion of the senior manager, who should be well informed on what the organisation's leaders consider to be classified information and what information is to be shared with their employees. For example, how the company is performing and what organisational changes are planned are issues that should be discussed openly with everyone who is likely to be involved throughout the process. On the other hand, the early stages of potential takeovers or sensitive issues involving individual staff members are better kept confidential. The increasing tendency for employees to regularly change employers must also be taken into account. Managers should consider the possibility that an employee will be working for a competitor in the future.

The disclosure regime imposed on any publicly listed company stipulates that certain executives are entrusted with information and then must make their own call about how much they wish to communicate. Therefore, managers must impress on their executive team what is important to employees and what should remain confidential.[4] Depending on the culture of the organisation, some managers may encourage open communication and share information that would typically be considered confidential, even to the point of discussing one another's salary levels and other employment incentives.[5]

Those senior managers who do have open, ongoing discussions with their staff may find it easier to gauge how much information to communicate. Regular two-way conversations with employees will not only encourage valuable input from all levels of the organisation but also tap into the internal grapevine, which can be a risky form of communication if left unchecked.[6] The internal grapevine will always operate in organisations, so it is important that issues raised on the grapevine are identified and reframed to reflect an accurate picture.

Barriers to interpersonal communication

Look back now to figure 13.1. Communication is not always perfect. Interference of some sort in the telecommunication process is called 'noise'. Given the rapid developments in telecommunications over the past 30 years, 'noise' due to technical faults is diminishing. Nonetheless, even today things can go wrong: telephone equipment does not always work; lines to exchanges still need to be repaired after underground flooding; calls can be misrouted through exchanges; and sometimes we need to redial because there is hissing or crackling on the line. Several less tangible barriers to communication relate directly to those people in the communication channel. For example, you will remember that earlier in the chapter we referred to the ever-increasing number of incoming and outgoing emails a manager is subjected to each day. While the development of technology can enhance the opportunity to communicate faster, particularly in a global market, this might not always be ideal. Therefore, managers should select the most appropriate channel of communication to get each message across to the recipient without distortion. For example, a recent survey found that few managers from the sample researched agreed that email was more persuasive than a face-to-face meeting, yet two-thirds of the same group researched reported that face-to-face communication skills had decreased as a result of email use.[7]

Noise still occurs in interpersonal communication in today's organisation; so to improve communications, it is important to understand the sources of noise. The most common sources of noise are physical distractions and cultural differences. Physical distractions include such things as a competing conversation being held in the office while you are trying to concentrate on an important telephone call. Environmental factors such as too much noise in open-plan offices, construction work going on outside the building or uncomfortable temperatures all fall into this category. Cultural differences can present a number of complications or obstructions to effective communication between individuals. The problems these blocks pose to managers are usually compounded by managers' deeply rooted orientations to life according to the pattern of their own society. While they may recognise that people from other cultures are different, they may find it hard to understand and adjust to the great variety of ways in which this difference manifests itself.

We need to recognise these sources of noise and to subject them to special managerial control. They are included in figure 13.1 as potential threats to any communication process.

Effective communicators not only understand and deal with communication barriers, they are also exceptionally good at active listening. Effective communicators recognise that being a good receiver is just as important, and often even more important, than being an accurate sender.

THE **Effective**Manager 13.1

The habits of good communicators

For good communication to occur people need to:

- speak clearly
- write clearly
- be aware of cultural differences
- listen attentively
- question precisely
- answer honestly
- pause for feedback signals.

Conflict and its effect on organisations

LEARNING OBJECTIVE 2

Conflict

Conflict is a universal phenomenon. It can facilitate learning, creativity and change, but for some people it makes their work day less enjoyable. For others, the frequency and intensity of workplace conflict makes them uncomfortable and impedes their effectiveness. Workplace conflict may reach such levels that people consider leaving the organisation.

Few people welcome conflict and many managers do not know how to manage it effectively. Yet successful conflict management is at the root of organisational effectiveness. Whether in the boardroom or at the 'coalface', conflict situations, infighting and internal disputes are commonplace. Conflict in the workplace can erupt at any time and at any level of the organisation. While much of the focus is on how to resolve conflict among employees at the lower levels of the hierarchy, just as many conflict situations can erupt in the boardroom. It is not uncommon to read in mainstream media about disputes and conflict among top managers in major organisations. Rational people, who otherwise appear to model appropriate managerial conduct, sometimes descend into brawls that take on a life of their own.[8]

What is conflict?

Conflict occurs whenever disagreements exist in a social situation over issues of substance, or whenever emotional antagonisms create frictions between individuals or groups.[9] Managers are known to spend up to 20 per cent of their time dealing with conflict, including conflicts in which managers are themselves directly involved.[10] In other situations managers may act as mediators, or third parties, whose job is to try to resolve conflicts between other people. In all cases, managers must be skilled participants in the dynamics of interpersonal conflict. They must also be able to recognise situations that have the potential for conflict, and deal with these situations to best serve the needs of both the organisation and the people involved.

Conflict subscribes to no rules. Petty disputes are common occurrences in all workplaces. Full-scale discord can always occur. Such conflicts cannot be predicted, nor can they be prevented, but they can be managed. Among the common reasons for conflict are differences in personal styles, values and job perspectives. Differing needs for personal success and variations in skill level can also cause conflict. Individuals in a conflict need to be listened to, because their anger is frequently a desire to see change effected. A manager needs to know how to resolve such interpersonal conflicts effectively. Where tension develops between individual managers or different management functions, the conflict can have a dramatic impact on organisational performance. Managers who understand the fundamentals of conflict and negotiation will be better prepared to deal with such situations.

If you listen in on some workplace conversations, you might hear the following:

'I don't care what you say, I don't have time to do it and that's that!'

'I no longer open my emails when I first get to the office. I get so many "fwd", it's an annoying start to the day.'

'The lines of communication are pretty bad around here.'

The very words used in these statements are important. They convey a sense of discord in the workplace and 'frame' the thinking of the people making them in a negative or adversarial way. This way of thinking is bound to affect the speakers' working relationships with the other people involved. It is also likely to affect their attitudes and work behaviours. At issue in each case is conflict. The ability to deal with such conflict successfully is a key aspect of a manager's interpersonal skills. Conflict must be effectively managed for an organisation to achieve its goals. Before it can be managed, conflict must be acknowledged and defined by the disputants. However, it may be difficult for the parties involved to agree on what is in dispute in a shared conflict, because they may experience, or frame, the same conflict in different ways.[11]

Substantive and emotional conflicts

Conflict in organisations can be as diverse as the people working there. While interpersonal conflict is natural and can actually spur creativity, the objective for managers is to manage it, often by preventing interpersonal differences from culminating in confrontations. As rational adults, we tend to expect that when we present an idea we will achieve consensus.

Conflict occurs when two or more people disagree over issues of organisational substance and/or experience some emotional antagonism with one another.

We believe others will see the logic of our views and support them, even when different cultures and backgrounds are apparent. However, because each of us has a different perspective we tend to support only those ideas and views that align with our own. To deal with conflict effectively, both objective and subjective elements contributing to the conflict need to be examined and addressed.

Two common examples of workplace conflict are a disagreement with your boss over a plan of action to be followed (for example, a marketing strategy for a new product); and a dislike for a coworker (for example, someone who is always belittling the members of an ethnic or identity group). The first example is one of substantive conflict — that is, a conflict that usually occurs in the form of a fundamental disagreement over ends or goals to be pursued and the means for their accomplishment.[12] When people work together day in and day out, it is only normal that different viewpoints on a variety of substantive workplace issues will arise. It is common for people to disagree at times over such things as group and organisational goals, the allocation of resources, the distribution of rewards, policies and procedures, and task assignments. Dealing successfully with such conflicts is an everyday challenge for most managers. The second example is one of emotional conflict — that is, a conflict that involves interpersonal difficulties that arise over feelings of anger, mistrust, dislike, fear, resentment and the like.[13] It is commonly known as a 'clash of personalities'. Emotional conflicts can drain people's energies and distract them from other important work priorities. They can emerge from a wide variety of settings and are common among coworkers as well as in superior–employee relationships. The latter is perhaps the most upsetting emotional conflict for any person to experience. Unfortunately, competitive pressures in today's business environment and the resulting emphasis on downsizing and restructuring have created more situations in which the decisions of a 'tough' boss can create emotional conflict.

Both types of conflict can have a positive influence on management performance. However, substantive (or task-oriented) conflict is likely to have the most positive effect, depending on how it is managed. Performance is what we typically think about when we consider effectiveness; it constitutes the decisions or solutions that affect productive output. Conflict can force managers to address some of their assumptions and override their attempts to achieve premature unanimity, thus leading to better performance. Managers engaged in substantive (task-oriented) conflict tend to direct their actions to their work, because the conflict forces them to concern themselves with task functions and related issues. By contrast, emotional conflict, although it affects the organisation's development and survival, is inward looking and thus offers a less positive effect on management performance. During such conflict, management actions are directed towards members' relations with each other, rather than with the organisation or the team agenda.

Substantive conflict is conflict that occurs in the form of a fundamental disagreement over ends or goals to be pursued and the means for their accomplishment.

Emotional conflict is conflict that involves interpersonal difficulties that arise over feelings of anger, mistrust, dislike, fear, resentment and the like.

THE **EffectiveManager** 13.2

Communication that can lead to conflict

The conflict911.com 'conflict help centre' warns that there are five types of communication that can lead to conflict. Managers should avoid:

- *Negative communication.* We all know a 'Negative Nigel/Nancy' in every team — they exist and we find it near impossible to remove them. But constant negativity drains the other team members of enthusiasm, energy and self-esteem.
- *Blaming communication.* Blamers spray blame around, effectively stopping reflection and scrutiny of their performance and behaviour. However, their impact can be reduced by fostering a learning environment, as well as the use of 'I messages', peer pressure and individual feedback.
- *Superior communication.* 'Superiors' frequently order people about, direct, advise and moralise. They are also very skilled at withholding information.

- *Dishonest communication.* Dishonest communicators frequently fail to practise listening to understand and fail to display empathy. They also display circumlocutory communication — also known as 'talking around the issue, not addressing it'.
- *Selective communication.* Selective communicators only tell what they think others need to know, hence keeping themselves in a position of power over the other team members. Such behaviour can be effectively addressed through assertive requests for having access to all the information.

Source: Extracts from Lee Hopkins, 'Minimising conflict with effective communication', http://conflict911.com/guestconflict/minimizingconflict.htm (viewed 4 January 2006).

Levels of conflict

It is possible to examine conflict from a number of different communication levels. In particular, people at work may encounter conflicts at four levels:

1. intrapersonal, or conflict within the individual
2. interpersonal, or individual-to-individual conflict
3. intergroup conflict
4. interorganisational conflict.

When it comes to dealing personally with conflicts in the workplace, how well prepared are you to encounter and deal with various types of conflict?

Intrapersonal conflict

Among the significant conflicts that affect behaviour in organisations are those that involve the individual alone. These intrapersonal conflicts often involve actual or perceived pressures from incompatible goals or expectations of the following types. *Approach conflict* occurs when a person must choose between two positive and equally attractive alternatives. An example is having to choose between a valued promotion in the organisation or a desirable new job with another organisation. *Avoidance conflict* occurs when a person must choose between two negative and equally unattractive alternatives. An example is being asked either to accept a job transfer to another town in an undesirable location or to have your employment with an organisation terminated. *Approach–avoidance conflict* occurs when a person must decide to do something that has both positive and negative consequences. An example is being offered a higher paying job, but one with responsibilities that will make unwanted demands on your time.

> **Intrapersonal conflict** is conflict that occurs within the individual as a result of actual or perceived pressures from incompatible goals or expectations.

Interpersonal conflict

Interpersonal conflict occurs between two or more individuals who are in opposition to one another; the conflict may be substantive or emotional in nature, or both. Two people debating aggressively over each other's views on the merits of hiring a job applicant is an example of a substantive interpersonal conflict. Two people continually in disagreement over each other's choice of work attire is an example of an emotional interpersonal conflict. Everyone has had experience with interpersonal conflicts of both types. It is a major form of conflict that managers face, given the highly interpersonal nature of the managerial role. We will address this form of conflict in more detail when we discuss conflict management strategies later in the chapter.

> **Interpersonal conflict** is conflict that occurs between two or more individuals.

Intergroup conflict

Another level of conflict in organisations occurs between groups. Such intergroup conflict can also have substantive and/or emotional underpinnings. Intergroup conflict is quite common in organisations, and it can make the coordination and integration of task activities very difficult. Consider this example of conflict between sales and production

> **Intergroup conflict** is conflict that occurs between groups in an organisation.

personnel in two plants of the same manufacturing company.[14] In one, a conflict relationship exists between the two departments; in another plant, the working relationship is cooperative. These differences are most apparent in terms of how group goals and the handling of information affects decision making in each setting.

Interorganisational conflict

Interorganisational conflict is conflict that occurs between organisations.

Conflict may also occur between entire organisations or independent units in large organisations. Such interorganisational conflict most commonly reflects the competition and rivalry that characterises organisations operating in the same markets. However, interorganisational conflict is really a much broader issue than that represented by market competition alone. Consider, for example, disagreements between unions and the organisations employing their members; between government regulatory agencies and the organisations subject to their surveillance; between organisations and those who supply them with raw materials; and between units within an organisation competing for organisational resources. If conflict between divisions in a company is ignored, the organisation will often be more concerned with internal competition than with external competition.

New organisational structures such as joint ventures, strategic alliances and networks have the potential to release conflicts, both between the new partners and also within the participating organisations. These latter conflicts were contained within the old structure or resolved by rules. The changes inherent in restructuring bring them to the surface, and such conflicts within the organisation and between organisations may result in the dissolution of partnerships.

OB in action

When organisations are faced with big decisions such as restructuring or forming strategic alliances, it is the CEO or head of the company who is the focal point of the decision-making process and who is ultimately responsible for the outcome. In difficult, sensitive or hostile environments, when tough decisions are to be made, who does the CEO turn to for advice or to act as a sounding board? His or her immediate staff or a consultant may be obvious choices, yet some CEOs are finding the backup support they need in syndicates: formal groups that meet outside the office.[15]

Take, for example, a situation in which a decision will ultimately result in conflict with one or more parties. The CEO is responsible for making the best decision for all parties, but in cases such as staff cutbacks or plant relocation the decision is never an easy one to make because people get hurt, so the potential for conflict can be huge. In such delicate situations, discussions with internal staff may not always be appropriate, whereas discussions in confidence with external peers who may have experienced or are likely to experience a similar situation may provide a good source of advice, and even comfort.

In Australia there are several syndicates that hold monthly round-table meetings at which CEOs meet with their peers from non-competing industries to discuss, in confidence, problems, failures and other demanding situations they face. As senior executives have little time to attend conferences, seminars and other educational forums to keep informed of current organisational issues, the syndicates provide an immediate viewpoint on a particular problem through open discussion among perhaps 15 similar people. Sharing of information across industries provides a learning environment for all involved.

Conflict and culture

Culturally diverse countries, such as Australia and New Zealand, are characterised by a wide range of traditions, languages, beliefs, values, ideas and practices. In addition, the increasingly international nature of organisations' operations brings people of diverse backgrounds together. As the Queensland University of Technology acknowledges,[16] 'Diversity is both an opportunity and challenge...Cultural, social and linguistic diversity are assets in an internationally competitive market and can broaden and enrich all teaching, research, curricula, community service, administrative activities and daily life, giving rise to new ways of conceptualising and addressing issues...It can be a source of tension, division or conflict within the University if difference is associated with exclusion, disadvantage or racism.'

In a multinational context, one of the key reasons for the early return of expatriates is the uncertainty and frustration resulting from poor cross-cultural adaptation. The result of this is an increase in the interpersonal conflict expatriates experience in the workplace abroad, caused by cultural differences.[17]

Constructive and destructive conflicts

Conflict in organisations can be dangerous. It is often upsetting both to the individuals directly involved and to others who may observe it or be affected by it. On an emotional level at least, many of us are more aware of its perils than its possibilities. A common byproduct of conflict is stress. It can be uncomfortable, for example, to work in an environment in which two coworkers are continually hostile towards each other. However, organisational behaviour recognises two sides to conflict — the constructive side and the destructive side (figure 13.2).

Constructive conflict results in benefits to the group or organisation. It offers the people involved a chance to identify otherwise neglected problems and opportunities; performance and creativity can improve as a result. Indeed, an effective manager is able to stimulate constructive conflict in situations in which satisfaction with the status quo inhibits necessary change and development. Such a manager is comfortable dealing with both the constructive and the destructive sides of the conflict dynamic. Another value of conflict is that it can prevent stagnation, stimulate interest and curiosity, and foster creativity.

Constructive conflict is conflict that results in positive benefits to the group.

When conflict arises, most people's first reaction is to become angry or distressed, and to seek to eliminate the problem. However, managers need to realise that if they can understand the issues that are causing the disagreement they will be in a better position to minimise the anger and distress and to use the conflict to the organisation's advantage. Conflict presents an opportunity for managers to become aware of substantive issues and to think of ways in which to resolve them. Members of a cross-functional team may have different information, ideas and perspectives about how the team should proceed, what the important issues are, how to solve problems facing the team and even what role each team member should play. An effective manager will seek to deal with these issues and the conflict will diminish.

Positive conflict can also help organisations become more innovative. Innovation can occur when different ideas, perceptions and ways of processing and judging information collide. Creative thinking can be a powerful tool in managing conflicts that result from personal disagreements and cognitive differences. Such conflict nurtures creativity. Various organisational members who see the world differently need to cooperate. Even when the parties have different viewpoints, managing those differences can be productive.[18]

Destructive conflict works to the group's or organisation's disadvantage. It occurs, for example, when two employees are unable to work together as a result of interpersonal hostility (a destructive emotional conflict), or when the members of a committee fail to act because they cannot agree on group goals (a destructive substantive conflict). Destructive conflict of these types can decrease work productivity and job satisfaction and contribute to absenteeism and job turnover. Managers must be alert to destructive conflicts, quickly acting to prevent or eliminate them, or at least minimise their resulting disadvantages. 'The effective manager 13.3' looks at ways to prevent destructive conflict.

Destructive conflict is conflict that works to the group's or organisation's disadvantage.

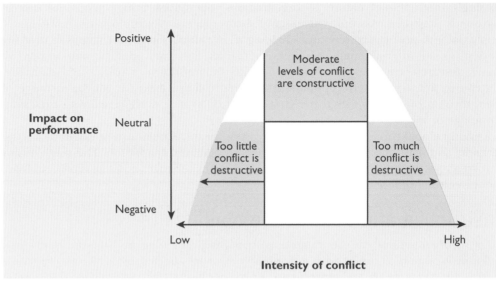

FIGURE 13.2 • The two faces of conflict: constructive and destructive conflict

How to prevent destructive conflict

- Listen carefully to employees to prevent misunderstanding.
- Monitor employees' work to assist them to understand and coordinate their actions.
- Encourage employees to approach you when they cannot solve difficulties with coworkers on their own.
- Clear the air with regular meetings that give employees a chance to discuss their grievances.
- Provide a suggestion box, check it frequently and personally reply to all signed suggestions.
- Offer as much information as possible about decisions to minimise confusion and resentment.
- Use employee surveys to identify potential conflicts that have not yet surfaced.

Conflict situations faced by managers

The very nature of the manager's position in an organisation guarantees that conflict will be a part of his or her work experience. The manager may encounter conflict in supervisor–employee relationships, in peer or intergroup relationships, and in relationships with senior management. The manager's ability to deal with such situations may in large part determine whether they have constructive or destructive impacts on the work situation. More specifically, an effective manager is able to recognise and deal with each of the following conflict situations.[19]

- *Vertical conflict* occurs between hierarchical levels, and commonly involves supervisor–employee disagreements over resources, goals, deadlines or performance results.
- *Horizontal conflict* occurs between people or groups at the same hierarchical level, and commonly involves goal incompatibilities, resource scarcities or purely interpersonal factors.
- *Line–staff conflict* occurs between line and staff representatives, and commonly involves disagreements over who has authority and control over certain matters, such as personnel selection and termination practices.
- *Role conflict* occurs when the communication of task expectations proves inadequate or upsetting, and commonly involves uncertainties of expectations, overloads or underloads in expectations, and/or incompatibilities among expectations.

Conflict becomes more likely in each of these situations when certain conditions exist. In general, managers should be aware that work situations with one or more of the following characteristics may be predisposed to conflict:[20]

- work flow interdependence
- power and/or value asymmetry
- role ambiguity or domain ambiguity
- resource scarcity (actual or perceived).

As discussed in chapters 8 and 9, the various parts of a complex organisation must be well integrated for it to function well. However, interdependencies among components can breed conflicts. When work flow interdependence is high — that is, when a person or group must rely on task contributions from one or more others to achieve its goals — conflicts often occur. You will notice this, for example, in a fast-food restaurant when the people serving the food have to wait too long for it to be delivered from the cooks. Good managers understand that the performance expectations and other aspects of such links must be handled carefully to ensure smooth working relationships. Indeed, one of the central precepts of total quality management is that 'internal customers' — other people or groups inside the organisation — should receive the same dedicated attention and service that external customers receive.

Power or value asymmetries in work relationships exist when interdependent people or groups differ substantially from one another in status and influence, or in values. Conflict due to asymmetry is prone to occur, for example, when a low-power person needs the help of a high-power person who will not respond; when people who hold dramatically different values are forced to work together on a task; or when a high-status person is required to interact with — and perhaps depend on — someone of lower status. A common example of the latter case occurs when a manager is forced to deal with another manager through his or her secretary.

When individuals or groups operate with a lack of adequate task direction or clarity of goals, a stressful and conflict-prone situation exists. In chapters 7 and 11 we discussed how role ambiguities may cause problems for people at work. At the group or department level, similar effects in terms of domain ambiguities can occur. These ambiguities involve misunderstandings over such things as customer jurisdiction or scope of authority. Conflict is likely when individuals and/or groups are placed in situations in which it is difficult for them to understand just who is responsible for what. It may also occur where people resent the fact that their 'territory' is being trespassed.

A common managerial responsibility is the allocation of resources among different groups. Actual or perceived resource scarcity is a conflict-prone situation. When people sense the need to compete for scarce resources, working relationships are likely to suffer. This is especially true in organisations experiencing the financial difficulties associated with a period of decline. As cutbacks occur, various individuals or groups will try to position themselves to gain or retain maximum shares of the shrinking resource pool; they are also likely to try to resist or employ countermeasures to defend their resources from redistribution to others.

Most conflicts develop in stages, as shown in figure 13.3. These stages include antecedent conditions, perceived and felt conflict, manifest conflict, conflict resolution or suppression, and conflict aftermath.[21] The conditions that create conflict, as discussed, are examples of conflict antecedents; that is, they establish the conditions from which conflicts are likely to develop. In addition, managers should recognise that unresolved prior conflicts help set the stage for future conflicts of the same or related sort. Rather than try to deny the existence of conflict or settle on a temporary resolution, it is always best to deal with important conflicts so they are completely resolved.

When the antecedent conditions actually become the basis for substantive or emotional differences between people and/or groups, such as those situations already described, the stage of perceived conflict exists. Of course, this perception may be held by only one of the conflicting parties. There is also a difference between perceived conflict and the stage of felt conflict. When people feel conflict, they experience it as tension that motivates them to take action to reduce feelings of discomfort. For conflict to be resolved, all parties should both perceive it and feel the need to do something about it.

Manifest conflict occurs when conflict is openly expressed in behaviour.

When conflict is openly expressed in behaviour it is said to be manifest. A state of manifest conflict can be resolved by removing or correcting its antecedents. It can also be suppressed through controlling the behaviour (although no change in antecedent conditions occurs); for example, one or both parties may choose to ignore the conflict in their dealings with each other. This is a superficial and often temporary form of conflict resolution. Indeed, we have already noted that unresolved conflicts — and a suppressed conflict falls into this category — may continue to fester and cause future conflicts over similar issues.

Unresolved conflicts of any type can result in sustained emotional discomfort and stress, and escalate into dysfunctional relationships between individuals and work units. In contrast, truly resolved conflicts may establish conditions that reduce the potential for future conflicts and/or make it easier to deal with them. Thus, any manager should be sensitive to the influence of conflict aftermath on future conflict episodes.

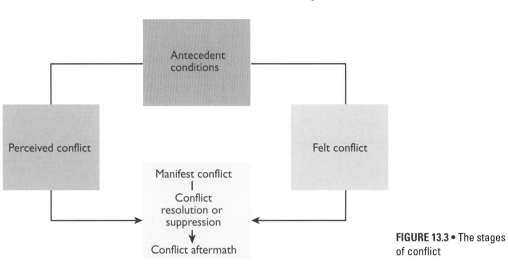

FIGURE 13.3 • The stages of conflict

Conflict-management approaches

Managing conflict

LEARNING OBJECTIVE 3

Conflict in organisations is inevitable. The process of managing conflict to achieve constructive rather than destructive results is clearly essential to organisational success. This process of conflict management can be pursued in a variety of ways. An important goal should always be to achieve or set the stage for true conflict resolution — that is, a situation in which the underlying reasons for a given conflict are eliminated.

Conflict resolution occurs when the reasons for a conflict are eliminated.

THE Effective Manager 13.4

What can be done to better manage workplace conflict?[22]

- Reinforce to managers their responsibility for managing conflict.
- Develop conflict management strategies.
- Ensure employees are familiar with the organisation's policy on interpersonal conflict.
- Facilitate discussion sessions to appropriately express workplace relationships and interpersonal tensions.
- Coach employees to effectively communicate to support the resolution of conflict.
- Appoint conflict contact officers to listen to concerns and help staff find ways to resolve them.
- Provide support services such as employee assistance programs that can be accessed on a confidential, self-referral basis.

Conflict-resolution styles

Research on the management of conflict shows that it depends to a great extent on the personality characteristics of individual managers. Blake and Mouton were the first to classify personality strategies or styles of conflict resolution into five basic types: forcing, withdrawing, soothing, compromising and problem solving.[23] Kenneth Thomas developed this line of analysis further by suggesting that the five basic styles could be compared in two aspects: assertiveness or self-confidence, which consists of a desire to serve one's own interests; and cooperativeness, where the tendency is to serve the interests of others.[24] Afzalur Rahim also points to five different personality styles, or strategies, in conflict resolution, which he analyses according to the orientation towards self or others. His five styles are: integrating, obliging, compromising, dominating and avoiding.[25]

Rahim draws attention to the fact that there is no one best style, because each has its advantages and disadvantages. The effectiveness of an application of a particular style depends on the situation. In everyday life people tend to show a preference for a certain conflict-resolution style; for example, a person with high affiliation needs will generally choose an obliging style and avoid a dominating style. It appears that in organisational life, the status of an organisational member could well influence the choice of conflict-resolution style;[26] for example, people may choose different strategies when dealing with a boss, an employee or a peer.

Most researchers share the view that an integrating style is best for managing conflicts in organisations, because this style is aimed at solving the problem, it respects the needs and interests of both sides, and is based on achieving a satisfactory outcome for each side.[27] However, choice of style needs to be contingent on the situation. A manager may choose a dominating style where the goals of the conflicting parties are incompatible, there has been a previous failure to reach agreement and a quick decision needs to be made.[28] In contrast, an integrating style would probably work best in a conflict caused by communication problems or in solving strategic problems linked to goals, policies and long-term planning in organisations. Research shows that managers believe that the frequent use of a compromising style hampers performance and the attainment of goals, but that they may endorse such a style in certain situations where mutual concessions are the only possible solution.[29] Research by Krum Krumov showed that the integrating style is used more often by women than men, and that its use increases gradually with age. In contrast, the compromising style is used equally by women and men, and its use tends to increase with age. However, the use of this style is more typical of employees than managers.[30]

Wayne Pace suggests that preferred ways of handling conflict occur because, when two people come together expecting to claim their share of scarce resources, they think somewhat habitually about themselves and the other person. Thus, conflict-resolution styles appear to be some combination of the amount of concern you have about accomplishing your own goals and the amount of concern you have about others accomplishing their goals. These concerns can be portrayed as two axes running from low concern to high concern. This paradigm results in a two-dimensional conceptualisation of personal conflict-resolution styles, as depicted in figure 13.4 and briefly described here. Unfortunately, when conflict occurs people have the tendency to do and say things that perpetuate the conflict.[31]

- Cell 1 — competitor or tough battler. People who employ this style pursue their own concerns somewhat ruthlessly and generally at the expense of other members of the group. The tough battler views losing as an indication of weakness, reduced status and a crumbling self-image. Winning is the only worthwhile goal and results in accomplishment and exhilaration.
- Cell 2 — collaborator or problem solver. People who employ this style seek to create a situation in which the goals of all parties involved can be accomplished. Problem solvers work at finding mutually acceptable solutions. Winning and losing are not part of their way of looking at conflict.

- Cell 3 — compromiser or manoeuvring conciliator. The person who employs this style assumes that everyone involved in a disagreement stands to lose and works to help find a workable position. A pattern of 'giving in' often develops.
- Cell 4 — accommodator or friendly helper. People who employ this style are somewhat nonassertive and quite cooperative, neglecting their own concerns in favour of those of others. The friendly helper feels that harmony should prevail and that anger and confrontation are bad. When a decision is reached, accommodators may go along with it and wish later that they had expressed some reservations.
- Cell 5 — avoider or impersonal complier. The person who employs this style tends to view conflict as unproductive and somewhat punishing. Thus, the avoider sidesteps an uncomfortable situation by refusing to be concerned. The result is usually an impersonal reaction to the decision and little commitment to future actions.[32]

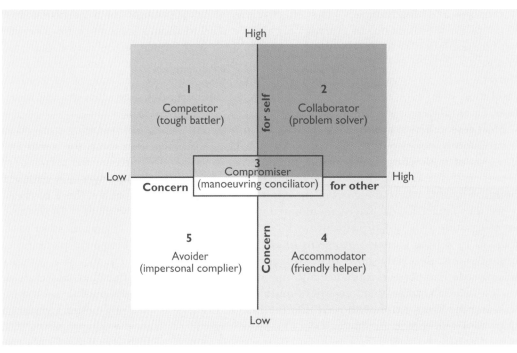

FIGURE 13.4 • Personal conflict-resolution styles
Source: R Wayne Pace and Don F Faules, *Organizational communication*, 3rd ed. (Boston, MA: Allyn & Bacon, 1994), p. 250.

Conflict resolution through hierarchical referral

Hierarchical referral uses the chain of command for conflict resolution; problems are referred up the hierarchy for more senior managers to reconcile.

Hierarchical referral makes use of the chain of command for conflict resolution; problems are simply referred up the hierarchy for more senior managers to reconcile. The managers involved will typically be those to whom the conflicting parties mutually report; they will be managers who ultimately have the formal authority to resolve such disputes by directive if necessary.

While hierarchical referral can be definitive in a given case, it also has limitations. If conflict is severe and recurring, the continual use of hierarchical referral may not result in true conflict resolution. For instance, managers may have the tendency to consider most conflicts a result of poor interpersonal relations. They may consequently seek outward signs of harmony as evidence of their conflict management skills, or they may act quickly to replace a person with a perceived 'personality' problem.[33] In so doing, they may actually fail to delve into the real causes of a conflict, and conflict resolution may be superficial. Employees may also learn that it is best not to refer any conflict upwards. Future conflicts may be kept from view until they finally erupt into major problems.

Conflict resolution and organisational design

When the organisational design allows groups, units and departments to operate in relative isolation from one another, conflict tends to be muted. But when work needs to be coordinated, when resources must be shared, and when other work flow interdependencies exist, conflicts often arise. Managers have a number of options available to reduce conflicts by adjusting the organisational design at such friction points.[34]

One option is decoupling the groups — separating them or reducing contact between them. In some cases, the tasks of the units can be adjusted to reduce the number of required points of coordination. The conflicting units can then be separated from one another and each can be provided with separate access to valued resources. While decoupling may reduce conflict, it may also result in duplication and a poor allocation of valued resources. Often the question is whether the conflict costs more than do the inefficiencies of resource allocation.

Buffering is another approach that can be used when the inputs of one group are the outputs of another group. The classic buffering technique is to build an inventory between the two groups so any output slowdown or excess is absorbed by the inventory and does not directly pressure the target group. Although it reduces conflict, this technique is increasingly out of favour because it increases inventory costs. This consequence is quite contrary to the practice of 'just-in-time' delivery that is now valued in operations management.

Conflict management can be facilitated by assigning people to serve as formal linking pins between groups that are prone to conflict.[35] People in linking-pin roles, such as project liaison officers, are expected to understand the operations, members' needs and the norms of their host group. Linking pins are supposed to use this knowledge to help their group work better with other groups to accomplish mutual tasks. Although expensive, this technique is often used when different specialised groups, such as engineering and sales, must closely coordinate their efforts on complex and long-term projects.

A variation of the linking-pin concept is the liaison group.[36] The purpose of such a group, team or department is to coordinate the activities of certain units and to prevent destructive clashes between them. Members of the department may be given formal authority to resolve disputes on everything from technical matters to resource claims or work assignments.

Decoupling involves separating or reducing the contact between two conflicting groups.

Buffering is a conflict management approach that sets up inventories to reduce conflicts when the inputs of one group are the outputs of another group.

Linking pins are people who are assigned to manage conflict between groups that are prone to conflict.

Liaison groups are groups that coordinate the activities of certain units to prevent destructive conflicts between them.

International **SPOTLIGHT**

Stakeholder engagement and conflict resolution

In order to minimise conflict and community objections to mining projects, some multinational mining corporations involve key external stakeholders. Community involvement means working in conjunction with communities to create acceptable processes for improving communication, managing conflicts and making appropriate decisions. Newmont Mining Corporation is a case in point.

> Newmont aims to engage, as much as possible, with its local communities to ensure interactions are relevant, conflicts are resolved quickly and to the mutual benefit of both parties and in such a way that stakeholders feel positive about their involvement with the Company.
>
> In Peru, for example, representatives of Yanacocha participate in two dialogue tables — one under the auspices of the Compliance Advisor/Ombudsman for the International Finance Corporation arm of the World Bank and the other through the Office of the President of Peru. These groups include elected officials, community leaders, non-government organizations and representatives from the mine discussing issues and concerns and seeking solutions and greater understanding.

(continued)

Negotiation and its role in organisations

LEARNING OBJECTIVE 4

Negotiation

Conflict between individuals, groups and organisations is a common phenomenon. When parties are involved in conflict, negotiation is frequently used to resolve differences. This section introduces you to negotiation as an important process in managing people and organisations.

Negotiation is the process of making joint decisions when the parties involved have different preferences.

Managers need to understand some of the key areas of negotiation in order to improve workplace effectiveness and performance. Negotiation is the process of making joint decisions when the parties involved have different preferences. In other words, negotiation can be considered a way of getting what managers want from others in the process of making decisions.

Negotiation is especially significant in today's work settings, where more people are being offered opportunities to be involved in decisions affecting them and their work. This may include the negotiation of individual employment contracts, which is increasingly becoming the norm in workplaces in Australia. As more people get involved in any decision-making process, so more disagreements are likely to arise over such diverse matters as wage rates, task objectives, performance evaluations, job assignments, work schedules, work locations and special privileges. Given that organisations are becoming increasingly participative, a manager's familiarity with basic negotiation concepts and processes is increasingly important for dealing with such day-to-day affairs.

Four types of negotiation situations

In the course of their work, managers may be faced with different types of negotiation situations. As shown in figure 13.5, there are four main types of situations with which managers should be familiar. These are:

- *Two-party negotiation.* The manager negotiates directly with one other person; for example, a manager and an employee negotiating a salary increase during an annual performance appraisal.
- *Group negotiation.* The manager is part of a team or group whose members are negotiating to arrive at a common decision; for example, a committee that must reach agreement on recommending a new sexual harassment policy.
- *Intergroup negotiation.* The manager is part of a group that is negotiating with another group to arrive at a decision regarding a problem or situation affecting both; for example, negotiation between management groups from two organisations to form a joint venture or strategic alliance.
- *Constituency negotiation.* The manager is involved in negotiation with other people and each individual party represents a broad constituency. A common example is a team representing 'management' negotiating with a team representing 'labour' to arrive at an agreement.

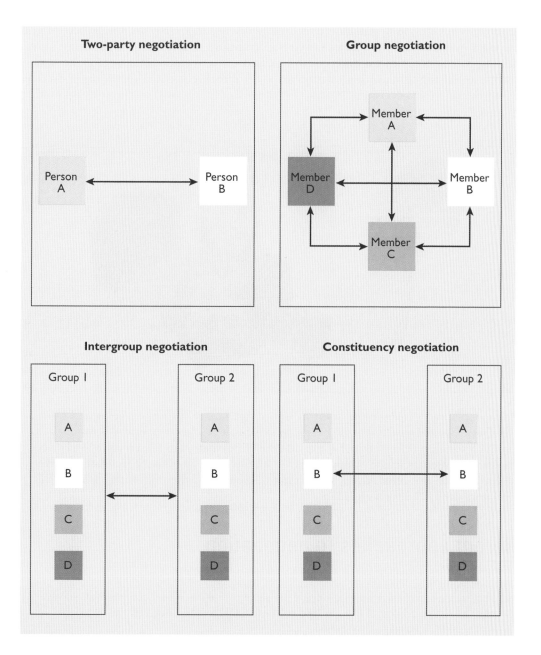

FIGURE 13.5 • Four types of negotiation situation faced by managers

Negotiation goals and outcomes

Two goals are at stake in any negotiation. Substance goals are concerned with outcomes relative to the 'content' issues at hand, such as the dollar amount of a wage agreement in a collective bargaining situation. Relationship goals are concerned with outcomes relating to how well people involved in the negotiation and any constituencies they may represent are able to work with one another once the process is concluded. An example is the ability of union members and management representatives to work together effectively after a contract dispute has been settled.

Unfortunately, many negotiations result in a sacrifice of relationships, as parties become preoccupied with substance goals and self-interest. In contrast, effective negotiation occurs when substance issues are resolved and working relationships are maintained or even improved.

Substance goals are concerned with outcomes tied to the 'content' issues at hand in a negotiation.

Relationship goals are concerned with how well people involved in a negotiation, and their constituencies, are able to work with one another once the process is concluded.

Effective negotiation occurs when issues of substance are resolved without any harm to the working relationships among the parties involved.

The parties involved in negotiation may find themselves at an impasse when there are no overlapping interests and the parties fail to find common points of agreement. But agreement in negotiation can mean different things, and the agreement may be 'for the better' or 'for the worse' for either or both parties involved. Effective negotiation results in overlapping interests and joint decisions that are 'for the better' of all parties. The trick is knowing how to get there.

Most people and organisations want to resolve workplace disputes quickly and fairly. The Queensland Department of Justice and Attorney-General operates a number of dispute-resolution centres that can provide skilled mediators to help resolve workplace disputes between managers, employees or unions. The mediators facilitate the discussion, but do not offer advice and do not take sides. At the end of the process, the mediators document the agreement.[37]

Different approaches to negotiation

Consider the following scenario. It illustrates an important point.

> Two employees want to book their holidays in the same period (during school holidays). However, the boss can only allow one of them to take holidays in that period. They begin to negotiate over who should take the holiday in that period.

For our purposes, the 'holiday' represents a valued outcome for both employees. The approach taken to the negotiation can have a major influence on its outcomes. It is useful to discuss two alternative approaches: distributive negotiation and integrative negotiation.[38]

Distributive negotiation

Distributive negotiation is negotiation in which the focus is on 'positions' staked out or declared by the parties involved, who are each trying to claim certain portions of the available 'pie'.

In **distributive negotiation**, the focus is on 'positions' that conflicting parties stake out or declare. Each party is trying to 'claim' certain portions of the available 'pie'. Distributive negotiation is sometimes referred to as competitive or positional negotiation. Returning to the holiday scenario, if the two workers adopted distributive bargaining approaches, they would each ask the question: 'Who is going to get the holiday at the requested time?' This question, and the way in which it frames subsequent behaviour, will have a major impact on the negotiation process and outcomes.

A case of distributive negotiation usually unfolds in one of two directions, neither of which yields optimal results. 'Hard' distributive negotiation takes place when each party holds out to get its own way. This leads to competition, whereby each party seeks dominance over the other and tries to maximise self-interests. 'Soft' distributive negotiation takes place when one party is willing to make concessions to the other to get things over with. In this case, one party tries to find ways to meet the other's desires. A soft approach leads to accommodation (one party gives in to the other) or compromise (each party gives up something of value in order to reach agreement).

In the case of the two employees wanting the same holiday period, the hard approach may lead to a win–lose outcome, in which one employee will dominate (perhaps by putting forth a stronger and more convincing case to the boss) and therefore wins the round. Or it may lead to an impasse, in which case neither employee will get the holiday. A soft approach (or compromise) may result in the holiday period being split equally between the two employees, where one employee gets half of the period and the second takes the other half. But here, too, dissatisfaction may exist because each employee is still deprived of what they originally wanted — the entire holiday period at the preferred time.

Integrative negotiation

In **integrative negotiation**, sometimes called principled negotiation, the focus is on the 'merits' of the issues. Everyone involved tries to enlarge the available 'pie' rather than stake claims to certain portions of it. For this reason, integrative negotiation is also sometimes referred to as problem-solving or interest-based negotiation. In the case of the employees, the integrative approach to negotiation would be prompted by asking the question: 'How can the available leave best be used?' Notice that this is a very different question from the one described for distributive negotiation. It is much less confrontational and allows for a broader range of alternatives.

The integrative approach to negotiation has much more of a 'win–win' orientation than does the distributive approach; it seeks ways of satisfying the needs and interests of all parties. At one extreme, this may involve selective avoidance, wherein both parties simply realise that there are more important things on which to focus their time and attention. In the holiday scenario, the two workers may mutually decide to forget about the holiday and to attend work. Compromise can also play a role in the integrative approach, but it must have an enduring basis. This is most likely to occur when the compromise involves each party giving up something of perceived lesser personal value to gain something of greater value. In the case of the workers, one may get the holiday this time in return for the other getting one during the next school holidays.

Finally, integrative negotiation may involve true cooperation. In this case, the negotiating parties engage in problem solving to arrive at a mutual agreement that truly maximises benefit to each. In the case of the holidays, this ideal approach could lead to both workers getting half the time off, and spending the other half working, but from home so they can still attend to their children. As you can see, this solution would be almost impossible to realise using the distributive approach because each worker would be preoccupied with getting the holiday. Only under the direction provided by the integrative approach — 'How can the available leave best be used?' — is such a mutually optimal solution possible. However, it is important to appreciate that the most effective negotiators will have a wide array of negotiation skills and will be able to use both approaches, mixing and matching them, depending on what they think works best for a specific issue or situation.

> **Integrative negotiation** is negotiation in which the focus is on the merits of the issues and the parties involved try to enlarge the available 'pie' rather than stake claims to certain portions of it.

Managerial issues in negotiation

Given the distinctions between distributive and integrative negotiation, it is appropriate to identify some negotiation issues of special relevance to managers — specifically, the foundations for gaining integrative agreements, classic two-party negotiation and communication problems in negotiation.

LEARNING OBJECTIVE 5 ✓ Managers' issues in negotiation

Gaining integrative agreements

Underlying the concept of 'principled' negotiation is negotiation based on the 'merits' of the situation. The foundations for gaining truly integrative agreements cover three main areas: attitudes, behaviours and information.[39] To begin with, there are *three attitudinal foundations of integrative agreements.*

1. Each party must approach the negotiation with a willingness to trust the other party.
2. Each party must be willing to share information with the other party.
3. Each party must be willing to ask concrete questions of the other party.

BATNA is the 'best alternative to a negotiated agreement', or each party's position on what they must do if an agreement cannot be reached.

As implied, the *information foundations of integrative agreements* are substantial; they involve each party becoming familiar with the BATNA, or 'best alternative to a negotiated agreement'. That is, both parties must know what they will do if an agreement cannot be reached. This requires that both negotiating parties identify and understand their personal interests in the situation. They must know what is really important to them in the case at hand, and they must come to understand the relative importance of the other party's interests. As difficult as it may seem, each party must achieve an understanding of what the other party values, even to the point of determining its BATNA.

Reaching this point of understanding is certainly not easy. In the complex social setting of a negotiation, things may happen that lead parties astray. An unpleasant comment uttered during a stressful situation, for example, may cause the other party to terminate direct communication for a time. Even when they return, the memory of this comment may overshadow any future overtures made by the offending party. In negotiation, all behaviour is important both for its actual impact and for the impression it leaves. Accordingly, the following behavioural foundations of integrative agreements must be carefully considered and included in any negotiator's repertoire of skills and capabilities:

- the ability to separate the people from the problem and to avoid letting emotional considerations affect the negotiation
- the ability to focus on interests rather than positions
- the ability to avoid making premature judgements
- the ability to judge possible agreements according to an objective set of criteria or standards.

Classic two-party negotiation

Figure 13.6 introduces the case of the new graduate.[40] In this case, a graduate is negotiating a job offer with a corporate recruiter. The example illustrates the basic elements of classic two-party negotiation in many contexts.

To begin with, look at the situation from the graduate's perspective. She has told the recruiter that she would like a salary of $45 000; this is her initial offer. But she also has in mind a minimum reservation point of $35 000 — the lowest salary that she will accept for this job. Thus, she communicates a salary request of $45 000 but is willing to accept one as low as $35 000. The situation is somewhat reversed from the recruiter's perspective. The recruiter's initial offer to the graduate is $30 000 and the maximum reservation point is $40 000; this is the most the recruiter is prepared to pay.

The **bargaining zone** is the zone between one party's minimum reservation point and the other party's maximum reservation point in a negotiating situation.

The bargaining zone is defined as the range between one party's minimum reservation point and the other party's maximum reservation point. In figure 13.6, the bargaining zone is $35 000–$40 000; it is a positive bargaining zone because the reservation points of the two parties overlap. Whenever a positive bargaining zone exists, bargaining has room to unfold. Had the graduate's minimum reservation point been greater than the recruiter's maximum reservation point (for example, $42 000), there would have been no room for bargaining. Classic two-party bargaining always involves the delicate tasks of first discovering the respective reservation points (your own and the other's) and then working towards an agreement that lies somewhere within the resulting bargaining zone and that is acceptable to each party.

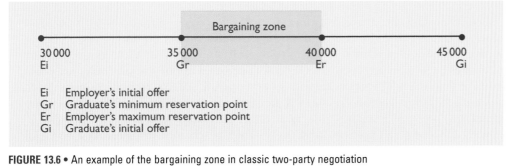

	Bargaining zone		
30 000	35 000	40 000	45 000
Ei	Gr	Er	Gi

Ei   Employer's initial offer
Gr   Graduate's minimum reservation point
Er   Employer's maximum reservation point
Gi   Graduate's initial offer

FIGURE 13.6 • An example of the bargaining zone in classic two-party negotiation

Underlying conflict

Olivia is a senior sales manager for VLC Software, where she has been employed for five years. VLC Software is a small software development company with 12 employees. Olivia was initially employed by VLC as a junior IT account support officer and has worked her way through the company hierarchy to the senior position she is in today. Olivia has a very good relationship with all the other employees, horizontal and vertical. Six people — five salespeople and one administration person — report to her as senior manager. All employees at VLC have a lot of respect for Olivia because of her background with the company. They feel she 'knows the ropes' and often consult her about professional and personal problems.

Unfortunately, over the past six months VLC has been losing market share. Industry trends suggest that software sales are consistent, so there do not appear to be any macro issues to account for the downturn in sales. Nelson, the CEO of VLC, is very concerned and feels that if VLC is falling below the industry average, then there is a chance the problem could be a human resource issue, either with his own staff or with the distributors.

(continued)

Because of Olivia's strong relationship with the other employees at VLC, and because it is easier to audit VLC than the external distributors, Nelson has asked her to prepare a confidential written report on the entire operation of VLC, identifying any weaknesses in systems and people. Olivia is concerned about the outcome, as over a period of time she has tried to deal with several operational and human resource problems but has ultimately failed. Olivia is aware of an underlying conflict between the five salespeople that is mainly due to the fact that sales territories are not clearly defined, and there are no firm incentive or reward schemes in place. As a result of this, some of the more experienced salespeople have been quietly operating outside their geographical areas, which is creating motivation problems among those who are staying within their boundaries.

Olivia is uncomfortable about how to conduct the audit because she is sensing something of an ethical dilemma. On one hand she feels it is her duty as senior manager to improve the operations and sales for VLC; on the other hand, she wants to remain loyal to her team. However, to prevent the underlying conflict from erupting, Olivia realises the time has come to conduct a complete audit and formally report her findings.

Questions

1. Should Olivia make it known to the employees at VLC that she is carrying out an audit? Explain why or why not.
2. If Olivia's findings suggest that the issue of underlying conflict among the salespeople is the reason for the downturn in sales, outline the process she should go through to counter that conflict. Bear in mind that Olivia's loyalty to all of the staff means she may need to draw on her negotiating skills to achieve a win–win outcome among the team.

It is too easy in negotiation to stake out your position based on the assumption that to gain your way, something must be 'subtracted' from the other party's way. This myth of the 'fixed pie' is a purely distributive approach to negotiation. The whole concept of integrative negotiation is based on the premise that the 'pie' can sometimes be expanded and/or used to the maximum advantage of all parties, not just one.

Parties to negotiations often begin by stating extreme demands, so the possibility of escalating commitment is high. That is, once 'demands' have been stated, people become committed to them and are reluctant to back down. As a result, they may be prone to nonrational escalation of conflict. Concerns for 'protecting your ego' and 'saving face' may enhance these tendencies. It takes self-discipline to spot this tendency in your own behaviour as well as that of others.

It is also common for negotiators to develop the belief that their positions are the only 'correct' ones. This is characterised by overconfidence and ignoring others' needs. In some cases, negotiators completely fail to see merits in the other party's position — merits that an outside observer would be sure to spot. Such overconfidence makes it harder to reach a positive common agreement. It may even set the stage for disappointment if the negotiation is turned over to a neutral third party for resolution. In **arbitration**, such as the salary arbitration now common in professional sports, this third party acts as the 'judge' and issues a binding decision after listening to the positions advanced by the parties involved in a dispute. Sometimes, a manager may be asked to serve as an arbitrator of disputes between employees, from matters as important as the distribution of task assignments to those as seemingly trivial as access to a photocopy machine.

Arbitration occurs when a neutral third party acts as judge and issues a binding decision affecting parties at a negotiation impasse.

Verbal disputes in sports

As we have seen in this chapter, some level of conflict is expected in organisations and may be tolerated. Sporting competitions provide a particularly interesting example of the tolerance of verbal disputes and abusive communication. Many sports, by their very nature, bring opposing parties into competition. All sports have a set of rules by which the players are expected to compete. One or more officials oversee the game to ensure compliance with the rules, but there is often much more flexibility than would be allowed in business organisations.

Some sports seem to accept, to varying degrees, heated verbal disputes, 'sledging' and intimidating body language between coaches or players and umpires or competitors. Prominent examples include rugby league, tennis, cricket, basketball and baseball. While such displays often embody a degree of theatre and strategy on behalf of the coach or player who pursues them, they also promote a culture of confrontation to participants and spectators, and acceptance of otherwise unsporting behaviour. Abuse of officials and organisers generally can be seen as a threat to the sport; in particular it threatens the ability of the sport to attract and keep officials willing to preside over competition.[41] Tennis and baseball are positioned at the very apex of this social phenomenon and as such struggle to maintain equilibrium between control, effective management of competitions and mutual respect of participants' roles.

Questions

1. Should verbal abuse be tolerated in sports? If so, to what degree?
2. What can sporting associations do in order to minimise and/or manage this problem?

Summary

Communication and its role in organisations

Communication in an organisation is a process by which organisational members share meanings by exchanging information. We communicate to inform, instruct, motivate or seek information, to achieve coordinated action throughout the organisation, to develop information for the benefit of the organisation, to express our feelings and emotions, and to explain respective job responsibilities, roles and expectations. The interpersonal communication process involves an intricate matching of information that is encoded, sent, received and decoded, sometimes with and sometimes without feedback, but always affected by noise. Communication is effective when both sender and receiver interpret a message in the same way. It is efficient when messages are transferred at a low cost. Communication channels include formal, informal and quasiformal relationships among members of the organisation. The organisation is a network of information and communication channels. The electronic age has provided organisations with new opportunities to link managers effectively. Barriers to communication include special sources of noise common to most interpersonal exchanges: physical distractions, cultural differences, the absence of feedback and status effects. Each of these sources of noise should be recognised and subjected to special managerial control. Managers can eliminate or reduce barriers through such techniques as wandering around, developing active listening skills, providing effective feedback to the sender of the communication, and articulating job roles and responsibilities.

Conflict and its effect on organisations

Conflict can be either emotional (based on personal feelings) or substantive (based on work goals). Both forms can be harmful in organisations if, as a result, individuals and/or groups are unable to work constructively with one another. Conflict situations in organisations occur in vertical and lateral working relations and in line–staff relations. Often, they result from work flow interdependencies and resource scarcities. Most typically, conflict develops through a series of stages, beginning with antecedent conditions and progressing into manifest conflict. The conflict may or may not be entirely 'resolved' in the sense that the underlying reasons for the emotional and/or substantive conflict are eliminated. Unresolved conflicts set the stage for future conflicts of a similar nature. When kept within tolerable limits, conflict can be a source of creativity and performance enhancement. Even when managers have different viewpoints, ongoing questioning and discussion about their differences may unleash more creative approaches to a situation as they are further probed. On the other hand, such situations can become destructive when these limits are exceeded and the hostility between individuals or groups continues. In this case, managers must be made aware of such conflicts and take appropriate action to resolve them.

Managing conflict

Conflict management should always proceed with the goal of true conflict resolution. Indirect forms of conflict management include appeals to common goals, hierarchical referral and organisational redesign. Direct conflict management proceeds with different combinations of assertiveness and cooperativeness on the part of conflicting parties. Win–win outcomes are achieved through cooperation and problem solving most often associated with high assertiveness and high cooperation. Win–lose outcomes usually occur through direct competition or authoritative command. Lose–lose outcomes are typically found as a result of avoidance, smoothing and compromise approaches.

Negotiation and its role in organisations

Negotiation in organisations occurs whenever two or more people with different preferences must make joint decisions. Managers may find themselves involved in various types of negotiation situations, including two-party, group, intergroup and constituency negotiation. Both substance goals and relationship goals are at stake. Effective negotiation occurs when issues of substance are resolved and human relationships are maintained, or even improved, in the process. To achieve such results, ethical conduct must be carefully maintained, even as negotiating parties represent viewpoints and preferences that differ greatly from one another.

Managers' issues in negotiation

Different approaches to negotiation can have very different results. In distributive negotiation, the focus of each party is on staking out positions in the attempt to claim desired portions of a 'fixed pie'. In integrative negotiation, sometimes called principled negotiation, the focus is on determining the merits of the issues and finding ways to satisfy one another's needs. The distributive approach is often associated with individual styles of competition (the 'hard' approach) or accommodation (the 'soft' approach). The integrative approach ideally leads to some form of cooperation or problem solving to achieve a mutually desirable solution.

Chapter 13 study guide

OB Key terms

arbitration, *p. 478*
bargaining zone, *p. 476*
BATNA, *p. 476*
buffering, *p. 471*
channels, *p. 455*
conflict, *p. 461*
conflict resolution, *p. 468*
constructive conflict, *p. 465*
decoding, *p. 456*
decoupling, *p. 471*
destructive conflict, *p. 465*
distributive negotiation, *p. 474*
effective communication, *p. 457*
effective negotiation, *p. 473*

efficient communication, *p. 457*
emotional conflict, *p. 462*
encoding, *p. 455*
feedback, *p. 456*
formal communication channels, *p. 457*
hierarchical referral, *p. 470*
informal communication channels, *p. 457*
information source, *p. 455*
integrative negotiation, *p. 475*
intergroup conflict, *p. 463*
interorganisational conflict, *p. 464*
interpersonal conflict, *p. 463*

intrapersonal conflict, *p. 463*
liaison group, *p. 471*
linking pins, *p. 471*
manifest conflict, *p. 468*
negotiation, *p. 472*
noise, *p. 456*
organisational communication, *p. 454*
quasiformal channels, *p. 458*
receiver, *p. 456*
relationship goals, *p. 473*
substance goals, *p. 473*
substantive conflict, *p. 462*
transmission, *p. 455*

OB Review questions

1. Describe the main sources of noise and disturbance in communication. Give examples.
2. Under what circumstances would conflict be accepted and considered to be positive? Give examples.
3. What are some of the most common strategies used in resolving conflict? Briefly explain why conflict in the workplace can be positive.
4. Describe some of the most common managerial issues in negotiations.

OB Application questions

1. Imagine you are the CEO of a large manufacturing company that has five factories in Asia employing a total of 5000 people. What are some of the ways you would select to communicate your company's vision throughout the organisation?
2. If, as a manager, you felt it necessary to criticise the productivity of one of your employees, what would be some of the important factors you would consider before approaching that person?
3. The text states, 'when conflict arises, most people's first reaction is to become angry or distressed, and to seek to eliminate the problem'. Provide an example in which you have been an *observer only* of a conflict situation. The example you describe could be from your workplace or a different environment, such as a bank or an airport. Write down how the reaction of the parties involved in the conflict appeared to an onlooker — in this case, yourself. Then explain how you would have handled the situation if you had been one of the parties in conflict, remembering to take into consideration the emotional aspect that can escalate conflict. *Note:* If more than one student is involved, each should have the opportunity to take the role of each of the parties involved.

4. According to the text, 'managers are known to spend up to 20 per cent of their time dealing with conflict, including conflicts in which managers are themselves directly involved'. What implications does this have for business school educators and new managers?
5. Using an example, explain how destructive conflict can have a negative impact on performance.

How would you remedy the conflict situation you have discussed?
6. Design a half-day awareness workshop aimed at teaching administrative staff the meaning of conflict and the various approaches to conflict resolution.

Research questions   OB

1. Access the web site of a large company with which you are familiar. Search the site with a view to identifying how the company:
   (a) communicates its commitment to new and existing employees and its external customers, such as yourself
   (b) addresses issues of conflict that are most common in the organisation (for example, bargaining with trade unions with a view to establishing enterprise agreements).

2. Select a well-known case of conflict involving multiple parties (including, for example, managers, customers, government and the community).
   (a) Examine the reasons for the conflict.
   (b) Outline how and why the conflict escalated.
   (c) Describe the approach(es) used in attempting to resolve the conflict.
   (d) Critically examine the effectiveness of these approach(es).

Running project   OB

Complete the following activities for your organisation.
1. Describe the formal communication channels likely to exist, based on the information on its organisational chart.
2. Find a job advertisement from your organisation (its web site is a likely source) and assess how well it communicates the job role. Apart from the job description, where else would you expect to obtain information about the expectations of the employer, both before and after joining the organisation?
3. What internal communication processes does your organisation use? Try to find examples of each and assess what criteria the organisation uses in choosing which communication channel to use. (For example,

why does it advertise its products in newspapers, but use its web site for job advertisements?)
4. Negotiation is especially significant in today's workplace, where more people are being offered opportunities to be involved in decisions. This can often lead to disagreements. If possible, arrange an interview with a manager or other person of authority in your organisation. Ask the manager what formal and informal processes the organisation has in place to deal with situations that may arise from intergroup conflict caused by any of the following issues: wage rates, task objectives, performance evaluations, job assignments, work schedules and locations, and special privileges.

Individual activity   OB

Disagreeing with your boss

Objective
To develop your understanding and application of different approaches to conflict resolution

Total time: 45–60 minutes
Procedure
First, think about the following scenario, then provide a solution or approach to the problem. Write down the approach you favour.

(continued)

Scenario

You work in the sales area of a software distribution company operating in the Asia–Pacific market. You have been working for the company for seven years and your income depends on the sales figures achieved by the company because you are given a very generous bonus based on these figures.

You and your supervisor, Frown, have not been getting along well for the past year or so. Frown is a domineering individual and does not seem to want your input on any major activities being undertaken in your sales unit. However, a major project has been assigned to your unit and Frown has instructed you to take responsibility for the project. The aim of the project is to develop a strategy for an effective market entry into a new geographical area in the region.

Frown gives directions for completing the project. You examine the situation and after some thought tell Frown that you have some ideas about how the project might be undertaken effectively. Frown responds, 'I am not interested in hearing your ideas. I get paid for having ideas and you get paid for following my directions.'

Against your better judgement you follow Frown's directions. Frown's ideas for the project are not sound and everything goes badly. The organisation loses a lot of money on the project and you predict that things are likely to get much worse if the project continues in the way being directed by Frown.

You are about to go to the regular Monday morning staff meeting, where you will be called on to report on the progress of the project. At this point, no-one is aware of how badly the project is going. You have mentioned it several times to Frown, who does not want to talk about it and says you are making excuses for your own incompetence. You are concerned about disagreeing with Frown. At the same time, you do not want to be embarrassed in front of your colleagues, who are also social acquaintances. Frown has the ability to greatly influence your career and basically controls your pay, promotional opportunities and other incentive rewards within the company for at least the next three years. Because of family obligations, you do not feel ready to leave the company.

OB *Group activity*

Conflict resolution

Preparation

You will be given the opportunity to role play handling a conflict you face or have faced. Select the conflict and write out the information for a class member who will play the role of the person with whom you are in conflict.

1. Define the situation and list pertinent information about the other party (that is, relationship to you, knowledge of the situation, age, background and so on).
2. State what you wish to accomplish during the conflict resolution.
3. Identify the other party's possible reaction to your confrontation (resistance to change).

Plan how you will overcome resistance to change using the problem-solving conflict management style. A good way to open the conflict resolution is to use an X (behaviour), Y (consequences), Z (feelings) statement: for example, 'When you smoke in my room (behaviour), I have trouble breathing and become nauseous

(consequences), and feel uncomfortable and irritated (feeling)'. Write out an XYZ statement to open your selected conflict resolution. During the role play, open with your XYZ statement, then allow the person to respond as you seek true satisfaction of everyone's concerns by working through differences, and finding and solving problems so everyone gains as a result.

Objective

To develop your conflict resolution skills[42]

Total time: *30–40 minutes*

Procedure 1

Break into groups of three. If there are any people not in a triad, make one or two groups of two. Each member selects the number 1, 2 or 3. Number 1 will be the first to initiate a conflict role play, then 2, followed by 3.

Procedure 2

1. Initiator number 1 gives his or her information from the preparation to number 2 (the responder) to read. Once number 2 understands, role play (see step 2 below). Number 3 is the observer.

2. Role play the conflict resolution. Number 3, the observer, writes his or her observation. Focus on what was done and how to improve.

3. Integration. When the role play is over, the observer leads a discussion on the effectiveness of the conflict resolution. All three should discuss the effectiveness. Number 3 is not a lecturer. Do not go on until told to do so.

Procedure 3

Same as procedure 2, only number 2 is now the initiator, number 3 is the responder and number 1 is the observer.

Procedure 4

Same as procedure 2, only number 3 is the initiator, number 1 is the responder and number 2 is the observer.

Case study: Conflict over new business strategies

Cory recently joined Executive Improvement Strategies (EIS), a small consulting firm specialising in training and development programs for senior managers. EIS is based in Auckland, New Zealand, with a small client base that takes in Australia. There are three other consultants working for EIS and one managing partner, Andrew, who started the firm five years ago.

Cory is highly experienced and well known in the corporate training arena; in fact, his credentials far exceed those of the other consultants, including Andrew, the managing partner. One of Cory's strengths is successfully targeting new business. Part of this can be attributed to his outgoing, gregarious personality, along with his rather non-traditional, casual approach to obtaining new business; however, it fits Cory's personality and it works.

As managing partner, Andrew has implemented a very rigid culture at EIS, particularly in relation to seeking new business. Since Cory has been with EIS, Andrew has not been particularly impressed with his approach to potential clients and on several occasions has had discussions with him about this, which have often resulted in conflict.

Cory has just learned of an excellent opportunity to move into the Asian market through one of his clients with whom he has had a long-standing relationship. Of course, Cory will be following through the Asian lead under the brand of EIS, so he is keen to meet with Andrew to brief him on his intentions.

Unfortunately, although the Asian opportunity is a good breakthrough for EIS, Cory's enthusiasm is dampened knowing that Andrew will have very set ideas about how to approach the Asian market, and that those ideas will be completely contrary to Cory's strategy. So what should be a positive meeting may ultimately turn into a disaster if it isn't handled correctly.

Questions

1. If you were to advise Cory about how to approach the meeting with Andrew in order to avoid initial conflict, what would you say?

2. In order to please Andrew, should Cory attempt to change his approach to potential new clients? Why, or why not?

3. Given that Cory and Andrew have very different approaches to obtaining new business, what processes can they put in place to ensure they can continue in a productive working relationship? Remember that Andrew is head of EIS, yet Cory has more experience and success.

Suggested reading

Max H Bazerman and Margaret A Neale, *Negotiating rationally* (New York: The Free Press, 1991).

Kirk Blackard, 'Assessing workplace conflict resolution options', *Dispute Resolution Journal*, vol. 56, issue 1 (New York, February/April 2001), pp. 57–62.

Jeanne M Brett, Debra L Shapiro and Anne L Lytle, 'Breaking the bonds of reciprocity in negotiations', *Academy of Management Journal*, vol. 41, no. 4 (August 1998), p. 410.

BJ Broome, S DeTurk, ES Krisjansdottir, T Kanata and P Ganesan, 'Giving voice to diversity: an interactive approach to conflict management and decision-making in culturally diverse environments', *Journal of Business and Management*, vol. 8, no. 3 (2002), pp. 239–64.

Cheryl Buggy, 'Empathy is the key to cultural communication', *Professional Manager*, vol. 8, no. 1 (1999), pp. 14–16.

Mely Caballero-Anthony, 'Mechanisms of dispute settlement: the ASEAN experience', *Contemporary Southeast Asia*, vol. 20, no. 1 (April 1998), p. 38.

Robert B Cialdini, 'Harnessing the science of persuasion', *Harvard Business Review* (October 2001), pp. 72–9.

Ross Dawson, 'Who shares wins', *Australian Financial Review BOSS Magazine* (November 2002), pp. 58–62.

Roger Fisher and William Ury, *Getting to yes: negotiating agreement without giving in* (New York: Penguin, 1983).

Winston Fletcher, 'Good listener, better manager', *Management Today* (January 2000), p. 30.

Andrew Gill, 'Drive out the fear', *HR Monthly* (November 1998), pp. 14–15.

Neal Q Herrick, *Joint management and employee participation: labor and management at the crossroads* (San Francisco: Jossey-Bass, 1990).

Carolyn Hirschmann, 'Someone to listen', *HR Magazine*, vol. 48, issue 1 (January 2003), pp. 46–51.

Deborah M Kolb and Judith Williams, 'Breakthrough bargaining', *Harvard Business Review* (February 2001), pp. 89–97.

Dorothy Leonard and Susan Straus, 'Putting your company's whole brain to work (how to address conflicts in an organization)', *Harvard Business Review*, vol. 75, no. 4 (July/August 1997), p. 111.

Colin McKenzie, 'Developing a CCO: conflict competent organisation', *New Zealand Management*, vol. 49, issue 2 (March 2002), pp 34–6.

EW Morrison, 'Newcomer information seeking: exploring types, modes, sources and outcomes', *Academy of Management Journal*, vol. 26, no. 3 (1993), pp. 557–89.

MA Mushref, 'Managing conflict in a changing environment', *Management Services*, vol. 46, no. 11 (2002), pp. 8–11.

Mary Power and Byron Rienstra, 'Internal communication in new corporate conglomerates: developing a corporate communication model for loosely coupled businesses in local government', *International Journal of Public Sector Management*, vol. 12, no. 6 (1999), pp. 501–15.

James K Sebenius, 'Six habits of merely effective negotiators', *Harvard Business Review* (April 2001), pp. 87–95.

Kathryn Tyler, 'Extending the olive branch', *HR Magazine*, vol. 47, issue 11 (November 2002), pp. 85–9.

PR Wayne, *Organization communication: foundations for human resource development* (Englewood Cliffs, NJ: Prentice Hall, 1983).

Holly Weeks, 'Taking the stress out of stressful conversations', *Harvard Business Review* (July/August 2001), pp. 112–19.

J Yates and W Orlikowsky, 'Genres of organizational communication: an approach to studying communication and media', *Academy of Management Journal*, vol. 17, no. 2 (1992), pp. 299–326.

Rachid M Zeffane and Bruce Cheek, 'The differential use of written, computer-based and verbal information in an organizational context: an empirical exploration', *Information and Management*, vol. 26, no. 1 (1995), pp. 101–21.

OB **End notes**

1. Thomas Dahle, 'An objective and comparative study of five methods of transmitting information from management to business and industrial employees', *Speech monographs*, vol. 21 (March 1954).
2. Edward G Wertheim, 'The importance of effective communication', Northeastern University College of Business Administration, http://web.cba.neu.edu/~ewertheim/interper/commun.htm (viewed 4 January 2006).
3. Deborah Tarrant, 'Talking heads', *Australian Financial Review BOSS Magazine* (July 2002), p. 58.
4. ibid.
5. John Case, 'When salaries aren't secret', *Harvard Business Review* (May 2001), pp. 37–9, 42–9.
6. Deborah Tarrant, op. cit., p. 58.
7. Tom Iggulden, 'A slap in the interface', *Australian Financial Review BOSS Magazine* (August 2001), p. 8.
8. Jane Walton, 'Board dynamics', *Australian Financial Review BOSS Magazine* (August 2001), pp. 60–1.
9. Richard E Walton, *Interpersonal peacemaking: confrontations and third-party consultation* (Reading, MA: Addison-Wesley, 1969).
10. Kenneth W Thomas and Warren H Schmidt, 'A survey of managerial interests with respect to conflict', *Academy of Management Journal*, vol. 19 (1976), pp. 315–18.
11. Robert Bolton, *People skills: how to assert yourself, listen to others, and resolve conflicts* (Sydney: Prentice Hall, 1986), ch. 12.
12. Richard E Walton, *Interpersonal peacemaking: confrontations and third-party consultation* (Reading, MA: Addison-Wesley, 1969).
13. ibid.
14. Richard E Walton and John M Dutton, 'The management of interdepartmental conflict: a model and review', *Administrative Science Quarterly*, vol. 14 (1969), pp. 73–84.

15. Rebecca Turner, 'Support team', *Australian Financial Review BOSS Magazine* (August 2002), pp. 30–1.

16. Queensland University of Technology (QUT), 'Cultural diversity policy', http://www.qut.edu.au/admin/mopp/A/A_08_10.html (viewed 4 January 2006).

17. See Avan Jassawalla, Ciara Truglia and Jennifer Garvey, 'Cross-cultural conflict and expatriate manager adjustment: an exploratory study', *Management Decision*, vol. 42, issue 7 (August 2004), pp. 837–49.

18. Dorothy Leonard and Susan Straus, 'Putting your company's whole brain to work', *Harvard Business Review*, vol. 75, no. 4 (July/August 1997), p. 111.

19. Developed from Don Hellriegel, John W Slocum, Jr and Richard W Woodman, *Organizational behavior*, 3rd ed. (St. Paul: West, 1983), pp. 471–4.

20. Developed from Gary Johns, *Organizational behavior* (Glenview, IL: Scott, Foresman, 1983), pp. 415–17; Richard E Walton and John M Dutton, 'The management of interdepartmental conflict: a model and review', *Administrative Science Quarterly*, vol. 14 (1969), pp. 73–84.

21. These stages are consistent with the conflict models described by Alan C Filley, *Interpersonal conflict resolution* (Glenview, IL: Scott, Foresman, 1975); Louis R Pondy, 'Organizational conflict: concepts and models', *Administrative Science Quarterly*, vol. 12 (September 1967), pp. 269–320.

22. Adapted from Roslyn Gaskell, 'How effectively is your organisation managing conflict?', *hrconnection*, vol. 8 (2003), <http://www.davidsontrahaire.com.au/upload/HR_Connection_Volume_8.pdf (viewed 12 September 2005).

23. Robert R Blake and Jane S Mouton, *The managerial grid* (Houston, TX: Gulf, 1964).

24. Kenneth W Thomas, 'Organizational conflict' in S Kerr (ed.), *Organizational behavior* (Columbus, OH: Grid, 1979), pp. 151–81.

25. M Afzalur Rahim, 'A strategy for managing conflict in complex organizations', *Human Relations*, vol. 38, no. 1 (1985), pp. 83–5.

26. Robert E Jones and Bonita H Melcher, 'Personality and preference for modes of conflict resolution', *Human Relations*, vol. 35, no. 8 (1982), pp. 649–58.

27. Paul R Lawrence and Jay W Lorsch, 'Differentiation and integration in complex organizations', *Administrative Science Quarterly*, vol. 12, no. 1 (1967), pp. 1–47.

28. Stephen P Robbins, '"Conflict management" and "conflict resolution" are not synonymous terms', *California Management Review*, vol. 21, no. 2 (1978), pp. 67–75.

29. Paul R Lawrence and Jay W Lorsch, *Organization and environment* (Cambridge, MA: Harvard University Press, 1967).

30. Krum Krumov, Snejana Ilieva, Sonya Karabeliova and Lyudmila Alexieva, 'Conflict resolution strategies in the transition to market economy', *Annals of the American Academy of Political and Social Science*, vol. 552, no. 10 (1997), p. 65.

31. Wayne Pace, *Organizational communication* (Englewood Cliffs, NJ: Prentice Hall, 1983), p. 145.

32. ibid.

33. Stephen P Robbins, *Organization theory: structure design and applications* (Englewood Cliffs, NJ: Prentice Hall, 1987).

34. See Jay Galbraith, *Designing complex organizations* (Reading, MA: Addison-Wesley, 1973).

35. Rensis Likert and Jane B Likert, *New ways of managing conflict* (New York: McGraw-Hill, 1976).

36. David Nadler and Michael Tushman, *Strategic organizational design* (Glenview, IL: Scott, Foresman, 1988).

37. Queensland Department of Justice and Attorney-General, 'Dispute resolution in the workplace', fact sheet D9 (September 2005), www.justice.qld.gov.au/mediation/about/D09workplace.htm (viewed 4 January 2006).

38. Following discussion based on Roger Fisher and William Ury, *Getting to yes: negotiating agreement without giving in* (New York: Penguin, 1983); Roy J Lewicki and Joseph A Litterer, Negotiation (Homewood, IL: Richard D. Irwin, 1985), pp. 315–19.

39. Roger Fisher and William Ury, *Getting to yes: negotiating agreement without giving in* (New York: Penguin, 1983), pp. 10–14.

40. This example is developed from Max H Bazerman, *Judgment in managerial decision making*, 2nd ed. (New York: John Wiley & Sons, 1990), pp. 106–8.

41. The Australian Baseball Federation, 'Addressing the problem of abuse of officials', http://www.baseball.com.au/site/baseball/abf/downloads/Addressing%20the%20Problem%20of%20Abuse%20of%20Official2.doc (viewed 13 Septepmber 2005).

42. Robert N Lussier, *Human relations in organizations: a skill building approach*, 2nd ed. (Homewood, IL: Richard D. Irwin, 1993), pp. 265–86.

CHAPTER 14

Organisational change and innovation

Learning objectives

After studying this chapter, you should be able to:

1. distinguish between radical and incremental planned change

2. discuss the forces favouring change and the targets of change in contemporary organisations

3. identify the change strategies used by managers

4. explain why people resist change and describe strategies to overcome resistance

5. discuss workplace stress in the context of change

6. explain why innovation is so important to organisations today and list the features you would expect to find in an innovative organisation

Domino's Pizza Australia owns the master franchise to the Domino's pizza brand in Australia and New Zealand. The chain has 387 stores across the two countries, employing more than 11 000 staff and making more than 40 million pizzas each year. The Australian Government chose to profile it on its National Innovation Awareness Strategy web site as an outstanding example of a business innovator.

Domino's Pizza (Australia) began in Red Hill in Brisbane in 1978 as Silvio's Dial-A-Pizza — the first store in Australia to offer home delivery. In 1993 Silvio's, which then operated 70 stores, bought the master Domino's Pizza franchise. Under its current growth strategy, the company aims to open 50 stores a year, reaching more than 500 stores by 2008.

Domino's Pizza has been able to grow in the competitive high-volume, low-margin takeaway food market through an innovative approach to research, marketing and human resource management.

The 36-year-old managing director of Domino's Pizza Don Meij says the pizza chain had a bumpy beginning, with three master franchisees failing during the first decade of Domino's introduction into Australia.

'In the early days we were trying to save our way to success by reducing our number of break-even stores by cutting our spending on research and marketing,' Don explained. 'Our customers could tell, and by cutting costs we were driving them away. We were a company of compromise but when we stopped compromising and looked at our unique attributes that set us aside from our competitors, we turned the corner and were a success.

'If companies compromise by cutting jobs, research and marketing they are putting themselves at risk. There are whole brands that do not exist today, or that are on the brink of not existing, because they have not been able to survive a cycle of adversity. Every business has cycles of downturns, but you have to come up with innovative strategies to survive these.'

In the case of Domino's Pizza, sound advice from a Domino's Pizza mentor in the United States resulted in a new way of thinking for the business. He advised the company to invest in research, marketing and training.

The company, following a series of mergers, now sells more pizzas than its competitors, and Don has been named Ernst & Young 2004 Entrepreneur of the Year.

Many of the innovations undertaken by Domino's Pizza are examples of product and process improvements...The company also researches trends overseas. [Don says] 'Research is very important, and it can be affordable...We keep re-investing our profit into future technology, products and training. We are very focused on staff training because if you have happy team members you will have happy customers.'

Moving into 2006 and beyond, Domino's had expanded through mergers with a number of other pizza companies including Big Daddy's Pizza in Melbourne, and Pizza Haven and Mad Dog Pizza in New Zealand.

Sources: Extract from the Department of Industry, Tourism and Resources National Innovation Council, 'Invest to create domino effect: Domino's MD', 30 March 2005, http://www.innovation.gov.au/index.cfm?event=object.showContent&objectID=A3B7DA79-65BF-4956-B87E6B34BA156C14 (viewed 27 September 2005); Domino's web site, www.dominos.com.au.

Introduction

As the experience of Domino's Pizza (Australia) indicates, in today's turbulent socioeconomic environment, business success depends heavily on a company's ability to adapt and innovate. We have truly entered an era in which increasingly greater premiums are attached to effective and positive approaches to innovation and change. The information revolution is transforming all before it, just as the industrial revolution did 200 years ago. The rules of the game have fundamentally changed: 'control' was important in the industrial era, but the information revolution demands innovation and flexibility as prerequisites for success. To survive and prosper in this dynamic setting, organisations must be willing and able to make substantial changes to ensure they remain economically competitive and responsive to the environment. For organisations, this means continual innovation. As our society becomes more technologically demanding, the need for change reaches all sectors of the economy, including industry, government, professional development programs and various institutional frameworks. This requires managers to reassess ways in which they develop and implement change strategies and encourage innovation. Even in the public sector, organisations face their greatest challenge in decades. There is relentless pressure to change the missions and innovative practices of these organisations.[1]

This chapter will help you understand the importance of change and innovation. It examines the various types of and approaches to change. We shall also deal with the increasingly important topic of innovation in an organisational context.

What is organisational change?

Radical versus incremental planned change

LEARNING OBJECTIVE 1

'Change' is the watchword of the day for most organisations. In organisational behaviour, 'organisational change' refers to organisation-wide change rather than to small changes such as adding a new person or making minor modifications to a process. Examples of organisation-wide change might include a change in mission, restructuring operations, the adoption of major new technologies, and mergers. Some experts refer to organisational transformation to designate a fundamental and radical reorientation in the way the organisation operates. Some of this change may be described as radical change.[2] This is change that results in a major make-over of the organisation and/or of its component systems. In today's business environments, radical changes are often initiated by a critical event, such as the arrival of a new chief executive officer, a new ownership brought about by a merger or takeover, or a dramatic failure in operating results. Radical change occurs infrequently in the life cycle of an organisation. However, when it does occur, this change is intense and all-encompassing. There may be times in an organisation's life when its survival depends on an ability to undergo successfully the rigours and demands of radical change. Radical change occurs when an industry's core assets and activities are both threatened with obsolescence, and knowledge and brand capital erode along with the customer and supplier relationships. It is most commonly caused by the introduction of new technologies or regulations, or by changing consumer preferences.

Radical change is change that results in a major make-over of the organisation and/or its component systems.

Another and more common form of organisational change is incremental change. This is change that occurs more frequently and less traumatically, as part of an organisation's natural evolution. Typical changes of this type include new products, new technologies and new systems. Although the nature of the organisation remains relatively unaltered, incremental change builds on the existing ways of operating and seeks to enhance them or extend them in new directions. The ability to improve continually through incremental change is an important asset to organisations in today's demanding environments.

Incremental change is change that occurs more frequently and less traumatically as part of an organisation's natural evolution.

The success of both radical and incremental change in organisations depends in part on change agents who facilitate and support the change processes. A change agent is a person or group who takes responsibility for changing the existing pattern of behaviour of another person or social system. It makes sense, therefore, that part of every manager's job in today's

Change agents are individuals or groups that take responsibility for changing the existing pattern of behaviour of a person or social system.

dynamic times is to act as a change agent in the work setting. This means being alert to situations or people needing change, open to good ideas, and able to support the implementation of new ideas into actual practice.

Planned and unplanned change

Changes in organisations can be planned or unplanned. Planned change occurs when an organisation deliberately attempts to make internal changes to meet specified goals or to pursue a set of strategies. For example, organisations often change their structures to meet given objectives or to pursue cost-cutting strategies. Also, an organisation may engage in major updating of its operational systems, which would mean engaging in some form of technological change.

Unplanned change is usually prompted by some external driver, such as market forces, economic crises, economic opportunities or social changes. Typically, organisations engage in organisation-wide change to respond to these forces and thereby evolve to a different level in their life cycle; for example, going from a highly reactive to a more proactive and planned development. However, not all change in organisations happens as a result of an intended (or change agent's) direction. Unplanned change occurs spontaneously or randomly, and without a change agent's attention. The appropriate goal in managing unplanned change is to act immediately once the change is recognised, to minimise any negative consequences, and maximise any possible benefits.

In this chapter we are particularly interested in planned change — that is, change that comes about as a result of specific efforts on the part of a change agent. Planned change is a direct response to someone's perception of a performance gap. This is a discrepancy between the desired and actual state of affairs. Performance gaps may represent problems to be resolved or opportunities to be explored. It is useful to think of most planned changes as efforts initiated by managers to resolve performance gaps to the benefit of the organisation and its members.

However, planned change often assumes that the future is predictable and there is an end state to be reached. In other words, managers tend to regard change as a once-only, major alteration to the organisation. In reality, in the vast majority of cases change occurs in an incremental way, reflecting the assumption that what worked in the past will also work in the future. However, with contextual dynamism and complexity being the new rule, any linear extrapolation is at best misleading. The line representing the link between past and future is at best dotted, and sometimes even discontinuous, with twists and thresholds everywhere.[3]

As Bowman has discovered, 'organisations are constrained by routines, but, paradoxically, routines are the very stuff of organisations; without routines organisations could not function. The problems start when routines get in the way of strategic thinking and strategic change'[4], and when routine thinking gets in the way of lateral/innovative thinking. Processes that challenge the taken-for-granted assumptions that underpin routine thinking are then needed for the organisation to progress.

Leadership of change

Most change initiatives, especially radical change, require effective leadership, not just on the part of the chief executive and other senior managers, but from leaders at all levels in the organisation.

The more recent Australian studies show that change processes that have the support of the workforce require good leadership, an appropriate model of change, some room for negotiation and compromise, and well-planned communication. In particular, a study focusing on six case studies in the Australian public sector found great support for the proposition that a prominent CEO role was important in 'driving' change, and in enlisting support for it.[5]

Unplanned change is change that occurs at random or spontaneously and without a change agent's direction.

Planned change is change that happens as a result of specific efforts on the part of a change agent.

The **performance gap** is the discrepancy between an actual and a desired state of affairs.

So what does the leadership of change involve? It encompasses many dimensions that need to be adapted to each situation. Initially, leadership involves preparing people for the change by challenging the status quo and communicating a vision of what the organisation can aspire to become. Next, it involves building the commitment of employees and change agents throughout the organisation, and enabling them to act by providing resources and training, delegating power, building change teams and putting appropriate systems and structures in place. Leaders then maintain the momentum of change through symbolic and substantive actions that reward progress and recognise the reaching of milestones, with themselves acting as effective role models.[6]

Robert Miles, a successful change management consultant and writer, has summarised the leadership of change in the following terms.[7] First and foremost, according to Miles, radical change is vision-led. That is, it involves the creation of goals that stretch the organisation beyond its current horizons and capacities. Secondly, it is based on a total-system perspective, wherein all major elements of the organisation are carried forward. And thirdly, it requires a sustained process of organisational learning so that people and processes develop synergistically. Figure 14.1 provides a picture of the four essential ingredients of a successful change process.

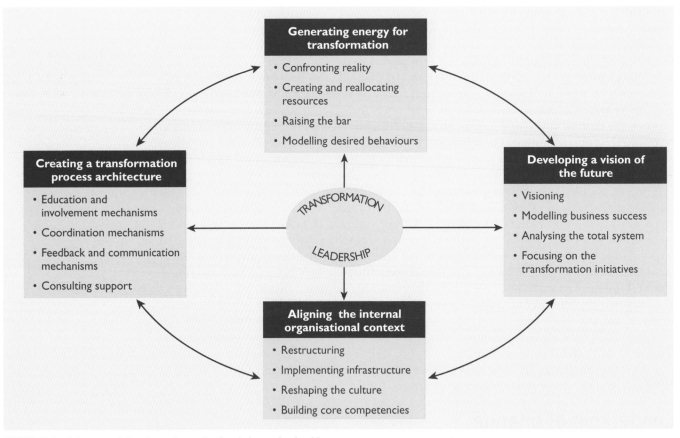

FIGURE 14.1 • A framework for planned organisational change leadership

Source: Robert H Miles, *Corporate comeback: the story of renewal and transformation at National Semiconductor* (San Francisco: Jossey-Bass, 1997), p. 6.

As figure 14.1 suggests, the process hinges on 'generating energy for transformation'. A key to this is in revealing to employees the shortfalls in current organisational performance — in essence, providing a reality check. One way to do this is by benchmarking the organisation against customer expectations, industry leaders or competitors. Another method is to diagnose internal strengths and weaknesses, for example, by conducting a skills profile of employees to gauge their capacity to work cross-culturally.

Based on such assessments, resources are released or reallocated to prepare the organisation and its staff for the next ingredient — 'developing a vision'. While 'generating energy' puts people into a frame of mind that supports change, the vision provides them with a sense of what the future organisation could be like and where they will be heading. A thorough organisational analysis is also needed as a basis for detailed planning of the change, which Miles describes as 'aligning the internal context'. The internal context consists of all the components that make an organisation what it is — its structure, culture, technology and so on. Any or all of these components can become targets for change. The final ingredient is 'creating a transformation process architecture'. Key words that express what this is about are education, involvement and communication.

While these ideas were specifically developed with radical change in mind, you will see from reading this chapter that they generally apply to incremental change as well. All planned changes require careful preparation to ensure that they achieve the results hoped for, and to reduce the likelihood that employees will resist change. You will also learn that there are several stages in the process of planned change, that there are at least four options of change strategy (the employee involvement strategy recommended by Miles is just one of these) and that managers must make careful choices about which aspects of the organisation to target for change.[8]

Forces of change

In any change process, certain forces tend to encourage or favour the process while others militate against it. Change demands that organisation members examine big-picture questions such as 'Who are we?', 'Where are we going?' and 'What do we want?' The major forces favouring organisational change are:

- a sufficient dissatisfaction with the existing situation, or state A
- a strong attraction to moving towards a more desirable position, or state B. (This position can frequently be described in a vision statement, or in an analysis of the company's goals and performance in comparison to those of competitors.)
- a desire to formulate a well-thought-out strategy that will realise the vision — that is, how the company can move from A to B.[9]

All three of these forces must usually be present for managers to feel compelled to seek change. In the absence of any one of the three, there is little or no motivation to galvanise managers into action. Associated with these factors are other elements such as strong leadership, effective communication, a tight alignment of people and organisational goals, and a clear definition of the compelling reasons to change.

OBJECTIVE 2 LEARNING

Forces favouring change and the targets of change

Effective and efficient change management

Effective change management requires three things:
- management commitment
- universal approval
- measures and rewards.

Efficient change management utilises two practices:
- strategic planning
- enterprise architecture engineering.

Enterprises can either manage change or be managed by change. Successful, competitive enterprises proactively and constantly manage change.

Source: Extract from Visible, 'Enterprise solutions, engineering the enterprise for excellence®', www.visible.com/Solutions/ (viewed 5 January 2006).

THE **Effective** Manager 14.1

Change may be triggered by internal or external forces. External forces include politics (for example, a change in government or government policy), laws (for example, anti-spam legislation), markets (for example, competition from foreign companies entering the home market) and technology (for example, the convergence of communications devices). Internal triggers include changes of ownership, products, services, process and measures of effectiveness that can happen in an organisational setting. Today's organisations must be able to react quickly and correctly to external change, while managing internal change effectively. External change is usually obvious and has immediate impact. In contrast, the need for internal change is often less obvious.

Cultural change

As we saw in chapter 11, organisational culture is the pattern of an organisation's shared beliefs, values, expectations and assumptions. Culture is a strong influence on people's thoughts and behaviour and affects all aspects of organisational life. It can significantly influence — positively and negatively — the outcomes of change so it cannot be ignored when considering a change initiative. Even the most rigid of organisational cultures can be subject to significant change under the right circumstances.

It is a massive task to achieve a major culture change, one in which new values are antagonistic to the old ones. Successful culture change, in which there is a change in the underlying values that drive behaviour, can take a long time, even years.[10]

THE **Effective**Manager 14.2

Pathways to effective cultural change

Gagliardi[11] recommends the following approach to culture change:
- Educate stakeholders as to why change is necessary.
- Communicate the new culture that is desired.
- Use value statements to embed the new cultural requirements.
- Give people the skills, knowledge and capabilities they will need to work differently.
- Create processes, systems and ways of working that enable people to put the new values into practice.
- Use performance management and rewards to enforce desired behaviours.

Organisational growth will engender change, and new companies tend to see a rapid evolution of organisational culture as they undergo consistent change. Established companies tend to be more structured and thus slower to undertake change. A long-established company may not seek change until change is forced upon it as the result of a merger or acquisition, adverse media attention or undeniable changes in the environment. When a merger occurs, the question of which partner's organisational culture will become dominant inevitably arises. Both companies may be able to allow a new organisational culture to emerge. Cultural change may also occur internally in an unplanned fashion as the result of a labour dispute, a scandal or an accident.[12]

OB in action

The merger of mining companies BHP and Billiton is an example of the coming together of very different organisational cultures. Billiton had a long history of operating in difficult markets and was an aggressive and tough operator. BHP had more of an Australian working class culture. Successfully merging the two would be a challenge.[13]

Technological change

The increased complexity of the business environment and of competition is due to a number of factors, but technology is a key driving force for change. Companies are generally receptive to technological change and are ready to accommodate further technological change in the future. Companies use sophisticated networks and information systems that have unprecedented capacity for meeting customer and other business needs. Business transactions take place nearly instantaneously via email and the Internet. These changes have increased the pace of business. This pace is another force of change with which managers must contend.[14]

Technological change that occurred slowly over centuries (such as the invention of the wheel) accelerated to change measured in decades (the impact of the car, for instance), which has now been transformed into continuous and pervasive change brought about by the computer chip and its successors.

Organisational targets for change

The forces for change are ever present in today's dynamic work settings.[15] They are found in the relationship between an organisation and its environment; mergers, strategic alliances and divestitures are examples of organisational attempts to redefine relationships with challenging environments. They are found in the life cycle of the organisation as it passes from birth through growth and towards maturity; changes in culture and structures are examples of organisational attempts to adjust to these patterns of growth. They are found in the political nature of organisational life; changes in internal control structures (including benefits and reward systems) are examples of organisational attempts to deal with shifting political currents.

Planned change based on any of these forces can be directed towards a wide variety of organisational components or targets. As shown in figure 14.2, these targets include organisational purpose, strategy, structure and people, as well as objectives, culture, tasks and technology.

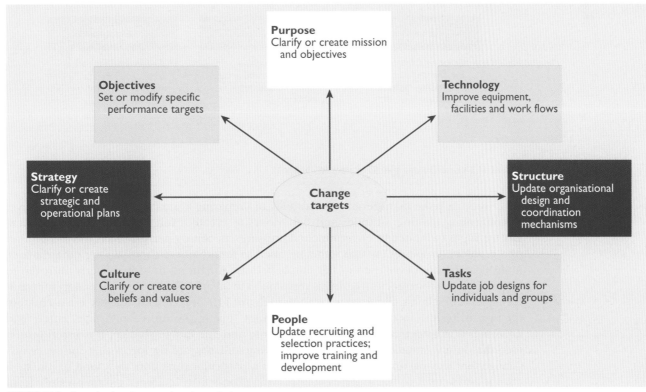

FIGURE 14.2 • Organisational targets for planned change

Sometimes, these targets for change are addressed mistakenly by management through 'fad' solutions that are offered by consultants and adopted by managers without much thought for the real situation and/or people involved. The logic of truly planned change requires a managerial willingness and ability to address problems concretely and systematically, and to avoid tendencies towards an easy but questionable 'quick fix'.[16]

Further, the manager must recognise that the various targets of planned organisational change are highly intertwined. For example, a change in the basic tasks performed by an organisation (that is, a modification in what it is the organisation does) is almost inevitably accompanied by a change in technology (that is, a modification in the way in which tasks are accomplished). Changes in tasks and technology usually require alterations in the structure of the organisation, including changes in the patterns of authority and communication as well as in the roles of members. These technological and structural changes can, in turn, necessitate changes on the part of the organisation's members. For example, members may have to acquire additional knowledge and develop new skills to perform their modified roles and work with the new technology.[17]

Phases of planned change

Kurt Lewin, a famous psychologist, recommends that any change effort should be viewed as a process that includes the phases shown in figure 14.3. Managers using Lewin's ideas will be sensitive to the need to ensure that any change effort properly addresses each of these three phases of change:[18]

1. unfreezing — getting people and things ready for change
2. changing — implementing the change
3. refreezing — making sure the change 'sticks' as part of new routines.

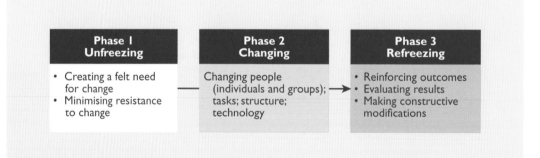

Phase 1 Unfreezing	Phase 2 Changing	Phase 3 Refreezing
• Creating a felt need for change • Minimising resistance to change	Changing people (individuals and groups); tasks; structure; technology	• Reinforcing outcomes • Evaluating results • Making constructive modifications

FIGURE 14.3 • Lewin's three phases of planned change

Unfreezing is the first stage of the planned change process in which a situation is prepared for change.

Unfreezing is the managerial responsibility of preparing a situation for change. It involves disconfirming existing attitudes and behaviours to create a felt need for something new. Unfreezing is facilitated by environmental pressures, declining performance, the recognition of a problem, or awareness that someone else has found a better way, among other factors. Many changes are never tried or fail simply because situations are not properly unfrozen to begin with. As a concept, unfreezing is very similar in meaning to 'generating energy for transformation', which was discussed in relation to figure 14.1. 'Force field analysis' is a useful tool for identifying the forces for and against change during the unfreezing stage. Force field analysis is a management technique to diagnose and encourage change. It is based on the idea that in any situation there are both driving and restraining forces that influence any change that may occur. Driving forces push in a particular direction; they tend to initiate a change and keep it going. In terms of improving productivity in a work group, pressure from a supervisor, incentive earnings and competition may be examples of driving forces.

Restraining forces restrain or decrease the driving forces. Apathy, hostility and poor maintenance of equipment may be examples of restraining forces against increased production. Changes occur when the driving and restraining forces are shifted out of equilibrium.[19] The basic steps are to identify the driving forces, identify the restraining forces, identify which forces can be changed, and weight those forces based on the degree to which they can be influenced and the likely effects of that influence.[20] You will find an exercise on force field analysis in the study guide at the end of this chapter.

Large systems seem particularly susceptible to the so-called boiled frog phenomenon.[21] This refers to a classic physiological proposition that a live frog will immediately jump out when placed in a pan of hot water; but when placed in cold water that is then heated very slowly, the frog will stay in the water until it boils to death. Organisations can fall victim to similar circumstances. When managers fail to monitor their environments, recognise the important trends, or sense the need to change, their organisations may slowly suffer and lose their competitive edge. The best organisations, by contrast, have managers who are always on the alert for 'unfreezing' opportunities.

The changing stage involves a managerial responsibility to modify a situation — that is, to change people, tasks, structure and/or technology. Lewin feels that many change agents enter this stage prematurely or are too quick to change things. As a result, they often end up creating resistance to change in a situation that is not adequately unfrozen. Changing something is hard enough, let alone having to do it without the proper foundations. Successful change requires sustained energy and clear goals to maintain the process.

> Changing involves a managerial responsibility to modify a situation — that is, to change people, tasks, structure and/or technology.

Successful change also depends on the degree of readiness to change, which suggests that two distinct forces act on people.[22] First, there are the forces within the individual. Second, there are the forces within the system, which (as we have discussed) include the type of leadership, the culture, the climate of the organisation and the perceived consequences of success or failure within the organisation. The combination of these factors affects the individual's degree of felt security. That is, if the degree of felt security is either high or low, then the efforts to introduce change will most likely be rejected. If people feel secure in their current work situation, then what need is there for them to change? If an individual's degree of felt security is very low, then anything you do to disturb that low state of security will be seen to be highly threatening. Thus, only in the middle ranges of felt security is the response to change most likely to be positive. Such positive response will be expressed through behaviours such as listening, clarifying, negotiating and a willingness to explore alternatives.

Refreezing is the final stage of managerial responsibility in the planned change process. Designed to maintain the momentum of a change, refreezing positively reinforces desired outcomes and provides extra support when difficulties are encountered. Evaluation is a key element in this final step of the change process. It provides data on the costs and benefits of a change, and offers opportunities to make constructive modifications in the change over time. Improper refreezing results in changes that are abandoned or incompletely implemented.

> Refreezing is the final stage of the planned change process in which changes are positively reinforced.

Change levers and change cycles

Managers may limit their capacity to manage change by focusing on a restricted set of organisational change levers. In other words, regardless of the nature of the problem that the change is meant to solve, they reach for the same levers every time. This means that the change process is viewed from only one perspective. It may be viewed as a technical problem, a political problem or a cultural problem that needs resolving. Noel Tichy argues that those who design, manage, and change organisations face the following three fundamental sets of problems, and effective change managers can recognise all three.

1. *Technical design problem.* The organisation faces a production or operational problem. Social and technical resources must be allocated to solve the problem and achieve a desired outcome.
2. *Political allocation problem.* The organisation faces an allocation of power and resources problem. It must determine how it will use its resources, as well as which parts of the organisation will benefit.
3. *Culture/ideological mix problem.* An organisation is held together by shared beliefs. The organisation must determine what values need to be held by what people.[23]

All of these problems tend to occur simultaneously in organisations. They therefore constitute the fundamental levers that prompt managers to contemplate strategic change. They form the basic parts of what could be described as the engine of change, as shown in figure 14.4. When these areas are considered over time, you can identify cycles in their relative importance. Attempts to resolve each set of problems give rise to new situations and hence new problems which in turn require new solutions.[24]

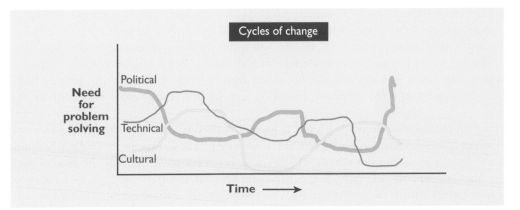

FIGURE 14.4 • The engine of change

Source: Adapted from N Tichy, *Managing strategic change: technical, political and cultural dynamics* (New York: John Wiley & Sons, 1983). Reprinted by permission of John Wiley & Sons Inc.

Seeing the change process as an engine allows us to understand some of the practical aspects of change. Managers may experience all of the problems outlined by Tichy, but to a varying degree. At some stage of organisational development, technical problems may be the most pressing. At another stage, cultural problems may need the most urgent attention. As with the oil or water that feeds an engine, none of these issues can be ignored if the engine of change is to run. All components of the engine need attention to ensure high performance. Change agents and participants often fail to understand this. Too often during a change process, one group becomes frustrated because their problems are not seen to be the most pressing. Managers need to understand that each group's problems are intertwined and that they must be dealt with simultaneously. In doing so, managers will find themselves addressing strategic change as shown in figure 14.5.[25]

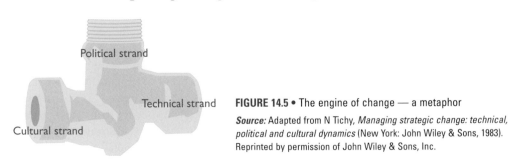

FIGURE 14.5 • The engine of change — a metaphor

Source: Adapted from N Tichy, *Managing strategic change: technical, political and cultural dynamics* (New York: John Wiley & Sons, 1983). Reprinted by permission of John Wiley & Sons, Inc.

'Resistance to change' revisited

The idea that people will naturally resist change, and that management must plan ways to overcome this, is firmly entrenched in the management literature. However, it was not always so. The term was coined by Kurt Lewin as recently as 1948, and its meaning has shifted since then. Dent and Goldberg[26] argue that current conceptualisations present resistance to change as the unproductive or inappropriate actions that people take to thwart the change efforts of management. It suggests an 'us and them' mentality and a tendency to blame employees for the failure of changes that would otherwise have been good for the organisation. In combating resistance, the focus is firmly on individuals and groups of employees. Managers are advised to be proactive in preventing or countering resistance — through education, communication, training and support, negotiation, cooptation and so on. Thus, the suggestion in the contemporary literature is that resistance can be prevented by anticipating employee-related reactions followed by early intervention to deal with them.

So what is the alternative to this conceptualisation of resistance? There are two points to consider here. First, people rarely resist change simply for the sake of doing so, and few are so entrenched in their habits and certainties that they will not contemplate another way of doing things. On the contrary, we normally resist things that are unpleasant or against our best interests — the possible loss of a job, loss of status, less favourable working conditions, new reporting arrangements or being railroaded into something we don't understand, for example. Even then, we will often accept short-term discomfort for longer-term advantages. The second point is that resistance to change is not simply a characteristic of individuals; it can come from any component of an organisational system, of which individuals are only one part. While it is certainly true that planned change is often less than successful, many factors could explain this. It seems unreasonable, therefore, to place undue emphasis on the individual employee.

To better understand this alternative view of resistance to change, we need to revisit Kurt Lewin's work. For Lewin, nothing much could change in an organisation as long as there was an equilibrium between the forces favouring change and the forces against change. To set off an unfreezing effect, the relative strengths of these two sets of opposing forces needed to change, either to weaken the barriers or to strengthen the drivers. Organisations were dynamic entities with many complex interconnections and effects. In short, resistance to change was 'a systems phenomenon, not a psychological one'.[27] If we take Lewin's original conceptualisation, the role of employees in moving change forward is through their full collaboration in planning and implementation processes. On the other hand, contemporary conceptualisations of resistance to change often imply that people are 'part of the problem' and that their education and participation is primarily for the purpose of securing cooperation in a process that rests firmly in the hands of management.[28]

Questions

1. How do you normally respond to changes in your life and work? Do you think that resistance to change is a normal response for yourself and others?

2. Explain the two different management rationales for employee participation in the change process that are implied in the last paragraph above.

Planned change strategies

Managers and other change agents use various means for mobilising power, exerting influence over others and getting people to support planned change efforts. As described in figure 14.6, each of these strategies builds from different foundations of social power (as discussed in chapter 10) and each has somewhat different implications for the planned change process. Among the change strategies commonly used by managers to bring about planned organisational change are:[29]

- *top-down approach to change* — using centralised power to force compliance with change directives
- *force-coercion* — using authority to force compliance with change directives
- *rational persuasion* — using logic and information to persuade people to accept change directives
- *shared power* — involving others in decisions identifying the need for change and desired change directions.

FIGURE 14.6 • Power bases, change strategies, management behaviours and predicted outcomes

Top-down approach to change

In pursuing the top-down (or directional) approach to change, executives and managers believe that one-way communication backed by the formal authority of their position is enough to implement change. This approach to change is very akin to the military model in its style and assumes that members lower down in the hierarchy will understand what is intended and follow through exactly as requested.

In many situations, this approach is problematic and ineffective, especially when the situation facing the organisation is complex and difficult to interpret.[30] With complex problems requiring change, top managers do not have a monopoly on expertise, information[31] and inputs. In such situations, having the additional perspectives of the lower-level managers and employees would be an advantage.

Given that members at the lower levels are generally on the firing line (that is, closest to the machinery, the consumer and the community), they are in an excellent position to observe problems and to provide varied and valuable inputs to any required changes. When a directive approach to change pervades the organisation, higher-level managers are unlikely to listen. Thus, the lower levels become increasingly frustrated and may even refuse to lend their cooperation. Further, the extent to which the change process requires member commitment for successful implementation suggests that the lower-level members may not comply automatically.[32] If members do not commit to the change process as intended, what finally is implemented may be a far cry from what top management had in mind.

Many eminent management scholars such as Tom Lupton have also voiced the idiosyncracies of authoritarian change. For instance, Lupton sees that change can be more successfully introduced from the bottom up than from the top down.[33] In general, individuals who are struggling to assert their autonomy tend to resist the efforts of people in authority to exercise control over them. By doing so, individuals do not necessarily reject the legitimacy of the authority, but rather seek to extend their own autonomy by working to control their interactions with the authority.

However, the 'bottom-up' (participative) approach to change is often not possible. In the case of public sector organisations, for example, the change process may be imposed on them by drastic changes in government policies and legislation. In this situation, change may be more directive and less participative.

Force-coercion and planned change

A force-coercion strategy uses legitimacy, rewards and/or punishments as primary inducements to change. That is, the change agent acts unilaterally to try to 'command' change through the formal authority of their position, to induce change via an offer of special rewards, or to bring about change via threats of punishment. People respond to this strategy mainly out of fear of being punished if they do not comply with a change directive, or out of desire to gain a reward if they do. Compliance is usually temporary and will continue only so long as the change agent remains visible in their legitimate authority, or so long as the opportunity for rewards and punishments remains obvious. If, as a change agent, you were to use the force-coercion strategy for bringing about planned change, the following profile might apply:[34]

> You believe that people who run things are basically motivated by self-interest and by what the situation offers in terms of potential personal gains or losses. Since you feel that people change only in response to such motives, you try to find out where their vested interests lie and then put the pressure on. If you have formal authority, you use it. If not, you resort to whatever possible rewards and punishments you have access to and do not hesitate to threaten others with these weapons. Once you find a weakness, you exploit it and are always wise to work 'politically' by building supporting alliances wherever possible.

Force-coercion strategy tries to 'command' change through the formal authority of legitimacy, rewards and punishments.

Rational persuasion and planned change

Change agents using a rational persuasion strategy attempt to bring about change through the use of special knowledge, empirical support or rational arguments. This strategy assumes that rational people will be guided by reason and self-interest in deciding whether to support a change. Expert power is mobilised to convince others that the cost–benefit value of a proposed change is high; that is, that the change will leave them better off than before. When successful, this strategy results in a longer-lasting, more internalised change than does the force-coercion strategy. If you use a rational persuasion strategy, the following profile may apply:

Rational persuasion strategy attempts to bring about change through persuasion based on empirical facts, special knowledge and rational argument.

> You believe that people are inherently rational and are guided by reason in their actions and decision making. Once a specific course of action is demonstrated to be in a person's self-interest, you assume that reason and rationality will cause the person to adopt it. You approach change with the objective of communicating, through information and facts, the essential 'desirability' of change from the perspective of the person whose behaviour you seek to influence. If this logic is effectively communicated, you are sure that the person(s) will adopt the proposed change.

Shared power and planned change

In order to minimise the likelihood of resistance, some of the best approaches to change put strong emphasis on involving all parties affected by the change. For example, a leader might meet with all managers and employees to explain reasons for the change, and generally how it will be carried out. A plan may be developed and communicated. Staff forums may be organised to give members the opportunity to express their ideas about the proposed change.

They are also given the opportunity to express their concerns and frustrations. This approach to change coincides with what is commonly known as a shared power strategy to change. This strategy actively and sincerely involves other people who will be affected by a change in planning and making key decisions in respect to it. Sometimes called a normative-reeducative strategy, this approach seeks to establish directions and social support for change through the empowerment of others. It builds essential foundations, such as personal values, group norms and shared goals, so support for a proposed change emerges naturally. Managers using this approach emphasise personal reference and share power by allowing others to participate in planning and implementing the change. Given this high level of involvement, the strategy is likely to result in a longer-lasting and internalised change. If you use a shared power strategy for bringing about planned change, the following profile may apply:

> You believe that people have complex motivations. You feel that people behave as they do as a result of sociocultural norms and commitments to these norms. You also recognise that changes in these orientations involve changes in attitudes, values, skills and significant relationships, not just changes in knowledge, information or intellectual rationales for action and practice. When seeking to change others, you are sensitive to the supporting or inhibiting effects of any group pressures and norms that may be operating. You try to find out their side of things and to identify their feelings and expectations.

On a final note, in a study examining the controversy between 'one best way' and contingent approaches to corporate change in 13 service sector organisations in Australia, Dunphy and Stace concluded that the 'one best way' models are inadequate because they do not capture the diversity of approaches actually used by these organisations. In particular, they concluded that the traditional organisational development model emphasising employee participation and shared power is unrepresentative of how change in many contemporary organisations is made. According to them, the model is also inadequate as a prescriptive model because different change strategies, some dramatically different from organisational development, resulted in successful financial performance.[35]

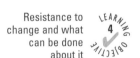

THE **Effective**Manager 14.3

Guidelines for effective change

Managers should keep in mind the following when planning change:
- consider using an expert consultant
- communicate the need for change
- gather as much information and feedback from employees as possible
- do not fall into the trap of change for change's sake
- study organisational change, including new forms and structures.[36]

Resistance to change

Typically, change initiatives are met by some resistance. This is because employees are often afraid of the unknown. Many of them may think things are already just fine and do not understand the need for change. Many may also be cynical about change. Some may even think that the proposed change goes against the values held by members in the organisation. That is why much organisational change is often discussed in conjunction with needed changes in the culture of the organisation, including changes in members' values and beliefs. In essence, resistance to change is often viewed by change agents as something that must be 'overcome' for change to be successful. This is not always the case. It is helpful to view resistance to change as feedback that can be used by the astute change agent to help accomplish his or her change objectives.[37] The essence of this notion is to recognise that when people resist change, they are defending something important that appears to be threatened by the change attempt.

Formally defined, therefore, resistance to change is any attitude or behaviour that reflects a person's unwillingness to make or support a desired change.

Resistance to change is any attitude or behaviour that reflects a person's unwillingness to make or support a desired change.

Both passive and active resistance work against organisational change. Passive resistance can include the widespread cynicism often found among workers exposed to frequent management change initiatives, where insufficient attention was paid to implementation and the effects on organisational members. Passive resistance can also occur where organisational members feel that the psychological cost of adjusting to new systems and processes is greater than any recommended or perceived benefits. Active resistance occurs where the redistribution of power threatens vested self-interest. This form of resistance can be dangerous for an organisation and can undermine even well-thought-out change programs.[38]

Why people resist change

There are several reasons for possible resistance to the introduction of a new management practice. People who directly report to a manager, for example, may resist the introduction and use of e-commerce (electronic commerce) in their workplace because:

- they are not familiar with online business and Internet use and wonder whether they could become familiar with it successfully (*fear of the unknown*)
- they may wonder if the manager is introducing e-commerce just to 'get rid' of some of the workers eventually (*need for security*)
- they may feel they are doing their jobs well and do not need the new facility (*no felt need for change*)
- they may sense that the manager is forcing e-commerce on them without first discussing their feelings on the matter (*vested interests threatened*)
- they may have heard from workers in other departments that e-commerce is being introduced to get more work out of people with no increase in pay (*contrasting interpretations*)
- they are really busy at the present time and do not want to try something new until the work slackens a bit (*poor timing*)
- they may believe that they will be left on their own to learn how to operate the new systems (*lack of resources*).

These and other viewpoints often create resistance to even the best and most well-intended planned changes. To deal better with these forces, managers often find it useful to separate such responses into resistance to change directed towards the change itself, the change strategy, and the change agent as a person.

Sometimes a manager may experience resistance to the change itself. A good manager understands that people may reject a change because they believe it is not worth their time, effort and/or attention. To minimise resistance in such cases, the change agent should make sure that the people affected by the change know specifically how it satisfies the following criteria.

1. *Benefit*. The change should have a clear relative advantage for the individuals being asked to change; that is, it should be perceived as 'a better way'.
2. *Compatibility*. The change should be as compatible as possible with the existing values and experiences of the people being asked to change.
3. *Complexity*. The change should be no more complex than necessary. It must be as easy as possible to understand and use.
4. *Triability*. The change should be something that people can try on a step-by-step basis and make adjustments as things progress.

Managers will always experience some resistance to their change strategy. Someone who attempts to bring about change via force-coercion, for example, may create resistance among individuals who resent management by 'command' or the threatened use of punishment. People may also resist an empirical-rational strategy in which the data are suspect or expertise is not clearly demonstrated, or a normative-reeducative strategy that appears manipulative and insincere.

Finally, managers may experience resistance to the change agent. In this case, resistance is directed at the person implementing the change and may reflect inadequacies in the personality and attributes of the manager as a change agent. Change agents who are isolated from other people in the change situation, who appear self-centred or who have a high emotional involvement in the changes are especially prone to such problems. Research also indicates that change agents who are different from other key people on such dimensions as age, education and socioeconomic factors are likely to experience greater resistance to change.[39]

How to deal with resistance to change

An informed change agent can do many things to deal constructively with resistance to change in any of its forms. In general, resistance will be managed best if it is recognised early in the change process. All things considered, the following general approaches for dealing with resistance to change have been identified:[40]

- *education and communication* — using one-on-one discussions, presentations to groups, memos, reports or demonstrations to educate people about a change before it is implemented and to help them see the logic of the change
- *participation and involvement* — allowing others to help design and implement the changes; asking individuals to contribute ideas and advice; forming task forces or committees to work on the change
- *facilitation and support* — providing socioemotional support for the hardships of change; actively listening to problems and complaints; providing training in the new ways; helping to overcome performance pressures
- *negotiation and agreement* — offering incentives to actual or potential resistors; working out tradeoffs to provide special benefits in exchange for assurance that the change will not be blocked
- *manipulation and cooptation* — using covert attempts to influence others; selectively providing information and consciously structuring events so the desired change receives maximum support; buying off leaders of resistance to gain their support
- *explicit or implicit coercion* — using force to get people to accept change; threatening resistors with a variety of undesirable consequences if they do not go along as planned.

Figure 14.7 summarises additional insights into how and when each method may be used by managers when dealing with resistance to change. When such resistance seems to be based on a lack of information or the presence of inaccurate information, education and communication are good managerial responses. Once persuaded that the change is for the best, people will often help implement the change. The downside is that the process of education and communication can be time consuming if too many people are involved. Participation and involvement is a good approach when the manager or change agent does not have all the information needed to design the required change. This is especially true if other people have a lot of power to resist. People who are allowed to participate in designing a change tend to be highly committed to its implementation. But, again, this process can be time consuming.

In cases where people are resisting the change because there will be adjustment problems, facilitation and support are recommended responses. In such circumstances, people are most likely trying hard to implement a change, but they are frustrated by external constraints and difficulties. Here a manager must play the 'supportive' role and try to make it as easy as possible to continue with the planned change. Of course, the manager must be able to invest the time and energy needed to provide this support and to gain needed commitments from the organisation. Negotiation and agreement tends to be most useful when a person or group will clearly lose something as a result of the planned change. When the person or group has considerable power, resistance can be particularly costly to the change effort.

Direct negotiation can sometimes prove a relatively easy way of avoiding or eliminating this form of resistance. This response requires a foundation of trust and may involve extra 'costs' in terms of any agreements that may be reached.

METHOD	USE WHEN	ADVANTAGES	DISADVANTAGES
Education and communication	People lack information or have inaccurate information	Creates willingness to help with the change	Can be very time consuming
Participation and involvement	Other people have important information and/or power to resist	Adds information to change planning; builds commitment to the change	Can be very time consuming
Facilitation and support	Resistance traces to resource or adjustment problems	Satisfies directly specific resource or adjustment needs	Can be time consuming; can be expensive
Negotiation and agreement	A person or group will 'lose' something due to the change	Helps avoid major resistance	Can be expensive; can cause others to seek similar 'deals'
Manipulation and cooptation	Other methods do not work or are too expensive	Can be quick and inexpensive	Can create future problems if people sense manipulation
Explicit and implicit coercion	Speed is important and change agent has power	Quick; overpowers resistance	Risky if people get angry

FIGURE 14.7 • Methods for dealing with resistance to change

There is no avoiding the fact that resistance to change can be — and is — managed at times through manipulation and cooptation. These responses may be used when other tactics just do not work or are too expensive. They may also make up a 'style' that a manager or change agent uses on most occasions. In some cases, manipulation and cooptation can provide a relatively quick and inexpensive solution to resistance problems. But a good manager understands that these approaches can also lead to future problems if people feel manipulated. A more extreme approach is explicit or implicit coercion. Coercion is often used when speed is of the essence or when the manager or change agent possesses considerable power. It is a fast response and can overpower resistance. It also runs the risk of offending people, however. People who experience coercion may feel angry at the manager or change agent, and be left without any true commitments to ensuring that the change is fully implemented. As Lewin might say, 'coercion may unfreeze and change things, but it does not do much to refreeze them'.

Regardless of the chosen strategy, managers must understand that resistance to change is something to be recognised and constructively addressed instead of feared. The presence of resistance typically suggests that something can be done to achieve a better 'fit' between the change, the situation and the people affected. A manager should deal with resistance to change by 'listening' to such feedback and acting accordingly.

Change and stress

More and more employers today are concerned about stress in the workplace. Organisational change can often be very stressful, although it is certainly not the only cause of stress. When experienced for a prolonged period of time, stress can lead to employee illness and even death. Employers and managers need be concerned not only for humanitarian reasons, but also because of the costs to their companies. Change of any sort in organisations is often accompanied by increased stress for the people involved. Hence managers and change agents alike need to understand the meaning and causes of stress as well as ways of preventing and managing it.

What is stress?

> Stress is a state of tension experienced by individuals facing extraordinary demands, constraints or opportunities.

Stress is a state of tension experienced by individuals facing extraordinary demands, constraints or opportunities.[41] Any look towards your managerial future would be incomplete without confronting stress as something you are sure to encounter along the way.[42] Consider this statement by a psychologist working with top-level managers with severe drinking problems: 'All executives deal with stress. They wouldn't be executives if they didn't. Some handle it well, others handle it poorly.' If you understand stress and how it operates in the work setting, you should be more likely to handle it well. This goes for both the stress you may experience personally and the stress experienced by persons you supervise.

Sources of stress

> Stressors are things that cause stress (for example, work, non-work and personal factors).

Simply put, stressors are the things that cause stress. One study of stress experienced by executives around the world reports that managers in mature industrialised countries worry about losing their jobs, about family and social pressures, lack of autonomy and poorly trained employees.[43] In contrast, managers in developing and recently industrialised countries worry about work overloads, interpersonal relations, competition for promotion and lack of autonomy. It is important for a manager to understand and be able to recognise these and other potential stressors, for they are the root causes of job-related stress. In turn, job-related stress influences work attitudes and behaviour. Figure 14.8 shows three categories of stressors that can act in this fashion: work, non-work and personal factors.

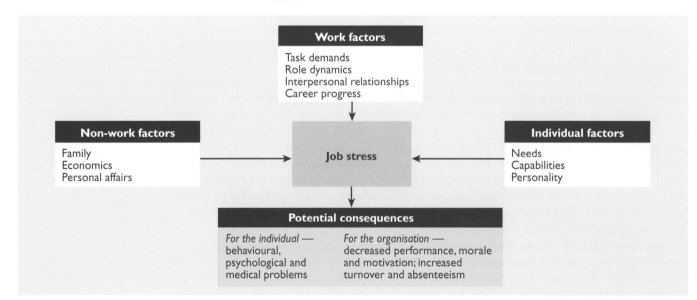

FIGURE 14.8 • Potential consequences of work, non-work and personal stressors for individuals and organisations

Preventing or coping with stress

Stress prevention is the best first-line strategy for dealing with stress. It involves taking action for yourself or others to keep stress from reaching destructive levels in the first place. In particular, stressors emerging from personal and non-work factors must be recognised so that action can be taken to prevent them from adversely affecting the work experience. Persons with type A orientations, for example, may exercise self-discipline; managers of type A employees may try to model a lower-key, more relaxed approach to work. At another level, family difficulties may be relieved by a change of work schedule; or the anxiety caused by family concerns may be reduced by knowing that your supervisor understands. Work stressors such as role ambiguities, conflicts and overloads can be prevented by good supervisor–employee communication, a willingness of employees to 'speak up' when role dynamics are creating difficulties, and sensitivity on the part of supervisors to behaviours or other symptoms indicating that employees are experiencing problems.

> **Stress prevention** involves taking action to prevent the emergence of stress that becomes destructive.

ETHICAL
Perspective

Long hours and stress at work

With the complexities of remaining competitive in the global market, and with lowered levels of job security, managers at all levels in organisations are working longer hours than ever before. The trend towards longer hours of work, both paid and unpaid, has been noted in Australia as well as among Asian countries. It is occurring in all sectors of the economy and not only in business organisations. In the short term, longer hours may increase the efficiency of the organisation,

but such gains may be negated by the longer-term effects on people. Unfortunately, the evidence is mounting that excessive hours of work are having severe repercussions for individual health and wellbeing, worker productivity and safety management.

Spending too many hours at work can lead to overtiredness and exhaustion or, in extreme cases, even worse. In Japan, for example, there is now a word for the situation when a person dies from overwork: *karoshi*.[44] It was estimated that up to 10 000 Japanese die of this condition each year! There is also a strong connection between the number of hours worked beyond the normal full working week — of around 40 hours — and increased levels of illness and injury from accidents. This relationship is based on the proposition that additional hours lead to fatigue, inattention and lack of sufficient care in hazardous situations. It is also the case that fatigue and emotional lows interfere with our capacity to make sound decisions, and this too can sometimes lead to accidents.

The consequences of stress from excessive working hours and other pressures have also been noted among senior executives around the world. The problem is so acute that the World Economic Forum held a discussion on the topic. The forum noted that chief executives increasingly suffer from stress, sleep deprivation, heart disease, failed personal relationships, loneliness and depression. In response, some commentators have argued that the high salaries and other benefits make executive jobs attractive, implying that the health risks are part of the package.[45] But should this be the end of the story? Are employers considering the long-term effect of long hours on worker productivity, or do they, in general, take a shorter-term view? How can organisations and their managerial employees (at all levels in the hierarchy) share the responsibility for individual health and welfare?[46]

Innovation in organisations

Innovation in organisations

LEARNING
6
OBJECTIVE

In order to survive and prosper, organisations need to build capabilities to make substantial changes to ensure they remain economically competitive and responsive to the environment. In most cases this means continual innovation. Innovation comes in many forms and degrees, but is typically defined as the creation of new and improved products and processes. There are various types of innovations: organisational innovation, market innovation, process innovation and so on. The simplest form of innovation is the variation of an existing idea or system (product, service or method of doing things) that may cause us to look at its function in a new way. The highest form of innovation is pure invention, where the product has no precedent. This must be considered to be a rare thing and unlikely to happen in our classroom.

The best organisations are able to 'innovate' on an ongoing basis; the best managers are able to help people use their 'innovative' talents to the fullest. Formally stated, innovation can be defined as the process of creating new ideas and putting them into practice.[47] It is the means by which creative ideas find their way into everyday practice in the form of new goods or services that satisfy customers, or as new systems or practices that help organisations better produce them. The former represents product innovation — innovation that results in the creation of a new or improved good or service. The latter represents process innovation — that is, innovation that results in a better way of doing things.

> **Innovation** is the process of creating new ideas and putting them into practice.

> **Product innovation** is innovation that results in the creation of a new or improved good or service.

> **Process innovation** is innovation that results in a better way of doing things.

Today's managers bear increasing responsibility for ensuring that both product and process innovation take place. They must be concerned with two main aspects of innovation as expressed in this equation:

$$\text{Innovation} = \text{invention} + \text{application}$$

In the equation, *invention* is the act of discovery, while *application* is the act of use. Both are critical to the innovation process. New ideas for improved products and services emerge from invention, but they achieve their full value only through application. In too many organisations invention occurs, but application does not. One key aspect of application is marketing.

THE **Effective** Manager 14.4

Promoting an innovation culture

To promote a culture of innovation throughout an organisation:
- define what a culture of innovation really is
- determine and communicate what it is that people have to change
- involve all levels of management in developing and implementing the cultural change plan
- train management and staff in the techniques of creative thinking
- develop a knowledge management system
- establish an evaluation and feedback system.

Source: Adapted from Australian Continuous Improvement Group, 'Leadership and innovation', http://www.acig.com.au/Services/service_leadership.htm (viewed 28 September 2005).

The innovation process

The various steps involved in a typical process of organisational innovation are shown in figure 14.9. These steps include:[48]
- *idea creation* — gathering new product or process ideas that arise from spontaneous creativity, ingenuity and information processing
- *initial experimentation* — examining new ideas in concept to establish their potential values and applications

- *feasibility determination* — conducting formal studies to determine the feasibility of adopting the new product or process, including the costs and benefits
- *final application* — producing and marketing the new product or service, or fully implementing the new process.

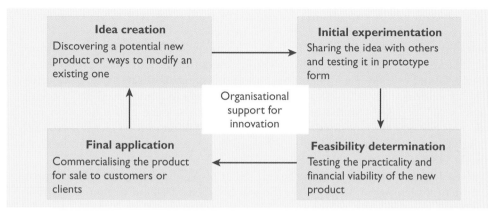

Idea creation
Discovering a potential new product or ways to modify an existing one

Initial experimentation
Sharing the idea with others and testing it in prototype form

Organisational support for innovation

Final application
Commercialising the product for sale to customers or clients

Feasibility determination
Testing the practicality and financial viability of the new product

FIGURE 14.9 • The innovation process: a case of new product development

Central to this view of the innovation process is the idea that any new product or process idea must offer true benefits to the organisation and/or marketplace. Further, the process is not complete until the point of final application has been reached.

Innovation in Australia's food and agriculture sector

International **SPOTLIGHT**

Innovation in Australia's food and agriculture sector is turning good ideas into commercial realities, backed by clean and environmentally-friendly agribusiness and ongoing successful government and industry partnerships.

Australia's agribusiness and food industries, like the people involved in them, are vibrant and diverse.

The sector incorporates many components: meat, poultry and seafood, fresh and processed fruits and vegetables, fibre, fodder and other agricultural support products, through to heavily processed foods and complex biotechnologies.

Australia has a well-deserved global reputation for producing clean, high-quality, environmentally-friendly agribusiness products, technologies and services. This has been achieved through innovation, the persistent application of sustainable agricultural and resource management practices, and ongoing successful government and industry partnerships.

The agribusiness sector is a dynamic growth area where opportunities abound for individuals and companies to grow and realise new business opportunities.

(continued)

Despite [several] challenges, Australian producers are among the world's most efficient because they realise the value of innovation. Innovation incorporates a range of business behaviours, including communication, intellectual property issues, networking, strategies, cooperation, marketing and planning at all levels. The formation and strengthening of supply chains, the uptake of technology and the commercialisation of research outcomes are all part of this process.

Australia is world-class in its research and development (R&D) and the uptake of innovation, but we can continue to improve when it comes to commercialising our ideas.

No-one should ever underestimate how important innovation is to the future of Australian agribusiness. In 2001, the Australian Government announced its 'Backing Australia's Ability' (BAA) initiative with A$3 billion for science and innovation programs. This has now been boosted with another A$5.3 billion in the successor package 'Backing Australia's Ability: Building Our Future through Science and Innovation'. In all, that's A$8.3 billion over a decade.

The New Industries Development Program (NIDP) is a good example of an Australian Government BAA program that bridges the gap between R&D and commercialisation.

The NIDP also promotes communication and the dissemination of lessons learned across agribusiness and related industries. Besides NIDP, the Government is funding many other programs to accelerate turning ideas into commercial realities.

To be successful, Australia must be determined to understand the process and able to follow the product through — from the original idea to commercialisation and marketing. We must continue to explore, develop and, in particular, commercialise our ideas, encouraging innovation among Australian businesses to continue their growth and prosperity.

The Australian Government continues to support programs through 'Backing Australia's Ability' that fill the gap between a good idea and a commercial reality.

Source: Excerpts from Peter McGauran, then Minister for Agriculture, Fisheries and Forestry, 'Food and agribusiness' in Innovation Australia, http://www.stroudgate.net/innovation/article/article.php?id=7,128 (viewed 28 September 2005).

Features of innovative organisations

Following are the major characteristics of highly innovative organisations like the CSIRO.[49]
1. Organisational strategy and culture support the innovation process.
2. Organisational structures support the innovation process.
3. The organisation is staffed to support the innovation process.
4. The organisation's top management supports the innovation process.

Although this list may seem straightforward and simple, it is a true management challenge to make sure that all four points are fulfilled in practice. To be innovative on a continual basis, an organisation's *strategies* and *cultures* must be built around a commitment to innovation. Chapter 9, on organisational culture, discussed many of the directions that are evidence of this commitment in today's workplaces. A common ingredient is the expectation that innovation will take place and that risk taking will be encouraged. This means that the organisational climate is one that tolerates mistakes or well-intentioned ideas that just do not work out as expected.

A study by the Australian Manufacturing Council set out to understand some of the features of organisations that successfully use product innovation as their competitive strategy. They took as a given that manufacturing is now an ideas-intensive activity. Australian organisations that are serious about manufacturing will therefore undertake research and development and will use current technology. One conclusion from the study is that exporting and innovativeness are closely intertwined. Innovative organisations are more likely to export, which provides opportunities, especially in gaining access to ideas essential for innovativeness. The study concentrated on organisations that use product innovation as a key competitive strategy.

However, when council researchers talked to these organisations they found that they used all sources of innovation (process, market, business system) to achieve competitive advantage. The message distilled from the broad database analysis was that organisations that are serious about manufacturing produce global products; use current technology; and undertake research and development. However, the study found that all types of organisations can be innovative. What most innovative organisations do can be distilled into three broad practices:

1. creating the need for new ideas
2. trawling the market for solutions
3. galvanising skilled people to deliver innovative solutions.[50]

Governments and industry groups can promote innovation by several means. The India Semiconductor Association (ISA), for example, has an initiative to promote technology and innovation in the Indian semiconductor industry. The initiative includes a series of awards to encourage the commercialisation of innovations from university research, as well as recognising innovation generally. The awards also operate at the school level, helping create a pervasive culture of innovation.[51]

In a highly innovative organisation, staffing is handled with a clear commitment to innovation. The organisation's strategies, cultures and structures support every member or employee, allowing them to use their creative talents to the full. This is what tends to happen in highly innovative organisations where managers tend to espouse a more flexible and open style of management, encouraging innovation and problem solving. In addition, managers in highly innovative organisations pay special attention to filling critical innovative roles as idea generators, information gatherers and project leaders.

Finally, an innovative organisation benefits from top-management support. Part of this responsibility involves setting a good personal example and maintaining a positive tone.

WhatWould **You**Do?

Trouble in the accounts department

Managers are often said to spend 20 per cent of their time dealing with interpersonal conflict. Sitting back in his chair, Ben Friedman reflected that it was more like 80 per cent, if his job was anything to go by! Since the company restructured the accounts department two months ago and appointed six new staff alongside nine others who had been around for some time, there had been nothing but trouble. Was it his imagination, or had Grace actually snarled at Phil when she passed him in the corridor yesterday? The staff had been grumpy and on edge for some time, but Ben had thought that people would settle in and develop smoother working relationships, given a bit of time. But it didn't seem to be happening.

Just last week, both Grace and Phil had contacted the same client and given conflicting advice about the costings of a new range of components that Ben's company was importing. Ben had no idea how this could have happened, as departmental policy was clear that clients would work with the one account manager, at least in the first instance. A different client had taken her business elsewhere when she had trouble identifying and contacting her new account manager. There had been similar 'mishaps' (paperwork not filed, people too busy to attend the weekly staff meeting, and so on) but luckily none was as damaging as the Phil and Grace fiasco. Reluctantly, Ben picked up the phone and spent some time talking to his friend and mentor Rachel from the advertising department. Towards the end of the conversation, she gave him this advice: 'Ben, it's time to get your people together and sort out just who is doing what in your department. It's not about personalities, and the problem won't just go away by itself.'

(continued)

Questions

1. What are the underlying causes of the problems that Ben is facing?
2. Put yourself in Ben's shoes, and design an intervention targeted at individual and/or team level to address the problems in the accounts department.

Management responsibility for innovation leadership further extends to putting the right strategies, cultures, structures and staffing in place, and keeping them updated. At any level of responsibility, such support for innovation begins with the ability to spot organisational 'barriers' to innovation.[52] But true management support for innovation goes further than mere recognition of potential barriers; it means being able to take the actions required to eliminate these barriers and to unlock the full innovation potential of the organisation. More specifically, it means decentralising authority and empowering people. It means redesigning work to create a sense of ownership for individuals and groups. It means making every effort to build a democratic workplace based on mutual trust. It means working with people to encourage experimentation and risk taking, and to eliminate the fear of failure. And, it means being willing to reward those who do experiment and take risks and who support change.[53]

Summary

LEARNING OBJECTIVE 1

Radical versus incremental planned change

Planned change is directed by managers and others acting as change agents. Radical change involves a significant transformation of the organisation and/or its objectives, systems and processes. It often occurs in response to a critical event such as the presence of a new chief executive officer, an emerging competitive threat, or a merger with another company. Incremental change is more gradual and involves an adjustment to the way things are currently done in one or a limited number of organisational departments. It is less disruptive and generally more frequent than radical change.

Forces favouring change and the targets of change

Within organisations, change is more likely to take place successfully when there is sufficient dissatisfaction with the way things are currently done, a strong attraction towards a more desirable state and a willingness to work towards a strategic approach to change. External factors in favour of change include increasing complexity in the business environment. Complexity is increased through globalisation, technological change, competition, and the need to be more efficient, innovative and responsive to customer demands. Organisational targets for planned change include purpose, strategy, culture, structure, people, tasks and technology.

Change strategies

Planned change strategies are the means used by change agents to implement desired change. Force-coercion strategies of change use aspects of a manager's position power to try to 'command' that the change will take place as directed. Temporary compliance is a common response of people who are 'forced' to change in this manner. Rational persuasion strategies of change use logical arguments and appeal to knowledge and facts to convince people to support change. When successful, this method can lead to more commitment to change. Shared-power strategies of change seek to involve other people in planning and implementing change. Of the three strategies, shared power creates the longest-lasting and most internalised commitments to the change.

Resistance to change and what can be done about it

Resistance to change is to be expected. Dealing successfully with resistance begins with an awareness that it represents 'feedback' that can be used by a change agent to increase the effectiveness of a change effort. People sometimes resist because they do not find value or believe in the change. They sometimes resist because they find the change strategy offensive or inappropriate. Sometimes they resist because they do not like or identify positively with the change agent as a person. Successful change agents are open to resistance and are capable of responding to it in ways that create a better 'fit' between the change, the situation and all the people involved.

Workplace stress

Stress is a state of tension experienced by individuals facing extraordinary demands, constraints or opportunities. Stress in the workplace is caused by work, non-work and personal factors (collectively known as stressors), including organisational change. Managers need to be able to minimise stress, cope with it themselves and help their employees cope with it.

Innovation in organisations

Innovation in organisations is the process of creating new ideas and putting those new ideas into practice. It is a process of 'invention + application' that turns creative ideas into products and/or processes of real benefit to people and organisations. Innovation is important to the private sector because it is so closely linked to competitiveness; that is, new or improved goods and services, or better ways of doing things ensure the financial viability of the enterprise. Innovation is also important in government business enterprises. Highly innovative organisations share certain features in common. They have supportive strategies, cultures, structures, staffing and top management. They tolerate mistakes and have a client-focused approach.

Chapter 14 study guide

OB Key terms

change agents, *p. 490*
changing, *p. 497*
force-coercion strategy, *p. 501*
incremental change, *p. 490*
innovation, *p. 508*
performance gap, *p. 491*
planned change, *p. 491*
process innovation, *p. 508*

product innovation, *p. 508*
radical change, *p. 490*
rational persuasion strategy, *p. 501*
refreezing, *p. 497*
resistance to change, *p. 503*
shared power strategy
   (normative-reeducative strategy),
   p. 502

stress, *p. 506*
stress prevention, *p. 507*
stressors, *p. 506*
unfreezing, *p. 496*
unplanned change, *p. 491*

OB Review questions

1. Explain the difference between planned and unplanned change. Give examples of situations where these occur.
2. Explain what managers can do to manage change and minimise resistance.

3. Explain the importance and benefits of innovation in organisations.
4. Discuss some of the things that managers can do to encourage and promote innovation in their organisations.

OB Application questions

1. Design a one-day training course targeting the mid-level managers of a medium-size organisation. There would be 20 participants coming from a diverse range of functions in the organisation, including production, design, administration, marketing, sales and product development. The aims of the program are to make participants aware of the meaning of 'cultural change', and also to gauge views on the current culture and potential required changes.

2. As a team leader in an organisation facing increasing competition from new entrants to your industry, you have been tasked with implementing changes within your unit. These changes are likely to disrupt current schedules, rosters and work processes significantly. Prepare a strategy for the unfreezing stage of the change process for your team, with a view to minimising resistance so that the changes can be implemented as smoothly as possible.

3. The best way to approach change is through the 'shared power' approach. Do you agree?

4. Discuss some of the work-related factors that can cause stress, then compare and contrast the following occupations in terms of the degree of stress they might generate: bus driver, call-centre operator, team leader and security guard. Choose one of these occupations and discuss the potential consequences of stress on the job holder and the organisation.

5. Many great ideas and inventions never achieve their full potential because of barriers within the organisational culture. Discuss.

6. You have developed a unique, simple-to-use and highly effective software package that will enable teachers to detect plagiarism from Internet sources in student assignments. As you have just completed your university degree, you are determined to set up your own business and market this product to universities around Australia. You also realise that, to build up

your business, you will need to create an organisation that encourages further innovation and product development. Based on the four features of an innovative organisation, describe the organisation that you would create to realise your dream of becoming a successful business entrepreneur.

1. Resistance to change is a complex response by employees when confronted with the possibility of unwelcome changes to their working lives. It is based on employee beliefs about the change (for example, there will be job cuts); emotions (such as anxiety, anger); and behaviours (for example, absenteeism, reduced work quality, undermining the changes). Conduct a search of the writing on the topic of resistance, identifying a range of employee response types emcompassing beliefs, emotions and behaviours. Where possible, identify organisations and situations in which these various responses occurred. What can you conclude about the way people respond to the possibility of unwelcome changes to their working lives? What can managers do to anticipate and minimise resistance to change?

2. What skills and competencies do good change agents have? Search the Internet to identify people who are presented as successful agents of change. You should find some good examples among the senior managers of large organisations in the business, public or community sectors. What skills and competencies do these people demonstrate? How have they used these skills and competencies to bring about change in their organisations?

Running project | OB

Complete the following tasks for your chosen organisation.

1. Identify factors that are driving change at your organisation. Try also to identify factors that are likely to produce a need for change in the near future.

2. (a) Choose one current factor from part 1 and explain the organisation's response.
   (b) Choose one future factor from part 1 and suggest an appropriate response. Does the organisation need to act now?

3. Referring to your answer to question 2(b), identify what resistance to change might be encountered, why it might arise and how it might be overcome.

4. How important is innovation to your organisation? Explain.

5. Identify factors in your organisation that (a) promote and (b) discourage innovation.

Individual activity | OB

Innovative attitude scale[54]

Introduction
Change and innovation are important to organisations. The following assessment surveys your readiness to accept and participate in innovation.

Instructions
Indicate the extent to which each of the following statements is true of either your actual behaviour or your intentions at work. That is, describe the way you are, or the way you intend to be, on the job. Use the following scale for your responses:

Almost always true	= 5
Often true	= 4
Not applicable	= 3
Seldom true	= 2
Almost never true	= 1

(continued)

1. I openly discuss with my boss how to get ahead.
2. I try new ideas and approaches to problems.
3. I take things or situations apart to find out how they work.
4. I welcome uncertainty and unusual circumstances related to my tasks.
5. I negotiate my salary openly with my supervisor.
6. I can be counted on to find a new use for existing methods or equipment.
7. Among my colleagues and coworkers, I will be the first or nearly the first to try out a new idea or method.
8. I take the opportunity to translate communications from other departments for my work group.
9. I demonstrate originality.
10. I will work on a problem that has caused others great difficulty.
11. I provide critical input towards a new solution.
12. I provide written evaluations of proposed ideas.
13. I develop contacts with experts outside my firm.
14. I use personal contacts to manoeuvre myself into choice work assignments.
15. I make time to pursue my own pet ideas or projects.
16. I set aside resources for the pursuit of a risky project.
17. I tolerate people who depart from organisational routine.
18. I speak out in staff meetings.
19. I work in teams to try to solve complex problems.
20. If my coworkers are asked, they will say I am a wit.

For an interpretation of your responses, turn to page 520.

OB *Group activity*

Force field analysis

Objectives
1. To improve your analytical skills for addressing complex situations
2. To show how force field analysis can aid understanding of change

Total time: 30–60 minutes

Procedure
1. Choose a situation in which you have high personal stakes (for example, how to get a better grade in a particular course, or how to get a promotion).
2. Using the following force field analysis form, apply the technique to your situation.
   (a) Describe the situation as it now exists.
   (b) Describe the situation as you would like it to be.
   (c) Identify the 'driving forces' — the factors that are presently helping to move things in the desired direction.
   (d) Identify the 'restraining forces' — the factors that are presently holding things back from moving in the desired direction.
3. Try to be as specific as possible in these descriptions of your situation. You should attempt to be exhaustive in your listing of these forces. List them all!
4. Now go back and classify the strength of each force as weak, medium or strong. Do this for both the driving and restraining forces.
5. At this point you should rank the forces on their ability to influence or control the situation.
6. In groups of three to four, share your analyses. Discuss the usefulness of and drawbacks to using this method for (a) personal situations and (b) organisations.
7. Be prepared to share the results of your group's discussion with the rest of the class.

Force field analysis form

Current situation

_____

_____

_____

_____

Preferred situation

_____

_____

_____

_____

Driving forces

_____

_____

_____

_____

_____

_____

_____

Restraining forces

_____

_____

_____

_____

_____

_____

_____

Case study: Planning for change at Alpha Metal Products `OB`

Herman Bent was appointed CEO of Alpha Metal Products during the early 1990s, at a critical point in the development of the Australian manufacturing industry. The government had announced a phasing-out of the high level of industry protection that had been in place for many years, resulting in much greater exposure to competition from overseas manufacturers. Alpha Metals, which produced a range of components used by carpenters and plumbers, was facing a difficult future, and Herman Bent had been employed by the board to save the company from ruin. During the first year of his tenure, Herman put considerable time into sizing up the situation facing the company, and by the end of the year was ready to brief the board on the situation. In the days leading up to that critical meeting, he reflected on what he had learned. Fortunately, the message he had for the board was not all bad. Certainly there were hard and uncertain times ahead, but with the right strategies in

place, Alpha Metals could emerge as a transformed but more viable company. He was confident that the board would support him, including the injection of funds needed over the next few years.

At that time the three manufacturing plants produced a range of products in steel, aluminium and plastics. Herman doubted that the steel products plant would survive in the global environment. Profit margins were already low and the plant and equipment were obsolete. He had decided to recommend that the plant be sold off to a BHP Billiton subsidiary. Aluminium, on the other hand, could be sourced locally at competitive prices, and the plant was relatively new. The environment for their aluminium components was relatively stable, and he did not anticipate big changes in the nature of demand or competitor activity over the next five years. Still, quality standards were disappointing and the plant manager, Stan, constantly complained of industrial problems and

(continued)

poor morale. Clearly, there was considerable scope to modernise management practices and maybe improve the product line and production efficiencies at the same time. Alpha Metals could come out well ahead with the aluminium products line if the situation was handled well.

The third division, plastics, was already doing quite well. Herman wanted to consolidate and build on the current setup, partly because of the future potential of plastics in the building industry. However, this would require an overhaul of operations and the discontinuation of some product lines that could be produced and marketed more cheaply by overseas competitors. Overall, the facility would need to be more innovative to ensure its future growth. He could see that to achieve this, considerable investment would be needed in research and development, and all plant managers and supervisors would need to build much closer links with the customer base. At present, the organisation structure was very traditional and employees at all levels generally lacked the full range of technical, management and marketing skills needed to run a modern manufacturing facility. However, from his discussions with the managers and staff from plastics, there was broad support for the changes that Herman had in mind.

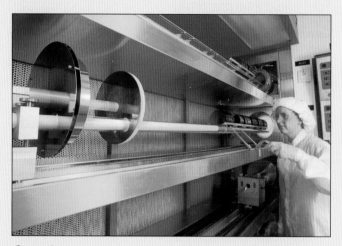

Questions

1. Discuss the pressures for change in the case of Alpha Metal Products.

2. Discuss the suitability of each of the planned change strategies in relation to Alpha Metal Products. Should Herman Bent adopt a different change strategy for the plastics and aluminium facilities?

3. Do you think that the employees will resist change? What can Herman Bent do to minimise any resistance?

OB *Suggested reading*

Nohria Beer (ed.), *Breaking the code of change* (Boston: Harvard Business School Press, 2000).

Wayne H Bovey and Andy Hede, 'Resistance to organizational change: the role of cognitive and affective processes', *Leadership and Organization Development Journal*, vol. 22, no. 8 (2001), pp. 372–82.

AJ Chopra, *Managing the peoples side of innovation* (Bloomfield, CT: Kumarian Press Inc, 1999).

Thomas Clarke and Stewart Clegg, *Changing paradigms: the transformation of management knowledge for the 21st century* (London: Harper Collins Business, 1998).

Daryl R Conner, *Leading at the edge of chaos: how to create the nimble organization* (New York: John Wiley & Sons, 1998).

Lynn Fossum, *Understanding organizational change* (Menlo Park, CA: Thomson Crisp Learning, 1989).

Keith Goffin and Rick Mitchell, *Innovation management* (New York: McMillan, 2005).

G Hamel and C Prahalad, *Competing for the future* (Boston: Harvard Business School Press, 1994).

Jean Helms Mills and Kern Mills, *Making sense of organizational change* (London: Routledge, 2003).

Craig C Kuriger, *Organizational change: case studies in the real world, 2004* (Boca Raton, FL: Universal Publishers, 2004).

Francis Stickland, *The dynamics of change: insights from the natural world into organisational transition* (London: Routledge, 1998).

Tudor Rickards, *Creativity and the management of change* (Oxford: Blackwell Publishing, 1999).

Michael A Roberto and Lynne C Levesque, 'The art of making change initiatives stick', *MIT Sloan Management Review*, vol. 46, no. 4 (2005), pp. 53–60.

Marvin Washington and Marla Hacker, 'Why change fails: knowledge counts', *Leadership and Organization Development Journal*, vol. 26, no. 5 (2005), pp. 400–11.

Rachid M Zeffane and David E Morgan, 'Organisational change and trust: can management be trusted to change', *International Journal of Human Resource Management*, special issue on Trust in the Workplace, vol. 14, no. 1 (2003), pp. 55–75.

1. Rachid M Zeffane, 'Patterns of organizational commitment and perceived management styles: a comparison of public and private sector employees', *Tavistock Institute Journal of Human Relations*, vol. 47, no. 8 (1994), pp. 13–27.

2. For more on the concepts of frame-breaking and frame-bending change see David Nadler and Michael Tushman, *Strategic organizational design* (Glenview, IL: Scott, Foresman, 1988).

3. Noel Tichy, *Managing strategic change: technical, political and cultural dynamics* (New York: John Wiley & Sons, 1983).

4. Cliff Bowman, 'Stuck in the old routines', *European Management Journal*, vol. 12, no. 1 (1994), p. 76.

5. Jenny Stewart and Paul Kringas, 'Change management — strategy and values: six case studies from the Australian public sector', Centre for Research in Public Sector Management, University of Canberra, http://www.blis.canberra.edu.au/crpsm/research/pdf/stewartkringas.pdf (viewed 5 January 2006).

6. F Graetz, 'Strategic change leadership', *Management Decision*, vol. 38, no. 8 (2000), pp. 550–62.

7. Robert Miles, *Corporate comeback: the story of renewal and transformation at National Semiconductor* (San Francisco: Jossey-Bass, 1997).

8. F. Graetz, op. cit.; Robert Miles, op. cit.

9. WE Deming, *Out of the crisis* (Cambridge, MA: MIT Center for Advanced Engineering Study, 1986).

10. See for example Sharon Parker, 'Tactical change' (2004), www2.agsm.edu.au/agsm/web.nsf/Content/AGSMMagazine-Tacticalchange (viewed 5 January 2006).

11. P Gagliardi, 'The creation and change of organisational cultures: a conceptual framework', *Organisation Studies*, vol. 7, no. 2 (1986), pp. 117_34, cited in Sharon Parker, 'Tactical change' (2004), www2.agsm.edu.au/agsm/web.nsf/Content/AGSMMagazine-Tacticalchange (viewed 5 January 2006).

12. J Silvester, NR Anderson and F Patterson, 'Organizational culture change: an intergroup attributional analysis', *Journal of Occupational and Organizational Psychology*, vol. 72, no. 1 (March 1999), p. 1.

13. Mark Bannerman, 'Shareholders react', transcript of Australian Broadcasting Corporation television program *Lateline*, broadcast 18 May 2001.

14. S Weston and J Harper, 'The challenge of change', *Ivey Business Quarterly*, vol. 63, no. 2 (Winter 1998), p. 78.

15. Rosabeth Moss Kanter, Barry A Stein and Todd D Jick, 'Meeting the challenges of change', *World Executive's Digest* (May 1993), pp. 22–7.

16. See for example Ralph H Kilmann, *Beyond the quick fix* (San Francisco: Jossey-Bass, 1984); Noel M Tichy and Mary Anne Devanna, *The transformational leader* (New York: John Wiley & Sons, 1986).

17. Robert A Cooke, 'Managing change in organizations' in Gerald Zaltman (ed.), *Management principles for nonprofit organizations* (New York: American Management Association, 1979). See also David A Nadler, 'The effective management of organizational change' in Jay W Lorsch (ed.), *Handbook of organizational behavior* (Englewood Cliffs, NJ: Prentice Hall, 1987), pp. 358–69.

18. Kurt Lewin, 'Group decision and social change' in GE Swanson, TM Newcomb and EL Hartley (eds), *Readings in social psychology* (New York: Holt, Rinehart and Winston, 1952), p. 4.

19. Accel Team, 'Team building', www.accel-team.com/techniques/force_field_analysis.html (viewed 5 January 2006).

20. Charles Sturt University, 'Managing change', NSW HSC online, http://hsc.csu.edu.au/business_studies/mgt_change/managing_change/Managechange.html#top (viewed 27 September 2005).

21. Tichy and Devanna, op. cit., p. 44.

22. Rachid Zeffane, 'Dynamics of strategic change: critical issues in fostering positive organizational change', *Leadership and Organization Development Journal*, vol. 17, no. 7 (1996), pp. 36–43.

23. Tichy, op. cit.

24. See Noel M Tichy, *Managing strategic change: technical, political, and cultural dynamics* (New York: John Wiley & Sons, 1983).

25. ibid.

26. E Dent and S Goldberg, 'Challenging "resistance to change"', *Journal of Applied Behavioral Science*, vol. 35, no. 1 (1999).

27. Dent and Goldberg, op. cit., p. 31.

28. Dent and Goldberg, op. cit., pp. 25–41.

29. Robert Chin and Kenneth D Benne, 'General strategies for effecting changes in human systems' in Warren G Bennis, Kenneth D Benne, Robert Chin and Kenneth E Corey (eds), *The planning of change*, 3rd ed. (New York: Holt, Rinehart and Winston, 1969), pp. 22–45.

30. Rachid M Zeffane, 'The downsizing paradox: problems in the quest for leaner organizations', *Journal of Industrial Affairs*, vol. 4, no. 1 (1995), pp. 45–8.

31. Rachid M Zeffane and Ferdinand Gul, 'The effects of task characteristics and sub-unit structure on information processing', *Information Processing and Management*, vol. 29, no. 1 (1993), pp. 21–37.

32. Rachid M Zeffane, 'Patterns of organizational commitment and perceived management styles: a comparison of public and private sector employees', *Tavistock Institute Journal of Human Relations*, vol. 47, no. 8 (1994), pp. 13–27; M Emery and M Emery, 'Participative design: work and community life' in M Emery (ed.), *Participative design for participative democracy* (Canberra: Australian National University, Centre for Continuing Education, 1992).

33. Tom Lupton, 'Organisational change: "top-down" or "bottom-up" management?', *Personnel Review*, vol. 20, no. 3 (1991), pp. 4–10.

34. The change strategy examples in this part are developed from an exercise reported in J William Pfeiffer and John E Jones, *A handbook of structured experiences for human relations training*, vol. II (La Jolla, CA: University Associates, 1973).

35. Dexter Dunphy and Doug Stace, 'The strategic management of corporate change', *Human Relations*, vol. 46, no. 8 (August 1993), pp. 905–20.

36. Carter McNamara, 'Basic context for organizational change', http://www.managementhelp.org/mgmnt/orgchnge.htm (viewed 27 September 2005).

37. Donald Klein, 'Some notes on the dynamics of resistance to change: the defender role' in Bennis et al. (eds), op. cit., pp. 117–24.

38. Kostas N Dervitsiotis, 'The challenge of managing organizational change: exploring the relationship of re-engineering, developing learning organizations and total quality management', *Total Quality Management*, vol. 9, no. 1 (February 1998), p. 109.

39. See Everett M Rogers and F Floyd Shoemaker, *Communication of innovations*, 2nd ed. (New York: The Free Press, 1971).

40. John P Kotter and Leonard A Schlesinger, 'Choosing strategies for change', *Harvard Business Review*, vol. 57 (March/April 1979), pp. 109–12.

41. Arthur P Brief, Randall S Schuler and Mary Van Sell, *Managing job stress* (Boston: Little, Brown and Company, 1981).

42. Portions of this treatment of stress developed from John R Schermerhorn, Jr, *Management for productivity*, 3rd ed. (New York: John Wiley & Sons, 1989), pp. 647–52.

43. Cary L Cooper, 'Executive stress around the world', *University of Wales Review of Business and Economics* (Winter 1987), pp. 3–8.

44. L Savery and J Luks, 'Long hours at work: are they dangerous and do people consent to them?', *Leadership and Organization Development Journal*, vol. 21, no. 6 (2000), pp. 307–10.

45. N Way, 'The fast lane speeds up', *Business Review Weekly* (11 June 1999), pp. 84–7.

46. Savery and Luks, op. cit.

47. See Edward B Roberts, 'Managing invention and innovation', *Research Technology Management* (January/February 1988), pp. 1–19.

48. John R Schermerhorn, Jr, *Management for productivity*, 4th ed.(New York: John Wiley & Sons, 1993), p. 661.

49. James Bryant Quinn, 'Managing innovation controlled chaos', *Harvard Business Review* (May/June 1985).

50. 'Product innovation', *Management* (May 1996).

51. Cyber India Online, 'ISA launches initiative to promote innovation', http://www.ciol.com/content/news/2005/105010703.asp (viewed 28 September 2005).

52. Based on Quinn, op. cit.

53. Based on Victor SL Tan, 'Change is the CEO's imperative', *New Straits Times* (22 May 1993), p. A1.

54. JE Ettlie and RD O'Keefe, 'Innovative attitudes, values and intentions in organizations', *Journal of Management Studies*, vol. 19 (1982), p. 176.

Interpretation of 'Individual activity'

To determine your score on the 'Innovative attitude scale', simply add the numbers associated with your responses to the 20 items. The higher your score, the more receptive to innovation you are. You can compare your score with that of others to see if you seem to be more or less receptive to innovation than a comparable group of business students.

Score	Percentile*
39	5
53	16
62	33
71	50
80	68
89	86
97	95

* Percentile indicates the percentage of the people who are expected to score below you.

Part 4 case study

THE UPS AND DOWNS OF NATIONAL MUTUAL/AXA

Introduction

National Mutual was established in Australia and New Zealand more than 100 years ago. Over the years, it became a very successful insurance company and by the mid-1980s was pursuing growth so aggressively that it overtook AMP to lead the market in winning new business.

To fund the growth strategy, National Mutual drew heavily on the financial reserves that it had accumulated over a century of successful operations. Specifically:

- National Mutual provided business development loans to its network of agents, many of whom spent the money on personal assets rather than investing it in their business. Therefore, of course, the productivity gains expected to come from this huge expenditure were never realised.
- National Mutual invested significant sums of money overseas in a bid to become a global player in funds management, life insurance and superannuation. However, the company did not have sufficient capital and operational capacity to back up its global ambitions.
- National Mutual offered customers higher returns than competitors. In doing so, though, it had to credit more money to its policyholder returns than it was receiving on its investments.

By the late 1980s, the company had severely undermined its solvency.

Facing up to the realities

The extent of the problem became apparent when it was found that National Mutual would not be able to meet the capital adequacy and solvency standards proposed in the draft 1992 Life Insurance Act. In addition, a proposed merger with ANZ Bank was disallowed,

partly due to government concerns about the underlying capital positions of both organisations.

National Mutual had a culture of pride, based on its 120 years of success and its prominent position in the Australian market, but its financial problems could not be denied. The company took several major steps in the 1990s to try to repair its balance sheet. In 1992 it undertook a capital restructuring. The following year, it sold off most of its international assets. In 1995, it demutualised (that is, it changed from being owned by its members to being owned by shareholders). French insurance company AXA acquired a 51 per cent shareholding. National Mutual listed on the stock exchange in 1996. In 1999, National Mutual was rebranded AXA.

Despite these significant changes within the company, National Mutual found that the newly deregulated Australasian market was changing even more. New players entered National Mutual's traditional markets, putting substantial pressure on pricing. There was significant growth and innovation in the retail investment and superannuation segments of the industry as competitors responded quickly to changing economic and demographic conditions.

National Mutual's business model was fundamentally unchanged. Its products were not competitive, its costs were 20 per cent above industry standards, and its distribution system was out of touch with the new model of financial advisers offering products tailored to individual needs. As a result, it had lost considerable market share in the profitable and growing retail investment and superannuation markets, but still had a large, unprofitable position in risk insurance. Over the decade of the 1990s, it had slipped to become a second-tier player.

Asian markets come to the rescue

While National Mutual had been forced to sell its US and European assets, the Asian interests it had retained had performed surprisingly well. Asia, in fact, would ultimately save National Mutual from financial failure.

(continued)

The international team in Melbourne adapted its low-cost Hong Kong approach to other Asian markets and by 1999, 75 per cent of profit was coming from Asia, compared to 25 per cent from Australia and New Zealand.

Leadership, structure and change

AXA decided the Asia–Pacific operation (now operating as AXA Asia–Pacific) required a major overhaul to improve the performance of the Australian and New Zealand businesses. It appointed a new chief executive officer in 2000, with the specific task of transforming the Australian and New Zealand operations.

Within a few months of arrival, the new CEO established an extensive, organisation-wide change program addressing every critical aspect of the business in Australia and New Zealand: distribution, marketing, product, e-commerce, customer service, human relations and others. The former head of the Asian businesses was appointed to oversee the three-year change program. This ensured the change program was not complicated by any existing vested interests in the Australian or New Zealand businesses. Most of the senior management team and the team at the next level down were replaced by new teams of internal and external people. This was necessary both to improve the company's management skills and to overcome resistance to change.

Central to the transformation program — known within AXA as 'K5' (5 key strategic objectives) — were five clear targets to be achieved within three years:

1. double the value of new business
2. enter the top five for net retail funds inflow
3. halve the management expense ratio
4. obtain a place in the top 25 per cent of ASSIRT/ AC Nielsen's service rankings (the ranking is based on aspects of service such as investment capability, investment team quality, investment performance, consistency and investment process quality)
5. rank in the top 25 per cent of AXA's global survey of employee satisfaction.

AXA realised that the company culture had to change, and that how the business changes were put in place would be as important as the changes themselves. To bring K5 to fruition, AXA engaged in a series of changes at the strategic and structural levels.

The company put a lot of effort into communication. Its communication program included a 'reality check' designed to create dissatisfaction with the present. This was combined with changes to the management group designed to communicate that the current poor business outcomes would not be accepted in the future. The communications program was recognised by the Public Relations Community of Australia's awards for employee communications.

A very strong governance and control process was implemented at the executive management level. It was overseen by a steering committee comprising the CEO, program director, chief financial officer, another executive and a consultant. A number of dedicated centralised project teams led the various facets of the change program such as project management, and training and development.

The company also looked to better match its capabilities to its needs. The problem of inadequate performance in investment management was solved by entering a joint venture for asset management with Alliance Capital, a company within the AXA Group with a first-class reputation in that field. In areas in which the company did not have the requisite skills internally — such as property management — it outsourced. AXA sold non-core assets such as trustee companies, payroll companies, and mortgage and commercial lending businesses. Core operating processes and systems that had previously been unreliable were stabilised, resulting in better customer service. Key products and key markets were analysed in depth. The analysis then informed significant upgrades and new product launches in retail investment and superannuation, designed to make the company more competitive in the market. The company restructured its relationship with distributors. It terminated unsatisfactory agency arrangements and created new agency terms designed to establish a stronger position, with advisers operating more modern and robust financial planning practices.

By the end of 2000, a new structure backed up by revitalised governance, leadership and management were firmly in place. The company had made a genuine attempt to address many of the problems it had been facing.

Improved outcomes

By mid-2002, results showed the company was clearly headed in the right direction to meet its K5 goals.

In relation to its first goal — to double the value of new business — AXA had achieved growth in new business sales in the sectors most important to its future, including investment, superannuation and master trusts.

In relation to its second goal — to enter the top five for net retail funds inflow — plans to refocus on more profitable retail investment products had caused some increase in outflows. Notwithstanding that, by mid-2000, for the first time in almost five years, the company experienced a net funds inflow. This had grown to almost A$2 billion for the 12 months to June 2002.

In relation to its third goal — to halve the management expense ratio — the company was doing extremely well. Recurring management expenses had been cut by more than one-third since the start of the program, against a backdrop of rising sales volumes. Part of the saving has been used to fund reinvestments in the business, with 20 per cent of all costs being business investments.

In relation to its fourth goal — to obtain a place in the top 25 per cent of ASSIRT/AC Nielsen's service rankings — AXA improved relative to its competitors across all the dimensions of service, but was still below the median for the market.

In relation to its fifth goal — to reach the top 25 per cent in AXA's world survey of employee satisfaction — by 2001 employee satisfaction had significantly improved, with the company just outside the top 25 per cent. By the next year, employee satisfaction was the highest of all AXA business worldwide.

Notwithstanding the improvement in all areas, there was a gap between where the company was and where it wanted to be by this stage of the program, particularly in relation to the second goal of net funds inflow.

Sustaining improvement

By the end of the three-year K5 transformation program, AXA had made enormous progress. It had achieved four of the K5 goals. The goal it did not achieve was to reduce the management expense ratio by 50 per cent. It had, however, made significant progress in that area too, achieving a 40 per cent reduction.

In April 2004, AXA launched a new set of objectives for Australia and New Zealand in a bid to increase the value of the Australian and New Zealand operations by 65 per cent. The three-year AXA 6 program included the goals:

1. double the value of new business
2. consistently be in the top five in the market in terms of net retail funds flow
3. double the value of funds under advice
4. reduce the cost to income ratio by one-third
5. consistently be in the top five in the market in terms of service to advisers
6. remain in the top 25 per cent of AXA's global survey of employee satisfaction.

By 2005, AXA's Australian operations had A$45.6 billion of funds under management and total gross inflows of almost A$10.8 billion. AXA's New Zealand operations had NZ$6.9 billion of funds under management and total gross inflows of over NZ$2.1 billion, and were in the top three in the wealth management and financial protection markets.

AXA's progress towards achieving its AXA 6 goals can be found in its annual reports, available from AXA's web site at www.axiaasiapacific.com.au

Sources: Adapted from Andrew Penn, 'Transformational change: a case study', Mt Eliza Business School, www.mteliza.com.au (viewed 27 October 2005); additional information from: AXA Asia Pacific Holdings Limited, 'Chairman's address', Annual General Meeting, 15 February 2001, www.axa-asiapacific.com.au (viewed 27 October 2005); AXA Asia Pacific Holdings Limited, 'Analyst compendium for the 6 months ending 30 June 2002', www.axa-asiapacific.com.au (viewed 27 October 2005), AXA Asia Pacific Holdings Limited, annual reports, www.axia-asiapacific.com.au (viewed 28 October 2005).

Questions

1. Explain some of the reasons for the decline of National Mutual from the 1980s to the end of the 1990s.
2. Analyse and describe the change strategy adopted by AXA to redress its problems.
3. What were some of the key ingredients of the resurgence of AXA's fortunes?
4. How would you describe the leadership style of the chief executive?

PART 5

CASE STUDIES

	PART/S CASE APPLIES TO			
	1	**2**	**3**	**4**
CASE STUDY 1 Solutions Software Company		✓	✓	✓
CASE STUDY 2 Teams at Fisher & Paykel		✓	✓	
CASE STUDY 3 Queensland Health crisis	✓	✓	✓	✓
CASE STUDY 4 Workout World	✓			✓
CASE STUDY 5 KD Transport	✓			✓

Case study 1

Solutions Software Company

VAL MORRISON

Jane Gordon is General Manager, Australia of Solutions Software Company (SSC), a leading international software company whose Australian division is based in Sydney. Jane is relatively new to the company — she has only been with them for three months — and she is having a bad day. On two separate occasions during the morning two of her senior sales consultants, Susan and David, have approached her asking for more flexible or, if possible, reduced working hours over the next few months. Jane thinks this is not a good time because, although sales have been steady and Susan and David are performing well, she has been getting pressure from head office to win more clients. Competition in the industry is at an all-time high and SSC's market share is constantly under threat.

SSC already has one of its senior sales consultants, Amanda, working flexible hours. Amanda has been with the company for two years and has an excellent track record and good client base. She is a single parent with two children at primary school and last year made an arrangement with Jane's predecessor to work more flexible hours in order to care for her children. While she still completes a full-time working week, Amanda is able to start later in the morning after taking the children to school then makes up her time by taking short lunch breaks and working occasional Saturdays.

SSC has always taken pride in being compassionate towards its employees and has adopted the philosophy that all employees should lead a balanced life between work and leisure. Families of employees are encouraged to take part in social activities, and management at SSC has been known to help out those employees who have suffered financial stress or experienced other personal setbacks.

Jane came to SSC from Hardware-Software, a Melbourne-based company that had a very different culture to SSC. The software industry is known to be tough and Hardware-Software would expect its employees to work long hours, take work home and be in the office at least one day during the weekend. Trying to take holidays was always an issue, especially as staff were not allowed to accumulate them from year to year. As a result, staff turnover was quite high and two years at Hardware-Software was considered a long-term appointment. Jane worked for Hardware-Software for five years before coming to SSC. She began as junior sales support and after 18 months was promoted to senior consultant. Two years later she became national sales manager. Jane had no problem with the long hours but always planned to move back to Sydney, her home town, which she loves. It was a difficult decision to make at the time but when the opportunity to be general manager of a software company came up, how could she refuse? Hardware-Software was actually Jane's first job after she left university and had really been her only working experience other than several short-term casual jobs in the hospitality industry during her years of study. Also, Jane was a later entry into university as she chose to travel overseas for 12 months after finishing high school.

For Jane, the cultural transition from Hardware-Software to SSC has not been easy so far. While she likes to consider herself a relatively easygoing, amiable type of person socially, her attitude to work is one of strict focus; achieving corporate goals is her first priority. Jane has always been single minded, and even while studying at university she was very focused and devoted many long hours working to gain her degrees. After completing her undergraduate studies, Jane stayed on to do honours, then a masters degree. Jane's single-minded attitude also resulted in her very quick progress up the corporate ladder at Hardware-Software. For a 28-year-old she has certainly achieved a lot and is in a very senior position compared to others of similar age. Because Jane lives alone and has only a small circle of friends and relatives in Sydney, she chooses to spend much of her supposed leisure time at the office. She does, however, intend joining a social club but hasn't decided exactly what that will be. Whatever interests she had when she was younger have seemed to become completely overtaken by her professional life.

Jane's appointment at SSC has not been particularly well received by some of the senior staff. Part of that is due to the reputation of Hardware-Software, and the fact that Jane worked there for five years clearly suggests to others that she is a workaholic with very few other priorities in her life. This perception was formed by the senior staff prior to Jane's arrival at SSC and, as she has only been with the company for a short time, there really has not been much opportunity for her to try to change that perception. Jane has been very preoccupied trying to orientate herself into the position as general manager and has not really spent much time developing the social aspect of the office environment.

Prior to Jane's appointment Susan had applied for the job as general manager and had total support from David and Amanda, as well as other members of staff at SSC. As well as being senior sales consultant, Susan is also supervisor of the entire sales department, which has a total of 14 employees. Susan has been with SSC for six years and is an excellent mentor for David and Amanda. Susan initiated a staff development program several years ago and has put many hours of her own time into counseling some of the younger members of the sales team. She is fully aware of the need to develop staff with a view to retaining them in the company as turnover in the software industry is high due to the competitive nature of the industry.

When Susan failed to get the position as general manager and Jane was brought in from another state, morale among the senior sales consultants dropped and Susan in particular began to question her role at SSC, using David and Amanda as 'sounding blocks' on many occasions. This, of course, did not help the overall acceptance of Jane's appointment and tended to add to the negativity which was already developing. Now, three months later, the friendly culture at SSC is certainly not what it used to be, even among the senior sales consultants who are seriously considering other options as their loyalty and motivation diminishes and priorities are reshuffled.

Since Jane's appointment, and with no other option for promotion in sight, Susan now wants to work flexible hours as she feels she is suffering burnout and would like to concentrate on her health so she can start a family. Even her doctor has said she works too many hours and should cut back. Susan's husband totally supports this and would really prefer that she gave up work altogether.

David has requested a more flexible, reduced workload so he can train for the Australian basketball selection game in three months time, as he wants to make the national team. He is a single man who is ranked in the top ten amateur basketball players in Australia. David has been with the company for five years and has an excellent track record and good client base.

Both David and Susan know of Amanda's flexible working arrangement and, although they appreciate SSC's philosophy towards families, they think this should apply equally to all employees wanting to lead a balanced lifestyle, not just those with children.

Jane has told both David and Susan that she will meet with them tomorrow to discuss their situations. Personally, Jane doesn't think either of them should be given more flexible hours, especially after her time spent with Hardware-Software and the sacrifices she has made in her career. Jane also doesn't think Amanda should be given preference, but that is something she inherited when she took over as general manager of SSC. Jane is concerned about the pressure from head office as all staff issues have to be approved by them and, once they find out that their entire senior team now seeks flexible working hours, she knows it will be difficult to support, especially as the pressure is on to increase the client base. However, Jane is also vaguely aware that, although there are only three senior sales consultants at SSC, there is a very good pool of second-tier sales people who are currently being developed by Susan and who could quite possibly be promoted should a vacancy suddenly become available. She makes a mental note to check this out before meeting with David and Susan tomorrow, just in case things get a little heated and she has to offer an ultimatum. Hopefully, it won't come to that.

Jane leaves the office that night knowing she will not sleep well. Tomorrow the situation has to be resolved. Fortunately, the meeting times with David and Susan have yet to be scheduled so Jane decides to meet with them both, separately, in the afternoon so she can spend the entire morning reviewing the staff situation at SSC and developing a sound strategy.

Questions

1. List and briefly describe each issue that Jane faces. Consider those things that are directly related to Jane as a manager, linking each of the issues to organisational behaviour theories and concepts.

2. Assuming Jane has no confidante at SSC, if you were a close friend of hers and that evening she called you and asked for advice on how to approach the meetings with David and Susan, what would you say? As a close friend it is expected that you will take into consideration Jane's personal and professional attributes when preparing your answer.

3. Assume that Jane has had a successful meeting with both David and Susan and they have agreed to consider a redesign of their existing roles to accommodate a flexible work arrangement. Bearing in mind that the outcome of this must be presented, by Jane, to SSC head office, how would you structure the redesign in order to benefit both SSC corporate goals and the satisfaction of the employees concerned? Remember to consider all employees at SSC, not just David and Susan.

This case is fictional.

Case study 2

Teams at Fisher & Paykel

MICHELE FROMHOLTZ

Background

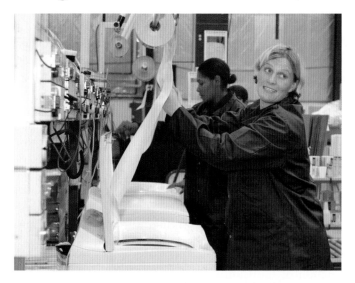

Fisher & Paykel is a New Zealand-based manufacturing company. It is best known for its range of household whitegoods but is also a successful manufacturer of healthcare products. The company's Range and Dishwasher Division is based at Mosgiel, near Dunedin, in New Zealand, and employs 400 people in manufacturing roles, along with 170 in support roles.

Fisher & Paykel had long enjoyed a reputation for teamwork, but the company had never formally defined its teams; rather, natural teams had developed around small, functional work areas. Over time, however, the company became concerned that there was too much emphasis on assembly skills and that the teams had little scope for self-direction. When export tariffs were removed and competitive products flooded the New Zealand market, the company considered innovation as an important way to differentiate its products rather than engaging in a price war. It set about enhancing the team culture to encourage improvement and creativity among all of its workers in a bid to maintain its innovation leadership.

Taking a team approach

Fisher & Paykel management was already influenced by studies of *kaizen*, an approach that emphasises continuous improvement. The company sent key operational staff on study tours to Japan's Kaizen Institute and on their return established pilot team projects. After several months, management decided to pursue team processes across the division and set up a 'planning project team' to demonstrate how 'team working' could be implemented throughout the organisation.

The vision was to manage the division through a network of work teams, each of which would be self-directing. They were to be trained and empowered to make improvements in their own workplaces. The company hoped the team-working approach would help achieve incremental gains in quality, control costs and facilitate employee acceptance of continuous change and market response.

Fisher & Paykel called its teams 'everyday workplace teams' (EDWT). These teams were built on the belief that team membership should be an integral part of employees' everyday work. An EDWT would encourage contributions from members, adopt a unified vision, understand and use quality tools, have a positive focus, operate within defined boundaries, be responsible for plans linked to goals and have a plan to develop the team, the members and the process. To support team development, four additional project teams were established: a 'communication team' to improve the communication systems to help the teams; an 'ideal training team' to look at training and members' individual development needs; a 'pay scale team' to look at how team skills could be rewarded within the competency-based pay systems; and an 'implementation team', set up to implement the entire team process and ensure that an understanding of the EDWT concept was communicated throughout the division, and to identify the boundaries for teams to operate within.

The EDWTs, built on the existing teams, had been based on functional boundaries. The challenge was to win the employees' support for cultural change while also challenging entrenched 'comfort zones'. Some past change projects had been seen as management fads that would not last. The implementation team pushed for training time in weekly team meetings, beginning with team-building activities then moving on to activities to improve work performance. Each team leader was to facilitate the sessions with the help of an interactive, activity-based workbook. Modules included communication skills, team building, working together and running meetings. Working on the workbook was part of the process of developing functional teams, developing and supporting team skills in individual team members, linking the team to divisional goals and prompting the team to work towards improving the operation of its work area. The company's commitment to the EDWT concept was demonstrated by stopping production to allow time for these sessions. All teams were to use the workbook over a 12-month period to develop a division-wide common understanding. Each team gave a presentation to management on its team development and improvement activities at the end of the process.

The members of the initial planning teams were the change agents (or champions of change). They reported that they were proud of the change, but they recognised that their own enthusiasm might have obscured some important considerations. They were stopped occasionally by reality checks and had to accept the lack of 100 per cent buy-in to change. Despite great improvements, they still see the change process as frustratingly slow.

Team leaders experienced the most significant change, as they had originally been charge hands or technical experts. Now they spend much less time on line activities and much more time utilising people-management skills, planning and facilitating team sessions, and coaching and developing team members. They also deal with developing business plans, monitoring production, problem solving and reporting.

Several team leaders chose to step down and return to the line. New people, mostly outside candidates, filled these roles. They are being supported by a leadership program with relevant training. Some of the new people found the role too challenging, or felt it did not offer them the future they wanted. Some felt ill-prepared for their new role, since they were used to taking instructions. Others quickly adapted to seeing themselves as translators of ideas, who made them usable and got them actually happening. These individuals have moved from the 'leave your brain at the door' mentality to become active participants, who must nonetheless still deal with resistance from within their teams. They see one of their roles as dealing with negativity among team members. Some, however, felt a lack of support from the company in dealing with those who did not subscribe to the team philosophy.

Team working is now well embedded. Most team members have accepted it, and many have developed skills beyond the duties of their operational jobs. Those who have embraced team working expect the company to take note of their suggestions for improvement and anticipate that the opportunities for their involvement will grow. Among those who have resisted team working, resistance has often been passive rather than active. Some labelled EDWT as 'every day waste of time'. Some professional and salaried teams felt the workbook was not designed to suit their needs. The level of team member buy-in seemed to depend on team leader enthusiasm.

Benefits and lessons for the future

Overall, the introduction of self-managed teams led to improvements that generated cost savings through fewer reject products, less wastage, better cycle times and lower rework times. The cumulative effect across the 31 teams was substantial. Teams are now able to organise their own work area and manage their own workloads, saving in the use of engineers, reducing downtime from changes to production processes or design, and achieving greater acceptance of changes.

Team members can take on specific roles, such as responsibility for maintenance of the work area or data collection. This is encouraged by the competency-based scale, but there is no 'sanction' for failing to develop team-working skills.

The company may in future do some things differently to facilitate change more effectively — for example, ensuring that the vision is matched by a clear plan for implementation, and that all objections and points of caution are debated before implementation. Better contingency planning for barriers to change could also have been more thoroughly considered. More time could have been spent consulting with and gaining commitment from team leaders, who were the individuals who had the most to lose or gain. Although the introduction of the team-working system has not been rapid, there is some acceptance that the slower introduction process may have allowed greater consultation, even at the expense of 'watering down' the vision. Reflecting a typical caution in the literature about teams, Fisher & Paykel has had problems matching the organisation's reward and control systems to its team-working endeavours. The changes to pay scales may not have gone far enough, and although linking the acquisition of generic skills to pay might be valid for lower-paid workers, it had less relevance for those who have reached the top through service and acquisition of manufacturing or assembly skills. The universality of the workbook approach might need review, with acknowledgement that specific issues may be relevant to some sections of the organisation.

It is not yet clear whether the investment of time, money and energy has delivered the hoped-for benefits. From the accounts given, however, it seems that the organisational climate has improved, and employees judge the process a success. Team working continues and is becoming embedded in the company. In the company's own words: 'We are proud of our devolved management processes and our flexible, open team environment where everyone plays a role in influencing and driving our progress as a global company'.[1]

Questions

1. Fisher & Paykel used 'natural teams' as the basis of the transition to the EDWTs. What are the differences between the natural teams and the new self-managing work teams, and how can these differences be explained in terms of what you have learned about groups and teams?

2. Fisher & Paykel did not isolate the introduction of self-managing work teams to the shop floor. Why did the organisation go to such lengths when introducing teams into their organisation?

3. In introducing the EDWTs, what team-building strategies were used at Fisher & Paykel?

4. How effective do you think the team processes have been at Fisher & Paykel, and what future do you see for the use of teams at the company?

End note

1. Adapted from M Mallon and T Kearney, 'Team development at Fisher and Paykel: the introduction of "Everyday Workplace Teams"', *Asia Pacific Journal of Human Resources*, vol. 39, no. 1 (2001), pp. 93–106; additional information from Fisher & Paykel corporate web site, www.fp.co.nz.

Case study 3

Queensland Health crisis

Introduction

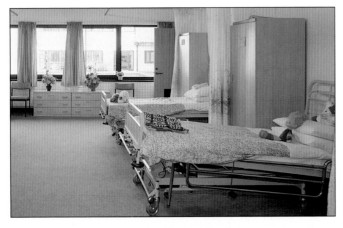

Queensland Health is the Queensland government body responsible for delivering public health care to Queenslanders. It provides hospital inpatient, outpatient and emergency care, aged care, health promotion programs, and community and mental health services to a diverse and growing population.[1] Its 2005–06 budget was A$5.4 billion.

In 2005, the Queensland Government initiated a wide-ranging inquiry into Queensland Health — the Queensland Public Hospitals Commission of Inquiry, headed by Geoffrey Davies. The inquiry was held in response to public, media and industry pressure after a series of bungled operations by surgeon Jayant Patel at Bundaberg Hospital, and to claims that hospital management had not appropriately responded to staff concerns about Patel. Various professional groups had alleged that the culture of Queensland Health was one of over-bureaucratisation, secrecy, bullying and intimidation — all to the detriment of health care.

A separate review of Queensland Health's systems — the Queensland Health Systems Review — was headed by Peter Forster of The Consultancy Bureau. The review observed and held discussions with several thousand staff, consulted with various stakeholders and received about 1300 formal submissions. The review's final report was handed down in September 2005; it was heavily critical of Queensland Health's culture and recommending wide-ranging changes to organisational structure, leadership, culture, job design and other factors. Most of the material in this case relates to the findings of the Queensland Health Systems Review. Some material also refers to the Queensland Public Hospitals Commission of Inquiry.

Findings and recommendations

The Queensland Health Systems Review report concluded that, in general, Queensland Health personnel were dedicated, professional and committed to providing the best possible care for patients and other customers. However, various aspects of the Queensland Health organisational structure, leadership, culture and job design prevented individuals and the organisation overall from delivering the high-quality service that was desired. The operation of Queensland Health is further complicated by the political importance and sensitivity of health care and the influence of the state government, particularly through the Minister for Health, who ultimately leads the organisation.

Organisational structure

Queensland Health's structure comprises 37 health service districts, public hospitals and various state-wide health services. These are supported by three 'zones' and a central corporate office. The review found that Queensland Health's hierarchical layers of decision making did not support a responsive and efficient health system. Responsibility for some 80 per cent of Queensland Health's resources lies with one position — the Senior Executive Director of Health Services — so it is little wonder bottlenecks are common in the decision-making process. The review found that the centralised and hierarchical structure contributed to the frustration of staff and customers (patients and others). Many Queensland Health staff felt angry, frustrated and resentful towards senior managers and some reported experiencing bullying and intimidation when seeking more funding to deliver patient care.[2] Formalised, centralised decision making is at odds with the reality of healthcare delivery, which is immediate and occurs between healthcare workers and their patients.

The report recommended Queensland Health be reorganised with a flatter structure that would devolve decision making and accountability to lower levels. This would allow clinicians — those directly responsible for patient care — rather than bureaucrats to make decisions.

Culture

The report identified several cultural problems in Queensland Health. These included bullying, intimidation and secrecy. The head of the review, Peter Forster, stated: 'An entrenched and negative feature of the Queensland Health culture is one of bullying, threat, intimidation, coercion and retribution on the one hand, and of secrecy, blaming and avoiding responsibility on the other. These values, attitudes and behaviours are not conducive to a cohesive staff environment or good patient care.'[3] Forster found that Queensland Health's focus on staying within budget (over the past decade it had moved from running deficits to operating within budget) had exacerbated the incidence of bullying and intimidation. He said Queensland Health had 'a culture of secrecy and cover-up', relying on claims of patient confidentiality to avoid the public release of information. The information being concealed included the true size of waiting lists. The review estimated that in fact almost 110 000 people were waiting for a consultation with a specialist in a public hospital and that about 25 000 of those would actually require surgery. More than 33 000 people were already on surgical waiting lists, and more than 20 per cent of those had been waiting for longer than medically appropriate. Some people needing elective surgery wait for more than a year. This problem itself was blamed on budget and workforce constraints, but the problem then led to cultural problems, including the concealment of such statistics.

Forster said: 'There is a real self-censoring that happens and it happens from the highest levels down. If I get the clear message budget integrity is what our priority is, I know even as a manager at a modest level that there's not much point asking for more money and not much point raising the problems. So we end up just acquiescing, being frustrated, not pursuing our goals. And if I am at the director-general level and the ministerial staff want to vet and read the newsletters I want to send to my staff, in the end I just lose interest in sending newsletters to my staff. There are all sorts of subtle influences in this public sector system that all add up to a self-censoring of real information that ministers desperately need to make appropriate decisions. It's not anyone's fault necessarily, just a systemic fault.'[4]

Health Commission inquiry head Geoffrey Davies recommended increased protection of those people who choose to make their concerns public (whistleblowers) and suggested that a central body be established to oversee public interest disclosures. Queensland Premier Peter Beattie rejected the suggestions.

Davies found that successive state governments had concealed elective surgery waiting lists and quality reports. He said this practice of suppression, in which he claimed at least one former health minister had been instrumental, had encouraged Queensland Health staff to act in a similar fashion. He said: 'It is an irresistible conclusion that there is a history of a culture of concealment within and pertaining to Queensland Health'.[5] He placed responsibility for the culture on the Beattie government,

saying it had encouraged such a culture for its own political purposes.

The review recommended that a new system of healthcare outcome monitoring and reporting be established, with public reports being issued several times a year.

A reluctance to share information was another feature of the Queensland Health culture. 'Silos', built around occupational groupings, are common in health care and had been reinforced by the pressures of workload and budget constraints. The review suggested that perhaps the most important aspect of cultural change would be to build trust between the people making up the multi-disciplinary teams that are integral to providing healthcare services. The report said the culture could only improve if there was participation in team problem solving, a redesign of the workplace, systems improvement and a focus on the patient when making decisions about care.

Leadership

The review found that leaders, managers and supervisors often failed to deal with complex problems, did not encourage staff participation in problem solving, did not engage with staff and did not properly manage non-performing staff. Many staff felt that non-performing staff were often transferred or promoted rather than appropriately managed. This had led to low morale, high stress and high absenteeism. The review recommended that Queensland Health 'address the most dysfunctional aspect of the organisation's culture through the appointment and development of leaders who can by example inspire staff and develop the attitudes, culture and beliefs desired'.[6] Leaders would need to be empowered and provide a positive model for others. There would need to be a significant focus on teamwork. Clinicians in particular would need to exhibit leadership based on a wider range of skills than just their technical, professional expertise.

Job design

The report found that clinicians themselves felt that much of their time was taken up with administration rather than patient care. Clinicians said much of the organisation (particularly the administrative functions) was based on the traditional Monday to Friday, 9 to 5 work week, but that this was not a realistic model for health care, which must provide a service around the clock every day of the year.[7]

The report recommended processes be reviewed to reduce the administrative workload and that administrative support be extended beyond the traditional work week so clinicians could focus on providing health care rather than paperwork.

The report also recommended that more clinical staff were needed and that they should be provided with flexible and family-friendly work arrangements, fair remuneration, and ongoing opportunities for professional development, in order to attract and keep them in the healthcare workforce. Measures such as providing secure and safe car parking for staff working at night were recommended. Queensland Health has often recruited doctors trained in countries with different standards of education and from developing countries, where those doctors are desperately needed. The review concluded that this was not appropriate and that every effort should be made to recruit locally trained doctors.

Conclusion

The review recommended that the challenges facing Queensland's health system were best resolved in 'an atmosphere of openness about the extent of the problems, likely options and consequences, and informed and meaningful public debate'. It recommended 'a more open and transparent public health system'.[8]

Specific recommendations included (among others) that Queensland Health should:

- 'ensure that the organisational arrangements that deliver health services are efficient and streamlined, and allocate as many resources as practical to frontline services, where clinicians work in teams and networks across Queensland to use scarce resources to best effect'
- 'implement systems and procedures to ensure the recruitment and retention of a well qualified and experienced clinical workforce, to reduce adverse clinical events and to support clinicians in their efforts to continually improve clinical practices'
- 'implement a range of systemic improvements relating to...the way in which the performance of the health service will be monitored and reported'
- 'improve avenues for members of the community and staff of the public health service to raise concerns about aspects of the service and have these concerns responsibly and appropriately addressed and resolved.'[9]

Questions

1. Use the performance equation (chapter 1) to briefly outline the factors affecting the job performance of clinicians at Queensland Health.
2. Use the information in this case to discuss the links between job satisfaction and job performance (see chapter 2).

3. One of the recommendations of the review was to empower those who deliver health care to make decisions. Discuss some of the risks that might be involved in adopting this recommendation. How could this empowerment help health organisations to deal with some of the structural problems they face, including centralised decision making, silos and over-bureaucratisation?

4. Queensland Health requires massive change. Some of the change is related to workforce behaviour. Discuss the relative merits of the four behaviour modification strategies in relation to the problems in Queensland Health.

5. One of the major problems facing all healthcare systems is the attraction and retention of nurses. Conduct further research to discover the reasons for this problem and then outline what flexible work arrangements could be implemented to help solve the problem.

6. Health care is often delivered by teams of clinicians with different skills as well as non-clinical staff. Outline the sources of power and influence of each member of a team that comprises a surgeon, a general practitioner, a radiographer (radiographers take X-rays and other medical images), a theatre nurse, a ward nurse, and a ward clerk (ward clerks undertake administrative duties). How might this affect communication and the decision-making process among the team members?

7. Explain how some of the shared cultural values, beliefs and behaviours emerged within the organisation and have become cultural problems.

8. One of the problems the review identified was a failure of leaders to manage non-performing staff. Remembering that there are labour shortages in many areas of health care, how could leaders go about improving the performance of staff?

9. Reforming Queensland Health will be a difficult task that will take a long time. If you were on the taskforce overseeing the reform process, what would your first step be?

End notes

1. Queensland Health web site, www.health.qld.gov.au (viewed 10 January 2006).
2. Queensland Health Systems Review, Final report, p. xi.
3. 'Budget constraints cause culture of secrecy', *The Courier Mail* (15–16 October 2005), p. 30.
4. ibid.
5. Hedley Thomas, Amanda Watt and Malcolm Cole, 'Condition critical', *The Courier Mail* (1 December 2005).
6. Final report, p. iv.
7. Final report p. xvii.
8. Final report, p. iv.
9. Final report, p. v.

Case study 4

Workout World

VAL MORRISON

Background

Workout World (WW) is a community fitness and leisure centre situated just outside Melbourne's CBD. WW was officially opened in January 2006 to coincide with the Commonwealth Games being hosted by Melbourne in March of that year. In the lead-up to that event, much of Australia and certainly Melbourne was embracing Commonwealth Games fever and, like many other sporting and non-sporting enterprises, WW used this as a way to gain extra exposure. As part of the grand opening public relations strategy, WW invited several elite sporting teams to stay at the facility prior to the commencement of the Games.

When the concept of WW was first proposed it was eagerly accepted by local government, which believed a multi-sport centre would provide a much needed boost to the area. It immediately donated some of the land on which WW is built. Although no formal agreement was entered into at that time, there was an unwritten understanding that local government would have a role in overseeing the operation of WW, in return for its generosity. Nothing was ever clearly documented.

This state-of-the-art leisure centre comprises a fully equipped gymnasium, two swimming pools, sports fields, a complete health and beauty spa, a sports science institute, 3-star apartment-style accommodation for 100 people, a bistro and a snack bar. There are also child-minding facilities operated by qualified staff. Because of the impressive facilities, part of WW's overall strategy is to attract elite national and international sports teams for off-season training camps, as well as targeting the local community. Teams from first division soccer in the United Kingdom and professional basketball in the United States, and international swimming teams are just a few of the high profile groups targeted by WW. To date this has been successful and the business is growing well.

Scenario

It is 7 am on Monday, 18 September 2006 and Peter Watson, General Manager of WW, is in his office struggling with a presentation in preparation for a meeting with all staff. The meeting is to commence at 8 am. Peter is feeling uncomfortable about the meeting and is not really sure what the outcome will be. What he does know is that it has to be positive, otherwise WW might be forced to close its doors by the end of the year.

Assisting Peter in the meeting is Ann Baker, a consultant in organisational behaviour. Ann has spent the last month working with Peter at WW, trying to resolve some of the issues that have arisen and slowly worsened over the past three months. Ann's report to Peter is what prompted the meeting. Ann was initially hired by Peter to try to find out why there is an obvious division between the departments at WW. For such a small facility, there is a huge bureaucracy developing and this is having a negative effect on members and potential customers due to the inconsistencies that have arisen across the different services offered by WW.

Peter stares out of the window and begins to think about the current situation at WW.

The current situation

There is a regular team of 44 staff working at WW. These people are split across five main business units, namely:
1. Sports science and physiotherapy (4 staff)
2. Residential accommodation, food and beverages (9 staff)
3. Health spa, fitness and sports centre (14 staff)
4. Swim centre (7 staff)
5. Sales, marketing, memberships and administration (10 staff).

Child care, maintenance and cleaning are run by contractors commissioned by the relevant local government departments. The people in those groups do not report directly to Peter as they have their own supervisors back at local government headquarters. However, they are required to liaise with Peter or one of his staff members about any problems they may encounter. Unfortunately this is not always the case; maintenance and cleaning staff in particular work mostly when WW is either at low occupancy or closed, to enable them to move freely around all facilities without inconveniencing the customers.

When the WW complex was built, four of the five business units were put out to tender to independent operators and were immediately acquired and run as four separate entities, but working under the brand of WW. The fifth unit — sales, marketing, memberships and administration — was maintained by WW. That is where the problems began. WW had the responsibility of sales and marketing, managing memberships and the general administration of the centre but had little control over the product delivered by the independent operators in the other four units. As the business developed, so the independent operators have become more isolated, although this may not necessarily have been intentional. Initially, everyone got on well together and although there is now a definite divide among the groups, this is something that has evolved because they are entirely separate entities rather than in a situation of conflict.

Peter's thoughts are interrupted by a knock on the door. It is Ann.

'Hi Peter,' says Ann as she walks into the office. 'How are you? Sorry to get straight to the point but I'd really like to go through some of the topics for discussion at today's meeting. This is a critical time for WW and if we don't approach the meeting in the correct way, it could be very uncomfortable for everyone concerned.'

Peter agrees. 'Yes, come in, we have about half an hour to go through the main issues.'

Ann sits opposite Peter at his desk and, without even looking at the agenda he was working on, she begins to reiterate her findings.

'Well Peter, in a nutshell, as you know there are several areas of concern for WW and if you don't communicate the potential problem areas to the staff today, then things will continue to deteriorate.'

'I know,' says Peter, 'but please bear in mind that although I'm GM of WW, my hands are somewhat tied when trying to coordinate, direct and motivate everyone towards the same goals. The four independent operators have become more and more isolated since we opened, to the point where they are communicating with our members and potential customers directly and are now even competing with each other on product offerings. This is very confusing for everyone.'

Peter continues, 'I know the situation doesn't look good, but I'm confident that we can solve the problems because when we first began everyone shared the same enthusiasm and commitment to WW. I think it is just that we have all become too involved in our own separate units and have forgotten about teamwork on a larger scale.'

Ann nods in agreement. 'What you have here are four separate, highly experienced teams who believe their way is right. Unfortunately, this is creating a lot of unnecessary bureaucracy and duplication, considering WW is a relatively small organisation. Peter, it is time for you to take back control and implement some sound strategies, but you have to do this without seeming too autocratic or overpowering.'

'Yes, but it won't be easy,' sighs Peter. 'These people signed a ten-year contract to operate independently. Now I have to try and take back some control. I'm partly to blame for this, trying to be everyone's friend and giving them autonomy, thinking that would create a good working atmosphere when, in fact, it is now becoming quite competitive and sometimes hostile.'

The problems

Leadership

Peter Watson has held the role of general manager for 15 years in several different companies. He has been extremely successful and is responsible for the growth of at least two large leisure companies. Prior to coming to WW, he was GM for a five-star resort in Western Australia and before that was with one of Australia's small private aviation companies serving the regional tourism market. WW was always going to be a challenge for Peter, given that he has a transformational leadership style and is not particularly forceful. However, his charismatic manner has usually ensured that people not only sit up and take notice but are also happy to work alongside him.

Communication

Because of the current structure of the business, ongoing and open communication between the separate business units has slowly ceased. When WW first opened, Peter held weekly breakfast meetings which everyone willingly attended and contributed to. However, as the business has grown and everyone has become more involved in their own area of operation, attendance at the meetings is sporadic and many of the staff don't contribute because they want the meeting over quickly so they can get back to their jobs.

Hours of operation

Although WW is open from 7 am to 7 pm seven days a week, not all facilities are operating during that time and often no prior notice is given. This is extremely inconvenient and confusing for the members who may want to use two of the four facilities, such as the swim centre and the gym, which are owned and operated by two different companies. This also presents a problem for the maintenance and cleaning contractors, who are never really sure when it is convenient for them to come in and carry out their work. The childcare centre is also affected by the lack of timetabling because it is not easy to roster on the correct number of staff required by government regulations to oversee the children.

Marketing and advertising

Although WW has an overall branding campaign and marketing communication strategy that incorporates all facilities within the centre, other promotional material is being mailed directly to members and potential customers from each of the independent operators who, not surprisingly, prefer to see their name behind their product, tending to drop the WW logo in favour of their own. Also, the content of the promotional materials is not shown to Peter prior to distribution, therefore the administration department at WW aren't informed about new products when members and customers ask for details.

Increasing memberships

WW is responsible for attracting new full-time members to the centre as well as short-term visiting groups from domestic and international markets. To date, while this has been relatively successful, coordination between the sales team and the four independent operators ensuring that product offering and pricing strategy fit with WW's overall plan is becoming more and more difficult to control.

Finding the solution

Ann looks at her watch. 'Peter, we are due in the conference room in less than an hour. Let's make the final changes to the agenda then head down there. It might be a good idea to get there before everyone else does so we can welcome them. It will get us off to a positive start.'

Questions

1. Obviously there are many potential problems associated with WW and the way it is structured. Clearly identify at least three problems that you think Peter is faced with, then go on to briefly describe the action he might take to overcome those problems you have identified.

2. It would appear that a conflict situation at WW is evolving between the five business units. What can Peter do to try and take control of this before they become even more isolated from each other?

3. Peter has less than an hour before the meeting begins and he is struggling with the agenda. Prepare a brief outline of the agenda and topics he should discuss at the meeting. Be sure to justify you answer and support this with OB theories and concepts.

This case is fictional.

Case study 5

KD Transport

RON FISHER

Background

John was the Managing Director of KD Transport, a long-established family company originally founded by his grandfather William more than 70 years ago. William had been a factory worker who had been seriously injured in a work accident that effectively ended his working life. Yet he was determined that he would lead an active and productive life as far as his injuries permitted.

With his brother, William established a small transport service delivering freight. Over the years the business grew, and when William died his daughter Marie took over the running of the business. Under Marie's guidance the business continued to prosper and grow, buying out a number of competitors along the way.

As managing director of the company, Marie continued the traditions of her father, including a philosophy of hard work and generous rewards for loyal staff. Rewards included a Christmas party for all employees and their families, together with large cash bonuses for key management staff. A few years ago Marie decided to retire and her son John became the new managing director of the business.

What John inherited was an organisation with over 150 vehicles and 250 employees. The business had four main depots, comprising the original depot established by William and three others that had originally belonged to competitors before being acquired by Marie when she was managing director. There was little in the way of overall company policies and procedures, each depot tending to be organised as a separate business unit, much as it had been prior to acquisition by KD Transport. John suspected that the lack of overall coordination was a major problem, but was unsure exactly what the issues really were or how to deal with them. What was obvious to him was the loyalty that employees showed to their particular depot and workmates, which was not mirrored at the overall company level.

Workforce relations

Marie, and in later times John, had tried to improve job satisfaction and productivity by offering incentives to employees, but these initiatives had mostly failed. John's view of this was that workers had low commitment and were not really interested in the company's fortunes. The view of the workforce was that management never followed anything through and usually broke any agreements that were made. An often-quoted example was an incentive scheme that had offered an all-expenses-paid holiday to the Gold Coast for the first staff member to generate new business beyond a predetermined annual amount. One employee had achieved the amount but John had refused to provide the prize, claiming that the employee had 'found a loophole in the incentive scheme'.

As managing director, John made all major decisions. Although each depot had a manager many operational decisions were also made by John. Managers had learned long ago that they would be held fully accountable for any of their decisions that went wrong. Consequently, any potentially contentious decisions were usually referred to John. For his part John enjoyed being portrayed as the main decision maker, basing many of his decisions on what he called 'gut feel'. He also tried to engender a spirit of competition between the depots as a means of improving productivity and morale.

John's wife and son also worked in the business, Ursula as an accounts clerk and Jeremy as a driver. Although John prided himself on his well-thought-out ideas and decisions, in reality most major decisions were thrashed out over the dinner table at the family home each night. When John changed his mind about business decisions, it was usually because Ursula had persuaded him to do so. She also had the final word on the appointment of all new employees. Jeremy's role in discussions was to provide feedback about the day-to-day operating activities of the business (what the drivers were saying and so on).

Business performance

John recently realised that the business was at a crossroads. Turnover and profitability had decreased over the past two years while levels of short-term debt had doubled, particularly over the past six months. The business now depended on an extensive overdraft facility in order to pay its way. Creditors were strung out as far as possible to the point where several suppliers were now demanding cash payments rather than providing goods on 30-day credit terms, which was normal industry practice. Levels of long-term debt were also high, mainly due to the cost of purchasing new vehicles. Maintaining a reasonable average fleet age was important in order to minimise maintenance costs and fuel consumption. Having a modern fleet was also important from the point of view of public perception.

The pressures of poor cash-flow and reduced profitability had also begun to affect the annual salary increases and bonuses that senior managers had come to expect. This year there would be no salary increases for anyone, and the payment of Christmas bonuses also seemed unlikely. Employees paid by the hour, such as drivers, mechanics and yard staff, were already being paid the minimum legal wage, therefore the only cutback they would suffer was the cancellation of the Christmas party. Overall, working for KD Transport was not the attractive proposition that it had once been.

The event that really worried John was recent notification from the bank that KD Transport's account had been placed into the debt recovery section of the bank. This meant that the bank would review company performance every six months. John knew that if the bank was not satisfied with his company's performance they could, and probably would, withdraw the overdraft facility, effectively putting the company out of business. In addition to losing the business that his grandfather had established 70 years ago there was another extremely important issue for John; all of his personal assets were held by the bank as security for the company's debts. If the company went out of business John and his family would lose everything.

John's plan

John believed that unless drastic action was taken there appeared to be little prospect of the business surviving. He and Ursula had discussed the company's situation extensively over the past few evenings. She was keen to rationalise the whole operation by closing one or possibly two depots and moving operations to one of the remaining depots. While this would mean longer distances to travel, and therefore higher fuel and maintenance costs, there would be major savings in operating costs through better utilisation of vehicles and larger (more cost effective) loads. Closing

two depots would also mean that about 25 per cent of the overall workforce could be retrenched, thereby providing major ongoing savings. A further benefit would be the possibility of selling the redundant depots and using the cash from the sales to bolster the company's cash position.

Communicating the change

In the days that followed John began to formulate his plan. As the managing director he would be responsible for implementing the changes that he and Ursula had planned. John decided that he would get the senior management of the company together and announce his plans. A two-day retreat for managers along with the company accountant was arranged. At the retreat he would present details of the company's position and his plans for change. At this stage he wasn't sure exactly of the finer details but he had spent several days with his personal assistant working on a PowerPoint presentation. John was confident that by getting his message through to the managers, effective change would follow.

Over the past few days Ursula and John had been discussing how the change program would be communicated to the workforce. Ursula had suggested that John should try to present a case for change based on reason and logic. However, John had decided that such an approach would probably not work. He favoured an approach where the workforce would just be informed of the situation, and at the latest possible time. As the most skilled communicator in the company, John was convinced that he would find a way to get the message across effectively. As far as John was concerned the business had to be operated more efficiently, therefore — apart from which individual stayed and which was retrenched — there was nothing to negotiate with the workforce. John expected that there would be a certain level of conflict resulting from the changes, but he was sure that he could 'ride out the storm'.

Questions

1. How is KD Transport structured? What are the major challenges arising from the present structure? How could these challenges be met?
2. How would you describe the culture of KD Transport?
3. What are John's strengths and weaknesses as a leader?
4. Discuss how power is distributed in KD Transport?
5. Discuss John's performance as managing director in terms of planning and decision making.
6. Is John a good communicator? How should John communicate the changes to the workforce?
7. What are the likely outcomes if John proceeds with his plan?

This case is fictional.

GLOSSARY

Ability is the capacity to perform the various tasks needed for a given job. *p. 45*

Absenteeism is the failure of people to attend work on a given day. *p. 58*

Achievement-oriented leadership is leadership behaviour that emphasises setting challenging goals, stressing excellence in performance and showing confidence in the group members' abilities to achieve high standards of performance. *p. 392*

Active management by exception involves watching for deviations from rules and standards and taking corrective action. *p. 397*

An **adhocracy** is an organisational structure that emphasises shared, decentralised decision making, extreme horizontal specialisation, few levels of management, the virtual absence of formal controls, and few rules, policies and procedures. *p. 296*

The **adjourning stage** is the fifth stage of group development, in which members of the group disband when the job is done. *p. 209*

The **affective components** of an attitude are the specific feelings regarding the personal impact of the antecedents. *p. 55*

Aptitude is the capability to learn something. *p. 45*

Arbitration occurs when a neutral third party acts as judge and issues a binding decision affecting parties at a negotiation impasse. *p. 478*

Artificial intelligence, or AI, studies how computers can be made to think like the human brain. *p. 436*

An **attitude** is a predisposition to respond in a positive or negative way to someone or something in your environment. *p. 55*

Authoritarianism is a personality trait that focuses on the rigidity of a person's beliefs. *p. 50*

Automation is a job design that allows machines to do work previously accomplished by human effort. *p. 151*

Autonomous work teams are teams given significant authority and responsibility over their work in contexts of highly related or interdependent jobs. *p. 245*

The **bargaining zone** is the zone between one party's minimum reservation point and the other party's maximum reservation point in a negotiating situation. *p. 476*

BATNA is the 'best alternative to a negotiated agreement', or each party's position on what they must do if an agreement cannot be reached. *p. 476*

The **behavioural components** of an attitude are the intentions to behave in a certain way based on a person's specific feelings or attitudes. *p. 55*

Behavioural decision theory refers to the idea that people act only in terms of what they perceive about a given situation. *p. 423*

Behaviourists study observable behaviours and consequences of behaviour, and reject subjective human psychological states as topics for study. *p. 114*

Beliefs represent ideas about someone or something and the conclusions people draw about them. *p. 55*

Brain drain refers to a characteristic of today's skilled workforce whose members are now more mobile and prepared to take their knowledge with them to their new workplaces as they pursue opportunities across the globe. *p. 18*

Brainstorming is a technique by which team members generate as many ideas as possible, without being inhibited by other team members. *p. 236*

Buffering is a conflict management approach that sets up inventories to reduce conflicts when the inputs of one group are the outputs of another group. *p. 471*

A **bureaucracy** is an ideal form of organisation whose characteristics include a division of labour, hierarchical control, promotion by merit with career opportunities for employees, and administration by rule. *p. 290*

Casual work is work where the number and schedule of work hours vary and there is little or no security of ongoing employment. *p. 26*

Centralisation is the degree to which the authority to make decisions is restricted to higher levels of management. *p. 280*

Certain environments are decision environments in which information is sufficient to predict the results of each alternative in advance of implementation. *p. 421*

Change agents are individuals or groups that take responsibility for changing the existing pattern of behaviour of a person or social system. *p. 490*

Changing involves a managerial responsibility to modify a situation — that is, to change people, tasks, structure and/or technology. *p. 497*

Channels are the media through which the message may be delivered. *p. 455*

Charisma is a dimension of leadership that provides vision and a sense of mission, and instils pride, respect and trust. *p. 398*

Charismatic leaders are those leaders who, by force of their personal abilities, are capable of having a profound and extraordinary effect on followers. *p. 395*

Classical conditioning is a form of learning through association that involves the manipulation of stimuli to influence behaviour. *p. 115*

Classical decision theory views the manager as acting in a world of complete certainty. *p. 423*

Coercive power is the extent to which a manager can deny desired rewards or administer punishment to control other people. *p. 346*

Cognitive abilities refer to our mental capacity to process information and solve problems. *p. 45*

The **cognitive components** of an attitude are the beliefs, opinions, knowledge or information a person possesses. *p. 55*

Cognitive dissonance is a state of perceived inconsistency between a person's expressed attitudes and actual behaviour. *p. 56*

Cognitive learning is a form of learning achieved by thinking about the perceived relationship between events and individual goals and expectations. *p. 117*

Cohesiveness is the degree to which members are attracted to and motivated to remain part of the group. *pp. 213, 240*

Common assumptions are the collection of truths that organisational members share as a result of their joint experiences and that guide values and behaviours. *p. 312*

A **compressed work week** is any scheduling of work that allows a full-time job to be completed in fewer than the standard five days. *p. 168*

Conflict occurs when two or more people disagree over issues of organisational substance and/or experience some emotional antagonism with one another. *p. 461*

Conflict resolution occurs when the reasons for a conflict are eliminated. *p. 468*

Conglomerates are organisations that own several unrelated businesses. *p. 292*

Constructive conflict is conflict that results in positive benefits to the group. *p. 465*

Consultative decisions are decisions made by an individual after seeking input from or consulting with members of a group. *p. 428*

Content theories offer ways to profile or analyse individuals to identify the needs that motivate their behaviours. *p. 82*

A **contingency approach** is the attempt by organisational behaviour scholars to identify how situations can be understood and managed in ways that appropriately respond to their unique characteristics. *p. 4*

Contingent rewards are rewards that are given in exchange for mutually agreed goal accomplishments. *p. 397*

Continuous reinforcement is a reinforcement schedule that administers a reward each time a desired behaviour occurs. *p. 122*

Contributions are individual work efforts of value to the organisation. *p. 11*

Control is the set of mechanisms used to keep actions and outputs within predetermined limits. *p. 274*

Controlling is the process of monitoring performance, comparing results with objectives and taking corrective action as necessary. *p. 13*

Coordination is the set of mechanisms used in an organisation to link the actions of its subunits into a consistent pattern. *p. 278*

Corporate social responsibility refers to the notion that corporations have a responsibility to the society that sustains them; is the obligation of organisations to behave in ethical and moral ways. *pp. 27, 274*

Countercultures are the patterns of values and philosophies that outwardly reject those of the larger organisation or social system. *p. 313*

Crafted decisions are decisions created to deal specifically with a situation at hand. *p. 420*

Creativity is the development of unique and novel responses to problems and opportunities. *p. 426*

A **cultural symbol** is any object, act or event that serves to transmit cultural meaning. *p. 315*

Decentralisation is the degree to which the authority to make decisions is given to lower levels in an organisation's hierarchy. *p. 280*

Decision making is the process of identifying a problem or opportunity and choosing among alternative courses of action. *p. 420*

Decoding is the interpretation of the symbols sent from the sender to the receiver. *456*

Decoupling involves separating or reducing the contact between two conflicting groups. *p. 471*

Demographic characteristics are background variables (for example, age and gender) that help shape what a person becomes over time. *p. 44*

Departmentalisation by customer is the grouping of individuals and resources by client. *p. 283*

Departmentalisation by geography is the grouping of individuals and resources by geographical territory. *p. 283*

Destructive conflict is conflict that works to the group's or organisation's disadvantage. *p. 465*

The **differentiation perspective** views an organisation's culture as a compilation of diverse and inconsistent beliefs that are shared at group level. *p. 322*

Directive leadership is leadership behaviour that spells out the what and how of employees' tasks. *p. 391*

Disruptive behaviour is any behaviour that harms the group process. *p. 196*

Distributed leadership is the sharing of responsibility for fulfilling group task and maintenance needs. *p. 212*

Distributive negotiation is negotiation in which the focus is on 'positions' staked out or declared by the parties involved, who are each trying to claim certain portions of the available 'pie'. *p. 474*

Division of labour is the process of breaking the work to be done into specialised tasks that individuals or groups can perform. *p. 6*

Divisional departmentalisation is the grouping of individuals and resources by product, service and/or client. *p. 283*

Divisionalised design is an organisational structure that establishes a separate structure for each business or division. *p. 292*

Dogmatism is a personality trait that regards legitimate authority as absolute. *p. 50*

Effective communication is communication in which the intended meaning of the source and the perceived meaning of the receiver are one and the same. *p. 457*

Effective groups are groups that achieve high levels of both task performance and human resource maintenance. *p. 197*

An **effective manager** is a manager whose work unit achieves high levels of task accomplishment and maintains itself as a capable workforce over time. *p. 9*

Effective negotiation occurs when issues of substance are resolved without any harm to the working relationships among the parties involved. *p. 473*

Efficient communication is communication at minimum cost in terms of resources expended. *p. 457*

Emergent behaviours are those things that group members do in addition to, or in place of, what is formally asked of them by the organisation. *p. 209*

Emotion management is exercising emotional self-control and self-regulation influenced by the context in which individuals find themselves *p. 46*

Emotional conflict is conflict that involves interpersonal difficulties that arise over feelings of anger, mistrust, dislike, fear, resentment and the like. *p. 462*

Emotional intelligence is a form of social intelligence that allows us to monitor and shape our emotions and those of others. *pp. 5, 46*

Employee involvement teams are teams of workers who meet regularly outside their normal work units for the purpose of collectively addressing important workplace issues. *p. 244*

Empowerment is the process by which managers delegate power to employees to motivate greater responsibility in balancing the achievement of both personal and organisational goals. *pp. 100, 359*

Encoding is the process of translating an idea or thought into meaningful symbols. *p. 455*

Environmental complexity is the magnitude of the problems and opportunities in the organisation's environment, as evidenced by the degree of richness, interdependence and uncertainty. *p. 271*

Equity theory is based on the phenomenon of social comparison and posits, because people gauge the fairness of their work outcomes compared with others, that felt inequity is a motivating state of mind. *p. 90*

ERG theory categorises needs into existence, relatedness and growth needs. *p. 84*

Escalating commitment is the tendency to continue with a previously chosen course of action even when feedback suggests that it is failing. *p. 435*

Ethical behaviour is behaviour that is morally accepted as 'good' and 'right' as opposed to 'bad' and 'wrong' in a particular social context. *p. 26*

The **ethical climate** is the shared set of understandings in an organisation about what is correct behaviour and how ethical issues will be handled. *p. 329*

An **ethical dilemma** occurs when a person must make a decision that requires a choice among competing sets of principles. *pp. 27, 439*

Existence needs are about the desire for physiological and material wellbeing. *p. 84*

Expectancy is the probability that the individual assigns to work effort being followed by a given level of achieved task performance. *p. 92*

Expectancy theory argues that work motivation is determined by individual beliefs about effort–performance relationships and the desirability of various work outcomes from different performance levels. *p. 93*

Expert power is the ability to control another's behaviour through the possession of knowledge, experience or judgement that the other person does not have but needs. *p. 349*

External adaptation is the process of reaching goals and dealing with outsiders. *p. 324*

Externals are persons with an external locus of control, who believe what happens to them is beyond their control. *p. 49*

Extinction is the withdrawal of the reinforcing consequences for a given behaviour. *p. 126*

Extrinsic rewards are positively valued work outcomes that the individual receives from some other person in the work setting. *pp. 96, 120*

Feedback is the process of telling someone else how you feel about something the person did or said, or about the situation in general. *p. 456*

Felt negative inequity exists when individuals feel they have received relatively less than others have in proportion to work inputs. *p. 90*

Felt positive inequity exists when individuals feel they have received relatively more than others have. *p. 90*

The **five key dimensions of personality** are extroversion–introversion; conscientiousness; agreeableness; emotional stability; and openness to experience. *p. 49*

Flexible working hours (flexitime) is any work schedule that gives employees daily choice in the timing of work and non-work activities. *p. 169*

Flexiyear or annual hours is a system whereby total agreed annual hours are allocated by workers as they see fit. *p. 169*

Force-coercion strategy tries to 'command' change through the formal authority of legitimacy, rewards and punishments. *p. 501*

Formal communication channels are communication channels that follow the chain of command established by the organisation's hierarchy. *p. 457*

Formal groups are 'official' groups that are designated by formal authority to serve a specific purpose. *p. 190*

Formal leadership is the process of exercising influence from a position of formal authority in an organisation. *p. 385*

The **formal structure** is the intended configuration of positions, job duties and lines of authority among the component parts of an organisation. *p. 268*

Formalisation is the written documentation of work rules, policies and procedures. *p. 277*

The **forming stage** is the first stage of group development, in which the primary concern is the initial entry of members to the group. *p. 206*

The **founding story** is the tale of the lessons learned and efforts of the founder of the organisation. *p. 314*

The **fragmentation perspective** views organisational culture as lacking any form of pattern as a result of differing meanings between individuals and within individuals over time. *p. 322*

Friendship groups consist of people with natural affinities for one another who may do things together inside or outside the workplace. *p. 192*

Functional departmentalisation is the grouping of individuals and resources by skill, knowledge and action. *p. 282*

Global management skills and competencies include understanding of international business strategy, cross-cultural management, international marketing, international finance, managing e-business and the Internet, risk management, managing sustainable organisations, re-engineering organisations, managing the virtual workplace, knowledge management, international economics and trade, and Asian languages. *p. 14*

Globalisation is the process of becoming more international in scope, influence or application. *p. 14*

Goal setting is the process of developing, negotiating and formalising an employee's targets and objectives. *p. 162*

Group decisions are decisions made by all members of the group, ideally with consensus being achieved. *p. 428*

Group dynamics are the forces operating in groups that affect group performance and member satisfaction. *p. 206*

Group inputs are the initial 'givens' in a group situation that set the stage for all group processes. *p. 199*

Group norms are the standards of behaviour that group members are expected to display. *p. 210*

Group outputs are the results of the transformation of group inputs through group processes. *p. 211*

Group roles are the sets of behaviours expected by the managers of the organisation and the group members for the holder of a particular position. *p. 210*

Groups are collections of two or more people who interact with one another for a common purpose. *pp. 190, 229*

Groupthink is the tendency of members in highly cohesive groups to lose their critical, evaluative capabilities. *p. 433*

Growth needs are about the desire for continued personal growth and development. *p. 84*

Heterogeneous groups are groups whose members have diverse backgrounds, interests, values, attitudes and so on. *p. 204*

Heuristics are simplifying strategies or 'rules of thumb' that people use when making decisions. *p. 425*

Hierarchical referral uses the chain of command for conflict resolution; problems are referred up the hierarchy for more senior managers to reconcile. *p. 470*

Higher-order needs are esteem and self-actualisation needs in Maslow's hierarchy. *p. 83*

Homogeneous groups are groups whose members have similar backgrounds, interests, values, attitudes and so on. *p. 204*

Horizontal loading involves increasing the breadth of a job by adding to the variety of tasks that the worker performs. *p. 152*

Horizontal specialisation is the division of labour through the formation of work units or groups within an organisation. *p. 281*

Human resource maintenance is the attraction and continuation of a viable workforce. *p. 9*

Human resources are the individuals and groups whose contributions enable the organisation to serve a particular purpose. *p. 7*

Hygienes (hygiene factors) are dissatisfiers that are associated with aspects of a person's work setting. *p. 88*

Incremental change is change that occurs more frequently and less traumatically as part of an organisation's natural evolution. *p. 490*

Individual decisions are decisions made by one individual on behalf of the group. *p. 428*

Individualised consideration is a leadership dimension by which the leader provides personal attention, treats each employee individually, and coaches and advises employees. *p. 398*

Inducements are what the organisation gives to the individual on behalf of the group. *p. 11*

Influence is a behavioural response to the exercise of power. *p. 345*

Informal communication channels are communication channels that do not adhere to the organisation's hierarchy. *p. 457*

Informal groups are groups that emerge unofficially and are not formally designated as parts of the organisation. *p. 192*

Informal leadership is the process of exercising influence through special skills or resources that meet the needs of other people. *p. 385*

Information power is the extent to which individuals have control over information needed by others. *p. 349*

An **information source** is a person or group of persons with a reason to communicate with some other person(s), the receiver(s). *p. 455*

The **initial integration stage** is the third stage of group development, at which the group begins to come together as a coordinated unit; it is sometimes called the norming stage. *p. 207*

Innovation is the process of creating new ideas and putting them into practice. *p. 508*

Inspiration is the communication of high expectations, the use of symbols to focus efforts, and the expression of important purposes in simple ways. *p. 398*

Instinct is made up of inherited patterns of unreasoned and unchangeable responses to particular actions and behaviours. *p. 48*

Instrumentality is the probability that the individual assigns to a level of achieved task performance leading to various work outcomes. *p. 93*

The **integration perspective** views organisational culture as a system of shared meanings, unity and harmony. *p. 321*

Integrative negotiation is negotiation in which the focus is on the merits of the issues and the parties involved try to enlarge the available 'pie' rather than stake claims to certain portions of it. *p. 475*

Intellectual stimulation promotes intelligence, rationality and careful problem solving. *p. 398*

Interest groups consist of people who share common interests, whether those interests are work or non-work related. *p. 192*

Intergroup conflict is conflict that occurs between groups in an organisation. *p. 463*

Intergroup dynamics are the dynamics that take place between groups, as opposed to within groups. *p. 214*

Intermittent reinforcement is a reinforcement schedule that rewards behaviour only periodically. *p. 122*

Internal integration is the creation of a collective identity and the means of matching methods of working and living together. *p. 325*

Internals are persons with an internal locus of control, who believe they control their own fate or destiny. *p. 49*

Interorganisational conflict is conflict that occurs between organisations. *p. 464*

Interpersonal conflict is conflict that occurs between two or more individuals. *p. 463*

Intrapersonal conflict is conflict that occurs within the individual as a result of actual or perceived pressures from incompatible goals or expectations. *pp. 129, 463*

Intrinsic motivation is a desire to work hard solely for the pleasant experience of task accomplishment. *p. 150*

Intrinsic rewards are positively valued work outcomes that the individual receives directly as a result of task performance. *p. 96*

Intuition is the ability to know or recognise quickly and readily the possibilities of a given situation. *p. 424*

The **job characteristics model** identifies five core characteristics (skill variety, task identity, task significance, autonomy and job feedback) as having special importance to job designs. *p. 155*

Job content refers to what people do in their work. *p. 88*

Job context refers to a person's work setting. *p. 88*

Job design is the planning and specification of job tasks and the work setting in which they are to be accomplished. *p. 151*

A **job diagnostic survey** is a questionnaire used to examine each of the dimensions of the job characteristics model. *p. 157*

Job enlargement involves increasing task variety by combining into one job tasks of similar skill levels that were previously assigned to separate workers. *p. 152*

Job enrichment is the practice of building motivating factors into job content. *p. 153*

Job involvement is the degree to which a person is willing to work hard and apply effort beyond normal job expectations. *p. 57*

Job rotation involves increasing task variety by periodically shifting workers among jobs involving different tasks at similar levels of skill. *p. 152*

Job satisfaction is the degree to which individuals feel positively or negatively about their jobs. *p. 57*

Job sharing is the assignment of one full-time job to two or more persons, who divide the work according to agreements made between themselves and the employer. *p. 170*

Job simplification is standardising work procedures and employing people in clearly defined and specialised tasks. *p. 151*

Jobs are one or more tasks that an individual performs in direct support of an organisation's production purpose. *p. 151*

Judgement is the use of the intellect in making decisions. *p. 425*

Key performance indicators are standards against which individual and organisational performance can be measured. *p. 165*

A **knowledge-based economy** is an economy in which the production, distribution and use of knowledge is the main driver of growth, wealth creation and employment across all industries — not only those classified as high tech or knowledge intensive. *p. 17*

Knowledge management focuses on processes designed to improve an organisation's ability to capture, share and diffuse knowledge in a manner that will improve business performance. *p. 17*

Laissez faire leadership involves abdicating responsibilities and avoiding decisions. *p. 397*

The **law of contingent reinforcement** is the view that for a reward to have maximum reinforcing value, it must be delivered only if the desired behaviour is exhibited. *p. 121*

The **law of effect** refers to Thorndike's observation that behaviour that results in a pleasant outcome is likely to be repeated; behaviour that results in an unpleasant outcome is not likely to be repeated. *p. 120*

The **law of immediate reinforcement** states that the more immediate the delivery of a reward after the occurrence of a desirable behaviour, the greater the reinforcing effect on behaviour. *p. 122*

Leaders provide inspiration, create opportunities, coach and motivate people to gain their support on fundamental long-term choices. *p. 384*

Leadership is a special case of interpersonal influence that gets an individual or group to do what the leader wants done. *p. 385*

Leading is the process of directing and coordinating the work efforts of other people to help them to accomplish important tasks. *p. 13*

Learning is a relatively permanent change in behaviour that occurs as a result of experience. *p. 114*

Least preferred coworker (LPC) scale is a measure of a person's leadership style based on a description of the person with whom respondents have been able to work least well. *p. 389*

Legitimate power is the extent to which a manager can use the internalised belief of an employee that the 'boss' has a 'right of command' to control other people. *p. 348*

Liaison groups are groups that coordinate the activities of certain units to prevent destructive conflicts between them. *p. 471*

Line personnel are work groups that conduct the major business of the organisation. *p. 281*

Linking pins are people who are assigned to manage conflict between groups that are prone to conflict. *p. 471*

Locus of control is the internal–external orientation — that is, the extent to which people feel able to affect their lives. *p. 49*

Lower-order needs are physiological, safety and social needs in Maslow's hierarchy. *p. 83*

Machiavellians are people who view and manipulate others purely for personal gain. *p. 50*

Maintenance activities are activities that support the emotional life of the group as an ongoing social system. *p. 212*

A **management philosophy** links key goal-related issues with key collaboration issues to come up with general ways by which the organisation will manage its affairs. *p. 319*

The **management process** involves planning, organising, leading and controlling the use of organisational resources. *p. 12*

A **manager** is responsible for work that is accomplished through the performance contributions of others. *p. 9*

Managers are concerned with making things happen and keeping work on schedule, engaging in routine interactions to fulfil planned actions. *p. 384*

Manifest conflict occurs when conflict is openly expressed in behaviour. *p. 468*

Material resources are the technology, information, physical equipment and facilities, raw material and money that are necessary for an organisation to produce some product or service. *p. 7*

A **matrix structure** is a combination of functional and divisional patterns in which an individual is assigned to more than one type of unit. *p. 286*

Mechanistic design emphasises vertical specialisation, hierarchical levels, tight control and coordination through rules, policies and other impersonal methods. *p. 279*

Merit pay is a compensation system that bases an individual's salary or wage increase on a measure of the person's performance accomplishments during a specified time period. *p. 131*

A **motivating potential score** is a summary of a job's overall potential for motivating those in the workplace. *p. 157*

Motivation to work refers to the forces within an individual that account for the level, direction and persistence of effort expended at work. *pp. 44, 78*

The **motivator–hygiene theory** distinguishes between sources of work dissatisfaction (hygiene factors) and satisfaction (motivators); it is also known as the two-factor theory. *p. 87*

Motivators (motivator factors) are satisfiers that are associated with what people do in their work. *p. 88*

Multiskilling helps employees acquire an array of skills needed to perform the multiple tasks in an organisational production or customer service process. *p. 161*

The **nature/nurture controversy** is the argument over whether personality is determined by heredity, or genetic endowment, or by one's environment. *p. 47*

The **need for achievement (nAch)** is the desire to do something better, solve problems or master complex tasks. *p. 85*

The **need for affiliation (nAff)** is the desire to establish and maintain friendly and warm relations with others. *p. 85*

The **need for power (nPower)** is the desire to control others, influence their behaviour and be responsible for others. *p. 85*

Negative reinforcement is the withdrawal of negative consequences, which tends to increase the likelihood of the behaviour being repeated in similar settings; it is also known as avoidance. *p. 124*

Negotiation is the process of making joint decisions when the parties involved have different preferences. *p. 472*

A **network organisation** is a de-layered organisation aligned around the complementary competencies of players in a value chain. *p. 297*

Noise is anything that interferes with the effectiveness of the communication attempt. *p. 456*

Non-routine problems are unique and new problems that call for creative problem solving. *p. 420*

Norms are rules or standards about the behaviour that group members are expected to display. *p. 239*

Observable culture is behavioural patterns that a group displays and teaches to new members. *p. 311*

Open systems transform human and physical resources received from their environment into goods and services that are then returned to the environment. *p. 7*

Operant conditioning is the process of controlling behaviour by manipulating its consequences. *p. 116*

Organic design is an organisational structure that emphasises horizontal specialisation, an extensive use of personal coordination, and loose rules, policies and procedures. *p. 279*

Organisation charts are diagrams that depict the formal structures of organisations. *p. 268*

Organisational behaviour is the study of individuals and groups in organisations. *p. 4*

Organisational behaviour modification is the systematic reinforcement of desirable work behaviour and the non-reinforcement or punishment of unwanted work behaviour. *p. 121*

Organisational commitment is the degree to which a person strongly identifies with, and feels a part of, the organisation. *p. 57*

Organisational communication is the process by which entities exchange information and establish a common understanding. *p. 454*

Organisational culture is a system of shared beliefs and values that guides behaviour. *p. 310*

Organisational design is the process of choosing and implementing a structural configuration for an organisation. *p. 268*

Organisational governance is the pattern of authority, influence and acceptable managerial behaviour established at the top of the organisation. *p. 367*

Organisational learning is acquiring or developing new knowledge that modifies or changes behaviour and improves organisational performance. *p. 135*

Organisational politics is the management of influence to obtain ends not sanctioned by the organisation, or to obtain sanctioned ends through non-sanctioned means of influence. *p. 362*

Organisational strategy is the process of positioning the organisation in the competitive environment and implementing actions to compete successfully. *p. 272*

Organising is the process of dividing the work to be done and coordinating the results to achieve a desired purpose. *p. 13*

Output controls are controls that focus on desired targets and allow managers to use their own methods for reaching defined targets. *p. 276*

Output goals are the goals that define the organisation's type of business. *p. 273*

Participative leadership is a leadership style that focuses on consulting with employees, and seeking and accounting for their suggestions before making decisions. *p. 392*

Passive management by exception involves intervening with employees only if standards are not met. *p. 397*

Perception is the process through which people receive, organise and interpret information from their environment. *p. 62*

Performance is a summary measure of the quantity and quality of task contributions made by an individual or group to the work unit and organisation. *p. 60*

Performance equation: Job performance = attributes × work effort × organisational support. *p. 5*

The **performance gap** is the discrepancy between an actual and a desired state of affairs. *p. 491*

Permanent formal work groups perform a specific function on an ongoing basis. *p. 191*

Personality is the overall profile or combination of traits that characterise the unique nature of a person. *p. 47*

Physical abilities refer to our natural and developed motor capacities for speed, strength, flexibility and so on, as well as our use of the five senses. *p. 45*

Planned change is change that happens as a result of specific efforts on the part of a change agent. *p. 491*

Planning is the process of setting performance objectives and identifying the actions needed to accomplish them. *p. 13*

A **policy** is a guideline for action that outlines important objectives and indicates how an activity is to be performed. *p. 276*

Positive reinforcement is the administration of positive consequences that tend to increase the likelihood of repeating the behaviour in similar settings. *p. 121*

Power is the ability to get someone else to do something you want done, or the ability to make things happen or get things done in the way you want. *p. 345*

Primary beneficiaries are particular groups expected to benefit from the efforts of specific organisations. *p. 273*

A **procedure (or rule)** is a more specific, rigid guideline that describes in detail how a task is to be performed. *p. 276*

Process controls are controls that attempt to specify the manner in which tasks will be accomplished. *p. 276*

Process innovation is innovation that results in a better way of doing things. *p. 508*

Process power is the control over methods of production and analysis. *p. 348*

Process re-engineering is the fundamental rethinking and radical redesign of business processes to achieve improvements in performance. *p. 13*

Process theories seek to understand the thought processes that take place in the minds of people and that act to motivate their behaviour. *p. 82*

Product innovation is innovation that results in the creation of a new or improved good or service. *p. 508*

Productivity is a summary measure of the quantity and quality of work performance that also accounts for resource use. *p. 9*

Programmed decisions are decisions that implement specific solutions determined by past experience as appropriate for the problems at hand. *p. 420*

The **psychological contract** specifies what the individual and the organisation expect to give to and receive from each other in the course of their working relationship. *p. 11*

Punishment is the administration of negative consequences or the withdrawal of positive consequences, which tends to reduce the likelihood of repeating the behaviour in similar settings. *p. 124*

Quality circles are groups of workers who meet periodically to discuss and develop solutions for problems relating to quality, productivity or cost. *p. 244*

Quality of work life refers to the overall quality of human experience in the workplace. *p. 10*

Quasiformal channels are planned communication connections between holders of the various positions within the organisation. *p. 458*

Radical change is change that results in a major make-over of the organisation and/or its component systems. *p. 490*

Rational persuasion strategy attempts to bring about change through persuasion based on empirical facts, special knowledge and rational argument. *p. 501*

The **receiver** is the individual or group of individuals that hear or read or see the message. *p. 456*

Referent power is the ability to control another's behaviour because the individual wants to identify with the power source. *p. 352*

Refreezing is the final stage of the planned change process in which changes are positively reinforced. *p. 497*

Relatedness needs are about the desire for satisfying interpersonal relationships. *p. 84*

Relationship goals are concerned with how well people involved in a negotiation, and their constituencies, are able to work with one another once the process is concluded. *p. 473*

Required behaviours are those contributions the organisation formally requests from group members as a basis for continued affiliation and support. *p. 209*

Resistance to change is any attitude or behaviour that reflects a person's unwillingness to make or support a desired change. *p. 503*

Resource dependencies occur when the organisation needs resources that others control. *p. 367*

Reward power is the extent to which a manager can use extrinsic and intrinsic rewards to control other people. *p. 346*

Risk environments are decision environments that involve a lack of complete certainty but that include an awareness of probabilities associated with the possible outcomes of various courses of action. *p. 421*

Rites are standardised and recurring activities used at special times to influence the behaviours and understanding of organisational members. *p. 315*

Rituals are systems of rites. *p. 315*

A **role** is a set of expectations for the behaviour of a person holding a particular office or position. *p. 240*

Role ambiguity is the uncertainty about what other group members expect of a person. *p. 240*

Role conflict occurs when a person is unable to respond to the expectations of one or more group members. *p. 240*

Routine problems are problems that arise routinely and that can be addressed through standard responses. *p. 420*

A **saga** is an embellished heroic account of the story of the founding of an organisation. *p. 314*

Satisficing means choosing the first satisfactory alternative rather than the optimal decision. *p. 423*

Schemas are cognitive frameworks developed through experience. *p. 63*

Self-concept is the concept that individuals have of themselves as physical, social and spiritual or moral beings. *p. 98*

Self-efficacy refers to a person's belief that they can perform adequately in a situation. *p. 100*

Self-managing teams are small groups of people empowered to manage themselves and the work they do on a day-to-day basis. *p. 245*

Shaping is the creation of a new behaviour by the positive reinforcement of successive approximations to the desired behaviour. *p. 122*

A **shared power strategy (or normative-reeducative strategy)** attempts to bring about change by identifying or establishing values and assumptions so that support for the change emerges naturally. *p. 502*

Shared values are the set of coherent values held by members of the organisation and that link them together. *p. 311*

A **simple design** is a configuration involving one or two ways of specialising individuals and units. *p. 288*

Situational constraints are organisational inadequacies which do not allow workers to perform adequately. *p. 44*

Situational control is the extent to which leaders can determine what their group is going to do and what the outcomes of their actions and decisions are going to be. *p. 389*

The **social information-processing approach** argues that individual needs, task perceptions and reactions are a result of socially constructed realities. *p. 160*

Social learning is learning that is achieved through the reciprocal interaction between people and their environments. *p. 117*

Social loafing is the tendency of people not to work as hard in groups as they would individually. *p. 196*

Socio-technical job design is the design of jobs to optimise the relationship between the technology system and the social system. *p. 160*

The **span of control** is the number of individuals reporting to a supervisor. *p. 281*

Staff personnel are groups that assist the line units by performing specialised services for the organisation. *p. 281*

Standardisation is the degree to which the range of actions in a job or series of jobs is limited. *p. 277*

Status is the indication of a person's relative rank, worth or standing within a group. *p. 204*

Status incongruence occurs when a person's expressed status within a group is inconsistent with his or her standing in another context. *p. 204*

Stimulus is something that incites action. *p. 115*

The **storming stage** is the second stage of group development, which is marked by a period of high emotion and tension among group members. *p. 207*

Strategic alliances are announced cooperative agreements or joint ventures between two independent organisations. *p. 296*

Stress is a state of tension experienced by individuals facing extraordinary demands, constraints or opportunities. *p. 506*

Stress prevention involves taking action to prevent the emergence of stress that becomes destructive. *p. 507*

Stressors are things that cause stress (for example, work, non-work and personal factors). *p. 506*

Subcultures are unique patterns of values and philosophies within a group that are not inconsistent with the dominant culture of the larger organisation or social system. *p. 312*

Sub-goal optimisation occurs when a group achieves its goals at the expense of the goals of others. *p. 198*

Substance goals are concerned with outcomes tied to the 'content' issues at hand in a negotiation. *p. 473*

Substantive conflict is conflict that occurs in the form of a fundamental disagreement over ends or goals to be pursued and the means for their accomplishment. *p. 462*

Substitutes for leadership are organisation, individual, or task-situational variables that substitute for leadership in causing performance/human resource maintenance. *p. 393*

Supportive leadership is a leadership style that focuses on employee needs and wellbeing, and promotes a friendly work climate; it is similar to consideration. *p. 391*

Synergy is the creation of a whole that is greater than the sum of its parts. *pp. 7, 196*

Systems goals are goals concerned with conditions within the organisation that are expected to increase its survival potential. *p. 274*

Task activities are the various things members do that directly contribute to the performance of important group tasks. *p. 212*

Task forces are temporary teams created to fulfil a well-defined task within a fairly short period of time. *p. 244*

Task performance is the quality and quantity of work produced. *p. 9*

A **teaching organisation** aims to pass on learning experiences to others, thereby allowing the organisation to achieve and maintain success. *p. 137*

Team building is a sequence of planned action steps designed to gather and analyse data on the functioning of a group, and to implement changes to increase its operating effectiveness. *p. 230*

Teams are small groups of people with complementary skills, who work together as a unit to achieve a common purpose for which they hold themselves collectively accountable. *p. 228*

Teamwork is when members of a team work together in a way that represents certain core values that promote the use of skills to accomplish certain goals. *p. 230*

The **technological imperative** is the idea that if an organisation does not adjust its internal structure to the requirements of the technology, it will not be successful. *p. 270*

Technology is the combination of resources, knowledge and techniques that creates a product or service output for an organisation. *p. 270*

Telework principles relate to work conducted remotely from the central organisation using information technology. *p. 172*

Temporary formal work groups are created for a specific purpose and typically disband once that purpose has been accomplished. *p. 191*

The **total integration stage** is the fourth stage of group development, which sees the emergence of a mature, organised and well-functioning group; it is also referred to as the performing stage. *p. 207*

Transactional leadership involves daily exchanges between leaders and followers, and is necessary for achieving routine performance on which leaders and followers agree. *p. 397*

Transformational leadership is a leadership style by which the followers' goals are broadened and elevated, and confidence is gained to go beyond expectations. *p. 397*

Transmission is the actual communication of a message from one person to another through a chosen channel. *p. 455*

Turnover is the decision by people to terminate their employment. *p. 58*

Uncertain environments are decision environments in which managers are unable to assign probabilities to the possible outcomes of various courses of action. *p. 421*

Unfreezing is the first stage of the planned change process in which a situation is prepared for change. *p. 496*

Unity of command is the situation in an organisation where each worker has a clear reporting relationship to only one supervisor. *p. 281*

Unplanned change is change that occurs at random or spontaneously and without a change agent's direction. *p. 491*

Valence represents the values that the individual attaches to various work outcomes. *p. 93*

Value congruence occurs when individuals express positive feelings on encountering others who exhibit values similar to their own. *p. 53*

Value-added managers are managers whose efforts clearly enable their work units to achieve high productivity and improve 'bottom-line' performance. *p. 10*

Values are global beliefs that guide actions and judgements across a variety of situations. *p. 53*

Vertical loading involves increasing job depth by adding responsibilities, like planning and controlling, previously held by supervisors. *p. 153*

Vertical specialisation is a hierarchical division of labour that distributes formal authority and establishes how critical decisions will be made. *p. 279*

Virtual organisations comprise individuals, groups and businesses that work together across time and space. *p. 297*

A **virtual team** is one whose members work interdependently towards the achievement of a common goal across space and time. *p. 247*

Voluntary reduced work time (V-Time or **time–income tradeoffs)** is a scheme by which workers trade income for additional leisure time that is packaged to suit their needs. *p. 170*

Work flow interdependency is the way work flows in an organisation from one group to the next. *p. 214*

Work teams or **units** are task-oriented groups that include a manager and his or her direct reports. *p. 9*

Workforce diversity means a workforce consisting of a broad mix of workers from different racial and ethnic backgrounds, of different ages and genders, and of different domestic and national cultures. *p. 18*

The **zone of indifference** is the range of authoritative requests to which an employee is willing to respond without subjecting the directives to critical evaluation or judgement — that is, the requests to which the employee is indifferent. *p. 354*

INDEX

ABC contingencies   116, 127
ability, defined   45
absenteeism
   defined   58
   reduction strategies   123
   relationship to job satisfaction   58–9
access and legitimacy paradigm,
      management of cultural
      diversity   314
accountability
   relationship to organisational
      governance   367
   of teams   250
achievement-oriented leadership   392
acquired needs theory
      (McClelland)   85–6
   meaning of pay   130
active management by exception   397
Adams, J. Stacy
   equity theory   90–2
      meaning of pay   130–1
adhocracies   296, 299
adjourning stage, group
      development   209
affective components, attitudes   55
age
   relationship to flexible work
      arrangements   167–8
   relationship to leadership   406
   relationship to performance   44
      perceptions   64
   workforce   20–1
agreeableness, dimension of
      personality   49
Alderfer, Clayton, ERG theory   84–5
ambiguity perspective see fragmentation
      perspective
amoebas (PS21 teams)   261
annual hours see flexiyears
applied focus, organisational
      behaviour   4
approach–avoidance conflict   130
approach conflict   129
aptitude, defined   45
arbitration   478
artificial intelligence (AI), use in decision
      making   436
attitudes   55, 66
   cognitive consistency   56–7
   components   55–6
   defined   55
   relationship to behaviour   56
attributes see individual attributes

attribution theory, leadership   385, 386
Australian Defence Force (ADF)
   organisational culture   327–8
   recruiting   303–4
authoritarianism, personality
      dimension   50
authority, relationship to
      obedience   352–3
authority decisions   428, 430, 431
autocratic decisions   431
automation   151
autonomous work teams   245
autonomy, job characteristic   155
average of members' opinions, decision-
      making process   431
avoidance see negative reinforcement
avoidance conflict   129–30

bargaining zone   476
BATNA   476
behavioural components, attitudes   55
behavioural decision theory   423, 442
behavioural theories, leadership   386–8,
      408
behaviourists   114
beliefs   55, 56
blaming communication   462
brain drain   18, 156
brainstorming   236, 435
branch offices   285–6
buffering   471
bullying see workplace bullying
bureaucracies   299
   defined   290
   dysfunctional tendencies   290
   growth   290
   mechanistic features, relationship to
      organic features   291–2
   organic features, relationship to
      mechanistic features   291–2

calculated risks   43
call centres, use of controls   277
casual work   167, 295
   defined   26
casualisation, of the workforce   26
centralisation   280
certain environments   421
challenging viewpoints, team
      building   235–6
change agents   490–1
change cycles   498
change levers   497–8

change management see organisational
      change, management
changing, phase in change process   497
channels   455
   see also communication channels
charisma   398
charismatic leaders   395–6, 408
   compared with inspirational
      leaders   395
   defined   395
chief executives, political actions   366–9
CICL   189
clash of corporate cultures   313
classical conditioning   115–16
classical decision theory   423, 442
codes of behaviour   277–8
coercive power   346–8
cognitive abilities   45
cognitive components, attitudes   55
cognitive consistency, attitudes   56–7
cognitive dissonance   56–7
cognitive learning   117
cognitive resource theory
      (Fiedler)   390–1
cohesiveness
   groups   213
   teams   240–2, 253
collective performance   229
Comcare   453
commitment, in learning
      organisations   136
common assumptions   312, 330
   relationship to management
      philosophy   319
communication   454, 480
   causes of conflict   462–3
   good habits   460
   process   455
   within groups   211
   see also interpersonal communication;
      organisational communication
communication channels   457–9
communities of competence   113
competency characteristics   66
competency differences   45–7
complaining, organisational culture   318
compressed work weeks   168–9
compromising style, conflict
      resolution   469
computer usage policies   329–30
conflict   460–8, 480
   defined   461
   levels   463–4

management   480
   relationship to culture   464–5
   stages of development   467–8
   types   461–2, 465–6, 466–8
conflict management
   approaches   468–72
   in teams   242
conflict resolution
   defined   468
   hierarchical referral   470
   relationship to organisational
      design   471
   stakeholder engagement   471–2
   styles   469–72
conglomerates   289, 292–3, 299
congruence, values   53
conscientiousness, dimension of
    personality   49
consensus
   achievement   432
   decision-making process   430, 432
constituency negotiation   472, 473
constructive conflict   465
consultative decisions   428
content themes, organisational
    culture   320
content theories of motivation   82,
   82–90, 102
   integration with process theories   96–7
context satisfaction, job design
    moderator   156
contingency approach, organisational
    behaviour   4
contingent reinforcement   121
contingent rewards   397
continual improvement, team
    building   237
continuous reinforcement   122
contributions (work inputs)   11
controlling, management process,
    defined   13
controls   274–8, 298–9
   defined   274–5
   use in battling fraud   277–8
coordination
   defined   278
   impersonal   279
   personal, styles   279
   personal methods   278
   styles   279
core–ring organisation   293–4, 299
corporate apparel   311
   see also dress codes

corporate culture
   clashes   313
   compared with organisational
      culture   322
corporate social responsibility   27, 274
countercultures   313
crafted decisions   420, 421
creativity
   in decision making   426–7
   defined   426–7
   relationship to emotion   426
CRG Medical Foundation   113, 137
cross-functional teams   249
cultural analysis, levels   311–12, 330
cultural change   494
cultural diversity   313–14
   relationship to conflict   464–5
cultural forms, research   320
cultural frames   419
cultural roles   317
cultural rules   317
cultural symbols   315–16
   defined   315
culture
   dimensions   19–20
   relationship to decision making
    436
   relationship to leadership   407
   see also multiculturalism; organisational
      culture
customer relationship marketing
   (CRM)   326

decentralisation   280
decision environments   421
decision making
   approaches   422–6
   choice of style   429–30
   current issues   436–41
   defined   420, 442
   ethical issues   437–41
   groups   211, 430–5
    improvement   434–5
   involvement strategies   428–9
   relationship to cultural
      differences   19, 436
   steps   422
   use of technology   436–7
decisions
   implementation   427–36
   types   420–1, 442
decoding   456
decoupling   471

defence force see Australian Defence Force
delegating style, leadership   393
Delphi technique   435
demographic characteristics   66
   defined   44
   effect on performance   44–5
deontology   438
departmentalisation
   by customer   283
   by division   283
    pros and cons   283–5
    see also divisionalised design
   by function   282–3
   by geography   283
   mixed forms   287–8
destructive conflict   465
   prevention   466
devil's advocate process   235
differentiation perspective,
    organisational culture   322
direction of effort   44, 78
directive leadership   391
discrimination and fairness paradigm,
    management of cultural
    diversity   314
dishonest communication   463
disruptive behaviours   196–7
distributed leadership   212
distributive justice, criterion for ethical
    political behaviour   371
distributive negotiation   474–5
   defined   474
diversity, in teams   250–2
division of labour   6–7
divisional departmentalisation   283
   pros and cons   283–5
divisionalised design, organisational
    structures   289, 292, 299
dogmatism, personality dimension   50
domain ambiguities   467
downsizing, and core–ring
    organisations   293
dress codes   317
   see also corporate apparel

effective change   502
effective communication   457
effective groups   197–8
effective managers   9
effective negotiation   473
effective teams   229–30, 232
efficient communication   457
ego involvement, group tasks   202

emergent behaviours, groups   209
emotion, relationship to creativity   426
emotional competence   46–7
emotional conflicts   462
emotional intelligence   5–6, 46
emotional stability, dimension of
    personality   49
emotional support   100, 101
emotions
    management   46–7
    within groups   211
empire building   368–9
employee-centred supervisors   387
employee involvement teams   244
employee rewards see rewards
employee rights   22
Employee Share Ownership Programs
    (ESOPs), and motivation   89
employer–employee relations,
    changes   22–6
employment opportunity   22
empowerment   78–81, 103, 373
    defined   100, 359
    implementation guidelines   361
    power keys   360
    process   99–102, 359–62
    in team development   250
encoding   455
ends agreement, group tasks   202
engine of change   498
environment
    influence on organisational
        design   271–2
    influence on personality   48
environmental branding   315–16
environmental complexity   271–2
environmental interdependence   271
environmental richness   271
equal pay   65
equity of earnings   22, 92
equity theory (Adams)   90–2
    meaning of pay   130–1
ERG theory (Alderfer)   84–5
escalating commitment   435–6
ethical behaviour
    defined   26–7
    relationship to personality traits   50–1
ethical climate   329
ethical dilemmas   27, 355, 439
ethics   26–7
    decision making   437–41
        framework   439–40
    of power and politics   370–1, 373

relationship to organisational
    culture   329–30, 331
    transformational leadership   398
ethnicity
    relationship to performance   44–5
        perceptions   65
everyday workplace teams   228
existence needs   84
expectancy, defined   92
expectancy theory (Vroom)   92–6
    equation   93
    managerial implications   94–6
    meaning of pay   130–1
expected silence   210
experiential activities, team
        building   235
expert based decision-making
        process   431
expert power   349–51
    defined   349
external adaptation
    defined   324
    organisational culture   324–5
externals, personality type   49–50
extinction (reinforcement strategy)   126
extrinsic rewards   96, 120–1
    organisational learning   114
    as positive reinforcement   124
extroversion–introversion   49

facilitators, role in team building   233
family-friendly workplaces   23
feedback
    in communication   456
    effect on goal setting   162–3
    empowerment strategy   100
    job characteristic   155
felt negative inequities   90
felt positive inequities   90
Fiedler, Fred
    cognitive resource theory   390–1
    leadership contingency theory   389–90
Fisher & Paykel   228, 527–9
five key dimensions of personality   49
flexible work arrangements   149, 165–8,
        174–5
    types   168–73
flexitime (flexible working hours)   169
flexiyears   169–70
force–coercion strategy, planned
        change   501
formal authority   348
formal communication channels   457

formal groups   190–1
formal leadership, defined   385
formal practices, organisational
        culture   320
formal retreats, team building   237
formal structures   268
formalisation   277
forming stage, group
        development   206–7
founding stories   314
fragmentation perspective,
        organisational culture   322–3
franchises   297–8
fraud, battling, use of controls   277–8
freedom to act   100
friendship groups   192
functional departmentalisation   282–3
fundamental interpersonal orientation
        (FIRO-B) theory   203–4

games, team-building activities   235
gender
    relationship to performance   44
        perceptions   64–5
    workforce profile   21
gender issues, and leadership   405–6
generation X
    values   54
    in the workforce   21, 53–4
generation Y
    response to punishment   125
    values   54
    in the workforce   21, 53
generational differences
    response to punishment   125
    in values   53–4
    workforce needs   21
glass ceiling see leadership, gender issues
global education groups   203
global management
    competencies   61–2
    skills and competencies   14–15
globalisation   14–16
    effect on recruitment   156–7
    and employer–employee
        relationships   22
    markets   272
GLOBE project   407
goal setting   162–5, 174
    defined   162
    effect on group effectiveness   199
    relationship to MBO   164–5
    see also organisational goals

goal statements   6
goals, in negotiation   473–4
group decisions   428
group negotiation   472, 473
group support systems   250
groups
   advantages and disadvantages
      194–5
   cohesion   213
   communication within   211
   compared with teams   228–9, 253
   complexities   213–14
   decision making   211, 430–5
   defined   190, 229
   development stages   206–9
   dynamics   206, 218
   effectiveness, relationship to group
      processes   206–11
   inputs   199–206, 218
      defined   199
   interdependence   214–15
   maintenance   196, 212–13, 218
   management   196–8, 218
   maturity, measurement   208
   norms   210
   as open systems   198
   outputs   211–14
      defined   211
   processes
      inputs   199–206
      relationship to effectiveness   206–
         11
   purposes   193–6
   relationship to needs
      of members   194
      of organisations   193–4
   roles of members   210–11
   size   205–6
   task performance   196–7, 212, 218
   types   190–3, 217
groupthink   433–4
   defined   433
   symptoms   433
growth-need strength, job design
   moderator   156
growth needs   84

hard distributive negotiation   474–5
heredity, influence on personality   48
Herzberg, Frederick
   two-factor theory   87–90
      job enrichment   153
      meaning of pay   130

heterogeneous groups   204
heuristics, defined   425
hierarchical referral, conflict
   resolution   470
hierarchy of needs theory (Maslow)   83–4
   meaning of pay   130
higher-order needs   83
HIH collapse   50–1
homogeneous groups   204
homophily   251–2
horizontal loading of tasks   152
horizontal specialisation   281–8, 299
   defined   281
hotgroups   244–5
House, Robert
   on charismatic leadership   395
   path–goal theory of leadership   391–2
human resources   7
   maintenance   10–12
      defined   9
hygiene factors   88
hygienes   88

idealised influence, transformational
   leadership   399
illumination, creative decision
   making   427
immediate reinforcement   122
impersonal methods, coordination   279
incentive pay, effect on motivation   61
incentives, as stimuli   117
incremental change   490, 512
incubation, creative decision making   427
individual attributes, effect on
   performance   42–3
individual decisions   428, 431
individual needs level, teams   229
individual performance equation   52, 65
individual rights, respect for, criterion for
   ethical political behaviour   371
individualised consideration,
   transformational leadership   398,
   399
individualism–collectivism
   cultural dimension   19
      relationship to decision
         making   436
inducements   11
   see also motivation
influence
   defined   345
   relationship to power   345–6, 357–9
informal communication channels   457

informal groups   192–3
informal leadership, defined   385
informal networks   364
informal practices, organisational
   culture   320
information, sharing   458–9
information power   348–9
   defined   349
information sources,
   communication   455
initial integration stage, group
   development   207
innovation   508–12, 513
   defined   508
   leadership by management   511–12
   process   508–10
inputs, into group processes   199–206
inspiration, transformational
   leadership   398, 399
inspirational leaders, compared with
   charismatic leaders   395
instinct   48
Instinctive Drive System™   41, 48
instrumentality, defined   93
insubordination   355
integrating style, conflict resolution   469
integration perspective, organisational
   culture   321
integration stages, group
   development   207
integrative negotiation   475
   agreements   476
intellectual stimulation, transformational
   leadership   398, 399
interdependence, groups   214–15
interest groups   192
intergroup competition   216–17
intergroup conflict   463–4
intergroup dynamics   214–17, 218–19
   defined   214
intergroup negotiation   472, 473
intermittent reinforcement   122–3
internal integration
   defined   325
   organisational culture   325–6
internals, personality type   49–50
international education, importance of
   groups   202–3
interorganisational conflict   464
interpersonal communication   454, 455–6
   barriers   460
interpersonal compatibilities, group
   development   203–4

interpersonal conflict   463
intragroup dynamics *see* groups, dynamics
intrapersonal conflict   129–30, 463
intrinsic motivation   150–1, 173
  defined   150
intrinsic rewards   96
intuition
  defined   424
  role in decision making   424–5
intuitive decision making   424–5

jargon   315
job characteristics model (Hackman & Oldham)   155–62, 174
Job Descriptive Index (JDI)   57, 58
job diagnostic surveys   157
job involvement   57
job satisfaction   66
  as an attitude   57–8
  defined   57
  facets   58
  relationship to performance   60–2
  relationship to workplace behaviour   58–62
job security   22, 78
  in core–ring organisations   293–4
jobs
  content   88
  context   88
  defined   151
  design   151–4, 174
    defined   151
    moderators   156
    social information-processing approach   160–1
  enlargement   152, 154
  enrichment   101, 153–4
    defined   153
  mastery   100
  migration   25
  program implementation   158–9
  rotation   152–3, 154
  sharing   170
  simplification   151, 154
judgement, defined   425
judgement heuristics   425–6

karoshi   507
key dimensions, personality   49
key performance indicators (KPIs)   165
knowledge and skill, job design moderator   156

knowledge-based economies, defined   17
knowledge management (KM), and nature of work   17–18

labour *see* workforce
labour shortages   79
laissez faire leadership   397
language, subcultures   315
law of contingent reinforcement   121
law of effect   120
law of immediate reinforcement   122
leaders
  accountability   404
  defined   384
leadership   1213, 384
  age and   406
  behavioural theories   386–8, 408
  charismatic approaches   395–6
  compared with management   384–6, 407
  and cultural differences   19
  culture issues   407
  current issues   405–7
  defined   385
  development theories   385–6
  emerging perspectives   395–400
  gender issues   405–6
  organisational change   491–3
  perspectives   385
  situational contingency theories   388–94, 408
  teams   231–2, 252
  traditional approaches   385, 386–8
  trait theory   386, 408
leadership contingency theory (Fiedler)   389–90
Leadership Grid®   387–8
learning
  approaches   114–15, 138
    see also classical conditioning; cognitive learning; operant conditioning; social learning
  compared with performance   115
  defined   114
  as modification of work behaviour   114–20
learning and effectiveness paradigm, management of cultural diversity   314
learning organisations   135–7, 139
  compared with teaching organisations   137

least preferred coworker (LPC)   389
legitimate power   348–9
  defined   348
level of effort   44, 78
liaison groups   471
line personnel   281–2
line–staff conflict   466
linking pins
  managerial function   191
  role in conflict resolution   471
listening skills, empowerment strategy   100
locus of control   49–50
long-term–short-term orientation, cultural dimension   20
lower-order needs   83

Machiavellianism   362
  personality dimension   50
machine bureaucracies   291
maintenance activities, in groups   212–13
maintenance level, teams   229
majority control, decision-making process   430, 432
management
  compared with leadership   384–6, 407
  functions   12–13
  with power and influence   355–9
management by exception   397
management by objectives (MBO), relationship to goal setting   164–5
management by wandering around   457–8
management philosophy   319
management process   12–13
managerial power   355–9
  acquisition   356–7
managers
  defined   9, 384
  effectiveness   9
  influence, relationship to trust   372
  innovation leadership   511–12
  linking pin function   191
  and political action   365
  role   28–9
  see also value-added managers
manifest conflict   468
masculinity–femininity, cultural dimension   19
Maslow, Abraham
  hierarchy of needs theory   83–4
    meaning of pay   130
material resources   7

maternity leave   171
   see also paid maternity leave
matrix structures   286–7
   defined   286
   pros and cons   286–7
McClelland, David
   acquired needs theory   85–6
      meaning of pay   130
means agreement, group tasks   202
mechanistic design, organisational
      structures   279, 289
membership characteristics, groups,
      effect on performance   202–3
mentors   117, 118
   hospitality industry   119–20
   legal profession   118
merit pay   131–2
   teaching profession   132–3
Michigan studies, leadership   387
Minnesota Satisfaction Questionnaire
      (MSQ)   57
minority control, decision-making
      process   430, 432
mobility, workforce   80
motivating potential score (MPS)   157
motivation   78–82, 99
   and cultural differences   19
   effect of incentive pay   61
   theories   82
      see also content theories; process
         theories
   to work   44, 78, 81–2
motivator factors   88
motivator–hygiene theory   87
motivators   88
multiculturalism
   management   313–14
   and the workforce   18–19
Multifactor Emotional Intelligence Scale
      (MEIS)   46
multinational corporations   15–16
multiskilling   161–2

nAch (need for achievement)   85, 86
nAff (need for affiliation)   85, 86
National Australia Bank
   leadership program   400
   organisational politics   368
nature/nurture controversy   47–8
need for achievement (nAch)   85, 86
need for affiliation (nAff)   85, 86
need for power (nPower)   85, 86
negative communication   462

negative reinforcement   124
negotiation   453, 472–5, 480–1
   approaches   474–5
   defined   472
   goals and outcomes   473–4
   managerial issues   475–8, 481
   types   472–3
network organisation   297
neutralisers, leadership   393
new leadership   385, 395–401
noise (communication)   455
   defined   456
nominal group technique   435
non-routine problems   420, 421
normative–reeducative strategy *see*
      shared power strategy
norms
   defined   239
   groups   210
   teams   239
nPower (need for power)   85, 86

obedience   352
   Milgram experiments   352–3
   relationship to acceptance of
      authority   353–4
   zone of indifference   354–5
observable culture   311
occupational stress   166–7
occupational subcultures   323
office politics   364
Ohio State studies, leadership   387
open-plan workspaces   200–1, 315
open systems   7
   BreadTalk   8
   groups   198
openness to experience, dimension of
      personality   49
operant conditioning   116–17
organic design, organisational
      structures   279, 289
organigraphs   269
organisation charts   268–9
organisational behaviour
   defined   4, 28
   modification
      defined   121
      strategies   139
      strategies summarised   127
      use of reinforcement   120–7
   need for understanding   27–8, 29
   relationship to job satisfaction
      58–62

organisational change
   case studies   222–3, 517–18
   defined   490
   forces favouring   493–4, 513
   leadership   491–3
   management   493
   phases   496–7
   relationship to stress   506–7
   strategies   500–2, 513
   targets   495–6, 513
organisational commitment   57, 58
organisational communication   454–60
   defined   454
organisational culture
   compared with corporate culture   322
   defined   310
   differing frames   419
   effect on group effectiveness   201
   management of   326–8, 331
   Mary Kay Cosmetics   316
   observable aspects   314–17, 330
   perspectives   321–6, 331
   relationship to
      ethics   329–30, 331
      national cultures   310–11, 330
      values   318–19
   research fields   320–1
   survival functions   324–6
organisational design   268–9
   building blocks   273–9
   defined   268, 298
   effect on employees   295
   effect on group effectiveness   201
   emerging forms   288–98, 299
   influencing factors   269–73, 298
   relationship to conflict resolution   471
   structures   279–88
organisational goals   273–4
organisational governance   367–8
   defined   367
organisational justice
   and punishment   126
   see also process theories
organisational learning   114
   defined   135
organisational politics   344, 362–9
   as compromise   363
   consequences   369–72
   defined   362
   ethics   370–1, 373
   National Australia Bank   368
   traditions   362–4
   unsanctioned and self-interested   362

organisational setting, effect on group
        effectiveness 199–201
organisational strategy 272–3
organisational support
    effect on performance 44
    in learning organisations 136
organisations
    key issues 29
    as open systems 7
    reasons for existence 6–7, 28
organising, management process,
        defined 13
outdoor experiences, team
        building 237–8
output controls 276, 299
output goals 273–4, 298
outsourcing 25, 156

paid maternity leave 23–4
participative leadership 392, 393
passive management by exception 397
path–goal theory of leadership
        (House) 391–2
pay
    creative practices 133–4
    as an extrinsic reward 130–4, 139
    meanings 130–1
    and motivation 88–9
perceptions 62–3
    about
        age relationship to performance 64
        ethnicity and performance 65
        gender relationship to
            performance 64–5
    defined 62
perceptual process 62–3, 66
    influencing factors 63
performance
    compared with learning 115
    defined 60
    factors 42–4
        dimensions 43
        predictability 5–6
    relationship to job satisfaction 60–2
performance equation 5, 42
    see also individual performance
        equation
performance gap 491
performance incentives, China 134
permanent formal work groups 191
persistence of effort 44, 78
personal coordination, styles 279
personal methods, coordination 278

personal power 349–52
    enhancement 357
personal values, versus team values 243
personality
    defined 47
    determinants 47–8
    differences 47–51
    key dimensions 49
    measurement 48
    traits 49–51, 66
        relationship to ethical
            behaviour 50–1
physical abilities 45–6
planned change 491, 512
    forces favouring 493–4
    leadership 492
    phases 496–7
    strategies 500–2
planning, management process,
        defined 13
policies, defined 276
political action
    by chief executives 366–9
    by managers 365
    relationship to subunit power 366
political behaviour
    analysis 371
    perceptions 363–4
political payoffs 365
pooled interdependency 214, 215
Porter–Lawler model, performance–
        satisfaction relationship 60
position power 346–9
    enhancement 356–7
positive conflict 465
positive reinforcement 121–2
    scheduling 122–4
power 344
    asymmetries 467
    defined 345
    ethics 370–1, 373
    relationship to influence 345–6,
        357–9
    sources 346–52, 372
    see also managerial power; obedience;
        personal power; position power
power-distance
    cultural dimension 19
        relationship to decision
            making 436
        relationship to leadership
            styles 407
precautionary principle 424

primary beneficiaries 273
principled negotiation 475
problem definition, creative decision
        making 427
problem-solving skills,
        improvement 429
problem-solving teams 244–5
problems, selection 427–8
procedures (rules) 276
process controls 276, 299
process innovation 508
process power 348
process re-engineering 13–14
process theories of motivation 82, 90–6,
        102–3
    integration with content theories 96–7
product innovation 508
production-centred supervisors 387
productivity, defined 9–10
professional bureaucracies 291
programmed decisions 420, 421
PS21 teams 261–3
psychological contracts 11–12, 354–5
    realignment 12
punctuated group development 209
punishment 124–6

qualitative research, organisational
        culture 321
quality circles 244
quality management 278
quality of work life (QWL) 10–11
quantitative research, organisational
        culture 320
quasiformal communication
        channels 458

radical change 490, 512
rational persuasion strategy, planned
        change 501
receivers (of messages) 455, 456
reciprocal interdependency 215
referent power 352
refreezing, change phase 497
reinforcement
    modification of behaviour 120–7, 139
    perspectives 127–8
relatedness needs 84
relationship goals, negotiation 473
remote working 171–3
required behaviours, groups 209
resistance to change 502–5, 513
    changing concepts 499